Date Due

DEC 12 '75			
JAN 6 '76			
APR 6 '77			
OCT 11 1985			

251

WESTERN POLITICAL THEORY

PART 2

FROM MACHIAVELLI TO BURKE

HARCOURT BRACE JOVANOVICH, INC.

New York • Chicago • San Francisco • Atlanta

WESTERN POLITICAL THEORY

PART 2
FROM MACHIAVELLI TO BURKE

LEE CAMERON McDONALD
Pomona College

ISBN: 0-15-595298-6

Library of Congress Catalog Card Number: 68–19235

Printed in the United States of America

Acknowledgments

Appleton-Century-Crofts—for excerpts from *The Statesman's Book of John of Salisbury,* translated by John Dickinson. Copyright by Alfred A. Knopf, Inc., 1927. Copyright, 1955, by Lindsay Rogers. Reprinted by permission of Appleton-Century-Crofts, Division of Meredith Corporation.

Barnes & Noble, Inc.—for excerpts from Thomas Aquinas, *De regimine principum* in *Selected Political Writings,* tr. by J. G. Dawson; ed. by A. P. D'Entreves, 1959.

Benziger Brothers, Inc.—for excerpts from Thomas Aquinas, *Summa Theologica,* English Dominican tr., copyright 1947 by Benziger Brothers, Inc.

Basil Blackwell & Mott Ltd.—for excerpts from Thomas Aquinas, *De regimine principum* in *Selected Political Writings,* tr. by J. G. Dawson; ed. by A. P. D'Entreves, 1959. For excerpts from Dante, *The Divine Comedy,* tr. by Geoffrey L. Bickersteth, 1965.

The Bobbs-Merrill Company, Inc.—for excerpts from David Hume: *Political Essays,* edited by Charles W. Hendel, copyright © 1953, by The Liberal Arts Press, Inc., reprinted by permission of the Liberal Arts Press Division of The Bobbs-Merrill Company, Inc.

Burns & Oates Ltd.—for excerpts from Thomas Aquinas, *Summa Theologica,* English Dominican tr., 1947.

Cambridge University Press—for excerpts from Robert Tucker, *Philosophy and Myth in Karl Marx,* 1961.

Clarendon Press, Oxford—for excerpts from *The Dialogues of Plato,* 4th ed., tr. by Benjamin Jowett, 1953, by permission of the Clarendon Press, Oxford. For excerpts from Plato, *The Republic,* tr. by F. M. Cornford, 1945, by permission of the Clarendon

Press, Oxford. For excerpts from *Nicomachean Ethics* in *The Works of Aristotle,* tr. and ed. by W. D. Ross, Vol. 9, 1925, by permission of the Clarendon Press, Oxford. For excerpts from Aristotle, *Politics,* tr. by Ernest Barker, 1958, by permission of the Clarendon Press, Oxford.

J. M. DENT & SONS LTD.—for excerpts from Plato, *Parmenides, Thaeitetos, Sophist, Statesman,* tr. by John Warrington, Everyman's Library Edition, 1961. For excerpts from Thomas Aquinas, *Selected Writings,* ed. by M. C. D'Arcy, Everyman's Library Edition, 1950, © revisions J. M. Dent & Sons Ltd. 1964. For excerpts from Thomas Hobbes, *Leviathan,* ed. by A. D. Lindsay, Everyman's Library Edition, 1950. For excerpts from John Locke, *Second Treatise* in *Two Treatises of Civil Government,* ed. by William S. Carpenter, Everyman's Library Edition, 1924.

E. P. DUTTON & CO., INC.—for excerpts from Plato, *Parmenides, Thaeitetos, Sophist, Statesman,* tr. by John Warrington, Everyman's Library Edition, 1961. For excerpts from Thomas Aquinas, *Selected Writings,* ed. by M. C. D'Arcy, Everyman's Library Edition, 1950. For excerpts from *Leviathan* by Thomas Hobbes. Introduction by A. D. Lindsay, Everyman's Library Edition. Reprinted by permission of E. P. Dutton & Co., Inc. For excerpts from John Locke, *Second Treatise* in *Two Treatises of Civil Government,* ed. by William S. Carpenter, Everyman's Library Edition, 1924.

HAFNER PUBLISHING COMPANY—for excerpts from Baron de Montesquieu, *The Spirit of the Laws,* tr. by Thomas Nugent; ed. by Franz Neumann, 1949. For excerpts from Jean-Jacques Rousseau, *The Social Contract,* tr. by G. D. H. Cole; rev. and ed. by Charles Frankel, 1947.

HARVARD UNIVERSITY PRESS—for excerpts reprinted by permission of the publishers from R. M. Gummere, translator, Seneca, *Epistulae Morales,* Cambridge, Mass.: Harvard University Press, 1953. For excerpts reprinted by permission of the publishers from W. A. Oldfather, translator, Epictetus, *Discourses,* Cambridge, Mass.: Harvard University Press, 1926. For excerpts from Dante, *The Divine Comedy,* tr. by Geoffrey L. Bickersteth, 1965.

INDIANA UNIVERSITY PRESS—for excerpts from *The Histories of Polybius,* tr. by E. S. Shuckburgh; Introduction by F. W. Walbank, 1962.

ALFRED A. KNOPF, INC.—for excerpts from Albert Camus, *The Rebel,* tr. by Anthony Bower, Random House, Vintage Books, 1956.

LUTTERWORTH PRESS—for excerpts from *Reformation Writings of Martin Luther,* tr. by Bertram Lee Woolf, 1952.

OXFORD UNIVERSITY PRESS—for excerpts from *Il Principe,* by Niccolo Machiavelli, translated by Luigi Ricci, revised by E. R. P. Vincent and published by Oxford University Press, 1906. Reprinted in *The Prince and The Discourses,* Random House, Modern Library, 1940.

RANDOM HOUSE, INC.—for excerpts from *Basic Writings* of *Saint Augustine,* ed. by Whitney J. Oates, 1948.

GEORGE B. SABINE—for excerpts from Cicero, *De republica* in *On the Commonwealth,* tr. by George H. Sabine and Stanley B. Smith, Bobbs-Merrill, n. d.

SCM PRESS LTD.—for excerpts from John Calvin, *Institutes of the Christian Religion,* I & II, tr. by Ford Lewis Battles; ed. by John T. McNeill, Library of Christian Classics, 1960.

THE UNIVERSITY OF CHICAGO PRESS—for excerpts from Karl Jaspers, *The Future of Mankind,* by permission of The University of Chicago Press. Copyright © 1961 by The University of Chicago. All rights reserved.

THE WESTMINSTER PRESS—for excerpts from *Institutes of the Christian Religion,* I and II, Library of Christian Classics, Vols. XX and XXI, edited by John T. McNeill and translated by Ford Lewis Battles. The Westminster Press. Copyright © 1960, W. L. Jenkins. Used by permission.

JOHN WILEY & SONS, INC.—for excerpts from David Easton, *A Systems Analysis of Political Life,* 1965.

To Claire

PREFACE

A book is what it is. Cut its pages properly and, inescapably, its virtues and vices are spread before all who can read and care to read. This makes the writing of prefaces a precarious enterprise, whether they are meant to serve as enticements or diversions. Should you therefore be overcome with curiosity about Plato, by all means proceed at once to page 5, where begins a well-meant chapter on that estimable sage. With or without prefatory preparation, you will find that if the chapter works you will want to read further—not just in McDonald, though that would be nice, but in Plato, which is even nicer.

This book, which examines the contributions of major Western political thinkers from ancient Greece to the present, includes a revision of my *Western Political Theory: The Modern Age,* which analyzed political thinkers from the seventeenth to the twentieth centuries. The present volume is thus a big book of commentary born in an age of small paperbacks and anthologies. In this sense, it is unconventional—influenced perhaps by the political philosophers in its pages who have questioned convention.

Some skeptics will wonder what can justify the attempt to compress more than two thousand years of political thinking into a few hundred pages. Their skepticism should be respected, for such sanity as the world knows is much in tempered skepticism's debt. In my 1962 preface I suggested that my aim was not to save the world or to make money (though, if the truth be known, I was opposed to neither aim), but rather to fulfill a "long-felt need in the author to write a book." That need having so long ago been met, I must find another justification for this second book. A second book, I am happy to report, is easier to write than a first book and provides even more pleasure in the writing. But it takes longer, because a second book is a less reliable excuse for avoiding service on committees. One way or another a decade of my life has spanned the writing of this book. Though I have tried to make the experience appear painful, I have in fact learned much of worth, much that I treasure, in writing this book. If others learn something in reading it, I shall be doubly grateful.

In the 1962 preface I most soberly thanked

a good many friends and scholars for manifold aid and comfort. Most of them should be thanked again for this volume. But instead I will merely mention a few others who have been generous with their expertise for the sake of this volume: Herbert Deane, Josiah Gould, Harry V. Jaffa, Harvey C. Mansfield, Jr., Leonard Munter, Frederick Sontag, and Theodore Waldman. Typists Mrs. Gladys Burton and Mrs. Shirley Martin each deserve special kudos. Thanks are due also to Pomona College and the Danforth Foundation for leave time and an Award, respectively, which made possible two periods of sustained research and writing in Cambridge, Massachusetts, and Claremont, California.

My youngest son—who at four months of age was induced to accept full responsibility for all errors of fact or interpretation in the 1962 book—is still my youngest son, but he is now six years old and a standout in first-grade research techniques. He stoutly refuses to shoulder additional burdens. I have no choice but to take the blame myself for the defects in what follows.

L. C. M.

Claremont, California

A NOTE ON THE PAPERBOUND EDITION

This volume is part of a variant printing, not a new or revised edition, of *Western Political Theory: From the Origins to the Present.* Some users of that book have requested a three-volume version that would enable them to fit the text into the particular patterns of their teaching and scheduling. To meet that request, the publishers have prepared this printing, consisting of three separate volumes that exactly reproduce the text of the one-volume version of *Western Political Theory: From the Origins to the Present.* Part One, now subtitled *Ancient and Medieval,* contains Chapters 1 through 7 of the original text; Part Two, *From Machiavelli to Burke,* contains Chapters 8 through 17; and Part Three, *Nineteenth and Twentieth Centuries,* contains Chapters 18 through 28. Since the variant printing is intended as a convenience to instructors and students, some of whom have had occasion to use the one-volume version, the original pagination, index, and list of selected readings are retained in the new printing. The difference between the one-volume and three-volume versions of the book is a difference only in form.

CONTENTS

11

HOBBES, *300*

12

LOCKE, *321*

13

THE EIGHTEENTH CENTURY, *339*

14

MONTESQUIEU, *369*

15

ROUSSEAU, *381*

WESTERN POLITICAL THEORY

PART 2

FROM MACHIAVELLI TO BURKE

8

MACHIAVELLI

Machiavelli has come to stand for a way of evil in politics, a way of clever and therefore mostly successful evil. A candidate consoles himself after an electoral defeat by saying, "I guess I'm just not Machiavellian enough." He means that his opponent will stop at nothing, whereas he will stop at something. "So you think the end justifies the means, eh?" we say with a slight sneer to the opportunist, thinking of the dark Florentine who must surely have resembled Simon Legree or the stock movie villain with the delicately waxed mustache.

Thus scholars must come forth and chip away at our misconceptions. They point out that, among other things, Machiavelli was simply a clear-eyed student of politics who saw life as it is rather than as it ought to be. He should not be blamed for injecting the toxin of "the end justifies the means" into the blood stream of the body politic, for the phrase goes back at least to the first century B.C. and the belief goes back even further. Machiavelli was, these scholars say, the first modern political scientist because he described rather than prescribed.

But did he only describe, other scholars ask? Was he not simply a representative of a long line of writers who inferentially told princes what they ought to do and what they ought to be? If so, he was not modern at all: he was a frustrated politician and a skilled writer who used his talent to produce the best but not a decisively original mirror-of-princes tract. Finally, as if to come full circle, another group of scholars tells us that Machiavelli was indeed what ordinary people have all along been told he was, a teacher of evil. Machiavelli was a Machiavellian—but one so subtle that we must study him deeply to know the depth of his evil.

Our work is cut out for us, for, while there is some truth in all these positions, some positions are better than others.

LIFE

Niccolo Machiavelli was born in Florence in 1469, the year Lorenzo de' Medici came to power. He was the son of a poor lawyer who, despite his modest livelihood, came from the Tuscan nobility. Niccolo had, apparently, an unexceptional education—one that emphasized Latin—but it seems he did not learn Greek. Of Machiavelli's early life, including his reactions to the momentous events in

Florence in the early 1490s, we know almost nothing. But in a letter to a friend in early 1498, he reveals that he was wholly unimpressed and even slightly contemptuous of the religious zeal of Savonarola, the reforming Dominican friar. About that time, Machiavelli was nominated for a public office but he was not elected. A month after Savonarola's execution later that same year Machiavelli was elected second chancellor of Florence.[1] He was twenty-nine years old and was to hold this position for fourteen years, until the fall of the republican regime in 1512.

His first year in office Machiavelli prepared his crisp *Report on the Pisan War,* a compilation of others' views that nevertheless suggested Machiavelli's early disenchantment with mercenary troops. (The intermittent war with Pisa would last almost a decade.) He went on an abortive diplomatic mission to Caterina Sforza, Countess of Imola and Forli, in hopes of securing the north and east approaches to Tuscany from attack. He learned much more when he accompanied the ailing Francesco della Casa as envoy to Louis XII of France on what turned out to be a rather humiliating mission: among the many Italian principalities importuning the French, money and arms were all that seemed to count and Florence had little of either.

The most successful Italian of the time was Cesare Borgia, who rampaged across Italy uniting papal lands by force and deception. In 1502 Machiavelli met Cesare Borgia at Urbino[2]—more to listen than to persuade—and was impressed by the man. Some think this ruthless man of power became a primary inspiration for Machiavelli's *The Prince (Il principe)*. "The Duke," wrote Machiavelli, "cannot be considered like other petty princes . . . but must be regarded as a new power in Italy."[3] On these and many similar missions, Machiavelli saw diplomacy from the seamy underside, learned the secrets of success and failure, and sent back to Florence reports that showed not only penetration but a remarkable detachment.

For some time Machiavelli had advocated a citizen army but commerce-oriented Florence was reluctant to make the necessary sacrifice and was needlessly suspicious of what Gonfalonier Soderini might do with such new power. But defeats of the ragged Florentine mercenaries (*condottiere*) by Pisa in 1505 led the council of eighty to approve the idea and to let Machiavelli take on the organizational job. The task was beset with trials because local mayors bargained for advantages, equipment was scarce, and citizen-soldiers from one town refused to serve with their counterparts from neighboring towns. A new department, the Nine of the Militia (*Nove di Milizia*), was organized in 1506 to direct the new force; provisional success followed. When, in 1509, the new *milizia* used blockades personally devised by Machiavelli to force Pisa to surrender, he was at the apex of his influence.

Machiavelli's political decline was, of course, tied to Soderini's political decline. Florence tried to maintain a precarious neutrality between Pope Julius II and Louis XII of France,[4] while discontent grew at home. Machiavelli was busily engaged in both diplomatic missions and militia recruitment. In 1512 came the downfall of the Florentine

[1] Lorenzo de' Medici, the Magnificent, grandson of the popular Cosimo de' Medici, had died in 1492. For two years an oligarchy floundered about. After Charles VIII of France invaded Italy in 1494, a revolt in Florence established a republic served by a great council of eighty, a first chancery of eight (headed by the chancellor, or secretary, of the republic) and a subordinate second chancery of ten to handle military and diplomatic affairs and some home-office functions. Machiavelli's position was, then, in reality that of first secretary to the second chancery.

[2] Machiavelli was an aide to Bishop Soderini, brother of Piero Soderini, the man who, as new permanent magistrate (*gonfalonier*) of Florence, would become Machiavelli's administrative superior and continuing benefactor.

[3] Letter dated November 8, 1502, quoted in J. R. Hale, *Machiavelli and Renaissance Italy* (New York: Macmillan, 1960), p. 69.

[4] Julius had formerly welcomed the challenge to Venetian power of Maximilian's Holy-Roman-Empire troops and Louis' French troops but now (1510) he saw them as too successful and signed a peace treaty with Venice. The Swiss, thanks to their sturdy Confederation, were able to maintain their independence, a fact that did not escape Machiavelli's attention.

militia and of Machiavelli. Julius, angered by the refusal of Florence to join his Holy-league troops in expelling the French from Italy, ordered them to suppress the republic and restore the Medicis and sent his troops down from the north. The Florentine militia made its major stand at the town of Prato and, though outnumbering the aggressors, its members broke and fled before the pope's trained mercenaries. Before a military assault on Florence was necessary, Soderini resigned, giving up the government to Medici partisans. Machiavelli did not follow his leader and, even after a staged riot had led to the transformation of the republic, he clearly hoped to stay on. He wrote an open letter to the Medicis, in effect commending himself to them but not in a fawning manner and not by renouncing the past.[5] But Machiavelli was purged in November and arrested and tortured in February, 1513, when his name appeared on a list of suspected republican conspirators. He was released in the general amnesty joyously proclaimed when Cardinal de' Medici was elected pope as Leo X. After a month of vainly trying to win employment from Giuliano de' Medici, the best prospect as patron, Machiavelli gave up and took his wife and four children to his villa at Sant' Andrea, between Florence and San Casciano.

Machiavelli relieved the frustrations of his enforced idleness occasionally by slipping off to Florence to visit his favorite prostitutes and drinking companions but mainly by writing long letters on current politics to his friend Francesco Vettori and by composing a treatise on politics called *De principatibus* (*On Principalities*), later called *Il principe* (*The Prince*). (Vettori, the friend who was in the best position to help Machiavelli win the favor of the Medicis, failed to do so—and probably did not try very hard. The voluminous correspondence ended in 1515 and Machiavelli did not write him again for twelve years.) Machiavelli stayed at Sant' Andrea for fourteen of the remaining fifteen years of his life, generally unhappy and always longing to get back into political circles. From 1515 to 1520 Machiavelli wrote most of his literary works: the *Discourses*;[6] *The Golden Ass*, a poem; *Dialogue on Our Language*; *Mandragola*, a well-wrought, bawdy play; *The Art of War* (*Arta della guerra*); *Life of Castruccio* (*Vita di Castruccio*); and probably also in this period *Belfagor*, a satiric *novella* on marriage. He wrote the *Historie fiorentine* from 1520 to 1525 under a stipend from Pope Leo X.[7]

During this period of maximum literary output, Machiavelli enjoyed the stimulus of

[5] The letter is reproduced in Pasquale Villari, *The Life and Times of Niccolo Machiavelli*, new ed., trans. by Linda Villari (New York: Scribner's, 1898), Vol. 2, p. 25. The original source is Machiavelli, *Opere* (Florence: Usigli, 1857), p. 1146.

[6] The younger and more northern scholars tend to argue that the *Discourses* was begun after completion of *The Prince*. See Felix Gilbert, "The Structure and Composition of Machiavelli's *Discorsi*," *Journal of the History of Ideas*, Vol. 14 (1953), pp. 136–56, and Hans Baron, "Machiavelli: The Republican Citizen and the Author of 'The Prince,'" *English Historical Review*, Vol. 76 (1961), pp. 217–53. The older and more southern scholars tend to argue that the *Discourses* was begun first then interrupted for *The Prince*. See Federico Chabod, *Machiavelli and the Renaissance*, trans. by David Moore (London: Bowes & Bowes, 1958), pp. 31–32, and Roberto Ridolfi, *The Life of Niccolo Machiavelli*, trans. by Cecil Grayson (Chicago: Univ. of Chicago Press, 1963), pp. 294–95. The argument turns in part on the character of Machiavelli's statement in Chapter 2 of *Il principe* that he will not speak of republics because he has dealt with them elsewhere at length. There is no clear evidence that a treatise on republics other than the *Discourses* existed before *The Prince*; neither is there clear evidence that Machiavelli began the *Discourses* first. But when evidence is clear scholars are denied the pleasures of argument. See E. W. Cochrane, "Machiavelli: 1940–1960," *Journal of Modern History*, Vol. 33 (1961), pp. 113–36.

[7] The grant, which came through Cardinal Giulio de' Medici, indicated that Machiavelli had finally won a measure of favor from the Medicis. He knew very well that his treatise could not be directly critical of the Medicis' role in Florentine history: "I cannot write this history . . . as I would write it if I were free from all obligations. The facts will be accurate and I will not leave anything out; I will simply avoid discussing the general causes of events. . . . Note well what I make his [Cosimo's] adversaries say, because that which I do not wish to say as coming from myself, I shall put in the mouths of his adversaries." This is a report by Donato Giannotti of Machiavelli's conversation with him expressed in a letter to Marcantonio Michieli, June 30, 1533, in Ridolfi, pp. 198–99. See also Villari, Vol. 2, p. 342.

the Oricellari circle, a gathering of literary connoisseurs and political expatriates led by the cultured cripple Cosimo Rucellai, whose grandfather had built the Oricellari Gardens in Florence. The circle members read and criticized the discourses as Machiavelli wrote them. Machiavelli dedicated the work to Cosimo and another member, Zanobi Buondelmonte. But the circle was shattered by the participation of many of its members (including Buondelmonte but not Machiavelli) in a conspiracy to assassinate Cardinal Giulio de' Medici that was discovered and foiled in 1522. The next year Giulio became Pope Clement VII.

In 1525 Machiavelli briefly entered the world of politics again when he went to Rome to attempt to convince Clement to organize a papal militia large enough to repel the Spanish and German troops of the encroaching Imperial (that is, of the Holy Roman Empire) Army. He seemed for a time to have the indecisive Clement's support but nothing happened. The next year, as chairman of a local committee, Machiavelli made a vital study of the decrepit fortifications for the city of Florence. His friendship with historian Francesco Guicciardini, a senior papal official, plus the spreading political chaos now also made possible some diplomatic excursions in a semiofficial capacity. In April and May of 1527 the marauding Imperial troops by-passed the tense defenders at Florence, headed straight for Rome, and sacked it. With Clement defeated and in hiding in Rome, the anti-Medici faction in Florence felt free to proclaim the old republic once again. They did so on May 16; on May 17 the Medicis left the city.

Machiavelli now had hopes for a post of importance in Florence but, ironically—as in 1512, when he had been tied to the Soderini —now he was identified with the Medicis, even though others less loyal to the republic but more wealthy won posts. Ten days after the republicans filled Machiavelli's old secretaryship with another man, Machiavelli, at fifty-eight, was dead, probably from an ulcer. It would be uncharitable to suggest that the mere loss of a job so aggravated Machiavelli's illness. He had learned by this time not to expect justice from life; but he was also worried about his family and the fate of a badly defended Florence.

During his lifetime, Machiavelli wrote many letters. They are most revealing of the man:

> His main topics are scandal and politics, but the tone constantly varies from boredom and depression, on the one hand, to exhilaration and conviction on the other, now relaxed and desultory, now indulging in flights of fantasy or burlesque. Lyrical and ardent in one place, foul-mouthed and off-hand in another, sensitive, changeable, self-conscious: it is in these letters rather than in his measured works that Machiavelli comes near to convincing us of one of his favorite themes: that human nature always remains the same.[8]

MACHIAVELLI, PHILOSOPHY, AND THE RENAISSANCE

We have outlined Machiavelli's life at some length because so much of his political writing is directed at the particular rather than at the general and, more for him than for most theorists, a proper understanding of his life seems bound up with a proper understanding of his writings. First, the ambiguity of Machiavelli's intention is an especially prominent problem in evaluating his work. Taking his known republican sympathies as a starting place, some say the dedication of *The Prince* to Giuliano de' Medici and, after Giuliano died, to Lorenzo de' Medici is a clue that what follows is but the work of an office-seeker.[9] Others go to the opposite ex-

[8] Hale, pp. 4–5.

[9] Giuliano, eldest son of Lorenzo the Magnificent (1449–92), ruled Florence after the expulsion of the Soderini in 1512 but without much enthusiasm. He became the Duke of Nemours in 1513. His successor was his young nephew, Lorenzo (1492–1519), who became Duke of Urbino in 1516. Machiavelli changed the dedication of *The Prince* in 1516, when Giuliano died. Though Machiavelli calls young Lorenzo the Magnificent in the dedication, he should not be confused with his grandfather. Machiavelli sent Lorenzo a copy of *The*

treme and say *The Prince* is nothing but an anti-Medici satire.[10] Still others have taken the content seriously but in a curiously different way. Some of his own zealously republican friends said after his death that Machiavelli wrote *The Prince* in hopes the Medicis would follow to their doom the policies it suggested![11]

Some find passionate, pugnacious, and sometimes bitter devotion to vigorous and even violent action more prominent than devotion to this or that form of rule in Machiavelli. (His friend Guicciardini, a more successful politician than Machiavelli, thought he took "an excessive delight in . . . violent remedies."[12]) These scholars admire Machiavelli's fierce style but find him predominantly parochial;[13] few consider him a philosopher. The Italian Renaissance did not neglect philosophy: Ficino and Pico della Mirandola made Florence under Lorenzo the Magnificent a center of Platonism. Their contemporary at Padua, Pietro Pomponazzi, propounded a sophisticated skepticism and materialism. He, in turn, was challenged by the orthodox Aristotelianism of Agostino Nifo at Bologna.[14] Machiavelli had no part in these movements of thought; he was apparently uninterested in traditional philosophy. Granting this, some would contend that he merely assumes the validity of most traditional philosophizing, whereas some would find him an insistent antiphilosopher, a subverter of tradition.[15]

The philosophical as well as the political atmosphere of the Renaissance, we must remember, was powerfully affected by more than a new-found delight in classical ideals. There were negative influences as well. Many people were reacting unfavorably to the corruption of the Roman Church, of which Alexander VI and his Borgia relatives are as representative as any.[16] The breakup of

Prince but it was never acknowledged, perhaps because, as one story has it, Lorenzo was far more interested in a gift of two greyhounds he received the same day.

10 See Garret Mattingly, "Machiavelli's *Prince:* Political Science or Political Satire?" *American Scholar,* Vol. 27 (1958), pp. 482–91. "Only in a satire can one understand the choice of Cesare Borgia as the model prince" (p. 490).

11 Herbert Butterfield, *The Statecraft of Machiavelli* (New York: Crowell-Collier, 1962), p. 74.

12 *Considerazioni sui discorsi del Machiavelli,* Bk. I, Ch. 26. Quoted in Federico Chabod, p. 113.

13 Butterfield finds Machiavelli doctrinaire, even eccentric, without significant linkage to ancient thought, and attached to the pathological in politics: ". . . his system of statecraft seems to imply the conditions of Renaissance Italy." Chabod finds the secret of Machiavelli's enduring appeal not in philosophical wisdom or historical accuracy but in the vitality of his brilliant but often vernacular style. Ironically, notes Chabod, "All the errors and defects of historical evaluation which had determined the creation and the practical ineffectiveness of *The Prince* . . . became the chief source of its immense vitality: if Machiavelli had judged the events of his time in a truly critical spirit he would not have written his treatise."

14 See Ernst Cassirer, *The Individual and the Cosmos in Renaissance Philosophy,* trans. by Mario Domandi (New York: Barnes & Noble, 1963); Paul Oskar Kristeller, *Renaissance Thought: The Classic, Scholastic, and Humanist Strains* (New York: Harper & Row, 1961); N. A. Robb, *Neo-platonism of the Italian Renaissance* (London: Allen & Unwin, 1935); and Ferdinand Schevill, *Medieval and Renaissance Florence,* Vol. 2, *The Coming of Humanism and the Age of the Medici* (New York: Harper & Row, 1963). In his *History of Florence* Machiavelli mentions Ficino only in passing as a member of Cosimo de' Medici's household. See Bk. VII, Ch. 6.

15 See Charles N. R. McCoy, "The Place of Machiavelli in the History of Political Thought," *American Political Science Review,* Vol. 37 (1943), pp. 626–41, and literature cited there. McCoy agrees with Allan Gilbert that Machiavelli is philosophically significant but disagrees sharply with Gilbert's thesis that *The Prince* is consistent with traditional thought and is merely typical of many medieval handbooks for kings. See Allan H. Gilbert, *Machiavelli's Prince and Its Forerunners* (Durham: Duke Univ. Press, 1938). McCoy would agree with Strauss that *The Prince* and the *Discourses* are of a piece but Strauss stands alone in finding an incredible systematization in Machiavelli. See Leo Strauss, *Thoughts on Machiavelli* (New York: Free Press, 1958).

16 Alexander made his illegitimate son Cesare a cardinal at the age of eighteen (he was never a priest) by means of a papal bull attributing his paternity to someone else. But when in 1498 Cesare wanted to give up the cardinalate for political reasons, which normally could not be done, Alexander convened a papal council that obligingly annulled the appointment by declaring Cesare the son of Alexander after all! The Borgias were not as vile as most historians have for centuries made them out to be and the scores of Spanish relatives at court were probably more of an irritant in Rome than the generally spurious allegations of sexual license. Machiavelli's estimate of Alexander in *The Prince* (Ch.

Western unity could be seen in the bewildering hodgepodge of shifting alliances and in the intrigue, deception, and warfare among the Western powers (not to mention the five major states of Italy alone—Venice, Milan, Florence, Naples, and the Papal States). The fall of Constantinople in 1453 to the Ottoman Turks ended a thousand years of Eastern Empire and caused great excitement in Europe and talk of new crusades. There developed a morbid fascination with oriental despots of the past, such as Genghis Khan and his descendant Tamerlane.) We are presented with the oddity of a pope, Pius II, writing a biography of Tamerlane.) Machiavelli's attitude toward religion is well known: he not only made light of it in general but blamed Christianity in particular for the division of Italy and the decline of military discipline.[17]

Antipathies alone, of course, cannot produce a body of thought as extensive as Machiavelli's. The rediscovery of classical Roman ideals helped shape the form in which Machiavelli's most general assertions were put—especially the pagan ideal of *virtù,* or manly strength; the heroic ideal of doing battle with *fortuna,* an almost personified fate; and a nonmystical adaptation of the Stoics' acceptance of *necessità:*

> The *virtù* of the conquering prince became the source of order, and since the Christian, transcendental order of existence had become a dead letter for the Italian thinkers of the fifteenth century, the *virtù ordinate* of the prince, the only ordering force experienced as real, acquired human-divine, heroic proportions. . . . The evocation of the mythical hero is at the center of Machiavelli's work in the same sense that the evocation of the philosopher king is at the center of Plato's work. Machiavelli had created a myth; this fact must be the basis of interpretation if we wish to avoid the misunderstanding of his theory of politics as the shallow insight that foul means are frequently more helpful than fair ones in acquiring political power.[18]

If generations of debate over Machiavelli's intention and even his significance have not settled the questions at issue, we cannot hope to settle them in these few pages; but we can try to cut through some of the confusion surrounding Machiavelli by looking at what he actually wrote.

THE PRINCE

The Prince is a short work of twenty-six chapters, compact and crisp, even tendentious in tone, but not rigorously systematic.[19] The dedication to Lorenzo (see p. 192, *n.* 9) has some superficial flattery but is scarcely fawning and is anything but modest. Machiavelli offers "that knowledge of the deeds of great men which I have acquired through a long experience of modern events [*cose moderne*] and a constant study of the past."[20] He prom-

18) is both uncharitable and inaccurate. See Maria Bellonci, *The Life and Times of Lucrezia Borgia,* trans. by Bernard Wall (London: Weidenfeld & Nicolson, 1953), and Rafael Sabatini, *The Life of Cesare Borgia* (New York: Brentano's, n.d.).

[17] On Machiavelli's general disregard for religion see his letter to Guicciardini written from Carpi on May 17, 1521, in Machiavelli, *Lettere familiari,* Edvardo Alvisi, ed. (Florence: Sansoni, 1883), p. 422, paraphrased in Hale, p. 205; Ridolfi, p. 190; and Villari, Vol. 2, p. 325. But in letters to friends and almost invariably in letters to his children Machiavelli nevertheless ended with *Christo ti guardi* (May Christ protect you). (*Chief Works and Others,* trans. and ed. by Allan H. Gilbert [Durham: Duke Univ. Press, 1965], Vol. 2, p. 915; written August 4, 1513.) The letter to Guicciardini referred to above, while usually treated as an attack on religion, nevertheless contains this passage: "I believe the true way of going to Paradise would be to learn the road to Hell in order to avoid it. Seeing besides this, how much credit a bad man has who conceals himself under the cloak of religion, I can easily conjecture how much of it a good man would have who in truth and not in pretense continued to tread muddy places like St. Francis." It seems clear that we are not entitled to be dogmatic on the issue of Machiavelli's religion or irreligion.

[18] Eric Voegelin, "Machiavelli's *Prince:* Background and Formation," *Review of Politics,* Vol. 13 (1951), p. 165. Voegelin is the source of the statements above about the oriental influence on Renaissance politics.

[19] Strauss would disagree. See p. 213 below.

[20] *The Prince and The Discourses,* trans. by Luigi Ricci, revised by E. R. P. Vincent, and Christian E. Detmold (New York: Random House, Modern Library,

ises that his work will be without the "superficial attractions and ornaments" that other writers use to adorn their works. This may be vain but it is not inaccurate. Following a dubious analogy about princes on the mountain peaks and those "of the populace" who comment on them while sitting in the valley, Machiavelli inserts what seems unabashed self-advertisement: "Should Your Highness gaze down from the summit of your lofty position toward this humble spot, you will recognize the great and unmerited sufferings inflicted on me by a cruel fate."

Republics and Principalities

Chapter 1 is a one-paragraph statement of the structure presupposed by the whole of *The Prince*. All states, says Machiavelli categorically, are either republics or principalities.[21] Machiavelli's knowledge of Polybius and through him of Aristotle's six-fold classification of governments makes his reduction of "all states" to the two forms all the more striking. (The *Discourses,* Book I, Chapter 2, describes the traditional six-fold classification.) Machiavelli presumably included democracies, aristocracies, and oligarchies under the label "republic" and despotisms as well as the traditionally legitimate monarchies under the label "principality." But in Chapter 1 Machiavelli does suggest two subcategories of principalities: hereditary states and new states; new states are either entirely new or are new dominions annexed to hereditary states, as Naples was united with Spain in 1504.

Chapter 2 is devoted to hereditary principalities, which the author points out are far more stable than new states. Perhaps for that reason Machiavelli is less interested in discussing them than he is in discussing new states, for this chapter is only three paragraphs long while Chapter 3, "Of Mixed Principalities," is fifteen paragraphs long. The opening sentence of Chapter 2 is of crucial importance, for it limits the coverage of *The Prince* to principalities, noting that the author has discussed republics earlier.[22] Machiavelli illustrates the stability of hereditary principalities by dubious reference to the Duke of Ferrara in 1484 and Pope Julius II in 1510. The chapter ends by noting that change can be assimilated into hereditary regimes because each change leaves an *addentellato* (the toothed wall left on a building) for future construction.

In new principalities, we are told in Chapter 3, it is different. Men change masters willingly in hopes of continually bettering themselves. Hence a conquering prince will have not only enemies in those he injures but untrustworthy allies in those whose expectations cannot be fulfilled. If he is to take possession of a province, he "will always need the favour of the inhabitants."[23] Winning this favor is easier if the prince shares the language of the inhabitants, if they are unaccustomed to freedom, and if the old ruling family is extinct. If the old ruling family is extinct, if the customs of the prince are similar to those of the new subjects, and if he makes no basic changes in laws or taxes, then he may be able to rule in absentia. But if the new language, laws, and customs are different, he must take up residence in the new state—or, even better, plant a colony of his people there. A mere garrison of troops is not enough, for "men must either be caressed or else annihilated; they will revenge themselves for small injuries, but cannot do so for great ones; the

1940), p. 3. Subsequent page references are to this edition. Mark Musa has translated and edited a useful new bilingual edition of *The Prince* (New York: St. Martin's Press, 1964).

[21] "Principalities" is a better translation of *principati* than the frequent "monarchies" is.

[22] We have already seen (p. 191, *n.* 6, above) how scholarly opinion divides on the question of whether this refers to the *Discourses*. The matter of dates is not as important as the amount of energy expended on the debate might make it seem, for none dispute that *The Prince* was written during one brief and concentrated effort or that some of the ideas found in the *Discourses* appeared in letters prior to *The Prince*.

[23] Musa translates *favore* as "backing" rather than as "favor."

injury therefore that we do to a man must be such that we need not fear his vengeance."

The Strategy of Survival

The proper strategy with reference to adjacent principalities is to lead and defend the weak neighbors and endeavor to weaken the strong neighbors (though the prince should not let them be invaded by an even stronger foreigner). A prince will thus be invited to intervene in disputes by those elements who are discontented "either through ambition or fear." The Romans in their captured provinces "always followed this policy." The Romans were sharp-eyed, too, at spotting disorders while they were still remote and nipping them in the bud. The action of Louis XII of France in Italy is an example of the opposite: he was invited in by the Venetians and his victories won him supporters but he imprudently helped Pope Alexander VI to occupy Romagna and thereby weakened himself. Machiavelli lists six mistakes Louis committed but the advice of the chapter boils down to two maxims: "One ought never to allow a disorder to take place in order to avoid war, for war is not thereby avoided, but only deferred to your disadvantage" and "whoever is the cause of another becoming powerful is ruined himself." In an "I was there" aside, Machiavelli informs his reader that when he was at Nantes in 1500 he told the Cardinal of Rouen that the French did not understand politics if they could allow the Church to become so powerful with impunity. This was very current history for Machiavelli[24] and we cannot believe that he is interested in generalization merely for its own sake. Even this early in *The Prince,* however, certain theoretical issues are implicit. Although ancient Rome is a chief source of examples for Machiavelli, his principal subject is the new state and the new state is a problem not known as such to Rome. As we saw in discussing the Stoics, the founding of Rome by Romulus at a fixed point in the mythical past was a source of stability or at least a symbol of stability. In his emphasis upon the founding of a new state Machiavelli is talking about—or, rather, implying—the recreation of a mythical past in the nonmythical present. This recreation has two implications about which we and Machiavelli will have more to say later: (1) the need for a powerful individual founder, one powerful enough to surmount the forces of historical necessity, and (2) the kind of moral vacuum that exists before an authoritative regime comes into being.

In Chapter 4 Machiavelli distinguishes two ways of governing kingdoms, however they may have been established. The first way is for the prince to be assisted in ruling only by his own servants; hence his authority [*autorità*] is complete; Turkey is Machiavelli's contemporary example. The second way is for the prince to rule with the aid of barons who have lands of their own and derive their position from the antiquity of their blood, as in contemporary France.

> Whoever now considers these two states will see that it would be difficult to acquire the state of the Turk; but having conquered it, it would be very easy to hold it. In many respects, on the other hand, it would be easy to conquer the kingdom of France, but there would be great difficulty in holding it.[25]

He then shifts to ancient examples. Darius III, King of Persia, ruled without dependence upon nobles. Hence Alexander, once he had conquered him, ruled securely. The Romans,

[24] At the time of writing, thirteen years later, Machiavelli still favored the French in Italy, though, curiously, his opinion is expressed with more perspective in a letter to Vettori (August 10, 1513) than in *The Prince:* "You do not want this poor King of France to have Lombardy again, and I do want it. I fear that your not wanting and my wanting have the same foundation of a natural affection or passion, which makes you say *no* and me, *yes.* You dignify your *no* by showing that there would be more difficulty in bringing about peace if the King were to return to Lombardy; I have shown in order to dignify my *yes,* that such is not the truth, and further that peace made in the method I indicate will be more secure and more solid" (*Chief Works,* Vol. 2, pp. 915–16).

[25] *The Prince,* p. 16. Strauss suggests that in his reference to France in this chapter Machiavelli is really referring to Italy. See Strauss, p. 66.

however, had trouble with Spain, France, and Greece, until "after the extinction of the old line of princes."

When a city or dominion has lived under its own laws, Machiavelli tells us in Chapter 5, it may be harder for a prince to win over its citizens. Living there himself and allowing them to keep most of their own laws may help but "there is no sure method of holding them except by despoiling them."

The New Order

When, in Chapter 6, Machiavelli turns to the individual models a prince should imitate, the result is apt to surprise us. Who are the "great men" (*uomini grandi*), the "most excellent" (*eccellentissimi*) ones, that Machiavelli offers as models for the "prudent" man who becomes a prince and who must rely on his own *virtù* rather than *fortuna?* Not Cesare Borgia (to whom tribute was paid in Chapter 7) but Moses, founder of post-exilic Israel; Cyrus, founder of the Persian Empire; Romulus, founder of Rome; and Theseus, founder of Athens. The last two are mythical figures and all four are colored with myth. They are "most excellent" presumably because of their compelling ability to lead and because of their courage to try wholesale reform, to build a "new order of things":

> there is nothing more difficult to carry out, nor more doubtful of success, nor more dangerous to handle, than to initiate a new order of things. For the reformer has enemies in all those who profit by the old order, and only lukewarm defenders in all those who would profit by the new order, this lukewarmness arising partly from fear of their adversaries, who have the laws in their favor; and partly from the incredulity of mankind, who do not truly believe in anything new until they have had actual experience of it.[26]

Therefore, unless they have great strength, such reformers fail; but if they can depend on their own strength and are willing and able to use force, "they rarely fail. Thus it comes about that all armed prophets have conquered and unarmed ones failed." Force is necessary not only for conquering but for "compelling believers to believe" after conquest, when belief begins to fail. The four men named were able to do this but, though he sought to be a sweeping reformer, Savonarola could not or did not compel belief and so his authority in Florence ebbed away.

Here we see emerging a favorite theme of Machiavelli, one that made him attractive to historians of the Croce school: history is moved by great men whose example exists for our imitation. Moreover, the great man is one who does not shrink from the methods necessary to succeed. Whatever the pretense, history honors those who succeed rather than those of pure motive who fail.

To the four "high examples" Machiavelli gives in this chapter he adds "a lesser one," Hiero of Syracuse, who, though of lower ability, became a prince without the aid of *fortuna* (apart from the opportunity). This reference provides a transition to Chapter 7, which concerns new dominions acquired by the power of others or by *fortuna*. In such a case the prince may rise to power rapidly and easily but get into trouble in trying to maintain his position once he has reached the top. Machiavelli employs the analogy of roots, which must grow deep or wide if the first storm is not to topple the plant.

From recent memory Machiavelli offers the examples of Francesco Sforza, who became Duke of Milan through his own ability, and Cesare Borgia, who became Duke of Valentine and ruler of the papal states by the influence of his father (see p. 193, *n.* 16, above) and then lost his power when that influence failed, "although every measure was adopted by him and everything done that a prudent and capable man could do." He continues: "I know of no better precepts for a new prince to follow than may be found in his actions; and if his measures were not successful, it was through no fault of his own but only by the most extraordinary malignity

[26] *The Prince,* p. 21. In *Chief Works,* a recent collection of Machiavelli's writings, references to Cyrus appear eight times; to Moses, five; to Romulus, five; and to Theseus, three. The references usually illustrate exactly what is illustrated above. See also Chabod, p. 69, *n.* 2.

of fortune." Machiavelli is quite inaccurate here, glossing over Cesare's role in his own ignominious decline. It is not the only time Machiavelli is inaccurate either out of carelessness or, as is probable here, for the sake of bolstering his argument with pseudofact.

But perhaps we miss the point if we focus in the wrong way on Machiavelli's flaws as a historian. In the summary of Cesare's actions in Chapter 7 there is little attempt to whitewash his ruthlessness. Cesare's aim was properly, says Machiavelli, to destroy ruling families who stood in his way. Machiavelli exaggerates both the amount of power left to Cesare after the death of his father and the effect of Cesare's illness in vitiating that power. That is to say, in making Cesare into a model hero he exaggerates his power rather than his humaneness. (This is what enables some to call *The Prince* a satire.) Machiavelli is neither an objective historian nor an apologist for local interests but a pleader for a general ideology of success.

Who Is Wicked?

The claim that Machiavelli is not really a Machiavellian, that he is not bereft of scruples, rests not only on the *Discourses,* which we shall examine shortly, but also on passages such as those found in Chapter 8 of *The Prince,* which examines princes who have gained their position by wickedness (*scelera*). Here, for example, he says, "It cannot be called virtue to kill one's fellow-citizens, betray one's friends, be without faith, without pity, and without religion; by these methods one may indeed gain power, but not glory."[27] Machiavelli is talking about Agathocles the Sicilian, who, after summoning the senators and rich people of Syracuse together for deliberations, slaughtered the lot of them. Yet Machiavelli's condemnation of Agathocles is highly equivocal. Cesare, who receives unstinted praise, was guilty of the same sort of murder by deception as Agathocles, though on a lesser scale. In Chapter 6 Machiavelli acknowledges at least Cesare's deception (Cesare "dissembled his aims so well . . ."), but he glosses over the messy consequences ("[the Orsini] fell into his hands. Having thus suppressed these leaders"). Moreover, in facing and surviving dangers, in "supporting and surmounting obstacles," and in "greatness of soul" (*grandezza dello animo*) Agathocles is inferior to no one. *Grandezza dello animo* is an important virtue—and sign of *virtù*—for Machiavelli throughout the whole of *The Prince,* so it is something of a surprise that he here bestows it upon the prime example of a wicked prince. Nevertheless, Agathocles' cruelty, inhumanity, and countless atrocities, says Machiavelli, "do not permit of his being named among the most famous men. We cannot attribute to fortune or virtue [*alla fortuna o alla virtù*] that which he achieved without either." Agathocles, an ancient and forgotten figure, cannot—certainly—be named among the famous. But Machiavelli leaves us wondering whether he is to be admired.

As if to pile example upon example, Machiavelli follows the ancient case of Agathocles with the modern case of Oliverotto of Fermo, who executed a *coup d'état* by means of the same kind of deception just described. Machiavelli does not stress but is clearly aware of the irony in the fact that this Oliverotto was himself subsequently deceived and strangled by Cesare.

The lesson of this chapter, in case it should seem by now a bit obscure, is that cruelties may be exploited "well or badly":

> Well committed may be called those (if it is permissible to use the word well of evil) which are perpetuated once for the need of securing one's self, and which afterwards are not persisted in, but are exchanged for measures as useful to the subjects as possible. Cruelties ill

[27] "Virtue" here is *virtù* used in its more moralistic sense. The same word is elsewhere translated *ingenuity, ability, vigor, worth, capacity,* and even *power.* The word "power" in this translation, however, is from *imperio* (*imperio ma non gloria*), which does not imply naked force but rulership with a degree of legitimacy. Hence the quotation is not the simple moral affirmation it seems. *Imperio* may, indeed, be beyond good and evil.

committed are those which, although at first few, increase rather than diminish with time.[28]

Hence cruelties and injuries should be done all at once "so that less tasted they will give less offense." But benefits should be confered little by little and over a period of time. This is a rule of thumb most able executives will follow. But the curious thing is that by the end of the chapter skillful cruelty comes to have a value of its own.

The Civic Principality

Sometimes a prince comes to power by favor of the people or by favor of the aristocracy rather than by crime and violence. This creates what Machiavelli calls a civic principality (*principato civile*). Such an accession to power does not depend on *virtù* or *fortuna* alone "but rather on cunning assisted by fortune."[29] The moral superiority of such an accession is not altogether evident; indeed Machiavelli never tries to clarify the qualitative distinction between the *principato civile* and other principalities. We are, in fact, led to doubt that he intended more than a superficial distinction between principalities established by force and those established with popular or aristocratic support. Later in Chapter 9 he speaks of a "civil prince" becoming an "absolute prince" too late to save his city. The implication is that the price of civility of this kind is generally too high. Before this, Machiavelli argues that in most cities the clash of two factions, popular and aristocratic, produces one of three effects: princely rule, liberty, or license. But true to the self-imposed limitation stated in Chapter 2, namely that this book deals only with principalities, Machiavelli saves discussion of aristocratic liberty and popular license for the *Discourses*.

Machiavelli is not consistent in all things but he does maintain the viewpoint of the prince throughout this work. He declares that if the prince is put in office by the aristocracy he is apt to have trouble because he is then surrounded by men who think they are his equals. The people, even when they are responsible for installing a prince, are more willing to obey and easier to satisfy. Moreover, "the aim of the people is more honest than that of the nobility, the latter desiring to oppress, and the former merely to avoid oppression." Hence it is easier to win the favor of the people but also more necessary to have their friendship in time of adversity. At such times, especially if the prince has relied too heavily on his magistrates, the magistrates may turn out to constitute an independent center of power. A prudent prince will not only keep his magistrates clearly subordinate; he will also refrain from relying too heavily on judgments of the loyalty of his people made during peacetime, when loyalty is easy, and will have coercive measures in reserve to insure the people's faithfulness at all times.

A prince who would be self-sustained will also attend to the fortification of his town—this was one of Machiavelli's bureaucratic specialties—and will keep a year's supply of food, drink, fuel, and arms in the storehouses. He will maintain a constantly high degree of military readiness. During a siege he will alternately bolster hope and instill fear of the enemies' cruelty. The citizens' military sacrifices on behalf of the prince and the loss of their fields to enemy action will not sour their loyalty, for "it is the nature of men to be as much bound by the benefits they confer as by those they receive."[30]

Popes as Rulers

The last chapter of *The Prince* nominally devoted to the different types of principalities is Chapter 11, on the "ecclesiastical principality." Like the others, says Machiavelli, ec-

[28] *The Prince*, p. 34.

[29] "Cunning assisted by fortune" is a translation of *astuzia fortunata* but surely *astuzia* is part of *virtù*. Machiavelli expands and contracts the content of *virtù* often in mystifying ways.

[30] The rule seems to hold in our own day: those individuals who have suffered most grievously from war have a greater tendency to support military solutions than those untouched by war. Gold-star mothers are not conspicuously pacifist.

clesiastical principalities are acquired by *virtù* or *fortuna* but unlike the others they can be maintained without either, for they are "sustained by ancient religious customs." Princes of the Church have states but need not defend them, have subjects but need not govern them. Since the subjects are not governed, they do not resent it and these principalities alone are "secure and happy."

Since ecclesiastical principalities are upheld by higher causes (*cogione superiori*) that the merely human mind cannot attain, says Machiavelli, it would be presumptuous to discuss them; he accordingly declines to do so. "However," he adds impishly, "I might be asked how it has come about that the Church has reached such great temporal power." He then proceeds to describe the background of the Orsini and Colonna factions in Rome and their methods of keeping the papacy weak until Alexander VI and his son Cesare "showed how a Pope might prevail by money and by force." After 1503 Julius II extended this power—gaining Bologna, putting down the Venetians, and driving the French from Italy. Hence Pope Leo X (Giovanni de' Medici, who became pope in 1513, the same year in which Machiavelli was writing) "has found the pontificate in a very powerful condition, from which it is hoped that as those Popes made it great by force of arms, so he through his goodness and infinite other virtues will make it both great and venerated."

The flattery of the previous sentence is conspicuous, since it is quite unlike the surrounding wordage in tone. The most striking thing about Chapter 11 is that although its title is "Of Ecclesiastical Principalities" its content is military history. Machiavelli promised not to speak of things ecclesiastical per se but he scarcely speaks of things political, for—unlike the preceding chapters, where history is used to illustrate general maxims of political rule—here, except for the last sentence quoted above, the history seems purely descriptive. Machiavelli's respect for popes like Alexander and Julius, who rule with "money and force" in a very unpapal manner, is evident but his feeling toward popes who rule in a proper papal manner remains carefully shrouded.

The Militia

Chapters 12, 13, and 14 record the Machiavellian enthusiasm for civilian armies and distaste for mercenary troops.[31] Both concepts are pronounced and both rest on an explicit assumption concerning the importance of arms—an assumption so sweeping it takes our breath away: "The chief foundation of all states, whether new, old, or mixed, are good laws and good arms. And as there cannot be good laws where there are not good arms, and where there are good arms there must be good laws, I will not now discuss the laws, but will speak of the arms." Why good arms "must" generate good laws Machiavelli nowhere attempts to demonstrate, yet the whole of *The Prince* gains its unity of purpose from this premise.

Machiavelli can scarcely say enough against mercenary troops:

> they are disunited, ambitious, without discipline, faithless, bold amongst friends, cowardly amongst enemies, they have no fear of God, and keep no faith with men. Ruin is only deferred as long as the assault is postponed; in peace you are despoiled by them, and in war by the enemy. The cause of this is that they have no love or other motive to keep them in the field beyond the trifling wage, which is not enough to make them ready to die for you. They are quite willing to be your soldiers so long as you do not make war, but when war comes, it is either fly or decamp altogether.[32]

Mercenary captains are either able men or not. If able, they are unreliable and will exploit you; if not able, they will ruin you. Hence, says Machiavelli, a prince must lead his own troops and a republic must send its own citizens to battle: ". . . it is seen by experience that only princes and armed republics make very great progress." Machiavelli saddled the Church with partial responsibility

[31] The theme is not confined to *The Prince* but is found in the whole corpus of Machiavelli's writings, public and private.

[32] *The Prince,* Ch. 12, p. 45.

for first depending upon mercenary troops, since its priests were not accustomed to bear arms. He gives discredit for being the first organizer of Italian mercenary troops to Como of Romagna, who died in 1409. Como and his successors restricted themselves almost completely to cavalry and discredited the infantry mainly for convenience' sake with, for Machiavelli, disastrous results. They fought by day only, took prisoners with excessive gentility, and "used every means to spare themselves." Machiavelli's bitter sarcasm almost explodes: ". . . the result of their prowess has been that Italy has been overrun by Charles, preyed on by Louis, and insulted by the Swiss. . . . they have reduced Italy to slavery and degradation." The passion of the last chapter of *The Prince,* which is often thought to set it apart from the more "objective" earlier chapters, is surely foreshadowed here.

Moreover, here as elsewhere the topical—even parochial—character of Machiavelli's historical examples is evident. They fall into two categories: classical references, sometimes used carelessly, and virtually contemporary and Italian references, such as those to Francesco Sforza of Milan, Paolo Vitelli of Florence, or, inevitably, Cesare Borgia. We sometimes suspect Machiavelli of spreading a thin patina of classical learning over conclusions of a very local sort.

Machiavelli called those troops borrowed from allies auxiliaries and considered them "as useless as mercenaries" but more dangerous because, being united under one command, they were more apt to be turned against their erstwhile employers: "In a word, the greatest danger with mercenaries lies in their cowardice and reluctance to fight, but with auxiliaries the danger lies in their courage."

If a prince is to be so preoccupied with military matters, we might well ask, how is he to have time for other things? Machiavelli does not shrink from answering this question and his answer is astounding: "A Prince should therefore have no other aim or thought, nor take up any other thing for his study, but war and its organization and discipline, for that is the only art that is necessary to one who commands."[33] In short, "there is no comparison whatever between an armed and a disarmed man."

How We Live and How We Ought to Live

A justification of sorts for this preoccupation with force comes in Chapter 15, in which Machiavelli promises to inquire into the methods and rules of a prince as regards his subjects and friends. Machiavelli boldly distinguishes his position "from the opinions of others" in that he will "go to the real truth of the matter" rather than expound "imagined republics and principalities." He explains, "for how we live is so far removed from how we ought to live, that he who abandons what is done for what ought to be done, will rather learn to bring about his own ruin than his preservation."[34] So many men are not good that a good man in their midst comes only to grief. Hence a prince with good impulses must actually "learn how not to be good."

Of course popular praise or blame attaches to certain qualities reputed to be in anyone so highly placed as a prince. Therefore, whatever his behavior, "he should be prudent enough to avoid the scandal of those vices which would lose him the state." Yet, Machiavelli cautions, prudence does not mean that simply to avoid scandal one should avoid those harsh actions that may be necessary to save the state: ". . . some things which seem

[33] Machiavelli continues: "Among other evils caused by being disarmed, it renders you contemptible," which recalls his plaintive dispatch of August 27, 1500, from the court of France, where Florence could get no hearing: "They call you Mr. Nothing" (*Ser Nihilo*) (quoted in Hale, p. 52).

[34] The imaginary republic Machiavelli derides no doubt includes Plato's, which was founded "in the realm of discourse . . . for it nowhere exists on earth" (*The Republic,* 592*b*, trans. by F. M. Cornford [New York: Oxford Univ. Press, 1945]). Strauss says that Chapter 15 of *The Prince* is where Machiavelli "begins to uproot the Great Tradition." The fact that this is the only chapter in *The Prince* without historical examples is, for Strauss, a tipoff.

virtues would, if followed, lead to one's ruin, and some others which appear vices result in one's greater security and well-being." On the one hand, for example (Chapter 16), it is often necessary to have a reputation for liberality, that is, generosity, even though the defense of the state may require niggardliness. But, on the other hand, a reputation for niggardliness is not so bad as, say, a reputation for rapacity, for the former at least does not produce hatred as the latter does. Likewise (Chapter 17), a reputation for mercifulness rather than cruelty is preferred—but not if cruel acts are necessary to preserve the state:

> one ought to be both feared and loved, but as it is difficult for the two to go together, it is much safer to be feared than loved. . . . Love is held by a chain of obligation which, men being selfish, is broken whenever it serves their purpose; but fear is maintained by a dread of punishment which never fails.
>
> Still, a prince should make himself feared in such a way that if he does not gain love he at any rate avoids hatred.[35]

At least superficially, Machiavelli is a predecessor of Hobbes in emphasizing a chain of obligation based on self-interest rather than altruism. But, as we shall see, Hobbes has the self-interest of all citizens in mind and Machiavelli has the self-interest of only the prince in mind: "Men love at their own free will, but fear at the will of the prince. . . . A wise [*savio*] prince must rely on what is in his power and not on what is in the power of others."[36]

Keeping Faith

"The experience of our times" indicated to Machiavelli that princes who have "done great things . . . have had little regard for good faith" and have overcome those who make loyalty a binding virtue. Fighting with laws is the way of men and fighting with force is the way of beasts but, since the first way is "often insufficient," a prince must learn how to act the beast—and more than one kind of beast: "One must . . . be a fox to recognize traps, and a lion to frighten wolves. Those that wish to be only lions do not understand this. Therefore, a prudent ruler ought not to keep faith when by so doing it would be against his interest."[37] Machiavelli offers a kind of reverse golden rule: do unto others as you fear they will try to do unto you. But he goes beyond even this: ". . . be a great feigner and dissembler . . . men are so simple and so ready to obey present necessities, that one who deceives will always find those who allow themselves to be deceived." This seems to go beyond mere prudence to extol the pleasure of exploiting the innocent. At any rate, necessity is always at hand to justify deception: ". . . it is well to seem merciful, faithful, humane, sincere, religious, and also to be so; but you must have the mind so disposed that when it is needful to be otherwise you may be able to change to the opposite qualities."[38]

Many who have never read Machiavelli or who could locate him only uncertainly in history will respond to his name with the

[35] *The Prince,* Ch. 17, p. 61. Yet Machiavelli wrote to Vettori in August, 1513, on the character of young Lorenzo and said, "He makes himself, in short, both loved and revered, rather than feared, which, as it is the more difficult to achieve, so it is more praiseworthy in him" (quoted in *Chief Works,* Vol. 2, p. 926).

[36] "The maxims of Machiavelli go beyond public welfare in this way and cater for the private purposes of an unscrupulous prince" (Butterfield, p. 83).

[37] Machiavelli was clearly not far from the political and moral standards of his day. Pope Julius II, conquering new lands in 1506, broke several papal treaties to do so and frankly admitted his disregard for the law. His only rationalization, as Machiavelli reports it from Cesena, was that necessity forced his predecessors to make the treaties and necessity explained his "correcting these things." Machiavelli reports that when His Holiness said this, "The ambassadors remained confounded and after a few words of reply they took their leave" (Second Mission to the Court of Rome, Dispatch No. 26, October 3, 1506, in *Writings of Niccolo Machiavelli,* trans. by Christian E. Detmold [Boston: Houghton Mifflin, 1891], Vol. 4, p. 55).

[38] The virtues in Italian are *pietà, fede, integrità, umanità,* and *religione*. Machiavelli's only example in this chapter is Alexander VI: ". . . no man . . . affirmed things with stronger oaths, and no man observed them less; however, he always succeeded in his deceptions"—hardly an accurate statement.

phrase, "The end justifies the means." Certain ironies attach to this response: In the first century B.C. Syrus said, "The end justifies the means"—and he was probably not the first. What Machiavelli actually said was, *e nelle azioni di tutti gli uomini, a massime de' principi, dove non è iudizio a chi reclamare, si guarda al fini,* which, in Musa's translation comes out, "with regard to the actions of all men, and especially with princes, where there is no court of appeal, we must look at the final result."[39] In other words, in the world of affairs results are what count. This may or may not justify any given means to those results, though for most men and for most means it seems to. But the final irony of Chapter 18 is that the thrust of the chapter really seems more perverse than the merely expedient ethics of this maxim of ill repute. As we have seen, Machiavelli seems to go beyond a prudent and amoral means-ends calculation to a positive delight in deception. The means become their own end—which is nothing new—but in this case a relatively degraded means becomes the end. This theme does not, of course, overshadow the more general theme of success at all costs but sometimes we suspect that success at the cost of being decent would be a price Machiavelli would pay without pleasure, for it is one thing to say, "Let us live by the standards of the world and shun otherworldly ideals"; it is another thing to say, "Let us live by the *worst* standards of the day." However cruel and vicious much of Renaissance life was, there were also hope and love and mercy in it. Yet Machiavelli takes men neither at their best nor at their average but almost at their worst. His skeptical friend Guicciardini perceptively objected to this debasement of human nature in the name of political success.[40]

Machiavelli begins Chapter 19 by saying that the most important qualities of the prince have already been discussed and he will now deal with the rest "briefly." But Chapter 19 is the longest chapter in *The Prince*. The prince is admonished to build a reputation sufficient to avoid the hatred of the mass of the people and is comforted by evidence that a conspiracy against entrenched power rarely succeeds. Not that there is much comfort in this fact: ". . . princes not being able to avoid being hated by some one" are constantly involved in difficult balancing acts. Machiavelli suggests the venerable maxim that a king should let others handle the unpopular duties while he takes personal charge of bestowing favors—a maxim no American governor or President forgets. For instance, the kings of France created a third arbiter (*iudice terzo*), namely parliament, to check the nobles and favor the people so that the monarchs could avoid some of the nobles' displeasure at their seeming to favor the people.

Machiavelli illustrates the need to avoid hatred by citing all the Roman emperors from Marcus Aurelius to Maximinus (161–238). This imperial cross section convincingly shows how little correlation there is between moral goodness and the avoidance of hatred. Indeed, "hatred is gained as much by good works as by evil." Pertinax and Alexander were humane and good men who "came to a sad end." Commodus, Caracalla,[41] and several others died bloody deaths but Commodus

[39] *Op. cit.*, p. 149. Allan Gilbert's translation is "As to the actions of all men and especially those of princes, against whom charges cannot be brought in court, everybody looks at their result" (*Chief Works,* Vol. 1, p. 67).

[40] See Butterfield, pp. 84–85. See also the *Discourses,* Bk. I, Ch. 3: "Whoever desires to found a state and give it laws must start with assuming that all men are bad and ever ready to display their vicious nature" (*The Prince and the Discourses,* p. 117; subsequent references to the *Discourses* are to this edition). In Chapter 18 of *The Prince* Machiavelli refers to the centaur Chiron—mythical tutor of ancient princes, including Achilles—and suggests this is a symbol of the half-human, half-animal nature a prince must have. Machiavelli thereby, says Strauss, "replaces the imitation of the God-Man Christ by the imitation of the Beast-Man Chiron" (*op. cit.*, p. 78). Wood puts a less eschatological interpretation on the symbol and notes that Chiron traditionally stood for the value of hunting as a preparation for war. See Neal Wood, Introduction to his edition of Machiavelli's *The Art of War* (Indianapolis: Bobbs-Merrill, 1965), p. XLIX.

[41] Machiavelli calls Caracalla by his other name, Antoninus.

was done in as much by his indignity as by his rapacity and the cruelty of Caracalla was ended by the fluke success of a lone assassin. Emperor Septimius Severus is Machiavelli's leading example of a new prince blessed with the aforementioned qualities of the lion and the fox. He "oppressed the people" but was able to "reign happily" because he kept the soldiers friendly and displayed qualities that "astonished and stupefied" the people.

Marcus Aurelius was a better emperor than Septimius, most of us would say, and Machiavelli, in one sentence, acknowledges the "great esteem" in which Marcus was held; but he was a hereditary prince and therefore "useless . . . to . . . imitate." Moreover, Machiavelli wants a more virile model for a new prince than Marcus provides. A new prince "must take from Severus those things that are necessary to found his state, and from Marcus those that are useful and glorious for conserving a state that is already established and secure."[42]

Princely Advice

In the next four chapters (20–23), amid many contemporary examples and one classical one, Machiavelli showers the new prince with advice:

(1) Arm your citizens.
(2) Do not foment factional divisions within cities under your dominion simply to keep them weak.
(3) If leading a rebellion, beware of allied rebels after the rebellion is over (even conservatives, opposed on principle to rebellion, will, later, be more trustworthy).
(4) Build fortresses only if you are afraid of your own people ("the best fortress is to be found in the love of the people").
(5) Always undertake enterprises "under the pretext of religion."
(6) Keep the minds of subjects "uncertain and astonished."[43]
(7) Avoid neutrality; but also avoid alliances with those more powerful than yourself.
(8) "Keep the people occupied with festivals and shows."
(9) Mingle with the different guilds and classes from time to time to display your humanity, but always do so with dignity.
(10) Select ministers with brains and of utter loyalty who do not flatter.[44]

A new prince can seem ancient if he prudently observes all these things, says Machiavelli at the start of Chapter 24. This is important, for a new prince is much more carefully watched than a hereditary prince. He will have double glory if he succeeds and double shame if he fails. Rulers who have "lost their position in Italy in our days" have done so because they committed the errors discussed above. They "must not accuse fortune for having lost them, but rather their own remissness," for the only good defenses are those "which depend on yourself alone and your own ability [*virtù*]."[45]

Fortuna

What is fortune (*fortuna*)? This is the subject of Chapter 25. Here, says Chabod, Machiavelli uncertainly confronts the vexing issue of historical possibility. Could this quite imaginary new prince actually create an Italy-wide militia and unite the fragmented Italian states? Could one man actually transform

[42] The "new prince" is a term Machiavelli uses with some ambiguity. It may mean a prince who seizes an established state (Sforza in Milan or Agathocles in Syracuse) or a founder of a new state, which, in turn, may be constructed in imitation of past states or be "wholly new" (Moses). See Strauss, pp. 70–71.

[43] This is in regard to Ferdinand of Aragon, "almost . . . a new prince." Recall that Septimius Severus kept his subjects "astonished and stupefied."

[44] But only ministers should have this freedom to speak the truth to the prince without flattery, for a prince loses status when just anyone can speak the truth to him.

[45] Strauss points out that Machiavelli uses the intimate form of you ("thou") when addressing the prince or the man of action and the nonintimate "you" when addressing others. See Strauss, p. 77.

weakness into strength? Machiavelli "realizes that he must bridge the gap at a single bound, without measuring the length of his flight."[46]

There has been an ambivalence in *The Prince* toward *fortuna,* goddess of the Renaissance. In Chapter 20 we find *fortuna* raising up enemies ripe for defeat to enhance the reputation of the ascendant prince; but in Chapter 24 Machiavelli says we cannot blame *fortuna* but only ourselves if we lose. How does *fortuna* help winners without hurting losers? If *fortuna* is a mindless and omnipotent fate, how can we avoid fatalism? If Machiavelli's dreams of Italian grandeur are to have any prospect of realization, he must find a basis for hope. He tries to save his reader-prince from fatalism by splitting responsibility with *fortuna* on a businesslike basis—fifty-fifty:

> It is not unknown to me how many have been and are of the opinion that worldly events are so governed by fortune and by God, that men cannot by their prudence change them, and that on the contrary there is no remedy whatever, and for this they may judge it to be useless to toil much about them, but let things be ruled by chance. This opinion has been more held in our day, and from the great changes that have been seen, and are daily seen, beyond every human conjecture. When I think about them, at times I am partly inclined to share this opinion. Nevertheless, that our free-will may not be altogether extinguished, I think it may be true that fortune is the ruler of half our actions, but that she allows the other half or thereabouts to be governed by us.[47]

But this neat formula is immediately muddied by contradicting metaphors: first *fortuna* is a river on a wild rampage that men are incapable of opposing but that, when quiet, enables men to build dikes to resist the assault of the next flood—a thoroughly defensive stance. Then *fortuna* is a woman waiting to be won by impetuous and bold action—indeed, even by force—an overwhelmingly offensive tactic.

A separate question is that of whether *fortuna* is God's action or mere chance. The swift transition from "governed by fortune and by God" to "ruled by chance" in the quotation above suggests the latter. But in Book II, Chapter 29, of the *Discourses* Livy, who identifies *fortuna* with heaven, is quoted as saying, "Fortune thus blinds the minds of men when she does not wish them to resist her power." Machiavelli comments "Nothing could be more true than this conclusion."[48] For great occasions *fortuna* selects as "her instrument" men of spirit and ability who know how to seize opportunities; to effect the ruin of states she puts into power men who hasten such ruin:

> I repeat, then, as an incontrovertible truth, proved by all history, that men may second Fortune, but cannot oppose her; they may develop her designs, but cannot defeat them. But men should never despair on that account; for, not knowing the aims of Fortune, which she pursues by dark and devious ways, men should always be hopeful, and never yield to despair.[49]

Machiavelli seems almost to be whistling in the dark here. His need for hope is powerful but the case for hope is not impressive, especially when we recall that in the Epistle Dedicatory of *The Prince* Machiavelli attributes his own trouble to *fortuna* and in Chapter 7 he says the failure of Cesare Borgia was not his own fault but the "extraordinary malignity of fortune." Fortune is generally a misfortune. The hope Machiavelli has is so improbable that it bothers him deeply, as he indicates in Chapter 25 of *The Prince,* where he tries once again to put responsibility on the individual's shoulders. *Fortuna,* he says, seems highly changeable but what actually changes is "time and circumstances." Hence we must look for the man who is infinitely responsive to external circumstances, who can shift the style of his approach to a given end

[46] Chabod, p. 21.

[47] *The Prince,* Ch. 25, p. 91. A close paraphrase of part of Chapter 25 is found in a letter to Piero Soderini written in January, 1512. See also the letter to Vettori written April 18, 1527, in which God seems to replace *fortuna.* See *Chief Works,* Vol. 2, pp. 895–97 and 1011.

[48] *The Discourses,* p. 382. See also Chabod, pp. 69–70, and Strauss, pp. 213–23.

[49] *The Discourses,* Bk. II, Ch. 29, p. 383.

quickly and easily, who can sometimes be impetuous—like Julius II, the only historical example of Chapter 25—and sometimes be cautious, "for if one could change one's nature with time and circumstance fortune would never change."

Yet is anyone's nature that malleable? Machiavelli recognizes that it is unlikely that any man can be impetuous and cautious in exact proportion to the demands of the environment and so says that when one cannot be both it is better to be impetuous. This somewhat frustrated conclusion is what precedes the *fortuna*-as-woman metaphor at the end of Chapter 25 and seems to lead to the rather impetuous patriotic plea of Chapter 26.

Liberate Italy?

Chapter 26 of *The Prince* is entitled "An Exhortation to Liberate Italy from the Barbarians." It is one of the most accurately descriptive chapter titles in *The Prince,* yet the chapter itself has posed an interpretive problem for many students of Machiavelli. Some say the chapter was added on later, that its passionate phrases do not match the detached prose of the rest of the work. Some say the professions of Italian patriotism show the real Machiavelli, while others say they are rhetorical window-dressing. Some find here simply another disguised plea for employment.[50]

In fact, the bulk of the chapter is not very passionate; what passion there is has been anticipated in earlier chapters—recall Chapter 12. Machiavelli begins by asking whether the time is now propitious for Italy to have a new prince who will introduce a "new system." And in what seems an exaggerated comparison, he says it was necessary that Israel, Persia, and Athens be reduced to weakness before Moses, Cyrus, and Theseus could display their greatness. Perhaps likewise "it was necessary that Italy be reduced to her present condition, and that she should be more enslaved than the Hebrews, more oppressed than the Persians, and more scattered than the Athenians." One cannot help but note that the occasion for the ruler to display greatness seems more important than the salvation of the state. There was a "gleam of hope," says Machiavelli that "some individual might be appointed by God" for the redemption of Italy but "he was thrown aside by fortune"—which raises the question again of whether *fortuna* can defeat God. The unspecified someone was presumably Cesare Borgia. At any rate, Italy now "prays God to send some one to redeem her from this barbarous cruelty and insolence." This plea is openly addressed to the Medici: "There is nothing now that she [Italy] can hope for but that your illustrious house will place itself at the head of this redemption."

Especially since *The Prince* as a whole is more concerned with military matters than any others, mention of redemption and a religious leader like Moses seems strange, although all three founders mentioned here, plus Romulus, had appeared in Chapter 6.[51] On the one hand, their deeds are certainly to be regarded as epoch-making. But on the other hand, the men whose great deeds are recounted in *The Prince,* says Machiavelli, were only men, and "each of them had less opportunity than the present, for their enterprise was not juster than this, nor easier, nor was God more their friend than He is yours." Machiavelli thereupon quotes Livy (Bk. IX, Ch. 1) to the effect that necessary wars are just and arms used of necessity are sacred (*pia*).

Though the evidence offered in *The Prince* would seem to indicate that the reorganiza-

[50] Hale notes that in a letter to Vettori on January 31, 1515, Machiavelli speculated about the influence of Vettori's brother Paolo on Giuliano de' Medici and the possibility of Giuliano becoming lord of a new state composed of Parma, Piacenza, Modena, and Reggio. In the letter he described the pitfalls facing such a new prince. Comments Hale: "It is possible that it was at this point that Machiavelli took up *The Prince* and on rereading it gained the impetus to crown it with the 'Exhortation to Liberate Italy from the Barbarians.' Here, at last, through Paolo's patronage, was the longed-for chance of employment with the Medici. Here was a concrete proposal which would call for talents such as his, and a situation to which much of the subject-matter of *The Prince* was directly relevant" (*op. cit.*, p. 166).

[51] See p. 197, *n.* 26, above.

tion of Italy would be difficult, Machiavelli now makes it seems easy: ". . . nor can there be great difficulty" if the new prince follows the methods Machiavelli has set up as targets.[52] Machiavelli paraphrases Exodus and Numbers to suggest that God has set up a situation ripe for reform: ". . . there is not lacking scope in Italy for the introduction of every kind of new organization." As individuals, Italians are superior in strength, dexterity, and intelligence, we are told; but when organized into armies they have fallen short. In a matter-of-fact way Machiavelli explains what new and superior military tactics can do. The Spanish fear cavalry, the Swiss fear infantry; so the Spanish beat the Swiss and the French beat the Spanish. But a new military system is possible, one in which attackers can get under the long pikes wielded by pikemen:[53] ". . . these are the things which, when newly introduced, give reputation and grandeur to a new prince."

This opportunity must not, therefore, be allowed to pass, so that Italy may at length find her liberator. I cannot express the love with which he would be received in all those provinces which have suffered under these foreign invasions, with what thirst for vengeance, with what steadfast faith, with what love, with what grateful tears. What doors would be closed against him? What people would refuse him obedience? What envy could oppose him? What Italian would withhold allegiance? This barbarous domination stinks in the nostrils of every one. May your illustrious house therefore assume this task with that courage and those hopes which are inspired by a just cause, so that under its banner our fatherland may be raised up, and under its auspices be verified that saying of Petrarch:

Valour against fell wrath
Will take up arms; and be the combat quickly sped!
For, sure, the ancient worth,
That in Italians stirs the heart, is not yet dead.[54]

[52] The target metaphor may reveal deliberate irony in Machiavelli's statement. In Chapter 6, he said that prudent archers aim above their target when it is far off.

[53] See Machiavelli's *The Art of War,* Bks. II and III.

[54] *The Prince,* Ch. 26, p. 98. The poem is from Petrarch, *Canzone,* st. 16, ll. 13–16.

Thus the justice of Machiavelli's cause is mentioned at the very end of *The Prince.* But nowhere is the quality of this justice made clear, even though we may assume that Machiavelli identifies justice with patriotism. The primary target of *The Prince* seems to be domination rather than judicious rule and the problems of organization are discussed in terms of military rather than political details. A negative program of sorts emerges in *The Prince:* Chapter 3 suggests exterminating princely lines; Chapter 4 says local loyalties must be destroyed; Chapter 5 tells a prince he must either reside in a conquered republic or lay it waste; Chapters 16–19 and 21 tell how reputations can be maintained. But most of the rest concerns military matters and alliances; the perpetuation of power rather than the purposes of rule is the subject matter of *The Prince.* This more than anything else is what makes the last chapter seem anomalous.

Strauss points out another anomaly: why does Machiavelli gloss over the factual lack of Italian patriotism, that fuel on which he would base all hope for change? Where were those capable of becoming Italian patriots? The new prince is to lead an all-Italian army that will look upon its leader as one of its own. But how in fact would a Venetian or a Milanese soldier look upon the Florentine Lorenzo?[55] Is this realism? Clearly it is not.

We may explain this basic unrealism of *The Prince* by saying: (1) *The Prince* is not representative of Machiavelli's serious thought but only a long-winded job-wanted advertisement sent to the Medicis. (2) Machiavelli was a rather foolish and inconsistent man. (3) The liberation of Italy was a cover story for a plot of greater magnitude. (4) Machiavelli's approach to politics was esthetic. Knowledgeable scholars may be found arguing for each of these views. Examination of the first argument obviously requires a look at Machiavelli's other work and such an examination is also a prerequisite to a consideration of the other three arguments.

[55] Strauss, p. 64.

THE *DISCOURSES*

How Similar to *The Prince*?

Limitations of space will not permit us to examine *Discourses on the First Ten Books of Titus Livius* in the detail with which we examined *The Prince,* which is but one-fourth its length. As a source of insight into the thought of Machiavelli, however, the *Discourses* is equal to and in many ways superior to *The Prince*. Whether or not the reference to a study of republics in Chapter 2 of *The Prince* is a reference to the *Discourses,* it is a companion effort—a treatise on republics as *The Prince* was a treatise on principalities—though in fact both works refer to both forms of government.[56] But does the *Discourses* reveal a more humane Machiavelli? That is the issue we mean to take up here.

Livy wrote forty-five books on the history of Rome but Machiavelli apparently intended to comment on only the first ten books, for it was republican Rome that interested him. He completed three books of commentary but may have intended more. The three books follow Livy in a very rough way internally but not in overall subject. That is, Machiavelli's first book discusses the domestic affairs of the Romans, his second their foreign and military affairs, and his third the actions of some of Rome's leading citizens. With each book Machiavelli returns again to Book I of Livy and starts afresh on the chronology. But there are many gaps and departures from Livy. Hale says of Machiavelli: "As he reads through Livy, associations from books or his own career come now in a flood, now sparsely, and he accepts the flow without seeking to adjust it to a uniform pressure. Some discussions are long essays which needed no passage from Livy to justify them, others are hardly more than brief notes on the text."[57]

Scholars who argue that there is a basic difference between *The Prince* and the *Discourses* point mainly to Machiavelli's enthusiasm for republicanism and creeping humanitarianism in the *Discourses.* This, supposedly, is the real Machiavelli. For example, Chapter 58 of Book I, titled "The People Are Wiser and More Constant than Princes," takes Livy to task for referring to the multitude as insolent and domineering. What is said of a multitude "does not apply to a people regulated by laws. . . . A people that governs and is well regulated by laws will be stable, prudent, and grateful, as much so, and even more, according to my opinion, than a prince."[58] Moreover, says Machiavelli, the defects of a prince can be remedied only by violence, whereas "words suffice to correct those of the people." An alliance with a republic is also more to be relied upon than one made with a prince. What appears as prevailing prejudice against the people results from the fact that it is easy to "speak ill of them in the mass . . . but a prince can only be spoken of with the greatest circumspection and apprehension."[59]

Machiavelli seems to have a concern for substantive justice in the *Discourses* that did not reveal itself in *The Prince,* though it is a naturalistic justice—such as Hobbes later adopted—rather than a transcendent justice that emerges. Justice arises from the need to punish law-breakers and law is originally but the command of the strongest. It was not until a people put such a strong man at their head for sheer self-defense that "they began to know the good and the honest," for out of gratitude for their protection came honor, hatred of evil, and law. "Such was the origin of justice. This caused them, when they had afterward to choose a prince, neither to look to the strongest nor bravest but to the wisest and most just."

It is easy to compile a list of humane

[56] This, of course, is not the only way to structure Machiavelli's political concerns. Wood argues that the two basic systems in Machiavelli's political thinking were not principalities and republics but ordered conflict and corrupt conflict, the first examined in the *Discourses* and the second in *Historie fiorentine*. See Wood, pp. LI–LII.

[57] Hale, p. 174.

[58] *The Discourses,* pp. 262–63.

[59] *Ibid.,* p. 266.

and prorepublican utterances from the *Discourses:* the people are less prone to the vice of ingratitude than princes, for, while fear induces ingratitude in the people, avarice as well as fear induces it in the prince (I, 29); Lycurgus deserves the highest praise for establishing a constitution in which the powers of prince, nobility, and people each keep the other in check (I, 2); more than founders of states, founders of religions deserve to be eulogized (I, 10); the "evil ambition to rule cancels the noblest qualities of mind and body"; a prince should be "fired with an intense desire to follow the example of the good" from studying the evil cruelties of ancient Rome.

But what do such professions mean? Passing tributes to virtue can be found in *The Prince,* too. And more striking than any superficial differences are the basic similarities in content between *The Prince* and the *Discourses.* Note first Machiavelli's emphasis in the *Discourses* on the need for cunning and ruthlessness in ruling and the disdain for conventional morality that is everywhere: seldom have men ever risen to high position without "force," "fraud," "cunning," and "deceit"; both for princes and republics government "consists mainly in so keeping your subjects that they shall be neither able nor disposed to injure you"; "one should never show one's intentions, but endeavor to obtain one's desires anyhow"; "whoever makes himself tyrant of a state and does not kill Brutus, or whoever restores liberty to a state and does not immolate his sons, will not maintain himself on his position long."[60] The list of quotations could be extended indefinitely.

In the second place, Machiavelli asserts as clearly in the *Discourses* as in *The Prince* that a ruler is to use religion rather than allow it to affect his choices. For example, the Romans are called wise rulers because they "made a show of observing religion even when they were obliged in reality to disregard it." In the *Discourses,* Christianity compares badly with pagan religion, for the former "places the supreme happiness in humility, lowliness, and a contempt for worldly objects, whilst the other, on the contrary, places the supreme good in grandeur of soul, strength of body, and all such other qualities as render men formidable." Christian principles "seem to me to have made men feeble, and caused them to become an easy prey to evil-minded men."

In the third place, Machiavelli's low view of human nature is fundamentally unchanged. Chapter 27 of Book I is entitled "Showing that men are very rarely either entirely good or entirely bad." But the content, a chronicle of an encounter between Pope Julius II and Giovonpaolo in which one is timorous and the other is cowardly, does not conform to even this degree of affirmation. Chapter 42 of Book I is more accurately titled "How Easily Men May Be Corrupted"; earlier Machiavelli says simply "mankind, being more prone to evil than to good." A less gloomy but hardly hopeful conclusion appears in the Introduction to Book II: "Reflecting now upon the course of human affairs I think that, as a whole, the world remains very much in the same condition, and the good in it always balances the evil; but the good and the evil change from one country to another." This concept of a moral ceiling or limited moral equation expresses Machiavelli's sense of moral issues as dynamic rather than static in human affairs, for in the same passage he says, "human affairs [is] in a state of perpetual movement, always either ascending or declining." Indeed, in Book III, Chapters 8 and 9, Machiavelli stresses that men of action must learn to adapt to constantly changing conditions. Successful men "suit their conduct to the time," difficult as that is.

We have not, by any means, exhausted the list of parallel themes in *The Prince* and the *Discourses* and we cannot try to do so. But it should be noted that in the *Discourses* the evil of mercenary troops and the value of a national army are not forgotten and Machiavelli's fascination with conspiracies is such that the chapter devoted to this subject

[60] Machiavelli here refers to what he has said "in another place" on the same subject. In Bk. III, Ch. 42, he refers to *The Prince,* this time by name, in support of the proposition that pledges may need to be broken at certain times.

(Bk. III, Ch. 6) is the longest in the whole work—as is its counterpart, Chapter 19 in *The Prince*.

Principality Versus Republic?

Discorsi does not argue in general terms the superiority of republics over principalities. Each is seen by Machiavelli to have strong points and weak points and to be fitted for certain occasions and not fitted for others:

> If republics are slower than princes, they are also less suspicious, and therefore less cautious; and if they show more respect to their great citizens, these in turn are thereby made more daring and audacious in conspiring against them.[61]

> Let republics . . . be established where equality exists, and, on the contrary, principalities where great inequality prevails; otherwise the governments will lack proper proportions and have but little durability.[62]

But, curiously, this evenhanded allocation of different tasks to principalities and republics does not eliminate from Machiavelli's discussion his admiration for the strong man who, defying the more malevolent assaults of *fortuna,* bends circumstances his way: ". . . to establish a republic in a country better adapted to a monarchy, or a monarchy where a republic would be more suitable, requires a man of rare genius and power."

Even in well-ordered republics the strong man is not superfluous: the "good . . . in a republic is due either to the excellence of some one man or to some law" and Machiavelli notes that it was the tribunes who "brought the Roman republic back to its original principles" by giving it good laws. ". . . to give life and vigor to those laws requires a virtuous citizen, who will courageously aid in their execution against the power of those who transgress them." This notion of a strong man leading the people back to original principles is one that occurs at several points and in several ways in the *Discourses.*

[61] *The Discourses,* Bk. III, Ch. 6, p. 431.
[62] *Ibid.,* Bk. I, Ch. 56, p. 257.

The New Republic

These two themes of the new strong man and the old recapturable principles are stated in a crucial way in Book I, Chapter 9, entitled "To found a new republic, or to reform entirely the old institutions of an existing one, must be the work of one man only." Though "many will perhaps consider it an evil example" that Romulus killed his brother and acquiesced in the death of Tatius the Sabine, Machiavelli reminds the reader that it is a general rule that neither a republic nor a principality is well founded or entirely reformed "unless it is done by only one individual." On these grounds Machiavelli explicitly justifies the killing of Remus and Tatius.

When a legislator of a republic has as his object the public good rather than his private interests, he "should concentrate all authority in himself." And if he employs "extraordinary means" to establish a new kingdom or republic "when the act accuses him, the result should excuse him"—which is but a close variation on the familiar "the end justifies the means." Machiavelli cites as corroboration for his views on one-man authority Moses, Lycurgus, Solon, and Agis—the last being a king of Sparta who "restored the laws of Lycurgus entirely" by the neat expedient of having all the ephors, or magistrates, slain.

Book I, Chapter 26, repeats the message for conquered states: "A new prince in a city or province conquered by him should organize everything anew." He should name new governors with new titles and new staff officers; he should make the poor rich and the rich poor. "Besides this, he should destroy the old cities and build new ones, and transfer the inhabitants from one place to another; in short, he should leave nothing unchanged" so that everything will be recognized as coming from him. Such wanton destruction would seem to require an impressive justification. What Machiavelli offers is, as indicated already, the return to original principles:

> There is nothing more true than that all the

things of this world have a limit to their existence; but those only run the entire course ordained for them by Heaven that do not allow their body to become disorganized, but keep it unchanged in the manner ordained, or if they change it, so do it that it shall be for their advantage, and not to their injury. And as I speak here of mixed bodies, such as republics or religious sects, I say that those changes are beneficial that bring them back to their original principles. For, as all religious republics and monarchies must have within themselves some goodness, by means of which they obtain their first growth and reputation, and as in the process of time this goodness becomes corrupted, it will of necessity destroy the body unless something intervenes to bring it back to its normal condition. Thus the doctors of medicine say, in speaking of the human body, that "every day some ill humors gather which must be cured."

This return of a republic to its original principles is either the result of extrinsic accident or of intrinsic prudence.[63]

Politics Above Morality

The truth is that Machiavelli is more concerned about the requirements of effective political and military action than about the ends of action, although—consciously or unconsciously—he seems to prefer those ends that, being sweeping and historically dramatic, give the best justification for drastic action. And the need for drastic action does not so much establish a new morality as simply make morality irrelevant:

where the very safety of the country depends upon the resolution to be taken, no considerations of justice or injustice, humanity or cruelty, nor of glory or of shame, should be allowed to prevail. But putting all other considerations aside, the only question should be, what course will save the life and liberty of the country?[64]

[63] *Ibid.*, Bk. III, Ch. 1, pp. 397–98. The notion of diseased humors that must be ruthlessly cured may be compared to Hegel's remark that war is a blowing of the wind that keeps the sea from foulness. See his *Philosophy of Right,* sec. 324A. Though it is not quite the same point, see also *The Discourses,* Bk. I, Ch. 4, where Machiavelli finds that liberty originates in conflict.

[64] *Ibid.*, Ch. 41, p. 528.

Referring to the wholesa
transfer of populations sp
26), Machiavelli says:

Doubtless these means are cr
of all civilized life, and nei
even human, and should be
one. In fact, the life of a pri … would be preferable to that of a king at the expense of the ruin of so many human beings. Nevertheless, whoever is unwilling to adopt the first and humane course must, if he wishes to maintain his power, follow the latter evil course.[65]

Machiavelli continues by explaining that most men follow neither course. They muddle along in the middle, neither good enough to be saints nor bad enough to be effective. At last we understand the meaning of the title of Chapter 27 of Book I—"That Men Are Rarely Either Entirely Good or Entirely Bad." The phrase is not offering mild words of comfort about the not-so-bad condition of most men; it is condemning men. The rare bird who is all good or all bad is alone worthy of praise. Machiavelli has led us into a Nietzschean transvaluation of values in which we are forced to ask: are our values really valuable and are our goods really good? Machiavelli seems to say that the rule of life is dominate or be dominated; take it or leave it but, in the name of Rome, please do not moralize about it.

INTERPRETATIONS OF MACHIAVELLI

Is Machiavelli Overrated?

It is not difficult to find scholars who argue that Machiavelli is a much overrated figure. Kraft, for example, finds most of Machiavelli's military proposals unsound, his psychological assumptions fallacious, and his historical accounts inaccurate. He calls Machiavelli a poet rather than a theorist in the

[65] *Ibid.*, p. 184.

sense.[66] Machiavelli repeatedly mis-ged the aims and instincts of the Medici amily whose favor he presumably sought. Perhaps his fame—and notoriety—stems from his daring in stating principles of politics that had been followed in every age of man but had not been openly avowed rather than from his political sagacity. But Hale, for one, is not much impressed even with this:

> Statesmen had been functioning efficiently on Machiavellian lines for centuries, and by begging them to be self-conscious about the motive for their actions, Machiavelli was not aiding but embarrassing their freedom of action. . . . It is as though Machiavelli's Prince had started life as an honest bourgeois, and needed constant reassurance that he need act no longer as a private citizen. The assumption that political action would be based on expediency was part of Machiavelli's novel approach to his subject; the laboring of this assumption a reminder that he brought to it a not altogether unconventional state of mind.[67]

Whether Machiavelli labored the need for expediency is open to serious question. But certainly we can agree that he was not scientific—if that implies suspension of normative judgments and careful weighing of evidence. For Machiavelli not only diagnosed the ills of Italy with a very narrowly focused vision but he set about to prescribe a cure for her and used the study of history as a coating for the pill. The prescription was arrived at in advance of the research. History was for him a storehouse of examples often wrenched out of context and "for him the Roman example is always the right one."[68] His aim was to provide inspiring examples for current imitation. Nor was his military judgment as good as he thought it was, though this was his forte. Moreover, his reliance on military solutions betrayed a lack of understanding of more complex economic, political, social, and religious causes behind Italy's division.[69] To the extent that he was a republican and a Roman partisan, he often seemed guilty of sentimentalism—which is not as rare a companion of cynicism as we might think.

Yet his weaknesses, many as they were, were perhaps essential to the unity of his prophetic mission of dignifying the way of power. Machiavelli was a prophet and we cannot use the same criteria in judging a prophet that we use in evaluating a technical scholar. Much of the argument for and against Machiavelli as the first modern political scientist is simply beside the point. The answer to our initial question must be yes: Machiavelli has often been overrated as historian, political scientist, and general savant. But, no, as poet and prophet he has not been overrated: his words have moved many people—some to heated opposition, some to secret delight.

The very unreality of Machiavelli's vision of a new prince bringing a wholly new system into being gives the conception the kind of urgency and passion that compels attention. That passion is at its height in *The Prince* and fades as Machiavelli grows older. Although, as Wood contends, the highly rational army structure described in *The Art of War* has some similarity to the well-ordered polity of *The Prince* and the *Discourses* and although the able general behaves much like the able prince, the hope of achieving such a system and such a man is slowly dissipated. At the very end of *The Art of War,* Machiavelli has Fabrizio, the chief proponent of military *virtù* in the dialogue, lament not only the shortage of modern examples of *virtù* and the failure of Italians to take such examples seriously but also his own aged incapacity to act:

> I cannot help complaining of fate, which either should not have let me know these things, or given me the power to put them in execution;

[66] Joseph Kraft, "Truth and Poetry in Machiavelli," *Journal of Modern History,* Vol. 23 (1951), pp. 109–21. A critical view of Machiavelli's military advice is found in Felix Gilbert, "The Renaissance and the Art of War," in Edward Meade Earle, ed., *Makers of Modern Strategy* (Princeton: Princeton Univ. Press, 1943). See also the references to Butterfield, Chabod, and Mattingly above.

[67] Hale, pp. 158–59.

[68] Butterfield, p. 56.

[69] See Chabod, pp. 85–93. Among other things, Machiavelli confuses the very special Italian *condottieri* with mercenary troops in general.

this is something I cannot hope for now that I am so far advanced in years. . . . If *Fortuna* had indulged me some years ago with a territory fit for such an undertaking, I think I should soon have convinced the world of the excellence of ancient military discipline.[70]

And in his *Life of Castruccio* Machiavelli "transports into the past that figure of a ruler which in *The Prince* he sought to impose on the future . . . all faith is lost, and despair is the keynote."[71]

Machiavelli as Subversive

We have so far concluded that *The Prince* does not stand as an aberration in Machiavelli's thought but rather that there is a unity to the whole of his writings. We have further concluded that Machiavelli's unifying mission is heavily tinged with parochialism: a new prince—who is much like idealized Roman warriors—is needed for a new Italy, which is not carefully drawn. This parochial content has been of continuing interest to readers of many generations in many lands. Is their interest explained by the vibrancy of Machiavelli's style, which transcends the limited content, or does the content itself contain riches we have not yet plumbed?

One who would surely opt for the latter interpretation is Leo Strauss, whose brilliant but evasive argument in *Thoughts on Machiavelli* must be noted here, even under the handicap of brevity. His approach to Machiavelli is similar to his approach to other political thinkers designated great. He assumes that premodern writers with any degree of prudence were obliged to conceal their basic teachings beneath a cover of conventionality, subtle inference, intentional "blunders," and judicious "silences." It is the business of scholars to penetrate, by the most meticulous analysis, the crust of exoteric doctrine to reach the esoteric doctrine. Applied to Machiavelli, the method reveals that the Florentine was interested in much more than Italy and that the frequency of his appeals to ancient practice is but a mask to conceal a revolutionary new teaching: ". . . all ancient or traditional teachings are to be superceded by a shockingly new teaching. But he [Machiavelli] is careful not to shock anyone unduly."[72] Machiavelli is not the patriot he pretends to be but shrewdly realizes "that the questioning of morality in the name of patriotism may go together with gravity, whereas the questioning of morality on other grounds is publicly indefensible."[73] Thus Machiavelli

[70] Wood, p. 212.

[71] Chabod, p. 108. Castruccio was a famous soldier of Lucca who was born in 1281 and who defeated the Florentines at Sarravalle.

[72] Strauss, p. 59. The intricate patterns Strauss finds, for example, in the "ascending" and "descending" phases of *The Prince,* in the use and nonuse of certain kinds of examples, in the numbering of chapters, or in the disjunctions between chapter title and chapter content and between generalization and illustration—all this is of necessity beyond comment here. But two observations may be made: (1) Renaissance scholars have pointed to a number of instances in which Strauss constructs an elaborate logical argument on a mistranslation of a sixteenth-century Italian phrase and they note that Strauss omits reference to any twentieth-century Machiavellian studies. See the reviews by Felix Gilbert in *Yale Review,* Vol. 48 (1959), pp. 465–69, and George L. Mosse in *American Historical Review,* Vol. 64 (1959), pp. 954–55. (2) Strauss is remarkably unperturbed by such criticism. The modern historian has, he says, "an immense apparatus supplying him with information which can be easily appropriated because it is superficial" (pp. 292–93). One suspects that Strauss is more concerned to promote a special way of reading the "classics" than in specific details of interpretation, however much effort he expends on details of interpretation, and those who respond to Strauss are virtually forced to read the original work with equal care if only to refute Strauss. Moreover, it appears that Strauss plays with his readers and indulges in the same game of esoteric silences—he is not unaware of twentieth-century Machiavellian studies—that he attributes to classical writers. Robert J. McShea is one of the few critics of Strauss to recognize this. See his excellent critique, "Leo Strauss on Machiavelli," *Western Political Quarterly,* Vol. 16 (1963), pp. 782–97, which, among other things, brings out Strauss's camouflaged opposition to theistic forms of natural law.

[73] Strauss, p. 285. The statement is made as part of Strauss's exegesis of Machiavelli's comic play, *La mandragola,* which is seen both as an allegory and as an example of "levity" in "the communication of truth." Levity provides a necessary counterpoint, parallel to the man-beast symbol, to the "gravity" that "belongs to the knowledge of truth" (*ibid.,* p. 290). See also Theodore A. Sumberg, "*La Mandragola:* An Interpretation," *Journal of Politics,* Vol. 23 (1961), pp. 320–40.

uses patriotism as a foil to undermine the "Great Tradition" of Western philosophy.

In the Straussian view, Machiavelli, though he praises the founder, in fact seeks for himself a higher glory than that available to the founder—namely the glory available to the teacher of founders, for, contrary to the opinion of the vulgar, the teacher's influence is more durable than that of any political ruler. Like Socrates, Machiavelli would found a city in speech, that is, he would found a political order. But as his use of the symbol of Chiron—half-man, half-beast—shows, Machiavelli "understands man in the light of the sub-human rather than the superhuman." Of Machiavelli's new prince established in a new state Strauss says, "not the one end by nature common to all which is visible in the sky—a pattern laid out in heaven—but the roots hidden in the earth reveal the true character of man or society. The teaching which derives from this principle is obviously opposed to that of classical political philosophy or of the Socratic tradition."[74] But, in fact, the earth rather than heaven as a source of truth is not so "obviously opposed" to classical political philosophy as Strauss here asserts; elsewhere he implies almost the opposite.[75] Strauss further asserts that Machiavelli's silence about Plato, Aristotle, and Cicero is evidence of his rejection of them. The classical philosopher Machiavelli does mention is Xenophon, who wrote a defense of tyranny. Rejecting the Platonic idea that there is a natural hierarchy of goods of the soul, Machiavelli implies that man is infinitely malleable. This belief has come to dominate the exercise of power in the modern world, which thereby gives modernity an essentially Machiavellian flavor.

We suspect that Strauss's opening assertion that Machiavelli is a "teacher of evil" is meant to conceal the degree of merit that Strauss actually finds in Machiavelli.[76] Nevertheless, it is necessary to refute the "teacher-of-evil" interpretation:

(1) Machiavelli's private letters are generally so much like his public writings that there seems little basis for saying that his real position was hidden in his public statements. Indeed, Machiavelli's frankness is all the more impressive in an age when frankness in political writing was uncommon and deprecation of one's work was the prevailing style. Machiavelli's counsel may be as evil as Strauss says it is but he scarcely conceals its wickedness as much as Strauss says he does.[77] Machiavelli often seems to delight in his own wickedness and thereby preludes what might have been a more significant tragic vision. Part of Machiavelli's popular appeal is exactly this brashness.

(2) Machiavelli was manifestly uninterested in Greek philosophy and traditional philosophic studies. He was, virtually all scholars agree, not well educated in classical philosophy. To find an attack on Plato, Aristotle, and Cicero in Machiavelli's silence about them strains one's credulity.

(3) Machiavelli's practical political motivations, that is, the desire to participate in the exercise of power in his own lifetime, while often exaggerated by commentators on Machiavelli, cannot be disregarded. Machiavelli never lost interest in the Italian politics of his own day and cannot be said ever to have fully transcended that particular genre of politics. It is unconvincing to see Machiavelli lifted out of his own age, put in direct dialogue with the ancients, and made a secret would-be counselor to all mankind.

(4) The application of Strauss's interpre-

[74] Strauss, pp. 297 and 290.

[75] *Natural Right and History* (Chicago: Univ. of Chicago Press, 1953), p. 8.

[76] That concealment is a characteristic of his work does not mean that we cannot learn from Strauss much about classical political philosophy and hence much about the contrasting assumptions of Hebraic-Christian and modern political thought. See his "Jerusalem and Athens," *Commentary*, Vol. 43 (June, 1967), pp. 45–57, and *What Is Philosophy?* (New York: Free Press, 1959).

[77] Strauss quotes a letter of Machiavelli to Guicciardini on May 17, 1521, where he boasts of his ability to lie (*Thoughts on Machiavelli*, p. 36). Strauss treats this as a clue to the deception in Machiavelli's whole literary output. But the passage is wrenched out of context, for Machiavelli is being jocular and referring to his ability to cope with the lies of the friars of Carpi, whom he was then visiting on a rather farcical mission. The complete letter is in *Chief Works*, Vol. 2, pp. 971–73.

tive devices to Machiavelli too often simply does not work. The "Scholastic" opening of *The Prince,* says Strauss, is "deliberately deceptive." But the opening is not Scholastic. The classificatory structure of chapters in which Strauss finds hidden meanings seems to be Strauss's rather than Machiavelli's. The "intentional" blunders on factual examples in Machiavelli seem quite unintentional and rather harmless. The "concealed" attack on the Church Strauss finds in one chapter of the *Discourses* is questionable given Machiavelli's open attack on the Church in the next chapter, which Strauss fails to cite. A vast expenditure of labor to demonstrate that Machiavelli was secretly saying what in fact he was asserting openly hardly seems worth the effort.

Machiavelli is indeed an important symbol of the fascination with power exercised for obscure ends that has characterized all too much of modern history. But however important he is as a symbol, Machiavelli cannot properly be regarded as the crucial, conscious instrument of the shift to an immoral rationale for governing men. He was, in the first place, not that conscious of a universal mission. In the second place, the problem of irresponsible power has by no means been a peculiarly post-Machiavellian phenomenon.

The State as a Work of Art

There remains one more special interpretation of Machiavelli's significance that we are obliged to look at. The German historian Jacob Burckhardt (in *Die Cultur der Renaissance in Italien,* 1860) was the first to help us see how the Renaissance state—which, with *le stato,* gave us our English "state"—could be visualized by its rulers as an artistic creation rather than as a moral object, as previous political orders had tended to be visualized. The humanism and secularism of Renaissance life put politics, like art, beyond good and evil. The Italian philosopher Benedetto Croce (in *Elementi di politica,* 1925) first spoke of Machiavelli as the discoverer of "the autonomy of politics," that is, the understanding that politics can be practiced for its own sake just as art is practiced for its own sake.[78]

Evidence that Machiavelli shared and perhaps extended this new Renaissance conception of the state stems not only from his own literary interests, which did not leave him even at the height of his diplomatic activity, but from his manner of referring to the ruler's task. A founder of a republic would, says the *Discourses,* do better with simple mountain folk than with corrupted city-dwellers, "as a sculptor finds it easier to make a fine statue out of a crude block of marble than out of a statue badly begun by another." In the Epistle Dedicatory of *The Prince,* we recall, the prince is said to be analogous to a landscape-painter who must put himself in the valley to draw the mountains and must ascend a prominence to paint the plains.[79]

Chabod is a distinguished Machiavelli scholar in the Croce tradition. He sees Machiavelli as an outstanding contributor to the theory of political autonomy but, with the help of recent historical scholarship, he is also able to see the degree to which prior Italian life and thought find a synthesis in Machiavelli:

> long before Machiavelli created the hero of politics the world had acclaimed the hero of art, a personage blind to every form of life save that of his own artistic imagination.
>
> And herein lies indeed the essential novelty of the Renaissance. As in art and literature, so in political theory and historiography, its so-called "realism and individualism," by means of a continuous process initiated by Alberti, carried on by Machiavelli and Ariosto, and brought to its logical conclusion by Galileo, led to the affirmation of the complete autonomy of art, politics, science and history. In other words, they lead to the abandonment of the typically mediaeval conception of the world according to which no branch of human activity could be

[78] A discussion of some of these conceptions in their sixteenth-century setting is found in J. H. Whitfield, "The Politics of Machiavelli," *Modern Language Review,* Vol. 50 (1955), pp. 433–43. See also Whitfield's book, *Machiavelli* (Oxford: Blackwell, 1947).

[79] Wood notes that Machiavelli uses similar analogies when referring to the separable but similar military art. See Wood, p. LIII.

considered independently of its relationship to life as a whole. The answer to allegory is the well-known precept of "art for art's sake." The two worlds are essentially different.

Art for art's sake, politics for politics' sake, and even, ultimately, science for science's sake —the results of Italian thought might well be summarized in these phrases.[80]

But Machiavelli's artistic amorality is maintained only by what amounts to a rather charming naiveté—young children are, after all, amoral, too. The rigorous cynic must take a position on the problem of politics and ethics but Machiavelli does not analyze the problem—he simply ignores it:

> This problem had remained outside the purview of the Florentine secretary, whose life was in very truth motivated by his political feeling, which burst forth with the impetuosity of a force of nature, of an underground spring that suddenly finds an outlet, expressing itself with a directness, a vivacity and, we might say, a natural innocence that have no parallel in the whole of modern history.[81]

Machiavelli leaves to his followers the difficult problem of establishing a rationale for a new morality of politics. This they did, as we shall see, under the rubric *raison d'état.*

Machiavelli's genius, thinks Chabod, is primarily a matter of style—"a complete expression of the predominance of imagination over pure logic." Again and again Machiavelli comes up with the "plastic image" that can wash over doubts and hesitations. Again and again Machiavelli displays "the manner and imagery of a great poet."[82] Without the poetry and without the tingling, if amoral, appeal of *grandezza dello animo,* Machiavelli is a collection of unresolved problems. He cannot be consistent, even in his humanism. Machiavelli's newly autonomous man struggles against *natura, fortuna,* and *necessità* as he heretofore had struggled against God and the Devil. Machiavelli, the most secular of thinkers, could not liberate himself from traditional religious patterns of thought. His hope for a new prince was like an eschatological expectation of a second coming. His pattern of constant human nature was like a belief in revealed truth. His appeal for a return to original principles was like a call to conversion. Machiavelli's friend Guicciardini was more "modern" than he, for Guicciardini rejected the search for patterns in history and the use of history to provide examples.[83] But that is the point. Machiavelli's art was that of poet and prophet rather than historian.

In Chabod's view Machiavelli, had he not been a bad historian, could not have become a universal influence. Can we say that art gained what political theory lost when in Machiavelli art for art's sake and politics for politics' sake became one?

CONCLUSION: MACHIAVELLI'S INFLUENCE

Nothing is more difficult than trying to measure the influence of one man's thought on other men's thoughts. Many attempts to do so—our own included, no doubt—fall short of helpfulness. "The Uses and Abuses of Machiavelli's Name" might be a better heading for this concluding section. Yet the prominence and the notoriety of that name require us to say something of the man's followers and detractors:

> In the porch of the sixteenth century stands the enigmatic figure of Niccolo Machiavelli, a figure that, for centuries to come, was sinister and a rock of offense. No writer, probably, has been so persistently used and abused or so little understood. From beginning to end of the six-

[80] Chabod, p. 184.

[81] *Ibid.,* p. 191.

[82] *Ibid.,* pp. 146 and 147.

[83] We must put "modern" in quotation marks, for, of course, the search for patterns in history is unending: witness Hegel, Marx, Spengler, and Toynbee. With an ironic twist, D'Entreves, in the Introduction to Chabod's book, cites "historical process" against the validity of the conception of the state as a work of art: ". . . the formula of the Renaissance state as 'a work of art' continued to enjoy credit long after the growth of the *signorie* had been shown to be the result of a slow historical process rather than the creation of the 'virtuous' Prince" (p. XI).

teenth century rolled over him a chorus of denunciation, which continued through the seventeenth and eighteenth centuries. Echoes of it are heard even now.[84]

"Machiavelli's theory," says another noted historian, "was a sword plunged into the flank of the body politic of Western humanity, causing it to shriek and rear up."[85] Some shrieked in genuine moral pain. But many rulers shrieked because Machiavelli seemed to be giving away trade secrets. On the one side, Frederick the Great, no stranger to the methods of Machiavelli, found it useful to write his *L'Antimachiavel* in 1740. On the other side, as late as 1942, Count Sforza, descendant of Machiavelli's Milanese allies and adversaries, wrote a book that tried to make Machiavelli into a democrat and could be only apologetic. Even Florence failed for centuries to honor one of its most famous sons.[86]

The anti-Machiavellian literature is truly mountainous—what Meinecke calls "catacombs . . . of forgotten literature by mediocrities." Most sixteenth-century criticism was, in fact, rather ignorant. The papal efforts to suppress Machiavelli's writings were quite effective: more people, at least, read *The Prince* outside than inside Italy. (*The Prince* was not published until 1532, with a French translation following in 1553, a Latin edition in 1560, and English and German versions not until the seventeenth century.)

Neither critics nor disciples of Machiavelli were required to read him and many who—reading nothing—simply conducted the kind of political skulduggery they had always known were branded disciples of Old Nick—a term that became a synonym for the Devil, although the name of Niccolo is apparently not the original source of that appellation. Most of the stories that tyrants from Catherine de' Medici to Benito Mussolini carried a copy of *The Prince* with them wherever they went are false; even if they had carried and read the work, such reading would not necessarily make Machiavelli their hidden tutor.

One of the first prominent Machiavelli-haters was Innocent Gentillet, a French Huguenot whose *Contre Nicolas Machiavel Florentin* (1576) was "clumsy, garrulous, and full of misconceptions."[87] He opposed Catherine de' Medici and foreign influences on France, which to him were linked with the evil Florentine. He somehow managed to find the cause of the massacre of St. Bartholomew (1572) not in religious fanaticism but in Machiavelli's supposed atheism. Yet the critics, though mostly ignorant of their target, were not altogether wrong. They often sensed correctly the central direction of Machiavelli's assumptions—power for power's sake—and their hostility, based on traditional conceptions of moral restraint, was consequently not entirely unfounded.

Apart from this hostility on moral grounds, the irrelevance of Machiavelli to the burning political issues of northern Europeans in the sixteenth century was a factor in the disparagement of him or at least in the failure to appreciate his work. The two most crucial issues of the sixteenth century were the proper relation between Church and state and the limits of the constitutional obligation of subjects to obey rulers. On questions of religious toleration and civic rights Machiavelli had nothing to say; the nature of legality and the rights of citizens did not interest him. This was true not only of Machiavelli but of Italian Renaissance thought generally: ". . . however much the quality of Italian political thought was changed in the course of the sixteenth century it remained throughout remote from the rest of Europe. Italian thinkers, to the end of the century, concerned themselves little, or not at all,

[84] J. W. Allen, *A History of Political Thought in the Sixteenth Century* (New York: Barnes & Noble, 1960), p. 447.

[85] Friedrich Meinecke, *Machiavellism: The Doctrine of Raison d'État and Its Place in Modern History,* trans. by Douglas Scott (New Haven: Yale Univ. Press, 1957), p. 49. Meinecke's work, an exercise in *Lebensphilosophie,* traces in almost Hegelian fashion—though with different sympathies—the clash of public and private morality from Machiavelli to World War I.

[86] See Ross Wilson, "Machiavelli and Florence," *Contemporary Review,* Vol. 197 (1960), pp. 164–65.

[87] Meinecke, p. 54.

with the questions that disturbed men elsewhere."[88]

Raison d'Etat

Machiavelli's central ideas entered the European consciousness in a more positive way through the doctrine of *raison d'état.* It might be more accurate to say that the phrase *raison d'état* signaled a new and generally Machiavellian attitude toward political morality. Though now remembered in its French form, the Italian phrase *ragion di stato* appeared in Francesco Guicciardini's *Dialogue Concerning the Government of Florence* (c. 1521); in correspondence he had earlier used the phrase *l'interesse dello stato.*[89] The phrase had little theoretical rigor in Guicciardini. He was so skeptical that he found little reason to formalize general rules or categories for anything, even though he did believe history was cyclical and repetitious.

Giovanni Botero's *Della ragion di stato* (1589)[90] helped popularize the phrase, though in the Epistle Dedicatory Botero himself says that in his visits to European courts he found everyone talking about reason of state and citing Machiavelli and Tacitus. Botero, a conservative Italian priest trained by Jesuits, posed as a critic of Machiavelli but he, like his opponent, "expresses the atmosphere of the Italy of his day . . . [and] makes very much the same assumptions, and appeals to the same kind of motives" as Machiavelli.[91]

Raison d'état was an important competitor with traditional natural-law assumptions as a formula for rationalizing political decisions. In operation it was not so much reason of state but the reason of the ruler—and probably not so much his reason as his intuition. No one outside a position of authority could really know what the interest of the state required. *Raison d'état* was *intuition de pouvoir.* As such it was loosely bound up with the secularization, the skepticism, the pragmatism, and the power orientation we associate with Machiavelli. This set of attitudes was reflected not only in Botero but in a number of subsequent writers, such as Lipsius, Raleigh, Bacon, Gentili, and Montaigne.

Of writers to be treated in the next chapter, Luther, Calvin, and Hooker ignored or were unaware of Machiavelli. Bodin, though he borrowed some military examples from Machiavelli, referred to him with high contempt. Neither the Christian nor the legal emphases of these writers had much in common with the glowing pagan prose of the Florentine secretary. Machiavelli stands by himself, neither wholly classical nor wholly modern. In him the admixture is unique, a strange blend of the parochial and the universal.

[88] Allen, p. 446.

[89] See Felix Gilbert, *Machiavelli and Guicciardini: Politics and History in Sixteenth Century Florence* (Princeton: Princeton Univ. Press, 1965), and Allen, pp. 495–501. Guicciardini's notebook (*Ricordi Politici e Civili*) has recently been published as *Maxims and Reflections of a Renaissance Statesman,* trans. by Mario Domandi (New York: Harper & Row, 1965). Though scoring, as we have noted, some telling points in his half-friendly comments on Machiavelli, Guicciardini was not always fair to him. Many later anti-Machiavellians would have been amazed to know that Guicciardini regarded his fellow Florentine as an optimistic dreamer who was much too careless with high-flown generalizations.

[90] Translated by P. J. and D. P. Whaley as *Reason of State* (New Haven: Yale Univ. Press, 1956). For a brief note on *raison d'état* in the seventeenth and eighteenth centuries see Ch. 10 and literature cited there.

[91] J. N. Figgis, *Political Thought from Gerson to Grotius, 1414–1625* (New York: Harper & Row, 1960), p. 97.

9

THE REFORMATION

Most institutions need reforming most of the time. Some institutions are reformed with gratifying regularity. Yet even in our supposedly secular age, the Western man in the street still knows that *the* Reformation refers to the Christian Church and to certain profoundly disturbing yet liberating events in sixteenth-century western Europe—events whose intellectual impact and political repercussions are with us still.

WHAT THE REFORMATION WAS

We may, nevertheless, still not understand why this event in the history of religion should also be an event in the history of politics. Even yet, as Figgis says, "Our politics are largely due to ecclesiastical differences which we are apt to despise, or to theological animosities which we ignore."[1] The Reformation symbolized a transfer of a good many of the powers and functions of the medieval Church to the secular state. But the most important shift, the shift in the loyalties of ordinary people, is the one hardest to describe. Nationalism is not the exact counterpart of religious devotion but nationalism as we know it was not possible until the pattern of religious devotion was altered. It is too simple to say that the Church as the agent of religious impulses declined and the new secular state filled the vacuum it left. On the one hand, the medieval Church was, as we have seen, also a government of sorts, with canon law a regulator of often quite practical matters. And the Church was always more than the priestly hierarchy. Both the secular prince and his subjects were assumed to be members of the same Church, the same communion of believers, as were the clergy. This meant that Christendom was not a body of communicants *within* a political order but a body of communicants *and* their political order.

In the initial stages of the Reformation, on the other hand, the secular prince, though still assumed to be a member of the faith by Protestant leaders, was credited with holding supreme power within his earthly and territorially limited jurisdiction. The medieval Church-state was conceived of as *universal,* or without fixed territorial frontiers and with

[1] J. N. Figgis, *Political Thought from Gerson to Grotius, 1414–1625* (New York: Harper & Row, 1960), p. 39.

mutually interdependent obligations. The Reformation state was a result of fragmentation and was territorially limited but legally all-powerful within its territory. Luther was not impressed by the virtue of secular rulers but he was not impressed by the virtue of ordinary citizens either; he saw it as necessary for practical as well as scriptural reasons to accept the power of secular law as coming from God. The Protestant "right of resistance" came, as we shall see, later.

The weakness at the center and the corresponding increase in the strength of smaller units of government were caused by more than the corruption of Rome. In strictly political terms, "the fifteenth century had seen a setback in the development of centralized government owing in part to the mutual exhaustion of France and England by the Hundred Years War, that premature movement of misdirected nationalism."[2] The overweening ambition of great and wealthy families, though pursued in the name of feudal ideals, was destroying the stability of earlier feudalism:

> the dying splendors of decadent chivalry were extremely expensive, though picturesque, and the later Middle Ages witnessed the bankruptcy, intellectual, moral, and practical, of the old-fashioned rulers and aristocracy. The beneficiaries of this carnival of arrogant incompetence and romanticism were the bourgeoisie and the surviving kings, who were driven into an alliance that proved more than a match for the great feudatories.[3]

The town-dwellers, or burghers, from which came the term "bourgeois," were also the beneficiaries of the growth in commerce resulting from the great explorations and the new trade routes, a growth that held a portent of an economic revolution whose consequences few could imagine.

The effect of the Reformation in England was simply to strengthen the already strong Henry VIII, who set himself against Rome[4] but who also wrote a tract condemning Luther. In Germany the local princes were not averse to using the religious upheavals to consolidate their power. But in France and England, where Church reform found support primarily in the nobility and in certain cities and provinces, the national religion remained Catholic in liturgy, if not in name.

FORERUNNERS OF THE REFORMATION

National feelings aroused against the Roman Church were not, obviously, unknown to Europe prior to the moment when Luther nailed his ninety-five theses to the door of the Wittenberg church in 1517. In the fourteenth century both the Germans and the English regarded the Avignon popes as untrustworthy allies of France. The protracted conflict between Louis of Bavaria and Pope John XXII (Louis was excommunicated and an interdict laid on his Germanic domains in 1324) had many nationalistic overtones. But politics alone will not explain the struggles either. Louis tried to get John XXII tried for heresy and his philosophical supporters—Marsilio of Padua and John of Jandun—echoed, we recall, the Albigensian and Waldensian preachers of an earlier era.

The Sects

As far back as the late twelfth century the followers of Peter Waldo (Waldensians) in the Alpine valleys and the Albigensians of Provence had moved in an anticlerical and

[2] John Bowle, *Western Political Thought* (New York: Barnes & Noble, 1961), p. 261.

[3] *Ibid.*, pp. 261–62.

[4] Pope Clement VII excommunicated Henry on July 11, 1533, after Henry had secured the passage of various anticlerical legislation, confiscated certain Church revenues, and induced Archbishop Cranmer to nullify his marriage to Catherine of Aragon and sanction his marriage to Anne Boleyn. The Act of Supremacy (November 11, 1534) may be taken as the start of the English Reformation, though at first there was no significant change in dogma or liturgy. Henry and his successors were declared Protector and Only Supreme Head of the Church and Clergy of England and the new national Church was named *Ecclesia Anglicana*.

antisacramental direction. In 1208 the not-so-innocent Pope Innocent III proclaimed a crusade against the Albigensians, who were cruelly crushed by King Louis VIII of France in 1226. The Waldensian movement lasted longer but eventually became entangled in Italian politics, lost its original orientation, and died out. But the ideas were not wholly lost: preaching in the vulgar tongues to the poor and outcast, these preachers believed in the spiritual equality of all believers—even women—and basing their religious practice on only what they could find in the Bible, they threw out the doctrine of purgatory, the buying of indulgences, the invocation of saints, and all the sacraments except baptism and communion. Some factions anticipated Luther's priesthood of all believers. Their ascetic piety, their emphasis on individual initiative and good works, bred, however imperceptibly, a new sense of individualism.[5]

Wyclif

Of more durability were the early reform movements of the north. John Wyclif (1320–84), professor of theology at Oxford, combined a stern faith in predestination that anticipated Calvin with a concept of a church opposed to the spirit of the world and hence poor in both spirit and material things. Jesus, he felt, intended his disciples to be propertyless. But Wyclif was cautious about drawing implications that would lead to social reform rather than Church reform. His attack on the wealth of the Church was shaped into a unique combination of natural law and scriptural legalism. Not altogether consistent with such legalism, perhaps, he also interpreted predestination in such a way that God's irrevocable grace flows not through institutions but directly to individuals. This had protestant, if not to say left-wing protestant, implications. Almost two hundred years before Henry VIII he proposed that England break away from the papacy. Wyclif's missionaries, called Lollards,[6] preached a minimum of worldly possessions and portrayed the Christian ideal as a communism of love.

Huss

Though the economic views of John Huss (1369–1415) were not as radical as those of Wyclif, the Hussite movement went further to advance them and their theological counterparts than had the Lollards. For refusing to renounce all Wyclif's forty-five articles that the Church had condemned as heretical, Huss, a preacher in Prague, Bohemia, was condemned by the Council of Constance in 1415 and burned at the stake. His death gave him a martyr's status and touched off a revolt in all of Bohemia and Moravia. (Huss's preaching in the cause of purifying the Church had been mixed with popular rhetoric appealing to Slavic patriotism and denouncing the Germans.) It is difficult to untangle the welter of motivations at work in the Hussite rebellion: the Bohemians wanted to get rid of German settlers; the nobles had their eye on the ample property of the Church; the middle class wanted to increase its power in the Prague Diet; the serfs wanted freedom and land; some of the lower clergy felt cheated and neglected by the hierarchy. One faction, the Taborites, whose genealogy went back to the Waldensians of the century before, smashed organs, altars, and church ornaments. They advocated the common ownership of property, ordinary dress for the clergy, and the elimination of all sacraments except baptism and communion. Their simple millenarian communism was an extension of Wyclif's tenets but their propensity toward violence and rebellion against

[5] See Ernst Troeltsch, *The Social Teaching of the Christian Churches,* trans. by Olive Wyon (New York: Harper & Row, 1960), Vol. 1, pp. 354–69. The Franciscan order, inspired by St. Francis of Assisi, shared some of these pietistic emphases but succeeded in being incorporated within the Mother Church rather than being cast out.

[6] Probably from the Middle Dutch *lollaerd,* from *lollen* (to murmur, mumble—hence prayers?). See Will Durant, *The Reformation* (New York: Simon and Schuster, 1957), p. 36 and Ch. 2, *passim.* On the subsequent influence of the Lollards, see George H. Williams, *The Radical Reformation* (Philadelphia: Westminster Press, 1962), pp. 401–03.

political order was quite alien to Wyclif's conception of Christian law.

Though difficult to measure, the influence of the Hussites on the Reformation is unmistakable. Though he had vigorously condemned the action of the Hussites after reading Huss's *De ecclesia,* Luther wrote in 1520: "Without being aware of it, I have now taught and held the whole doctrine of John Huss, and John Staupitz has taught the same things in ignorance. In short, we are all Hussites without knowing it, and therefore Paul and Augustine are literally Hussites."[7]

Erasmus

Because he wanted above all else to maintian Christian unity, Desiderius Erasmus (1467–1536), the Dutch "prince of humanists," must be called a forerunner of the Reformation rather than a reformer; but his careful criticism of the doctrine and practice of the Church was widely read in the sixteenth century and was enormously influential. Erasmus, "the cautious Humanist, who possessed a special talent for mildly deriding what struck him as being wrong (small, human, he said), and who would never launch a revolution, prepared more than anyone else a deep change in the religious ideas of very many people."[8] Erasmus gained the reputation as a humanist for the display of classical learning in his *Collectanea adagiorum* (1500), a compilation of adages, mainly of classical authors, with Erasmus' commentary; but his best known work was *In Praise of Folly* (1509), written in the Bucklersbury home of Sir Thomas More and titled with a pun on his host's name (*Encomium Moriae*). For obvious reasons, the work was published anonymously. In it Folly (*Moria*) speaks in her own name and shows why she and not the Virgin is the idol of the world. Princes,[9] courtiers, and mankind in general are made fun of but the theologians and priests take the brunt of Erasmus' wit. Theologians

> live in the third heaven, adoring their own persons and disdaining the poor crawlers upon earth. They are surrounded with a bodyguard of definitions, conclusions, corollaries, propositions explicit and propositions implicit. Vulcan's chains will not bind them. They cut the links with a distinction as with a stroke of an axe. They will tell you how the world was created. They will show you the crack where Sin crept in and corrupted mankind. They will explain to you how Christ was formed in the Virgin's womb; how accident subsists in synaxis without domicile in *place*. The most ordinary of them can do this. Those more fully initiated explain further whether there is an *instans* in Divine generation; whether in Christ there is more than a single filiation; whether "the Father hates the Son" is a possible proposition; whether God can become the substance of a woman, of an ass, of a pumpkin, or of the devil, and whether, if so, a pumpkin could preach a sermon, or work miracles, or be crucified. . . . Like the Stoics, they have their paradoxes—whether it is a smaller crime to kill a thousand men than to mend a beggar's shoe on a Sunday; whether it is better that the whole world should perish than that a woman should tell one small lie. Then there are Realists, Nominalists, Thomists, Albertists, Occamists, Scotists—all so learned that an apostle would have no chance with them in argument.[10]

Despite all this, he continues, "Still they are Folly's servants, though they disown their mistress."

If the learned are foolish, the ignorant are not wise. Of mendicant friars Erasmus says:

> They call it a sign of holiness to be unable to read. They bray out the Psalms in the churches like so many jackasses. They do not understand a word of them, but they fancy the

[7] In *Briefwechsel*. Quoted by Williams, p. 216.

[8] H. A. Enno van Gelder, *The Two Reformations in the Sixteenth Century* (The Hague: Nijhoff, 1961), p. 133.

[9] In 1516, after becoming privy counselor in the royal court at Brussels, Erasmus hastily wrote a mirror-of-princes-type tract, *Institutio principis Christiani* (*The Education of a Christian Prince*), an unexceptional collection of princely advice. He favored monarchy on traditional grounds and opposed the concentration of wealth. Most striking, perhaps, was his strong advocacy of more schools for popular education and his almost pacifist opposition to war.

[10] In J. A. Froude, ed., *The Life and Letters of Erasmus* (New York: Scribner's, 1894), pp. 130–31.

sound is soothing to the ears of the saints. . . . They pretend to poverty, but they steal into honest men's houses and pollute them, and, wasps as they are, no one dares refuse them admittance for fear of their stings. They hold the secrets of every family through the confessional, and when they are drunk, or wish to amuse their company, they let them out to the world. If any wretched man dares to imitate them they pay him off from the pulpits, and they never stop their barking till you fling them a piece of meat.[11]

We are puzzled by repeated descriptions of such a writer as cautious. But Erasmus did have a delicate sense of limitation and his wit was so welcome that Pope Leo X could read *Praise of Folly* with shrugging tolerance, while Luther could acknowledge it as an important precursor of his own work. Erasmus was popularly said to have laid the egg that Luther hatched. In fact, Erasmus' more sober work had a less spectacular but equally significant influence. About the same time that *Praise of Folly* came out, Erasmus, who was more than anything else a philologist, published his Greek New Testament with accompanying Latin translation. His critical work on the text of the Bible laid a foundation for modern biblical criticism. Attention to the context within which biblical utterances occur not only ultimately changed the character of religious belief but made possible a modification of the institutional power of a Church that had long held an official monopoly on biblical interpretation.[12]

Despite his satirical writings on religion, Erasmus hoped to see a Church still based in Rome but sufficiently different from the new Lutheran churches to be called a Third Church. His disagreement and eventual break with Luther came partly from theological and partly from temperamental sources. Erasmus did not like the belligerence of the Lutherans and he opposed their predestinarianism on grounds set forth in *Diatribe de libero arbitrio* (*A Plea on Behalf of the Free Will*, 1524). After reading Luther's hostile rejoinder, *De servo arbitrio* (*On the Slave Will*), the following year, Erasmus declared, "I shall bear therefore with this [the medieval] Church until I shall see a better one."[13] A man caught in the middle, able to see both sides too clearly, Erasmus revealed his anguish in a letter written to Adrian VI, the new pope, in 1523: "One party says I agree with Luther because I do not oppose him; the other finds fault with me because I oppose him. . . . I advised him to be moderate, and I only made his friends my enemies."[14]

Erasmus typifies the perennial plight of the man of thought in a time of crisis, aware that men of power are using his own ideas and judgments in ways he never intended while he is able only to watch helplessly.

More

Because Sir Thomas More (1478–1535) became a martyr for the Catholic Church by being executed by Henry VIII[15] and because he vigorously opposed Luther, there is a tendency to mark him down as a conservative or to say that his early writings, including the famous *Utopia* (1516), do not represent his

[11] *Ibid.*, p. 132.

[12] Another sober and influential work of Erasmus was *Enchiridion militis Christiani* (*A Handbook of Militant Christianity*, 1503), a devotional handbook that reveals the influence on Erasmus of the Stoics, Florentine Neo-Platonism, and Thomas à Kempis. See van Gelder, pp. 134–35. Van Gelder's long chapter on Erasmus is especially helpful.

[13] Quoted in Williams, p. 11.

[14] Froude, p. 310.

[15] He was beheaded for refusing to swear allegiance to Henry VIII as head of the Church. The charge of treason was based on perjured evidence. One story has it that, putting his head on the block, he asked the executioner to allow him to lay aside his beard, as "*that* had never committed any treason" (H. V. S. Ogden, in the Introduction to his edition of More's *Utopia* [New York: Appleton-Century-Crofts, 1949], p. VII). Subsequent page references are to this edition. Apocryphal or not, the story reflects the cheerful equanimity with which More faced life as well as death. His son-in-law, William Roper, in his *Lyfe of Sir Thomas More* (c. 1556), reports that as the lieutenant was helping More up the scaffold, More said, "See mee safe upp, and for my cominge downe lett mee shift for myselfe" (quoted in J. Rawson Lumby, ed., *Utopia* [Cambridge, Eng.: Cambridge Univ. Press, 1952], p. LV).

real convictions. But this would unfairly deny him credit for a degree of consistency quite remarkable for a man who exercises power as well as writes and who is, besides, beset by tremendous pressures.

A man of parts, More was a student at Oxford, became a barrister at Lincoln's Inn, studied Greek, and made friends with the great Erasmus before being elected to Parliament in 1504. He was subsequently undersheriff of London, undertreasurer of England, and, in 1529, he succeeded Cardinal Wolsey as Lord Chancellor. He resigned in 1532 because of his inability to serve as the king's agent in the divorce of Catherine of Aragon and in 1534 incurred Henry's fatal enmity by refusing to acknowledge his headship of the Church.

More began *Utopia*,[16] his claim to fame among political philosophers, during a diplomatic mission to Flanders in 1515. He described it as a trifle. His delight in telling a clever tale accounts in part, but only in part, for the form of the work, for a careful camouflage of some of its political implications was necessary. Written in Latin, the book was first published on the continent and an English translation did not appear until long after More's death. In the work More tells of meeting a Portuguese sailor named Raphael Hythloday (from *hythos,* or nonsense), who had traveled with Amerigo Vespucci on his explorations and found an isle near Persia where life, if not perfect, was unusually well regulated. By bringing his friends George Temse and Peter Giles into Book I—which was written last—More evoked an air of realism convincing enough to induce at least one missionary to vow that he would go to Utopia and convert the Utopians. Book I contains a description of More and Hythloday's initial encounter. The longer Book II, which is in the words of Hythloday, is a description of the institutions of Utopia.

Utopia is an island two hundred miles in breadth with fifty-four cities. The capital city is Amaurot (from the Greek *amauros,* or uncertain). Each city is surrounded by farm households of at least forty men and women under the direction of a master and mistress. A magistrate directs the work of thirty farm households. Likewise, in the city a magistrate, or phylarch (originally called a syphogrant), is in authority over each thirty households and a chief phylarch, elected annually, is over every ten phylarchs. There are two hundred phylarchs in all. They constitute an assembly and elect a prince for life, though he is subject to removal for despotic behavior. The island as a whole is governed by a senate consisting of three representatives from each city. As in the British House of Commons, measures introduced in the senate may not be debated on that day and votes are taken only after a measure has been considered on three different days.

There is no private property in Utopia, yet the people take great interest in the beauty of their homes. Houses have two doors, never locked: one opens onto the spacious street—twenty feet wide—and the other opens onto the gardens. There is considerable rivalry between residents of different streets to see which street can become most attractive. Every ten years all residents change houses by lot. Every city has four hospitals and all persons are well cared for. "No city desires to enlarge its bounds, for the inhabitants consider themselves husbandmen rather than landlords." People, including women, work but six hours a day. Farm work is somewhat harder but everyone is assigned to farm work for a two-year stint once in his life. Those who prefer farm work may stay on longer than two years. Each person has his own special trade or skill. In each of four districts of a city are a market and warehouses where products are brought and stored and where the head of each household can be issued whatever his household needs. There is no money: "Men and animals alike are greedy and rapacious from fear of want. Only human pride glories in surpassing others in conspicuous consumption. For this

[16] *U topos* is Greek for "no place." The original title was *Nusquama,* or "nowhere." It is not known when or how the title came to be changed.

kind of vice there is no room whatever in the Utopian way of life." Those few who show "an extraordinary capacity and disposition for learning in boyhood" are excused from labor to devote themselves to learning and literature. One of the few occupations closed to citizens is slaughtering, for this tends to brutalize those engaged in it. Bondsmen, who are usually criminals and are always chained, are used for this work. Citizens, soothed by music, eat in common dining halls. They are not forbidden to eat in their own homes but this is rarely done. They are, however, forbidden to travel out of their own district without a passport. Because Utopians "hate and detest" war, they hire mercenaries at considerable expense to do their fighting for them.

One may note many features of *Utopia* that seem unrealistic: the lack of money and greed, the lack of alliances with other nations and the propensity to defend the property of neighboring nations more vigorously than Utopia's own, the universal love of simplicity and beauty. ". . . the fashion of clothing never changes." No one is ever idle. ". . . no loafing is tolerated, and there are no pretexts for laziness, or opportunities. There are no taverns or ale houses, no brothels, no chances for corruption, no hiding places, no secret meetings." Marriages are broken only by death.[17]

Yet, for one so opposed to war More is remarkably detailed in his descriptions of warfare. And his passage on how kings have calculated to win Flanders, The Brabant, and Burgundy is worthy of Machiavelli. Moreover, there is an obvious danger in identifying all of the Utopians' preferences with More's preferences. At the very end More prudently inserts a general disclaimer: "I admit that not a few things in the manners and laws of the Utopians seemed very absurd to me: their way of waging war, their religious customs, as well as other matters, but especially the keystone of their entire system, namely, their communal living without the use of money." Nor could More easily accept the women priests of Utopia, an institution suggestive of Plato's *Republic*. In Part I More even engages in a brief debate with Hythloday over the role of philosophy in the state. The debate, however, seems double edged. It sets More apart from Hythloday but also sets him apart from Henry VIII: ". . . do not," he says, "force unheard of advice upon people when you know that their minds are different from yours. You must strive to guide policy indirectly, so that you make the best of things, and what you cannot turn to good, you can at least make less bad." Knowledge of More's relations with the domineering Henry makes this a poignant passage.

It is not difficult to see More's own historical situation and a good many of his own viewpoints reflected in the text of *Utopia*. Hythloday says that the English economy supports many superfluous trades, many, that is, that feed only the spirit of "luxury and wantonness." The English system makes people thieves and then punishes them severely for it. More shared Erasmus' gentle skepticism about modern logicians and their grand speculations on man-in-general; this was paralleled in the practical bent of the Utopians, whose philosophic concern was ethics, not ontology. Indeed, they, like More himself, understood religion to issue in happiness and even pleasure. And King Utopus, early lawgiver of Utopia, might well have been speaking for More in both the extent and the limits of his religious toleration:

> He did not venture to make dogmatic decisions in regard to religion, perhaps from some idea that God likes and inspires a variety and multiplicity of worship. He deemed it foolish and insolent for anyone to try to make all men accept his own beliefs by force and by threats. If one religion is true, and the others false, and if men use reason and moderation, he clearly foresaw that the truth would prevail by its own strength. But if men fight and riot, as evil and headstrong men will do, then the best and holiest re-

[17] Under proper auspices, a woman and her suitor are presented to each other naked before marriage so that some hidden deformity may not jeopardize the marriage.

ligion in the world will be crowded out by the emptiest superstitions, like wheat choked by thorns and briars. So he imposed no one religion on his people, and left each man free to believe what he would, with one exception. He made a solemn and severe law against any who sink so far below the dignity of human nature as to think that the soul dies with the body, or that the universe is carried along by chance without an over-ruling providence.[18]

More can be regarded as a spokesman for the new humanism in his tolerance, optimism, and rationalism; but there is much old-fashioned Thomism in this position as well. Aquinas, too, was optimistic and cheerful. The Utopians, says More,

define virtue as living according to nature. We have been ordained, they say, by God to this end. To follow nature is to conform to the dictates of reason in what we seek and avoid. The first dictate of reason is ardently to love and revere the Divine Majesty, to whom we owe what we are and whatever happiness we can reach. Secondly, reason warns us and summons us to lead our lives as calmly and cheerfully as we can, and to help all others in nature's fellowship to attain this good.[19]

A better claim to modernity, some say, can be made on the basis of More's attack on property. "I am persuaded that unless private property is entirely done away with, there can be no fair distribution of goods, nor can the world be happily governed." "In other places where they speak of the common good, every man is looking out for his own good. But in Utopia where there is no private property and where they zealously pursue the public business, there the name of commonwealth is doubly deserved." This is what made More attractive to latter-day socialists like Kautsky.[20]

More's imagination and cogency more than his profundity strike a spark. It is true that More dealt with two of the major problems of modern times—war and the distribution of property—but his framework remained thoroughly medieval and his communism was closer to monasticism than to the socialism of the future, with one important exception. As Ames argues,[21] More's humane sympathies led him to make acute and harsh observations on the condition of the English working people and he found the explanation of their misery not in human nature or fate or moral weakness but in their material conditions. In Book I More poignantly describes the suffering of the poor turned into wandering beggars by the enclosure of pasture lands. This sensitivity partly explains his opposition to the Reformation as well: in England in his time the Reformation meant the confiscation of Church and guild properties, "which were the chief social security of craftsman and peasant."[22]

Opposed to the Reformation, More was nevertheless a reformer not only of economic relationships but of religion as well. A conservative could not have made Hythloday say that Christ's commandments

disagree with our way of living far more than my discourse does. . . . Seeing that men will not fit their ways to Christ's pattern, the preachers have fitted His teaching (as though it were a leaden rule) to human customs, to get agreement somehow or other. The only result that I can see is that men become more confirmed in their wickedness.[23]

More was at once medieval and modern, a reformer and a traditionalist, a man of thought and a man of action, a man of wit and a man of utter seriousness. He fits easily into no category, except perhaps that of saint, which is itself a questionable category.

[18] *Utopia*, p. 72.
[19] *Ibid.*, p. 48.
[20] See Karl Kautsky, *Thomas More and His Utopia*, trans. by H. J. Stenning (New York: Russell & Russell, 1959). But, not surprisingly, Kautsky found More to be basically bourgeois in his outlook. See also Frederic Seebohm, *The Oxford Reformers* (New York: Dutton, Everyman's, 1914).

[21] Russell Ames, *Citizen Thomas More and His Utopia* (Princeton: Princeton Univ. Press, 1949).
[22] *Ibid.*, p. 178.
[23] *Utopia*, p. 24.

LUTHER

Life

Martin Luther, the first of the seven children of Hans and Grethe Luther, was born in Eisleben, a small town northwest of Leipzig, in 1483. Hans Luther, an upward-moving miner of stubborn and domineering temperament, hoped that Martin would become a lawyer and accumulated sufficient means to send him to school. In 1505, the year Martin received an M.A. degree at the University of Erfurt, he decided to become a monk. The decision followed a strange and frightening experience in a thunderstorm when Martin was jolted by a bolt of lightning and vowed to St. Anne—who, ironically and significantly, was his father's patron saint—that he would become a monk.[24]

In 1508 young Luther was assigned to the Augustinian monastery in Wittenberg and became instructor in logic and physics at the University of Wittenberg. He later became professor of theology, a position he retained for most of his life. A visit to Rome in 1510 revealed no outburst of indignation in Luther but in succeeding years his hostility to certain papal policies, especially the abuse of indulgences, grew. On October 31, 1517, Luther nailed his famous ninety-five theses to the door of the Castle Church in Wittenberg, the church of Frederick the Wise, Elector of Saxony. Luther knew that each November 1, All Saints' Day, the Elector displayed his grandiose collection of saintly relics and so he expected a large crowd to read his theses. Moreover, he sent a copy to the archbishop. Yet the significance of the theses could hardly have been seen to be what we now, with hindsight, attribute to them. Few of Luther's remarks could be classed as outright heresy and even on the chief item of complaint, indulgences, a moderate tone generally prevailed:

> (41) Papal indulgences should only be preached with caution, lest people gain a wrong understanding, and think that they are preferable to other good works: those of love.
>
> (43) Christians should be taught that one who gives to the poor, or lends to the needy, does a better action than if he purchases indulgences.
>
> (47) Christians should be taught that they purchase indulgences voluntarily, and are not under obligation to do so.
>
> (48) Christians should be taught that, in granting indulgences, the pope has more need, and more desire, for devout prayer on his own behalf than for ready money.[25]

One can find a sharpness in the wording of some of Luther's theses, however, that is a foreshadowing of the vitriol that is to come:

> (79) It is blasphemy to say that the insignia of the cross with the papal arms are of equal value to the cross on which Christ died.
>
> (86) Again: Since the pope's income today is larger than that of the wealthiest of wealthy men, why does he not build this one church of St. Peter with his own money rather than with the money of indigent believers?
>
> (87) Again: What does the pope remit or dispense to people who, by their perfect penitence, have a right to plenary remission or dispensation?
>
> (90) These questions are serious matters of consequence to the laity. To suppress them by force alone, and not to refute them by giving reasons, is to expose the church and the pope to the ridicule of their enemies, and to make Christian people unhappy.[26]

[24] For a fascinating and wise account of the intricate relations between Martin and his father and their effect on his later life and thought, see Erik Erikson, *Young Man Luther, A Study in Psychoanalysis and History* (New York: Norton, 1962). See also Preserved Smith, *The Life and Letters of Martin Luther* (Boston: Houghton Mifflin, 1911) and Roland H. Bainton, *Here I Stand* (New York: Abington-Cokesbury Press, 1950).

[25] *Reformation Writings of Martin Luther,* trans. by Bertram Lee Woolf (London: Lutterworth Press, 1952), Vol. 1, pp. 36–37. Unless noted, further quotations from the theses *An Open Letter, De captivitate Babylonica,* and *On the Freedom of the Christian Man* are from this volume of this edition. Technically, an indulgence is the remission of punishment, either on earth or in purgatory, following the forgiveness of sin through the sacrament of penance.

[26] *Ibid.,* pp. 40 and 42.

There followed a debate in writing and of growing acrimony between Luther and Tetzel, Dominican friar and leading money-raiser (mainly by selling indulgences) for Albrecht of Brandenberg, Archbishop of Mainz. Albrecht needed the money to pay Pope Leo X for arranging his confirmation as archbishop and Leo needed the money to finish building the Basilica of St. Peter in Rome. At this point Luther became an apparent pawn in the power struggle between the German princes and the Italian papacy as they fought over the dubious economic burdens entailed by loyalty to the pope. The moderate Leo, sensing political difficulties, rescinded a summons to Luther to appear in Rome and instead ordered him to appear before Cardinal Cajetan in Augsburg in October, 1518 to answer charges of indiscipline and heresy. Luther refused to recant and the venerable but undiplomatic Cajetan asked Frederick the Wise to send Luther to Rome. Frederick refused. In Luther's account of this episode the term "reformation" first came to be used, though Luther certainly had not yet imagined that reformation would mean more than internal improvement led from within the Church.

A papal emissary, struck by the growing antipapal feeling in Germany, managed to induce Luther to write a letter of complete submission to Leo. Leo replied in a friendly spirit, inviting Luther to Rome. But the ambivalent Luther refused to go. Later that year, when Luther debated Dr. Johann Eck in Leipzig, defending Huss and questioning the primacy of the bishop of Rome in early Christianity, his heresy was made overt and his position appeared beyond the point of retreat. Eck recommended excommunication.

In 1520, Leo issued *Exsurge Domine* (*Rise, O Lord*) condemning forty-one statements by Luther, ordering the public burning of his writings, and ordering him to come to Rome and make a public recantation within sixty days or be excommunicated. Luther replied with his *An den christlichen Adel Deutscher Nation von Standes Besserung* (*Open Letter to the Christian Nobility of the German Nation Concerning the Reform of the Christian Estate*),[27] after which came his excommunication. In the same year, 1520, Luther wrote two more politically significant tracts, *De captivitate Babylonica ecclesiae praeludium* (*The Babylonian Captivity of the Church*)[28] and *Von der Freyheit eynes Christen Menschen* (*On the Freedom of the Christian Man*). We shall discuss these three works in a moment. In the elation of revolutionary fervor, Luther publicly burned the writings of the pope in December, 1520, and, matching extremity with extremity, declared that no man could be saved unless he renounced the papacy.

To cope with growing dissension, young Emperor Charles V called together a Diet at Worms with leading nobles, clergy, and representatives of free cities. Luther was summoned to answer the resolution proposing his condemnation. On April 18, 1521, after one day of equivocation, Luther answered in German the Latin charge of putting his own will ahead of the Church: ". . . my conscience is captive to the Word of God. I cannot and I will not retract anything."[29]

Condemned by Charles and a divided Diet, Luther was spirited away by Frederick the Wise to the castle of Wartburg, where he stayed a year, until the Protestant rebellion in Wittenberg became so disorderly that Luther felt obliged to return and preach order. From there—writing, preaching, teaching—abetted by his young wife Katie and growing family, he helped to change the religious consciousness of the Western world. Luther's power was the power of words—words now spread more widely than ever,

[27] Also translated as *An Address to the German Nobility* or (by Woolf) *An Appeal to the Ruling Class*, among other English titles.

[28] Translated by Woolf as *The Pagan Servitude of the Church, a First Inquiry*. See *Reformation Writings*, Vol. 1, pp. 201–307.

[29] *Luther's Works*, Jaroslav Pelikan and Helmut T. Lehmann, eds. (Philadelphia: Muhlenberg Press, 1955–), Vol. 32, p. 112. The most famous part of Luther's statement—"Here I stand. I can do no other. May God help me. Amen."—was added to the Latin text in German and may be spurious. Luther probably said only, "May God help me." See Roger A. Hornsby's footnote at p. 113.

thanks to the invention of the printing press. He invested his words with intellectual honesty, moral conviction, and an engaging Christian spirit, for he could be humble and humane despite, and almost along with, the excesses of his all-too-human anger.

An Open Letter to The Christian Nobility

Politics was always incidental to Luther and his political thought must be gleaned from the interstices between theological arguments. Perhaps because of its essential simplicity, Luther's political thought can nevertheless be illustrated by reference to a few representative expressions of it.

In his famous *Sermon on Good Works* (May, 1520) Luther had addressed a few short passages to secular rulers calling on them to attack the real Turk, that is, the papal establishment. In August, 1520, he extended this theme in *An Open Letter to the Christian Nobility*. The egalitarian implications of the tract were far reaching and influential.

Luther begins by battering at the "three walls" by which "the Romanists have very cleverly surrounded themselves." The first is the claim that secular authorities had no justification to rule over them. The second, used when Scripture was quoted against them, is the claim that only the pope was competent to interpret Scripture. The third, used when threatened by a council, is the claim that only the pope could summon a council. "May God now help us, and give us one of those trumpets with which the walls of Jericho were overthrown; that we may blow away these walls of paper and straw, and set free the Christian." The development of the attack on the first wall led Luther to a basic Protestant principle, the priesthood of all believers. Whatever the work we are called to do, says Luther, whether we are priests, farm-workers, or princes,

> we have one baptism, one gospel, one faith, and are all equally Christian. For baptism, gospel, and faith alone make men religious and create a Christian people. When a pope or bishop anoints, grants tonsures, ordains, consecrates, dresses differently from laymen, he may make a hypocrite of a man, or an anointed image, but never a Christian or a spiritually-minded man. The fact is that our baptism consecrates us all without exception, and makes us all priests. As St. Peter says, "You are a royal priesthood, and a realm of priests."[30]

Priests are selected to perform special functions but only as a convenience. The priest acts on behalf of all Christians, "of whom all have the same authority." "It would be similar if ten brothers, kings' sons and equal heirs, were to choose one of themselves to rule the kingdom for them. All would be kings and of equal authority, although one was appointed to rule." Note that there is no implication here that kings should be elected by all citizens, for in the analogy one is elected by his brother heirs. The point is that all Christians are brother heirs in the spiritual kingdom. Luther's religious egalitarianism was not matched by a political egalitarianism.

Nor was there any hint of what twentieth-century man would call the separation of Church and state: "Those who exercise secular authority have been baptized like the rest of us, and have the same faith and the same gospel; therefore we must admit that they are priests and bishops. They discharge their office as an office of the Christian community, and for the benefit of that community." Or, again, "since the secular authorities are ordained by God to punish evil doers and to protect the law-abiding, so we ought to leave them free to do their work without let or hindrance everywhere in Christian countries."

Luther was unquestionably naive in neglecting restraints on secular rulers other than inclusion within the Christian fold and in fact in the years to follow some rulers were all too eager to exploit Luther's position to justify their own expansion of power at the

[30] *Reformation Writings*, pp. 112–13. *Anointed image* (*oelgotzen*) has a double meaning: literally, an idol smeared with oil; figuratively, a half-wit, or dummy. The scriptural reference is I Peter 2:9.

expense of the Roman Church. Yet it is not hard to understand how Luther, who in 1517 had wanted only to reform the Church and not split it or society asunder, should now be overcautious in his support of the forces of law and order. Citing once again the ubiquitous Romans 13 Luther continues:

the social corpus of Christendom includes the secular government as one of its component functions. This government is spiritual in status, although it discharges a secular duty. It should operate, freely and unhindered, upon all members of the entire corpus, should punish and compel where guilt deserves or necessity requires, in spite of pope, bishops, and priests.[31]

Luther complained that if a priest is killed a whole country is placed under interdict and asks why a priest's being killed should be so different from a farmer's being killed. He found no scriptural basis for such special privilege and power to the clergy but he did find a scriptural—as well as a practical—basis for the power of secular rulers. Luther was really medieval in his view of secular government but his vigorous antipapal polemics shattered the institutional checks that could make that view viable. His powerful intellect and personality were never brought squarely to bear on the sociological implications of his religious reform:

Luther would never shirk a mundane task such as exhorting the elector to repair the city wall to keep the peasant's pigs from rooting in the villagers' gardens, but he was never supremely concerned about pigs, gardens, walls, cities, princes, or any and all of the blessings and nuisances of this mortal life. The ultimate problem was always God and man's relationship to God. For this reason political and social forms were to him a matter of comparative indifference.[32]

With characteristic enthusiasm, sarcasm, and wit, Luther proceeded in *An Open Letter* first to knock down the three walls and then to attack the system of cardinals and the Roman bureaucracy and its pomp, extravagance, and corruption. He lists twenty-seven "proposals for improving the state of Christendom," including: abolishing the infamous indulgences, allowing the clergy to marry, surrendering most papal lands in Italy, abolishing mendicancy "everywhere," reducing the number of special masses, and taking away from Rome "annates" paid by German cities and the right to bestow benefices in Germany. He also ridiculed kissing the pope's feet and carrying him about in a sedan chair when he was perfectly capable of walking. Proposal 24 would invite the Hussites to join "us"—meaning the Roman Church, of which Luther still felt himself a member.

Proposal 25 was directed to universities, who were attacked, surprisingly, not so much for their subservience to Rome as for their subservience to ancient Greece. Although Luther had taught Aristotle at both Erfurt and Wittenberg, he was sharply critical of the emphasis on Aristotle rather than the Scriptures in the universities where

the blind pagan teacher Aristotle is of more consequence than Christ. In my view, Aristotle's writings on *Physics, Metaphysics, On the Soul,* and *Ethics,* hitherto regarded as most important, should be set aside along with all others that boast they treat of natural objects, for in fact they have nothing to teach about things natural or spiritual.[33]

"Without pride," Luther adds, he can say he understands Aristotle better than Aquinas or Scotus did—which may be quite accurate, since Aquinas and Scotus read Aristotle in a Latin translation from the Arabic and Luther read him in the original Greek.

Luther commended the study of Latin, Greek, Hebrew, mathematics, history, medicine, and law as well as theology but he wanted all these freed from the restrictions of canon law, which contained but "the arbi-

[31] *Ibid.*, p. 117.
[32] Bainton, p. 216.

[33] *Reformation Writings,* p. 184. Luther's critique of classical philosophy is brilliantly exemplified in his *Lectures on Romans* (1515–16). See the Wilhelm Pauck translation in the Library of Christian Classics, Vol. 15 (Philadelphia: Westminster Press, 1961), pp. 335–37 and 414–19.

trary choices preferred by the pope and his lickspittles." Even here, Luther's irritation with political complexities is evident:

The temporal law! God help us, what a rank growth that has become. Although it is much better, wiser, and more proper than the "spiritual law," in which nothing is good except the name, nevertheless there is far too much temporal law. Surely there would be quite enough law if there were but wise rulers side by side with the Holy Scriptures.[34]

Luther would have appeals to common law and the customs of each people as the basic line of legal guidance, with resort to imperial law only rarely. Lest it be thought that Luther was interested only in reducing the quantity of legal education to increase the quantity of theological education, it ought to be noted that he proposed to reduce the number of required books on theology. Reading many books, he said, does not make a man learned; but reading a good book often may. He would throw out the degree Doctor of Holy Scripture, for no man is worthy of it and it had been debased.

Proposal 26 (added in the second edition) attacks the legal fiction of the Holy Roman Empire—an attempt, thought Luther, to preserve the shadow of Roman authority in Germany without a legitimate and substantial base. By design, the Romanists took the name of the empire—no longer viable in application to the lands of the old Empire—and by crowning Charlemagne in Rome in 800 set up a new Germanic empire, which, piece by piece, was given away in the form of feudal states. "Thereby we (the Germans) became the pope's feudatories, and there is now a second Roman empire, one built by the popes, but on German foundations." This was rank political injustice: Germans had been deceived and misused. Nevertheless, said Luther, "So be it. For God, the Lord, it is a small thing to toss empires and principalities to and fro. He makes so free with them that sometimes He gives a kingdom to an errant knave, and takes it from one of a religious mind."

Here are the seeds of the political quietism that has marked the whole of Lutheran history down to the time of Hitler. Politics is not very important to God, so it should not be too important to the Christian. But Luther's rage at the pope leads to prophetic outbursts that seem to contradict his advice to suffer tyrants cheerfully:

We must let the Romanists see for once what it is that we have received from God through them. So be it and be it so! Let the pope give us the Roman empire and all it means, but let our country be free from his intolerable taxes and frauds. Give us back our freedom, our power, our honor, our bodies and souls; and let us be an empire as an empire ought to be, and let there be an end of his word and claims.[35]

But it soon becomes explicit that the "us" of "let us be free" is a collective "us." The German emperor should be free of papal taxes but nothing is thereby implied about the political freedom of the emperor's subjects. And the "let" of "let us be free" is a moral and not a political imperative. That is, Luther is making a prophetic and unilateral appeal to the pope's conscience rather than suggesting procedures for inducing bilateral transfer of political authority. The verbal abuse Luther continually heaped upon the pope was, to be sure, more likely to arouse anger than conscience and could be seen as a kind of political invective, a kind of incitement, albeit largely unpremeditated.

To divide Luther's thought in any way between political and religious aspects is artificial, yet some such distinction may be invoked in comparing the way Luther uses terms like "the Romanists" or "Romish despotism" when attacking papal institutions and the way he uses "us" to designate members of the Christian community, from which not all followers of Rome would be excluded. To put it another way, although all of Luther's writings were religious rather than political in motivation, insofar as he attacked certain institutions of Church organization, finance, and control he could be said to be

[34] *Ibid.*, p. 187.

[35] *Ibid.*, p. 194.

waging a political war within the Church and against the secular power of the Church.

The last of the twenty-seven proposals of *An Open Letter* is the only one that is not devoted to the transgressions of the clergy; one out of twenty-seven may be an index of Luther's secular interests. This section, a "consideration of temporal failings," is a quite revealing catchall:

(1) People of means are wearing too many fancy clothes. They dress in silk and velvet when they should stick to wool and linen.

(2) There is too much foreign commerce. "I do not see many goodly habits which have been introduced into the country by commerce."

(3) The traffic in annuities (a way of getting around antiusury regulations) is traffic with "a device of the devil."[36]

(4) The Fuggers' banking house and similar companies "we must surely bridle."[37]

(5) The abuse of eating and drinking is "a special failing of ours."

(6) Finally, houses of prostitution ought to be closed down.

In all these areas the secular government would need to take a hand. Luther expresses a genuine sympathy with rulers who had to take on such burdens: "Everyone might learn from this what a fearful responsibility it is to sit on high and to act as a ruler." Then Luther slips into a remarkable digression in which he expresses the need for more young men to marry and to enter secular vocations. Of men going into the priesthood he says,

> I fear that not one in a hundred has any other reason than need of a livelihood, plus doubt about being able to support himself as a married man. Hence they first lead very disorderly lives, and sow their wild oats, and are sated; but experience shows they tend to sow them within. I think it is a true proverb which says, "Most of the monks and priests are doubters." So things go on, as we see.[38]

So Luther commiserates with the young, who have no one to guide them, for neither priest nor ruler pays attention to their real duties. "They want to exercise authority far and wide, and yet they are of no use. Oh, what rarities will lords and rulers be in heaven on this account."

From his sympathy with rulers Luther has quickly moved to doubts of their salvation. Perhaps suddenly aware of his rambling, he breaks off as one would at the end of a personal letter: "Enough for the present." Yet he cannot relinquish the pen even now without one or two more barbs thrust at Rome. He knows that many will feel he has spoken too harshly but, he explains, he has had to speak and God, not man, will judge him. "My great concern and primary fear are that my case may remain uncondemned; that would show me it was not yet pleasing to God."[39] Here are all the Lutheran traits—brashness, color, honesty, disdain of earthly authority, and a combination of human sympathy and righteous anger that do not always mix smoothly but that engage us irresistibly.

De Captivitate Babylonica

This tract contains even fewer political references than *An Open Letter* does, but it

[36] See Luther's essay on *Trade and Usury* (1524), trans. by Charles M. Jacobs, in *Luther's Works,* Vol. 45, pp. 233–310. Luther could not know that the high prices and growing disparity in wealth he saw were a portent of great economic transformations to come. Nor did he seem aware that they were partly a result of the discovery of America and an all-water route to India. To him they were the result of simple greed, of which he had ample evidence. His condemnation of usury was not much different from those of the Scholastics or Aristotle. See *Nichomachean Ethics,* 1133^{a-b}. See also F. E. Cranz, *An Essay on the Development of Luther's Thought on Justice, Law and Society* (Cambridge, Mass.: Harvard Univ. Press, 1959), and Gustav Wingren, *Luther on Vocation* (Philadelphia: Muhlenberg Press, 1957).

[37] The banking house of Fuggers had a monopoly of papal finances in Germany and supervised the collection of indulgence money. It had loaned money to Albert of Brandenburg to pay Pope Leo X to finish rebuilding St. Peter's. See Bainton, pp. 74–76.

[38] *Reformation Writings,* pp. 198–99.

[39] Part of Luther's winsomeness is shown by the fact that he can speak of hoping to displease "my friends the papists" and not make "friends" sound utterly satirical.

reinforces the latter's egalitarian thrust, primarily by means of another case for the priesthood of all believers. The essay concerns sacramental doctrine and expresses the position that was to become, with a few exceptions, standard doctrine for the Reformed churches. Only two of the seven sacraments of the Roman Church, namely baptism and communion, it argues, should be retained because only these are sanctioned by the Scriptures, although confession is encouraged by the Scriptures and Luther was willing to give the sacrament of penance an acceptable but secondary status. But confirmation, matrimony, holy orders, and extreme unction were not to be regarded as divinely ordained sacraments. *De captivitate Babylonica* produced *A Defense of the Seven Sacraments* by no less a personage than King Henry VIII of England. This earned him the title of *Defensor fidei* in a bull by Leo X (October, 1521).

The critique of holy orders was another vehicle for asserting the priesthood of all believers. It is worth noting that this doctrine is even today generally understood in a one-sided way. It meant, to be sure, that individual men may have a direct relationship to God and do not need the mediation of a priest but it also meant, paradoxically, that every man is obliged to be a mediator, a priest, to every other man. No man needs an official priest; every man ought to be an unofficial priest. "According to what Scripture teaches us, what we call priesthood is a form of service." The implications of this doctrine for the communal organization of man's life on earth were great but were, as we shall see, developed more fully in Calvinism than in Lutheranism.

There is a common sense here as elsewhere in Luther that can explain much of his dramatic popular impact. On ordination he says,

> My point is, not that I wish to condemn a rite which has been celebrated ever since the church was founded; but that I refuse to place a man-made fiction among things divine; I refuse to construe anything as if it were of divine institution when it has not been divinely ordained. Otherwise, we shall appear ridiculous to a hostile critic.[40]

But common sense is not the same as surrender to common opinion (*De captivitate Babylonica* was written in Latin precisely because its audience was not to be a popular one, though Luther's enemies immediately translated it into German) and Luther does not shrink from the difficult and subtle question of how the mind can take the Scriptures as an ultimate source of truth if it rejects the Church—or any other agency—as an ultimate source of truth. He does not, of course, examine questions of historical validity that more modern thinkers might raise but his response to the question of the nature of knowledge is by no means crude:

> as Augustine says . . . the mind is so laid hold of by the truth itself, that by virtue of that truth, it is able to reach certainty in any judgment. Nevertheless, the mind is unable to judge the truth as such, although it is compelled to say, when entirely confident, this is true. For example, the mind declares with infallible assurance that three and seven make ten, and yet it cannot adduce any reason why that is true, although it cannot deny its truth. The fact is that, rather than being itself the judge, the mind has been taken captive, and has accepted a verdict pronounced by the Truth herself sitting on the tribunal. Similarly by the illumination of the spirit, when doctrine comes up for decision and approval, the church possesses a "sense" whose presence is certain, though it cannot be proved. Just as no philosopher attempts to appraise the conceptions of common sense, but is rather judged by them, so, among ourselves, there is a spirit of which we are aware, which judges all things, but is judged by none, as the apostle says. But I digress.[41]

Luther is able to speak as a philosopher even when arguing the limits of philosophy and yet to do so in such a way that the minds of ordinary persons are honored: ". . . the common man received his own dignity, not so much because of the doctrine of the priesthood of all believers, inestimably

[40] *Reformation Writings*, p. 308.
[41] *Ibid.*, p. 309.

important though that was, but because he was led to respect his own powers of moral judgment."[42]

On the Freedom of The Christian Man

This was written in October, 1520, and published the following month. Luther wrote the first version in Latin but also prepared a less polished but perhaps more influential German version. He sent a copy of the Latin version to Leo along with his *Open Letter to Pope Leo X* in November.

The title is somewhat deceptive, for the crucial content is not the old free-will-determinism controversy, as might be thought, but an exposition of the theory of justification by faith—or, more accurately, justification by grace. This theory constitutes a Protestant tenet of equal significance to that of the priesthood of all believers.[43] The doctrine derives rather directly from Paul,[44] however, and cannot be called exclusively Lutheran. Its institutional significance is that it puts salvation beyond the reach of any prescribed set of rituals, laws, or institutions. The doctrine that one is justified by faith rather than by works must not be crudely interpreted to mean that (1) good works are unimportant or (2) believing a thing hard enough will make it so. Good works are important but they are the fruits of divine grace, not a way of earning divine grace. Scriptural commandments, observes Luther, prescribe many good works that we ought to perform, "but this does not mean that they are fulfilled by us. They give good instructions, but no assistance. They teach what man should do, but give no power to do it."

Luther never explicitly defines the two key words in this exposition, faith and works, but he leads us to see that faith involves three interrelated ideas: basic trust, active obedience, and grace. Faith is much more than mere intellectual assent for both Paul and Luther. It is commitment of the whole self. One can follow certain procedures that can make him receptive to grace if it comes but only God can give it. The Church is called the bride of Christ because, like a bride, it can prepare for conception but cannot conceive without the sperm of the divine groom.[45] After a man's pride is lost and he acknowledges his inability to fulfill God's commandments on his own, another word of God comes, not of command but of covenant—the promise of faith. God "alone commands and alone fulfills." When faith comes,

> all commandments and laws are like broken chains; and if [a man's] chains are broken, he is assuredly free. That is Christian freedom, gained by faith alone. It is wrong to think this means that we can either be idle or do evil; rather it means that we have no need to perform works of merit in order to attain godliness and salvation.[46]

Though primarily concerned with the inner man, Luther did not ignore the outer man. Though such a conception of freedom can—and often did—induce indifference to earthly affairs and even passivity, it need not. Writers who blame Hitler on Lutheran quietism oversimplify a good deal. On the one hand, the man blessed with Christian freedom is a slave to no man, only to God. Hence he can almost literally tell the most exalted kings and pontiffs to go to hell—an exercise Luther, in the case of pontiffs, was almost too delighted to perform. On the other hand, the free Christian seeks to be the servant of every man—to perform those good works most needful for the welfare of others, rich or poor, humble or mighty,

> For a man does not live alone in his own body,

[42] Woolf, in the Introduction to his translation of *De captivitate Babylonica* in *Reformation Writings*, p. 201.

[43] Not that the doctrine of the priesthood of all believers was neglected in *On the Freedom of the Christian Man:* it was discussed there even more explicitly than in *De captivitate Babylonica*.

[44] See I Corinthians 9:19; Romans 1:1, 7:15–24, 8:21, and 10:4. See also Luther's early *Lectures on Romans*, pp. 3–8, 202–59, 288–93, and 365–66.

[45] Man's inability to earn grace by his own efforts is not too unlike his inability to see the vision of truth by his own efforts in the Platonic view of things. See Plato's Seventh Epistle.

[46] *Reformation Writings*, pp. 361 and 362.

but among other men in the world. Therefore he cannot remain without works in his contacts with others; he must speak to and cooperate with them, although none of these actions is necessary for his own godliness or salvation. In all such works his will should be subject to no constraint, and should only be directed to the way in which he may serve other people, and be helpful to them.[47]

The point Luther is making in all of this is, as always, a theological and not a political one, namely that such service should be seen as the fruit of the good tree of grace and not as the means whereby men produce good trees. Freedom is not a permit for lawlessness but a state of motivation that represents obligations well beyond the law.

Concerning Temporal Authority

The man touched by grace can leave law behind. But what about the mass of mankind who have not known Christian freedom or who know it only very imperfectly? Is not political law a necessity for them and is not their obedience to that law a necessity for the maintenance of an orderly civil society? The answer to this question for Luther was, of course, affirmative, as it was for most of the writers we have so far studied. But Luther was forced by his unique position to approach this question with mixed feelings. Having held that the Roman Church should in all cases obey secular authority, he nevertheless refused the command of the Diet of Worms, a secular authority, to recant and cease writing his heretical treatises. And what exactly were the duties of princes sympathetic with Lutheran doctrine but also feeling the weight of legal bonds tying them to Charles V? Many were asking questions about these matters and Luther finally agreed to address himself to them in writing. Thus came *Von welltlicher Uberkeytt wie weytt man yhr gehorsam schuldig sey* (*Temporal Authority: To What Extent It Should Be Obeyed*, 1523).[48]

The treatise is in three parts. The first upholds the divine origin of temporal authority, the second traces the limits of temporal power, and the third gives some pastoral advice to princes. According to the first, true Christians do not need secular law. But there are not very many true Christians in the world:

If all the world were composed of real Christians, that is, true believers, there would be no need for or benefits from prince, king, lord, sword, or law. They would serve no purpose since Christians have in their heart the Holy Spirit, who both teaches and makes them do injustice to no one, to love everyone, and to suffer injustice and even death willingly and cheerfully at the hands of anyone.[49]

Take away law and there would be no change in these people's behavior. But take away law from most men and it is like "loosing the ropes and chains of the savage wild beasts and letting them bite and mangle everyone." It is like putting wolves, lions, eagles, and sheep in the same fold. Hence secular law has been sanctioned by the Scriptures and "laid down for the sake of the lawless."[50]

But how can the awesome power of constables, judges, and executioners be reconciled with other scriptural commandments from Jesus Himself to "love thy enemies" (Matt. 5:44) and to "resist not evil" (Matt. 5:38)? This, says Luther, is advice for Christians and not, he seems to say, sound public policy. Christ sanctioned the sword but did not wield it and neither should Christians simply for their own sake. A Christian should never resort even to a court of law to protect his own interests, even though courts of law are necessary for society. The Christian should obey the law not for himself but to help his non-Christian fellow men learn peace. This

[47] *Ibid.*, p. 375.

[48] Also translated *Concerning Temporal Authority* and *On Secular Authority*. Subsequent quotations are from *Luther's Works*, trans. by J. J. Schindel, rev. by Walther I. Brandt. Vol. 45, pp. 75–129.

[49] *Ibid.*, p. 89.

[50] See Romans 13:1–2; I Timothy 1:9; I Peter 2:13–14. From these sources Luther concludes that civil law "is in the world by God's will and ordinance."

is not possible "unless the governing authority is honored and feared." The Christian serves his government not for himself but for others: "You have the kingdom of heaven; therefore, you should leave the kingdom of the earth to anyone who wants to take it." With unconvincing logic Luther denies that this is a "council of perfection" and chastises the "sophists" who say that it is. *All* Christians are obliged to love enemies and resist no evil. What is ambiguous here is the term "Christians." At one time it refers to all who acknowledge Jesus as the Christ; at another time it refers to those few who are models of loving behavior. Luther does not—perhaps cannot—state this distinction clearly and stick to it.

So long as one serves the interests of others and not simply private self-interest, there is nothing to prevent a Christian from being a hangman, a constable, a jurist, a lawyer, or a prince. But these people are put in a curious and tension-filled position: "You suffer evil and injustice, and yet at the same time you punish evil and injustice; you do not resist evil, and yet at the same time, you do resist it." Christians in civil authority, if Luther is correct, are split personalities, the innocent victims of evil-doers in their private selves and the powerful scourges of evil-doers in their public selves. It is not surprising, if this is true, that there should be so few Christian rulers.

In the last paragraph of Part I Luther takes up the question that twentieth-century man might think most significant in this whole area of political obligation and dismisses it curtly: if the use of the sword in the interests of others rather than in the interests of self is the criterion that justifies the actions of official rulers, why could not a private individual pick up the sword on his own properly motivated initiative? "Answer: such a miracle is not impossible, but very rare and hazardous."[51] From the time of Luther on, we are likely to say, it is less rare, though no less hazardous.

Part II of *Concerning Temporal Authority* tries to demonstrate that there are clear moral limits to the power that secular rulers may exercise. In brief, secular law is unjustified in trying to control conscience or thought. "We want to make this so clear that everyone will grasp it, and that our fine gentlemen, the princes and bishops, will see what fools they are when they seek to coerce the people with their laws and commandments into believing this or that." They have "no power over souls." In trying to make judgments on the conscience of others, rulers are like judges making a decision on evidence that is neither seen nor heard. Only God can judge souls.[52]

But rulers do have proper authority over property, including the bodies of subjects. Luther—basing his comments on actual events in Meissen, Bavaria, and the Mark—could be quite explicit in drawing the boundaries between citizen cooperation and resistance. If troops search one's house to confiscate one's Bibles or forbidden books, one is to stand by and permit it to be done. But one is not to "lift a little finger" to cooperate with those who would suppress God's word; one "should not turn in a single page, not even a letter" to them. Cooperation in lawful acts of authority and nonresistance in unlawful acts of authority should be followed even when one knows "that since the beginning of the world a wise prince is a mighty rare bird, and an upright prince even rarer." We must simply accept the fact that when God puts a wise prince in power it is a precious

[51] The issue was not dismissed quite as curtly as this sounds. Luther gave as an example of such a miracle the case of Samson harassing the Philistines.

[52] Romans 13:1, "Let every soul be subject unto the higher powers," gave Luther some trouble. But here (*Luther's Works*, pp. 110–11) he says the passage refers to only those governmental powers that fit the standards he is presently discussing, namely those of proper "human ordinance" (I Pet. 2:13). This gives grounds for citizen resistance, which Luther does not explore. It is interesting that Luther dropped the word "soul" (*seele*) in the 1522 edition of his German Bible, as does today's Revised Standard Version: "Let every person be subject to the governing authorities." The Greek is *psyche*.

miracle, for most often He has chosen to put "gaping fools" in authority. Such men may try to defeat heresy by the sword but "God's word must do the fighting."

The final part of *Concerning Temporal Authority* is like a very un-Machiavellian *The Prince.* It is un-Machiavellian because it addresses itself to Christian princes, a "rare prize in heaven," and also because—by contrast with the subtle deceptions Machiavelli elucidates—Luther displays more clearly here than elsewhere what Wolin has so aptly called the simplistic imperative.[53] There are difficulties but few subtleties in the rule Luther is talking about. His faith is ingenuous. A prince should "in his heart empty himself of his power and authority, and take unto himself the needs of his subjects, dealing with them as though they were his own needs. For this is what Christ did to us; and these are the proper works of Christian love."[54]

The advice is neither comprehensive nor very helpful. Princes should pray, sacrifice play to duty, avoid false counsel, punish firmly but justly, take nothing by force that belongs to another, but defend the property of subjects by force if necessary. Princes should go easy on debtors if the debtors are poor and not be rigid in requiring restitution, for the law of love is more important than any rights. The prince is to be reasonable. To illustrate reasonableness Luther tells how Charles the Bold, Duke of Burgundy, dealt with the case of a wronged woman. Written laws are important, but "we should keep written laws subject to reason, from which they originally welled forth as from the spring of justice. We should not make the spring dependent on its rivulets or make reason a captive of letters."

[53] Sheldon Wolin, *Politics and Vision* (Boston: Little, Brown, 1960), p. 162.

[54] The "proper" works of love are contrasted with the "strange" works of love. In a just war, for example, "it is both Christian and an act of love to kill the enemy without hesitation, to plunder, and burn" in order to win (p. 125). The only thing proscribed, apparently, is the violation of wives and virgins. See *ibid.*

Murderous and Thieving Hordes

The peasant rebellions in Thuringia, Franconia, Saxony, and elsewhere (1524–25) arose largely out of economic issues that preceded the religious Reformation. There had been long-festering grievances over tax burdens and the management of farm lands. Peasants resented having to pay for the new princely bureaucracies and the growing imposition of Roman law and its concept of private property was jeopardizing the peasant's reliance on the common use of woods, streams, and meadows. When the plundering of castles and cloisters began, the motivations of the plunderers were various: some wanted a peasant dictatorship, some a classless society, some a return to feudalism. Many simply wanted food, wine, and women. There were Catholics and Lutherans on both sides but Luther's name was popular with peasants, and Catholic princes without exception seemed to hold Luther somehow responsible for the uprisings.

Luther's support for the princes in their often ruthless suppression of the peasants is most sharply expressed in *Wider die mordischen und reubischen Rotten der Baveren* (*Against the Murderous and Thieving Hordes of Peasants,* 1525).[55] The work's very sharpness has clouded his reputation as a humane reformer. Luther was under some pressure to take up the sword, figuratively if not literally, and provide the leadership for a popular political movement. From the views already summarized we can see why, as a Christian theologian, he found this course repugnant. The Reformation he sought was to be of the spirit and through the word.

[55] Also translated as *Against the Robbing and Murdering Horde.* The text will be found in *The Works of Martin Luther,* H. E. Jacobs, ed. (Philadelphia: Muhlenberg Press, 1915–32), Vol. 4, pp. 247–54. Two other tracts of Luther address this problem: The earlier *Admonition to Peace* (April, 1525) is more calm and pastoral. The later *Open Letter Concerning the Hard Book Against the Peasants* expresses traces of dismay that the "devils" of destruction had now entered the princely victors but the hard line against rebellion was not fundamentally modified.

Political leadership concerned itself with a realm of affairs Luther did not wish to inhabit and scarcely wished to acknowledge. Luther regarded religiously minded, fanatic peasant leaders like Muntzer as "false prophets" who were twisting the doctrine of the priesthood of all believers into unjustified secular uses.

Princes, he counseled in *Murderous and Thieving Hordes,* should exceed their duty in offering terms to the rampaging peasants. But if they declined,

> If the peasant is in open rebellion, then he is outside the law of God, for rebellion is not simply murder, but it is like a great fire which attacks and lays waste a whole land. Thus, rebellion brings with it a land full of murders and bloodshed, makes widows and orphans, and turns everything upside down like a great disaster. Therefore, let everyone who can, smite, slay, and stab, secretly or openly, remembering that nothing can be more poisonous, hurtful, or devilish than a rebel. It is just as when one must kill a mad dog; if you don't strike him, he will strike you, and the whole land with you.[56]

The one phrase "smite, slay, and stab" hurt Luther's reputation as much as anything else, though we recall language in defense of civil power only slightly less strong in *Concerning Temporal Authority.* With better arms and professional military leadership, the princes butchered thousands of peasants. Unfortunately, Luther's tract was published just at the height of the butchery. In the long run the economic and physical loss by the peasants may have been less significant than the political loss: for three centuries thereafter German peasants had no political voice.

Luther was not antipeasant. He was antirebellion and anti-offensive war. He not only opposed the Peasants' War but had opposed the rebellion of knights in 1522 (the Sickingen war) and a new crusade against the Turks. But politically minded men could not always understand his position and would not let him theologize above the battle. Ironically, the Catholicism of Bavaria and Austria probably stems more from a reaction against the "Lutheran" Peasants' War than from the success of the Counter Reformation. Nevertheless, despite the failure and the confusions of the Peasants' War, the religious side of the Reformation continued as a popular movement.

Conclusion

We have devoted more attention to an essentially antipolitical figure than might seem appropriate in a study of political thought. But apolitical thinking can produce some powerful political by-products. In this case the by-product is something called modern individualism. Modern individualism is, of course, the product of more influences than we can easily catalog or even know. But Luther's radical new confidence in individual conscience is woven into the cultural foundations of Western participant-oriented political systems.

Luther's individualism is represented as much by his splendid German Bible for the masses as it is by his defiant stand at Worms, although the two are not unrelated. Luther's "freedom of conscience," being severely restricted to the inner man, is not our "freedom of conscience." Indeed, even within the Christian fold, agreement between individuals on the meaning of the Scriptures is not as easily reached as Luther assumed. But his religion was conscience religion and every man's right to search for truth and to think his own thoughts in his own way owes much to Luther.

Luther's acceptance of the political *status quo,* deriving from his political indifference, allows us to call him medieval in his political views. Curiously, however, his belief in individuals became so intense that it resulted in a bias against institutions—against religious institutions, of course, but even more against political institutions. His faith in individual

[56] Quoted in Bainton, p. 280. On Luther and the peasant wars see also Franz Lau, *Luther,* trans. by Robert H. Fischer (Philadelphia: Westminster Press, 1962), pp. 113–21, and Gerhard Ritter, *Luther: His Life and Work,* trans. by John Riches (New York: Harper & Row, 1963), pp. 147–78. Lau's book has an excellent annotated bibliography.

conscience when transferred to politics became faith in individual rulers—a sometimes desperate faith, for Luther's innate honesty forced him to admit that "a wise prince is a rare bird." He succeeded to a degree in depoliticizing the Church. He also wanted to, but could not, depoliticize politics. Wolin has insightfully described the paradox that "as Luther's Church became less political in concept, it became increasingly political in its dependency on secular authority."[57] The consequent tension remained for Calvin to dissolve.

CALVIN

Life

To many twentieth-century Americans John Calvin (1509–64) is a villain. To them Calvin means Calvinism and Calvinism means blue laws, emotional repression, capitalist greed, and burnings at the stake. It means hell in the name of heaven. In fact, however, neither he nor it was quite that bad.

Calvin, the son of an ambitious, self-made lawyer who was secretary of the local bishopric, was born Jean Cauvin in Noyon, Picardy. As an arts student at the University of Paris, fourteen-year-old Jean mastered Latin but suffered under the musty and eminently orthodox instruction in theology. He concurred agreeably with his father's counsel to give up theology and study law. Transferring to Orléans and visiting the city of Bourges, he learned not only law but Greek and tasted in both places the new Renaissance spirit that had not yet penetrated Paris. Even now, however, there was in the frail boy little levity but much self-criticism combined with a terribly rigorous self-imposed regimen of studies.

Finding the possibility of the practice of law distasteful, Calvin returned to Paris to pursue the life of the free-lance humanistic scholar on the model of Erasmus, whom he admired. In 1532, at the age of twenty-two, he published a commentary on Seneca. Sometime during this second Paris stay—the details are not known—Calvin was converted to Protestantism. Not quite two years later he was forced to flee Paris with Nicholas Cop, rector of the University, when the latter was charged with heresy for a sermon Calvin may have helped compose. For two years he wandered, ending up in Basel, where he promptly took up the study of the Hebrew language and composed the remarkable *Christianae religionis institutio* (*Institutes of the Christian Religion*). He was twenty-six years old when the work was published in 1536. The early publication did not mean that Calvin was eager to be rid of the work—he could scarcely stop revising it. The *Institutio* went through seven more editions, growing each time, until the final version in 1559 was five times the size of the original.

Going to Strasbourg after a visit to Noyon in 1536, Calvin was forced by imperial troops fighting the French in the third Hapsburg-Valois war to detour by way of Geneva. His friend William Farel had been having difficulties organizing a church in this newly reformed city and asked Calvin to stay and help. Calvin tried to beg off but Farel said God would curse him if he put his own scholarly pursuits ahead of the Lord's work in the Church. Calvin yielded to this "dreadful adjuration" and stayed, spending most of the rest of his life in Geneva.

Geneva was so important for Calvin's political consciousness—as later it would be for Rousseau's—that we must digress for a moment to examine its peculiar government. For years the city had been subject to three different authorities—the bishop, the counts of Savoy, and four syndics, or magistrates, elected annually by the citizens. Tensions had led to warfare between the bishop and the counts of Savoy and, in 1530, between the citizens and their supposed allies in Bern and Freiburg; all of this was part of a larger struggle between France and Savoy. By the time Calvin appeared on the scene, the bishop and the Savoyard counts had been expelled and the government was operating under

[57] Wolin, p. 147.

three councils. The General Council, consisting of all the heads of households in the city, elected the four syndics. The Little Council, which was composed of the four syndics, the city treasurer, and twenty others elected by the Council of Two Hundred, chose the Council of Two Hundred. This circularity in elections tended, of course, to allow power to gravitate to the syndics.

Most of the Swiss cantons had accepted Zwinglian Protestantism. Farel had helped make Protestant Bern in 1528, Neuchâtel in 1530, and Orbe and Grandson in 1531. Geneva was next. In the revolt of 1535 Protestants had won over the Council of Two Hundred after a public dispute over whether a Catholic woman had tried to poison Protestant leaders. Mobs pillaged Catholic churches and in August the General Council forbade Roman priests to say mass and expelled them from the city. Farel's men controlled the councils and began imposing ordinances requiring church attendance and regulating personal morals. These measures, usually associated with Calvin, thus began before his arrival in town. And Geneva, by now a bustling commercial city of seventeen thousand, was notorious for its violence and prostitution.

Calvin was never an ordained pastor. His position was reader in Holy Scripture in the Church of Geneva. He first lectured on the Book of Romans and only later became a regular preacher. Farel, a success as an *agent provocateur,* desperately needed the help of Calvin's orderly legal mind. The first order of business was to write *Articles Concerning the Government of the Church,* which was promulgated on January 16, 1537. Calvin based the *Articles* on his *Institutio,* and their aim was to establish a systematic discipline among all citizens (citizen and church member now became almost synonymous). To discover papists, a confession of faith was required of all citizens. Only "worthy members" of the Church could participate in the Lord's Supper. The young were to receive a thorough instruction in the fundamentals of the Christian faith in order to prepare them for confession and useful Christian citizenship. A civil commission was established to judge matrimonial questions according to the word of God. The government appointed lay officials in each of twenty-six wards with the power to excommunicate sinners. The reformers' aim was to have a church that was at one and the same time an established church and a confessional church—which was probably the same as wanting to eat one's cake and have it too.

The burghers of Geneva were not at all happy with the *Articles.* The councils accepted them but did little by way of enforcement. In 1538, after a squabble over the manner of celebrating the Lord's Supper, the councils banned Farel and Calvin from the pulpit. They went ahead and preached, for which they, along with their ally Elie Corauld, were banished from the city. Calvin, planning to resume the scholarly life, went back to Basel. But once again came an opportunity that Calvin first refused but then accepted as an inescapable call from God: he took the job of preacher to a congregation of French Protestants and professor of theology in Strasbourg. There he married but suffered the death of an infant son and, after a few years, that of his wife. The liturgical forms Calvin worked out for the Strasbourg church provide the basic structure for Calvinist churches to this day.

Meanwhile, back in Geneva, dissension and street fighting plagued the city. Finally, Jean Phillippe, the man who had led opposition to Calvin and Farel, was executed for homicide and some began to demand Calvin's return. He returned in 1541 and set about to make Geneva a "City of God," an undertaking pursued with somewhat greater personal moderation than characterized his earlier Genevan adventure but with a stern countenance and a firm hand nevertheless. His work load was quite incredible: he preached several times a week and was a professor of theology, a kind of superintendent of churches and schools, and permanent advisor to the municipal government. In late 1541 he was chairman of a commission of five clergymen and six counselors to draw up the *Ordonnances ecclesiastiques,* which established four divinely sanctioned offices in the church—pastors, teachers, elders, and deacons—terminology still used by Reformed churches. The clergy were declared ineligible for civil office but, since the Bible was declared to be the law of the Christian state and the clergy the proper interpreter of the Bible, the Calvinist clergy had secular power of great magnitude.

Calvin was head of the Consistory, a body composed of five pastors and twelve lay elders that took upon itself the task of supervising the morals of every resident of Geneva. Citizens could be examined, summoned before the Consistory, publicly reproved, and excommunicated. The Church-state relationship was so intimate as almost to merge. The Consistory would admonish and for this the Little Council would punish. Hence, in addition to punishments expected in that age, records show imprisonments for laughing during a sermon, for playing cards on Sunday, for swearing, for saying the pope was a good man, for saying there is no devil or hell, and for dancing (which usually involved kissing). The severity of the moral regulation was possibly matched by Geneva's earlier reputation for licentiousness. This is not to say that the regulation changed Geneva's character altogether: in 1546, at Calvin's instigation, the Council closed down the local taverns and substituted five abbayes where wine could be served[58]—provided no one got drunk—and cards could be played for one hour at a time. Dancing and obscene songs were forbidden. Grace was to be said before drinking, religious conversation was to be encouraged, and nine o'clock was closing time. Patronage was less than spectacular and after three months the taverns reopened.

The grimness of Geneva should not be exaggerated, even though grimness and tragedy there were. Between 1542 and 1546 seventy-six persons were banished and fifty-eight put to death, thirty-four for witchcraft.[59] The last figure was largely the result of the general panic that accompanied the plague of 1543, which almost everyone thought had been spread by witches. Calvin should not be blamed for all this. He was called a dictator in his own day but his personal power in Geneva was not fully consolidated until 1555, nine years before his death. The Council found a number of occasions to demonstrate that Calvin was not its master. Over his protest the Council in 1543 took away from the Consistory the right of excommunication. He was once censured for his language, censored in his writing, and several times overridden on policy proposals. But the government was more cooperative than many others in Geneva. A faction called the *Patriotes* resented Calvin's French origins, named their dogs after him, and insulted him in the streets. Possibly it was they who shot at him. The *Libertins* believed in liberty of conscience but Calvin charged them with moral laxity and transformed the meaning of "libertine." One of their great clashes with Calvin came over whether slashed breeches might be worn.

Many vigorous challenges to Calvin came on religious grounds—from the Catholic Balsec, the Lutheran Westphal, the Unitarian

[58] Calvin was not a teetotaler: ". . . we have never been forbidden to laugh, or to be filled, or to join new possessions to old ancestral ones, or to delight in musical harmony, or to drink wine" (*Institutes of the Christian Religion,* 1559 ed., Bk. III, Ch. 19, sec. 9, trans. by Ford Lewis Battles, in John T. McNeill, ed. [Philadelphia: Westminster Press, Library of Christian Classics, 1960], Vol. 1, p. 841.) Subsequent quotations from *Institutio* are from this edition. The original edition had seven chapters, the first four following the organization of the traditional catechism of his day—the Ten Commandments, the Apostles' Creed, the Lord's Prayer, and the sacraments. Then came two chapters on "false sacraments" and a concluding chapter covering Christian liberty, ecclesiastical government, and civil government. The last edition was organized into four books: Father, Son, Holy Ghost, and Holy Catholic Church—each with from seventeen to twenty-five chapters.

[59] Georgia Harkness, *John Calvin* (New York: Holt, Rinehart and Winston, 1931), pp. 29–30. These biographical remarks have been derived primarily from Miss Harkness' work and from Durant, John T. McNeill, *The History and Character of Calvinism* (New York: Oxford Univ. Press, 1954), and Thomas H. L. Parker, *Portrait of Calvin* (Philadelphia: Westminster Press, 1955). For further references see John T. McNeill, "Thirty Years of Calvin Study," *Church History,* Vol. 17 (1948), pp. 207–40.

Socinus, and the humanist Castellio. The most famous clash was with Michael Servetus, able Spanish physician and critic of Trinitarian doctrine. He escaped a death sentence from the French Inquisition, traveled through Geneva on his way to Italy, and was recognized while listening to one of Calvin's sermons. Tried for heresy without right of counsel, he was, on order of the Council, burned at the stake in 1553. Calvin sought a more humane execution but he had drawn up the indictment and clearly favored Servetus' death.

In 1555 the Council returned the power of excommunication to the Consistory. A riot against the influx of Calvinist refugees from France, England, Scotland, and Italy was the occasion for crushing the *Libertin* party with a number of beheadings. From that point until his death in 1564 Calvin's authority was not seriously threatened. The year 1559 was a banner one: the University of Geneva (then the Academy) was founded with Theodore Beza as rector; Calvin was, at long last, formally made a citizen; and the final edition of the *Institutio* was published.

Luther is attractive to the modern temper—note the popularity of Osborne's play, *Luther*—because, though he was capable of great rage against his enemies, he was also capable of self-doubt. Calvin's corresponding unattractiveness lies in the fact that from the age of twenty he always seemed a bit too sure that he was right and the spokesman of God. As on everything, he could theologize even on this sense of rightness:

> Calvin never openly discountenanced Luther's lifelong agonizing for faith, but the following passage might have been directed against it. Calvin declared, "It is not possible to serve God without a tranquil mind, for those who labor in inquietude, who dispute with themselves as to whether He is propitious or offended, whether He will accept or reject their prayers, those who in consequence waver between hope and fear and serve God anxiously can never submit themselves to Him sincerely and wholeheartedly. Trembling and anxiety cause them to hate God and wish it were possible that His very existence might be wiped out." For Calvin the doctrine of election was an unspeakable comfort because it eliminated all such worries and freed man from concern about himself in order that he might devote every energy to the unflagging service of the sovereign Lord.[60]

What made this certitude tolerable in Calvin were his personal generosity, his utter lack of concern for money or for his own personal comfort, his lack of ostentation, and his sympathy for members of his flock—however ruthless he could be with heretics. Sometimes he could even confess to limitations. Just before his death, the Little Council visited him at his sickbed and he said,

> I thank you exceedingly for having conferred so many honors on one so plainly undeserving of them, and for having borne so patiently with my numerous infirmities. . . .
>
> I earnestly entreat that if in anything I have not done what I ought, you will attribute it to want of ability and not to want of will, for I can truly declare that I have sincerely studied the will of the state. Though I have not discharged my duty fully, I have always tried to promote the public good; and if I did not acknowledge that the Lord has sometimes made my labors profitable, I should be guilty of dissimulation. . . .
>
> I also acknowledge that in another matter I am greatly indebted to you; namely, for having borne patiently with my vehemence, which was sometimes carried to excess. My sins in this respect have, I trust, been pardoned also by God.[61]

That these almost last words should eulogize the "interests of the state" and the "public good" is a sign of what, for our purposes, may be of deeper significance than merely temperamental differences between Luther and Calvin. Calvin believed in political organization in a way Luther never could. He did so for reasons that were both practical and theological. The practice we have examined; let us now look at the theology.

[60] Roland H. Bainton, *The Reformation of the Sixteenth Century* (Boston: Beacon Press, 1952), p. 117.

[61] *Joannis Calvini Opera*, Vol. 9, p. 887, and Vol. 21, p. 164. Quoted in Harkness, pp. 57–58.

The *Institutio*

The ground of authority

Perhaps the most fundamental question of political theory is the character of authority and the role we ascribe to it, for in the problem of authority is united the problem of persons' obligations to others and a political order's obligation to persons. As the form of the good was Plato's authority, or nature was the Stoics' authority, or grandeur of soul was Machiavelli's authority, God in Christ was the authority for the leaders of the Reformation. But, whereas Aquinas could count on God's will being authoritatively interpreted by the Church (whether as the natural law of reason or the divine law of Scriptures), the reformers preached a God found in self-authenticating Scriptures. The seat of such authority is the conscience of individuals.[62]

Yet neither Luther nor Calvin could be comfortable with what must have seemed to them the anarchic implications of this position. Luther liked to quote Acts 5:29, "We ought to obey God rather than men." But was every man competent to know what God commanded for his own situation? Luther believed that every man was at least more competent to apply the Scriptures to his own particular situation than was a cumbersome and ingrown bureaucracy. That is why he worked so hard on a German edition of the Bible. In this special sense, then, Luther moved away from reliance on outer rule to reliance on inner spirit, from law to grace, from works to faith. He was not a mystic who believed that religious truth is incommunicable. For Luther, to be justified by faith was not to be excused by faith but to be made just by faith—"The just shall live by faith" (Rom. 1:17).

Nevertheless, though Luther did not quite abandon the external life of man to the devil, he did remain skeptical of the external, institutional life of man. Calvin, more skeptical of the inner life, regained a measure of confidence in social institutions. For Luther's call to salvation he substituted a system of ethics. For a Lutheran Church that would not interfere with secular rulers, he substituted a Calvinist Church that would guide secular rulers. Grace was not ruled out but law returned.

Reason, corruption, and grace

Calvin had to rely more on reason in corporate law than on reason in individual men because men seemed to him so hopelessly corrupt that even their reason was affected. Luther tended to identify natural law with scriptural command. But one meaning of natural is "uncorrupted" and for Calvin mere access to Scripture was not enough to control corrupt man: "I do not say, as Cicero did, that errors disappear with the lapse of time and that religion grows and becomes better each day." In their perversity, "through the stupid hardness in their minds," men are engaged in one recurring headlong flight from God and continually seek "to corrupt the worship of him." He writes,

> Experience teaches that the seed of religion has been divinely planted in all men. But barely one man in a hundred can be found who nourishes in his own heart what he has conceived; and not even one in whom it matures, much less bears fruit in its season. Now some lose themselves in their own superstition, while others of their own evil intention revolt from God, yet all fall away from true knowledge of him. As a result no real piety remains in the world. But as to my statement that some erroneously slip into superstition, I do not mean by this that their ingenuousness should free them from

[62] This is not the same as saying that the conscience of individuals is self-authenticating. Contrary to Stoic or Kantian belief in universal moral laws of conscience, Protestantism holds that a very particular and outrageously specific book is the bearer of God's truth. Moreover, even Protestants put the Holy Spirit within individuals as members of the Church and not as autonomous beings, in the manner of modern scientific liberalism. See James H. Nichols, *The Meaning of Protestantism* (London: Collins, Fontana, 1959), Chs. 7 and 8. On the credibility of the Scriptures apart from the judgment of the Church and on the basis of human reason, respectively, see Calvin's *Institutio,* Bk. I, Chs. 7 and 8. It should be noted also that neither Luther nor Calvin believed, as do modern fundamentalists, that the Bible is inerrant in every detail.

blame. For the blindness under which they labor is almost always mixed with proud vanity and obstinacy. Indeed, vanity joined with pride can be detected in the fact that, in seeking God, miserable men do not rise above themselves as they should, but measure him by the yardstick of their own carnal stupidity.[63]

Men who believe there is no God are those "who, by extinguishing the light of nature, deliberately befuddle themselves." Though they "furiously repell all remembrance of God" suggested by the inward feelings of nature, even they "are compelled to recognize some god" and so they fashion "dead and empty" idols to follow.

In these passages Calvin asserts that it is man's quest for God that distinguishes him from the beasts; but later, in Book II, he affirms the classical assertion that reason is what separates man from beast:

Since reason, therefore, by which man distinguishes between good and evil, and by which he understands and judges, is a natural gift, it could not be completely wiped out; but it was partly weakened and partly corrupted, so that its misshapen ruins appear. John speaks in this sense: "The light still shines in the darkness, but the darkness comprehends it not" (John 1:5). In these words both facts are clearly expressed. First, in man's perverted and degenerate nature some sparks still gleam. These show him to be a rational being, differing from brute beasts, because he is endowed with understanding. Yet, secondly, they show this light choked with dense ignorance, so that it cannot come forth effectively.[64]

The fall of Adam planted the seeds of sin in all men, argues Calvin, and hence all men, even infants, are condemned unless God chooses to elect them and thereby save them from hell.[65] That some men should be eternally damned was an almost conventional belief and rarely challenged in Calvin's day. On this point as on many other points concerning sin and grace, Calvin followed Augustine. But he went Augustine one better with his idea of double predestination, that is, God not only failed to elect certain men to salvation (hence damning them), He also specifically designated the ones not elected as reprobates (hence damning them again) —a double check, one might say. "The decree is dreadful indeed, I confess." It does and should make us tremble. Yet that men are so condemned is a "just but inscrutable judgment of God to show forth his glory in their condemnation." Although Calvin employs ponderous scriptural scholarship and leans heavily on Paul to support this claim, he does not make clear how an action of God that is inscrutable can be known by men as just, except perhaps by definition. At least Calvin does not claim absolute clarity: "Despite the fact that we do not clearly grasp the reason for this, let us not be unwilling to admit some ignorance where God's wisdom rises to its height."

Election and vocation

God is as unrestricted in electing men to salvation as He is in condemning them to reprobation. One is elected to be holy; one is not elected because he has been holy. God has foreknowledge of all things. But we cannot say that God elects a man because of His foreknowledge of that man's merit, for to say that would imply a man has merit without election. Despite all this, "predestination rightly understood brings no shaking of faith but rather its best confirmation." No man can be sure of his election (to pray to God, "I have been chosen, hear me," would be, says Calvin, "preposterous"), yet, paradox-

[63] *Institutes,* Bk. I, Ch. 4, sec. 1, p. 47.

[64] *Ibid.,* Bk. II, Ch. 2, sec. 12, p. 270. Rousseau, another child of Geneva, makes less of natural reason but much of uncorruption in describing man in the state of nature. Sin corrupts Calvin's natural man; society corrupts Rousseau's natural man. See Ch. 15, pp. 385–89, below.

[65] Contrary to popular opinion, Calvin does not dwell upon hell. He devotes only one section of the *Institutio* to it (Bk. III, Ch. 25, sec. 12). Moreover, he conceives of hell as alienation from God and says that the fire-and-brimstone images are only metaphors for a spiritual condition "figuratively expressed to us by physical things." This interpretation makes infant damnation somewhat less ridiculous. For Calvin, infants were not necessarily saved (as for Zwingli) but the unbaptized were not necessarily damned.

ically, there are outward signs of election, including an air of assurance. One of the most important blessings of the elect is that they are freed from gnawing anxiety. This does not mean that they will display "haughtiness, arrogance, and contempt of others." Quite the contrary, their manner is marked by simplicity, charity, and quiet confidence.

We are apt today to individualize Calvin's doctrine of election too much and by doing so perhaps to miss its political significance. To be sure, only individuals can be of the elect or the damned. But the elect are not so much set apart as infused into the body of Christ, the true Church. They are compared by Calvin to Israel as the "saving remnant" and share both the joys and the suffering of Christ as they work side by side with other humans who may be—and in Geneva virtually had to be—formal members of a church. One should not even ask too many questions about nor dwell upon the problem of one's own election: "Christ . . . is the mirror wherein we must, and without self-deception may, contemplate our own election. . . . It is into his body the Father has destined those to be engrafted whom he has willed from eternity to be his own."

What we now call our vocation or calling without religious overtones was for Calvin intimately related to the effects of election and the spiritual life generally. What one does in this life is tied to one's status in the next. Indeed, Calvin talks more of this life than the next and this concern for the activity of the spirit within the common affairs of men may be a chief point of difference between him and Augustine, matched only by their differences over the nature of the Church. This life was not, for Calvin, just a veil of tears to be gotten through: "The firmness of our election is joined to our calling."

There are two kinds of call, general and special. The general call is the outward preaching of the word whereby all are invited into the fold. The special call is the "inward illumination" given to the individual believer.

In his *Protestant Ethic and the Spirit of Capitalism* Max Weber[66] provoked wide-ranging discussion by his analysis of the relationship between the Calvinist doctrine of vocation and the rise of capitalist enterprise. Without Calvin's sense of divine blessing on thrift, hard work and prudence, the argument goes, northern European city-dwellers (rural inhabitants tended to be Lutherans, southern Europeans Catholics) would not have been able to work as hard as they did, forego present pleasures for future gain, amass capital, and thereby build the capitalist system whose technology we now all know. We will need to come back to this issue later, as it relates to Calvin's descendants, but we may note now that one difficulty with this view applied to Calvin himself is that he says very little about the duty to labor. There is no question that Calvin prized industry, regarded idleness as a vice, and was himself incredibly hard-working. But he never looked upon riches as a sure sign of election: some may be rich as a sign of God's favor but others may be rich as a terrible example of the sin of avarice.

By his life as well as in his writings he upheld the ideal of hard labor. But he also warned against working too much simply to acquire material possessions. He called avarice "a disease of the mind":

> For we see that the avaricious grow weary, as their cupidity ever excites them, for they are like an oven: and since they are hot, if an hour is lost, they think that a whole year has passed away; they calculate the very moments of time. "How is it," they say, "there is no merchant coming? I have now rested one day and I have not gained a farthing."[67]

Moreover, to make too much of the potentialities for economic self-advancement in Calvinism exaggerates its individualistic character. Calvin could not be said to hold an individualistic theory of social ethics. For him, membership in the religious communion automatically entailed social duties.

[66] Translated by Talcott Parsons (New York: Scribner's, 1930).

[67] *Commentary on Amos 8:5,* in *Calvini Opera,* Vol. 43, p. 145. Quoted in Harkness, p. 170.

Speaking of the meaning of holy communion, he said:

> We shall benefit very much from the Sacrament if this thought is impressed and engraved upon our minds: that none of the brethren can be injured, despised, rejected, abused, or in any way offended by us, without at the same time, injuring, despising, and abusing Christ by the wrongs we do . . . that we cannot love Christ without loving him in the brethren; that we ought to take care of our brethren's bodies as we take care of our own; for they are members of our body.[68]

Christian freedom

Calvin's chapter on Christian freedom[69] is quite reminiscent of Luther's tract *On the Freedom of the Christian Man.* Both men are, of course, at pains to make it clear that they are not talking about political freedom but spiritual freedom. Calvin makes three points:

(1) Freedom is above the law, that is, the letter of scriptural commandment, and a man cannot therefore be free simply by obeying the law. Even though, in fact, perfect obedience to the law is itself too difficult for us to achieve, were we perfectly obedient we would not necessarily know spiritual freedom. ". . . the question is not how we may become righteous, but how, being unrighteous and unworthy, we may be reckoned righteous." The answer is to forget about works, to "turn our attention from ourselves, and to look only to Christ," to throw ourselves on God's mercy.[70]

(2) Being freed from the yoke of the law, from compulsion, the Christian conscience nevertheless yields a voluntary and newly joyous obedience to it. Calvin uses the analogy of servants and sons (the Allen edition translates it "slaves" and "children"). Servants, being under law, must do as they are told; they strive anxiously to fulfill every last direction out of fear of their master. Sons of a gracious father, secure in the knowledge that their father will accept and value even their imperfect work, perform their tasks no less ably but willingly and cheerfully. Christians who think that they may sin with impunity because they are freed from law should understand that this freedom "has nothing to do with them."

(3) Christian freedom is indifferent to external things—to what shall be eaten and how or what shall be worn and when. If one takes these things too seriously, his conscience becomes trapped in an infinite regress of dubious formal standards, a "pit of confusion." If to show virtue one abstains from delicate food, then why not brown bread? If one abstains from good wine, then why not poor wine or even all but the rankest water? Immediately we are struck by the apparent contrast between this tolerant and casual attitude toward externals and the reality of Calvin's Geneva, where even dresses a bit too gay or overfancy hair styles were forbidden.

If we read on, however, we find an admonition not to let Christian indifference to external things be a justification for luxury or gluttony. Interestingly, the argument for moderation is based fundamentally on social obligation, on the need to respect the sensibilities of others. Calvin quotes I Corinthians 10:28–29 to the effect that, though our consciences be free to do many things, we should nevertheless avoid doing them if they would give offense to another. He excoriates those who take spiritual freedom "as an excuse for their desires that they may abuse God's gifts to their own lust and by those who think that freedom does not exist unless it is used before men, and consequently, in using it, have no regard for weaker brethren."[71]

[68] *Institutes,* Vol. 2, Bk. IV, Ch. 17, sec. 38, p. 1415.

[69] John McNeill has brought together this chapter and the chapter "On Civil Government" plus some of Calvin's commentaries and published the collection as *On God and Political Duty* (New York: Liberal Arts Press, Library of Liberal Arts No. 23, 1950). The translations are from the nineteenth century but the collection is most useful and about the only inexpensive edition readily available. The John Allen translation in this edition speaks of Christian liberty rather than Christian freedom.

[70] Calvin relies heavily in his argument on Galatians 1–3.

[71] Passages like this as well as Genevan practice enabled Tawney to argue against Weber that Calvinism, given the right socioeconomic setting, could have evolved

From a somewhat different angle, Calvin argues that the indifference to external things means "that under coarse and rude attire there often dwells a heart of purple, while sometimes under silk and purple is hid a simple humility. Thus let every man live in his station." A political egalitarian could find little comfort here; but just to make sure no one misunderstands, Calvin later explicitly contrasts Christian freedom with political freedom:

the former resides in the inner mind, while the latter regulates only outward behavior. The one we may call the spiritual kingdom, the other, the political kingdom. Now these two . . . must always be examined separately. . . . There are in man, so to speak, two worlds, over which different kings and different laws have authority.

Through this distinction it comes about that we are not to misapply to the political order the gospel teaching on spiritual freedom, as if Christians were less subject, as concerns outward government, to human laws, because their consciences have been set free in God's sight; as if they were released from all bodily servitude because they are free according to the spirit.[72]

On civil government

The radical separation of the temporal from the spiritual, these "two worlds," makes a coin with two sides, of course. One side is the subservience of the individual Christian to civil law, however constituted; the other side is subservience of civil law to ecclesiastical authority acting in defense of the faith. Hence Calvin cannot simply dismiss civil government as beneath notice—as Luther often seemed tempted to do—and at the end of this chapter on Christian freedom he promises to discuss civil government "in another place." The other place is, significantly, the last chapter of the whole *Institutio.* Strange—or is it?—that a massive treatise on abstruse theology should end with politics.

into a collectivist dictatorship just as easily as it did into an intense individualism. See R. H. Tawney, *Religion and the Rise of Capitalism* (New York: New American Library, Mentor, 1950).

[72] *Institutes,* Vol. 1, Bk. III, Ch. 19, sec. 15, p. 847.

Calvin saw himself in the middle between the too "worldly" Jews and the too "otherworldly" Anabaptists. A casual acknowledgement of the importance of politics might seem a surrender to the "Jewish vanity" ("folly" in the Allen translation), which includes the spiritual kingdom "within the elements of this world." The kingdom of Christ does not, he insists, "consist in" what kind of a government a man lives under. "Yet," Calvin rushes on, "this distinction does not lead us to consider the whole nature of government a thing polluted, which has nothing to do with Christian men."

Among the most useful functions of civil government is "to cherish and protect the outward worship of God"; but also of great use is "to form our social behavior to civil righteousness, to reconcile us one with another, and to promote general peace and tranquility":

. . . if it is God's will that we go as pilgrims upon the earth while we aspire to the true fatherland, and if the pilgrimage requires such helps, those who take these from man deprive him of his very humanity. Our adversaries claim that there ought to be such great perfection in the church of God that its government should suffice for law. But they stupidly imagine such a perfection as can never be found in a community of men.[73]

There follows a kind of mirror-of-princes tract addressed to Christian magistrates that includes abundant scriptural references to sustain their authority. But Calvin has already introduced elements of pluralism uncongenial to older writers, for he discusses the system of civil government as involving three parts or branches—magistrates, laws, and people.

From his other writings we know that republican Calvin has a certain tendency to disparage kingship even when borne on the shoulders of biblical kings: "For kings are pleased with their own greatness and wish their own pleasure to be treated as an oracle. . . . No virtue is so rare in kings as mod-

[73] *Ibid.,* sec. 2, p. 1487.

eration and yet none is more necessary."[74] The first edition of the *Institutio,* dedicated to Francis I, was a plea on behalf of persecuted evangelicals in France. Calvin could not have forgotten that Francis was a persecuting king. He signed the dedication on August 23, 1535. His friend and coreligionist Étienne de la Farge had been burned to death in France on February 15, 1535.

Only at the end of the *Institutio* do we begin to see the potentialities for political theory that flowered under a later generation of Calvinists. On the one hand, we find a sense of the value of government under plural headship. On the other, we find a sanction—but only potentially—for civil resistance through reliance on ephors, or inferior magistrates. By contrast with Augustine and Luther, civil government in Calvin occupies not merely a necessary but a high position: "To think of doing away with it is outrageous barbarity. Its function among men is no less than that of bread, water, sun and air; indeed its place of honor is far more excellent."[75] Moreover, civil government does not require the unifying center of a prince or king:

> . . . if the three forms of government which the philosophers discuss be considered in themselves, I will not deny that aristocracy, or a system compounded of aristocracy and democracy, far excels all others: not indeed in itself, but because it is very rare for kings so to control themselves that their will never disagrees with what is just and right; or for them to have been endowed with such keenness and prudence, that each knows how much is enough. Therefore, men's fault or failing causes it to be safer and more bearable for a number to exercise government, so that they may help one another; teach and admonish one another; and, if one asserts himself unfairly, there may be a number of censors and master to restrain his willfulness.[76]

Calvin now uses even freedom (*libertas*) in a wholly political rather than spiritual context and calls for its defense: ". . . the magistrates ought to apply themselves with the highest diligence to prevent the freedom (whose guardians they have been appointed) from being in any respect diminished, far less violated." The fact remains, of course, that Calvin wanted a republic of *ordered* liberty, which in Geneva meant a city of true believers; and, as he repeats here, because God would seem to prefer variety in government—kingdoms here, republics there—as individuals "it is our duty to show ourselves compliant and obedient to whomever he sets over the place where we live."

The esoteric reference to the ephors a moment ago was prompted by Calvin's own esoteric reference to ephors in the last chapter of the *Institutio.* For reasons partly of historical accident his apparently innocuous statement has been linked to various theories of political resistance to authority soon to be examined—those of Francis Hotman; George Buchanan; the anonymous *Vindiciae contra tyrannos* (*A Vindication Against Tyrants,* 1579), Johannes Althusius; and, perhaps most spectacularly of all, John Knox.[77]

To the end of the *Institutio,* Calvin has,

[74] *Commentary on Daniel,* Lecture 29. In McNeill, ed., *On God and Political Duty,* p. 93. Daniel is justified in transgressing against King Darius because he could not obey him without losing his piety. See Lecture 30, pp. 101–02.

[75] Thus, contrary to Luther, Calvin found nothing amiss with Christians resorting to courts of law. See *ibid.,* sec. 17. In general, Calvin's view of law was compatible with traditional natural-law views, that is, although the implementation would vary from place to place and from situation to situation, a single set of underlying principles of justice was universally valid. See John McNeill, "Natural Law in the Teaching of the Reformers," *Journal of Religion,* Vol. 26 (1946), pp. 179–82.

[76] *Institutes,* vol. 2, Bk. IV, Ch. 20, sec. 8, pp. 1493–94. The word translated "democracy" is, in Latin, *politia,* or Aristotle's best form of the government of the many.

[77] On the Spartan ephors see Ch. 4, pp. 93–94, above. On Althusius see Ch. 10, pp. 277–79, below. For the rest see the section following. See also J. W. Allen, *A History of Political Thought in the Sixteenth Century,* 3rd ed. (New York: Barnes & Noble, 1951), Part I, Ch. 6, and Part III, Chs. 3–6, and R. H. Murray, *The Political Consequences of the Reformation* (New York: Russell & Russell, 1960), Ch. 5. In his treatise *Der Hirt* (*The Pastor,* 1524) Ulrich Zwingli had referred to pastors as similar to the Spartan ephors, guarding the people against the depredations of higher rulers. Calvin may have known this passage. See *Institutes,* Vol. 2, p. 1519, *n.* 54.

when the issue is raised, stressed obedience to even wicked rulers. The political right is vindicated not by subjects but by God: ". . . it is not for us to remedy such evils . . . only this remains, to implore the Lord's help." God answers such prayers in unexpected and unpredictable ways, often through "unwitting agents." It was thus, says Calvin in an astonishing twist of emphasis, when God "broke the bloody scepters of arrogant kings and when he overturned intolerable governments. Let the princes hear and be afraid." Obedience and suffering apply to

> . . . private individuals. For if there are now any magistrates of the people, appointed to restrain the wilfulness of kings (as in ancient times the ephors were set against the Spartan kings, or the tribunes of the people against Roman consuls, or the demarchs against the senate of the Athenians; and, perhaps, as things are now, such power as the three estates exercise in every realm when they hold their chief assemblies), I am so far from forbidding them to withstand, in accordance with their duty, the fierce licentiousness of kings, that, if they wink at kings who violently fall upon and assault the lowly common folk, I declare that their dissimulation involves nefarious perfidy, because they dishonestly betray the freedom of the people, of which they know that they have been appointed protectors by God's ordinance.[78]

Fittingly enough, the last scriptural references in a book full of them call for obedience to God; but in the context of a discussion of kings and the grounds for opposing them, such references as "We must obey God rather than men" (Acts 5:29) take on new meanings.

Rebellion is wicked and impious unless led by duly authorized magistrates who, in the name of God *and* the people, can claim a right higher than kingship. Calvin could not have seen fully how useful this doctrine would be for rebels.

Conclusion

In John Calvin we find a rationale both for powerful government and for vigorous restraints on government. The assumed unworthiness of men requires that they be trained to self-discipline and ruled with a firm hand; but since the rulers, too, are but men, they should command no excessive veneration. A collective rule that puts no man ahead of the whole community is best. Finally, if a solitary impious ruler goes too far, the spokesmen of the whole community may rightfully put him down. The strait-laced prophet of spiritual order had given his disciples a precious loophole through which they might justify a righteous political disorder.

DOCTRINES OF RESISTANCE AND TOLERATION

Knox

John Knox (1505?–72) was the leader of the Scottish Reformation and the man who first conspicuously broke away from Calvin's adjuration to civil obedience. A year of cruel treatment as a French galley slave during which he stubbornly refused to bow before the Virgin Mary had prepared Knox for his battle against Catholicism, a battle that had already produced a number of Scottish martyrs. When Mary Stuart, lately Queen of France, came home to be Queen of Scots after the death of her husband, Francis II, the Geneva-trained Knox was ready. With the help of Queen Elizabeth of England and the Calvinist Church in Scotland (The Faithful Congregation of Jesus Christ in Scotland), Knox was able effectively to frustrate Mary's political ambitions. But the seeds of popular revolt could be found in Knox well before his clash with Mary Stuart in 1561. In a note to a French translation he made in 1557 he said that, if princes either maintain idolatry or persecute "God's chosen children," then "what must follow hereof, but that either Princes be reformed and be compelled to also reform their wicked laws or

[78] *Institutes,* Vol. 2, Bk. IV, Ch. 20, sec. 29, p. 1519.

else that all good men depart from their service and company."[79]

When Mary challenged Knox in 1561—"Think ye that subjects having power may resist their princes?"—Knox boldly replied, "If their princes exceed their bounds."[80] By the time of the Treaty of Edinburgh in 1560 it was Knox's view on rebellion rather than Calvin's that tended to prevail among Calvinists. One difficulty was that Knox was not much interested in systematic theorizing and propounded a rather confused theory of the Scottish constitution that made the nobles civil magistrates so that they might qualify as ephors and hence be legitimate rebels. Beyond that, at one point in his *Appellation* (1558) he seems to argue that it is the duty of all men, not merely nobles, to repress blasphemous kings: ". . . the punishment of such crimes as idolatry, blasphemy, and others that touch the Majesty of God, doeth not appertain to Kings and chief rulers only, but also to the whole body of the people, and to every member of the same, according to the vocation of every man."[81] But even talk of "every man" did not mean that Knox thought of popular democracy in the modern sense. In the first place he was talking about some kind of organized communal action—not political free enterprise—and in the second place he assumed the action was aimed at putting down idolatry—not at making public policy in general.

Nevertheless, in his narrow, even fanatical, way Knox had taught rulers that traditional respect could no longer be counted on. And his Genevalike organization of the Scottish Church gave the world another example of a multiheaded political organism.

The *Monarchomachs*

The political problem of the Reformation, viewed from the standpoint of political authority, was whether the old system of one land, one Church could be abandoned without social chaos. Social chaos threatened ominously because the duty to persecute seemed to almost everyone an essential attribute of religious conviction. The most devout men viewed a policy of toleration as immoral. Yet, obviously, religious minorities could survive only under a policy of toleration or by claiming a right to resist those rulers they regarded as heretical. In sixteenth-century France the *Monarchomachs* represented an important group of resisters and the *Politiques* represented an important group of tolerators.

In the Holy Roman Empire, the peace of Augsburg (1555) maintained the principle of territoriality (*cujus regio ejus religio*). The two confessions, Lutheran and Catholic, were declared legal in their respective spheres. Only Zwinglians, Calvinists, and Anabaptists were excluded. On this basis Lutheranism spread through eastern Germany and Scandinavia in alliance with political power. In France, however, no such resolution was possible. The vigorous Calvinist minority, called—for reasons unknown to us—Huguenots, were demanding religious liberty from strong monarchs of a different religious communion. Whether religious liberty could exist under political absolutism was an open question, one that stimulated political speculation. Only with hindsight do we see how much "Political liberty is the residuary legatee of ecclesiastical animosities."[82]

[79] Quoted in Allen, pp. 108–09.

[80] Quoted in Murray, p. 120. One of Knox's best known works is *The First Blast of the Trumpet Against the Monstrous Regiment of Women* (1558) in which he attacks Mary of Lorraine, Mary Tudor (Cursed Jezebel of England), Mary Stuart, Catherine de' Medici, and all women rulers as contrary to the Scriptures and the laws of nature. After the common front against Mary Stuart, Knox assured Queen Elizabeth he did not really mean to include her!

[81] Quoted in Murray, pp. 119–20. Knox and his cohorts had expected that the confiscated Catholic properties in Scotland would be used to support the new Church but the nobles were more interested in land for themselves than in theology and would give up little of the spoils. This, as much as doctrine, turned Scottish Presbyterianism against the aristocracy and led it in the direction of popular government.

[82] Figgis, p. 154. As Miss Harkness points out, a new religion preaches submission when it is very weak or very strong. "Only in the intermediate stage, when it is strong enough to rebel but not to dominate, is it likely to encourage resistance."

The rulers of France were generally more political than religious and, when at long last it became clear that Catholicism could be maintained as the compulsory faith only at the expense of the stability of France itself, a policy of toleration won out. Toleration was a *politique* position to assume and its defenders were called *Politiques;* we shall examine some of their thought in the next section. But from 1562 to 1572 there was intermittent fighting, with atrocities on both sides. Catherine de' Medici, the queen regent, favored a policy of toleration but was caught up in a network of political, familial, and religious struggles that tragically led to an abortive coup and the massacre of St. Bartholomew (1572), in which thousands of Huguenots were slaughtered in Paris and the provinces. In the subsequent round of assassinations, Henry of Navarre, a Protestant, became heir to the French throne. But after a decade of battering at the Parisian stronghold of his enemies, he became Henry IV only by becoming a Catholic. His often-quoted "Paris was well worth a mass" may have been lighthearted cynicism but may also have been tired resignation. Henry IV gave France the Edict of Nantes (1598), which gave the Huguenots the right to worship (except in Paris), full civil rights, and control of two hundred fortified towns. It lasted until Louis XIV disastrously annulled it eighty-seven years later.

The massacre of St. Bartholomew provoked a rash of tracts arguing the need to resist tyrant kings. Among the best known were *Franco-Gallia* (1573), written by Francis Hotman of Paris, Bourges, and Geneva; *Du Droit des magistrats sur les sujets* (*On the Right of Magistrates over Their Subjects,* 1574), probably written by Theodore Beza; and *De jure regni apud Scotos* (*On the Law of Rulership as It Pertains to the Scots,* 1578), written by the Scots-Frenchman George Buchanan.[83] Hotman's assertion that the Estates was superior in authority to the king and his implicatiton that ultimate sovereignty rested in the people were put in the form of bad history rather than systematic argument; but his rhetoric was powerful. Beza, Calvin's learned successor at Geneva, was led by the massacre to a reversal of his earlier orthodox-Calvinist position of nonresistance. Buchanan's lopsided dialogue attempted to demonstrate that the king is but an agent of the community who must be bound by law and by an implied contract with his people.

The "Vindiciae"

The most famous *Monarchomach* tract, *Vindiciae contra tyrannos,* was published under the pseudonym Junius Brutus.[84] We shall look at it more closely.

The *Vindiciae* asked four questions:

(1) Whether Subjects are bound and ought to obey Princes, if they command that which is against the Law of God.

(2) Whether it be lawful to resist a Prince

[83] For a discussion of these and other *Monarchomach* tracts see Allen, Part 3, Chs. 4–5; Murray, Ch. 5; Figgis, Ch. 5; and Bainton, *Reformation,* Ch. 12. Allen also discusses the precursors of these resistance arguments found in earlier sixteenth-century writings: Marius Salamonius, *De principata* (*On Beginning Principles,* 1544); the anonymous tract *Bekenntnis Unterrich und Vermanung* (*Confession, Instruction, and Admonition*) of Magdeburg (1550); John Ponet, *A Shorte Treatise of Politicke Power* (1556); and Christopher Goodman, Knox's English associate, *How Superior Powers Ought to be Obeyed* (1558). The text of the Ponet work may be found as an appendix to Winthrop S. Hudson, *John Ponet* (Chicago: Univ. of Chicago Press, 1942).

[84] The authorship of the *Vindiciae* has long been disputed, with most scholars arguing either for Hubert Languet or Philippe Duplessis-Mornay and some for both. On this issue see George Sabine, *History of Political Theory,* 3rd ed. (New York: Holt, Rinehart and Winston, 1961), p. 377, *n.* 4; Murray, p. 202, *n.* 2; Harold Laski's Introduction to his edition of *A Defense of Liberty Against Tyrants* (London: Bell, 1924); and Ernest Barker, "The Authorship of the *Vindiciae contra Tyrannos,*" *Cambridge Historical Journal,* Vol. 3 (1930), pp. 164–81. Subsequent quotations are from the Laski edition. Allen, finding too many irreconcilable views hidden beneath the label *Monarchomach,* questions its value. See Allen, p. 342. The actual name was invented by divine-right theorist William Barclay in his *De regno et regali potestate* (*On Rulership and Royal Dominion,* 1600) and so was not contemporaneous. As Barclay used it, it did not mean, necessarily, opposition to kingship per se but assertion of the right to resist kings.

which doth infringe the law of God, or ruin the Church. By whom, how, and how far is it lawful.

(3) Whether it be lawful to resist a Prince which doth oppress or ruin a public State, and how far such resistance may be extended. By whom, how, and by what right or law it is permitted.

(4) Whether neighbor Princes or States may be, or are, bound by Law to give succour to the subjects of other Princes, afflicted for the cause of true religion, or oppressed by manifest Tyranny.[85]

The answers, to make a long story too short, are no, yes, yes, and yes. What is important is not the answers but the argument, which is clearly a *pièce d'occasion* with veiled references to Catherine de' Medici but is also set in a larger framework than most of the other resistance tracts. The work's historical significance lies in its transformation of the idea of religious covenant into a libertarian contract.

The answer to the first question, which relies mainly upon Scripture, is simple in its conclusion:

If then Saul, although he were a king, ought to obey God, it follows in all good consequence that subjects are not bound to obey their king by offending God. Briefly those who . . . seek to enthral the service of God with a necessary dependence on the will of a mutable man, and religion of the good pleasure of the king, as if he were some God on earth, they doubtless little value the testimony of Holy Writ.[86]

The answer to the second question is more innovative. The Old-Testament covenant experience is made political and double:

Now after that kings were given unto the people, there was so little purpose of disannulling or disbanding the former contract, that it was renewed and confirmed for ever. We have formerly said at the inaugurating of Kings, there was a double covenant treated of, to wit "between God and king"; and "between God and the people."[87]

The obligation to maintain the contract is mutual, so that if a king should "follow after strange gods" and Israel does not "withdraw him from his rebellion . . . they make the fault of their king their own transgression." Moreover, there should be institutions capable of holding kings to account, for it is a poor contract that does not grant to the parties to it "power to perform the conditions covenanted." The response to offending kings should, of course, be restrained and measured: "If their assaults be verbal, their defense must be likewise verbal; if the sword be drawn against them, they may also take arms."

The author of the *Vindiciae* was not a democrat. He did not go so far as Buchanan and identify the will of the people with the will of the majority. Nor did he wish to make every man responsible for restraining tyrants; this responsibility should fall on the ephors: ". . . private persons, they have no power; nor any calling to unsheathe the sword of authority." If they draw it, "they make themselves delinquents." Nevertheless, he quotes what Theopompus, king of Sparta, said after the "controllers of the king," the ephors, were instituted, to the effect that the more who watch over the affairs of the kingdom, "the more safe and happy shall be the state."

In his answer to the third question Brutus traces the history of the election of kings through Scriptures, ancient Rome, France, and Germany and observes "so much as none were ever born with crowns on their heads, and sceptres in their hands . . . no man can be a king by himself." He quotes Aristotle, Cicero, Seneca, and Augustine to build up an impressive weight of tradition and pays tribute to the majesty of law, which binds subject and monarch alike. This is "by nature"; there are hints of English thought of the seventeenth century in such statements as that men are born "by nature loving liberty."[88]

[85] Laski, Table of Contents. Laski's long Introduction is characteristically dazzling.

[86] *Ibid.*, p. 84.

[87] *Ibid.*

[88] That Brutus aimed to restore respect both for natural law and ancient liberty is suggested by the dedication, which implies that the whole work is a defense

The careless or confused avoidance of the theoretical issue posed by making kings simultaneously agents of God and agents of the people keeps the *Vindiciae* out of the first rank of political treatises; but its influence was great, especially on Locke. The author's reliance on legal precedent plus a distaste for arbitrary power make its tone quite Whiggish. Murray finds an unbroken line running from Luther's liberty of conscience to the political liberty of the Declaration of Independence. This line goes through Calvin, Knox, Duplessis-Mornay, Milton, Locke, and Hamilton.[89] That seems to stretch things a bit, but reading the *Vindiciae* does make the reader conscious of the element of continuity in what we are likely to call all too casually the Western political tradition.

Ligueurs, Politiques, and Jesuits

The Catholic League

However much the Huguenots would deny that they were rebels, most French Catholics could not help but see them as such. The formation of the Catholic League in 1576 with the support of the Duke of Guise, was, among other things, an effort to counter the divisive effects of the postmassacre Huguenot pamphlets. The expedient conversion of Henry of Navarre back to Catholicism may even have owed something to the League's influence.

The spirit of the League was not of necessity absolutist in politics; especially after the treacherous assassination of the Duke of Guise by Henry III in 1588, the League's writers came to share some of the constitutional arguments of the *Monarchomachs.* They were united only on the virtue of a common Catholic faith and in this "only a mind with a strong Protestant bias could suppose that the League writers were, on the whole, less sincere than those on the Huguenot side."[90] With Huguenot heir Henry of Navarre approaching the French throne and Anglican Elizabeth sitting on the English throne, they knew, however, that they could not rely simply on hereditary right and were disposed to toy with ideas of sovereignty in the people so long as papal authority was maintained.

The most forceful writer of the Catholic League was Jean Boucher (1551–1646), a preacher and teacher at the Sorbonne and the author of *De justa abdicatione Henrici tertii* (*On the Rightful Abdication of Henry the Third,* 1598). Though forceful, this *ligueur* was untroubled by consistency—he declared that since the people "constitute" the kingship they can depose kings but also maintained the limitless power of the pope to create and depose kings. This was enough to make Barclay attack him as a Catholic *Monarchomach.*

The Politiques

The *Politiques,* who were mainly Catholics, were nevertheless opposed to ultramontane views such as Boucher's. A Huguenot *Monarchomach* like Hotman made a greater appeal to the *Politiques* because his work *Franco-gallia* aroused a strong sense of national patriotism—a patriotism that, at the pope's expense, could possibly save France from its bitter religious warfare. The *Politiques* came to feel not that religious toleration was a virtue but that it was a necessity. (Only a few rare souls in the sixteenth century believed in toleration as a matter of principle: Calvin's opponent Castellio was one and Browne in England was another.) It would not be quite correct, therefore, to say of the *Politiques* that for them the religion of the state had replaced the religion of the Church, although it is sometimes put that way. They were willing to concede—and recollection of Luther is inescapable here—that religion is an individual matter and that civil power rather than the Church is the proper unifying agent for society.

---

of natural law against the seditious doctrines of Machiavelli's *The Prince.*

[89] Murray, p. 105.

[90] Allen, p. 345.

De L'Hopital. The spirit of the *Politiques* goes back before their time to Michel de L'Hopital, a noble and learned man who was chancellor under Catherine de' Medici until he was forced to retire for his advocacy of toleration. He worked for the reconciling purposes of the Edict of Nantes long before its fruition. His *Traité de la reformation de la justice* (*Treatise on the Reform of Justice*) lamented that equality before the law was not a reality in France and argued for a strong and just monarchy guided by divine justice (*la justice divine*) and natural law (*le droit naturel*) as the only agency that could remedy the sordid corruption of the courts.[91]

Gregoire. Perhaps a typical *Politique* was Pierre Gregoire of Toulouse (1540–96?), author of *De republica* (1586), a devout Catholic who nevertheless would have limited the secular power of the pope and granted an independence to civil authority in controlling most of the functions we associate with the modern state. He was not as modern as Bodin, however, for he modeled his work along the lines of classical treatises, defended the natural origin of politics in the manner of Aristotle, and dressed the power of the secular ruler in a shadowy organismal, group-being idea in which the personality of the people—which *is* the *republica*—is to some degree absorbed into the personality of the ruler.[92] The most important of the *Politique* writers was, without question, Jean Bodin. His work so transcends the events of his time that we will need to devote a separate section to it following our discussion of the Jesuits.

Barclay. The fear of anarchy is what unites the *Politiques* more than anything else. Even a conservative like William Barclay (1546–1608), who parades all the stock divine-right arguments for placing unquestioned sovereignty in the monarch, has a utilitarian streak not far beneath the surface: "Rate the evils of misgovernment as high as you will, still they are less than those of anarchy."[93]

The Jesuits

The Society of Jesus, organized only in 1534, provided the intellectual thrust of the Counter Reformation. Politically, the Jesuits often sounded more constitutional and even more democratic than time proved them to be. Mostly Spanish—like their founder, St. Ignatius Loyola—their political loyalties tended to be with Philip II of Spain. For this Henry III of France was against them. Hence they were sometimes uneasy allies of the *Monarchomachs,* even though, ironically, the *Politiques* were the Catholics. The Jesuits did not wish to attribute to secular rulers power direct from God in the manner of the old Gelasian two-swords notion and they were too prudent to claim absolute secular power for the pope. Hence they tended to minimize religious in favor of constitutional arguments.

Bellarmine. Chief controversialist of the Counter Reformation was Robert Cardinal Bellarmine (1542–1621). Others were Juan de Mariana (1537–1624), and Francisco Suarez (1548–1617). In that part of his compendium *De controversiis* (*On Controversy*) devoted to the source of political authority,[94] Bellarmine defends a modified two-swords doctrine: the pope's authority comes directly from God; the king's authority comes indirectly from God through the consent of the

[91] See Murray, pp. 156–57, and Allen, pp. 292–96.

[92] See Otto Gierke, *Natural Law and the Theory of Society, 1500 to 1800,* trans. by Ernest Barker (Boston: Beacon Press, 1957), pp. 51, 59–60, and 67.

[93] *De regno,* p. 119. Quoted and trans. by Figgis, p. 139. Like his chief opponent, Buchanan, Barclay was a Scotsman transplanted to France. Other divine-right theorists of monarchy at that time were the Scottish-French Blackwood, the French Le Roy and De Belloy, and the Italian Zampini. See Allen, Part 3, Ch. 7, and J. N. Figgis, *The Theory of the Divine Right of Kings,* 2nd ed. (Cambridge, Eng.: Cambridge Univ. Press, 1914).

[94] Translated by Kathleen Murphy as *De Laicis* (*On the Laity*) or *The Treatise on Civil Government* (New York: Fordham Univ. Press, 1928). The Introduction, by M. F. X. Millar, S.J., attempts to relate Bellarmine to the principles of the American Constitution. *De controversiis,* though written earlier, was published in 1620.

people. The consent, however, is filtered through traditional communal structures, which Bellarmine justified by reference to Scriptures and the natural gregariousness of man rather than by any acknowledgement of the legitimate power of public opinion. Indeed, the last section of *De controveriis* is devoted to the dangers of liberty of opinion.

Mariana. Mariana's treatise *De rege et regis institutione* (*On Rulership and the Royal Institution,* 1599) goes beyond most of the Jesuit tracts in both systematization and profundity. He begins with a description of a state of nature out of which government arose—a unique foreshadowing of Rousseau. He defends tyrannicide with abundant historical examples. He shows monarchy to be the most efficacious system of government but also shows that it needs a checking institution such as the Estates in which, of course, the bishops can play their proper role. Book III of the work is a mirror-of-princes treatise, which, Dunning has shown, involves a bit of borrowing from Machiavelli.[95]

Suarez. Suarez, in *Tractatus de Legibus ac Deo Legislatore* (*Treatise on Law and the Precepts of God,* 1611), went furthest in separating the monarch from religious control. Theology seems almost incidental in Suarez: "Civil power springs from natural right; but the determination of the measure and the form of government of this power is left to the will of men."[96] Suarez was a link with the Jesuits of the seventeenth century and with Grotius and Pufendorf, who, abandoning traditional expectations of domestic religious restraints on the consciences of kings, labored in the vineyard of a rationalistic international law in hopes that this institution might prove to be the vehicle whereby God's will for newly self-conscious nations might be recognized. Even the twentieth century has not seen the end of this hope.

95 William Dunning, *A History of Political Theory from Luther to Montesquieu* (New York: Macmillan, 1905), pp. 74–75.

96 Bk. III, Ch. 4, sec. 1. Quoted in Murray, p. 230.

BODIN

Life

Jean Bodin (1530–96), the son of a master tailor, was born in Angers, France. He was admitted to the Carmelite order and under its tutelage studied philosophy, Greek, and Hebrew in Angers and Paris. For reasons not fully known—he may have flirted with Calvinism—Bodin left the Carmelite order, studied law at Toulouse, and taught there. Coming to Paris in the early 1560s as an advocate, he published the humanistic work *Methodus and facilem historiarium cognitionem* (*Method for the Easy Comprehension of History*),[97] in which appropriate methods of study are applied to the three basic areas of knowledge—things human, natural, and divine. Bodin used this classificatory scheme throughout his life. That his aim was no less than to fit all knowledge into a system of universal law is shown by another work, *Juris universi distributio* (*Law Apportioned to All Men*). A third publication of this period was *La Réponse à M. de Malestroit,* in which he effectively refuted the view that the debasement of currency was the cause of the sixteenth century's inflation.

In 1569 Bodin was imprisoned, probably for heresy.[98] Despite this he became counselor to the Duke of Alençon, the king's youngest brother, in 1571. But the abortive plot to put the duke on the throne when the king, Charles IX died, left Bodin in seclusion

97 Translated by Beatrice Reynolds (New York: Columbia Univ. Press, 1945). This work was influenced by the anti-Aristotelian—or at least revisionist—teachings of Ramus at the University of Paris. See Kenneth D. McRae, "Ramist Tendencies in the Thought of Jean Bodin," *The Journal of the History of Ideas,* Vol. 16 (1955), pp. 306–23.

98 The first biographer to document this fact is Kenneth D. McRae in the Introduction to his recent and indispensable edition of Bodin's *The Six Bookes of a Commonweale,* trans. by Richard Knolles (Cambridge, Mass.: Harvard Univ. Press, 1962). Most of the above biographical data are taken from McRae, pp. A3–A13. Subsequent quotations are from this edition.

at Laon, where he composed most of the *Six Livres de la république* (*Six Bookes of a Commonweale*), first published in Paris in 1576. The same year that the *République* appeared, Bodin was chosen representative of the third estate for Vermandois at the Estates-General of Blois, where he aroused the ire of the king by opposing his revenue measures. Again in the service of Alençon, Bodin traveled to England and Flanders, where his observations may have led to some of the changes in the Latin version of the *République* Bodin published in 1586. Bodin succeeded his brother-in-law in the office of *procureur du roi* for Laon in 1567; to keep this post during the uprisings against Henry III following the assassination of the Duke of Guise in 1588, Bodin collaborated with the Catholic League, even though his sympathies remained those of a royalist and *Politique*. His religious sympathies remain something of an enigma, for his will requested a Catholic burial but he also clearly believed in the privacy of religious belief, and in the dialogue *Heptaplomeres* (*Seven Questions*) he analyzed Christianity in a manner to shock both Catholics and Protestants. Yet he was a devout person, a learned person, and, curiously, as his writing on witchcraft (*De la Démonomanie des sorciers*, or *On the Demonology of Sorcerers*) shows, a gullible person.

Six Livres de la République

Bodin's great work, though clearly conditioned by the politics of the day, stands apart from the other *Politique* works by virtue of its magistral scope. Though Bodin's fear of anarchy appears in his Preface and elsewhere, he intended his *République* as a textbook on government and it was soon used as such at Cambridge and elsewhere. However much Bodin criticized Aristotle, he was inspired by the example of Aristotle's encyclopedic approach to knowledge and by the hope for a universal juridical science, a hope unevenly tinged with the mentality of modern secularism and progressivism. ". . . the natural law theory of the state finally won the day when Bodin in his *De République* emancipated the theory of public law from the classical tradition and made the modern concept of sovereignty the pivot of his argument."[99]

The content of the work was not, unfortunately, always equal in quality to its ambitious structure; even the logical sequence of topics became disarrayed at the secondary level. Moreover, literary felicity was not one of Bodin's virtues: "Changelessness, coherence, and confusion are the characteristics of Bodin: the changelessness is in thought, the coherence in idea, and the confusion in expression."[100] A partial listing of the contents of the *République* will suggest both its range and its emphasis: Book I discusses the state, the family, domestic authority, slavery, and sovereignty; Book II covers the three types of state—monarchy, aristocracy, and democracy—the "mixed state," and tyranny; Book III includes senates, councils, magistrates, colleges, corporations, and universities; Book IV treats states and historical change, astrology, the role of the sovereign, and factions; Book V considers climate, property, reward and punishment, military problems, and treaties; and Book VI examines censorship, the treasury, coinage, monarchical succession, and principles of justice.

Sovereignty

Bodin begins Book I with a definition—which is characteristic—and with a definition that hides a logical dilemma—which is also characteristic:

> A Commonweale is a lawful government of many families and of that which unto them in common belongeth, with a puissant soveraigntie. This definition, omitted by them which have written of a Commonweale, wee have placed in the first place. . . . For a definition is nothing else than the very end and scope of the matter propounded.[101]

[99] Gierke, pp. 36–37.

[100] Murray, pp. 130–31.

[101] *Six Bookes*, Bk. I, Ch. 1, p. 1. The first sentence in the Latin version (1586) reads: "A state is an association of families and their common affairs, governed

A definition is not the very end but only the beginning. This was part of Bodin's problem: he had a clear definition but not a clear end for the state beyond peace and order. Hence the question arises whether a state defined by a powerful sovereignty needs anything but power to make it lawful. Bodin says that a band of robbers is not a state even though it has an all-powerful chieftain. This is not only because a sovereign's power must be used justly and sanctioned by God but because this power is durable. Practically speaking, a robber's power is not durable, whereas a sovereign's must be "perpetual": "Soveraigntie is the most high, absolute, and perpetual power over the citizens and subjects in a Commonweale." Or again, "Sovereigntie is not limited in power, charge, or time certaine."[102] But how can any man's power be absolute, perpetual, and subordinate to none but "the immortall God alone"?

We shall return to the problem of absoluteness in a moment. But first let us acknowledge that the modern mind is apt to take less seriously than would Bodin the effectiveness of the ruler's sense of subordination to God. We must remember that, on the one hand, Bodin believed not only that divine retribution should but in fact did fall with awesome consequences on evil rulers. The sovereign's obligation to God was not a trivial matter. On the other hand, dependence on this relationship did not make Bodin a conventional divine-right theorist. And precisely at this point Bodin's modernity appears: sovereigns must have absolute and perpetual power under God but—almost incidentally—sovereigns do not have to be kings:

> Let us grant an absolute power without appeal or controlement to be granted by the people to one or many to mannage their estate and entire government: shall wee therefore say him or them to have the state of Soveraigntie, when as hee only is to bee called absolute Soveraigne who next unto God acknowledgeth none greater than himself? Wherefore I say no soveraigntie to be in them, for a certaine time, which once expired, they are bound to yeeld up their authoritie.[103]

Bodin certainly preferred monarchy—the special brand he called royal monarchy—but sovereignty is the characteristic of any state, monarchy or not.

Sovereignty, family, and property

Whether individual or collective, Bodin's sovereign is under God. But, at least initially, this individual or collective sovereign would seem to be as free from restrictive human obligations as Hobbes's sovereign would later seem to be. The immunity of Bodin's sovereign is a function of his necessity and his necessity looms large in the eyes of *Politiques* weary of the bloodshed caused by those who put sectarian religious allegiance ahead of public order. Nevertheless, Bodin was psychologically unable to suppress certain feudal loyalties that, defended in the *République,* tended to undermine the bold assertion of absolute and perpetual power in the sovereign.

The family—thought Bodin, like Plato and Aristotle—is the basis and origin of the state. It is "the true seminarie and beginning of every Commonweale, as also a principall

---

by a supreme power *and by reason* [our italics]" (trans. by Francis Coker in his *Readings in Political Philosophy,* rev. ed. [New York: Macmillan, 1938], p. 370). Some think the italicized addition is a concession to traditionalist critics; but it could be explained as easily by the mellowing in Bodin's own outlook that took place between the two versions. By 1586 Bodin was out of public life and more detached and humane in his stance, though it is needless and futile to speculate on which version best expresses the real Bodin.

[102] Coker's translation of the Latin version is, "Sovereignty is supreme power over citizens and subjects unrestrained by laws" (*op. cit.*), p. 374. Excerpts from the French version in a more up-to-date translation than Knolles's may be found in W. T. Jones, ed., *Masters of Political Thought* (Boston: Houghton Mifflin, 1949), Vol. 2, pp. 53–84.

[103] *Six Bookes,* Bk. I, Ch. 8, p. 86. Though not a divine-right theorist, Bodin produced some passages that, out of context, could be made to sound very much like the work of a divine-right theorist. He called kings God's lieutenants on earth and said, "he which speaketh evill of his prince unto whome he oweth all dutie, doth injurie unto the majestie of God himselfe, whose lively image he is upon earth."

member thereof." But this does not mean that the king is simply a superfather. In fact, Bodin made a sharp separation between the public authority of sovereigns and the private, domestic authority of heads of families—a separation so sharp that we are led to wonder how the family can give birth to the state yet be so different from the state. A further difficulty is the apparent limitation on sovereign power arising from the necessity of protecting the family. Bodin's rationale here was that by natural justice and long practice it is the duty of the state to protect property and property is an essential attribute of family existence.

The question of property illustrates the war in Bodin's mind between feudal conceptions of obligation and modern conceptions of state power. Bodin's support of the Salic Law of royal succession is another example of the same difficulty: it was a dictate of reason, French customary law, and God that royal succession did not go through the female line; and no sovereign, however absolute, could tamper with that. (God, as someone observed, changed His mind while crossing the English Channel, for the English succession could go through the female line.) Another fundamental law Bodin assumed to be inviolable held that kings could not alienate lands that were part of the public domain. These laws illustrated what Bodin called *leges imperii,* laws so fundamental that they were part and parcel of kingship itself. In swearing their oath of office before God French kings bound themselves of their own will to such laws, even though no other mortal had legal superiority to insure that their obligation would be fulfilled.

We must be careful, however, not to make too much of the word "absolute" and hence make too much of Bodin's "contradictions," as some writers do. Bodin was partly under the sway of the Middle Ages, to be sure, but

> the middle ages made some distinctions which we have lost or ignored. The power of a king was "absolute" and practically irresponsible but it was not "arbitrary." The medieval king was an autocrat *de jure,* but he was not a despot, and if he abused his lawful power he might become a tyrant, something different from either.[104]

To be bound by the laws of God, nature, and custom—which often merged—was more than verbal window-dressing. The "absolute power" of Bodin's sovereign, as we have seen, meant, in his own explanation, unchecked by higher *human* authority. Part of the confusion may stem from our understanding of "absolute" as wholly unconditioned, immutable, and unaffected. The French source of this English word in the 1577 edition was *puissance absolue.* McRae argues[105] that the Latin of the 1586 edition was more considered and more precise: *potestas legibus soluta* suggests unrestrained or independent legal power. Even this does not end the relevance of linguistic considerations, for we need to remember that talk of contradictions between all-powerful kings' law and all-powerful natural law, or God's law, rests upon the single English word "law," when actually two different sets of terms and two different levels of meaning are involved. To Bodin, God's law, or natural law, meant *droit* in French or *jus* in Latin, whereas kings' law was *loi* in French or *lex* in Latin. Today's legal positivist would most likely say that the latter is real law, the former only morality. But this is a judgment that would be uncongenial if not incomprehensible to Bodin. Both levels refer to real law, he would probably say to his English-speaking friends, and both involve morality.

However much this may soften the theoretical problem, such conclusions do not, in truth, help much to overcome the practical difficulty within the terms of Bodin's system that arises when a property owner, citing natural law, withholds his consent to be taxed and a king decides to collect the tax anyway. Yet even here Bodin was trying to be consistent with the reality of French prac-

[104] Charles H. McIlwain, *The Growth of Political Thought in the West* (New York: Macmillan, 1932), pp. 364–65.
[105] Introduction to *Six Bookes,* p. A15.

tice and his own experience. His parliamentary behavior as representative for Vermandois shows us that he was capable of acting on the assumption that the Estates-General and the regional estates were guardians of a natural law that a sovereign could be induced to recognize. Whatever their sixteenth-century behavior, we know that later kings were not this respectful even of settled doctrines of natural or customary law. Nor should we in our superior historical knowledge make Bodin out to be wholly ingenuous in his defense of either absolute sovereignty or customary law. In making the best case he could in behalf of order in a troubled time, he was capable of a lawyer's tactics. McRae notes that, although the origins and validity of the Salic Law were an issue much disputed in Bodin's day, Bodin prudently made no mention of such disputes in the *République* lest it open doors to unwelcome arguments.[106]

There is, nevertheless, a paradox in the belief that a commonwealth, to exist at all, needs rulers of unlimited power who will also operate within prescribed limits. But if Bodin did not resolve the paradox, neither can it be said that modern advocates of majority rule or modern advocates of minority rights have wholly resolved it.

States and governments

In Book II Bodin reviews the writings of Plato, Aristotle, Herodotus, and Polybius and mentions Cicero, More, and Machiavelli, among others, on the forms of the state. He reaches the conclusion that the forms of government—monarchy, aristocracy, and democracy—are not really different forms of state. The state is the commonweal as it was defined in Book I, Chapters 1, 8, and 10—a community under a sovereign. And a sovereign is always one. It follows that the age-old quest for the mixed state is a chimera: "I answere that such a state was never found, neither that such a state can bee made, or yet well imagined, considering that the markes of soveraigntie are indivisible."[107]

What Bodin sees, albeit incompletely, at this point is that the modern nation-state can never be a Greek *polis*. Its basis, whatever outward form its government may take, must be different. Hence citizen participation, which was essential to Aristotle's idea of the *polis,* is not essential to Bodin's idea of the commonwealth. Thus the unity of public and private happiness (*eudaemonia*) Aristotle sought in the good *polis* is not a viable goal for modern states. The modern state is big, diverse, pluralistic, and must be ruled by a dominant central power. Bodin's commonwealth is not a cultural entity, as the *polis* was, and that is why Bodin must distinguish it from corporations, colleges, estates, universities, and other cultural communities: "Now a familie is a communitie naturall; a college is a communitie civill, and a commonweale . . . is a communitie governed by a soveraigne power."[108]

A commonwealth cannot exist without families, for without families it would have no subjects. It can, at least in theory, exist without lesser civil societies, for it, too, is a civil society. But Bodin concedes that most of the cultural values of the smaller community are lost to the larger. The Greeks, he said, called their cities *philitia* [sic] from *philia* (friendship); but friendship is not the distinguishing mark of the commonwealth, with its multiplicity of often hostile religious groups. Indeed, religious communities often pose a threat to the very survival of the commonwealth. Bodin prudently chooses to illustrate this truth by reference to Rome rather than to France. In periods of such turmoil early ideals must be deferred or by-passed, "In which case the best advised princes and governors of Commonweales do imitate the wise pilots, who when they cannot attain unto the port by them desired, direct their course to such port as they may." This quotation may serve as a sign not only of Bo-

106 *Ibid.*, pp. A18–A19.

107 Bodin earlier says that Aristotle did not understand the marks of a commonwealth.

108 See Gierke, p. 64.

din's difficulty of finding clear ends for the new nation-state, barred from the old Greek ports, but of the difficulty faced by all modern, pragmatic, ruler-pilots.

Conclusion

Bodin is a tantalizing mixture of the old and the new. He argued that the state grows naturally out of family relationships in the manner of the ancients; yet in opposing the *Monarchomachs'* contract idea, he also argued, somewhat in the manner of nineteenth-century theorists of power, that the state may be a product of sheer force. He possessed an almost modern belief in progress—a confidence in the benefits to mankind that would result from the invention of the printing press, gunpowder, and the nation-state—yet this was combined with a bizarre confidence in medieval numerology and astrology.

Bodin's sociological interest in the effect of climate on national character foreshadowed Montesquieu, and his approach to economic questions showed a cool empiricism; yet this particularism was counterbalanced by an often uncritical acceptance of a natural-divine law working in all things to bring about unity and harmony. (His last chapter is devoted to a defense of a universal "harmonic justice," which is set against the geometric justice of aristocracies and the arithmetical justice of democracies.) He was, of course, an advocate of religious toleration and believed that religious belief was a personal and not a public concern; yet he assumed that government would be and should be controlled according to the tenets of revealed religion.

Bodin contributes in three ways to themes that have become central to Western political thinking. The first two are often overlooked in the large shadow cast by the third. In the first place, Bodin—however quaint his numerology and astrology—does, in Book IV, attempt to theorize about the process of historical change in states and thereby to move beyond the cyclical theories of the ancients. His general lack of success should not obscure the importance of his effort.

In the second place, Bodin gives the sovereign the power to make law and not simply to adjudicate, administer, and enforce preexisting law. This legislative power becomes the chief function of sovereignty: ". . . the first and chiefe marke of a soveraigne prince [is] to be of power to give lawes to all his subjects in general, and to everie one of them in particular." That Bodin would keep this power out of the hands of representative assemblies is secondary in importance to the basic assertion of a conception of *made* law, a conception without which modern parliaments and modern legislation would not be possible.

Finally, of course, the conception of sovereignty itself—a conception more remarkable than any specific content Bodin may have given it—stands as a monument to the rise of the modern state. This is the contribution conventionally attributed to Bodin and in this case convention is right.

With Bodin the Roman conception of world order and the medieval conception of a unified Christian society were abandoned. The basis of the nation-state was laid down. It now remained for Grotius, Hobbes, and a host of other theorists to enlarge and refine it.

HOOKER

Like Bodin, Richard Hooker (1554–1600) was a link between the medieval and the modern. Students of the seventeenth century will have been introduced to him through the pages of Locke, who used and perhaps misused him to gain respectability for a revolutionary doctrine. "The judicious Hooker" was understandably a touchstone for any Englishman who valued judiciousness.

Life

Hooker was born near Exeter to a yeoman family and was educated at Oxford, thanks to an uncle and the bishop of Salisbury, both of whom admired his scholarly talents. In 1577 he became a fellow of Corpus Christi College, where he lectured on logic and Hebrew, and took holy orders sometime before 1581. As master of the Temple Church, London, after 1585, Hooker began a notable preaching duel with Walter Travers, reader of the Temple, who was a Presbyterian. Out of this contest between Anglicanism and Presbyterianism, the intensity of which troubled the quiet and modest Hooker, came the attempt to put in writing what he could less well articulate in speech. The attempt became his magnum opus, for Hooker's whole reputation rests on the magistral *Laws of Ecclesiastical Polity,* written to defend the Anglican polity against Puritan claims. Of the eight books in the work, the first four appeared in 1593, the fifth in 1597 —Hooker was now, by choice, a country parson in Bishopsbourne, near Canterbury—and the last three posthumously. Book VIII, on Church and state, was not printed until 1628.

Hooker died in 1600 at the age of forty-six. He had been for nearly all his life an obscure Oxford don or a humble parish clergyman, unprepossessing in appearance and almost pathologically bashful. Yet his book is of major importance in the history of religion and thought: it might well be called the earliest philosophical masterpiece written in the English language.[109]

Laws of Ecclesiastical Polity

Reason and nature

Forgetting how medieval Hooker was, we are apt, on the one hand, to read too many modern assumptions into him. On the other hand, the very extent to which he drew on medieval sources may conceal from us the degree of his originality. Neither is the leisurely organization or elliptical style of his work calculated to focus our attention:

> Hooker consciously avoids symmetry. His prose-style is not an Elizabethan prose-style, but a baroque prose-style. . . . This style expresses the mental attitude which lay behind his work: an attempt to reconcile, rationally, facts and viewpoints which are actually contradictory, and which can, however, be grasped intuitively as so many variations of one magnificent theme.[110]

Working with the legacy of Marsilio of Padua, Hooker argued for the unity of Church and state resting on a base of common consent. Working with the rich materials of Aquinas, Hooker argued for the harmony of nature with the supernatural. Through these writers Hooker went back to the Stoic idea of universal moral law and finally to Aristotle, whose systematic, rational quest for truth he much admired. To Puritans who ridiculed his Scholastic affections Hooker replied: "If Aristotle and the Schoolmen be such perilous creatures, you must needs think yourself an happy man, whom God hath so fairly blest from too much knowledge in them."[111] Morris suggests that Hooker was more of a Renaissance man than a Reformation man; but Munz argues more compellingly that Hooker, "living in a thoroughly medieval world," failed to understand Renaissance Platonism.[112]

Hooker was a Protestant, as his doctrine of salvation shows, but he valued tradition, authority, good order, and law too highly to be any kind of a rebel; yet his tolerance exceeded that of his age—especially were the Calvinists shocked when he suggested that even a pope might be saved. "The corruption of our nature being presupposed," he nevertheless rejected the Calvinists' belief in the total depravity of man and he modified their

[109] Christopher Morris, *Political Thought in England, Tyndale to Hooker* (London: Oxford Univ. Press, 1953), p. 175. For biographical data see Raymond A. Houk, ed., *Hooker's Ecclesiastical Polity, Book VIII* (New York: Columbia Univ. Press, 1931), Introduction and Ch. 2; F. J. Shirley, *Richard Hooker and Contemporary Political Ideas* (London: Society for Promoting Christian Knowledge, 1949), Ch. 2; and Izaak Walton, *Life of Hooker* (1825), in John Keble, ed., Hooker's *Works,* 7th ed. (Oxford: Clarendon Press, 1888), Vol. 1.

[110] Peter Munz, *The Place of Hooker in the History of Thought* (London: Routledge and Kegan Paul, 1952), p. 173.

[111] Quoted in Shirley, p. 72.

[112] Munz, p. 171. Cf. Morris, p. 196.

total dependence upon Scripture by arguing that God is capable of revealing Himself in many different ways. According to his sometimes unreliable biographer, Walton, Hooker once said that what we perceive by sense is more certain than what we hear as the word of God. Above all, in rather Thomistic fashion he relied upon the innate reason of men, that "infallible knowledge imprinted in the minds of all the children of men, whereby both general principles for directing human actions are comprehended, and conclusions derived from them."[113] But Hooker moved beyond Thomas by separating almost in Kantian fashion the law of reason as it is found in men and the law of nature as it applies to the orderly working of physical processes.

Hooker saw instinct as another part of God's law and he followed Aristotle in believing that man is a naturally gregarious creature. Though he agreed up to a point with Augustine that government was made necessary by the sinfulness of man, he found more reason in and for government than Augustine did: ". . . in a word all public regiment of what kind soever seemeth evidently to have risen from deliberate advice, consultation, and composition between men, judging it convenient and behoveful." Hence, although Hooker has a kind of state-of-nature concept—two generations before Hobbes—it refers to an environment so primitive that no man would or could return to it. Though the present days are full of evil compared to the days "wherein there were no civil societies . . . as yet no manner of public regiment established . . . we have surely good cause to think that God hath blessed us exceedingly." Men saw early that government was necessary for "peace, tranquility, and happy estate."

Law

Book I of the *Laws of Ecclesiastical Polity* is Hooker's outline of the hierarchy of law in the universe.[114] It is a treatise on political science but much more than that, for it deals also with ontology and ethics. Divine law, Hooker argues, is supreme and unchangeable; and precisely because it is unchangeable it does not bind "things indifferent," areas of man's existence that may be quite important to him but are not bound by necessity or essentiality. Hence arise the great variety of laws and customs around the world, because "one kind of laws cannot serve for all kinds of regiment." But this does not mean that reason can bring no judgment to bear against human law, for the adaptation of general rules to local circumstance is precisely the area where human rationality is most needed.

Hooker distinguished between one kind of human law, which is so "mixedly" with what "plain and necessary reason" demands, and "merely human" law, which binds no man until it is enacted by civil authority. Prohibitions against bigamy and incest are examples of the former, the rule of primogeniture is an example of the latter. As this example suggests, Hooker found a much greater latitude for variety, that is, found many more laws "merely human," than the typical establishment theorist of his day. The third category of human law, says Hooker, is the law of nations, which transcends the body of domestic law of any particular state yet is not divine law strictly speaking. The law of nations is not only negative—what Hooker called secondary—that is, "arising from the conditions created by man's depraved nature," of which an example would be the laws of arms, it is also affirmative, or primary—that is, conducive to intercultural communication, "the courteous entertainment of foreigners . . . commodious traffic, and the

113 *Laws of Ecclesiastical Polity,* Bk. II, Ch. 8, sec. 6, in *Works,* Vol. 1, pp. 272–73. Except for quotations from Book VIII, subsequent quotations are from this edition.

114 Books II and III deal with the tenets of Puritanism; Books IV and V are a defense of the Church of England against charges of creeping Catholicism; Book VI concerns the role of the laity in the Church and Book VII the authority of bishops; Book VIII discusses Church-state relations. In his long introduction to his edition of Book VIII, Houk takes up the question of the authenticity of Books VI–VIII—the posthumous books—and finds compelling evidence that Hooker wrote them. See *Hooker's Ecclesiastical Policy, Book VIII,* pp. 67–90.

like." These laws spring from the same motive that led Socrates to profess himself a citizen of the world. However comfortable our own polity, we are not satisfied until we "have a kind of society and fellowship even with all mankind."

Like Aristotle, Hooker thought of law as collective reason purged of individual passion and therefore more reliable than dependence upon the will of any one man. His law seems almost to have a life of its own. It animates the soul of the body politic:

We see then how nature itself teacheth laws and statutes to live by. The laws which have been hitherto mentioned do bind men absolutely even as they are men, although they have never any settled fellowship, never any solemn agreement amongst themselves what to do or not to do. But foreasmuch as we are not by ourselves sufficient to furnish ourselves with competent store of things needful for such a life as our nature doth desire, a life fit for the dignity of man; therefore to supply those defects and imperfections which are in us living single and solely by ourselves, we are naturally induced to seek communion and fellowship with others. This was the cause of men's uniting themselves at the first in politic societies; which societies could not be without Government, nor Government without a distinct kind of Law from that which hath been already declared. Two foundations there are which bear up public societies; the one a natural inclination whereby all men desire sociable life and fellowship; the other an order expressly or secretly agreed upon touching the manner of their union in living together. The latter is that which we call the Law of a Commonweal, the very soul of a body politic, the parts whereof are by law animated, held together, and set on work in such actions as the common good requireth.[115]

Consent

Hooker is credited with articulating ideas of contract and consent that were profoundly to influence English political thought, especially as they flowed through Locke's work. While this observation is generally correct, it is important to note that Hooker's conception of society was far more organic than those of either Hobbes or Locke. He spoke of "contract" but his meaning of the term was closer to a religious covenant that binds all men together in mutual obligation than to a legal arrangement. He spoke of "consent" but he was referring to the response of the whole community to basic institutions and not to a device whereby an affected minority—or majority—may exercise a veto power. Hooker influenced Burke as well as Locke; certain passages in the *Laws of Ecclesiastical Polity* seem to be echoed almost in duplicate in Burke's oratory: ". . . to be commanded we do consent, when that society of which we are part hath at any time before consented, without revoking the same after by the like universal agreement. . . . Corporations are immortal; we were then alive in our predecessors, and they in their successors do live still."

Later theorists of popular sovereignty needed not only Hooker's notion of consent but Bodin's theory of sovereignty; the latter was conspicuously absent in Hooker. His sovereign is not one whose will becomes law but one who exists to enforce preexisting law: "The lawful power of making laws to command whole politic societies of men belongeth so properly unto the same entire societies" that for a prince to arrogate such power to himself "is no better than mere tyranny." The medieval tenor of this assertion is obvious. Although Hooker left open the possibility of "express commission" of a ruler by God, he assumed a normal harmony of the agencies of common consent and the will of the ruling sovereign. An infant can hence be king without diminishing the authority of the office of kingship. The sovereign is the king-*in*-parliament, not the king as an isolated person.

This very doctrine of organic consent, however, separated Hooker from the divine-right theorists, who, as Filmer would soon attempt, tried to equate the authority of kings with the authority of fathers. Not so for Hooker:

[115] *Laws of Ecclesiastical Polity,* Bk. I, Ch. 10, sec. 1, p. 184.

To fathers within their private families nature hath given a supreme power; for which cause we see throughout the world even from the foundation thereof, all men have ever been taken as lords and lawful kings in their own houses. Howbeit over a whole grand multitude having no such dependency upon any one, and consisting of so many families as every politic society in the world doth, impossible it is that any should have complete lawful power, but by consent of men, or immediate appointment of God; because *not having the natural superiority of fathers,* their power must needs be either usurped, and then unlawful; or, if lawful, then either granted or consented unto by them over whom they exercise the same, or else given extraordinarily from God, unto whom all the world is subject.[116]

Hooker's view of both consent and tyranny, then, was medieval, which meant that tyranny, although condemned by God, was less dangerous than anarchy; therefore individuals were denied the right to resist tyrants.

Church and state

One of the ironies of Hooker's position is that in the name of medieval values he was more tolerant of diversity than his modern Puritan critics. The forms of both political and ecclesiastical organization fall into his category of "things indifferent" or "things arbitrary" in the sight of God. That man needs some kind of government "the law of nature doth require; yet the kinds thereof being many, nature tieth not to any one, but leaveth the choice as a thing arbitrary." Likewise, natural law prescribes that virtue be rewarded and vice punished but the particular way in which this is done is left to the ingenuity of human reason working within the limitations of time and place. Finally, even within the Church, though natural law and the Scriptures prescribe certain things that must be done of necessity,

nevertheless, by reason of new occasions still arising which the Church having care of souls must needs take order for as need requireth, hereby it comes to pass that there is and ever will be great use even of human laws and ordinances, deducted by way of discourse as conclusions from the former divine and natural, serving for principles thereunto.[117]

One exception to this latitude for innovation strikes us with particular force, however. Even though monarchy is not an absolutely required form of government for Hooker, if a monarch rules and the society is Christian, the monarch simply must be a Christian. Hooker could not imagine any other arrangement. His whole mission was to defend what he regarded as a Christian constitution of England. Toward this object he could be

apologist or critic: but, Hooker's nature being what it was, there was never a real choice for him. He had to become its apologist. It appears, to begin with, that to disapprove of existing conditions would have smacked to Hooker of impiety towards God. For Hooker was profoundly Christian in his interpretation of human history as the work of divine providence.[118]

Helping to explain but also complicating this providential view of English government is Hooker's deep conviction that, at bottom, the government of the Church and the government of the commonwealth are one. After a lengthy discussion of the different functions of civil government and ecclesiastical government, Hooker nevertheless concludes,

The Church and the commonwealth therefore are . . . personally one society, which society being termed a commonwealth as it liveth under whatsoever form of secular law and regiment, as church as it hath the spiritual law of Jesus Christ; for as much as these two laws contain so many and so different offices, there must of necessity be appointed in it some to one charge, and some to another, yet without divid-

[116] *Ibid.,* sec. 4, p. 187.

[117] *Laws of Ecclesiastical Polity,* Bk. VIII, Ch. 6, in Houk, p. 229. Subsequent page references to Book VIII will be to this edition.

[118] Munz, p. 69. Munz illustrates the point with Hooker's discussion of how the Christian diocese grew out of the Roman province. Instead of finding in this relationship a secular origin for religious institutions, Hooker found that Roman institutions were part of God's plan for the furtherance of Christianity. See *ibid.*

ing the whole, and making it two several impaled societies.[119]

For this position Hooker is sometimes called an Erastian, that is, one who would subordinate Church authority to state authority. But this is a misnomer. He would not, like Erastus or Hobbes, allow the sovereign to define right religion and he applied his theory of communal consent to both Church and commonwealth. Aquinas and Marsilio of Padua might have subscribed to this view but Queen Elizabeth would not have been happy had Book VIII been published in her lifetime. Perhaps it was his awareness that defense had become criticism that caused Hooker's life work to remain unfinished at his death.

Conclusion

Hooker is a suitable figure with which to end a chapter on the Reformation, for he carries us forward and backward. He revealed the value of the old hidden in the new and also managed to remind men that reformations need reforming. His was an Aristotelian search for the mean—a mean between Puritan "liberty" with "every man his own commander" and patriarchal divine-right orthodoxy, a mean between unquestioned authority and the consent of the governed, a mean between theocracy and Erastianism. He cannot be said to have succeeded in finding a wholly satisfactory mean. We credit him not so much with a doctrine as with an attitude. He was not worldly enough to be a Renaissance man and not righteous enough to be a Reformation man. He was a medieval man confronting problems of a modern, pluralistic world with mixed hope and dismay but with enough appreciation of the complexities of man's social existence to provide a bridge over the years to thinkers as diverse as Locke and Burke.

[119] *Laws of Ecclesiastical Polity,* Bk. VIII, Ch. 1, p. 160. Hooker did concede that "the Church and the commonwealth are names which import things really different; but those things are accidents, and such accidents as may and should always lovingly dwell together in one subject." Hooker later suggests the interlocking character of the relations between clergy, people, and ruler when he says that the power of the clergy originating outside the political sphere "resteth nevertheless unexercised except some part of the people of God be permitted them to work upon" and "in a peaceable environment, for which all men subject to a Christian king, depend in that respect on him also."

CONCLUSION: THE REFORMATION AND THE MODERN AGE

Somewhere along the route that stretches between Luther's nailing his theses to the door of the Wittenberg church in 1517 and the Treaty of Westphalia in 1648, the modern age began. It is an age, we know, characterized by the rise of the centralized nation-state, individualism, and experimental science. Largely inadvertently,[120] the Protestant Reformation contributed to all three phenomena, even as its own evolution was reciprocally influenced by all three.

This is not the place to open the complex historical issues attending an adequate understanding of nationalism, individualism, and what for lack of a more graceful term we are compelled to call scientism.[121] What

[120] Even Hooker inadvertently contributed to the pluralism he deplored by what Bainton calls the solution of *comprehension,* or putting as many people as possible within a single church "by making minimal and ambiguous demands" on them. See *Reformation,* p. 183.

[121] On nationalism see Lord Acton, *Essays on Freedom and Power* (Boston: Beacon Press, 1948); Carlton J. H. Hayes, *Essays on Nationalism* (New York: Macmillan, 1926); Hans Kohn, *The Idea of Nationalism* (New York: Macmillan, 1944); and Boyd C. Shafer, *Nationalism, Myth and Reality* (New York: Harcourt, Brace & World, 1955). On individualism see Harold J. Laski, *Liberty in the Modern State* (New York: Harper & Row, 1930); E. Harris Harbison, *The Age of Reformation* (Ithaca: Cornell Univ. Press, 1955); Johan Huizinga, *The Waning of the Middle Ages* (New York: Longmans, Green, 1948); and H. M. Robertson, *Aspects of the Rise of Economic Individualism* (Cambridge, Eng.: Cambridge Univ. Press, 1933). On scientism see Marie Boas, *The Scientific Renaissance, 1450–1650* (New York: Harper & Row, 1966); E. A. Burtt, *The Metaphysical Foundations of Modern Physical Science,* rev. ed. (Garden City, N. Y.: Doubleday, Anchor, 1954); Herbert

we can do before moving into the fascinating seventeenth century, where political theory—especially English political theory—so colorfully illustrates all three phenomena, is to pause and ask three questions arising out of the Reformation era that may have relevance to our own day:

(1) Where persons of opposed fundamental beliefs clash in great numbers, is civil liberty possible without the eventual privatization of those fundamental, that is, religious, beliefs?

(2) If fundamental beliefs become private, if they are removed from the public domain, is political power then exercised without the benefit of being channeled and informed by a commonly understood moral authority?

(3) If political power is exercised without being informed by a commonly understood moral authority, is it likely to become prey to expedience and can the body politic then sustain itself as a body politic?

Butterfield, *The Origins of Modern Science, 1300–1800* (New York: Macmillan, 1962); Arthur Koestler, *The Sleepwalkers* (New York: Macmillan, 1959); and Thomas S. Kuhn, *The Structure of Scientific Revolutions* (Chicago: Univ. of Chicago Press, 1964).

10

THE SEVENTEENTH CENTURY

A magnificent century, the seventeenth, and nowhere more magnificent than in England. In France the monolithic rigidities of absolutism under Louis XIII and Louis XIV seemed to freeze political speculation. England, by contrast, was going through her great national travail: from Tudor absolutism, to Stuart would-be absolutism, to revolution, to the Commonwealth, to the Restoration, and finally, in the Glorious Revolution of 1688, to the establishment of Parliamentary supremacy on an enduring basis. Such contention seems to force national self-examination and serious political thinking. America's Revolution and Civil War were, in like fashion, her great periods of political speculation. England was perhaps more fortunate than she knew in having to work out her political adjustment to modernity earlier than most nation-states and fortunate, too, in that she was able to do so. England's island isolation rather than some mystique of national character is perhaps most responsible for this happy state of affairs—although the behavior of Englishmen, displayed in situations such as their lone stand against the Nazis in 1940, will often inspire admiration for English national character even in those who do not believe in the concept.

In political thought, the seventeenth century was indeed England's century. Yet we must not let national political history crowd out theory. The theoretical questions asked in the seventeenth century that are especially significant for us seem to be four in number. These can usefully serve as the framework of this chapter: (1) How can obedience to autocratic rulers be justified? (2) How can constitutional restraints on rulers be justified? (3) How can a popular basis for political authority be justified? (4) How do leaders respond to the need for reliable moral standards for political rule when religious standards are beginning to break down?

THE POLITICAL OBLIGATION OF SUBJECTS

One of the first practical and theoretical problems any political order must wrestle with is how to sustain a sense of political obligation on the part of the mass of citizens. We say "sustain" rather than "establish" because a sense of political obligation is of such a primal quality that social life can scarcely exist unless it is present. Dissolve the bonds of political obligation and one is close to dissolving the responsibility of one man to another, or vice versa. Social responsibility and political responsibility are intimately bound together—as any mayor, monarch, or prefect can testify. When both are gone, anarchy results; and in practice anarchy has generally meant looting, pillage, rape, and casual murder. This *state of nature,* or the condition of man as he might be outside political society, was a concept that fascinated many seventeenth- and eighteenth-century thinkers. Such fascination was prerequisite to so-called social-contract theories, for, if the state of nature was a condition from which man needed to escape, what more logical way (to those living in a society where the commercial contract was becoming more and more important[1]) than to enter a contractual relationship that established a joint partnership called government? Thomas Hobbes and John Locke are the most famous contractualists and so important are they that we must devote separate chapters to them. Before the contractualists held sway, however, the conspicuous theorists were those who denied that man had been or could be free of his primeval obligation to rulers.

Divine Right

There is irony, perhaps only the irony of all historical development, in the fact that, while the divine ordination of monarchical rule was taken for granted for centuries, divine right as a well-articulated theory became conspicuous only when monarchy itself was under attack. During that period, concern for the problem was intense: "From 1528, when Tyndale's book was issued, until the appearance of Hobbes' *De cive* in 1642, political thought exhausted itself almost wholly on *The Obedience of a Christian Man.*"[2] As a basis for this political obligation of subjects the theory of divine right was most generously stated in seventeenth-century England by King James and by Sir Robert Filmer.

James I

"The wisest fool in Christendom," as James I (1566–1625) was known, came to the throne upon the death of Elizabeth in 1603. He was thirty-seven. Vain, slovenly, devout, widely learned, caustically humorous, shrewd, but erratic and explosive—these adjectives help to portray the man and, along with his unyielding view of monarchical supremacy, explain much of his trouble with Parliament. James had been born into an atmosphere of pervasive and often bloody intrigue. His father, Henry Stuart, earl of Darnley, was murdered in 1567, the year that the infant James became James VI, king of Scotland. It was one husband, several years, and several conspiracies later that his mother, Mary, Queen of Scots, was executed at Fotheringhay. Although James's accession contravened the will of his great-uncle Henry VIII, he won out over his rivals, Lady Arabella Stuart and William Seymour, in part because of Elizabeth's wishes and in part because he was acceptable to all parties. Anglican churchmen knew he would support them ("No bishop, no King" was his often-quoted maxim), Catholics expected at least toleration from the son of Mary Stuart, and Presbyterians took heart from the fact that he had been brought up in the tenets of the Scottish Kirk. All but the Anglican churchmen were destined to be disappointed.

The young king's tutor had been George Buchanan, the Prince of Humanists, whose treatise *De jure regni apud Scotos* (1578) espoused the view, popular in Scotland, that a king's authority derived solely from the people. This view reflected the Huguenot influence in Scotland. But James, whose grandmother had been Mary of Guise, was more affected by another French influence on Scot-

[1] See C. B. Macpherson, *The Political Theory of Possessive Individualism: Hobbes to Locke* (New York: Oxford Univ. Press, 1962).

[2] Charles H. McIlwain, ed., *The Political Works of James I* (Cambridge, Mass.: Harvard Univ. Press, 1918), p. xx. Subsequent quotations from James are from this edition. See also J. N. Figgis, *The Theory of the Divine Right of Kings,* 2nd ed. (London: Cambridge Univ. Press, 1914).

land, that of the *Politiques,* a group of French Catholic promonarchists. James owed a debt of sorts to two early divine-right theorists, Scotsmen transplanted to France, William Barclay and Andrew Blackwood.[3] Barclay and Blackwood were Catholics and *Politiques* but other Catholics, especially the English Jesuits, were at this time developing antimonarchical doctrines that put them in an uncomfortable alliance with the Puritans, as the English Presbyterians, among others, were called. James would have no truck with either Catholics or Puritans as such.

James's principal political works were written before he became king of England. They include *Basilicon Doron, or His Majesty's Instructions to His Dearest Son, Henry the Prince* (first published in 1599) and *The True Law of Free Monarchies* (1598). A free monarchy, for James, was one free of meddlesome parliamentarians. A number of his speeches to Parliament later follow the same theory. In the *Basilicon Doron* James admonishes one who would be king to serve God and God alone and accepts the traditional distinction between the God-fearing king and the tyrant who feels no responsibility to God. The work reveals a rigorous conception of a king's duty to his people. But James also waxes indignant over those who dare challenge a king's sovereign authority: "I was oft times calumniated in their popular sermons not for any evil or vice in me but because I was a king. . . . Sometimes they would be informing the people that all kings and princes were naturally enemies to the liberty of the Church. . . . Take heed, therefore (my son), to such Puritans, very pests in the Church and Commonwealth." His son would do well to study history with care, but "not of such infamous invectives as Buchanan's or Knox's Chronicles."

The True Law of Free Monarchies was a more systematic treatise. The core of the argument rested on no more than the analogy between a father's authority over his children and a king's authority over his people. Relying heavily on scriptural references to kingly power in ancient Israel, James finds a similar power implied by the coronation oath of Scotland, "as well as of every Christian Monarchy": "By the Law of Nature the King becomes a natural Father to all his Lieges at his Coronation: And as the Father of his family is duty bound to care for the nourishing, education, and virtuous government of his children, even so is the King bound to care for all his subjects."

The dependence on analogy so important in divine-right theories meant, of course, that opponents could simply deny the validity of the analogy, which they did. Where James attempted more logical explications, they generally failed. For example, when the law of nature was read into the law of primogeniture as a sign of God's preference for hereditary monarchy, one was faced with the practical problem of reconciling its operation in France, where female lines were excluded, with that in England, where women had their chance at the throne.

Logical arguments failing, James's tendency was to invoke an element of mystery in a somewhat arbitrary way and thunder at his opponents. Thus, in his famous speech in Star Chamber (1616) James says, "It is atheism and blasphemie to dispute what God can do: good Christians content themselves with his will revealed in his word. So, it is presumption and high contempt in a subject, to dispute what a king can do, or say that a king cannot do this or that; but rest in that which is the King's revealed will in his law."

But James came a generation too late to act effectively on such sentiments. Neither common-law judges nor the Puritans in Parliament were prepared to receive warmly his argument that God's law as interpreted by the Church of England, "most pure . . . and . . . sureliest founded upon the word of God, of any church in Christendom," stands above the law of nature, which itself takes precedence over the common law and statutory law. James agreed to maintain the common law, but "as to maintain it, so to purge it. . . . For I will never trust any interpretation that

[3] See J. W. Allen, *A History of Political Thought in the Sixteenth Century* (London: Methuen, 1928), Part II, Ch. 10; Part III, Ch. 7.

agreeth not with my common sense and reason, and true logic. . . . As for the absolute prerogative of the Crown, that is no subject for the tongue of a lawyer, nor is lawful to be disputed."

The Puritans did not object to the theological flavor of James's statements. If anything, their arguments were more heavily theological than his. Rather they objected to the finality with which he assumed power for himself and the Church of England. The logical possibility that a king's power might come from God indirectly *through* the people was scarcely entertained by divine-right theorists of this time. Moreover, the Lutheran doctrine forbidding resistance to tyrants was simply assumed by them to be a part of the divine-right position, even though there was no logically necessary connection between it and what James was talking about. The divine-right theory was a popular theory rather than a systematic theory with philosophic roots. We might properly call it ideological in character.

Filmer

The ideological use of divine-right theory is best illustrated by noting the fate of *Patriarcha: A Defense of the Natural Power of Kings against the Unnatural Liberty of the People*[4] by Sir Robert Filmer (c. 1588–1653). Filmer, the eldest son of a family of eighteen children, was educated at Trinity College, Cambridge, and received legal training at Lincoln's Inn but devoted most of his life to the duties of a country gentleman at the family estate in Kent. These duties included service as a county magistrate. His circle of friends embraced a rather distinguished group of lawyers, clerics, historians, and businessmen, many of whom later made their mark on the colony of Virginia. Members of this group often wrote manuscript treatises on current intellectual questions for circulation to one another and to their sons and cousins in London. Such was Filmer's discourse on usury (c. 1630) and such was the *Patriarcha,* written sometime between 1635 and 1642 to defend the royal prerogative. Though not active in pursuing the Royalist cause during the Puritan Revolution, Filmer was imprisoned from 1643 to 1645. It was only in his last years that any of Filmer's writings were published and by his own request the *Patriarcha* was never published during his lifetime. It was resurrected in 1680 as an ideological weapon in a battle somewhat different from that for which it was written. Noting the judicious and critical wit displayed in some of Filmer's other writings, Laslett observes, "The worst of the injustices which have been done to him is that he should have been judged almost exclusively on *Patriarcha* alone." Another, of course, is that most people have seen Filmer only through the scathing critique administered to him by Locke in *The First Treatise of Civil Government.*

What Filmer adds to the basic analogical argument of James I is an attempt at historical justification of divine right. His complete faith in the literal historical truth of the Bible is striking. In much the same way that the divinity of twentieth-century Japanese emperors has been traced back to the origins of man, Filmer traced the divine authority of European kings back to Adam. As the first man on earth, Adam was given authority by God over his wife, Eve, over his children, and over all the possessions of the earth. Adam, then, was the first king.

> And indeed not only Adam, but the succeeding Patriarchs had, by right of Fatherhood, royal authority over their children. . . . I see not then how the children of Adam, or of any man else, can be free from subjection to their parents. And this subordination of children is the fountain of all regal authority, by the ordination of God himself.[5]

As do biblical fundamentalists today, Fil-

[4] See Peter Laslett, ed., *The Patriarcha and Other Political Works* (Oxford: Blackwell, 1949). This section rests heavily on Laslett's fine edition, which served to resurrect Filmer from the oblivion into which Locke's attacks had cast him. Subsequent quotations from Laslett and Filmer are from this edition.

[5] *Ibid.,* Bk. III, p. 57.

mer believed that all the races and kingdoms of man descended from the three sons of Noah—Shem, Ham, and Japheth—to whom the continents of earth were parceled out by their father, like field-work assignments, after the Flood. The biblical command to political obedience was thus simple and clear: it was identical with the Fifth Commandment's enjoinder to parental obedience. Filmer, of course, could not actually trace genealogical lines back to Noah and he had to admit the reality of various usurpations of kingly power and some disturbing breaks in hereditary lines. He came closest to granting the validity of election in stating that, if the eldest male descendant of Adam could not be found in any given society, then the chief heads of families might establish the new royal house. But this provision was thought in no way to weaken the one true basis of governmental authority, namely paternalism.

On the negative side, Filmer's argument was directed against "The natural freedom of mankind, a new, plausible and dangerous opinion," and turned on the anarchic implications of any doctrine of individual consent. If consent were to be the moral basis of authority, it would be manifestly impossible to gather together all individuals to consult them or to achieve unanimity were they gathered. Even in the so-called mixed monarchy, fundamental disputes must be resolved by the will of one man, the sovereign monarch. The liberties of parliaments are "not from nature but from the grace of princes." In the assumption of the necessity of unitary sovereignty, Filmer was following Bodin quite closely. Moreover, secure in his own understanding of history, he could with some confidence deny the historicity of any genuine democratic society.

While the role of Adam and Noah in this argument no doubt strikes us as absurd—as it did Locke—we must not let incongruity lead us astray. The fact is that English society more nearly corresponded to the patriarchal image of Filmer than to the individualistic image of the liberals and radicals of that day:

> It was simply not true that authority was being exercised by consent. How could it be pretended that the son consented to being commanded by the father? What conceivable sophistry could justify the obedience of the apprentice in going to church at his master's bidding, or the submission of the schoolboy to a beating, on the ground that they had given their assent? If authority could be exercised without consent, if in fact it was perpetually being so exercised, then there must be some other source of obligation. This other sort of obligation could only be by nature, not by choice, and observation showed that it was patriarchal.[6]

Today we think it strange that political power should be handed down from father to son, but not so with economic power: we still accept with equanimity the right of inheritance applied to property. Filmer took largely for granted the assumptions appropriate to his position as master of a huge household in East Sutton Park, Kent. Lesser patriarchs like Filmer were, of course, a minority of the population. "Nevertheless, in most of the places where the word 'people' is mentioned in the political writings of the time, even in such authors as Milton himself, it is possible to substitute the word 'patriarchs' or 'heads of households.' "

Filmer is a curious mixture of realism and unreality. There is a certain mystique that surrounds all political authority. It was Filmer's destiny to contribute to the mystique of monarchy and to capture the imagination of monarchical supporters through his use of the Genesis stories. We should not expect their acceptance to be tempered with critical reservations; many people in the seventeenth century still believed in the power of kings to heal scrofula by touching. Had Filmer been more critical, he would have been less effective. Nor was his argument held lightly by supporters of the king. Just before his death on the scaffold in 1649, Lord Capel affirmed the core of Filmer's divine-right argument: "I die for keeping the Fifth Commandment, given by God himself and written

[6] *Ibid.*, p. 31 (Laslett's Introduction).

with His own finger. It commands obedience to parents, and all divines, differ as they will on other points, agree in this, and acknowledge that it includes the magistrates."[7]

Bossuet

The seventeenth century was not a great period for political speculation in France. The atmosphere under the absolute rule of Louis XIII and Louis XIV could hardly have been less congenial for inquiries into the nature of the good state and most literary efforts were confined to the writing of panegyrics on the regime. The best-known political writer of the seventeenth-century France was Jacques Bossuet (1627–1704), Bishop of Meaux and colorful funeral orator, who, as might be expected, furnished ideological fuel for the defense of absolute monarchy. Had he not been appointed tutor of the Dauphin in 1670, he might never have bothered with political studies; but with this responsibility he felt an obligation to train his charge in the political wisdom of the past. The Dauphin was an indifferent student; but the cause of refuting rebellious Protestant *Monarchomachs* was enough to keep Bossuet at his task, even in the face of such unpleasant diversions as mediating clashes between the pope and Louis XIV.

Bossuet's principal political work was *La Politique tirée de l'Écriture Sainte* (*Politics Based on Holy Scripture*), published posthumously in 1709. He began with the same assumptions as had Filmer—the literal truth of the Bible, the patriarchal line from Adam to the present, and the rest. In his use of scriptural references to support detailed arrangements of the *status quo,* Bossuet outdid Filmer. Louis' lavish court, for example, was justified by reference to Solomon's extravagance: God, it seems, was using both courts to breed respect for monarchy. Bossuet made a problem for himself by arguing that one and only one ideal polity—monarchy—could be distilled from the Scriptures yet maintaining the tradition (not accepted by the Jesuits) that resistance to any government was unjustified. This argument placed the believer living under a form other than monarchy in an ambiguous position. Filmer had rather naïvely assumed that monarchies had always existed and would always exist, with alternative forms being only transient, anarchic aberrations. Bossuet, writing at the end of the century, could not so confidently take for granted the historical normality of monarchy; but in essence, like Filmer, he simply sidestepped the problem:

> We have seen that, by order of the Divine Providence, the monarchical constitution was in its origin the most conformable to the will of God, as declared by the Scriptures. We have not overlooked therein the fact that other forms of government flourished in antiquity, of which God gave no special command to the human race, so that each people ought to accept as divinely ordained the form of government established in its country.[8]

Much influenced by the rationalist Hobbes's treatment of the horrors of the "state of nature," Bossuet was able to adopt the description but felt obliged to modify the explanation. It was the fall of man, the Augustinian concept of man's sin and corruption, rather than Hobbes's mechanistic psychology that explained the need for an all-powerful sovereign ruler:

> Far from the people being sovereign in this condition, as yet there is no such entity as a people. . . . There cannot be a people, since the existence of a people presupposes already some bond of unity, some settled behavior, and some established law; which things cannot exist until the multitude have begun to escape from this unhappy state of anarchy.[9]

While for Hobbes the authority of the

[7] Quoted by W. E. H. Lecky, *History of the Rise and Influence of the Spirit of Rationalism in Europe* (New York: Appleton-Century-Crofts, 1888), Vol. II, p. 181.

[8] *La Politique tirée de l'Écriture Sainte,* Bk. II, Art. 2. Quoted in Norman Sykes, "Bossuet," Ch. 2 in F. J. C. Hearnshaw, ed., *The Social and Political Ideas of Some Great French Thinkers of the Age of Reason* (London: Harrap, 1930), p. 55.

[9] *Cinquième avertissement,* sec. 50. Quoted in Sykes, p. 53.

sovereign was analogous to the central nervous system of the Leviathan, for Bossuet the analogy was the relationship of God to his whole creation:

> If God withdrew His hand the universe would fall into annihilation. So if the authority of the King ceased in the Kingdom all things would fall into confusion. . . . Behold an entire nation united in the person of a single ruler; consider this sacred, paternal, and absolute authority; behold the hidden counsel which governs the entire body of the State, residing in one single head. Thus the image of God may be seen in Kings and the idea of their royal majesty.[10]

Bossuet composed a careful delineation of the differences between absolute monarchy, which he was defending, and arbitrary government, which he was not. But even as he wrote, the excesses of his own monarch dissolved the line in practice. Theories, even eloquent theories, that lose contact with the practice of men soon lose force and become anachronisms. Such was the fate of divine-right theories in the seventeenth century. But other theories dealing with the political obligation of subjects were destined to fare better. Of these, the theory of sovereignty lasted longest.

Sovereignty

Should the general precede the particular or the particular precede the general? Strict logic might demand that we say nothing about such concepts as natural law, the social contract, the state of nature, and sovereignty until they can be spelled out in some detail. Such detail will appear in the subsequent chapters on Hobbes, the greatest political thinker of the seventeenth century, and Locke, the most influential. Yet perhaps we can avoid doing either Hobbes or ourselves an injustice if we first see him reflected in the speculations of lesser men. In the seventeenth century to set forth a theory of sovereignty was to explain, in more legalistic and less emotional terms than those of divine-right thinkers, why the citizen ought to accept the fact of a determinate center of governmental power in every society. (It is significant that, while Locke's aversion to Hobbes led him to avoid the term "sovereignty," he could not avoid talking about "supreme power.") But Hobbes's tremendous impact is recorded in the fact that, despite all differences of ability and nationality, pre-Hobbesian writers on sovereignty were more superficial on the topic than post-Hobbesian writers. In the former category are Bacon and Grotius, in the latter Spinoza and Pufendorf.

Bacon

An enthusiast and theoretician for the new world of science, Francis Bacon (1561–1626) was at the same time a practitioner and theoretician of an old world of politics. As Attorney General under James I he was thrust into the difficult position of defending the royal prerogative against the challenge of Chief Justice Coke. Bacon responded to the challenge with resourcefulness. While he did not sanction James's basic hostility to Parliament, it is probably correct to say that he was sincere in defending a strong royal prerogative. But his use of the concept of sovereignty was loose and unsystematic. When "there be other bands that tie faster than the band of sovereignty, kings begin to be put almost out of possession." Without much analysis, however, he takes for granted that there can be other such bands. "The wisest princes need not think it any diminution to their greatness . . . to rely upon counsel. . . . Sovereignty is married to counsel." He seems to identify sovereignty with personal rulership in general rather than to see it as a concept of supreme power, which would make the problem of whether to accept counsel almost irrelevant. Yet in his warning to the common-law judges Bacon placed sovereignty beyond the law: "Let judges also remember that Salomon's [*sic*] throne was supported by lions on both sides: let them be lions, but yet lions under the throne; being circumspect that

[10] *La Politique,* Bk. IV, Art. 4, Prop. 1. Quoted in *ibid.*, p. 60.

they do not check or oppose any points of sovereignty."[11] But he did assume that, somehow, sovereignty itself could be checked. Submission to monarchy was as natural for Bacon as a child's submission to his parents but he elaborated neither a sociological nor a legalistic theory of sovereignty. Brilliant man that Bacon was, his political engagements and even more his political frustrations seemed to dry up the theoretical potential he possessed. As his contemporary Abraham Cowley wrote in a poem dedicated to Bacon, "For who on things remote can fix his sight/ That's always in a Triumph, or a Fight."

Grotius

The Dutch jurist Hugo Grotius (1583–1645) was a far more systematic student of politics than Bacon; but his study of sovereignty was incidental to his basic purpose of formulating the law of nations. His concern with sovereignty was mainly for the sake of determining which governments could rightly be parties to war and he did not depart significantly from Bodin. Grotius' legalism is well displayed in Chapter 14 of his great work *De jure belli et pacis* (*On the Law of War and Peace*), entitled "Of the Promises, Contracts, and Oaths of Sovereigns," which concerns the lawful power kings have over their own actions, their subjects, and their successors. An ambivalence in Grotius between wanting to give the sovereign absolute power and wanting to impose on him moral obligations is reminiscent of Bodin; and the confusion of public authority with patrimonial power in land ownership is hardly modern. In modern usage, Grotius' sovereign is not really sovereign. True, a king is not bound by his own laws. No subject is legally wronged if the king revokes a law. And the king may bind his successors but "this does not go to an infinite extent. For an infinite power of imposing such obligations is not necessary, in order rightly to exercise the government: as such power also is not necessary for a guardian or a Tutor; but only so much as the nature of the office requires."[12] Moreover, "if a free People had made any engagement, he who afterwards should receive the sovereignty in the fullest manner, would be bound by the engagement." Nor can sovereignty be received by usurpation: "Usurpers have no authority to bind the People" (or the "Legitimate Sovereign"). Private contracts of the sovereign do not have the standing of laws for all the people. The degree to which such contracts bind subjects is to be determined not by the consequences but by an inquiry—by whom?—into "the probable reason for doing the thing; if there be such a reason, the People itself will be bound."

These quotations are useful only because they convey the legalistic flavor of Grotius' concern with sovereignty and his disinclination to pursue the philosophic implications of the subject. Despite the distinction made in the Prolegomena to *De jure* between sovereignty in the body politic as a whole and sovereignty in the government, for Grotius the possibility of a systematic general theory of sovereignty was defeated by his concentration on a mass of details about the powers of specific governments.

After Hobbes no such evasive treatment of the problem of sovereignty was possible. And it *is* a problem, which, briefly stated, is this: if, as Bodin said, sovereignty is what makes a state a state and if sovereignty is that power to make and enforce law that is itself above law, then anything a sovereign chooses to do in the state is by definition lawful. Despite the obviousness of the conclusion, Hobbes was the first man to draw it and hold to it. Even today the stark conclusion is repugnant to many. The way the boldness and vigor of Hobbes's formulation affected later seventeenth-century writers on sovereignty is shown by the examples of Spinoza and Pufendorf.

[11] The three quotations are from Bacon's *Essays or Counsels, Civil and Moral,* 5th ed. (London: Dent, 1906), Nos. 15, 20, and 56, respectively.

[12] The quotations in this paragraph are from *De jure belli et pacis,* Bk. II, Ch. 14, sec. 12, trans. by William Whewell (Cambridge, Eng.: Cambridge Univ. Press, 1853), Vol. II, pp. 121–22.

Spinoza

The modest scholar Benedict Spinoza (1632–77) ranks as one of the major philosophers of modern times. A resident of Amsterdam, he was a descendant of persecution-driven Spanish Jews. But Spinoza bore a double burden: persecuted by Gentiles because he was a Jew, he was also excommunicated by Amsterdam Jewry because he was a nonconformist. His great work was produced during a rather short life, while working full time as a lens grinder, since scholarly occupations were closed to him. A highly systematic thinker, he poses something of a problem for one who would extract only the political elements of his system without distorting them in the process. A further problem is that we can easily exaggerate Spinoza's dependence on Hobbes simply because they share the same vocabulary:

> As far as political theory is concerned, Spinoza is often described as a follower of Hobbes, and it is true that he borrowed many ideas and arguments from his great predecessor. But when he remarked that, unlike Hobbes, he kept natural right intact, he was not pointing to a minor deviation, but to a disagreement on fundamentals.[13]

The point made about natural right in the passage just quoted is that Spinoza goes one step further than Hobbes in maintaining a purely deterministic system. For Hobbes man has a natural right to do all he can to preserve himself. This concept of natural right is far different from the definition that holds that man has a natural right to those things that are discovered by reason to be good by the standards of a universal moral order; but it still rules out a fairly wide range of behavior—aggression, assault, murder, et cetera—that may not be justified by self-preservation. For Spinoza, man has a natural right to do all that he can do—without qualification. Natural right is at last purged of any moral overtones and becomes simply a description of nature. It is a given of Spinoza's system that *every* human act is related to self-preservation. By this standard the Hobbesian qualification of natural right is irrelevant, if not inconsistent. Moreover, while Hobbes limits natural right to God, man, and beasts, Spinoza grants it to all nature. In effect, then, for Spinoza the power of nature and the right of nature are identical.

Another way of putting this position is that Hobbes retains at least a slim distinction between what contemporary man would call natural behavioral laws and moral commands—what the theologian would call the existential and essential realms—both of which are willed by God. How much Hobbes personally believed in the latter is the subject of much argument but the degree of his belief does not nullify the distinction. For Spinoza there is no such conflict: God wills what man does and what he ought to do simultaneously. It is impossible for Spinoza's man to break the law of nature.

This union of the natural and the moral in Spinoza bears directly on the questions of sovereignty and the social contract. For Hobbes the presence of the sovereign is what gives a people unity. The duty of the subject to obey stems directly from his duty to preserve himself, a duty that can best be accomplished under conditions of peace. But having contracted to accept an all-powerful sovereign for this end, the subject has bound himself to obey the sovereign's commands without reservation—or rather with one reservation: he can resist a direct threat to his own life. And since "covenants without the sword are mere words," the sovereign can maintain the contract through continual force and threats of force. The contract has a prudential origin for Hobbes (it is established to save men from the anarchic state of nature) but it does not seem to have a prudential terminus. Once established it is fixed.

But Spinoza—who was more favorably disposed to republicanism than was Hobbes—does not give the same sanctity to contract that Hobbes does. The duty of the subject to obey the sovereign is purged of the last shred of moral obligation that remains in Hobbes. It is simply the inexorable workings

[13] A. G. Wernham, in the Introduction to his translation of Spinoza's *Political Works* (Oxford: Clarendon Press, 1958), p. 35.

of the laws of nature that, if a sovereign misuses his power, his subjects will rebel and he will have destroyed himself. Since it is assumed that the people can in some fashion pick a new king, there must be a greater degree of unity in the absence of a sovereign than Hobbes would grant. For his own sake, then, Spinoza's sovereign takes on a greater burden of persuading his subjects that it is to their advantage to obey.

In the *Tractatus theologico politicus* (*Treatise on Political Theology,* 1670) Spinoza agrees with Hobbes that all states had to begin with a contract, a contract that was a historical fact, a point in time. By the year of the *Tractatus politicus* (*Political Treatise,* 1677) he had modified his views to the extent of not even mentioning this contract. He sounds almost Aristotelian:

> Since men, as I said, are led more by passion than by reason, their natural motive for uniting and being guided as if by one mind is not reason but some common passion; common hope, or common fear, or a common desire to avenge some common injury. . . . But since all men fear isolation, because no isolated individual has enough power to defend himself and procure the necessaries of life, they desire political society by nature, and can never dissolve it entirely.[14]

While the position of the sovereign in Hobbes's state would not be particularly enviable, even less so would be that of Spinoza's sovereign. In the face of the fact that—as for Hobbes—"men are by nature enemies," Spinoza's sovereign had the difficult task of bringing about in the state "a union or agreement of minds"—a task not altogether consistent, perhaps, with Spinoza's fervent advocacy of religious toleration.

It is not surprising that Spinoza, as the greatest of Hobbes's followers, was also the one who most modified and extended his thought. Given Spinoza's naturalistic-deterministic orientation, sovereignty became more than merely a legal or moral concept. It became a principle of natural unity in the state itself, in whose service an individual monarch might be only an instrument.

[14] *Political Works,* p. 315.

Pufendorf

The German jurist Samuel Pufendorf (1632–94) was probably more famous than Spinoza, though certainly less notorious, during their parallel lifetimes.[15] Since then, Spinoza's reputation has steadily grown and Pufendorf's has steadily receded. But this first professor of international law can serve as a further illustration of Hobbes's impact on political thought. Pufendorf had opposed the German versions of Bossuet's divine-right ideas especially as expressed in the writings of Johann Horn. He also was assailed by Leibnitz for his attempt to separate natural law from theology. Pufendorf was noted for his rationalism both in content and style, that is, he avoided the citation of scriptural and classical authorities so characteristic of writing in his time. By his pedantic manner and continual qualification he managed to avoid offending anyone; but these qualities also vitiated much of his argument.

Pufendorf faced the task of attempting to reconcile Grotius' limited, moralistic sovereignty with Hobbes's absolutist sovereignty. Sovereignty was, for Pufendorf, the highest earthly power but it was also to be limited by natural law and by custom. The unique element in his theory of sovereignty was his explicit distinction between absolute and restricted sovereignty. First distinguishing between authority over one's self and one's own things (which authority he called liberty) and authority over others and the things of others (which authority he called sovereignty), Pufendorf designated sovereignty as *absolute* "when its acts cannot be rendered void by any third person who is superior, nor be refused obedience on the part of those over whom sovereignty is exercised, upon the basis of some right which has been sought or retained by a pact entered into at the time when the sovereignty was established." Sovereignty was *restricted* "when one or the other, or both of

[15] An item in *The New York Times* (July 14, 1954), reported that the Jewish synagogue board of Amsterdam had refused to repeal the three-hundred-year-old order excommunicating Spinoza, as had been suggested by Prime Minister Ben-Gurion of Israel.

those, can take place."[16] By contrast with Hobbes, Pufendorf argued that citizens, upon agreeing to place themselves under a sovereign, may at the moment of entering the contract make "the express reservation that they are unwilling to be bound by his orders in certain things. Such restriction is not at all repugnant to nature." If it is the contract that makes a sovereign sovereign and if the signatories have free will, it rests with them to determine the degree to which they will admit to control over them. Individuals, however, do not have rights that could stand in the way of a public sovereign acting for the general welfare. In this argument there is obviously a tinge of "consent of the governed" but it is stated in too abstract a form to have any practical effect.

Part of Pufendorf's popularity was based on the fact that his law of nature seemed full of pleasantly moral sanctions, yet not so many as to be an interference with strong government. The core of Pufendorf's system is a heavy weight of duty on sovereign and subject alike: on the one hand, "The general law of rulers is this: The welfare of the people is the supreme law. . . . They ought . . . to believe that nothing is to their private advantage, if it is not also to the advantage of the State." To this end, he must restrict his own "pleasures, delights and empty employments" and keep flatterers and triflers at a distance.[17]

"To the rulers of the state a citizen owes respect, loyalty, and obedience. This implies that one acquiesce in the present regime, and have no thoughts of revolution. . . . A good citizen's duty towards the whole state is to have nothing dearer than its welfare and safety, to offer his life, property, and fortunes freely for its preservation."[18]

Pufendorf's prescriptive-moralistic qualifications are enough to show that theorists of sovereignty are not necessarily absolutists; yet the fact remains that the most vigorous and systematic theorists of sovereignty—Hobbes and Spinoza—carried the concept in the direction of absolutism. The admonitions of a Pufendorf could in practice mean very little to a monarch unrestrained by any superior or even competing earthly power. Acutely aware of this weakness, other theorists were meanwhile working out theories that would not depend on the moral self-restraint of rulers but could justify institutional restraints on governing power. Such restraints are the essence of constitutionalism.

RESTRAINTS UPON RULERS: CONSTITUTIONALISM

Community: Althusius

A leading commentator on Johannes Althusius (1557–1638) has called him "the most profound political thinker between Bodin and Hobbes."[19] Althusius was, however, a much-neglected thinker until the publication of Otto von Gierke's *Johannes Althusius und die Entwicklung der naturrechtlichen Staatstheorien* (*Johannes Althusius and the Development of the Political Theory of Natural Law*, 1880). The reason for this neglect appears to be that Althusius' theory of federalism had little application to France and England, where the reputations of political thinkers tended to be made and unmade for the next two centuries. Today we see his theory of federalism as highly relevant to modern political organization, and regard his definition of *popular sovereignty* (ultimate political authority residing inalienably in the whole people) as one of the earliest and

[16] *Elementorum juris prudentiae universalis* (1660), trans. by William A. Oldfather (New York: Oxford Univ. Press, Carnegie Classics of International Law, 1931), p. 56.

[17] *De officio hominis et civis* (1673), trans. by Frank Gardner Moore (New York: Oxford Univ. Press, Carnegie Classics in International Law, 1927), p. 121.

[18] *Ibid.*, p. 144.

[19] Carl J. Friedrich, in the Introduction to his edition of Althusius' *Politica methodice digesta*, 3rd ed. (1614) (Cambridge, Mass.: Harvard Univ. Press, 1932), p. xv. An abridged translation of this edition by Frederick S. Carney has been published as *The Politics of Johannes Althusius* (Boston: Beacon Press, 1964).

clearest. That these two concepts should be related at all may seem remarkable. Even today—and all the more so in the seventeenth century—sovereignty signifies unity, while federalism signifies diversity. In the United States, where we have managed to live with and under a system of unity in diversity (*e pluribus unum*), we perhaps take too much for granted the kind of achievement our "dual sovereignty" represents. Only with a concept of sovereignty such as Althusius', divorced from any single ruler or government, can one visualize a federal allocation of powers that can maintain any higher degree of unity than that achieved by a mere alliance of separate, sovereign powers.

Althusius' place in time and space can, of course, be given credit for part of his orientation. A devout Calvinist, he had visited Geneva and studied at Basel, where he received his doctorate in law in 1586. He shared the Calvinists' doctrine of resistance to tyrants through the use of the ephors, or lesser magistrates,[20] and shared, as well, the early Calvinists' strong sense of civic duty and community discipline. He left a professorship at Herborn in 1604 to become city attorney in Emden, East Friesland, in what is today northwest Germany. The nearness of the United Netherlands was significant—in practice because its troops protected Emden during the Thirty Years' War and in theory because Althusius could observe and admire the federational elements in that body politic.

Althusius was a unique mixture of medieval and modern. The same comment is often made about Bodin and about Richard Hooker, the great English divine. But the label, while no less applicable, has a somewhat different meaning for Althusius. Bodin was for repudiating the pluralism of the Middle Ages in favor of a sovereign monarchy but he retained a medieval conception of abstract natural law. The result was an authoritarian yet individualistic society. Althusius retained or went back to the pluralism—Friedrich would say dualism—and corporateness of the Middle Ages, yet his theory was more naturalistic, in the modern scientific sense, than those of legalistic contemporaries such as Grotius, or especially Bodin. Like other Calvinists, Althusius identified natural law with the Decalogue but this was the most superficially handled part of his thought. Like almost all except divine-right theorists in the seventeenth century, Althusius used the idea of a social contract. But in his hands it became less of a legal fiction and more of a description than in the hands of perhaps any other theorist of the time.

The key to Althusius' system was the conception of the basic social group: the *consociatio symbiotica,* or a community living together by nature. The "sociological" orientation of Althusius is shown by his definition of *politics:* ". . . the science of those matters which pertain to the living together."[21] Man is a political *and* a social animal. In fact Althusius' *consociatio symbiotica* and Aristotle's *koinonia* would not be very far apart. According to Friedrich, Althusius is the first man to use the term *symbiotica* (living together) with political connotations. This concept is at the heart of his contribution to the theory of contract, sovereignty, and federalism.

The *consociatio symbiotica* was not simply the political community. It was the generic form of a whole range of human associations. Thus marriage in later editions of the *Politica methodice* (*The Politics,* 1614) became *consociatio symbiotica conjugum*. The *consociatio collegium* referred generally to the guilds; the *consociatio symbiotica universalis,* or *civitas,* or *respublica,* referred to the state; and so forth. *Any* such community is marked by the operation of two kinds of law, one that establishes the pattern of relationships among members and the other that creates and limits the supreme authority in the group. The idea of a constitutional political order involves both these aspects of law but modern constitutional theories are especially grounded in the latter.

The basic types of *consociatio* boiled down to five: the family, local voluntary corpora-

[20] See p. 248, above.

[21] Althusius, *Politica,* p. 15.

tions (*collegia*), the local political community, the province, and the state. At each level the members were related to one another by a contract—or rather contracts, for the formation of a community was clearly a two-stage matter. The first contract established the society itself (and the first kind of law); the second entrusted powers to specific leaders, or governments. In Locke we shall find the same division between the social contract proper and the governmental contract but not stated so clearly. In addition to this network of contracts, there are also contracts relating each of the five levels to the next highest. Each community, therefore, bears rights and obligations vis-à-vis the others. The state itself results from the contracting not of individuals but of lesser communities. While comparable to the medieval network of feudal rights and obligations, and, of course, evolved from them, Althusius' scheme is also a somewhat rationalized structure suggestive of the modern constitution-building mentality.

If a sense of community is essential to the constitution-making process, so is a sense of law, which no one exemplified more dramatically than did Coke.

The Common Law: Coke

The common law is that body of judge-made law, supposedly common to all of England, that began to take shape during the thirteenth century with the rise of a legal profession, the development of systematic teaching of the law, and the secularization of the courts. Its primary characteristic is the rule of *stare decisis,* or the adherence to precedence in the decision of cases. It derives its authority not from the acts or decisions of one lawmaker or one judge but from the collective effect of a long line of judges and justices of the peace. It is accretive law. General rules are not formulated at one moment and codified, as under Roman-law systems, but rather are extracted from the pattern of precedents discoverable in a long series of concrete cases. It may therefore seem anomalous to single out one man to illustrate the role of English common law in modern constitutionalism. Nevertheless, if any one man can be credited with preserving the integrity of the common law at a critical moment in history, that man would be Sir Edward Coke (pronounced Cook, 1552–1634), "the oracle of the common law."

More than most men, Coke felt the weight of precedent on his shoulders. Perhaps this was indeed a prerequisite to his extensive contributions to the common law. The law of the land was available to him in the decisions of past courts, in Magna Carta (1215), and in the writings of former judges: the twelfth century's Ranulf de Glanville, the great Justice Henry Bracton (whose thirteenth-century treatise *Of the Laws and Customs of England* was frequently quoted by lawyers), Chief Justice Sir John Fortescue (*De laudibus legum Angliae* [*In Praise of English Law*], written in the late fifteenth century), and Judge Sir Thomas Littleton (*Treatise on Tenures,* on which Coke wrote a distinguished commentary). Despite these sources, Coke's *Institutes* (published in four parts between 1628 and 1644) and *Reports* (published in thirteen parts between 1600 and 1659) were the first systematic collation of English sources and precedents. The *Institutes* was the first work that could be used effectively as a textbook in teaching English law. During Coke's day, legal instruction in London's four Inns of Court was largely oral. (Oxford and Cambridge taught no English law whatever and did not until Blackstone's first professorship in 1758.) Coke's works were loaded with more medieval references than most people cared to handle and it came to be tacitly agreed among English lawyers that one did not seek to go behind Coke's authorities. Thus Coke the writer became almost as binding as first-hand judicial precedent.

It would appear so far that Coke was primarily a scholar; but this designation would hardly fit his colorful career. Solicitor General, then Attorney General under Elizabeth, he was knighted by King James and elevated to the posts of Chief Justice of Common Pleas and Chief Justice of King's Bench, successively. For his stubborn resistance to James's attempts to extend the royal prerogative at the expense of the common law, Coke was removed from office in 1616. The specific issue was whether the king could command the common-law courts to desist from hearing a case. At the showdown his fellow judges gave ground but Coke stood fast. "Tough old Coke," Carlyle called him, and the appellation fits. After various skirmishes and reconciliations, Coke got himself elected to the Parliament of 1621. Although hardly friendly to the republican sentiments then growing in Parliament, Coke immediately became such a strong leader of the Parliamentary opposition to James that in December of that year he was arrested and put in the Tower of London, only to be released when Parliament was dissolved in January. A subsequent attempt by James to get Coke out of England by giving him an important post in Ireland failed when Coke refused to go. Upon ascending the throne in 1625, Charles I prevented Coke from being elected to Parliament by the neat trick of making him sheriff of Buckinghamshire. But by the Parliament of 1628 Coke was able to get himself elected as knight of the shire for Bucks. In that year he drafted the Petition of Right, which Parliament forced Charles to sign. This, along with Magna Carta and later the Bill of Rights, became one of the great charters of England.

The two theories of greatest importance to which Coke contributed are, first, the general principle of the supremacy of the common law and, second, the argument for "artificial reason" in the law, an argument that Coke used against James and against Francis Bacon. The general argument for the supremacy of common law was enshrined in Bonham's case (1610). The Royal College of Physicians had arrested Dr. Thomas Bonham for practicing medicine without a certificate. The court denied the right of the college to make the arrest on the grounds that it was acting as judge and party in the same case, a practice forbidden by the common law. Yet the authority of the College of Physicians existed by virtue of a parliamentary statute: ". . . it appears from our books," wrote Chief Justice Coke of the Court of Common Pleas, "that in many cases the common law will control acts of Parliament and sometimes adjudge them to be utterly void; for when an Act of Parliament is against common right and reason, or repugnant, or impossible to be performed, the common law will control it and adjudge such Act to be void."[22] There is some ambiguity in the statement because at this time an Act of Parliament could mean judicial decisions as well as statutory enactments. Moreover, the statement was attacked as an obiter dictum. But the intrinsic weight of the argument was far overshadowed by the historic uses to which it was put. John Adams, James Otis, and Patrick Henry were only three of the Americans who, almost two centuries later, found the Coke of Bonham's case a useful revolutionary ally. Actually, of course, Coke was anything but a revolutionary; the common law for him was a means of preserving the past. The monarchy may have been a barrier to change for Americans in 1776 but monarchical power seemed a threat of change to Coke in 1610.

We do not grasp Coke's essential contribution if we merely quote Bonham's case. Even Bacon had said, "The common law is more worthy than the statute law." The burning question of the day was the relation of common law to the king's prerogative. The battle had begun when, as Chief Justice of Common Pleas, Coke had issued writs of prohibition against Archbishop Bancroft's Ecclesiastical Court of High Commission, which James favored and which did not follow common-law procedures.

He was asked to discuss the matter with the clergy in the presence of King James November 13, 1608, and he roundly asserted that he would not be able to accept the Romanist interpretation of the clergy. James, taking exception to this dogmatic view, declared that he was the supreme judge, and that under him were all the courts. To this Coke replied: "The common law protecteth the king." "That is a traitorous speech,"

[22] Quoted in Catherine Drinker Bowen, *The Lion and the Throne* (Boston: Little, Brown, 1956), p. 315.

King James shouted back at him in great anger; "the king protecteth the law, not the law the king. The king maketh judges and bishops." He then proceeded to denounce Coke so vehemently, shaking his fists at him, that Coke "fell flat on all fower," before the King and humbly begged his pardon.[23]

Coke was subsequently removed to the King's Bench, a lower-paying job, but the conflict continued—now against Lord Chancellor Ellesmere's Court of Chancery, which used Roman-law procedure, then against Attorney General Bacon, who theorized about the Roman law of nature, or the rule of right reason, as a part of the king's prerogative. To the claim of James and Bacon that the natural reason of the king was sufficient to establish law, Coke countered with a concept of artificial reason, which he claimed could be produced only by the esoteric training of the Inns of Court:

Reason is the life of the law, nay the common law itself is nothing else but reason; which is to be understood as an artificial perfection of reason, gotten by long study, observation and experience, and not as every man's natural reason. . . . By the succession of ages [the law of England] has been fined and refined by an infinite number of grave and learned men, and by long experience grown to such a perfection, for the government of this realm, as the old rule may be justly verified of it, that no man out of his private reason ought to be wiser than the law, which is the perfection of reason.[24]

The strength of the common law can be thought of as legal strength. But we would err if we concluded that legal checks in a formalistic sense guarantee what we have come to call constitutional government. There is a spirit in Coke's stubborn resistance to James that could hardly be called legalistic. It was scarcely even judicious. (In his courtroom oratory against such victims as Essex and Raleigh, Coke was noted for surprise and caustic invective rather than calm, judicial demeanor.) This spirit, rather, involved an almost worshipful respect for tradition, a disposition that opposed yielding any one person too much power, and the courage to speak up when power became unduly personalized. We must admire this spirit even as we recognize that Coke's own conception of sovereign law was too divorced from political reality to operate as he hoped it would. Coke, making the law into a person, felt that real persons ought to keep their petty hands off it. "Magna Carta," he wrote in the *Institutes,* "is such a fellow that he will have no sovereign." But what this would mean in practice, as Gooch observes, is that not the rule of law, but the rule of lawyers would replace the rule of king and Parliament.[25]

Puritan Constitutionalism

Virtually any restraint upon a ruler, if we follow Friedrich, will be constitutional if it is effective, regularized, and public in character. The very idea of contract is such a restraint.

No single Puritan thinker can provoke us to as searching a reflection on the specific problem of contract as can Hobbes or Locke. The Puritan writers were not "social contractualists" as the term came to be used. Nevertheless, the Puritan movement as a whole, a fascinating mixture of thought and action, conveys to us one unique dimension of contractualist thought. We might call it the covenant idea. We can recall from Althusius that the idea of contract does not necessarily presuppose individualism. We can infer from Hobbes ("covenants without swords are mere words") that the idea of contract does not necessarily presuppose consent. Moreover, Coke ought to be enough to remind us that not all legal, constitutional re-

[23] Carl J. Friedrich, *Constitutional Government and Democracy,* rev. ed. (Boston: Ginn, 1950), p. 105. Compare the more extended description of this famous incident in Bowen, pp. 303–06, pieced together from a variety of sources. Despite the necessity of humbling himself before James on this Sunday, on the Monday morning following Coke issued another writ of prohibition against the High Commission.

[24] Quoted in *ibid.,* p. 105.

[25] G. P. Gooch, *Political Thought in England from Bacon to Halifax* (London: Butterworth, 1914), pp. 64–65.

straints on rulers presuppose contract. The common law, for Bracton as well as Coke, was above both king and people, not a contract between them. For Puritans covenants were not simply contracts in the prudential, expedient, business usage—the final confirmation of a deal, a practical means of holding people to account—but rather the ordination of a *sacred* obligation shadowed over by the countenance of God Himself.

The idea of a covenant is, of course, Hebraic in origin.[26] God's covenant with Abraham and the children of Israel was the promise that gave meaning to the whole of Hebrew history, justifying the trials of the past and compelling Israel to look forward to an ultimate consummation in history. If the children of Israel are faithful to God, God will protect them. In any event, He will use them for His divine purposes. Puritans shared similar convictions. Moreover, they could and did draw from the early Calvinists powerful senses of social concern, of hard discipline, of duty to the community. They made the religious sphere penetrate all things, even the activity of money-making. Their religious destiny might not be fulfilled on earth; but it had to be worked out on earth.

To this day there is something of the covenant flavor in our conception of a constitution. It is not, to American eyes, a mere contract, as Justice Marshall reminded us in the great case of *McCulloch v. Maryland* (1819). "We must never forget," he said, "it is a *constitution* we are expounding." A constitution implies solemnly held rights and duties, a sense of enduring fundamental law that casts a veil of sanctification over lesser, more expedient statute law. And in solemnity and sanctity the Puritans had no peers. The form was there even when the content was not. Note such magnificent names of the period of the Puritan Revolution as "The Solemn League and Covenant," between Parliament and Scotland (1643), and "The Solemn Engagement of the Army" (1647). No name was more symbolic than "Puritan" itself.

The term "Puritan" came from the Latin *puritas* and originally designated the rather diverse assortment of Englishmen who wished to "purify" the Church of England along Calvinist lines, to de-Romanize it further than had been done under Elizabeth. Worship in the Anglican Church was, in fact, not much different from what it had been before the break with Rome. The Puritans objected to the use of images and altars, the wearing of the surplice, the observance of saints' days, Archbishop Cranmer's *Book of Common Prayer,* and ceremonialism in general. The more unruly sometimes broke into Anglican services and forcibly ripped the surplices off the priests' backs.

Loosely speaking, "Puritan" was equated with "Nonconformist" and "Dissenter" and thus came to refer to anyone, English or American, who objected to the practices of the Church of England—not only to those who wished to purify the Church but even to those who wished to leave it entirely.

Woodhouse classifies the Puritans of the period of the English Revolution into three groups:

(1) *The Presbyterians,* the only group to whom, strictly speaking, "Puritan" applied, wanted to organize the Church of England according to Calvinist principles. They could be called the right wing of the Revolution. They stood for support of The Solemn League and Covenant negotiated with the Scots by Sir Henry Vane, Parliamentary representative, in 1643. By this agreement Scotland agreed to come to the aid of Parliament in the Revolution and, a bit reluctantly, Parliament pledged the "reformation of religion in the Kingdoms of England and Ireland, in doctrine, worship, discipline and government, according to the Word of God, and the example of the best reformed churches, and that popery and prelacy should be extirpated."[27] The Presbyterians tended to dominate Parliament but the alliance of the Pres-

[26] See John F. A. Taylor, *The Masks of Society: An Inquiry into the Covenants of Civilization* (New York: Appleton-Century-Crofts, 1966).

[27] Quoted in Godfrey Davies, *The Early Stuarts, 1603–1660* (Oxford: Clarendon Press, 1937), p. 134.

byterian faction with the Scots "was its potential military strength and its actual political weakness, for in moments when national feeling ran high its majority in Parliament became a minority."[28]

(2) *The Independents,* or Separatists, or Congregationalists, as they were later called (including the Plymouth Pilgrims), believed in leaving the control of church matters in the hands of local congregations. Distrustful of the Presbyterians' conception of an established church, they were nevertheless forced to cooperate with them to maintain a united front against the king. Despite their minority position in Parliament, the Independents, as the most consistent party of toleration, had considerable support among the general populace and especially in the city of London. The officer corps of the revolutionary army tended to be made up of Independents and it was their scheme for settlement, called the Heads of the Proposals, that was presented to King Charles by the Army in 1647. This proposal had some interesting features: the king was to surrender control of the militia for ten years and a Council of State was to conduct foreign policy for seven years. Both the Episcopal (Anglican) and Presbyterian ecclesiastical systems were to be sanctioned and there was to be general religious toleration—except, of course, in the case of Catholics. Parliaments were to be biennial and were to be made more representative by reforms that would abolish the so-called rotten boroughs.

(3) Various *Left-wing sectarians and radicals* can be sharply divided into two categories: the somewhat secular radicals, interested in democratic reform—the Levellers, the Diggers, and so forth—and the religious fanatics and doctrinaires, such as the Anabaptists and the Fifth-Monarchy men. The more secular groups were especially representative of the rank and file of the Army.

Outside the Puritan category altogether were the Erastians, named or misnamed for Thomas Erastus, the sixteenth-century Swiss theologian who came to symbolize the position that the Church should be subordinate to state authority. Despite the fact that "Erastian" was something of an epithet, the Independents in Parliament often worked with the Erastians and were close to them.

Divided and quarreling as these groups were, they were nevertheless held together by a sense of divine mission and, to a greater or lesser degree, by—what is even more important to constitutionalism—a sense of history. "I cannot but see," said Army leader Oliver Cromwell,

> but that we all speak to the same end, and the mistakes are only in the way. The end is to deliver this nation from oppression and slavery, to accomplish that work that God hath carried us on in, to establish our hopes of an end of justice and righteousness in it. We agree thus far. Further too: that we all apprehend danger from the person of the King and from the Lords.[29]

This remark is taken from the so-called Putney debates, the rare and remarkable record of a revolutionary army debating its principles. Each regiment sent representatives, or "agitators," to meet with the Army Council and express rank-and-file sentiment. Out of these debates (and later debates) came *An Agreement of the People,* which we will look at more closely in a moment. It was a revolutionary document, drafted by the radical element in the Army known as the Levellers; but it was also a constitutional document, written with an eye toward the potential despotism of Parliament as well as the actual despotism of the king.

Cromwell and his son-in-law Ireton were moderates, at least within the group context of the Army itself, and did not at all like the business of extending the suffrage. (Cromwell, like Pym and many other leaders of the Revolution, was, after all, a member of the landed-gentry class.) The point at issue here,

[28] A. S. P. Woodhouse, in the Introduction to his edition of *Puritanism and Liberty, Being the Army Debates (1647–9) from the Clarke Manuscripts* (Chicago: Univ. of Chicago Press, 1951), p. 15. "But English Presbyterianism," Woodhouse continues, "is not to be confounded with Scottish. Few indeed wished to see the Scottish church duplicated in England."

[29] *Ibid.,* p. 104.

however, is neither Leveller hopes nor Cromwellian motives. The point is that the arguments that Cromwell and especially Ireton used against the *Agreement* were arguments of constitutional precedent. For example, to the question of giving the Commons extensive powers over the Lords, Ireton said, "I would fain know this: [since] that a Lord is subject to the common law, how can we take away that right of peers to be for the matter of fact [i. e., to decide] whether guilty or not guilty of the breach of such a law, when that it is a point of right for the Commons to be tried by *their* peers." Ireton was an institutionalist, whereas the Levellers placed the subjective "inner light" of God's commands to them ahead of any institution.

With Colonel Rainborough, a Leveller, Ireton engaged in a spirited debate involving fine points of the status of monarchy before the Norman conquest, the position of the Commons under Edward I, and like topics:

RAINBOROUGH: [I think it well for us] to consider the equality and reasonableness of the thing, and not to stand upon [a] constitution which we have broken again and again. . . . Besides the oath he [Ireton] found, [I would add] that one of the main articles against Richard the Second was that he did not concur with, and agree upon, those wholesome laws [that] were offered him by the Commons for the safety of the people. . . .

IRETON: You would have us lay aside arguments of constitution, and yet you have brought the strongest that may be. I have seen the Articles of Richard the Second, and it is strange that the Parliament should not insist upon that.

RAINBOROUGH: That is not the thing that I would consider of.

IRETON: I suppose no man will make a question that that may be justice and equity upon no constitution, which is not justice and equity upon a constitution. . . . I wish but this, that we may have a regard to safety—safety to our persons, safety to our estates, safety to our liberty. Let's have that as the law paramount, and then let us regard [the] positive constitution as far as it can stand with safety these. . . .

WILDMAN: I could wish that we should have recourse to principles and maxims of just government, [instead of arguments of safety] which are as loose as can be. [By these principles, government by King and Lords is seen to be unjust.]

IRETON: The government of Kings and Lords is as just as any in the world, is the justest government in the world. *Volenti not fit injuria.* Men cannot wrong themselves willingly and if they will agree to make a king and his heirs [their ruler], there's no injustice. . . . Any man that makes a bargain, and does find afterward 'tis for the worse, yet is bound to stand to it.[30]

It is surprising to find a conservative, contractualist argument boldly stated in the midst of a revolutionary-army debate. The vigor of English constitutional tradition could hardly have a better testimonial. After Charles was beheaded in 1649, more and more people began to entertain the idea that perhaps a king was fairly useful, after all. Following the final defeat of the Royalist forces in 1651, it became evident that the "rule of the saints" under a Council of State left something to be desired. *The Instrument of Government,* England's only operative or partly operative written constitution, was then (1654) set up, for all practical purposes creating a monarchy under a different name. Cromwell was established as Lord Protector, to rule with a Council of State and a one-house Parliament. What has come to be a cardinal principle of sound constitution-making, the invulnerability of the basic law to easy legislative amendment, was well enough known to be attempted in the *Instrument* (as, in fact, had been planned in *The Agreement of the People*). Unfortunately, Parliament was unimpressed by this restraint and tried to amend the unamendable; this effort brought about the dissolution of Parliament by Cromwell in 1655. The sole basis of right, Ireton had argued, was that "wee should keep covenant with one another." But how difficult to remain one big, happy family when the children are many, ambitious, and without a common enemy.

In the American colonies, where no revolutions were to be fought for a while, the

[30] *Ibid.*, pp. 115 and 120–22.

impact of the covenant view on constitutional structure could be seen even more dramatically than in England. At the very beginning of the colonial experiment, in the Mayflower Compact (1620), the tone was set:

> We . . . having undertaken for the Glory of God, and Advancement of the Christian Faith, and The Honour of our King and Country, a voyage to plant the first colony in the northern part of Virginia; do by these Presents, solemnly and mutually in the Presence of God and one another, covenant and combine ourselves into a civil Body Politick, for our better Ordering and Preservation and furtherance of the Ends aforesaid.[31]

The Fundamental Orders of Connecticut (1639) strikes a similar note.

The close-knit, congregational community paralleled to a considerable degree the town-government structure in New England, with the covenant relationship affecting both. While there was a theoretical, and to some degree a practical, separation of Church and state, secular authority was to take on the responsibility for punishing religious offenses—including idolatry, blasphemy, and heresy—and public taxes were to be used for church support. *The Platform of Church Discipline* adopted by the General Court of Massachusetts Bay in 1649 declared of church and civil government, "both stand together and flourish, the one being helpful unto the other, in their distinct and due administrations."

The constitutional element in the Massachusetts theocracy resided more in the selection of officials than in the subsequent control over them, although church officers "in case of manifest unworthiness and delinquency" might be removed by the membership. John Winthrop, governor of the Massachusetts Bay Colony until his death in 1649, once drew the analogy between the citizens' freedom to select civic officials and the freedom of a woman to select a husband: the initial freedom may have been genuine; but the relationship so chosen was more covenantal than contractual, for once the choice had been made, the wife was duty bound to obey the husband. Winthrop described the extant form of government as mixed, neither tyranny nor "mere democracy"—"the meanest and worst of all forms of government."[32]

Individual Liberties

The idea of individual liberties is perhaps implicit in every modern constitution that tries to restrict the powers of centralized authority. But every concrete claim for liberty—and every right is, in the last analysis, a claim—ultimately rests not upon the invocation of a constitutional rule but upon the appeal to moral principle. Apart from contractual arguments, apart from legal-traditional arguments, stand those arguments that attempt to speak for the individual and his right to freedom. Whenever an articulate spokesman is bold enough to make such claims, either on behalf of himself as a highly visible specimen or on behalf of an abstract category—the individual—the powers that be feel the pressure of constraint from below. It is important to distinguish this kind of pressure from that operating only by virtue of the democratic or republican representational principle, which we will consider in a moment. Whatever the basis for the selection of the ruler, whatever the legal basis for his continuance in office, a cry for justice, an appeal to be let alone, or an outburst in the name of freedom, can be regarded as a contributor to constitutional restraint, even though no claim for formal representation is made. It is hard to separate these appeals from democratic or republican representational arguments, for most often one author is voicing both. But there is a distinction: put crudely, it is the distinction between libertarianism and egalitarianism. In the former the individual is seeking the freedom to be

[31] H. S. Commager, ed., *Documents of American History,* 3rd ed. (New York: Appleton-Century-Crofts, 1943), pp. 15–16.

[32] *A Modell of Christian Charity* (1630). Quoted in Alan P. Grimes, *American Political Thought* (New York: Holt, Rinehart and Winston, 1955), p. 29.

different from others; in the latter he is seeking to be treated the same as others.

Williams

One of the outstanding seventeenth-century spokesmen of religious toleration and individual liberty was Roger Williams (1604–83). Always a religious seeker, he fought for the right of others to be the same. A protégé of Coke, he was an Anglican priest but became a Puritan, later a Baptist, and still later a freethinker. He came to the Massachusetts Bay Colony in 1631, having known its leaders Cotton and Hooker in England. But life was not tranquil in New England for one so courageous, obstreperous, and morally sensitive as Williams. He made an issue of the fact that for the sake of maintaining their charter from Charles I the Massachusetts Puritans had never officially repudiated Anglicanism. He also had the audacity to stand up for the Indians, to point out that England really had no right to take their land away from them. Cver two hundred years later, liberty-minded Americans—not to mention heroes of the Wild West—were still callous to this kind of argument. And finally Williams insisted that a religious oath should not be imposed on anyone not voluntarily subscribing to the religious tenets implied by it. This was as clear a threat to the Puritan theocracy as his general advocacy of the separation of Church and state. Enough was enough and Williams was banished in 1636.

Williams moved south and set up the Rhode Island colony, the Providence Plantations, remarkable for both its religious tolerance and its democratic constitutional structure. "Wee agree," stated the Plantation Agreement at Providence (August 27, 1649), "as formerly hath been the liberties of the town, so still, to hould forth liberty of Conscience." Williams returned to England to seek a royal charter and in 1644, amid the strife of civil war, Williams and his friend Milton each wrote tracts for the times in behalf of individual liberties, tracts that have endured beyond their times. Williams' great tract was *The Bloudy Tenent of Persecution for Cause of Conscience Discussed;* Milton's was the *Areopagitica.* Unlike Milton's work, Williams' was directed to the religious problem of the day, the toleration of religious deviation. Though perhaps less relevant to our own day, it was certainly more urgent for his own than Milton's plea for an unlicensed press. Williams' concern for conscience was not a product of religious indifference but quite the reverse:

> An enforced uniformity of religion throughout a nation or civil state confounds the civil and religious, denies the principles of Christianity and civility, and that Jesus Christ is come in the flesh. . . . Whether thou standest charged with ten or but two talents, if thou huntest any for cause of conscience, how canst thou say thou followest the Lamb of God, who so abhorred that practice? . . . Without search and trial no man attains this faith and right persuasion. I Thes. v (21). . . . In vain have English Parliaments permitted English bibles in the poorest English houses, and the simplest man or woman to search the scriptures, if yet against their soul's persuasion from the scriptures, they should be forced, as if they lived in Spain or Rome itself without the sight of a bible, to believe as the church believes.[33]

Milton

The work of John Milton (1608–74) on divorce had been published without conforming to the Law of 1643 requiring that all books be passed on by an official censor and registered with the Stationers' Company. The *Areopagitica* (from Areopagus, the law court of ancient Athens) is Milton's plea to Parliament to repeal the law.[34] In form it is not so much a defense of the individual's rights as of the right of truth itself, or, to follow Milton's personification, *her*self: ". . . though all the winds of doctrine were let loose to play upon the earth, so Truth be in the field, we do injuriously, by licensing

[33] Quoted in A. T. Mason, ed., *Free Government in the Making* (New York: Oxford Univ. Press, 1956), pp. 63–64.

[34] It failed to achieve its purpose but was so popular that the law was not enforced.

and prohibiting, to misdoubt her strength. Let her and falsehood grapple; who ever knew Truth put to the worse, in a free and open encounter?"[35] The strength of this faith in the power of truth to win, so characteristic of the liberal mentality in the past three centuries, has perhaps been shaken a bit in recent times, for we have seen what we take to be truth downed by a muscular falsehood even in "free and open encounter"; nevertheless, like the truth it refers to, this doctrine has a gratifying resiliency. Milton, however, like any first-rate pamphleteer, uses not only this but all available arguments. He is pragmatic in pointing out the intellectual accomplishments of free England by contrast with a policy that has "damped the glory of Italian wits." He invokes religious apprehension in saying, ". . . as good almost kill a man as kill a good book. Who kills a man kills a reasonable creature, God's image; but he who destroys a good book, kills reason itself, kills the image of God, as it were in the eye." He is critical, in the highest sense, in showing the logical consequences of his adversaries' position: "I cannot praise a fugitive and cloistered virtue, unexercised and unbreathed, that never sallies out and sees her adversary, but slinks out of the race. . . . Assuredly we bring not innocence into the world, we bring impurity much rather; that which purifies us is trial, and trial is by what is contrary." He is also critical in the lesser sense of one who casts barbs at foolishness: "How many other things might be tolerated in peace, and left to conscience, had we but charity, and were it not the chief stronghold of our hypocrisy to be ever judging one another?"

From his literary fame John Milton might seem to belong in the company of distinguished political theorists. But the regrettable fact is that apart from the *Areopagitica* he never produced a work of political theory of sufficient depth and consistency to grant him membership among the greats. His treatises against the bishops and his pleas for liberalized divorce had earned him a reputation for radicalism before he ever turned to strictly political subjects. Thus he was called a republican before his writings indicated as much. *The Tenure of Kings and Magistrates* (1649) was a bold defense of regicide and the right of revolution but contained nothing on republicanism. Power, he argued, belongs in the people; but this view entailed no concept of popular sovereignty and in fact was supported with little analysis of any kind. In his next political work, that same year, Milton turned against the people. The *Eikon Basilike* (*King's Book*), a forgery by John Gauden, was a eulogy to the recently executed Charles that captured the imagination of a wide host of readers. Milton, named by the Council of State to produce a reply, turned out *Eikonoklastes* (*The Iconoclast*), a bitter, inaccurate attack on Charles. In it the people were now seen as "an inconstant, irrational and hapless herd, begotten to servility." Nevertheless Milton became an avowed, if somewhat aristocratic, republican in the *Defensio populi anglicani* (*Defense of the English People,* 1651), a reply to Royalist Salmasius of Leyden. On the two efforts, Hobbes commented, "They are very good Latin both, and hardly to be judged which is better; and both very ill reasoning, hardly to be judged which is worse." Though once praising Cromwell to the skies, Milton later was disturbed by his autocracy and in his most extreme of all polemical political writings, and his last, he lashed out at the evil of government by *any* one man. But his allegedly republican alternative to a lord protector or a restored monarch was a lifetime council of wise oligarchs![36]

The lesson we learn from Milton's example is that, while Bacon may have been suffocated by too much practical political experience, Milton was rendered impotent by too little. A great poet, a master of the English language, a brilliant man, Milton was never at

[35] *Areopagitica* (London: Dent, Everyman's Ed., 1927). This and the immediately following quotations are from pp. 36, 25, 5, and 37, respectively. Like many other spokesmen for "toleration" in his day, Milton was unable to go so far as to favor freedom for Catholic or Unitarian views.

[36] *The Readie and Easie Way to Establish a Free Commonwealth* (1660).

home with politics or in touch with common people. He possessed a burning passion for freedom and boldly identified himself with the great issues of his day in its service; but he had no understanding of the subtleties of power and of the compromises men must make to achieve a tolerable stability. Great political theory requires more than right ideals and a quantity of information. It requires a sense of politics.

The Levellers and the Independents—to be discussed shortly—are best examined in connection with egalitarianism. But it ought to be noted here that libertarianism as well as egalitarianism was flowing through the Army ranks, not as forcefully perhaps, and not without conflict, for libertarianism and egalitarianism are as often at odds as they are allies. *The Agreement of the People* opposed conscription as "against our freedom"[37] and asserted general immunity against being "questioned for anything said or done in reference to the late public differences, otherwise than in execution of the judgments of the present representatives, or House of Commons." It asserted a general principle of equality before the law—at least a negative freedom: "That in all laws made, or to be made, every person may be bound alike, and that no tenure, estate, charter, degree, birth, or place, do confer any exemption from the ordinary course of legal proceedings, whereunto others are subjected." In the area of worship there is a slight ambivalence: while denying that the ways of God's worship are to be entrusted to any human power, "nevertheless the public way of instructing the nation (so it be not compulsive) is referred to their [Parliamentary representatives] discretion."

The anonymous Leveller tract *The Ancient Bounds* (1645) is more explicit than this:

> I contend not for variety of opinions; I know there is but one truth. But this truth cannot be so easily brought forth without this liberty; and a general restraint, though intended but for errors, yet through the unskilfulness of men, may fall upon the truth. And better many errors of some kind suffered than one useful truth be obstructed or destroyed. . . . Moses permitted divorce to the Jews, notwithstanding the hardness of their hearts; so must this liberty be granted to men (within certain bounds) though it may be abused to wanton opinions more than were to be wished.[38]

But none, perhaps, could match Milton in his forthrightness: "I have shown that the civil power neither hath right nor can do right by forcing religious things. I will now show the wrong it doth by violating the fundamental privilege of the Gospel, the new birthright of every true believer, Christian liberty. 2 Cor. 3. 17: *Where the spirit of the Lord is, there is liberty.*"[39] That Milton was quite clearly twisting Paul's meaning of "liberty" in II Corinthians, giving it a social rather than a psychological meaning, is beside the point. The point is that as a spokesman for the libertarians, Milton was obliged to fight first of all on the front against religious suppression. Later in the century, so also would Locke in his *Letters Concerning Toleration*.

Bayle

France does not have much to offer in the area of the theoretical defense of individual liberties in the seventeenth century. The best known defender of "toleration" was Pierre Bayle (1647–1706), who was anything but systematic. A French Calvinist who was converted into the Jesuit fold only to relapse again, he was persecuted from right and left. After his banishment from France he settled in Rotterdam and, even in that tolerant spot, he was hounded out of his professorship by a zealous Huguenot for his defense of atheists. His great work was the *Critical Dictionary* (1696–97). Skeptical, rambling, deliberately labyrinthine in order to fool the censors, and betraying a fascination with the

[37] *The Agreement of the People,* in Woodhouse. This and the immediately following quotations are from the Appendix, pp. 443–45.

[38] *The Ancient Bounds,* in Woodhouse, p. 247.

[39] *Of Civil Power in Ecclesiastical Causes* (1659), in Woodhouse, p. 226.

small fact, the work nevertheless communicated Bayle's critical curiosity. His penchant for examining all prejudices made him "the spiritual father of Voltaire." "Errors are none the better," said Bayle, "for being old."

His defense of libertarian principles is best stated in the *Commentaire philosophique* (1681), directed against policies of forcible conversion, especially the "conversion by dragoon" of Louis XIV. Bayle was anything but irreligious, however. Though the term "Enlightenment" as the symbol of the eighteenth-century rationalist movement came from Bayle, he was less secular in his interests than most of the eighteenth-century Enlightenment thinkers:

> There is a vivid, natural light which enlightens all men from the first moment that they open the eyes of their minds and convinces them irresistibly of its truth. From this we must infer that it is God himself, the essential and substantial truth, who then gives us this direct enlightenment and causes us to contemplate in essence the ideas of the eternal truths. . . . God's will has given the soul an unfailing resource for discerning true and false; this resource is the natural light.[40]

Although this could not be called a metaphysical basis for individual liberty—in its naturalism it is almost antimetaphysical—it is nevertheless a philosophical base. God does not ration his natural light. Opinions ought to be free because they naturally gravitate toward truth. Milton personified truth fighting her own battles against falsehood and wanted to assure her a fair match. For Bayle, as De Jouvenel illustrates it, truth is more like a target at which all men are trying to aim. While no man may hit it, all men should be allowed to shoot, for the more shooting, the more the arrows will tend, by the operation of God's natural light, to bunch around the bull's-eye.

Williams, Milton, and Bayle spoke for the doubting individual and the subtlety of truth. They found doubt inescapable and useful and rebelled against systems of orthodoxy that tried to forbid doubt. Their cry for justice was a cry to let the individual speak out. Parallel theories were devoted to letting the people have power.

THE GROUND OF POLITICAL AUTHORITY: POPULISM

Among the many arguments for giving the ordinary man more power three would seem to be basic: (1) Healthy government requires a condition in which no one group has too much power. Unless ordinary people have a considerable degree of power, the few, the elite groups, have too much. Since power corrupts, it ought to be spread around as much as possible. (2) Since the ordinary man's fate is often decided by government, he has a moral right to be consulted, to affect by his consent or lack of it what government does. (3) The ordinary man is capable of a kind of wisdom that even the well-intentioned expert does not possess. Wise government therefore must be popular government. No flesh-and-blood theorists can be put in one or the other of such neatly divided categories without injustice. Nevertheless, Harrington is close to the first position, the Levellers in general are close to the second, and one Leveller in particular, Walwyn, is close to the third.[41]

Harrington

Though he was a friend and counselor of Charles I, through his own historical studies and travels James Harrington (1611–77) be-

[40] Quoted in Bertrand de Jouvenel, *Sovereignty*, trans. by J. F. Huntington (Chicago: Univ. of Chicago Press, 1957), p. 282.

[41] In France at this time there was virtually nothing that could be called populistic or democratic thought. Perhaps the closest approximation was the work of Claud Joly, an obscure opponent of Cardinal Mazarin. Bishop François Fénelon is sometimes regarded as a liberal because he was a man of Christian charity and kindly tolerance and because his *Télémaque* anticipated some of Rousseau's ideas on education. But Fénelon was certainly not a republican, let alone a democrat.

came a confirmed republican. He had been especially impressed by the Venetian Republic. But he took no sides in the Puritan Revolution and had to use various wiles to prevent Cromwell from suppressing *Oceana,* despite the tributes the author paid him in the work. It was finally published in 1656. This utopia was a thinly disguised description of England in which James I was Morpheus, Oliver Cromwell was Olphaus Megaletor, Hobbes was Leviathan, Westminster Hall was the Pantheon, and so on. Originally a monarchy, the country of Oceana had suffered a civil war because the constitution and the economic facts of life were out of adjustment. The commonwealth that replaced it was built upon a representative system of checks and counterchecks, what Harrington called liberated sovereignty.

What separated Harrington's theory from traditional mixed-government theories was the originality of his distinction between the external principles of government derived from the economic position of the nation and the internal principles derived from the nation's intellectual resources (we might speak of them as material and psychological causal factors). The former was the foundation of any political society, the latter was the superstructure; but it was not a superstructure in the Marxian, deterministic sense, for man retained considerable capacity to affect his environment. "The principles of government then are in the goods of the mind, or in the goods of fortune. To the goods of mind answers authority; to the goods of fortune, power or empire."[42] Harrington contrasts his distinction between authority and power with Hobbes's identification of them. Without quite disparaging power so conceived (for it is basic to his conception of economic influence), Harrington seemed to identify the neglect of true authority with monarchialism, Hobbism, and rule for lesser interests than the common good. Harrington's attachment to the classical republican ideal no doubt accounts for the moral quality he gave to authority. His chief distinction, however, is his persuasive argument for the proposition that political power follows economic power—an argument that combines the insights of Aristotle and Machiavelli. In illustration of this view, Harrington indicated that the ongoing shift in property ownership from the nobles to the people meant, inevitably, that the people would gain political power. What he did not see was that in the England of his own day the economic power of land was being replaced with the economic power of commerce.

The internal principle, the intellectual resources of a people, was the clue to the freshness and vitality of any political system. The principle was applied, or perhaps enhanced, by rotation in office, one of Harrington's favorite reforms. Like the circulation of the blood, he felt, it was good for the system. Not that one man was as good as the next. Harrington was no democrat. He believed in a "natural aristocracy" of ability and implicitly identified it with the gentlemen of the realm, excluding servants and wage-earners (but not yeomen) from citizenship. But he did not impose restrictive property qualifications on political participation. The aristocratic element in his utopia would be represented in a senate, which would deliberate and propose policies. Its power would be balanced by an assembly of the people with power of veto. The magistracy, whose operation was outlined in overwhelming detail, would execute the laws. Harrington made no mention of a judiciary but we have here, nevertheless, a system of separation of powers a hundred years before Montesquieu. All sorts of questions, including the choice of a poet laureate, were to be decided by popular vote. The people were to have the advantage of widespread public education. Liberty of conscience was guaranteed by the absence of all religious qualifications or penalties—except, as always, for Catholics, Jews, and "idolaters." The key to Harrington's balanced system was the prevention of an overconcentration of wealth. This end would be

[42] *Oceana,* in Henry Morley, ed., *Ideal Commonwealths* (London: Colonial Press, 1901), p. 185. See Charles Blitzer, *An Immortal Commonwealth: The Political Thought of James Harrington* (New Haven: Yale Univ. Press, 1960).

accomplished by the abolition of primogeniture and entail and the limitation of the value of land that any one man could own to that providing an annual income of £2,000.

Harrington's optimistic neglect of man's capacity to derail even so neatly balanced a system as this can be, and was, subjected to much criticism; but the whole effort was nevertheless grounded in an impressive knowledge of historical examples. This concern for historical detail can be credited in part to Harrington's reading of Machiavelli, just as his interest in deterministic causality was stimulated by Hobbes—however much he criticized Hobbes.

Callously imprisoned after the Restoration, Harrington was driven insane and died in obscurity; but his work had a considerable effect on many subsequent thinkers, including the American founding fathers.

The Levellers

Although they were indefatigable tract writers, the Levellers were reformers first and theorists second. The moral urgency of their cause continually overshadowed their analytical tendencies. Yet the vitality, cogency, and prophetic relevance of their missives give them a special significance—perhaps, if we are honest, a sentimental significance. The term "Levellers," coined probably by Charles I or Cromwell, was an epithet intended to suggest that the purpose of the movement was to cut down every mark of status or privilege and level the nation to a flat and common uniformity. With justice, the Levellers insisted that this was not their aim: they had no designs at all on economic inequalities but were interested in equal political representation. Their appeals above human law to the natural law, which sanctioned every man's right to participate in government, and their assumption of natural equality in the ability of citizens did, however, contain some of the anarchic implications attributed to them.

The rapid rise and fall of the Leveller movement suggests the pattern of almost all revolutions: at a certain point a wave of revolutionary feelings brings the radicals to the fore; the moderates are reluctantly induced to support the radicals by the increasing repressions of the now fearful government. Once the revolution occurs and the symbols of the past have been removed, however, the forms of the past creep back and conservatism is once again in the saddle.

Lilburne

The most famous Leveller leader was John Lilburne (1614–57). A lieutenant colonel in Manchester's army, he became the civilian leader of the movement after the debate on *The Agreement of the People* in the Army councils had come to naught. The fluidity of his ideas is shown by the fact that, when first arrested by the House of Lords, he asserted the sovereignty of the House of Commons. When later imprisoned by the House of Commons, he simply transferred sovereignty to the whole people. There, at least, it seemed to stay for Lilburne. For his attack on Cromwell and Ireton in 1649 he was tried and acquitted, after making a strong popular impression with his courageous speeches. He was banished in 1652, returned the next year only to be arrested again. His second trial generated intense public interest. Again he was acquitted and again banished. He returned in 1657 only to die, a leader without a movement, a few days before Cromwell himself.

The nature of Lilburne's appeals, the source of his support, is perhaps best indicated by his dramatic trials rather than by any of the many pamphlets he wrote. With great skill the amateur lawyer put the court on the defensive by challenges to its legality and won the crowd with references to the historic liberties of Englishmen, the laws of nature, and the laws of God. After his eloquent final plea to the jury at his first trial —"My honest jury and fellow citizens, who . . . by the law of England . . . having . . . alone the judicial power . . . you judges that sit there being no more . . . but ciphers to pronounce the sentence"—"the People with a lowd voyce, cried Amen, Amen" and more soldiers had to be rushed into the courtroom.[43] Here is the authentic voice of the demagogue.

In 1648 the various factions in the revolutionary army formed a tenuous alliance in resistance to Parliament. Involved were the "center party" of Independents under Ireton, the Fifth-Monarchy men under Harrison (see below), and the Levellers of Lilburne and Overton. Lilburne was made head of a committee to revise *The Agreement of the People* for presentation to Parliament. The new version proposed a Parliament of four hundred members chosen by all men over twenty-one who were not servants or recipients of relief. No member could sit for two successive Parliaments. Parliament was forbidden to legislate in the field of religion and could not grant monopolies or tax food. Prisoners were to be allowed counsel, tithes were to be abolished, and local congregations were to be free to make their own arrangements with ministers. These proposals were too radical for the Independent officers; they made further modifications before submitting the new version to Parliament, which was impressively unimpressed. Harrison was his usual millennial self and said, "God intends its failure." Lilburne was disgusted and, as usual, appealed to the people, publishing the text of the original version of the *Agreement* in his *Foundations of Freedom* (1648).

Rainborough

Perhaps no utterance of the Levellers has been quoted more frequently than that of Colonel Thomas Rainborough (?–1648). In defending the first *Agreement of the People* in the Putney debates of 1647, he said, "For really I think that the poorest he that is in England hath a life to live, as the greatest he; and therefore truly, sir, I think it's clear, that every man that is to live under a government ought first by his own consent to put himself under that government."[44] Rainborough continues on to draw a revolutionary conclusion from this premise, namely that citizens are not *presently* bound to the government unless they have given it their consent, a conclusion with immediate anarchic consequences. Behind both the premise and the conclusion is an assumption about the natural reason of man that seems to anticipate Locke. Replying to Ireton's rejoinder, Rainborough says,

> I do hear nothing at all that can convince me, why any man that is born in England ought not to have his voice in election of burgesses. It is said that if a man have not a permanent interest, he can have no claim. . . . I do think that the main cause why Almighty God gave men reason, it was that they should make use of that reason. . . . And truly, I think that half a loaf is better than none if a man be hungry: [this gift of reason without other property may seem a small thing], yet I think there is nothing that God hath given a man that any [one] else can take from him. . . . I do not find anything in the Law of God that a lord shall choose twenty burgesses, and a gentleman but two, or a poor man shall choose none; I find no such thing in the Law of Nature, nor in the Law of Nations.[45]

If this natural law is above all constitutions, asks Ireton rather sarcastically, what is to keep you people from taking away all property? To this Rainborough replies with some heat that God's law certainly does not take away property. It assumes property, "else why [hath] God made that law, Thou shalt not steal? . . . As for yourselves, I wish you would not make the world believe that we are for anarchy." At this point Cromwell himself, in characteristic role, leaps into the fray as a soothing mediator, albeit a somewhat paternal one. He assures Rainborough and his Leveller friends that no one is calling them anarchists. It is only that their argument "tends to anarchy, must end in anarchy." But the important thing for the moment is that "we should not be so hot one with another."

[43] Joseph Frank, *The Levellers, A History of the Writings of Three Seventeenth-Century Social Democrats —John Lilburne, Richard Overton, William Walwyn* (Cambridge, Mass.: Harvard Univ. Press, 1955), p. 221.

[44] Woodhouse, p. 53.

[45] *Ibid.*, pp. 55–56.

Although they did not develop a formal contract theory, it is clear from this and other passages in the Leveller literature—unusually spontaneous, grass-roots literature—that the idea of the consent of the governed was a basic Leveller tenet: men had a moral right to choose their own government. A second tenet was the essential equality of men by nature. Again, without constructing an extensive natural-law theory, they continually appealed to the natural equality of men, especially with reference to their reason. Despite the religious overtones of much of their writing, compared to the millenarians and some of the Independents, the Levellers were almost rationalistic in their point of view, stressing what the eighteenth century would come to call self-evident truths. Finally, they clung firmly to the belief in liberty of conscience. In this they followed closely Roger Williams' argument and often quoted him.

The Fifth Monarchy

We have already made passing reference to the Fifth Monarchy men. A further note may be useful because the mere existence of this group illustrates the intricate intermixture, if not confusion, of religion and politics at this particular period. If a populistic or democratic theory is one that places ultimate authority in the people, then it is likely to be a secular theory, since for the man of religion ultimate authority must be placed in God. In this sense, then, the Fifth Monarchy men were more theistic than populistic. They regarded Christ alone as the source of ultimate authority; but unlike other Christians they expected Him to assert this authority by setting up an earthly rule (the Fifth Monarchy) in a particular place (England) at a particular time (soon).

Their numbers included millenarian preachers John Canne and William Aspinwall, and Army leader Colonel Thomas Harrison. The ablest writer of the lot was John Rogers, whose best work was *Sagrir, or Doomesday Drawing Nigh* (1653). Laws are necessary, he argued, but they may be disobeyed when they do not conform to man's natural reason perfected by the light of God's word in the Scriptures. The principal purpose of law ought to be to restrain the lusts of the great and rich. This purpose, he said, had been perverted in England (and elsewhere) and explains why God, through the revolutionaries, was now striking down the great and rich of England.[46] The Fifth Monarchy men ardently supported Cromwell until he dissolved the Barebones Parliament, which contained many of their members, whereupon he was denounced as the Anti-Christ.

Two items suffice to convey the spirit and temper of this group. These men anticipated with much eagerness the year 1656, which was thought to be the year of the Second Coming, when England would be radically transformed and Christ would at last be set upon an earthly throne. The reason? The ages of the patriarchs in Genesis, if added up, come to 1,656 (although Rogers somehow calculated 1,666!). In 1661, after the Restoration, a group of Fifth Monarchy men, in one of their last organized actions, broke into St. Paul's Cathedral and asked the first person they saw whom he was for. "For King Charles," he replied. "We are for King Jesus," they said and shot the poor fellow dead.

The Diggers: Winstanley

In 1649 a strange little band went out from London to St. George's Hill, Surrey, to cultivate a patch of land in common and to share a communal existence. These were the so-called Diggers; their leader was Gerrard Winstanley (1609–52). The experiment in communism was a dismal failure, if for no other reason than the hostility of nearby landlords and the action of troops who pulled down the two houses in which the group was living. But Winstanley's ideas were precocious, whether or not they were influential.[47]

[46] For a good statement of Fifth Monarchy views, see Perez Zagorin, *A History of Political Thought in the English Revolution* (London: Routledge and Kegan Paul, 1954), Ch. 8.

[47] See Gerrard Winstanley, *Works*, George H. Sabine, ed. (Ithaca: Cornell Univ. Press, 1941).

Winstanley was a cloth merchant ruined by the depression of 1643 (ruined, he said, by the "cheating art of buying and selling") who moved through a tortuous religious odyssey. Beginning as a Baptist, he became an antinomian chiliast, then a somewhat mystical pantheist, and ended up as a Quaker. His philosophic communism, coinciding with his pantheism, bore seeds of the Enlightenment in its identification of God with nature and its stress on indwelling reason.

It was this that gave his radicalism its far-reaching implications. More than any man of his time he refused to admit the permanent and unalterable fact of a fallen world, and looked to the reintroduction of the pristine good. When this unyielding quest for an absolute justice was united to a philosophy whose ultimate bearings must . . . be regarded as naturalistic, we have a synthesis unlike anything in its day, a synthesis which essentially looks forward to the enlightenment and beyond.[48]

Winstanley's tract of 1649, *The True Levellers Standard Advanced,* challenged "the powers of England" and "the powers of the world" who by their actions denied that "the great creator Reason made the Earth a common treasury for beasts and man." Every landlord was a living violation of the commandment "Thou shalt not steal." "You Pharaohs, you have rich clothing and full bellies, you have your honours and your ease; but know the day of judgment is begun and that it will reach you ere long. The poor people you oppress shall be the saviours of the land."[49] Despite the fact that the small handful of men working on St. George's Hill was peaceably occupying unused crown lands, it is not surprising that they were repudiated by one and all and their leaders arrested, fined, and forbidden to speak. Conservatives, not disposed to make fine distinctions among their enemies, regarded Winstanley as just another Leveller. And with some cause: "'The poor shall inherit the earth.' I tell you," he wrote, "the scripture is to be really and materially fulfilled. You jeer at the name Leveller. I tell you Jesus Christ is the head Leveller." But the Levellers themselves did not welcome his company and in the second *Agreement of the People* any attempt to establish communism was made a penal offense.

Winstanley's major work is *The Law of Freedom* (1652), a utopia on a scale comparable to those of More, Campanella, and Harrington. Private property, wage labor, even money itself is abolished. Each worker has his quota to be produced for the common store. Education is universal. All offices are elective and of one year's duration. Everyone over twenty is eligible to vote; everyone over forty is eligible to be a candidate to Parliament. In place of the usual Christian worship, every Sunday shall see "gathered instruction" in moral precepts, laws of the society, and current affairs. (One is reminded of Rousseau's "civil religion.") At first Winstanley felt that repressive laws would be unnecessary once private property was abolished; but in the *Law of Freedom* he felt it necessary to provide a code of penalties, including the physical branding of anyone who was impious enough to declare that a piece of land was "owned" by someone.

Of Winstanley's later days little is known. His last work, *The Saints' Paradise* (1658), struck a more placid, quietistic tone that seems to confirm his supposed adoption of Quakerism.

For all his anachronisms in thought and action, Winstanley gets the prize for being most radical of the seventeenth-century radicals. For centuries private property had been regarded as the inevitable consequence of, and adjustment to, the fact of man's sinful nature. Winstanley turned the whole proposition upside down: now it was the existence of private property that had made men sinful. Moreover, he pushed beyond the merely political reforms, which constituted the horizon of most reformers' vision, to fundamental economic relationships and with simplicity and directness sought to put what he believed into practice, in itself a mark of uncommon radicalism.

[48] Zagorin, p. 47.
[49] Quoted in Gooch, p. 126.

Walwyn

One of the few reformers—he repudiated the label "Leveller"—to carry his argument beyond the level of moral exhortation to somewhat systematic analysis was William Walwyn (1600–?). Early studies of the revolutionary period scarcely mention him but recent scholarship has done much to enhance his reputation. He was not the typical Leveller in either background or outlook. Grandson of a bishop, son of a country gentleman, himself a successful cloth merchant, he brought to the movement a breadth of view and an inquiring intelligence far surpassing those of the more famous Lilburne. Lacking Lilburne's or Overton's directness and brashness in making mass appeals, Walwyn had a greater consistency that nevertheless made his a more fundamental radicalism. Against Lilburne's somewhat romantic rendering of English history and self-righteous identification with the principles of Magna Carta, we have Walwyn's sardonic view of Parliamentary history:

> See how busie they have been about the regulating of petty inferior trades and exercises, about the ordering of hunting, who should keep Deere and who should not, who should weare cloth of such a price, who Velvet, Gold and Silver, what wages poore Labourers should have, and the like precious and rare business, being most of them put on purpose to divert them from the very thoughts of freedome suitable to the representative body of so great a people. And when by accident or intollerable oppression they were roused out of those waking dreams, then whats the greatest thing they ayme at? Hough wth [how with] one consent cry out for Magna Carta . . . calling that messe of pottage their birthright, the great inheritance of the people, the great Charter of England.[50]

Walwyn's pamphlet *The Power of Love* (1643) was a defense of liberty of conscience and the use of reason in examining all religious opinion. Now that the Bible was in English, he argued, every individual Englishman, whatever his capacity, had the means of religious enlightenment and ought to be allowed to employ it. History shows that the most learned men have been "the troublers of the world. . . . The poore and unlearned Fishermen and Tent-makers were made choyce of for Christ's Disciples and Apostles."[51] Walwyn was an antinomian, that is, one who believed that salvation depended on faith rather than on conformity to law, and held that to true faith the dogma of the churches was largely irrelevant. He also believed in universal redemption—that God's grace had been granted to all and not withheld for the elect few. Thus if God so bestowed his favor on all men, the state at the very least should grant due respect and the right of participation to all men regardless of station.

Despite his consistent religious orientation, on matters of political policy Walwyn tended to be pragmatic. Again his attitude on Magna Carta is indicative. If it does not provide protection for those rights deemed important in the present, then, said Walwyn, simply draft another charter. Perhaps one of his most pragmatic tenets—in the twentieth-century sense of that word—was the proposition that continual discussion is the basis of free government: nothing "maintains love, unity and friendship in families: Societies, Citties, Countries, Authorities, Nations; so much as a condescension to the giving, and hearing, and debating of reason."[52]

Compared with their emphasis on the virtues and rights of the common man, constitutionalism was a marginal element in the Levellers' thought. But they were just Calvinists enough to question their own faith in the perfectibility of man and, in so doing, grant that a constitutional balance of power might be a necessary restraint on man's sin. Walwyn, at least, made the point:

> 'tis urged, That if we were in power we would bear ourselves as Tyranically as others have done: We confesse indeed that the experimentall defections of so many men as have succeeded

[50] *Englands Lamentable Slaverie* (1645). Quoted in Frank, p. 65.

[51] Quoted in Frank, p. 38.

[52] *The Fountain of Slaunder Discovered* (1649). Quoted in Zagorin, p. 29.

in Authority, and the exceeding difference we have hitherto found in the same men in low and in an exalted condition, make us even mistrust our own hearts, and hardly beleeve our own Resolutions to the contrary. And therefore we have proposed such an Establishment, as supposing men to be too flexible and yielding to worldly Temptations, they should not yet have a means or opportunity either to injure particulars, or prejudice the Publick, without extreme hazard and apparent danger to themselves.[53]

Despite Walwyn's touch of realism, Wolfe is probably correct in summing up the Levellers as "last-ditch idealists, born centuries too soon, impatient, impulsive, unwilling or unable to gauge the barriers that barred the way to their utopian England."[54]

NATURAL LAW, REASON OF STATE, AND COMPARATIVE POLITICS

The bulk of this chapter has been concerned with prescriptive and ideological theory, for this was the character of most seventeenth-century theorizing. But what we might call descriptive and methodological theory was not wholly absent. The self-consciously nonvaluational element in theory will become increasingly important as we move toward the scientific twentieth century. But we can briefly note at this point three seventeenth-century currents affecting descriptive theory: a new methodology applied to natural law, reason of state, and comparative political studies.

[53] *A Manifestation* (1649). Quoted in Frank, p. 202. This tract was written by Walwyn in the Tower of London and signed by himself and three fellow prisoners —Lilburne, Overton, and Thomas Prince. The incarceration was distinguished by a protesting march of a crowd of Leveller women, petition in hand, on the House of Commons, perhaps the first such participation of women in English politics.

[54] Don M. Wolfe, quoted in Frank, p. 203. See Wolfe's long Introduction to his edition of *Leveller Manifestoes* (New York: Nelson, 1944), pp. 1–108.

Grotius and Natural Law

In our recent discussion of sovereignty we saw that Grotius' concept of sovereignty was addressed to particulars rather than stated in the form of a general theory. It was at once both legalistic and moralistic. But Grotius made two other noteworthy contributions. First, he is the "father of international law." Though consciously following a long line of theologians and jurists—Victoria, Ayala, Suarez, Gentili, and others—who had contributed to the law of nations, the comprehensive and systematic character of his great work *De jure belli et pacis* won for international law general acceptance as a field. Second, and more central to our interests here, he introduced into the ancient natural-law tradition a new method that later did much to stimulate its secularization.

Grotius' break with the Scholastic tradition of natural law was not sharp. He was a dedicated Christian and took pains to avoid impiety. But his contemporaries and especially his follower Pufendorf saw what was new in Grotius. It was his rationalistic method. He sought to make law a science, modeled on mathematics, with clarity, self-evidence, and coherence the pervasive standards. His rationalism is most forcefully stated in his often-quoted statement: "Natural Law is so immutable that it cannot be changed by God himself. For though the power of God be immense, there are some things to which it does not extend. . . . Thus God himself cannot make twice two not be four; and in like manner, he cannot make that which is intrinsically bad, not be bad."[55] This position was not meant to be irreligious. It can be compared to the traditional Christian view that the just is just not because God wills it but because God is just. But in the hands of Pufendorf and others this position becomes the vehicle of an extensive secularization characteristic of many modern natural-law theories. "What Grotius had put forth as a

[55] *De jure belli et pacis*, Bk. I, Ch. 1, sec. 5, trans. by William Whewell (Cambridge, Eng.: Cambridge Univ. Press, 1853), Vol. I, p. 12.

hypothesis has become a thesis. The self-evidence of natural law has made the existence of God perfectly superfluous."[56] Spinoza, as we have seen, identifies natural law with man's natural behavior. If not superfluous, God for Spinoza has at least become synonymous with nature.

Thus the concept of natural law that entered the seventeenth century as a fairly uniform set of transcendental moral standards, the "right reason" of the Stoics and the Scholastics, had by the end of the seventeenth century taken off in a somewhat new direction. The old tradition was still in evidence, to be sure, but along with it was a new conception of an immanent (i.e., not transcendental), naturalistic standard. As we shall see, this new emphasis is a conspicuous part of the thought of both Hobbes and Locke.

Reason of State

On a somewhat different level, a more practical level, the concept of reason of state also became an alternative to older conceptions of natural law. The doctrine of reason of state (or, as a result of its association with the *ancien régime, raison d'état*) postulates a rational standard for political action in the interests of a state, a standard supposedly recognizable by rulers and those who bear responsibility but not visible to others. The doctrine is not an offspring of the seventeenth century; the sixteenth century was its real parent. The term was first used in Italy in Francesco Guicciardini's *Dialogue Concerning the Government of Florence* (c. 1521). By the second half of the sixteenth century it was a catchword. Giovanni Botero published his influential *Ragion di Stato* in Rome in 1589.[57] Later Don Quixote would be discussing *razón de estado* with his Spanish priest and barber. But considering the secularization and nationalization of politics that took place in the seventeenth century, one can say that, if the doctrine was not a child of the age, it was at least a stepchild.

Friedrich has pointed out with some insight how the concept of reason of state served as a tool for transferring religious allegiance from its traditional objects to a newly deified state. Understanding this ulterior function of the concept will help explain the loose way in which the concept was used in the sixteenth and seventeenth centuries. Reason of state ("principle" is perhaps a shade closer to *ragion* than "reason") was associated with any discussion of statecraft that followed nonethical or Machiavellian lines. Botero was simply formulating principles of statecraft in the mirror-of-princes tradition. Later the doctrine came to be an alternative or perhaps foil to natural-law theories. Before Grotius lifted it into the realm of mathematics, the problem of natural law had always been the problem of how to explain a history in which wrong seems to triumph just as often as right. Theories that looked unblinkingly at the historical facts of political life and either explained or tried to justify political necessity or acts of expediency were called reason-of-state theories. They were at once both more empirical and less rational than natural-law theories.

In the hands of rulers, harried or unharried, the phrase became a useful piece of obfuscation implying "father knows best." In England, in Darnel's case (1627), Attorney General Heath was arguing for the Crown when he said that reason of state might justify the arrest and detention of men innocent of any breach of the law who nevertheless were dangerous to the state. That master of *raison d'état,* Louis XIV, wrote in his memoirs,

> It is always worse for the public to control the government than to support even a bad government which is directed by Kings whom God alone can judge. . . . Those acts of Kings that

[56] Alexander Passerin d'Entrèves, *Natural Law* (London: Hutchinson's Univ. Library, 1951), p. 53.

[57] See *The Reason of State,* trans. by P. J. and D. P. Whaley (New York: Yale Univ. Press, 1956); Friedrich Meinecke, *Machiavellism, The Doctrine of Raison d'État and Its Place in History* (1924), trans. by Douglas Scott (London: Routledge and Kegan Paul, 1957); Carl J. Friedrich, *Constitutional Reason of State* (Providence: Brown Univ. Press, 1957).

are in seeming violation of the rights of their subjects are based upon reasons of state—the most fundamental of all motives, as everyone will admit, but one often misunderstood by those who do not rule.[58]

Here reason of state is not so much a theory of government as it is a privileged and probably impenetrable motive of rulers.

Reason of state has not been a characteristic feature of Anglo-American political thinking. During a House of Commons debate of 1621 one of the members protested James's use of the phrase and suggested petitioning the king to define what he meant by it. Doughty old Coke stood up and offered a definition of his own: "Reason of state is often a trick to put us out of the right way; for when a man can give no reason for a thing, then he flieth to a higher strain and saith it is a *reason of state*."[59] Yet even so perceptive and cautious a student of politics as George Savile, first marquis of Halifax, saw in the drive toward national self-preservation a fundamental principle of politics that has a kind of morality of its own, to which he applied the venerable phrase:

there is a Natural Reason of State, an undefinable thing, grounded upon the Common Good of Mankind, which is immortal, and in all Changes and Revolutions, still preserveth its Original Right of saving a Nation when the Letter of the Law perhaps would destroy it; and by whatsoever means it moveth, carrieth a Power with it, that admitteth of no opposition, being supported by Nature.[60]

Reason of state thus became in the seventeenth century a naturalistic law able to hold its own with the more ancient natural law.

The Growth of Comparative Political Data

If reason of state implied a concern for the empirical realities of politics, even more was this concern implied by the striking growth of comparative political data in the seventeenth century. While not, strictly speaking, a part of political theory, the development is worth noting. In England Sir William Petty, who has been called the first man to apply statistics to public affairs, was specializing in population studies. Harrington, as we saw, relied heavily on historical data of a sociological type. In France, Pierre d'Avity in 1614 brought together and published a mass of political and anthropological data on the *"empires, royaumes, estats . . . et principautez du monde."* Dutch firms published some fifty treatises on the different states of the world and in Germany one Werdenhagen mirrored the new interest in comparative politics with his *Introductio universalis in omnes respublicas* (*Introduction to All Commonwealths,* 1632).[61] Bacon's advice to "consult only things themselves" had penetrated even to the world of politics.

CONCLUSION

What is important in the seventeenth century? England, for one thing, is important. England was the dramatic center and remains the scholarly center of the seventeenth-century political transformations characteristic of the modern age. But issues, ideas, concepts—which of these are important? These seven are especially worth remembering:

(1) *Divine right,* because, unrealistic as most divine-right theories were, they assumed a reverential, majestic, "given" quality in political authority, a quality that often came closer to describing people's actual attitudes toward authority than the consent theories that replaced divine right.

(2) *Sovereignty,* because the major political theories for the next three hundred years

[58] Quoted in C. Northcote Parkinson, *The Evolution of Political Thought* (Boston: Houghton Mifflin, 1958), p. 70.

[59] Bowen, p. 436.

[60] *The Character of a Trimmer* (1684), in Walter Raleigh, ed., *The Complete Works of George Saville, First Marquess of Halifax* (Oxford: Clarendon Press, 1912), p. 60.

[61] See G. N. Clark, *The Seventeenth Century* (Oxford: Clarendon Press, 1929), pp. 213–14.

would be inextricably bound up with the moral dilemmas it posed.

(3) *Constitutionalism,* because the ideas of common law, covenant, and contract served as restraints on rulers at a time when economic and nationalistic forces were encouraging a lack of restraint.

(4) *Religious toleration*, because the civil liberties we may today take for granted, especially freedom of expression, had to be fought for and established in a context of intense religious conflict and intolerance.

(5) *Populism,* because the common man as distinguished from a metaphorical "the people" came closer to the seat of power in the Puritan Revolution than ever before. He won no prizes but the seeds of popular elections, universal suffrage, mass education, and perhaps even social security were planted there.

(6) *Natural law,* because at this time natural law was rationalized and made deductive in a new way.

(7) *Reason of state,* because it reminds us that divine right can take many forms, even the form of secularism.

11

HOBBES

The combination of an apparently hardheaded, power-centered conception of politics with an elaborately logical display of system-building accounts for the impact Thomas Hobbes still makes at first reading. The expedient as well as the moral difficulties surrounding present-day schemes of power politics account for the continuing relevance of Hobbes, a master political theorist by almost universal agreement.

LIFE

Most of what is known about Thomas Hobbes's early life comes from his autobiography, composed in Latin couplets at the age of eighty-four, and from the *Brief Lives* of John Aubrey, who was least brief about his friend Hobbes. Neither source is infallible. Hobbes's mother was supposedly fearful of the invasion of their town of Malmesbury by the threatening Spanish Armada and so gave birth to Thomas prematurely. He and terror were thus born twins, said Hobbes. His abiding passion for peace he attributes to his early timidity, which is somehow connected with his birth. His father, vicar of Charlton and Westport, was probably not so ignorant or unlearned as Aubrey said he was—but who would want to question the story of how the senior Hobbes once fell asleep in church after a Saturday night of cards and shouted out that clubs are trumps? There is no question that he did strike a man with his fists and had to flee Malmesbury because of it. He went somewhere "beyond London" and disappeared forever. Thomas and his older brother and sister were brought up by their uncle Francis Hobbes, a glover.

Scholar and Tutor

Thomas went to school at the Westport church and was an able student. Later he had the good fortune to be taught at the school of Robert Latimer, a classicist and an unusually able teacher for the time and place. Latimer worked Thomas long and hard and in 1603, not quite fifteen years of age, Thomas set off for Magdalen Hall, Oxford. He was "tall, sallow, handsome, delicate . . . [with] hazel eyes that shone like 'a bright live-coal' " and such black hair that he had been nicknamed the crow. He did not like Oxford, according to his elderly reflections, because of the arid medieval curriculum; but possibly at the time it was the inept and somewhat degenerate tutors who more displeased him. "Athletic sports had not yet organized idleness," said biographer Stephen, "but Hobbes . . . found sufficient excuses for not attending lectures." He much preferred, Aubrey notes, to visit bookshops and "lye gaping on mappes."

After Hobbes received his bachelor's degree in 1608, the principal of Magdalen, who must have known talent even when divorced from industry, recommended him as tutor for William Cavendish, later the second earl of Devonshire. Thus began an association of immense importance to Hobbes's future. He lived as a member of the family until the earl died in 1628. Devonshire House was more stimulating than a university. Nowhere, said Hobbes, was it easier "to study the liberal arts liberally." In 1610 Hobbes and his pupil and friend made the grand tour of Europe, where Hobbes learned French and Italian. Back home, he hunted, played the bass viol, and wrote a translation of Thucydides. Possibly he served as an occasional secretary to Francis Bacon.

With the death of the earl, Hobbes, now forty, somewhat reluctantly became traveling tutor to the son of Sir Gervase Clinton. It was during this time that Hobbes made his first acquaintance with geometry. Once, when in a gentleman's library, he noticed Euclid's *Elements,* opened to Proposition 47. Hobbes read the proposition and said, "By God, this is impossible." So he read the demonstration of it, which referred to another proposition, which referred to another, and so on, until he was convinced of its mathematical certainty. From that point on he was "in love with geometry." This love was to have a deep effect on his political theory. In 1631 he went back to Devonshire House, now as tutor to the third earl. Traveling with the earl in France, he became a good friend of Marin Mersenne, a Franciscan monk, who was close to Descartes and a leader in scientific circles. In 1634 or 1636 Hobbes met Galileo; but it is probably apocryphal that Galileo was the first to implant in his mind the idea that geometry might be applied to ethics.

Work and Politics

Back again in England, Hobbes developed an interest in politics. In the *Elements of Law,* which circulated in manuscript form in 1640, Hobbes wrote of the indissolubility of sovereignty in the king and made the first of his several cases for absolutism. The tract occasioned much talk and even resulted in threats on his life. " 'Tis time for me to shift myself," said Hobbes, and went back to France. There has been much discussion of whether this was an act of cowardice. It is probable that the intellectual congeniality of Mersenne and Paris was as much a factor in his move to France as was the hostility of London on the eve of revolution. Hobbes spent eleven years in France this time. He disputed with Descartes, wrote the *De cive* (*On the Civic Order,* 1642), and then wrote the *Leviathan,* which Oakeshott has called "the greatest, perhaps the sole, masterpiece of political philosophy written in the English language." It is said that he carried an inkhorn in the head of his cane and while on walks continually wrote in a notebook that had been subdivided into the sections of the proposed *Leviathan.*

Hobbes was about to run out of money when among the bedraggled Royalist refugees flooding into Paris appeared the young Prince of Wales (who later became Charles II). Hobbes secured a position as his tutor in mathematics. Even this association alarmed some of the court who frowned at Hobbes's reputation as an atheist and skeptic. He was sternly advised to stick to mathematics and not to attempt any instruction in politics. However, the publication of the *Leviathan* (1651) stirred up so much trouble that his situation at the exiled English court became impossible. On the one hand, the Royalists said that the *Leviathan* was an endorsement of the Cromwellian *status quo;* some even claimed that it was but a deceitful expression of support for Cromwell, written so that Hobbes might go home in safety. On the other hand, supporters of the Commonwealth did not like his apparent irreligion and his association with monarchists. In any event,

Hobbes did return to England the next year, to stay there for the rest of his life. That the *Leviathan* was not anti-Cromwellian seems suggested by Hobbes's boast in 1656 that the work had "framed the minds of 1000 gentlemen to a conscientious obedience to the present government." As against this, however, he said it had been the distrustful French clergy rather than the exiled English court that had made him want to leave Paris. The evidence on Hobbes's underlying political loyalties justifies no more than a tentative conclusion. But it seems clear that he was more faithful to the practical implications of his theoretical tenets, namely that *any* strong government was preferable to anarchy, than either Royalist or Cromwellian could understand.

In 1655 Hobbes published his *De corpore* (*On Body*), an exposition of scientific materialism. Unfortunately he led himself up a blind alley by claiming to have squared the circle. This assumption provoked the long and bitter, if not insulting, controversy between Hobbes and John Wallis, the Oxford mathematician. Although never admitting his own errors, Hobbes was on the defensive in this fray. Perhaps hardest of all for him to accept was being outdone in mathematics by a mere minister. Other antagonists in the continuing forensic battles in which Hobbes was engaged were Seth Ward, professor of astronomy at Oxford, who, in his *Vindiciae academiarum* (*Vindication of the Academy*, 1654), claimed that Hobbes had no understanding of what English universities were doing, and Bishop Bramhall, with whom Hobbes had been engaged in debate in Paris on the question of free will. The untimely release of some of Hobbes's statements rekindled this controversy in England during the fifties. Despite the support of Sir William Petty, who called him one of the great men of the age, Hobbes was never elected to the Royal Society, which was organized in 1662. The opposition of Wallis, Ward, Wren, and Boyle was too much to overcome. Although Hobbes was not without distinguished friends—the poets Cowley and Davenant, the scientists Harvey and Sorbière, and the brilliant classicist Selden—he had virtually no philosophical defenders and a host of critics. Some even said it was he who had brought down God's wrath in the London plague of 1665–66 and the great fire of 1666. Nothing recedes like success.

Reputation

After the Restoration Hobbes finally won the favor of his former pupil. Charles II liked Hobbes's repartee and likened him to a "Beare to be bayted." From Charles he received an annual pension of £100, which apparently was paid most of the time for the rest of his life. But the Church continued its rumblings against his "atheism." Samuel Pepys noted in his diary in 1668 that he had to pay twenty-four shillings for an eight-shilling copy of the *Leviathan,* since the bishops had forbidden its reprinting. Charles himself forbade the publication of *Behemoth, or the Long Parliament,* as much to protect Hobbes as for any other reason. (It was published posthumously in 1682.) In 1675 Hobbes left London to retire to Chatsworth and Hardwick. There he died in 1679, at the age of ninety. According to Southwell, he died a "very good Christian." In any but a liturgical sense of "Christian," no one is qualified to make this kind of judgment about another person. All we can do is point to externals: Hobbes was overtly anticlerical and had a strong distaste for sermons. Yet he is known to have traveled a mile to take the Eucharist according to the Anglican rite. His cosmology and political theory stand on wholly secular assumptions, yet he went to great lengths to find scriptural support and preserve the appearance of piety.

Throughout his long life Hobbes was noted for having sharp wit and genial sarcasm and for being, as he called himself, timorous. "There was not much poetry in him," as Lindsay has said.[1] Nor was he ever modest: "Natural philosophy is therefore but

[1] A. D. Lindsay, in the Introduction to his edition of Thomas Hobbes's *Leviathan* (New York: Dutton, Everyman, 1950), p. XIII.

young," he wrote, "but civil philosophy yet much younger, as being no older (I say it provoked, and that my detractors may know how little they have wrought upon me) than my own book *De Cive*."[2] In his old age he was said to be more "peevish," conceited, and disparaging of others than ever. But even his enemies admired his spirit. He was handicapped by palsied fingers, yet his nimble mind kept working. In his eighties he translated the *Iliad* and the *Odyssey* not, he said, because his translation was better than previous ones but because it would give his critics something to work on and divert them "from showing their folly on my more serious writings." At his death he left unfinished a critique of Coke aimed at showing him excessively worshipful of precedent.

Hobbes was something of a health faddist, seeking to perspire as profusely as possible on the theory that "old men were drowned inwardly by their own moisture." To this end he played tennis until he was seventy-five and had rubdowns after his daily walk. He also felt that ventilation of the lungs was important and accomplished this by closing all the doors, getting into bed, and singing at the top of his voice.

For a man of his literary distinction, Hobbes died with a rather small library. A favorite theme of his was that most men read too much and cluttered up their minds. He early discovered, reports Bayle's *Dictionary*, that most books are simply quotations from other books and for this reason preferred the established classics.

Despite a life of probity, Hobbes's personal reputation suffered abuse. There was a time in England when all things evil were given the label Hobbist. "A tract of 1686 describes the 'town-fop' as equipped with three or four wild companions, 'half a dozen bottles of Burgundy, and two leaves of *Leviathan*.'"[3] It was not until the end of the century that Hobbes ceased to be the standard whipping boy for controversialists.

MOTION AND MATTER, GEOMETRY AND POWER

One of the first things to be said about the content of Hobbes's political theory is that, substantial as it is, it may be less important than the assumptions upon which it proceeded. Hobbes was probably the first modern political theorist to assert that "civil philosophy" and "natural philosophy" could not be treated in separate compartments but were indissolubly bound together. This is a contention honored in theory or in practice by most of the modern authors in this book but by almost none of Hobbes's contemporaries. Indeed, it was this position that made Hobbes so dangerous to orthodoxy. Francis Bacon was a great exponent of the new science, but of an inductive science. He was willing to let general principles take care of themselves while the great search for data went on. His name could be invoked by the pious scientists of the new Royal Society without fear of being branded heretics by religious or political authorities. But the science that Hobbes championed was deductive science. He cared very little for the gathering of empirical data but wanted most of all to establish principles that should be right and logically consistent. He was passionately devoted to building a complete system, one that tied together physics, psychology, politics, and ethics. Any such devotion to logical completeness is a threat to orthodoxy; and Hobbes's unfortunate mixture of conceit and timidity compounded the threat. "Intellectual audacity combines awkwardly with personal timidity," Stephen rightly observed. Hobbes "shrank from no convictions to which his logic appeared to lead him; and he expounded them with a sub-

[2] *De corpore,* Epistle Dedicatory, in *The English Works of Thomas Hobbes,* Sir William Molesworth, ed. (London: Bohn, 1839–45), Vol. I, p. IX. Subsequent quotations from *De corpore* are from this volume of this edition. Quotations from *De cive* are from Volume II of this edition.

[3] Sir Leslie Stephen, *Hobbes* (London: Macmillan, 1904), p. 68.

lime self-confidence, tempered, indeed, by his decided unwillingness to become a martyr. Of course, like most men in whom the logical faculty is predominant he was splendidly one-sided."[4]

Motion

The one universal phenomenon, the basic principle of all things for Hobbes, is motion. "Galileus in our time," he writes in *De corpore,* ". . . was the first that opened to us the gate of natural philosophy universal, which is the knowledge and the nature of *motion.*" This statement means that the overriding task for scientists and philosophers—Hobbes would make little distinction between them—is to provide a mechanical explanation of the universe, including its political aspects. Audacious is the only word for it. But, more precisely still, what does Hobbes mean by calling motion ultimate? The world, for Hobbes, is reducible to particles—atoms—far beyond the threshold of human perception. These ultimate particles cannot be grasped or known; only the results of their interaction can be known. In themselves they have no properties, only motion: ". . . motion produces nothing but motion."[5] What we can know, then, is how one state of motion passes into another, the laws of change. And for this knowledge geometry is the only tool: "They that study natural philosophy," says Hobbes, "study in vain except they begin at geometry; and such writers and disputers thereof as are ignorant of geometry do but make their hearers and readers lose their time."[6] Thus the irreducibility of motion and faith in geometry are welded together.

Hobbes is not called a "motionalist," though he could be if there were such a word. He is called a materialist. What is the relation of motion as a fundamental principle and matter as a fundamental principle? Hobbes simply asserts with very little argument that the material world is the only world. Thought is a species of motion. Spirit is a species of motion. And only *things* can move: ". . . the whole mass of things that are is corporeal, that is to say, body; and has the dimension of magnitude, namely, length, breadth, and depth . . . and that which is not body is no part of the universe." All existence is simply matter in motion. But of course it is not so simple. Descartes agreed with Hobbes on the fundamental character of geometrical laws of motion—though the two men were never eager to agree with each other—but he was no materialist. *Cogito ergo sum—Je pense, donc je suis*—"I think, therefore I am." Thought, for Descartes, was separable from and prior to the corporeal. He also denied Hobbes's contention that motion itself is the object of sense. We need not go into these arguments. The point is that motion and matter may be more separable than Hobbes imagined.

How does Hobbes explain thought, imagination, dreams, and spirit in bodily terms? The best way to answer this is to summarize the first few books of the *Leviathan.* The union of the physical and the political, the geometrical and the social, is seen at once in the first words of Hobbes's Introduction:

> Nature (the art whereby God has made and governs the world) is by the art of man . . . imitated, that it can make an artificial animal. For seeing life is but a motion of limbs . . . why may we not say that all *automata* (engines that move themselves by springs and wheels as does a watch) have an artificial life? For what is the heart, but a spring; and the nerves, but so many strings; and the joints, but so many wheels giving motion to the whole body, such as was intended by the artificer? Art goes yet further, imitating that rational and most excellent work of nature, man. For by art is created that great Leviathan called a COMMON-WEALTH, or STATE (in latin CIVITAS) which is but an artificial man . . . in which the sovereignty is an artificial soul, as giving life and motion to the whole body.[7]

[4] *Ibid.,* pp. 56, 71.

[5] *Leviathan,* Ch. 1. Subsequent quotations from the *Leviathan* are from the Lindsay edition. Punctuation, spelling, and capitalization have been modernized. The results may be compared with Michael Oakeshott's edition (Oxford: Blackwell, 1946).

[6] Quoted in Stephen, *Hobbes,* p. 81.

[7] *Leviathan,* Introduction, p. 3.

Man is both the matter and the artificer of this artificial beast, the state. And he is very much the same in both capacities, for Hobbes, unlike almost all other political absolutists, assumes a natural equality of mankind. Although the objects of passions are diverse, the passions themselves are similar. By looking into ourselves we can see the passions of all other men: "He that is to govern a whole nation, must read in himself, not this or that particular man; but mankind." This is hard to do, "harder than to learn any language or science," but it must be done.

Sense and Thought

Chapter I of the *Leviathan* begins with a discussion of sense. All thoughts, every mental conception, are but representations of sense impressions, singly or in train. "The cause of sense is the external body, or object, which presses the organ proper to each sense." The qualities of sense—light, color, sound, odor, heat—are all forms of motion. Sight is caused by motion, not by something in the object itself—though this fact is unrecognized by the Aristotelian universities, says Hobbes disparagingly. Imagination is "nothing but decaying sense" and is identical with memory, which can be simple or compounded, as when a man puts together the image of a horse with the image of a man to conceive a centaur. Much memory is called experience. The law of inertia forbids that motion itself decay, so Hobbes says that sense decays when one form of motion is overshadowed by another—a greater, closer, or more recent form —as when the sun's light blots out the stars' light without extinguishing it. Imagination during sleep is called dreaming. Hobbes's dream interpretations are not quite Freudian but they are colorful. From the inability to distinguish between dreams and vision arose "the greatest part of the religion of the gentiles." Hobbes prudently exempts Christianity from this interpretation of religion but does note the way "crafty ambitious persons abuse the simple people" with "this superstitious fear of spirits."

Hobbes belongs, partly at least, in the camp of English empiricists in that he denies the existence of any innate ideas in the mind apart from those ideas that derive from experience. "There is no other act of man's mind . . . naturally planted in him." Thus nothing beyond what is finite can be conceived, "therefore the name of God is used, not to make us conceive him; (for he is incomprehensible; and his greatness, and power are unconceivable;) but that we may honour him." If, however, we identify empiricism with experimental science, then Hobbes is not an empiricist. He was committed to deduction, or, as he called it in *De corpore,* the synthetical, rather than the inductive. But there is no doubt about his being a nominalist: "there being nothing in the world universal but names." Through the misuse of words and names, especially through metaphor, thinks Hobbes, men are apt to deceive themselves and others into believing that what is fictional really exists. He anticipates twentieth-century semanticists in insisting "a man that seeks precise truth, had need to remember what every name he uses stands for . . . else he will find himself entangled in words, as a bird in lime-twigs." Thus, settled definitions that can be used with geometrical precision are essential to truth. "For true and false are attributes of speech, not of things." The common-sense use of words is not often "excellently wise" but, then, neither is it "excellently foolish," as in the case of Schoolmen who value words "by the authority of an Aristotle, a Cicero, or a Thomas." Many statements based on false inference are called erroneous, says Hobbes, when they ought to be called absurdities, or senseless speech. In Chapter 5 of the *Leviathan* he gives some quite sophisticated examples of seven types of such absurdities.

Will, Free or Determined?

In animals there are two kinds of motions, one called vital (pulse, breathing, nutrition, etc.), the other called voluntary (speech, motion of limbs, etc.). The "interior beginnings" of the latter are called the passions, or endeavor. Endeavor toward something is desire; endeavor "fromward" something is aversion. Desire and love are the same and aversion and hate are the same. Contempt is the stationary middle, "an immobility, or contumacy of the heart." That which we desire is good. That to which we have an aversion is evil. In ethics Hobbes is a complete subjectivist: the good is a product of motions having their center in the individual and is wholly relative to the individual. The words "good" and "evil" "are ever used with relation to the person that uses them: there being nothing simply and absolutely so; nor any common rule of good and evil to be taken from the nature of the objects themselves." Already we can begin to see the rationale for strong government. If there is no objective standard of good, men cannot be expected to cooperate in serving it or get anywhere in trying to communicate rationally what it is. The only way men can adjust their differences is to balance their desires or, more accurately, to establish a tolerable harmony of behavior despite their subjective desires. This can be done only by an external unifying force, which, as we shall see, is for Hobbes the sovereign.

Hobbes rejects the Scholastic definition of will as rational appetite. *Will* for him is simply the *last* desire or aversion pertaining to a given act. Will is therefore not free but determined. Moreover, "no discourse whatsoever can end in absolute knowledge of fact, past or to come. For, as the knowledge of fact, it is originally sense; and ever after, memory. And for the knowledge of consequence, which I have said before is called science, it is not absolute, but conditional." We have, then, a picture of man moved by passions beyond his ultimate control, unable to achieve any fixed, absolute knowledge of anything because all life is in flux. He is restless because happiness is never assured. Happiness resides in having (not in having had) a desired object. But "because the constitution of a man's body is in continual mutation, it is impossible that all the same things should always cause in him the same appetites and aversions: much less can all men consent in the desire of almost any one and the same object." Life is thus highly dynamic, uncertain, and naturally competitive.

A superficial reader may feel that Hobbes is inconsistent when later he talks of men *voluntarily* contracting with one another. How can a determined will act voluntarily? Hobbes effectively surmounts this difficulty by saying (in Chapter 21) that his conception of liberty or freedom is simply the absence of "external impediments to motion." A free man is one "not hindered to do what he has a will to," whatever the source of that will. "When the words *free* and *liberty* are applied to anything but bodies, they are abused." Thus, "fear and liberty are consistent," as when a man pays a debt only for fear of landing in jail. He had liberty (i.e., physical liberty) to do otherwise. Thus, "liberty and necessity are consistent." In fact, "to him that could see the connection of . . . [all] causes, the necessity of all men's voluntary actions would appear manifest." Hobbes's determinism remains unshakable. If we were to say that men's thoughts are determined but that the movement of their bodies is free, we would not be far from Hobbes's meaning. This position does not actually reconcile liberty and necessity so much as it puts them in different compartments or at different levels of meaning. Liberty pertains to the superficially descriptive. Necessity pertains to underlying causes. Such a "consistency" does not give much cheer to defenders of free will.

Hobbes does not often provide what we would call experimental evidence on how men behave. He is, as we have stated before, not inducting but deducting. He is saying that, *if* the nature of the universe is matter in motion, then men *must,* by and large, behave in a certain way. The "by and large" is important. We are familiar with theoretical models in contemporary physics and economics but we are only beginning to use them in sociology and political science. Hobbes was constructing a theoretical model. That an individual acted altruistically here and there—as Hobbes himself did: he was notably generous to charitable causes—did not invalidate the system. Economists can assume that men will buy as cheap and sell as dear as they can and build a fairly workable predictive model on the assumption, even though some men do not behave this way. Hobbes was doing much the same thing for the political order and we are not being altogether fair if we dismiss him because our best friend has —apparently—unchanging, uncompetitive, altruistic values.

Power and Politics

In a few chapters of the *Leviathan* Hobbes has moved from the cosmological to the psychological and ethical. In Chapter 10 he enters upon the more strictly political with a discussion of power: "The power of a man (to take it universally) is his present means to obtain some future apparent good. . . . The nature of power is . . . like to fame, increasing as it proceeds; or like the motion of heavenly bodies, which the further they go make still the more haste."

"The greatest of human powers is that which is compounded of the powers of most men, united by consent in one person. . . . Therefore, to have servants is power; to have friends is power." But, above all, the sovereign of a commonwealth has power.

Hobbes does not miss the subtle psychological factors in power: "Reputation of power is power; because it draws with it the adherence of those that need protection. So is reputation of love of a man's country (called popularity) for the same reason. . . . Good success is power; because it makes reputation of wisdom. . . . Reputation of prudence is power. . . . Eloquence is power; because it is seeming prudence." No one who has watched the political hacks hustle away from a loser to cluster like bees around the winner can doubt Hobbes's realism at this point. But Hobbes tends to go further and make the esteem derived from political power the only esteem: "The value or worth of a man is, as of all other things, his price; that is to say, so much as would be given for the use of his power: and therefore is not absolute; but a thing dependent on the need and judgment of another." High and low honor therefore has meaning only "by comparison to the rate that each man sets on himself." That power is a fundamental concept for Hobbes may be indicated by one of the most famous statements in the *Leviathan:* "I put for a general inclination of all mankind a perpetual and restless desire of power after power that ceases only in death." This is not because man is incapable of being content with moderate power, "but because he cannot assure the power and means to live well which he has present, without the acquisition of more." And so, the kings whose power is greatest are those who most seek additional power. The twentieth century can provide not a few confirmations of this tenet.

THE STATE OF NATURE AND NATURAL LAW

The subjective basis of the good and the dominance of the passions over the rational have denied to Hobbes's world the possibility of easy cooperation between men. But this does not make Hobbes an elitist in the usual sense of the word. Hobbes is that rare creature, the egalitarian autocrat.

The State of Nature

"Nature has made men so equal in the faculties of body and mind as that though there be found one man sometimes manifestly stronger in body, or of quicker mind than another; yet when all is reckoned together, the difference between man and man is not so considerable as that one man can thereupon claim to himself any benefit to which another may not pretend as well as he." And he thinks that by and large there is greater equality between men's mental faculties than there is in physical strength. We are not often aware of this because of "a vain conceit of one's own wisdom, which almost all men think they have in a greater degree than the vulgar, that is, than all men but themselves and a few others whom . . . they approve." Out of this equality of ability "arises equality of hope in the attaining of our ends"; but equality of hope means that when men desire the same ends, as they often do, they become natural enemies. They seek gain, or safety, or reputation and this "is far enough to make them destroy each other." "Hereby it is manifest that during the time men live without a common power to keep them all in awe they are in a condition which is called war, and such a war is of every man against every man." This condition does not mean continual fighting but the continual threat of it, as foul weather may include the gloomy period between two showers of rain. If this is a startling thesis, Hobbes notes in one of his lapses into practical empiricism, let us look at our own experience. Do we not lock our doors and even our chests at night? In so doing, does not a man "as much accuse mankind by his actions, as I do by my words?" Hobbes also pays brief, and quite erroneous, homage to the savage races of America, who are supposed to illustrate the historicity of the natural war of all against all, the state of nature in which the life of man is "solitary, poor, nasty, brutish, and short."

Where does justice lie in this kind of situation? Hobbes's answer is, Nowhere: "Where there is no common power, there is no law: where no law, no injustice." This point is of utmost significance. For centuries men had assumed that there was a level of justice behind or higher than men's daily practice of justice in punishing offenders. The Platonic form, or ideal, of justice might be greatly at variance with what the men of power were doing in the law courts; but the former stood as an immutable standard whereby the latter could be judged. The *jus naturale* of the Roman lawyers was thought to have a more immediate relevance to practice, in that the right reason of the judges could bring into operative law, especially the *jus gentium,* the tenets of the more exalted natural law. For Aquinas positive law was not true law unless it conformed to natural (rational) or divine (scriptural) law. Different as they are, all these positions assume that there is a higher law, a higher justice, which either guides or condemns what rulers do. Hobbes wipes away this distinction. Without organized power in society, justice simply does not exist. It is the product of power and not the guide or judge of power. The concept of natural law remains but it is transformed. It is not what men of right reason *ought* to do to live properly; it is what reason shows men of passion *must* do to stay alive. The difference can hardly be exaggerated.[8]

Natural Law

We noted in the preceding chapter that Spinoza is even more thoroughgoing than Hobbes in pushing obligation out of natural law, for there is in Hobbes the injunction that a man is obliged to preserve his own skin and to permit others to do likewise. Not a very exalted moral obligation, most of us would say, but it is at least something. "The right of nature, which writers commonly call *jus naturale,* is the liberty each man has to use his own power, as he will himself, for the preservation of his own nature; that is to say, of his own life; and consequently of doing anything which in his own judgment and reasons he shall conceive to be the aptest means thereto." From this one basic "right of nature" Hobbes derives a general "law of nature": "The right [*jus*] is the liberty to do or forbear; the law [*lex*] determines and binds." They are two sides of a coin. The law of nature forbids a man to do that which is destructive of his life. From this premise Hobbes logically derives some fourteen subsidiary laws of nature and hints at others.[9]

The first and most fundamental of these laws has two branches: first, "to seek peace

[8] A traditional natural-law formulation will also, as indicated above, stress "must" and minimize "ought"—or, rather, deny the distinction between them. There is an element of necessity in all natural-law thinking. But we might say it is long-run, even ultimate necessity that leaves man free to make a moral choice in day-to-day life. The necessity in Hobbes's natural law is immediate, practical, and, because he is a determinist, seems scarcely a matter of moral choice at all. How *much* morality resides in Hobbes's system we shall examine in a moment.

[9] *De cive,* Chs. 2–3, lists twenty laws of nature.

and follow it" and, second, "by all means we can, to defend ourselves." In Hobbes's view the two are simply positive and negative corollaries. The second law is to be content with as much liberty as one is willing to grant other men against oneself. This sounds like the golden rule and indeed Hobbes cites the Scriptures on the point, later suggesting that, if his deductions on natural law are too subtle, the golden rule is "one easy sum, intelligible even to the meanest capacity." But the chief burden of his argument at this point is to justify the basic concept of the covenant by which men give up control of all but one basic liberty to the government. This covenant is divested of all the religious overtones the term held for the Puritans. It is a purely secular arrangement. In fact, Hobbes specifically excludes covenants with God from his discourse: "To make covenant with God is impossible, but by mediation of such as God speaks to, either by revelation supernatural, or by his lieutenants that govern under him, and in his name. For otherwise we know not whether our covenants be accepted or not." The supernatural and the natural were not to be dealt with in the same terms. This was one of the several bases of the charge of atheism cast at Hobbes. But atheism and amorality are not synonyms. Some of the other laws of nature derived from the basic tenet of self protection have unmistakable moral overtones. They include the following prescriptions:

(3) Men should perform covenants made.

(4) No man should show ingratitude for those gifts that are bestowed upon him from another by "mere grace." Ingratitude "has the same relation to grace that injustice has to obligation by covenant."

(5) ". . . every man [should] strive to accommodate himself to the rest." This is the law of "compleasance."

(6) ". . . a man ought to pardon the offenses past of them that repenting, desire it. For pardon is nothing but granting of peace" and aversion to peace is contrary to the law of nature.

(7) In taking revenge, returning evil for evil, men should look to the good that will follow the action rather than to the evil that is past. Revenge without respect to the profit to come is "vainglory, and contrary to reason, and to hurt without reason tends to the introduction of war, which is against the law of nature."

(8) Because signs of contempt or hatred provoke fighting, no man "by deed, word, countenance, or gesture, [should] declare hatred or contempt of another." The breach of this precept is "contumely."

(9) Every man should acknowledge other men as his equal by nature. The breach of this precept is "pride."

(10) Upon entering into the condition of peace, no man should reserve to himself any right he is not content "should be reserved to every one of the rest."

These precepts, it is clear, are "shoulds." They are not laws in the same sense as the law of gravity. There is genuine moral content in them, yet they are but deductions from a precept that, given a nontheistic bias, has a kind of inexorability similar to that of the law of gravity: if a man does not preserve himself, he ceases to exist. Hobbes's earthbound, prudential, mechanistic ethics would seem to justify its designation as a-theistic, though not necessarily with all the diabolical connotations his seventeenth-century critics attached to the label atheism.

COVENANT, COMMONWEALTH, AND SOVEREIGN

The term "covenant" was a fairly technical one for Hobbes. In Chapter 14 he spells out the conditions of valid and invalid covenants. On the one hand, for example, covenants are invalid if they are against the civil law, if they require the parties to do the impossible, if they take away from the individual the right to defend his own life when directly threatened, if the individual has already covenanted away the thing to be pledged by a previous valid covenant, and so forth. On the other hand, "Covenants entered into by fear, in the condition of mere nature, are obligatory." There is a fine distinction between mere promises, words that do not bind, and covenants, which are more intractable. "The force of words being . . . too weak to hold men to the performance of their covenants, there are in man's nature but two imaginable helps to strengthen it, and those are either a fear of the consequences of breaking their word, or a glory or pride in appearing not to need to break it. This latter is a generosity too rarely found to be presumed on." Thus Hobbes regards oaths as superfluous, adding nothing to the obligation incurred.

So central is the concept of covenant that justice itself rests upon it: ". . . the definition of injustice is no other than *the not performance of covenant.* And whatsoever is not unjust is *just.*" The third of Hobbes's laws of nature, you recall, is that men should perform the covenants they have made. Men are therefore obligated to do what they probably would not do in the absence of fear and that is all they are required to do as far as society is concerned.[10] Hobbes's society—state and society are virtually synonymous for Hobbes—begins where fear begins and ends where fear ends. Society, it would seem, is perennially walking a tightrope of fear strung between the terror of a state of nature and a genuinely moral community.

Hobbes's concept of the valid covenant was a general concept applying to every aspect of life outside the state of nature. But by far the most crucial application of it was to the establishment of a commonwealth, for there could not be *any* valid covenants prior to that one. By the same token, social life could not last for long after a commonwealth expired, for "covenants without the sword are but words, and of no strength to secure a man at all. Therefore, notwithstanding the laws of nature . . . if there be no power erected . . . every man will and may lawfully rely on his own strength and art for caution against all other men."

> The only way to erect such a common power . . . is [for men] to confer all their power and strength upon one man, or upon one assembly of men, that may reduce all their wills, by plurality of voices, unto one will. . . . This is more than consent or concord; it is a real unity of them all, in one and the same person, made by covenant of every man with every man, in such a manner, as if every man should say to every man, *I authorize and give up my right of governing myself to this man, or to this assembly of men, on this condition, that thou give up thy right to him, and authorize all his actions in like manner.* This done the multitude so united in one person is called a COMMON-WEALTH, in latin CIVITAS. This is the generation of that great LEVIATHAN, or rather (to speak more reverently) of that *mortal god,* to which we owe under the immortal *God,* our peace and defence.[11]

What is created by this act is an artificial person, who (or which) acts in the name of every individual who is a party to the covenant: ". . . he that carries this person is called SOVEREIGN, and said to have *sovereign power;* and every one besides, his SUBJECT."

Let us examine some of the key phrases in this central declaration of Hobbes and note some of the problems they raise. The covenant is more than "consent or concord." The social contract is no romantic picture of individuals agreeing in the sweet light of reason to follow a certain course as long as it suits their fancy. It is no game. It is "a real unity," a hard and inescapable unity in which diverse wills are ground into one by the stark terror of diversity and the sheer power of the surrogate. Not that Hobbes is able to make this transaction literal. There is still the *"as if* every man should say to every man." It is a legal fiction of sorts but still real, made real by the untenability of any alternative interpretation of why men must and do accept government over them. "Generation," of course, refers to the process of begetting and not to the historical age. The Leviathan has

[10] In his argument against "breach of promise," however, Hobbes does seem to depart from his consistent egoism by calling the truly just man one who keeps his covenants without the need of fear. Hobbes would appear to be gratuitously praising a "higher" motive. But such a man is, in any case, so rare as not to upset the overall mechanistic system.

[11] *Leviathan,* Ch. 17, p. 143.

always gobbled up its subjects. But few before Hobbes dared to call it a mortal god, which, despite passing reference to the immortal God, seems to be the overriding center of allegiance for mortal man. The multitude is "united in one person." We may be confused by the statement that this person can be an assembly of men. A person for Hobbes is an entity "whose words or actions are considered as . . . representing the words or actions of another man. . . . When they are considered as his own then he is called a natural person. And when they are considered as representing the words and actions of another, then he is a feigned or artificial person."[12] In the same way our corporations today are persons in the law.

The sovereign created by this original covenant or contract is thus an artificial person. He personates—not impersonates—every member of the commonwealth who formerly made up the headless multitude. It is important to note that as the creation *of* the contract he is not a party to it. The contract is between each and every subject. Therefore there is no legal way by which the subjects can call the sovereign to account. His existence is the condition of their peace. Yet he speaks for them with a voice of his own; he is not a representative in the democratic sense of one who mirrors public opinion on all issues. Only by understanding this unique position of the sovereign can we make sense of Hobbes's controversial statement, "The law of nature and the civil law contain each other and are of equal extent." He means that neither can become operative until the commonwealth comes into being. The sovereign is the sole source of civil law, yet because he personates all his subjects they are the authors of his every act, even the unwise ones, even the ones they disapprove of. This, as someone has said, seems a clear triumph of logic over common sense.

[12] Hobbes's failure to distinguish carefully enough between authorization and representation and the consequences of this failure for his whole theory of obligation are exquisitely examined by Hannah Pitkin in "Hobbes' Concept of Representation," *American Political Science Review,* Vol. 58 (1964), pp. 328–40 and 902–18.

For all Hobbes's skepticism, common sense does often seem to be crowded out of his system. Yet we must always keep in mind that Hobbes is—or thinks he is—dealing with the *ultimate* basis of political obligation, which is fear. A man is *afraid* to disobey the sovereign for fear of the anarchy he might precipitate in a kind of chain reaction of disobedience. Remove the common tie of obedience to the sovereign and an explosion results. Since men's fearful nature and drive toward self-preservation are presumed to be basically the same from one man to the next, Hobbes's citizen can logically feel that, if he does not obey, no one else will obey. In a sense, then, it is fair to say that this man has accepted and made his own the sovereign's command, even though it would not have been his command had he been sovereign. The questions this conclusion raises for us are not so far fetched. How much of our so-called morality does in fact rest on fear? Should we be thankful for any system that keeps our "natural" selves in check? Plato raised the same kind of question in the *Republic* with Glaucon's fable of the magic ring of Gyges, which made a man invisible at will and opened all sorts of possibilities for unpunished mischief. Would we be our present decent selves if we could get away with anything?

MORALITY IN THE STATE OF NATURE

In Hobbes's setting this question becomes that of the existence of morality in the state of nature. There is no justice or injustice in his state of nature. Is there no morality either? If none, if man is but an animal without a government over him, how can we expect him to live like a moral creature even with a government? Not surprisingly, these are the very issues that most divide contemporary Hobbes scholars. While we cannot do justice to the subtlety of their arguments here, the vitality of their disagreements helps to wash away any merely antiquarian attitude we might have toward Hobbes.

The arguments of these scholars fall basically into three categories. The first position is that there is little morality anywhere in Hobbes's system. Of the older commentators, Stephen[13] seemed to hold the view that when Hobbes used the term "obligation" he used it in either a descriptive or, in some cases, a deceptive, sense rather than with truly moral connotations. Sabine states that Hobbes "is saying merely that in order to cooperate men must do what they dislike to do, on pain of consequences which they dislike still more. In no other sense is there logically any obligation whatever in Hobbes' system."[14] The obligation here seems dependent *only* on the avoidance of punishment. Likewise, De Jouvenel asserts that moral conduct for Hobbes rests solely "on the fear of repression—and on nothing else." He grants that Hobbes's sovereign will employ his wiles to keep this fear in the background of men's minds but doubts that it thereby gains any moral stature:

> It is by means of the desire to avoid the punishment that the will is made up against the prohibited act. This desire to avoid punishment forms by degrees good habits, with the result that the punishment becomes no longer present to the mind and the law comes to be obeyed from a respect now second nature. Let us note that this is to assimilate the training of citizens to the training of dogs.[15]

The second position is that man, for Hobbes, becomes moral only in the commonwealth—that morality is not natural but artificial, a product of social organization. Lamprecht, for example, finds that "Hobbes is insisting that any significant morality is social in character and presupposes the occurrence of regularized procedures. Morality is not significantly present when men are considered in their separateness as atomic individuals,"[16] even though there are "the beginnings of morality" in the state of nature. "Hobbes never maintained, as Hobbism attributed to him, that law creates moral distinctions by fiat." Oakeshott is another who argues that the concept of obligation in Hobbes is genuinely moral but that it does not come into being until civil society is founded. By declining to label as moral an obligation stemming from rational self-interest alone, Oakeshott avoids making an easy but empty case. One

> kind of obligation, which we will call *moral* obligation, is not the effect of superior power, or of the rational perception of the consequences of actions, but of Authority. . . . An Authority is a will that has been given a Right by a process called authorization. . . . the only sort of action to which the term moral obligation is applicable is obedience to the commands of an authority authorized by the voluntary act of him who is bound. The answer to the question, Why am I morally bound to obey the will of the Sovereign? is, Because I have authorized this Sovereign, "avouched" his actions, and am "bound by my own act."[17]

As Oakeshott interprets Hobbes, physical, moral, and rational (self-interested) obligations are all necessary to preserve civil society. The mixture of the three Oakeshott calls *political* obligation.

The third position is that for Hobbes morality is an attribute of man in both the state of nature and the commonwealth, morality under the commonwealth being merely a new form of that which existed before. Taylor, for example, has argued that because Hobbes's laws of nature may be known by the use of reason they have the same kind of obligatory character as Kant's categorical imperatives.[18] In a tightly reasoned book War-

[13] *Hobbes.*

[14] George Sabine, *History of Political Theory* (New York: Holt, Rinehart and Winston, 1937), p. 469.

[15] Bertrand de Jouvenel, *Sovereignty,* trans. by J. F. Huntington (Chicago: Univ. of Chicago Press, 1957), p. 242.

[16] This and the immediately following quotations are from the Introduction to Sterling Lamprecht's edition of Thomas Hobbes's *De cive* (New York: Appleton-Century-Crofts, 1949), pp. XXIII–IV. See also Lamprecht's "Hobbes and Hobbism," *American Political Science Review,* Vol. 34 (1940), pp. 31–53.

[17] Michael Oakeshott, in the Introduction to his edition of *Leviathan,* pp. LIX–LX.

[18] A. E. Taylor, "The Ethical Doctrine of Hobbes," *Philosophy,* Vol. 13 (1938), pp. 406–24. Kant's formula-

render has examined with great care everything Hobbes has to say about obligation. He asserts, "A moral obligation . . . to obey the civil law cannot logically be extracted from a system in which man has *no* moral obligations before or apart from the institution of that law. Any view that assumes otherwise contains a hiatus in the argument that cannot be surmounted, and if, in fact, this is Hobbes' position, he must be held to have failed in his main enterprise."[19] Warrender does not think Hobbes has failed. He finds that Hobbes relies upon two types of obligation, that which results from physical coercion and does not implicate the individual's will and that which is voluntary and does implicate his will. The former is physical and the latter is political, or moral. The sovereign, the source of civil law, has, it turns out, relatively little physical power: ". . . the power of the sovereign is primarily the reluctance of his subjects to break natural law."[20] Their reluctance to break the natural law is never wholly divorced from fear of physical threats; but neither is it typically divorced from their own conception of duty. Says Hobbes in *Behemoth:* "For if men know not their duty, what is there that can force them to obey the laws? An army, you will say. But what shall force the army? Were not the trained bands an army? Were they not the janissaries, that not very long ago slew Osman in his own palace at Constantinople?"[21] The capacity and the willingness of men to do their duty is, then, a necessary, though not a sufficient, condition for the existence of society.

Strauss is another who affirms the moral if not the moralistic characteristic of Hobbes's thought. In tracing its evolution he finds that the fear of death (to be distinguished from the fear of mere punishment) becomes for Hobbes the most significant of men's legitimate, moral motives and is set against pride and vanity. One obeys the law because the existence of law is the alternative to death:

> Hobbes distinguishes no less precisely than other moralists between legality and morality. Not the legality of the action but the morality of the purpose makes the just man. That man is just who fulfills the law because it is law and not for fear of punishment or for the sake of reputation. . . . In believing that the moral attitude, conscience, intention, is of more importance than the action, Hobbes is at one with Kant and the Christian tradition. He differs from this tradition at first sight only by his denial of the possibility that just and unjust action may be distinguished independently of human legislation.[22]

In the state of nature every action is permitted because every individual is his own judge; but even there Hobbes does not approve every *intention,* only the intention of self-preservation.[23]

OBLIGATION IN HOBBES SUMMARIZED

What can we say in summarizing Hobbes's difficult theory of obligation? First of all, de-

tion is "Act only on that maxim whereby thou canst at the same time will that it should become a universal law." One should bind oneself, in other words, to the same standard that one would impose on others. Compare Hobbes's second law of nature: "That a man . . . be contented with so much liberty against other men as he would allow other men against himself." (*Leviathan,* Ch. 14.) In both cases the rules are categorical in the sense of being offered as dictates of universal reason. In neither case are they categorical in the sense of being inescapable. See J. W. N. Watkins, *Hobbes' System of Ideas: A Study in the Political Significance of Philosophical Theories* (London: Hutchinson, 1965).

19 Howard Warrender, *The Political Philosophy of Hobbes; His Theory of Obligation* (Oxford: Clarendon Press, 1957), p. 6.

20 *Ibid.,* p. 317.

21 *Behemoth,* Ferdinand Tonnies, ed. (London: Simpkin, Marshall, 1889), p. 59.

22 Leo Strauss, *The Political Philosophy of Hobbes, Its Basis and Its Genesis,* trans. by Elsa Sinclair (Oxford: Clarendon Press, 1936), p. 23.

23 A fourth position might be that of John Laird, who cites quotations from Hobbes that would substantiate *both* positions two and three above and says, "I cannot see how these views can be reconciled." He further notes, "Very probably Hobbes would not have restricted his ethical theory to the problem of deliverance from civil tumult had the calamities of his own England weighed less heavily on his spirit" (*Hobbes* [London: Oxford Univ. Press, 1934], pp. 184 and 188).

spite what many people casually say about him, Hobbes is not a might-makes-right man. He says in *De cive* that even in the state of nature, though external forces push us like animals, "pride, ingratitude, breach of contracts (or injury), inhumanity, contumely, will never be lawful, nor the contrary virtues to these ever unlawful, as we take them for dispositions of the mind, that is, as they are considered in the court of conscience, where only they oblige and are laws." In the commonwealth, these good motives can be more safely externalized. It is the sovereign's specific moral obligation to provide for the safety of the people and to make good laws. In the *Leviathan* he asks, "But what is a good law? By a good law, I mean not a just law; for no law can be unjust. . . . A good law is that which is *needful,* for the *good of the people,* and withal *perspicuous.*" True, no one but God can enforce this obligation on the sovereign and, when we remember Hobbes's theology, this is not much of a restraint; but it is further evidence refuting the charge of amorality against Hobbes.[24]

Second, the fear of death is not for Hobbes a despicable human motive but rather a motive of some moral significance. A man can seek the preservation of life with some dignity and rationality—more dignity than when he merely seeks to avoid punishment and more rationality than when he seeks preferment for the sake of pride and vanity. We think of the fear of death as anxiety-ridden, irrational, egoistic. It is that, in part, no doubt. But Hobbes sometimes seems to make a much more positive affirmation of this passion for safety. At one point in *De cive* he says, "By safety must be understood, not the sole preservation of life in what condition soever, but in order to its happiness. For to this end did men freely assemble themselves, and institute a government, that they might, as much as their human condition would afford, live delightfully." This interpretation gives promise of an expanded and more positive hedonism than we usually associate with Hobbes. Of course, it may well be that any form of hedonism, if widely and rigorously followed in a society, would tear it apart rather than hold it together as Hobbes expected. The contention here is not that Hobbes's morals are either adequate or realistic, only that they existed.

Third, Hobbes does have a theory of duty, closely identified with his natural-law principle of keeping covenants. Constraint is necessary to extract dutiful obedience from most men; but, as noted above, Hobbes does seem to concede moral superiority to the man who does his duty without constraint. To give his sense of duty Kantian overtones is, however, a bit strained. For Hobbes duty is not the universal ethical principle it is for Kant, either in scope of application to subject matter or in its place in a hierarchy of values. Duty is a function of, and therefore subordinate to, the obligation to obey the sovereign.

Fourth, we cannot say that for Hobbes all morality was a product of society. Some of the evidence has been adduced above, and it seems ample, to indicate that goodness and rightness and even conscience have a place in the state of nature. In addition we would do well to recall that Hobbes is an individualist, a very thoroughgoing individualist for whom society is an artificial, even if necessary, creation. This position would seem to follow from his cosmology of atomic particles and his subjectivist epistemology. But more concretely we can see in his advice to the sovereign in the *Leviathan* all sorts of individualistic assumptions: the wise sovereign would issue relatively few commands; unnecessary laws do no good—they are but "traps for money"; the purpose of the sovereign is "not to bind the people from all voluntary actions but to direct and keep them in such a motion as not to hurt themselves by their own impetuous desires." Indeed, Hobbes's major purpose seems to be to establish conditions for the safe pursuit of individual ends. He was close in many ways to the later laissez-faire school in matters of practical economics. All this is enough to show that those who call

[24] The influence of the Puritan idea of covenant on Hobbes is discussed by Herbert W. Schneider in the Introduction to his edition of *Leviathan,* Parts I and II (New York: Liberal Arts Press, 1959).

Hobbes an early totalitarian do not know what they are talking about. The essence of totalitarianism is the absorption of the individual into the mass and the destruction of his privacy. Hobbes wanted to protect his privacy and was manifestly unmoved by high-flown collective ideals.

REVOLUTION

We must pass by many of the subjects Hobbes discusses in the *Leviathan:* the rights of the sovereign (Chapter 18); the nature of sovereignty under monarchy, democracy, and aristocracy (Chapter 19); the functions of public ministers (Chapter 23); the economy (Chapter 25); and others. The book qualifies as a major work on grounds of comprehensiveness as well as originality. But two problems, both related to sovereignty, are enough to command our attention for the rest of this chapter. The first is that of revolution.

If one contends that there is no moral obligation in Hobbes, then the difference between the state of nature and the commonwealth is simply one of centralized force. This would seem to be an open invitation to continual rebellion and violence. We have rejected such a view of Hobbes but problems remain. One problem is the general unsettlement produced by Hobbes's radical, atomic individualism. The core of Hobbes's critique of Coke was directed against Coke's confidence in the wisdom embodied in the accidents of the historical past. Coke gave custom an authority superior to that of any living lawmaker. Such an exalted view of custom would inhibit the sovereign and Hobbes had to reject it. To the sovereign Hobbes gave the power to eliminate undesirable customs at will. Thanks in part to the anthropologists, we now know more fully than Hobbes how absolutely inescapable is the authority of custom in any functioning society. To treat customs lightly or bend them to suit a sovereign's will is to invite rebellion. Hobbes the antirevolutionary is in this sense as revolutionary as anyone. Granted that Hobbes's advice to the sovereign is to rock the boat as little as possible, Hobbes could not guarantee that a sovereign would follow his advice.

A second weak spot stems from Hobbes's distinction between sovereignty by institution and sovereignty by acquisition. In the former men come together and by formal contract establish a sovereign; in the latter the sovereign simply takes over by conquest. The two differ "only in this, that men who choose their sovereign do it for fear of one another and not of him whom they institute: but in this case [acquisition] they subject themselves to him they are afraid of. In both cases they do it for fear." Whatever the method of establishment, afterward the power and authority of the sovereign are identical. Yet it would seem from our earlier discussion of obligation that the requisite pattern of duties would be much more easily maintained by an instituted sovereign than by a conquering sovereign. Recall Hobbes's statement in *De cive* about safety meaning more than bare surviving, but rather living "delightfully." This was the end for which men did "institute a government." This position certainly loses conviction if one says, "Living delightfully is the end for which men yield to a conqueror." Moreover, if elected sovereigns and bullying sovereigns have identical status, is this identity not an encouragement to the bully to foment rebellion wherever and whenever he can? You, too, can become a sovereign. Why delay? Though a moralist, Hobbes could not conceive of any moral grounds that could limit a sovereign's general grant of power, for such a conception would shatter the logic of his whole rationale for government. Thus, again, he seemed to invite the very revolution he hated.

Finally, a more practical problem: once a revolution has in fact started, how does a subject know who is the sovereign? The problem was not altogether academic for Hobbes. He takes up the question at the very end of the *Leviathan,* in the appended "Review and Conclusion": ". . . the point of time, wherein a man becomes subject to a conqueror, is that point, wherein having liberty to submit to him, he consents, either by express words, or by other sufficient sign, to be his subject." Obligation to the former sovereign ends "when the means of his life is within the guards and garrisons of the enemy." A civilian can rightfully yield sooner than a soldier. As long as the old sovereign still has troops in the field, the soldier should be loyal to him. But even the soldier has no obligation beyond the point where the old sovereign can protect and nourish him. If a mess wagon blows up, this could presumably mean a change of sovereigns for a hungry foot soldier. If either soldier or civilian is thrown into jail by the conqueror, there is no obligation to the authority that does it. Every man, it seems, has a natural right to try to get out of jail. What constitutes the crucial difference between a predatory sovereign's protection when one is in jail and his protection when one is out of jail Hobbes does not elucidate. Yet there are times, after all, when a man will be better fed in jail than out.

LESSER CORPORATIONS, RELIGION, AND THE "KINGDOM OF DARKNESS"

We see what Stephen meant in talking about Hobbes's "splendid one-sidedness" when we look at his view of organizations that might stand between the individual and the sovereign. The idea of social stability being maintained by a balance of power between social organizations of less extent than the state was utterly alien to Hobbes's frame of mind: ". . . to leave to a [subordinate] body politic of subjects to have an absolute representative to all intents and purposes were to abandon the government . . . contrary to their peace and defence." Hence his strong antipathy to factions: ". . . leagues of subjects . . . are, in a Commonwealth . . . for the most part unnecessary and savour of unlawful design; and are for that cause unlawful, and go commonly by the name of factions, or conspiracies." Adopting an organic metaphor, Hobbes likened lawful corporations to muscles serving under the higher organs of the sovereign officials; but unlawful corporations were "wens, biles, and apostems."

Hobbes was thoroughly consistent in disparaging institutional forms that jeopardized his conception of sovereignty. The traditional mixed-state idea, for example—the balance of king, aristocracy, and people—Hobbes regarded as impossible. In *De cive* he wrote: ". . . power is either without limit, or is again restrained by some other greater than itself; and so we shall at length arrive to a power which hath no other limit. . . . that same is called the supreme command." Hobbes's hostility to Presbyterianism, best expressed in *Behemoth,* is at least partly related to its mixed and therefore ambiguous form of ecclesiastical government, with neither the bishops of Anglicanism nor the congregational autonomy of the Independents.

Religion in general, however, is a subject of special concern for Hobbes. About one-half of the *Leviathan* is devoted to scriptural exegesis and the subject of religion. Yet, paradoxically, the greater Hobbes's attention to religion, the more secular his thought became. Strauss has traced this concern as it developed through the pages of the *Elements of Law* (1640), the *De cive* (1642), and the *Leviathan* (1651). The trend is consistently toward greater but more critical attention to the Scriptures, toward a more rigid political absolutism, and away from "natural theology" (i.e., the discovery of God's will through reason) toward revealed theology. The *Elements of Law* had three chapters on religion, the *De cive* had four, and the *Leviathan* seventeen. Yet, while the *De cive* devoted two chapters to the scriptural proof of natural law, the *Leviathan* gave two paragraphs to the same subject. While in all three works Hobbes affirms that belief that Jesus is the Christ is all that is necessary for salvation,[25] the basis

[25] Strauss, who is very sensitive to the pressures on writers in turbulent times to avoid extreme unorthodoxy if they are to live, regards this affirmation as merely conventional and in no way proof of Hobbes's Christianity or even his theism. See *Natural Right and History* (Chicago: Univ. of Chicago Press, 1953), p. 198*n*. Oakeshott, on the other hand, notes that Hobbes died

of religious authority shifts from the *Elements,* where it is the Church, to the *De cive,* where it is personal belief in Jesus, to the *Leviathan,* where it is the political sovereign who permits certain beliefs. After the *Elements,* says Strauss, "That scripture vouches for priestly rule is from now on not an argument for priestly rule, but an argument against scripture."[26]

Hobbes's aim, of course, is not to eliminate religious belief but to make it a tool of the state—the so-called Erastian position. To this end he discusses angels, miracles, the sacraments, redemption, the "office of our blessed savior," and, in the longest chapter of the book, Chapter 42, "power ecclesiastical." His advice to those who wish to make religion rational has become classic: "For it is with the mysteries of our religion, as with wholesome pills for the sick, which swallowed whole have the virtue to cure; but chewed, are for the most part cast up again without effect."

The long, involved, and heavily scriptural argument of Chapter 42 can be summarized quite briefly: "Preachers . . . have not magistral but ministerial power"; they are rightfully concerned only with faith and "faith has no relation to or dependence upon compulsion." Compulsion is within the province of the sovereign, who, in the interests of peace, may find it necessary to exert compulsion that affects teaching and the externals of worship.

The last part of the *Leviathan,* the "Kingdom of Darkness" (Chapters 44–47), is a biting, savage indictment of the "confederacy of deceivers that, to obtain dominion over men in this present world, endeavor by dark and erroneous doctrines to extinguish in them the light both by nature and the gospel, and so to dis-prepare them for the Kingdom of God to come." The Church of Rome took the brunt of this attack but by no means all of it. These deceptive clergymen, the "children of darkness," were compared to the fairies who "inhabit darkness, solitudes and graves. . . . What kind of money is current in the kingdom of fairies is not recorded. . . . But the ecclesiastics in their receipts accept of the same money that we do." It is only toward the end of the *Leviathan,* after Hobbes's Erastianism becomes overwhelming, that one is likely to go back to the beginning and note a short but incredibly audacious statement in his catalogue of passions: "Fear of power invisible, feigned by the mind, or imagined from tales publicly allowed, RELIGION; not allowed, SUPERSTITION." This is surely the ultimate power of the sovereign, the power to define religion out of existence.

CONCLUSION: THE PROBLEM OF SOVEREIGNTY

Shakespeare would not be Shakespeare if he were not an Elizabethan. But neither would he be Shakespeare if he were *only* an Elizabethan. He is read both because he reflects his age and because he transcends his age. The same can be said for Hobbes. He, too, is a fascinating mixture of the old and the new, the parochial and the universal. We said that modernity was characterized by individualism, the nation-state, and the new science. Hobbes's thought can be hung on these three hooks with not much left over and in each case the old is blended with the new.

Hobbes was an individualist in the extreme. As the atoms bounced back and forth within the individual, individuals were seen to carom off each other as each went his way in pursuit of individual ends. Despite his absolutism, Hobbes caught the spirit of laissez faire. The individual in his system was liberated from a wide variety of constraints. The natural law became a kind of background regulating principle comparable to what the economics of a subsequent century would call the invisible hand. There was very little by

"in mortal fear of hell-fire" and credits him with a more genuine concern with religion. To judge Hobbes personally an atheist seems quite unwarranted, even though the consequences of his writings would be no different were such a judgment warranted. Perhaps this is all that Strauss means.

[26] *Political Philosophy of Hobbes,* p. 74.

way of restrictive allegiances standing between allegiance to self and allegiance to the sovereign. The medieval *corpus mysticum* was thoroughly shattered. Yet Hobbes did not depart from the basic forms of medieval political speculations. He kept the concept of natural law and twisted it to his own ends. He did not repudiate the distinction between objective natural law and subjective natural right—he simply nullified it: the concept of sovereignty was preserved but made precise and concrete; the people were still to be reckoned with but as individuals, not as a community; the Scriptures were to be followed but under new Erastian interpretations. He did not turn his back on earlier theorists. As Laird expresses it, "he beat them at their own game."

In his victory Hobbes erected a state that was absolute not merely in the sense of supreme social power but also in the sense of supreme religious authority. In the *Leviathan* he wrote that obedience to God's laws "is the greatest worship of all" but the same natural reason that reveals these laws requires us to entrust their application to the sovereign: "It follows that those attributes which the sovereign ordains in the worship of God, for signs of honor, ought to be taken and used for such by private men in their public worship." Hobbes sometimes despaired that any sovereign would in fact use the system of secular obligation he had developed in this way: "I am at the point of believing this my labour, as useless as the Commonwealth of *Plato*." But remembering that Plato's philosopher-king had to know mathematics whereas the Hobbesian sovereign had to know only Hobbes's own "science of natural justice," Hobbes found hope that some unprejudiced sovereign could someday take the *Leviathan* and "convert this truth of speculation into the utility of practice." This is something new, at least in the postclassical period. Before Hobbes the state of nature was a theological term. Hobbes made it a political term, with civil society replacing the state of grace. Oakeshott says that he consciously or unconsciously went back to the Roman period in erecting a "civil theology."

Strauss points out that, despite Hobbes's scientific interests, his basic thesis grew out of a moralistic rather than a scientific tradition. He did not, on the one hand, limit himself to the naturalistic observations characteristic of modern science, that is, he did not merely describe what in his day was called natural appetite. Nor, on the other hand, did he adhere to traditional natural law, which sought to define an objective moral order. Hobbes was interested in natural right, a basis for subjective, juridical claims. His individualism and his political absolutism, thus, were not anomalous tenets but at root were one. This philosophy is hedonism, for there is no good beyond the individuals' desires that can give a basis for community values. He does not stress wisdom, courage, or the "severe virtues" but rather the "liberal virtues": "Just as Machiavelli reduced virtue to the political virtue of patriotism, Hobbes reduced virtue to the social virtue of peaceableness." The elimination of any standard but the subjective meant, says Strauss, the elimination of God, in fact if not in name: ". . . political atheism and political hedonism belong together. They arose together in the same moment and in the same mind."[27] Oakeshott gives a more positive construction to the virtue of peaceableness and denies that Hobbes is a hedonist. "Felicity" is the end of Hobbes's state, thinks Oakeshott. It seems rather arbitrary of Strauss to deny God access to the subjective; but whether a grubby sort of peace or a more elevated felicity is the highest of Hobbes's social goals, there is no doubt that neither of them transcends the secular. As author of a sovereign power and a social policy that owes nothing to the authority of transcendent values, Hobbes is a fit symbol for all that is secular in the modern state.

While undoubtedly a secular moralist, Hobbes was still very much involved with the new science. The extent of this involvement has been sketched above. The interweaving of science, morals, and practical politics in Hobbes's mind is succinctly registered

[27] *Natural Right and History*, pp. 187, 169.

in the beginning of *De corpore:* ". . . from the not knowing of civil duties, that is, from the want of moral science, proceed civil wars." A good case can be made that Hobbes's interest in building an indestructible political *science* preceded his concern with validating absolute sovereignty as such. Strauss shows how Hobbes built his system by fusing parts of Platonic idealism with Epicurean hedonism. He retained Plato's concern for the political system, the ideal—or ideational—polity but he rejected Plato's transcendental perfectionism. He substituted for it the rather worldly Epicurean goal of the pleasant life but rejected Epicurus' antipolitical bias. The combination is what has been referred to above as political hedonism. It should not be understood as merely one more expression of what constitutes the good life. Hobbes thought he was constructing a scientific model of the political world as exact as any geometrical model. Given a cooperative sovereign—a flaw in the system, as we shall see—Hobbes could do what the Greeks had failed to do, *produce a political science that works*. A good many twentieth-century political scientists, especially in America, seem to be animated by very much the same kind of hope.

The mold into which all these ingredients —individualism, absolutism, and scientism— were poured was sovereignty, the union of many into one, a center for earthly allegiance, the very foundation of law. The American economist and social theorist Bentley once said of sovereignty, ". . . as soon as it gets out of the pages of a lawbook or the political pamphlet it is a piteous, threadbare joke." From Bentley's hardheaded, no-nonsense position it may well be a joke. But it is no joking matter to a diplomat in the United Nations who is invoking the concept in order to keep a UN inspection team out of his country, to a Southern senator defending states' rights, or to anyone fighting to keep a state senatorial district from being abolished. "Sovereignty" has permeated our political vocabulary so deeply that we take "popular sovereignty" for granted. In this case, to say there is no sovereign, no single source of law, is akin to saying the people do not rule. We are accustomed to say that democracy is the only legitimate regime. By this we imply that legitimacy is not determined by the purposes to be served by the state but only by the locus of final social power, that is, by the sovereign. Thus, if we deny the concept of sovereignty, we deny our only principle of political legitimacy; we are left adrift with no criteria of the good and the bad state. The theory of sovereignty bequeathed to us by Hobbes has, in our generation, made the legitimacy of majoritarian democracy dependent upon its form rather than its content. When majorities become inflamed or hysterical, we are uncomfortable with the theory. But we have not yet produced another theory powerful enough to displace it.

Apart from the overriding significance of the concept of sovereignty itself, what, for us, is true and false in Hobbes's system? Let us be more modest and ask instead where Hobbes fell down and what may be salvaged for present use.

At least six failures may be noted:

(1) In trying to describe and prescribe at the same time Hobbes used the word "natural" to mean two different things, which he did not or could not distinguish. On the one hand, the natural was what reason would show to be necessary for our self-preservation; on the other hand, the natural was the consequences of our spontaneous passions. On the one hand, it was what gave some men power over other men; on the other hand, it was what prescribed the rights all men were to observe. In the early nineteenth century Bentham and Austin were to propound a conception of sovereignty and law (the command of the sovereign) virtually identical with Hobbes's while deriding both natural-law conceptions and the social contract. By this time the rationalistic trappings had fallen off.

(2) Although revolution was forbidden by Hobbes's interpretation of natural right, by giving "sovereignty by institution" and "sovereignty by acquisition" equal standing and by giving the subject no voice in the determination of lines of succession Hobbes would

seem to have made revolution virtually inevitable.

(3) As a thoroughgoing egalitarian Hobbes endowed his sovereign with no greater skill or wisdom than anyone else, yet he admits in the *Leviathan* that to function the commonwealth needs "the help of a very able architect." When a state breaks up, it is the fault of the sovereign: ". . . the fault is not in men, as they are the *matter* but as they are the *makers*." Hobbes is not reluctant to tell the sovereign what a difficult job he has—he must pick good counselors, be popular, reward and punish skillfully, avoid unnecessary laws, and much more. The mathematical probabilities that this almost accidentally selected sovereign will botch the job are overwhelming.

(4) Even if it put the most elevated construction on Hobbes's conception of self-preservation, a political system without sympathy, self-sacrifice, and compassion anywhere in it quite probably would fly apart like a smashed atom.

(5) By questioning the legitimacy and minimizing the importance of human associations intermediate between individual and sovereign, Hobbes was working with an image of a society unlike any that has ever existed or probably ever will exist. Since the next two centuries made the same mistake, we should not be too harsh with him for this weakness.

(6) Finally, Hobbes did nothing to extend the logic of his analysis to the world scene. If avoidance of war is the dominant aim of life and an absolute sovereign is essential to this end, then a world sovereign would seem essential. Yet by giving each nation its own absolute sovereignty, Hobbes would—and history has—made worldwide conflict all the more likely. Yet, ironically, the natural law that has created this tense, warlike world is telling subjects everywhere to seek peace as hard as they can and as soon as possible.

The parts of Hobbes's system in no way add up in significance to the whole; but these insights do seem relevant to our situation:

(1) Moral obligation does require a degree of security. Without society, government, laws, and other restraints, men would probably be worse creatures than they are. International morality is as weak as it is in part because nations are their own masters and rarely have a common bond of security sufficient to risk trusting other nations. Though he made too much of the need for security and the fears that make men natural enemies, Hobbes is an invigorating antidote to some of the more romantic notions of brotherhood always with us.

(2) Those of us who lean toward egalitarianism like Hobbes's frank assertions about man's humanity and frailty, even, or especially, when these assertions undermine his own theory of sovereign rule. This is a negative contribution to the so-called liberal tradition but it is by no means the least desirable element.

(3) The implications of the theory of sovereignty are manifold and, from this writer's point of view, not all of them are good. Hobbes's logic, his constant pushing toward the extreme case, at least make us aware of some of the implications of the theory of sovereignty that later defenders have overlooked. For one thing, a consistent application of it requires an Erastian view of Church-state relations. For another, it would treat as a *non sequitur* the theory of dual sovereignty, which prevails in American constitutional law. Hobbes, as De Jouvenel has pointed out,[28] is often more logical than his critics. If we are going to play around with the theory of sovereignty, we would at least do well to pay heed to its greatest exponent.

[28] De Jouvenel observes that we often take our image of "economic man" from Hobbes because it fits the economic model and simultaneously select a happier, more rational "political man" to fit our democratic theories. We cannot have it both ways, says De Jouvenel. If man is really as Hobbes described him, some form of absolutism is inevitable. See *Sovereignty,* pp. 239–41.

12

LOCKE

The portraits of John Locke display a man with a long face; a long, humped nose; a high, scholarly forehead; large, heavy-lidded eyes; and a large but well-contoured mouth. One receives an impression of reserve, of quiet, undefiant pride. Here is a man of moderation and of balanced judgment who was suspicious of "enthusiasm" and complacency alike. Here is a man of caution and wit whose influence insinuates rather than provokes, as did Hobbes's.

LIFE

There are several parallels between the lives of Locke[1] and Hobbes. Both were born in small towns in the southwest of England—Wrington in Somerset was Locke's birthplace. Both were Oxford undergraduates, disgruntled with the medieval curriculum, and both were lifelong bachelors. Some differences are conspicuous, too. Hobbes's relationship with his father was nonexistent; Locke's father was important to him in several ways. The elder Locke, a Puritan, was an attorney and clerk to Alexander Popham, the deputy lieutenant of Somerset County. Between 1634 and 1640 it was the senior Locke's unpleasant duty to collect King Charles's hated ship money; then came the Revolution and, outfitted as a captain, he followed Popham into battle in the Parliamentary cause—with little success and less glory. The practical significance for young John Locke of his father's exploits stemmed from a result of the Revolution. The Long Parliament took over the distinguished Westminster School in London. This event gave Mr. Popham, member of Parliament from Bath, the right to nominate candidates for enrollment. In 1647 he rewarded his friend and counselor, the elder John Locke, by naming his fifteen-year-old son to the school, thus launching a famous scholarly career.

The Young Locke

Despite the Puritan victory, Westminster School was decidedly Royalist, due largely to its great headmaster, Richard Busby, called by Gladstone "the master of the public school

[1] The bulk of this biography has been drawn from Maurice Cranston, *John Locke; A Biography* (New York: Macmillan, 1957), a model of what historical biography should be.

system." The conflict between this new environment and his Puritan background was both disturbing and stimulating to Locke. In 1652, at the age of twenty—older than the typical undergraduate—Locke left London for Christ Church College, Oxford. He had won a scholarship, though he was at the bottom of a list of six winners. At Oxford he developed an interest in experimental science not as a result of the curriculum, for it was still basically medieval (Aristotle and Galen were the principal authorities for the professors of medicine), but more in rebellion against it. Dissection, experimentation, and the teaching of new clinical techniques went on in the private homes of scientists, only some of whom were connected with the university. Locke was drawn into this remarkably distinguished group of men. He was not much of a practical experimenter himself but he was fascinated by the principles upon which experiment proceeded. He was reacting against the excessive reliance on tradition that he associated with the Royalists as well as against the moral emotionalism—enthusiasm, he called it—of the Puritans. By age twenty-four, the year he received his Bachelor of Arts degree, the empiricist in Locke was evident.

He was not yet, however, a liberal in politics. He felt, for example, that Catholics, Quakers, and various other dissenters were too dangerous to be tolerated. His grounds for this position were essentially practical: the fear of anarchy. In 1658, the year Cromwell died, Locke received his Master of Arts degree. The general uncertainty as to the future of the Commonwealth left their mark on young Locke. His letters reveal that he was gloomy about the future of England, despairing of mankind, and unsure what to do with his life. When the Restoration came, it was a cause for great rejoicing. Locke simultaneously welcomed the "happy return of his Majesty" and disparaged the "popular asserters of public liberty." The myth that Locke was at this stage of his life as much a "liberal" as he was later rested for centuries on the mistaken attribution to him of an essay written in 1661 by Walter Moyle. What Locke was writing in that year is more typically revealed by his reply to a pamphlet of Edward Bagshawe. Repudiating the latter's argument for religious toleration, Locke said that the magistrate "must necessarily have an absolute and arbitary power over all indifferent actions of his people."[2] In this and other writings Locke clearly borrowed heavily from the ideas of Hobbes, whose *Leviathan* Locke had read in his twenties. Yet he never acknowledged his debt to Hobbes; in fact he even denied it on at least one occasion, perhaps to avoid the distasteful label "Hobbist."[3]

Scientist and Diplomat

In 1661, shortly after his election to a lectureship in Greek at Christ Church, Locke was saddened by the death of his father.[4] The lawyer Locke left to his eldest son enough land around Pensford to provide him with a modest income for the rest of his life. But for all his gentleness, Locke tended to be an impatient and sharp-eyed landlord.

During his period as Oxford tutor, Locke became a close friend of Robert Boyle, the father of chemistry, whose High Street home was the center for much scientific research. It is significant that Locke, like Boyle, brought no clearly formed metaphysical conceptions about nature to his and Boyle's experimental work. They were above all following Bacon's advice to examine *things.* It was only after this period that Locke read Descartes and began to speculate on the philosophy of inquiry.

With the encouragement of his friend John Strachey, Locke decided that he needed travel to round out his education. The diplomatic service was the tool to this end. In 1665 he left England to be secretary to the mission to Brandenburg, having learned shorthand to

[2] From the Locke manuscripts in the Bodleian Library. Quoted in Cranston, p. 60.

[3] A letter from John Aubrey to Locke in 1673 commending to him both the works and the person of Thomas Hobbes suggests the possibility that the two great philosophers met at least once. But Locke's reply to Aubrey is lost and the occurrence of meeting is purely conjectural.

[4] Locke's mother, of whom he spoke rarely but with affection, died when he was twenty-two. His younger brother, Thomas, died in 1663.

fit him better for the post. What soon impressed Locke in the town of Clèves was that Calvinist, Lutheran, and Roman Catholic religions were all tolerated. In a letter to Boyle he wrote, "They quietly permit one another to choose their way to heaven; and I cannot observe any quarrels or animosities amongst them on account of religion."[5] The practical possibility of a policy of toleration was beginning to change Locke's political orientation. But he had less admiration for the food, church singing, and merchandise of Clèves. The characteristic Lockean sense of humor crops out in a letter to Strachey where he notes that he had spent three days finding a pair of gloves to buy and the next two days trying to put them on.

Locke's success as a diplomat led to two subsequent offers of employment—one with the ambassador to Spain, the other a like post in Sweden—when he returned to England in 1666. After anxious ponderings, Locke refused both. He had decided to study medicine. Locke and a friend opened a small laboratory in Oxford and solicited funds from interested scientists to keep it going. The evidence indicates that Locke was primarily interested in applied medicine, in drugs and herbals. In 1667 he met and began to collaborate with Thomas Sydenham, the greatest English physician of his day and a pioneer of the clinical method. Locke had made an even more important friendship the year before, when Lord Ashley, later earl of Shaftesbury and Lord High Chancellor, met Locke on a trip to Oxford to drink mineral waters. Locke operated on Ashley for a cyst of the liver in 1668. Fortunately, the operation was a success and Locke thereby won a lifelong patron. It was Shaftesbury's intervention with the king that gave Locke tenure at Christ Church without the necessity of taking holy orders, which Locke wished to avoid. He had earlier sought a Doctor of Medicine degree in order to teach there but had been denied it by the suspicious medical faculty: they granted that he had done the requisite advanced work but noted sternly that he had no Bachelor of Medicine degree. Able to teach, but not to teach medicine, he had won a hollow victory.

About this time Locke began to read Descartes. He welcomes Descartes' advocacy of systematic doubt but rejected his deductive, rationalistic reconstruction. He did not go so far as Hobbes and assert that matter or body is everything but he did question whether more could be known of mind than of matter, as Descartes believed. In 1668, at the age of thirty-six, Locke was elected a fellow of the Royal Society. He had already moved to London to live in Lord Ashley's palatial establishment. That same year he became secretary to the Lords Proprietors of Carolina and later had a hand in drafting the *Fundamental Constitution* of that colony, a document carefully designed to avoid the dangers of "democracy." The colonists themselves had other ideas and the constitution was never put into effect.

Whig Man of Affairs

As Shaftesbury moved higher and higher in the government, Locke moved with him. When Shaftesbury was made Lord Chancellor, Locke continued to serve him from the relatively obscure post of secretary of presentation, a position involving ecclesiastical relations. But after Shaftesbury found out about King Charles's secret pro-Catholic Treaty of Dover with France, he could scarcely conceal his disillusionment. In spite of his earlier policy of toleration, he became increasingly anti-Catholic. His usefulness to Charles faded and he was dismissed. Locke, meanwhile, had prudently obtained a somewhat more secure job as secretary to the Council of Trade and Plantations; but a reorganization, ostensibly for economy, cut him out of this post in 1675. Displaying a breadth barely comprehensible to specialized, twentieth-century man, Locke had been all the while continuing his medical studies and in the same year received a Bachelor of Medicine degree from Oxford and a "faculty" to practice as a physician.

We shall later consider the tangle of Whig politics as a backdrop for the publication of

[5] Cranston, p. 82.

the *Two Treatises of Government* (1689). Suffice it to say at this point that Locke's financial journals reveal that he purchased a copy of Filmer's *Patriarcha* and *Inquest* for four shillings, sixpence on February 3, 1680. It is very probable that he began composing a reply shortly thereafter. There is no evidence that Locke wrote the treatises after the Glorious Revolution of 1688, as was believed for years. Shaftesbury, forced by his plottings of 1682 to flee England, went to Holland, where he died of "gout of the stomach" in early 1683. After the Rye House Plot (June, 1683), several Whig writers were arrested and Locke felt it expedient in the late summer to follow the example of his now-deceased patron and journey to Holland. Some said that among the papers he burned before leaving was a full-length biography of Shaftesbury.

The first lonely winter in Amsterdam (part of the time he felt it necessary to go under the assumed name Dr. van der Linden) Locke spent working on his *Essay Concerning Human Understanding*. He also wrote extensively to his English friends. His letters to Edward and Mary Clarke contained much advice on raising children; some were published as *Thoughts Concerning Education* (1693). In November, 1684, by express order of the king Locke's name was stricken from the rolls of Christ Church. Locke was in Utrecht in 1686, working on the fourth book of the *Essay Concerning Human Understanding,* when he took time out to write his influential *Letter on Toleration,* published in Latin in 1689. For two years, beginning in 1687, Locke was a paying guest in the Rotterdam home of Benjamin Furly, a famous, radical, and somewhat eccentric Quaker who undoubtedly nourished Locke's spirit of toleration.

In 1685 Charles II died suddenly and was succeeded by Catholic James II. Protestants were somewhat consoled by the fact that James had no heir and Protestant Mary of Orange was the heir presumptive to the throne. But in June, 1688, the birth of a son to the queen shattered these hopes. The English public was now receptive to a Lockean kind of political theory, that is, a theory of limited monarchy, as it had not been in 1683. Encouraged by the change in public temper, William of Orange set sail from Holland for England with four hundred ships under Admiral Herbert. On November 5, 1688, they landed at Brixham and the insurgent forces moved toward London under Lord Mordaunt[6] with scarcely any opposition and much support. James subsequently fled to France.

Writer of Parts

In February, 1689, Locke joined Lady Mordaunt and Princess Mary in the expedition taking them to England to their husbands and, in Mary's case, to the throne. Locke went to live with a friend in London. He declined an appointment as English ambassador to the Elector of Brandenburg on grounds of health, noting, among other things, that he could not keep up with the "warm drinking" of the Germans, a diplomatic challenge that would be unavoidable. He declined other offers as well, and finally settled for the position of Commissioner of Appeals, a nondemanding post if not quite a sinecure. Although he wanted to regain his place at Christ Church "as acknowledgment that he had been wronged," Locke withdrew the request when he learned it would mean displacing another and concentrated on seeing his *Essay Concerning Human Understanding* through the printers. Meanwhile, he rejoiced over the Act of Toleration passed by Parliament. With his three most important books on press, 1689 was by any measure a big year for Locke.

To escape the debilitating London air, the asthmatic Locke in 1691 went to live at Oates, the country estate of his long-time friend and correspondent, Lady Masham, who was more than gracious in giving Locke the run of the place. The same year saw the publication of his book *Some Considerations of the Consequences of the Lowering of Interest, and Raising the Value of the Money,* which dealt with the highly pressing prob-

[6] Whose wife, in Holland, was at this time carrying on a genteel flirtation with Locke.

lems of interest rates and the practice of "clipping" the edge off unmilled coins. Except for advocating a recoinage to cope with the latter problem, Locke favored minimal governmental interference with supply, demand, rates of interest, and the use-value of money. His economics as well as his politics were clearly Whiggish.

In 1692 Locke edited and in large part rewrote his late friend Robert Boyle's *History of the Air;* that year he also wrote his own *Third Letter for Toleration.* In 1695 the Act for the Regulation of Printing was repealed, in part because of the weight of Locke's arguments against it fed through his friends on the House of Commons committee considering the matter. In Locke's memorandum the heaviest weight was given to the practical, even commercial, values of liberty of the press: "Unlike Milton, who called for liberty in the name of liberty, Locke was content to ask for liberty in the name of trade; and unlike Milton, he achieved his end."[7] This year also saw the anonymous publication of *The Reasonableness of Christianity.* Critics tried to prove that the author was a Socinian (in present-day language, Unitarian) and that all Socinians were atheists. Although he did not remove the cloak of anonymity, Locke was provoked into a reply. He more effectively refuted the latter charge than the former.

Last Years

Despite illness, in 1696 Locke surprisingly accepted an appointment to a new Board of Trade, designed to deal with the threatening rise of Dutch trade, the disintegration of colonial administration, the problem of piracy, and other pressing matters. Locke moved back to London and, though he was ailing and the duties were arduous, he clearly dominated the work of the board. During a convalescent absence at Oates, however, he began to write (though he never completed) *The Conduct of the Understanding.* Despite its title, the book attacked a problem somewhat different from that of the *Essay,* namely the nature of prejudice and its opposite, "clear thinking." In one passage he takes to task those who prefer to deal with only one sort of man and those who prefer books to any sort of man. The experience of practical politics, of coming to grips with a variety of strong viewpoints expressed by a variety of strong personalities, is, he felt, essential training for anyone who would seek truth. This passage helps to explain why Locke the truth-seeker would interrupt his scholarship to take on a heavy burden of public service. It is also a testament to the vitality of his questing spirit.

In 1697 Locke prepared a report for the Board of Trade on the problems of unemployment and pauperism. Although the report was not adopted, Locke's severe proposals for the treatment of beggars, including imprisonment and impressment into sea duty, suggest the limits of his "liberalism." Fortunately for the ailing bachelor, Locke had managed to draw full pay while spending a good part of his winters at Oates. In the spring of 1700, however, Lord Chancellor Somers, the man who had induced Locke to take the Board of Trade position, was removed from office by the exposure of Captain Kidd's Whig-approved piracy and Locke felt it was expedient to resign.

He spent his last days at Oates, carrying on a wide correspondence, replying to critics, writing a commentary on the epistles of St. Paul, and conversing with visitors who came, he gently complained, all too infrequently. John Locke, a great philosopher, died on October 28, 1704, at the age of seventy-two.

THE TWO TREATISES: POLITICAL PHILOSOPHY OR TRACTS FOR THE TIMES?

The second of Locke's *Two Treatises of Government*[8] is so famous that fame has become

[7] Cranston, p. 387.

[8] The full title is *Two Treatises of Government. In the Former the False Principles and Foundation of Sir*

a barrier to its understanding. The phrases "life, liberty, and property," "consent of the governed," "the majority have a right to act and conclude the rest," have become commonplaces in the political vocabulary of the West, if not the world. If we were not aware of his originality, we would say the man was using clichés. Students of the American Constitution will find the phrase "life, liberty, and property" familiar because it refers to the rights singled out for protection against arbitrary federal action in the Fifth Amendment and against state action in the Fourteenth Amendment. In his natural-rights assumptions, his moderation, and his reasonableness, Locke was an intellectual godparent of James Madison, the Father of the Constitution. In 1783 Madison and two other congressmen compiled for their colleagues a list of books, which they titled "The American Statesman's Library." Locke's name was one of the most prominent on the list. (If today's congressmen have not read Locke, they have probably not read many of the other authors on the list either.) The polemical duties taken up by Madison and Locke were in many ways similar. Both were interested in making a case for the legitimacy of a government that either had been or would be born of rebellion. Even more obviously did this task fall to Thomas Jefferson in writing the Declaration of Independence. The weight of natural-rights terminology hung heavily on the Declaration and the meaning of "life, liberty, and the pursuit of happiness" in the Declaration is not so different from Locke's "life, liberty, and property" as is often believed. Locke's defense of a sensible revolution, a reasonable revolution, was so congenial to the American situation and the American mentality that his ideas can be regarded as an important weapon in the defeat of his own countrymen four generations after he wrote.

Locke's skill as a polemicist may lead us to wonder if he was *only* a polemicist. Certainly the *Second Treatise* has none of the logical cohesion of the *Leviathan*. If it is only a tract for the times, perhaps we should leave it to the historian of ideas and not bother to seek profound political theory in it. Actually, the *Second Treatise,* like many important works of political theory, can be dealt with on different levels and the obvious meaning is not always the most important.

Let us first look at the *Second Treatise* as a tract for the times, as a weapon wielded in the Whig cause of Parliamentary supremacy. Will this point of view not explain Locke's reluctance to draw logical conclusions? Will this not make clear why a highly intelligent writer could tolerate inconsistencies? We have noted above that the *Two Treatises* were written in or about 1681 as a reply to Filmer's *Patriarcha.* The dispute that was the occasion of these writings was called the Exclusion Controversy. Locke's patron, Shaftesbury, was the leader of the Country Party, in general the ideological successors of the Roundheads of the Cromwellian period. Above all they feared a Catholic monarch and wished to remove the Catholic duke of York (the future James II) from the line of succession. A thoroughly unscrupulous and nefarious fellow named Titus Oates invented the elaborate Popish Plot, complete with falsified documents, claiming that the Jesuits were going to murder Charles and put James on the throne. Shaftesbury was willing to exploit the resulting furor in an attempt to remove James from the line of succession. An Exclusion Bill, as it was called, would have passed in 1679 had not Charles prorogued and then dissolved Parliament. A second bill the next year was defeated only by action of the House of Lords. The conservatives, including most of the Anglican clergy, feared this assault on the king's prerogative. Desperate for ammunition, they resurrected Filmer's tract on monarchy and circulated it widely. The next year, 1681, Charles called Parliament to meet in Oxford in order to avoid Shaftesbury's "London mobs." But the London Whigs, as they came to be called,[9] simply moved into Oxford with

Robert Filmer and His Followers are Detected and Overthrown. The Latter is an Essay Concerning the True Origin, Extent, and End of Civil Government.

[9] For a time the Shaftesbury men were called Peti-

ribbons on their hats. "No Popery. No Slavery," the ribbons said. Locke was there and described the tumultuous scene in a letter. Charles subsequently dissolved the Parliament. Four years of repressive monarchical autocracy followed until his death in 1685.

Within a few months of the publication of Filmer's tract three of the ablest Whigs were at work on a refutation—Locke's historian friend James Tyrell; Algernon Sidney, the dean of statesmen of the "old cause"; and Locke himself. Charles's rage over Sidney's moderately republican *Discourses Concerning Government* led to Sidney's execution in December, 1683. Locke, who was by this time, as we have seen, in Holland, prudently held up publication of his own reply until 1689 and even then printed it anonymously.

With cutting polemical skill Locke, in the *First Treatise,* dissected Filmer's claim that the authority of kings could be traced to the primeval authority of Adam and thence to God. Locke sneered at Filmer's

> Description of his Fatherly Authority, as it lies scatter'd up and down in his Writings, which he supposes was first vested in *Adam,* and by Right belongs to all princes ever since. . . . If he has . . . any where in the whole Treatise, given any other Proofs of *Adam's Royal Authority* other than by often repeating it, which, among some Men, goes for Argument, I desire any body for him to shew me the Place and Page, that I may be convinced of my mistake.[10]

The tone of the debater is unmistakable. The demolition was so complete that for centuries Filmer had the disadvantage of being known principally through Locke's critique of him. The historical argument was easy to discredit; but as Laslett has pointed out,[11] Locke did not really come to grips with the fundamental problem posed by Filmer's writings: is not social authority, in the broadest sense, "natural" and is not political authority inevitably bound up with social authority?

EQUALITY AND THE STATE OF NATURE

Locke begins the *Second Treatise* with a summary of his critique of Filmer, then explains that it is now his task to "find out another rise of government, another original of political power."[12] In a direct manner that would seem consistent with his stress on precise definition in the *Essay,* Locke defines political power: "Political power . . . I take to be a right of making laws with penalties of death and consequently all less penalties for the regulating and preserving of property, and of employing the force of the community . . . *and all this only for the public good* [our italics]." Note that Locke does not take what the twentieth-century political scientist might call an empirical, nonvaluational approach to political power. Presumably laws with penalty of death made and enforced without regard to the public good would not only be a bad exercise of power but not power at all—a definition that seems to bring true power close to justice. Locke's later discussion of the abuses of power, however, ignores this definition. On the one hand, we could infer that he is merely planting a seed in the read-

---

tioners because of the petitions to the king they drew up protesting the dissolution of Parliament; the Royalists, the successors of the Cavaliers of the English Revolution, were called the Abhorrers because of their counter-petitions abhorring Shaftesbury's interference with the royal prerogative. It was during the Exclusion Bill debates that the terms "Whigs" and "Tories" came into use. Both were pejorative terms, as have been many party labels. Three theories have been suggested for the origins of the name "Whig": (1) that it was a derivative of "whey"—for the sour-milk faces of Scottish parliamentarians; (2) that it was derived from the slogan "We Hope In God"; (3) that it came from "Whiggem" —the call of Scots drivers to their horses. Any one is probably as reliable or as dubious as the others. The term "Tory" has a more certain origin: the outlaws who hid in the bogs of Ireland were called tories.

[10] *Two Treatises of Government,* I, Peter Laslett, ed. (London: Cambridge Univ. Press, 1960), pp. 165 and 168.

[11] Peter Laslett, in the Introduction to his edition of *The Patriarcha and Other Political Works* (Oxford: Blackwell, 1949).

[12] *Two Treatises of Civil Government,* II, Ch. 1, sec. 1, William S. Carpenter, ed. (New York: Dutton, Everyman, 1924). Subsequent quotations from the *Second Treatise* are from this edition.

er's mind, a standard by which tyranny can later be recognized and judged. On the other hand, this troublesome sentence could be but an unconscious mixing of the moral flavor of medieval Scholasticism with the antiseptic definitionalism of modern science.

In Chapter 2, entitled "The State of Nature," Locke leans heavily on Richard Hooker, the great English divine who wrote *The Laws of Ecclesiastical Polity* (1594). "The judicious Hooker," Locke called him, and so has everyone else since. Hooker gives us, and Locke adopts, a kind of legalized golden rule, which simultaneously invokes the concept of nature and asserts a moral obligation concerning the equality of citizens. "My desire . . . to be loved of my equals in nature as much as possible may be imposeth on me a natural duty of bearing to themward fully the like affection; from which relation of equality between ourselves, and them that are as ourselves, what several rules and canons natural reason hath drawn for direction of life no man is ignorant."[13] By quoting Hooker, Locke gives his egalitarianism the sanctity of age and revered authority and identifies it with a tradition of natural law that goes back to the ancient Stoics. That Locke has the motives of a debater rather than a scholar, however, would seem to be indicated by what he omits from Hooker. Neither Hooker nor the preceding natural-law tradition uses a concept of the state of nature. In Hooker the "several rules and canons [of] natural reason" operate on man seen as a naturally social creature. But Locke uses Hooker to bolster his argument *for* the state of nature.

The heart of any state-of-nature argument is that government is artificial rather than natural, that government is a human contrivance, a convention, and is not necessarily ordained of God (or a demiurge) by His work of creation. It is not prior to the individual either in the sense of being a prerequisite to birth and life or in the Aristotelian sense of being essential to the individual's true fulfillment of himself. The device could be used, as in Hobbes, to remove government from criticism by theological standards or, as in Locke, to justify criticism of arbitrary power by pragmatic standards. In one case it bolstered arbitrary government, in the other it undermined it. Hobbes and Locke could disagree as they did about government and the characteristics of the state of nature only because they agreed that there was a state of nature.

Locke answered early and specifically the question raised in our discussion of Hobbes about the moral obligations existing in the state of nature: "The state of nature has a law of nature to govern it, which obliges every one; and reason which is that law, teaches all mankind who will but consult it, that being all equal and independent, no one ought to harm another in his life, health, liberty, or possessions." Locke broadens the range of protection of natural law beyond Hobbes's domain of self-preservation and gives the possibility of natural cooperation greater weight. Self-preservation comes first but man has at least the negative obligation not to "harm another in his life, health, liberty, or possessions." Life in the state of nature is not filled with the stark terror it was for Hobbes, only with "inconveniences" arising from the facts that every man has the right to judge and punish offenders and "self-love" sometimes interferes with the perception of or obedience to natural law: ". . . yet it is certain that there is such a law . . . as intelligible and plain to a rational creature and a studier of that law as the positive laws of commonwealths."

Locke often finds it necessary to forget his ostensible target, the Kentish patriarch, for the sake of a dig at the Malmesbury sage—who is never named. For example, after granting that the creation of civil government is the "proper remedy" for the "inconveniences" of the state of nature, Locke admonishes those who are bothered by the thought of men being judges in their own cases "to remember that absolute monarchs are but men. . . . And if he that judges judges amiss in his own or in any other case, he is an-

[13] *The Laws of Ecclesiastical Polity,* Bk. I. Quoted in Locke, *Second Treatise,* Ch. 2, sec. 5.

swerable for it to the rest of mankind." In such passages Locke's common sense washes refreshingly over Hobbes's forced logic.

Though Hobbes pays only indifferent attention to the problem of the historicity of the state of nature, Locke characteristically brings the question down to the everyday level. Since there is no common government over them, independent nations may be said to be in a state of nature with each other. Yet they do get along, somehow: "The promises and bargains for truck, etc., between two men in Soldania, in or between a Swiss and an Indian in the woods of America, are binding to them, though they are perfectly in a state of nature in reference to one another. For truth and keeping of faith belong to men as men and not as members of society."

In Chapter 3 Locke takes an even more pointed thrust at Hobbes when he notes the confusion of some who have identified the state of nature with a state of war. One puts oneself in a state of war with another man, says Locke, only when one uses force and seeks absolute power over him. And all men do not seek such power at all times. At the expense, perhaps, of his theory of natural equality Locke observes that even in a state of war "when all cannot be preserved, the safety of the innocent is to be preferred." The innocent are the most worthy. It is not surprising, then, that Locke the "liberal" Whig places on government a special moral obligation to protect the innocent. Not simply preservation of life is essential, as Hobbes seems to say, but preservation of a certain quality of life, which is related to the individual's right of self-determination. Hobbes had made the state of nature an inescapable category for political theorizing for the next century; but Locke was reluctant to accept Hobbes's dilemma: take the chaos of the state of nature or take absolute government, for there is no other choice. Both sides of this equation are too extreme for Locke. The state of nature is not hell and the power of government need not be absolute. The pressures to escape one's natural condition are not so terrible and the threat of dissolution of government is therefore not so terrible. Whether in a state of nature *or* under a government, Locke feels, "freedom from arbitrary power is so necessary to, and closely joined with, a man's preservation, that he cannot part with it but by what forfeits his preservation and life together."[14] Arbitrary power is clearly Locke's bête noire.

Thus a state of slavery is but a state of war between master and slave. And slavery is not natural either in the state of nature or under government. A man must consent to the power over him or it is arbitrary. If he is not in a position to give his consent, then by definition the power over him is illegitimate. Here is the crux of the distinction between Locke and Hobbes or even Filmer: for the latter two the need for power or the fact of power was its justification; for Locke the subject's consent was its justification.

PROPERTY

We shall return in a moment to the problem of consent. At this point Locke's theory of property intrudes, for it is closely related to his ideas on the state of nature, arbitrary power, and the ends of government. In Chapter 5 of the *Second Treatise,* Locke analyzes what seems at first glance to be an extraneous subject in a work on government, the origins of property.

Locke is an early defender of the labor theory of value, a theory held by most of the classical economists and by Karl Marx but rejected by almost all contemporary economists. Stated simply, the theory holds that the value of a product is measured by the amount of labor invested in it: a ton of coal dug by five men in one hour is worth one half as much as a ton of copper dug by five men in two hours or by ten men in one hour. Locke also sees labor as the explanation of the origin of property itself: God gave the

[14] Richard H. Cox in *Locke on War and Peace* (New York: Oxford Univ. Press, 1960) argues that Locke's state of nature, though initially disguised, is in fact, as in Hobbes, a state of war.

world to men in common; but whatever a man "removes out of the state that nature hath provided and left it in, he hath mixed his labour with, and joined to it something that is his own, and thereby makes it his property." This argument does not mean, however, that a man should accumulate as much property as is physically possible in this way. God has given us goods to enjoy: "As much as any one can make use of to any advantage of life before it spoils, so much [a man] may by his labour fix a property in; whatever is beyond this, is more than his share, and belongs to others. Nothing was made by God for man to spoil or destroy." Thus, even—or especially—in the state of nature, a man has no natural right to what exceeds his own or his family's capacity to consume. The essentially agrarian basis of Locke's thinking is suggested by the fact that the same standard is applied to land ownership: a man has a natural right to as much land as he can personally cultivate for the sake of his own and his family's needs.

Certain highly imperishable commodities, however, are virtually exempt from the problem of waste. Things hard to come by—like gold, silver, diamonds, "things that fancy or agreement have put value on more than real use"—in time come to stand in the place of perishable produce. Plums that rot in a week are traded for nuts that last a year, which are traded for pieces of metal that last a lifetime. "And thus came in the use of money—some lasting thing that men might keep without spoiling, and that, *by mutual consent* [our italics], men would take in exchange for the truly useful but perishable supports of life." Observe that the possession of money rests upon mutual consent and not on natural right. The natural rights of property relate to what is directly useful to the support of biological life. All possessions beyond this and all property in money rest on consent, that is, on social right and not on natural right. Those, therefore, who make speeches about the natural rights of property with reference to, say, corporate profits, are being, whether they know it or not, quite un-Lockean.

Practical political applications can be read into Locke's chapter on property as easily as into other parts of the *Second Treatise*. On the one hand, men of property must know that "consent" not "nature" gives worth to their money. Economic position no more than political position is certified and fixed by divine sanction. On the other hand, since waste is the primary criterion by which violations of natural law are judged and since money can be stored up indefinitely without waste, men of great wealth need not fear that they are violating natural law simply because of their wealth. There is in this an ingenious mixture of egalitarianism and aristocracy. Here is an attack upon privilege that, nevertheless, as far as economic classes are concerned, does not rock the boat. If we recall Locke's own rather penurious landlordism and the severity of his attitude toward paupers, we know that he was no economic do-gooder. Locke's theory of property, like his politics, was nicely suited to the Whig man of affairs.

Finally, however, we must recognize that beneath Locke's equivocal yet practical assertions lies an emphasis that is fundamental to an understanding of his political theory. Far from being marginal to politics, Locke's theory of property implies what man's chief aim in life is and should be and therefore what standard should guide government. Property, which is something more than mere physical estate, is at the heart of his conception of the good life and the good state, "the GREAT end of men's entering into society being the enjoyment of their properties in peace and safety."

CONSENT

Consent is obviously an important concept for Locke. But what did he mean by consent of the governed? Even the most rabid of present-day majoritarians would not contend that each individual must have an opportunity to approve or disapprove every governmental act that might affect him. Among other things, it would be difficult to collect income taxes were this the practice. Here again we find that, whatever else he was, Locke was not a doctrinaire. What Russell said of his philosophy is applicable to his politics: "Locke aimed at credibility and achieved it at the expense of consistency. Most of the great philosophers have done the opposite."[15]

There are at least three vital qualifications that Locke imposed on his theory of consent. The first is that the equality of subjects is not to be taken in a literal, mechanical sense:

> Though I have said above (Chapter II) that all men are by nature equal, I cannot be supposed to understand all sorts of equality. Age or virtue may give men a just precedency. Excellency of parts and merit may place others above the common level. Birth may subject some, and alliance or benefits others, to pay an observance to those whom nature, gratitude, or other respects may have made it due. And yet all this consists with the equality which all men are in, in respect of jurisdiction or dominion, one over another; which was the equality I there spoke of as proper to the business in hand, being that equal right that every man hath to his natural freedom, without being subjected to the will or authority of any other man.[16]

Children, for example, "are not born *in* [our italics] this full state of equality, though they are born *to* [our italics] it," and are subjects of their father rather than the state until they come of age. Not *all* persons are equal and therefore not all persons are consent-givers.

The second is that giving consent is relevant only to a restricted function, "the business in hand," which is the *establishment* of the government itself. We might call this giving consent the constituent authority residing in a people. Locke was no closer than Hobbes to saying that government should not make a man do what he might not want to do. Consent is not necessarily involved in the making of ordinary statutes and is certainly not involved in their enforcement. The question Locke is raising and answering is, Upon what fundamental base must the whole governmental structure rest if it is to be legitimate? Shall it be the mystique of divine right, the fear of death, or rational consent of naturally equal men? If we take Locke's question at face value and the three alternative answers available in his time, we shall no doubt be with Locke rather than with Filmer or Hobbes. Yet we must also recognize the circularity involved in the basic rationale for his answer: men are naturally equal, which is to say they are equal mainly in their constituent capacity. Why are they equal in their constituent capacity? Because they are naturally equal. It could be said that the empirical case goes to Filmer by default.

The third qualification is that, putting aside the difficulty of natural equality, how often does the average citizen have a chance to give or withhold his consent to the whole governmental structure? How do we know when people are consenting and when they are not? Since such clear-cut occasions arise rarely, Locke was forced to make a distinction between express consent and tacit consent. The distinction—or at least Locke's application of it—was one of the more slippery elements in his theory: "I say that every man that hath any possession or enjoyment of any part of the dominions of any government doth thereby give his tacit consent and is as far forth obliged to obedience to the laws of that government as any one under it." The possession may be as substantial as a large piece of land or as transient as the right to travel freely on the highway. In either case, consent is assumed to have been given. This interpretation would seem to render the moral basis of the theory of consent rather empty, for who can exist in a country without some "possession" thus broadly conceived? The view also offers an ambiguous distinction between the kinds of duties falling upon those who give one or the other kind of consent: since tacit consent rests upon some possession or other, if that possession is abandoned, says Locke, the obligation ends. The

[15] Bertrand Russell, *History of Western Philosophy* (New York: Simon and Schuster, 1945), p. 613.

[16] *Second Treatise,* Ch. 6, sec. 54.

subject "is at liberty to go and incorporate himself into any other commonwealth. . . . Whereas he that has once by actual agreement and any express declaration given his consent to be of any commonwealth is perpetually and indispensably obliged to be and remain unalterably a subject to it." This burden on, and discrimination against, the express-consent people (e. g., those who take an oath in support of the government) seems oppressive. It also contradicts Locke's earlier statement that Filmer's idea of the natural, historical right of patrimony is discredited by the fact that many monarchies are scattered over the world and would not have existed "if men had not been at liberty to separate themselves from their families and their government, *be it what it will* [our italics], . . . and go and make distinct commonwealths and other governments as they saw fit." At this point the freedom to pack up and leave is given the blessing of natural law. If the freedom issues from natural law, it is hard to see how the mere form in which consent is expressed can be allowed to nullify it. Moreover, when later discussing tyranny and the dissolution of government, Locke does not seem particularly concerned to deny those who have given their express consent[17] to the regime the right to rebel against it when it becomes tyrannical.

Part of the confusion is cleared up when we realize that rebellion against a ruler did not mean for Locke rebellion against the social order. There is the definite implication of *two* contracts—one between individuals as individuals, which establishes the social order, and another between individuals as members of a majority and a particular government. Thus those entering civil society by express consent may be indissolubly bound to that society and can never revert to the state of nature, although they *can* reject a particular ruler: ". . . the power that every individual gave the society when he entered into it can never revert to the individuals again as long as society lasts, but will always remain in the community, because without this there can be no community, no commonwealth."

Locke certainly does not tax himself to make clear this distinction between the two contracts, however. In Chapter 8, where the key statement on contract appears, he first states that a man leaves the state of nature "by agreeing with other men to join and unite into a community." The community would seem to be more fundamental than a particular government. In the same paragraph, however, he continues, "When any number of men have so consented to make one community *or government* [our italics], they are thereby presently incorporated, and make one body politic, wherein the majority have a right to act and conclude the rest." It would appear that the individual is the agency of choice in the first instance only. After that the majority alone possesses the right of rejecting an offending government: ". . . every man, by consenting with others to make one body politic under one government, puts himself under an obligation to every one of that society to submit to the determination of the majority, and to be concluded by it; or else this original compact . . . would signify nothing."

[17] If Locke was not perfectly clear as to the proper range of consent, how clear are we? Present-day pollsters can testify that the practical problem of measuring consent is by no means simple. Where is the line between consent and acquiescence? between acquiescence and complete indifference? There are moral questions that plague us as well. How important is the "intensity factor" in the worth of a citizen's choice? Assuming measurement were possible, should the involved voter's vote count more heavily than the apathetic voter's vote? These are questions our society has scarcely raised, let alone answered. Locke, at least, was aware of the apathy of most citizens. Indeed, he found it a useful contributor to political stability. It is no doubt also fair to say that Locke was not really trying to look at the community as a sociological fact but as a legal entity. Two important present-day discussions of consent and obligation are John Plamenetz, *Consent, Freedom and Political Obligation* (London: Oxford Univ. Press, 1938) and Joseph Tussman, *Obligation and the Body Politic* (New York: Oxford Univ. Press, 1960).

THE MAJORITY

Why does the majority rather than some other more select (or more extensive) group have such conclusive authority? Locke's answer is strictly utilitarian, even mechanistic: "For that which acts any community being only the consent of the individuals in it, and it being one body must move one way, it is necessary the body should move that way whither the greatest force carries it, which is the consent of the majority; or else it is impossible it should act or continue one body, one community."[18] If, on the one hand, we agree that one man with his vote is roughly equal to another man with his vote, we are entitled to ask for more than a simple majority; but this demand is impractical, because if we wait for more than a simple majority to coalesce, we may wait too long. The community may move in no direction at all; it may simply stand still and be broken by the tide of events. If, on the other hand, we settle for less than a simple majority, the few become unequal in power, since they are pushing the many in a direction they do not want to go. If one asks, "But why precisely 50.01 percent?" one can always answer, "Why not?" Do we really have any more exalted reason than this for advocating majority rule?

The term "majority rule," of course, raises the well-known dilemma concerning minority rights: if the majority rules, minority rights are not absolute. If minority rights are absolute, the majority does not really rule. Locke simply avoided raising the question in this form and, by and large, so has American society. If we listen to a speech by the President, watch a well-run Congressional-committee hearing, or sit in a small-town planning commission, we discover that American political leaders tend to be impressed by both goals but unimpressed by the logical conflict between them. The illogic of Locke is possibly one clue to his continuing political relevance and the illogic of our Anglo-American political system one clue to its continuing success.[19]

By citing his majoritarian passages, Kendall has been able to argue that Locke is at heart a collectivist rather than an individualist. Kendall also contends that Locke's treatment of the individual himself is nonindividualistic: Locke's individuals "always prove, upon examination, to be highly socialized individuals . . . and the rights he claims for them, even in the state of nature, are the rights which have their origins in social needs."[20] Kendall's study served to draw attention to a major defect of Locke's liberalism and perhaps all liberalism—a term, incidentally, that was not applied to politics until several generations after Locke—the too easy identification of individual interests with society's interest. The term "collectivism," however, is a twentieth-century concept with but a strained relationship to seventeenth-century problems. Locke and his Whig brethren were certainly against one kind of collectivism, namely feudal corporativism. They wanted to "liberate" the individual from a rigidly hierarchical social order, hallowed by an official Church and sanctified by mystery.[21]

Actually, the issue of individual versus majority was almost irrelevant to the burning issue of the day, which was majority versus king, or, to be more realistic, Parliament versus king. James II was very unpopular and the anti-Jacobite Whigs had two-thirds of the votes in the House of Commons. Locke was giving the Whigs a political theory

[18] "Acts" is a verb.

[19] Whether cause or effect, the areas in which majority rights vis-à-vis minority or individual rights have been most precisely defined in American society have tended to be the areas most troublesome to us, for example, racial segregation and free speech for radicals.

[20] Wilmoore Kendall, "John Locke and the Doctrine of Majority Rule," *University of Illinois Studies in the Social Sciences*, Vol. 26 (1940–42), p. 66.

[21] Ironically, though he scorned medieval superstition and mystery, Locke was a great lover of mystery, inventing a code for his diary, cutting the signatures off letters he received, using various *noms de plume* in correspondence with friends—especially women friends. Such eccentricities have not made easier the historian's task.

that was persuasively antimonarchical and pro-Parliament. The preferred position that Parliamentary power had in Locke's theory is conspicuous. Parliament alone would seem to be the vehicle of the majority. In a given government "there can be but one supreme power, which is the legislative." It must, at least indirectly, control both the executive and the *federative,* or that which concerns "the power of war and peace, leagues and alliances." There is a residual power in the people, the community, to save themselves from the possible wicked designs "even of their legislators" but "this power of the people can never take place till the government be dissolved." The right of society or the community to break its bonds with an unjust monarch is discussed at length; the possibility of the legislative branch being tyrannical is barely mentioned. At the very end of the *Second Treatise* Locke repeats for emphasis what he had stated earlier: ". . . when the society hath placed the legislative in any assembly of men to continue in them and their successors, with direction and authority for providing such successors, the legislative can never revert to the people whilst that government lasts."[22]

Thus the sovereignty—or, for Locke, "supreme power"[23]—of the people never comes into play until all government is dissolved. This is the extreme case, what Locke calls the appeal to heaven. Meanwhile, the Parliament can be fairly well assumed to have the situation in control. In any practical application the Parliament is the people in Locke's theory. This was a theory of popular government, popular at least in the sense that ultimately "the people shall be judge." It seems less popular when we consider how thoroughly unrepresentative of the common man was the English Parliament of that time. In his incisive study of Locke's political theory, Gough gives us an assessment that reflects a healthy sense of realism:

> He appears to state his political theory in general philosophical terms, as if it were a purely logical deduction from general principles, but if we read between the lines we recognize the historic features of the English seventeenth-century constitution. . . . Locke's real starting point was not a mass of right-possessing individuals in a state of nature. . . . What he was really doing, under the guise of erecting a form of government on the basis of freely consenting individuals, was to describe the operation of the traditional English constitution in terms of the political philosophy current in his age.[24]

CONCLUSION: POLITICS AND PHILOSOPHY

One can hardly blame a tract-writer for couching his arguments in the most respectable philosophic trappings, even though they are only marginally relevant. Nor can one expect Locke to analyze at a sophisticated theoretical level the possible tyranny of legislatures when the king was the immediate enemy and the legislature was the ally in a good cause. But was Locke only a tract-writer? If so, why is the *Second Treatise* invariably excerpted in anthologies of the political greats? Could it be that the *Second Treatise* has been carried along all these years by the reputation of its author as a philosopher and the popularity of his political ideas with succeeding generations? Cobban once described Locke as "the writer whose influence pervades the eighteenth century with an almost scriptural authority." Yet the *Second Treatise* contains a number of passages that can best be described as carelessly written and suggestive of a less than devoted preparation. Many, in fact, would study Locke only as a "political prophet"—to use Parkinson's phrase—whose ideas reflected the

[22] Locke does, however, again mention the possibility of forfeiture of legislative authority, in which case it "reverts to the society" and the people "continue the legislative in themselves."

[23] Probably because it was used by both Hobbes and Filmer, the term "sovereignty" was never mentioned in the *Second Treatise*. It was used in reference to Filmer's theory in the *First Treatise*.

[24] John Gough, *John Locke's Political Philosophy* (Oxford: Clarendon Press, 1950), pp. 70–71.

seventeenth and influenced the eighteenth centuries. We can and have studied him in this way. But such study must inevitably have a slightly antiquarian flavor to a student of contemporary politics. How can Locke's politics clarify our own politics? This is the more urgent question.

Locke can help us understand the relationship between our own philosophical beliefs and our political beliefs. By themselves, Locke's political beliefs may appear to be historically limited, outdated. But his general philosophical position is more likely to be seen as relevant to the twentieth century. If the political corollaries of this philosophy can be recognized without their expression in seventeenth-century language, we may better see how close we are to Locke, after all. Although not universally recognized, there are, in fact, a number of parallels between Locke's epistemology and his politics.[25] Let us look first at his epistemology.

Locke's Epistemology

A primary objective of Locke's *Essay Concerning Human Understanding* is to undercut the argument for *innate ideas,* or universal principles in the mind of man discoverable by a priori reasoning. If this seems an essentially negative task, Locke is characteristically modest about it: ". . . everyone must not hope to be a Boyle or a Sydenham; and in an age which produces such masters as the great Huygenius, and the incomparable Mr. Newton . . . it is ambition enough to be employed as an under-laborer in clearing the ground a little, and removing some of the rubbish that lies in the way to knowledge."[26]

[25] See Walter M. Simon, "John Locke: Philosophy and Political Theory," *American Political Science Review,* Vol. 45 (1951), pp. 386–99. Simon sets out to disprove George Sabine's contention that there is no clear connection between Locke's philosophy and his political thought. See the latter's *History of Political Theory* (New York: Holt, Rinehart and Winston, 1937), pp. 528–31.

[26] *An Essay Concerning Human Understanding,* Epistle to the Reader, in *Works of John Locke,* J. A. St.-John, ed. (London: Bell, 1883), Vol. I, p. 121. Subsequent quotations from the *Essay* are from this edition.

In the Introduction to the *Essay* he makes a lucid plea for us to be content with the limits of our knowledge, to employ our minds for those purposes that may be of most use to us, and to avoid the futility of perplexing ourselves "out of an affectation of an universal knowledge." He insists we should not seek certainty "where probability only is to be had and which is sufficient to govern all our concernments."

Actually, of course, Locke does more than offer us reminders of our limitations: he offers us a new way of thinking; he lays the groundwork of British empiricism. And toward the end of the *Essay* he even forgets his disparagement of enthusiasm and his desire for universal maxims and, setting forth a prospect of synthesis worthy of Hobbes, rather ironically becomes most enthusiastic in stating the possibility of a universal mathematics of morals:

> They that are ignorant of algebra cannot imagine the wonders in this kind [sic] are to be done by it; and what farther improvements and helps, advantages to other parts of knowledge, the sagacious mind of man may yet find out, it is not easy to determine. . . . "Where there is no property there is no injustice" is a proposition as certain as any demonstration in Euclid. . . . I can as certainly know this proposition to be true as that a triangle has three angles equal to two right ones.[27]

The basic contention of British empiricism is contained in Locke's famous assertion:

> *All ideas come from sensation or reflection*—Let us then suppose the mind to be, as we say, white paper,[28] void of all characters, without any ideas; how comes it to be furnished? Whence comes it by that vast store which the busy and boundless fancy of man has painted on it with an almost endless variety? Whence has it all the materials of reason and knowledge? To this I answer, in one word, from experience.[29]

[27] *Ibid.,* Bk. IV, Ch. 3, sec. 18, Vol. II, pp. 154–55.

[28] Here and elsewhere Locke used the image of white paper as a symbol for the human mind at birth rather than the *tabula-rasa*—blank-slate—metaphor that is perennially attached to him. The latter term apparently became identified with Locke as a result of Leibnitz's constant use of it in criticizing him.

[29] *Essay,* Bk. II, Ch. 1, sec. 2, Vol. I, p. 205.

There are, to put it briefly, no innate ideas.

In their rejection of innate ideas both Locke and Hobbes might be called empiricists. In the customary sense of the term, however, Locke was empirical and Hobbes was not: Locke trusted to observation and experiment, or what is generally called the inductive method, rather than the logically deduced, rationalistic system preferred by Hobbes. There were, however, even in Locke residues of Cartesian rationalism: the passage quoted above about the certainty of geometry and the principles of justice is one example; the quest for the "true idea," fixed and clear, is another. There is something of the rationalistic spirit in Locke's famous distinction between primary and secondary qualities. Locke regarded primary qualities as those attributes of bodies wholly independent of our sensation: ". . . solidity, extension, figure, motion or rest, and number." He regarded secondary qualities as those arising in the perception of an object yet ultimately being merely reflections, in the perceiver, of primary qualities. He thought the secondary qualities included bulk, texture, colors, sounds, and tastes.[30]

The whole trend of Locke's thought, however, was away from abstract systematization and toward the particularization of ideas and words. Our ideas are produced in the reflection that follows perception. Complex ideas are but a compound of simple ideas. Very much as Robert Boyle put atoms together to make molecules and molecules together to make up more complex structures, Locke assembled the world of ideas: "Ideas of substances are nothing else but a collection of a certain number of simple ideas, considered as united in one thing." Like Hobbes, Locke could be called an atomist, although he avoids drawing the extreme case, as Hobbes was prone to do, and he does not carry the whole of experience back to matter in motion. Also like Hobbes, Locke is a nominalist: "Words in the primary or immediate signification stand for nothing but the ideas in the mind of him that uses them" and at root their signification is arbitrary. One of the great sources of human error is that through force of habit men "often suppose their words to stand for the reality of things," especially when dealing with the general nature of phenomena, "this whole mystery of *genera* and *species* which make such a noise in the schools." Actually, "general and universal belong not to the real existence of things; but are the inventions and the creatures of the understanding, made by it for its own use, and concern only signs, whether words or ideas. . . . When therefore we quit particulars, the generals that rest are only creatures of our own making."

[30] Although Bishop Berkeley later pointed out that everything Locke said about secondary qualities could also be said about primary qualities and thereby demolished the distinction, practical physics followed Locke for generations.

Epistemology and Politics

Locke's vivid analysis of the limits of abstract knowledge would seem to work against the success of any general theory applicable to a field as dynamic and complex as politics. Indeed, it is interesting that he chooses to call the loose words of ordinary conversation civil words as distinguished from more precise and exact terms, or philosophical words.

The parallels that obtain between Locke's political thought and his philosophy are probably significant not so much for the direct causal relation one bears to the other—though this is not to deny that there is such a relation—as for the suggestion they contain of a parallel between the prevailing *Weltanschauung* of the post-Lockean West and its political thought. Political thought is always a reflection of something more than simply the political. In this case a scientific world view is reflected in "liberal" politics. For example, the atomism of Locke's physics fits his view of the way complex ideas are compounded of simple ideas, which in turn corresponds to his picture of individuals coming together to form a state. Note also the mechanistic language in Locke's rationale for majority rule: a "body should move that way whither the greater force carries it." Again, his epistemological skepticism seems to be reflected in his nominalist view of the state. The good state for Locke is one that protects individual rights. But in the last analysis the rights are defined (by the legislature) subjectively rather than by reference to any objective standard of the good. To say this is to bring into question the whole concept of natural law as Locke uses it, and so we must do.

There is sometimes thought to be a contradiction between Locke's repudiation of innate ideas in the *Essay* and his stress on natural rights in the *Second Treatise*. The contention is that one cannot deny the force of a priori ideas in one place and affirm them in another; or again that men cannot have the same natural rights if they all have different experiences and all knowledge comes from experience. Gough has effectively shown that such an argument misinterprets Locke's understanding of natural rights, the law of nature, and the relationship between them. A key phrase for understanding Locke at this point is the "light of nature," an expression we encounter in the thought of Bayle. The *light of nature* is, for Locke, a "combination of the interdependent faculties of sense perception and reason. . . . The law of nature is not innate; what is knowable by the light of nature is the kind of truth at which a man may arrive, by himself and without extraneous help, through the right use of the faculties with which he was endowed by nature."[31] There is little doubt that, by themselves, men can arrive at a kind of truth and can base legitimate claims—natural rights—upon it; but insofar as this represents the operation of a law of nature, such a law appears to be almost procedural in character, that is, without a universal content that specifically commands certain acts. This position is a departure from traditional forms of natural law, which assume a universal, *objective*, moral order discoverable by the right use of reason.

If we recall the quotation from the *Essay* stating that "where there is no property there is no injustice" is as certain "as any demonstration in Euclid," we know that Locke hoped for a natural law as demonstrable as Euclid. But Locke could never elaborate natural law so conceived into a politically relevant code of particulars because he ran into the theological problem: being a Christian, Locke felt that natural law came from God and must ultimately rest on otherworldly sanctions. But he could not honestly say that reason demonstrates the existence of the other world. Thus it was that in 1695 he published anonymously *The Reasonableness of Christianity*, which tried to show not the reasonableness of belief in God or the other world but the reasonableness of New-Testament law. For this effort, as we saw, he was attacked—rightly, as being a Socinian and, wrongly, as being an atheist. His argument for a distinction between "the law of works," which was "the law of nature, knowable by reason," and the "law of faith," which was belief in God and Jesus as the Christ, could not be validated by reason. In defending the reasonableness of the Scriptures he was led to repudiate the doctrine of original sin, the Athanasian Creed, and other Trinitarian expressions and to try to rationalize the "simple teaching" of Jesus, "free from the corrupting and loosening glosses of the scribes and Pharisees."

But Locke is forced to grant that strict obedience to the law of works in the New Testament is not necessarily rewarded with political success. How many successful political—or other—leaders can consistently "turn the other cheek," "walk the second mile," "take no thought for their lives," "judge not," et cetera? Really fundamental virtue, it seems, must rest on otherworldly sanctions; and the law of reason that has bearing on success and happiness in this world is therefore what Strauss has called a partial law of nature, closer to Hobbes's ideal of self-preservation than to the New Testament's command of self-sacrifice. Thus, in the last analysis, Locke's major political tenets—government by consent, majority rule, the rights of property, and even the whole idea of the state of nature—are but dimly related to the law of nature Locke set out to establish. In the end he was left with fideism rather than the "reasonableness of Christianity." Is Locke's persistence in using nat-

[31] Gough, p. 14. It is probably safe to say that Jefferson's "inalienable" rights are not "innate" in the traditional sense, either.

ural-law terminology in his political theory therefore but a sign of his confusion and ineptness? If so, does he deserve to be placed among the great political theorists?

It is Strauss's conclusion that the inconsistencies "are so obvious that they cannot have escaped the notice of a man of his rank and his sobriety."[32] Locke probably knew very well that he was deviating from traditional natural law toward a more utilitarian standard. Locke was a man of great prudence and caution who knew that revolutionary ideas cannot always be put forth in bold-faced terms. Recall that he held up publication of the *Two Treatises* until 1689, when the political revolution he defended would be acceptable to the victorious Whig revolutionaries, and even then he chose to remain anonymous. But the deeper intellectual-moral revolution, the shift from transcendent to utilitarian standards of political morality, might not be acceptable even to Whig revolutionaries, who would have liked to think that they were acting with God's blessing.

Thus, while there were major inconsistencies both within Locke's political thought and between his political thought and his philosophical writings, at the level of greatest significance there is a close correlation between the *Essay*'s admonition to rest content within the modest limits of our knowledge, to let probability "govern all our concernments," to eschew universal knowledge and improve life within the frame of observation and experience and the optimistic, common-sense, utilitarian conclusions to be drawn from the *Second Treatise*.

Those of us who live in modern, Western, "democratic" societies are indeed Lockeans but not simply because we believe that man came out of a state of nature to form government by mutual consent or that natural law dictates what that government and its citizens should do. If we think about these things at all, it is probably with little conviction. We are Lockean because, however unsure we are about natural law, we feel God, or nature, or life has given us certain *rights*. It was Locke even more decisively than Hobbes who transformed natural law into natural rights. He replaced faith in a universal, objective moral order with belief in the validity of subjective claims for earthly happiness. Locke's theory of property bears this out as much as any other aspect of his thought: it is labor that produces the value of everything. In a sense, then, man can by labor create his own world; the role of government is simply to enable him to do so without necessarily involving him in the problem of defining the common moral ends of production.

We like Locke because he seems to be an individualist but we are not sure individualism is relevant any more. We are beginning to have doubts about Locke's optimistic conclusions concerning a rights-oriented society. We are not quite Lockean any more but we are not yet anything else. We still think of ourselves as citizens of a secularized, rights-claiming, theoretically individualized, economy-oriented world. This is Locke's world. But we are not sure that we can or should expect it to last much longer.

[32] Leo Strauss, *Natural Right and History* (Chicago: Univ. of Chicago Press, 1953), p. 220. It is Professor Strauss's great contribution to our understanding of historical political theory to remind us of an author's need to conceal his true intent in much political writing of the past. Political theory is often more than meets the eye. Sometimes, however, as a result of making consistency an almost inevitable attribute of the theorist, Strauss is led to regard simple human mistakes as part of a grand esoteric design. But the application to Locke seems pertinent.

13

THE EIGHTEENTH CENTURY

In political theory the eighteenth century belongs to France as surely as the seventeenth century belongs to England. Germany was beginning to be heard from and a tiny group of American colonies produced some well-tailored constitutional speculations. But when we think of the eighteenth century, we think of the Enlightenment and, when we think of the Enlightenment, we think of France. As England's international and colonial power rose, the fertility of her political thought declined. In France, the reverse order obtained.

Political theory in the eighteenth century can be organized around five new developments that provide us with the structure of this chapter: (1) a new philosophical orientation called the Enlightenment, stressing faith in the unity of nature, human reason, and a secularized natural law; (2) the birth of laissez-faire economics; (3) a new emphasis on a progressive order of history; (4) a new concern with constitution-making; (5) a set of data for theorizing about revolution.

THE ENLIGHTENMENT

The Enlightenment is the name we give to the philosophical movement that put its faith in reason by pitting reason against faith. Despite many antecedents in the seventeenth century, the movement is identified with the eighteenth century because that century produced a self-conscious rejection of religion as the guiding authority in art, morals, politics, and scholarship. A new spirit of critical inquiry, "reason," took religion's place. This movement had political causes as well as political effects. The eighteenth century was a period of intense struggle between dynastic sovereigns for control of colonies and heretofore semiautonomous provinces. By contrast with England, the Continental representative assemblies were the refuge of reaction, the seat of feudal privilege. In their struggle to gain ascendancy over them, such sovereigns as Frederick the Great of Prussia, Joseph II of Austria, and Catherine the Great of Russia adopted the antifeudal ideology of the Enlightenment, thus becoming enlightened despots, much admired by French intellectuals.

The *philosophes,* or popular philosophers of France, applauded anyone, king or commoner, who attacked the old order. Their bitterness toward the Church was especially deep. Their success was phenomenal:

> In the middle of the eighteenth century they constituted a literary clique in Paris, barely known outside of its walls; by 1789 it might be

said that virtually the entire body of educated opinion was now on their side. A revolution in ideas had taken place. . . . In their war against the Old Regime the *philosophes* succeeded, in a remarkably short time, in completely discrediting its institutions and ideals. In religion they spread incredulity and indifference, even more than hostility.[1]

As the Church bureaucracy lost power, the state bureaucracy gained it. A by-product of the monarchs' drive for control was the growth of centralized governmental administration, which fixed itself on the land with a permanence known only to bureaucracies. While designed primarily to prevent local magistrates from having their own way with loose interpretations of customary law, eventually the proliferations of bureaucratic rules came to operate as a check on the whims of the autocrat himself. By 1741 Hume was able to observe, not with complete accuracy, "It may now be affirmed of civilized monarchies what was formerly said in praise of Republics alone, *that they are a government of laws not of men.*"[2] As economic prosperity came to commercial interests, monarchs identified their own good fortune with governmental centralization and increased opportunity for individuals and they identified both these tendencies with the victory of "reason" over the shackles of the past. In England the Whig party represented a happy compromise of commercial interests with the country nobility. Their triumph in 1688 foreshadowed a relatively placid eighteenth-century domestic scene. But in France the antagonism between the commercial interests and the nobility festered until it erupted in the Revolution.

But along with the political tensions ran an infectious sense of discovery and intellectual excitement. Let one of the *philosophes* describe it:

the discovery and application of a new method of philosophizing, the kind of enthusiasm which accompanies discoveries, a certain exaltation of ideas which the spectacle of the universe produces in us—all these have brought about a lively fermentation of minds. Spreading through nature in all directions like a river which has burst its dams, this fermentation has swept with a sort of violence everything along with it which stood in its way. . . . from the principles of the secular sciences to the foundations of religious revelation, from metaphysics to matters of taste, from music to morals, from the scholastic disputes of theologians to matters of trade, from the laws of princes to those of peoples, from natural law to the arbitrary laws of nations . . . everything has been discussed and analyzed.[3]

Voltaire and the *Philosophes*

The central vision of the *philosophes* was the unity of nature under an overarching natural science. Denis Diderot, who with Jean d'Alembert edited the great French *Encyclopédie,* ranks with Bacon as a popular exponent of experimental method. Like Bacon, whom he helped restore to prominence, Diderot was uninterested in abstract mathematical systems but rather stressed the practical and technological side of science. The *Encyclopédie* was filled with drawings of industrial devices and gadgets. Voltaire played with science, collecting specimens of this and that to no particular end. Mixed with this practical, unspiritual bent, however, was an enthusiasm that took on an almost religious quality of its own. Diderot read Bayle and was stimulated by his faith in man's "inner light." Baron Paul Henri Dietrich d'Holbach, whose *System of Nature* was the most extreme and clear-cut statement of Enlightenment materialism and atheism, closes the work with a glowing devotional to nature, "the sovereign of all beings."[4]

All these men followed Locke's sensationalist psychology and epistemology,[5] and none

[1] J. Salwyn Schapiro, *Condorcet and the Rise of Liberalism* (New York: Harcourt, Brace & World, 1934), p. 34.

[2] David Hume, "Of Civil Liberty," in C. W. Hendel, ed., *Political Essays* (New York: Liberal Arts Press, 1953), p. 106.

[3] Jean d'Alembert, *Elements de philosophie* (1759). Quoted in Ernst Cassirer, *The Philosophy of the Enlightenment,* trans. by F. C. A. Koelln and J. P. Pettegrove (Boston: Beacon Press, 1955), p. 4.

[4] The passage may, however, have been written by Diderot.

[5] Étienne Bonnot de Condillac tried to extend Locke's

more enthusiastically than Voltaire (François Marie Arouet, 1694–1778). Voltaire spent the years between 1726 and 1729 in England and returned home Locke's ardent disciple. Locke, he felt, had done for the human mind what Newton had done for nature. Voltaire's mission in life became that of using his magnificent powers of ridicule to advance Lockean ideas. But Locke's politics tended to accompany his epistemology. It was ironic that, while in England Locke's political theory was mainly a rationale for established interests, in France it became a radical attack on the *status quo*. Voltaire, who became famous as a radical reformer, never intended to be a political revolutionary. Like most *philosophes,* he considered enlightened despotism an acceptable (though not necessarily ideal) avenue of reform; and he was, for a while, a good friend of Frederick the Great. Moreover, most of the *philosophes* preferred talking to acting. While the political discussions in the Paris salons were scintillating, there was nevertheless an air of artificiality about them. No one was much moved to march out into the streets to organize the unsavory masses.

Voltaire, however, cannot be said to have been timid. His honest fear of the mob was mixed with his forthright hatred of oppressors. He served time in the Bastille, was chronically in exile for his attacks on revered authority, and saved a number of lives by virtue of his intervention on behalf of the unjustly condemned. That he was not a revolutionary cannot be blamed on either lack of courage or lack of intelligence. Voltaire had both. He simply could not sustain a really optimistic position. He hoped to make the world only a little better: "It is impossible in our melancholy world to prevent men living in society from being divided into two classes, one the rich who command, the other the poor who obey. . . . Equality, then, is at the same time the most natural and the most chimerical thing possible."[6] Candide's resigned, somewhat bitter advice at the end of Voltaire's novel may have been the author speaking: ". . . let us cultivate our garden."

How, then, did the *philosophes* come to be known as revolutionary figures? Part of the answer may come from their attitude toward religion. Voltaire's position could best be summed up by saying that the mass of men ought to believe in some religion so that they will behave themselves. Metaphysics, for most of the *philosophes,* was wholly subordinate to morals. But men cannot long believe in a God who is but a tool of expedience. The persistent efforts of the *philosophes* to lead men away from traditional faith and their inability to replace it with something else in time bred the passionate religion of the state that became the soul of the French Revolution. What began as indifference ended as hostility: "Nowhere except in France had irreligion become as yet an all-prevailing passion, fierce, intolerant, and predatory."[7]

Yet the Enlightenment supposedly was a period of great optimism. What of the religion of reason as a substitute for orthodox religion? For some men, such as Condorcet, the new faith could support continuing evangelism. Voltaire, however, was too much of a realist to be carried away by high hopes. His sense of new knowledge that could save the world was continually being mixed with disgust that the world was rejecting it. It was Carl Becker in his now-classic *Heavenly City of the Eighteenth-Century Philosophers* (1932) who, seeing the paradox of skepticism

epistemology to more rigorous limits than Locke had done and traced "reflection" to language rather than simply to a "power" produced by sensation. His psychology was both systematic and influential.

6 "Equality" in *The Philosophical Dictionary,* trans. by William F. Fleming, in Lord Morley, ed., *The Works of Voltaire* (New York: Dingwall-Rock, 1927), Vol. IV, Part II, pp. 262 and 264.

7 Alexis de Tocqueville, *The Old Regime and the French Revolution* (1856), trans. by S. Gilbert (Garden City, N. Y.: Doubleday, Anchor, 1955), p. 149. De Tocqueville has also shown how the absolutism of the *ancien régime* made Frenchmen more and more like each other at the same time that citizens were erecting façades of separate interests to preserve their pride. Only by understanding this phenomenon, said De Tocqueville, can we understand "how it was that a successful revolution could tear down the whole social structure almost in the twinkling of an eye."

and faith, drew a parallel between the thirteenth and the eighteenth centuries:

There were, certainly, many differences between Voltaire and St. Thomas Aquinas, but the two men had much in common for all that. What they had in common was the profound conviction that their beliefs could be reasonably demonstrated. In a very real sense it may be said of the eighteenth century that it was an age of faith as well as of reason and of the thirteenth century that it was an age of reason as well as of faith.[8]

But Voltaire's faith was scarcely untroubled. Touched by the suffering of men, he could be magnanimous: "What is toleration?" he wrote in the *Philosophical Dictionary*. "It is the appurtenance of humanity. We are all full of weakness and errors; let us mutually pardon each other our follies—it is the first law of nature."[9] More often he was incapable of pardoning others' folly: *Candide* was a classic of biting satire on the follies of extreme optimism; the parody of Leibnitz' philosophy that "all is the best possible" becomes a whip to lash the reader with a consciousness of man's persistent stupidity.

This disjuncture of hopes and reality helps to explain Voltaire's failure to produce a systematic political theory. It is too simple merely to attribute this failure to the fatal flaw of a mind "discursive and tangential rather than orderly and concentrated."[10] His hopes were at once too high and too low to produce a rounded political theory. The same kind of hopeless hopefulness, militant fatalism, and passionate dispassion is evident in Diderot: "Self-interest has produced priests, priests have produced prejudices, prejudices have produced wars, and wars will continue as long as there are prejudices, prejudices as long as there are priests, and priests as long as self-interest calls them into being."[11]

The closest thing to an orderly theoretical development in Voltaire comes in the *Essai sur les moeurs* (*Essay on Customs*), where he speaks of the two empires, the Empire of Nature, which reveals itself in the unity of all mankind, and the Empire of Custom, which accounts for the great diversity among groups, sects, and nations.[12] From a similar assumption of ultimate human uniformity Hume and Montesquieu are led to place great weight on the causal influence of institutions in creating diversity. Voltaire would seem to share this view, yet he always stresses the spirit rather than the form. He is interested only marginally in such things as the proper construction of constitutions. Abstract theories could never crowd out Voltaire's concern with questions of practical morals. Nevertheless, he thought it was the task of the philosopher to reconcile these two empires, to make custom conform to the more fundamental empire of nature. Thus, against legal codes he put natural law, against traditional Christianity he put natural religion, and against the cramped privileges of the *ancien régime* he put natural rights.

He did pay enough attention to legal problems to deride the corpus of modern civil and criminal law. He compared it to the uneven, squalid, ramshackle growth of the large, unplanned cities. The law could be, he felt, as orderly and acceptable as the rules of chess if it were constructed rationally in the interests of the player-citizen. At that time it con-

[8] Carl L. Becker, *The Heavenly City of the Eighteenth-Century Philosophers* (New Haven: Yale Univ. Press, 1932), p. 8. See also R. R. Palmer, "Thoughts on *The Heavenly City*," in R. O. Rockwood, ed., *Carl Becker's Heavenly City Revisited* (Ithaca: Cornell Univ. Press, 1958), pp. 123–28. A criticism of Becker's emphasis on the rationalism of the Enlightenment is well made by Peter Gay in "The Enlightenment in the History of Political Theory," *Political Science Quarterly*, Vol 69 (1954), pp. 374–89. See also Peter Gay, *Voltaire's Politics, the Poet as Realist* (Princeton: Princeton Univ. Press, 1959), and his *The Enlightenment: An Interpretation* (New York: Knopf, 1966).

[9] *Works*, Vol. VII, Part II, p. 100.

[10] J. B. Black, "Voltaire," in F. J. C. Hearnshaw, ed., *The Social and Political Ideas of Some Great French Thinkers of the Age of Reason* (London: Harrap, 1930), p. 136.

[11] *La Promenade du sceptique* (1747), Discours Prélim., in *Oeuvres complètes* (Paris: Garnier, 1875), Vol. I, p. 183. There is more consistency to this pessimistic element in eighteenth-century French thought than is often recognized. See Henry Vyverberg, *Historical Pessimism in the French Enlightenment* (Cambridge, Mass.: Harvard Univ. Press, 1958) and Gay, *Voltaire's Politics*.

[12] Ch. 197, *Oeuvres complètes* (Paris: Lefebvre, 1829), Vol. XX, pp. 307–25. See Black.

sisted of the irrational accretions of generations of special interest. In great impatience he argued for wiping away *all* existing law, this baggage from the dead past. Give to contemporaries the task of formulating a simple, logical system of laws. Almost any group of reasonable men could do it. Coke would have shuddered. Yet not too many years later the Napoleonic Code came close to what Voltaire hoped for.

Voltaire's support of Locke and natural rights, however, did not make him a believer in a state of nature. Man, he felt, was naturally gregarious and, indeed, owed natural duties to the state.[13] Nor did inequality of possessions bother him. The *philosophes* were neither pie-in-the-sky optimists nor radical egalitarians. In the last analysis, however, we must mark these men down for optimists and for liberals whose optimism marred their liberalism. They were great admirers of the English Constitution because it protected individual property rights. They were disturbed by autocracy in France because individuals suffered. Political problems that had dimensions other than the individual did not interest them. Even attacks on the Church were based primarily on the argument for individual freedom.[14] In one sense, there was no problem of society for these men, only problems of individuals. From them, in part, came the preoccupation of liberalism with the individual and the neglect of groups of which he must necessarily be a part. From them, in part, came liberalism's unbounded faith in education. Freedom is everything and knowledge is freedom: "In fact, what does it mean to be free? It means to know the rights of man, for to know them is to defend them."[15]

Utilitarianism: Helvetius

By *utilitarianism* we mean a general predisposition to judge social policies in terms of their utility, or use-value, rather than by other presumably more metaphysical standards. We also mean, more specifically, a school of thought originating in England and France that accepted as a basic explanation of human behavior the desire to gain pleasure and avoid pain and extended this principle into a general definition of the *good*: to maximize pleasure and minimize pain.

Despite his Lockean psychology, Voltaire remained largely the rationalistic moralist to the end. Diderot moved in the course of his life away from natural-law thinking toward utilitarian ethics. Claude Adrien Helvetius (1715–71), an important influence on Bentham, moved even further in this direction. Helvetius, a wealthy farmer-general whose salon was a frequent meeting place for the *philosophes,* is best remembered for the famous utilitarian standard, "the greatest good for the greatest number," a standard that theoretically could be applied to ethical questions without reliance on natural law or natural rights. He also propounded what Halévy has called "the principle of the artificial identification of interests,"[16] that is, that men can be assumed to act only in their own self-interest but a well-regulated system of punishments will enable the legislator to channel these interests toward the public good. Helvetius' aim was to "treat morals like any other science and to make an experimental morality like an experimental physics."[17]

The concept of interest was the key to this science, comparable to the laws of motion in the physical universe. The laws of interest were at one and the same time the key to how

[13] See Constance Rowe, *Voltaire and the State* (New York: Columbia Univ. Press, 1955).

[14] See Diderot, *Memoirs of a Nun,* trans. by Francis Birrell (Chester Springs, Pa.: Dufour, 1959).

[15] Voltaire. Quoted in Cassirer, p. 251.

[16] Elie Halévy, *The Growth of Philosophic Radicalism,* trans. by Mary Morris (Boston: Beacon Press, 1955), p. 19. This may be compared to Bernard de Mandeville (1670–1733) in *The Fable of the Bees,* who found in the world a natural identification of individual and public interests. If people were left alone, "private vices" would become "publick virtues." The connection between this view and the assumptions of the laissez-faire economics of Adam Smith is important. See p. 351, below.

[17] *De l'esprit,* Preface. Quoted in Halévy, p. 19. The similarity here to Hobbes is striking, a similarity Halévy overlooks.

men behaved and how they ought to behave. Since the union of is and ought cannot be as simple as this concept would seem to assume, a distinction appeared in Helvetius between a misunderstood interest and a man's true interest, which it was the business of the legislator and the educator to point out to the individual. Here are the seeds—some of them, at any rate—of the welfare state. The importance of education and legislation in helping individuals achieve their own best interest is an important tenet in the liberal tradition. But so is the belief that, despite this helping hand, the individual's interests are still his own. And each man's—and woman's; Helvetius was a feminist—interest was worth about as much as any other man's. Even at this date the egalitarian drive inherent in utilitarian ethics was manifest. It was not the omnipotence of man, however, but the omnipotence of the environment that was ostensibly confirmed by Helvetius' theories. Man was a product of his environment—except that some men, the legislators, somehow transcended this limitation and were able to modify the environment. "Make good laws; they alone will naturally direct the people in the pursuit of the public advantage, by following the irresistible propensity they have to their private advantage. . . . It is of little consequence that men be vicious; it is enough that they be intelligent. . . . Laws do all."[18] In this way were the gates to limitless historical progress opened.

The shift from natural law to a simple pleasure-pain explanation of man appears to be fundamental and, indeed, it is. But Helvetius was too much affected by the eighteenth-century environment to see this shift as we might. He shared with others the common faith in the unity of nature, the permanence of truth, and even the Cartesian ideal of a universal mathematics as the "alphabet of nature." In these ways he was closer to the natural-law tradition than most twentieth-century empiricists would be. He began not so much with the method of scientific inquiry as with a metaphysical notion of "nature"—in whose name he attacked metaphysics. Moreover, Helvetius had no real psychology. His understanding of interests was largely external and his tendency was to think in terms of manipulating individuals rather than understanding their inner motivations. He measured an individual's enlightenment more by action than by motive. In this way freedom itself became externalized. Yet the free individual is still important enough to Helvetius to make him spar with the problem: ". . . the freedom of man consists in the free exercise of his power; I say *his* power, because it would be ridiculous to regard as non-freedom our inability to pierce the clouds like an eagle, live under the water like a whale, or make ourselves kings."[19] This comes dangerously close to saying that man is free to do what he is free to do.

The certitude, simplicity, and mechanical qualities of Helvetius' utilitarianism fitted well into the *philosophes'* political program—or, rather, their political lack of a program—namely enlightened despotism, for, if the calculation of social goods is as scientific as Helvetius' utilitarianism would make it appear to be, then obviously lawmaking is a matter for expert determination rather than for bargaining and compromise. Father knows best has been the attitude of all autocracies. In recent times scientific authority—the expert knows best—has been added to the other sources of strength in the autocratic arsenal—sometimes with peril to the autocrat. In the history of ideas seen from a Western vantage point Helvetius' utilitarianism has often been put in the democratic ledger because of its influence on egalitarian thinkers. But its logic can just as easily lead in the opposite direction.

Godwin

The principal English interpreter of the French Encyclopedists was William Godwin

[18] *Treatise on Man,* II, 300–301. Quoted in Charles Frankel, *The Faith of Reason, The Idea of Progress in the French Enlightenment* (New York: King's Crown Press, 1948), p. 58.

[19] *De l'esprit,* Disc. I, Ch. 4, in *Oeuvres complètes* (Paris: Garnery, 1793), Vol. I, pp. 298–99.

(1756–1836). He was trained as a Calvinist clergyman but, after he had spent five years as a pastor in a country parish, his faith was shaken when he read Holbach's *System of Nature*. He left his parish, no longer a Tory and no longer a Calvinist, but something of the Calvinist's stern moral discipline remained with him always.[20] Although he wrote novels, essays, histories, and other works in great profusion, Godwin's major work was *An Enquiry Concerning Political Justice*. Begun in 1791 and finished in 1793, it was a great statement of faith in the French Revolution—or at least in the ideals of the French Revolution, for Godwin himself was opposed to revolutions.

Specifically, Godwin can be regarded as a disciple of Helvetius, sharing his view of the universe as a vast chain of cause and effect, a Newtonian mechanistic world, although Godwin could not go as far as Holbach and declare himself a materialist. The key argument —and, in fact, the core of his life's work—was on behalf of the perfectibility of the human species. Education can remake man. His character is not, as Montesquieu believed, formed by climate, nor, as Burke believed, cramped by dark, ineradicable passions. The vice in man results from error, which reason can correct.

Two quite different strains were at work in Godwin. On the one hand, he was a rationalist, declaring for a justice higher than any government and a reason higher than any positive law. Political institutions "to be good must have constant relation to the rules of immutable justice . . . [which] uniform in their nature, are equally applicable to the whole human race."[21] Most laws should be abolished, for "Reason is a thousand times more explicit and intelligible than law; and when we are accustomed to consult her, the certainty of her decisions would be such, as men practiced in our present courts are totally unable to conceive." On the other hand, Godwin adhered to a much more low-level, Helvetian pleasure-pain psychology: "The points in which human beings resemble are infinitely more considerable than those in which they differ. We [all] have the same senses. . . . Sensual pleasure on the one hand, or intellectual on the other is, absolutely speaking, the highest and most desirable."

But of the two strains, the rationalist emphasis seems clearly to dominate. Take his discussion of forms of government, for example. The moralistic tone is overwhelming. Monarchy as a form of government is "essentially corrupt." It is "founded in imposture." Aristocracy, too, is "in direct opposition to all sound morality, and all generous independence of character." Both rest on deceitful assumptions of natural inequality. So-called mixed governments are likewise mere "imposture." Only democracy is in any way acceptable to Godwin and he is scarcely enthusiastic about that. Like Rousseau he felt that representative arrangements involved unwarranted abnegations of individual judgment; but unlike Rousseau he worried over the protection of minorities—the argument had a close parallel to that of John Stuart Mill's "On Liberty"—and he was not at all taken in by *vox populi*: ". . . the voice of the people is not, as has sometimes been ridiculously asserted, 'the voice of truth and God' . . . universal consent cannot convert wrong into right."[22]

Godwin was an extreme egalitarian who

[20] This Calvinist rectitude may appear to have deserted Godwin in his relationship with Mary Wollstonecraft, handsome and famous defender of the rights of women. She was thirty-seven, he was forty when they met. It was love at first sight—"the purest, most refined state of love," said Godwin—whereupon they lived together without benefit of marriage until shortly before the birth of their only child. But this was a matter of moral principle, not immorality, for Godwin had already attacked the institution of marriage on moral grounds. The experience of marriage helped change his mind as to its value and, indeed, the short but blissful relationship with Mary affected his whole philosophy, leading, he said, to a reexamination of the "empire of feeling." Mary died tragically a few days after childbirth. See C. Kegan Paul, *William Godwin* (London: King, 1876), Vol. I, p. 294.

[21] *An Enquiry Concerning Political Justice,* 3rd ed., Bk. V, Ch. 1, in F. E. L. Priestly, ed. (Toronto: Univ. of Toronto Press, 1946), Vol. II, p. 2. Subsequent quotations from the *Enquiry* are from this edition.

[22] See David Fleisher, *William Godwin: A Study in Liberalism* (London: Allen & Unwin, 1951).

permitted property in his system only that it might be given away. Yet he was not a communist, for he did not like the thought of organized group cooperation either. About all that is left is anarchism, so we call Godwin an anarchist. He did believe in anarchism but not in anarchy. The distinction is fundamental and may be Godwin's most striking contribution: *anarchy* to Godwin meant every man free to do as he liked, a condition he despised; *anarchism,* by contrast, meant society functioning without a government. This Godwin dearly desired. But such a condition could not be achieved as a result of every man going his own way; it required the voluntary self-regulation of each individual for the public good. Here Calvinist discipline and duty come again to the fore. Godwin's ringing demand was for a spirit of "universal benevolence," attainable only by education. It was the aspiration to this universal benevolence, each man a brother to every other man, that led him for a time to advocate elimination of the family.

Godwin is fascinating because he marvelously combined the worst and the best in Enlightenment faith. With a mechanical psychology that trampled on moral subtleties and with a dogmatic conviction that science would conquer evil as it conquered nature, he blended a simple faith in man's capacity to reason, to improve himself, and to feel the tides of "universal benevolence" out of which comes duty to the common good. Though we cannot make Godwin into a great political theorist, we must admit that he was a good and courageous man whose aspirations reveal some of the positive values that have given liberalism as a movement emotional force.

ECONOMICS AND POLITICS

Politics and economics always go hand in hand. Tender souls repelled by crass money matters sometimes hold this against politics, apparently believing that if legislators talked more about the good life and less about the gross national income we would be better off. They may be right. The simple fact remains, however, that politics is particularly tied to common concerns—the things that bother most people—and staying alive and eating well have always bothered more people more insistently than knowing the truth or contemplating the beautiful. Even totalitarian dictators must see that people are fed and bridges are built before turning to the esthetics and morals of the party line. Economics is fundamental.

But there was a time, the feudal period, when economic relationships were welded to a status system that scarely changed from one generation to the next. The ratio of births to deaths was stable. Geographic explorations were few. Economics was still basic but economic questions were fixed because, relatively speaking, the society was static. By the sixteenth and seventeenth centuries neither economics nor politics was static; we can recall the theoretical interest in economics displayed by students of government, such as Harrington and Locke. But it was not until the eighteenth century that economic turmoil and the Enlightenment faith in science joined to produce a new "economic science." Whether the Physiocrats, or the Kameralists, or Smith should receive the trophy as founder of modern economics is a moot point. All of them made their contribution.

The Physiocrats

The founder of the school known as the Physiocrats was François Quesnay, a court physician to Louis XV who specialized in royal mistresses. Although he had written two articles for Diderot's *Encyclopédie* in the 1750s, it was late in that decade, when he was well into his sixties, before Quesnay published anything in economics. The birth of the Physiocratic school dates from an interview Quesnay had in July, 1757, with Victor Riqueti, Marquis de Mirabeau, author of *Ami des hommes* (*Friend of Man*). The next year Quesnay published his *Tableau oeconomique* (*Economic Table*), an elaborate chart of the economy modeled on the human circulatory system and not unlike some of the flow charts we see in introductory economics textbooks. The group, which originally was called simply *Les Économistes,* included, in addition to Quesnay and Mirabeau, Jean de Gournay, Mercier de la Rivière, Dupont de Nemours, and, though he disliked the label, Jacques Turgot. As Minister of Finance, Turgot in 1774 tried to put Physiocratic theories into practice, without much success.

The Physiocrats symbolize four phenomena: a reaction against the past, some economic axioms, a practical political program, and a set of philosophic assumptions. The reaction against the past was directed at feudal inefficiencies and mercantilist restrictions. Tolls, monopolies, privileged hunting—any of the feudal vestiges that were wasteful, choked off trade, or inhibited consumption—were opposed. In France, mercantilism was most closely identified with the policies of Louis XIV's great finance minister Jean Colbert. It connoted strict state control of the economy, protective tariffs, centralized taxation, economic exploitation of colonies, and subordination of agriculture to commerce and manufacturing. Wealth, mercantilists felt, consisted in bullion and nations could prosper only at each others' expense. It is not surprising that the Physiocrats opposed such policies. What followed these policies and therefore seemed to be caused by them was the economic malaise of France. Wars, fantastic monarchical extravagance, and the expulsion of Protestants had increased the debt and reduced the population. The French merchant marine had been ruined by the Seven Years' War. The population had declined by four million between 1660 and 1715. Two-thirds of the tax revenues were being consumed by the cost of collection; agricultural production had fallen off precipitously.

The basic economic axiom that the Physiocrats hurled against mercantilism was the view that ultimately only agriculture can generate economic value. Though mistaken, their conclusion is understandable not only on the basis of the economic facts just mentioned but from the world scene as the French saw it. England, where there had been recent great strides in agriculture, was prosperous. Commercially oriented Holland was declining. Spain was declining, possibly because she had tried to develop her marine power at the expense of agriculture. Quesnay was aware that money was important to France but its importance to him was mainly as a stimulus to agriculture. Agriculture is the "surest source of revenue" for the state, since only agriculture can produce a surplus profit for the owner. By contrast, the Physiocrats saw trade and industry, operating on a narrower margin, as sterile. In criticizing the shortcomings of Locke's labor theory of value, they went so far as to make human labor wholly subsidiary to land as the source of economic value.[23]

But if the land was to be productive, several requirements needed to be met: wastefulness and parasitical commercial elements had to be eliminated; large capital investments in land had to be encouraged (the larger the landowner, the greater the surplus profit); and a free market for goods had to be provided. Hence came a policy and with it a name graven deeply into the Western consciousness: *laissez faire, laissez passer*. The government was to keep its hands off trade.[24] The Physiocrats had no direct concern with such political questions as the right of suffrage or the proper construction of constitutions. Apart from questions of trade and colonialism they could not be said to be antigovernment. But their program had all

[23] See G. Wenlersse, "Physiocrats," in *Encyclopaedia of the Social Sciences* (New York: Macmillan, 1931), Vol. V, pp. 348–51; and Henry Higgs, *The Physiocrats* (New York: Macmillan, 1897).

[24] But their use of the term "laissez faire" did not mean the Physiocrats foreshadowed all that it came to mean: "Quesnay's *Maximes* were intended to provide [an omniscient] government with the viewpoints necessary to translate into practical policy the principles of the *Tableau* on the basis of statistical data which he offered to have furnished periodically. The idea of a self-regulating system of markets had never as much as entered his mind" (Karl Polanyi, *The Great Transformation* [Boston: Beacon Press, 1957], p. 135). The Physiocrats favored government protection of agriculture to such an extent that their position has been called an inverted, agrarian mercantilism.

sorts of political consequences. They defended various liberties regarded as corollaries of the right of private property, for example, the right freely to sell one's services and the property in one's person and the right to sell one's goods unchecked even by international conventions. This point of view assumes a legal equality of sorts, though it also takes for granted existing inequalities among participants in the economic process.

The philosophical underpinnings given these views probably came after the fact rather than before. These men were reacting more to conspicuous economic conditions than to subtle theories, which makes all the more impressive the degree to which they could bring the basic Enlightenment assumptions to bear on their policy. Employing the characteristic Enlightenment mode of geometric reasoning, they felt they had a hold on fixed a priori laws of nature concerning economic relations, laws that would stand forever. Government was not as irrelevant to the natural harmony of the universal order as it was to Smith's concept of the "invisible hand" guiding market transactions but there is no doubt that the Physiocrats believed in such an order.

Turgot

Jacques Turgot (1727–81) was the most philosophically inclined Physiocrat. Possibly for that reason he was separated somewhat from the rest. He carried furthest the idea of inevitable progress. Indeed, his faith in the "ubiquity of reason," to use Frankel's phrase, led him to the most un-*philosophe* extreme of lecturing in 1750 on the contribution Christianity had made to progress. "Turgot found continuity everywhere, and wherever he found continuity he inferred progress."[25] Thus every shred and tatter of history, however soiled, contributes something to the advance of mankind. Every "mutation" brings some advantage. Willy-nilly such reasoning brought Turgot to the dilemma of every monistic system: either every act of history is directed and we are but pawns, or no act of history is directed and chance makes progress meaningless.

But men do not have to be good philosophers to make a contribution to political theory and the Physiocrats did make a contribution. They took Locke's individualism but rejected his labor theory of value. They took faith in a natural order from the *philosophes* and applied it to economics, where it has remained alive longer than in most other areas. (Examine, for example, the speeches of Herbert Hoover.) By focusing on the concrete problems of France they helped push beyond the Anglomania of the *philosophes*. But, above all, their serious attempt at economic analysis gave birth to a science. Though more deductive than inductive, though mislabeled "moral and political science," their discipline was an important ancestor of nineteenth- and twentieth-century political economy. By no means the least of their descendants was Marx, who, with different materials and different results, also built a theory on surplus value and sought to exorcise the parasites from the economic order.

The Kameralists

In the states of Austria and Germany during the mid-eighteenth century there arose a school of political economists who came to be known as the Kameralists (from *Kammer*, or chamber where the royal treasure was stored). The personalities of these men are, for most of us, hidden beneath a heavy veil of anonymity. Who has heard of Schröder, Hornick, Dithmar, Gasser, von Justi, or Sonnenfels? They were mercantilists rather than free-traders and hence differed sharply from the Physiocrats. But whereas further west mercantilism was focused especially on the need for colonial expansion, in Germany it was identified with the need for industrial and governmental centralization. The Kameralists were against freedom of trade on the grounds that population and food supply varied in direct relation to each other and that governmental stimulation was necessary

[25] Frankel, p. 122.

to attract aliens, enlarge industry and agriculture, and achieve a balanced population.

The significant aspect for our purposes is the degree to which the Kameralists relied on the same philosophic tenets as the Physiocrats to achieve different ends. The Kameralists, too, invoked a doctrine of natural law but, following Pufendorf, used it to justify the extension of state power rather than individual rights. Along with this principle, and with some inconsistency, they postulated a kind of utilitarian general happiness of subjects toward which state action is directed. But, most important, they tried to develop an administrative and economic science, making significant contributions to the use of statistics in public finance.

In Germany the Enlightenment had the advantage of somewhat more enlightened enlightened despots. By contrast with the conceited extravagance of the Louises or the dull stodginess of the Georges, governmental efficiency was sought after and rewarded. If efficiency is not necessarily enlightened, it is at least on the way to being "scientific." In Prussia, under Frederick the Great, candidates for the civil service had to study Kameralism in the universities. (Dithmar of Frankfurt was appointed to the first university chair of Kameralism by Frederick William I.) Maria Theresa of Austria centralized tax-collecting and effectively reorganized the royal exchequer as a national treasury. The ends were already becoming out of date; but the means had the marks of the new.

Adam Smith

Even those who have never studied economics know the name of Adam Smith (1723–90). The name itself has a basic quality to it: what is more primeval than Adam or more common than Smith? Given the stimulus "Adam Smith," almost anyone can respond, "*Wealth of Nations* (1776)." Americans feel that their wealthy nation born in 1776 must have some connection with this work, even though Smith was a Scotsman. And rightly so: after 1776 "all of the Western World became the world of Adam Smith: his vision became the prescription for the spectacles of generations. . . . he gave the world the image of itself for which it had been searching."[26]

Adam Smith, a lecturer in moral philosophy at the University of Glasgow, was famous for his friendliness, his halting delivery, and his unbelievable absent-mindedness. He had already written *The Theory of Moral Sentiments* (1759) when he went to France as tutor to the duke of Buccleuch. There he met Voltaire, Turgot, and Quesnay. He was much impressed with Quesnay's *Tableau oeconomique,* even though he could not accept the Physiocrats' reduction of all productive value to land. Of the Physiocrats Smith once said, "[their] system with all its imperfections, is perhaps the nearest approximation to the truth that has yet been published on the subject of political economy."[27] While in France, Smith set to work on his *Wealth of Nations,* which, when published years later, would far overshadow the Physiocrats' efforts.

Smith's work was clearly an eighteenth-century creation—rambling, digressive, sweeping in subject matter and approach. It thoroughly incorporated the familiar Enlightenment belief in the natural order of history. Nor was its economic orientation new. The free-trade arguments of men as far back as Sir Dudley North in *Discourses on Trade* (1691) anticipated much of Smith's argument. But *The Wealth of Nations,* which was much more a description than a proposal for reform, reflected, at one place and time, the realization of a completely new world of capitalistic economics and a new faith in the future of a system of competitive enterprise that was already here. The market-oriented society was a fact and now it had a philosophic rationale.

The Wealth of Nations begins with a description of the principle of specialization of

[26] Robert Heilbroner, *The Worldly Philosophers* (New York: Simon and Schuster, 1953), p. 32. Chapter 3 is a good summary of Smith's economics. See also Joseph Cropsey, *Polity and Economy: An Interpretation of the Principles of Adam Smith* (The Hague: Nijhoff, 1957).

[27] Quoted in Higgs, p. 2.

labor, the key to modern industrial society. One man working alone can make, perhaps, twenty pins a day. Ten men working together can make 48,000 pins a day. But this great leap in productivity requires a market capable of absorbing it. Smith sought for and found the laws of this market, the laws we have since labeled supply and demand. If the market is left free, the economic self-interest of thousands of isolated consumers and hundreds of isolated producers will unconsciously direct the system toward ends that are best for the economic welfare of the whole society. The driving force is called competition. To illustrate: if the price of commodity A becomes too high, two results automatically occur. Consumers begin buying other commodities, creating greater demand in those sectors, which will then require more labor, thereby absorbing some of the workers laid off or reduced in wages in industry A. Moreover, other producers rush in to take advantage of the consumer dissatisfaction with the present producers of commodity A, thus forcing the price down again. This process was a kind of balancing act but it was seen as doing more than merely creating a static balance analogous to the national balance of trade the mercantilists sought. Smith put into the system two dynamic factors, which made progress a viable ideal. The system was continually expanding in such a way that the capitalist could accumulate surpluses and these accumulations could and should be reinvested to tap an ever expanding market. Smith opposed the use of accumulated capital for charitable purposes (which would only stimulate idleness) *or* for pretentious luxury for the capitalist. The great competitive machine would tolerate neither sloth nor ostentation.

The corollary of this law of accumulation was the law of population. The supply of laborers would, like the supply of goods, vary with the demand. As wages went up, not merely would the number of workers for a particular industry go up but the *total* number of workers would increase. And the converse if wages went down. "The liberal reward of labour, therefore, as it is the effect of increasing wealth, so it is the cause of increasing population. To complain of it is to lament over the necessary effect and cause of the greatest public prosperity."[28] If this relationship between wages and the existence or nonexistence of human beings seems a bit strained, we must remember that

> In Smith's day infant mortality among the lower classes was shockingly high. . . . In many places in England, half the children died before they were four, and almost everywhere half the children only lived to the age of nine or ten. Malnutrition, evil living conditions, cold and disease took a horrendous toll among the poorer elements. Hence although higher wages may have affected the birth rate only slightly, it could be expected to have a considerable influence on the number of children who would grow to working age.[29]

The perfect competitiveness of the system, the inability of any one producer to affect prices or demand, the complete mobility of labor, the rationality of consumers—all these assumptions upon which the system rested were not facts of Smith's day any more than they are facts of our own day. But, though he may have exaggerated man's innate "propensity to barter, truck and exchange" and though he missed the vital role of credit, Smith's model nevertheless approached the reality of his day much more closely than it does the economic reality of our day. This was still a period of relatively small producers and of workers so close to starvation that they *had* to move if wages shifted. Certainly there is no greater mistake than to make Adam Smith a defender of giant corporate enterprise in the twentieth-century sense, a sense he could, after all, scarcely imagine. The "exclusive privileges of corporations, statutes

[28] *The Wealth of Nations,* 6th ed., Bk. I, Ch. 8. Quotations from this work are taken from Bohn's Standard Library Ed. (London: Bell, 1896). The Reverend Thomas Robert Malthus, in *An Essay on the Principle of Population as It Affects the Future Improvement of Society* (1798), took a less optimistic view of increasing population. Pointing out that, while people multiply, the land does not, he concluded that the misery of bare subsistence would be the perennial lot of most of mankind.

[29] Heilbroner, p. 57.

of apprenticeship, and all those laws which restrain . . . the competition to a smaller number than might otherwise go into them . . . are a sort of enlarged monopolies [sic]" and, for Smith, monopolies are most unhealthy: "The price of monopoly is upon every occasion the highest which can be got. The natural price, or the price of free competition, on the contrary, the lowest which can be taken . . . for any considerable time together." The former is "the highest which can be squeezed out of the buyers. . . . Such enhancements of the market price may last as long as the regulations of police which give occasion to them." We can see in this statement the basis of Smith's antipathy to government. It is the "police" whose power, alone among powers, can artificially prop up monopolies. This assumption, of course, is what makes Smith relevant to political studies.

We must, however, again remember that the police who upset the market price represented not the welfare state of the twentieth century but the mercantilist state of the eighteenth. It is true that Smith had little use for "that insidious and crafty animal, vulgarly called a politician or statesman"[30] but neither was he opposed to every conceivable act of government, as Spencer very nearly was a few decades later. Smith, for example, granted the desirability of public education, admitted the possibility of some governmental action to cope with the more inhumane aspects of the factory system, and, indeed, charged government with the all-important responsibility of actively blocking threatening monopolies, collusions, and trade barriers. He supported government economic activity on behalf of defense or other requirements of national interest. On one occasion he urged that direct, government rule would be better for India than the exploitive rule of the private East India Company. There was, however, in the late eighteenth century a general absence of economic legislation, the kinds of measures that make up the bulk of today's Parliamentary work, and Smith certainly did not favor a fundamental change in this respect.

In Adam Smith the acid of counting, calculating, clanking industrialism has gone a long way toward dissolving the feudal mystique of the community, the common bond of allegiance to the group, an influence that still held some sway in Locke's use of "the people." Locke's somewhat inconsistent identification of the individual's interest with society's interest has by this time become a consistent and conscious identification of particular, private interest and general, public interest. The individual "neither intends to promote the public interest, nor knows how much he is promoting it. . . . By directing . . . industry in such a manner as its produce may be of the greatest value, he intends only his own gain, and he is in this, as in many other cases, led by an invisible hand to promote an end which was no part of his intention." The mystique of the feudal community has been ironically replaced by an even more esoteric power lurking behind the mechanical, impersonal economic system. The invisible hand—or at least its imaginary shadow—did, at least, buoy up the optimistic spirit of economists and businessmen during the rigors of industrial expansion, even though, being invisible, it afforded considerably less solace to tired and hungry laborers.

Although Smith himself was a goodhearted soul with a genuine concern for public welfare, there were in his system the seeds of callousness, some of which came to fruition in Malthus and Ricardo. Neither he nor many of his successors were so addicted to material production that they hoped everyone would be prosperous; nor were they far enough away from Calvinism to regard happiness as a legitimate fruit of prosperity. On the one hand, the poor would benefit by the continuing upward spiral of the productive system; but there would always be the poor.[31] And since happiness is in large part an inner

[30] H. J. Laski, *Political Thought in England, Locke to Bentham* (London: Oxford Univ. Press, 1920), p. 194.

[31] The problem of poor relief was not great in 1776; but only a decade later it was acute. This helps explain some of Smith's optimism, which otherwise would be inexplicable.

state of grace anyway, the poor are not necessarily less happy than the rich and need not, certainly, be pitied as a class. On the other hand, while all men are basically equal both by nature and even in the all-important ability to produce goods, the rich—at least the rich entrepreneurs—had become so by virtue of stout character, by will and fortitude, which had enabled them to use their more or less equal talents while others' talents lay idle through sloth. The result was an egalitarian system run by an elite.

The roots of industrial and colonial paternalism went deeper and deeper. The managerial class could go about its work without the ostentatious trappings of the nobility yet with a sense of mission that had, and still has, a strong moral content. And by separating government from economics it could conceal even from itself the degree to which it was running the government.[32] By leaning on necessity it could beg the question of the good life. By sticking to business it could make business stick to everything.

Economics and Politics in the Eighteenth Century: A Summary

Three conclusions may be drawn from this section. First, the eighteenth-century economists, even mercantilists like the Kameralists, were participants in the general fascination with the order of nature and with geometrical system. Economists have worked with abstract systems ever since. In order to make the system work, it appears as if Smith abstracted the one motive of economic self-interest and made this the only motive of life. Actually, he did not. His central concern, at least in *The Wealth of Nations,* was with the way a system behaved not the way individuals behaved. By assuming a sufficient degree of economic self-interest in the individual cogs to make the machine work, he had a theoretical system that, in fact, was not too far from reality. Although increasingly bothered by "nonclassical" and only partially calculable influences—such as advertising, group cohesion values in labor unions, the pressure of public opinion, the desire to maintain good will on the part of big companies, government tax policies, and other imponderables—this is the system economists still believe in. They do not say that every man is driven to seek out the lowest price and the highest wage; but they assume most men do, make predictions accordingly, and are right often enough to continue to do so. What this assumption does to the mentality of the average citizen is more a sociological and a political question than an economic one; to this question we must return later.

It is sufficient at this point to note that for the last hundred years—from Auguste Comte to David Easton—some political theorists have felt that they were at the same point as the economists of the eighteenth century, that is, ready to offer the world a political system that could rationalize a complex set of factors and make possible predictions about future political behavior. This effort, too, will engage our subsequent attention.

Second, economic theorizing in the eighteenth century shared the vision of change, development, and progress manifest in political thought, narrowly conceived. The dynamic had won a clear-cut victory over the static. The open-endedness of the world ahead, both an effect and a cause of industrialization and individuation, came to be taken for granted. Quesnay's flow chart and Smith's law of accumulation testify to the hopeful, dynamic, expanding character of the era. Said Smith, with considerable accuracy and characteristic matter-of-factness, "it is not the actual greatness of national wealth, but its continual increase, which occasions a rise in the wages of labour."

Whatever the proper labels for the economic systems that are competing for dominance in the twentieth century—*capitalism, communism, socialism, welfare economics*—

[32] Joseph Schumpeter has pointed out, however, the degree to which capitalists were dependent upon the "protecting strata" of the nobility in the advance of industrial society. For a richly insightful account of the social context of capitalist development, see his *Capitalism, Socialism, and Democracy,* 3rd ed. (New York: Harper & Row, 1950), Part II.

it is highly significant that they all share the progressive assumptions of eighteenth-century thought. A lag of a mere two centuries should not, by this time, surprise the student of political theory.

Third, the most cursory glance at the economic theorizing of the eighteenth century will confirm what we noted at the beginning of this section: there is always a relationship between political and economic theory. But there is some irony in the fact that modern thinkers became least concerned about this relationship at that moment when they were most concerned to separate the two spheres of politics and economics. From ancient times men had assumed a close relationship between politics and economics but felt no need to develop a separate discipline of economics. Plato and Aristotle would no more have thought of omitting economic matters from their discussion of politics than they would have tried to discuss economics apart from politics. The *polis* embraced both—and more. But partly because men in the eighteenth century had a new vision of material progress and partly because they felt that to be scientific meant to compartmentalize, a political-economic theory came into being; and as a result, one set of phenomena was newly illuminated while another set was obscured. What were obscured were the degree to which the market economy was a political invention[33] and the degree to which the commercial classes influenced governmental policy. The breakthrough of this separation was engineered by Marx, who turned more than Hegel upside down. In the early liberal creed politics was not supposed to affect economics. In Marx politics was nothing but a branch of economics. It is premature to expand on Marx here. The point is simple: to theorize means to theorize *about* something. Therefore, because politics and economics are never wholly separable, political theory and economic theory are never wholly separable. The laissez-faire theorists forgot this and their forgetting helps us to remember.

[33] See Polanyi, especially Ch. 12.

HISTORY AND POLITICS

France: Condorcet

In a way that is not easy for the more disillusioned residents of the twentieth century to comprehend, the eighteenth-century *philosophes* were deeply aroused by the prospect of radical change in the course of history. A new way of thought was closing the door of the past and opening up a future of unlimited potentialities. It was more than simply a vision of a changed human environment —we, too, can construct our science-fiction cities of the future. It was, especially for the lesser *philosophes,* a vision of a wholly new, beatific quality of life.

In the list of *philosophe* historians—a list that would include Chastellux, Abbé Raynal, von Grimm, and many others—the best-developed yet typical philosophy of history belongs to Condorcet (Marie Jean de Caritat, Marquis de Cordorcet, 1743–94). Condorcet's biography can tell us much of the *philosophes's* political environment. He was the son of an impoverished army officer of noble birth and a mother of wealthy bourgeois background. The union, a conjunction of class decay and class ascendancy, was not atypical of eighteenth-century France. Condorcet was educated at a Jesuit college: "The man who was to become a skeptic in religion, a pacifist, and a democrat was brought up in the environment of priests, soldiers, and nobles."[34] Showing brilliance in mathematics and hating the profession of arms, Condorcet offended his father's family by choosing to live in Paris on a small allowance sent by his widowed, overprotective mother. His mentor in mathematics was the great D'Alembert and Condorcet was soon drawn into the intellectual life of the salon. Despite his timidity, the list of friends he made in this circle reads like an eighteenth-century *Who's Who:* Helvetius, Lafayette, La Rochefoucauld, Franklin, Jefferson, Paine, Diderot, Holbach, Quesnay, Smith, and, above all, his "masters," Voltaire and Turgot, both of whom he honored with

[34] Schapiro, p. 67.

biographies. Condorcet scandalized this set by his prosaic puritanism: he fell in love, married happily, and never took a mistress. He wrote ably in mathematics but turned to economics after Turgot appointed him inspector of the mint in 1774. When Necker and mercantilism returned to the saddle in 1776, Condorcet resigned. In politics he could be called a constitutional monarchist before the Revolution, a democrat after. With Lafayette, the younger Mirabeau, and others he helped organize and later became president of the Friends of the Negroes, an antislavery society. He also worked diligently for woman suffrage.

Condorcet's role in the French Revolution was not decisive but it was significant because he was the only *philosophe* to be an active participant—indeed, he was so active it cost him his life. A member of the National Convention, Condorcet was chairman of the committee to draw up a constitution in 1793. The document,[35] a product of years of reflection, meant as a model for all mankind, was coolly received by the Convention and was falsely labeled a Girondist scheme by the Jacobins. When Condorcet wrote a pamphlet attacking the hastily contrived Jacobin constitution, the Convention called for his arrest. For nine months he hid out, painfully but patiently writing his most famous work, *Outlines of an Historical View of the Progress of the Human Mind,* one of the most optimistic works ever written. When finally arrested, footsore and half-starved, he had only a copy of Horace in his pocket. He died his first night in prison—from self-administered poison, according to one report, from exposure, according to another. In either case, it was a sordid end for the last of the *philosophes.*

This last work gained some of its fame from the peculiar circumstances of its writing —almost as if readers were repaying the *philosophes,* intellectual godfathers of the Revolution, for the way the Revolution treated them. Its basic assumption was "that the perfectibility of man is absolutely infinite" and it set out to show that "the course of this progress may doubtless be more or less rapid, but it can never be retrograde."[36] Condorcet traced nine epochs in the history of mankind, beginning with men who lived in animal-like hordes and continuing through the pastoral state, the era of first agriculture, the glory of Greece, and so on. Each age had to fight off and struggle through the "seductive influences" of prejudice. In the Middle Ages man was "plunged into darkness" by superstition; but apparently this plunge did not qualify as a retrograde movement, only a temporary delay in the upward spiral of history. The ninth epoch spanned the period from Descartes to the French Republic. The tenth stretched out into the limitless, bountiful future. Only in his own day, Condorcet felt, had man finally arrived at the knowledge of the true rights of man, deduced from a single principle: man "is a being endowed with sensation, capable of reasoning upon and understanding his interests, and of acquiring moral ideas."

Condorcet's naiveté strikes us as incredible. Without being aware that he was dealing in paradoxes as difficult as, and not dissimilar from, those of Christian theology, he described an omnipotent process of history that yet had given man consciousness of his freedom from historical limitations. He gave us a point in time, his own day, beyond which evil would be timelessly overcome. He gave us a new morality, which is man's understanding of his own interests.

Despite Condorcet's practical interest in constitutions, his theory of government seems almost wistfully divorced from practice. He cited Sidney, Locke, and Rousseau on the equality of all men but waved away any contractual theory that would bind people to

[35] It proposed a unicameral legislature elected annually by direct manhood suffrage—women were sacrificed to expediency, presumably—with nominees to come from "primary assemblies" in each *département.* The *départements* were to nominate three times the number of candidates to be elected and a preferential ballot was to be used. Although this scheme does not reflect it, Condorcet had closely studied and much admired American state and Federal constitutions.

[36] *Outlines of an Historical View of the Progress of the Human Mind* (Philadelphia: Carey, Rice, Orwood, Bache & Fellows, 1796), p. 11.

their government in perpetuity. No man can be bound except by himself; even acts of the majority can be validated only by the free acceptance of the individual, for the individual can never yield up his own reason to a majority if the result might be violation of individual rights. The practical result of this position would seem to be anarchy. But Condorcet preferred to think of it not as anarchy but rather as a universal reign of harmony and peace.

Condorcet has often been called the perfect ideologue. He was the "man of principle," one who actually operated on certain social assumptions—the natural goodness of man, the evil effects of inherited institutions, the inevitability of progress—as if they were geometric axioms. If the facts did not conform, so much the worse for the facts. For Condorcet, as for most of the *philosophes,* "the individual" was one of the most abstract of the abstractions. "History" was another. And because they were abstractions, Condorcet could forget that individuals are *in* history as a fish is in water and that they cannot, however exhilarating a new flash of self-consciousness may be, foresee the tides and currents of the far future.

And yet, reflecting on Condorcet's almost childlike trust in men and the devotion that led this shy, diffident man to enter the political fray for the sake of the people, we cannot be too harsh with him for his naiveté. As with Godwin, it is not his logic but his impulsive departures from logic that lead us to admire this "theologian of political rationalism." It was at the expense of some of these impulses that Montesquieu was able to give us deeper insights into the nature of politics and history.

England: Bolingbroke

In England in the eighteenth century, the greatest insights into history and politics—or, rather, to be more precise, into the political uses of history—are given to us by conservatives: Bolingbroke, Hume, and Burke. Hume and Burke are important enough to deserve separate treatment in Chapters 16 and 17, respectively. Bolingbroke is in no way a political theorist of the first rank but the combination of his political writings and his political action can tell us something about the relationship of history to ideology.

Henry St. John, first Viscount Bolingbroke (1678–1751), was "a man of headlong vehemence, a born partisan, whose gifts were all for fighting, and to whom it came naturally to seek reconciliation with an enemy by injuring a friend."[37] One of the organizers of the new Tory party, Bolingbroke was a political power while still young and spent most of his later years plotting to regain his earlier glory. A member of Robert Harley's two moderate Tory cabinets between 1704 and 1714, he overshadowed and outmaneuvered the older Harley. But in 1715, after the accession of George I, Harley and Bolingbroke were impeached by the new Whig majority in Parliament for their Jacobite sympathies. Bolingbroke fled to France. Pardoned in 1723, he returned to England but was kept from power by Robert Walpole, the new leader of the Whigs. Frustrated, Bolingbroke turned to writing. His three chief works are *A Dissertation on Parties* (1734), *The Study and Use of History* (1735), and *The Idea of a Patriot King* (1738).

We read Bolingroke, if at all, less to discover great insights than to see what relationship his active life in politics bore to his writings. It is a case of the ancient problem of the man of thought versus the man of action. His felicitous style and his air of dispassion conceal what some of his letters reveal, the deep cynicism that lay behind much of what he did and wrote. We might suspect this cynicism upon considering the spectacle of Bolingbroke, a professed Deist, brilliantly arguing in the House of Lords in 1714 for an act that forbade Dissenters to act as tutors or schoolmasters. It happened to be expedient for Tories to support this particular measure of the queen and Bolingbroke was just the man to make the Established Church sound very good indeed—without, apparently,

[37] G. N. Clark, *The Later Stuarts, 1660–1714,* 2nd ed. (Oxford: Clarendon Press, 1955), p. 235.

believing a word of what he was saying. In the *Dissertation on Parties* this most ardent of partisans argued against parties, at least against the only kind of parties that were known to history. Somewhat as in the case of the early Federalists in America, the *raison d'être* of Bolingbroke's faction was to get rid of factions. We still have, of course, pressure groups working to save us from pressure groups. Bolingbroke's early use of the concept of the separation of powers made this doctrine a conservative weapon against the centralization of ministerial power in Walpole's evolving cabinet system.[38]

The *Patriot King* was at once a plea for the dissolution of factions out of common loyalty to a monarch and a statement of the ideal of a monarch fully loyal to the English Constitution—the rule of a man, yet the rule of law, the best of two worlds. Given such a man and such a system, "concord will appear, brooding peace and prosperity on the happy land; joy sitting in every face, content in every heart; a people unoppressed, undisturbed, unalarmed."[39] Bolingbroke once admitted that such a monarch would be "a sort of standing miracle," which led Laski to observe than no other comment was needed. But it is of passing interest that, while Bolingbroke's conception of monarchy would have earlier fitted nicely into the divine-right mold, by this time divine-right arguments had little ideological usefulness and Bolingbroke was obliged to say, "A divine right to govern ill is an absurdity."[40]

Of greatest relevance to our present interest is Bolingbroke's *The Study and Use of History*. The book was a demonstration more than an explanation of how history may be used for political purposes. Notwithstanding some subtle insights, as, for example, in his treatment of self-love as a motive for the study of history, Bolingbroke's political generalizations, directed toward "a constant improvement in private and public virtue . . . to make us better men and better citizens" are fairly vacuous and rest on random and arbitrary historical examples. Indeed, the examples are often clear, while the principles they are supposed to illustrate are not. But toward the end, recent history comes to the fore and Bolingbroke's partisan spirit shows its hand. The reader is swiftly carried from Olympian observations on universal history to complaints about local taxes.[41] Is this simply sophomoric sloppiness, in which case Bolingbroke is unworthy of our attention, or are these the wiles of a professional politician who knows how to use words in all sorts of contexts to further his ends? The latter would seem to be true—although, of course, we can never be completely sure of the degree of self-consciousness in Bolingbroke's deceptions. The use of words is a form of power; indeed, it is one of the chief forms of power for the politician. He, unlike the scholar, uses words, ideas, and principles as weapons of combat rather than as tools for the discovery of truth; and it is perhaps only the conceit of the scholar that believes the former requires less intelligence than the latter. That Bolingbroke had the power to sway is indicated not only by the response to his writings in his own day but by the fact that George III, Chatham, and Disraeli were moved by them, especially by the image of the "patriot king."

The problem of the relationship between the man of action and the man of thought is as old as Plato and as young as the RAND Corporation. The problem of the political use of history is as old as Thucydides and as young as *Pravda*. The problem is whether and to what extent truth and power can be joined together. It is more than the schism between thinkers and doers. Condorcet was a politician, though a bad one, who sincerely thought he had historical truth by the tail. Hume, as we shall see, was an academic philosopher who wrote polemical history. Burke, and possibly Montesquieu, came closest to resolving the dilemma in one man. Whether

[38] See *A Dissertation on Parties*, 10th ed. (London: Davies & Cadell, 1775).

[39] *The Idea of a Patriot King*, new ed. (London: Davies, 1775), p. 217.

[40] *Ibid.*, p. 79.

[41] See *The Study and Use of History*, new ed., corrected (London: Cadell, 1770), pp. 381–82.

they succeeded is one of the questions awaiting us in later chapters.

Italy: Vico

Against the dominant progressive-optimistic-intellectualistic mood of the eighteenth century one man stands like a boulder in a stream. The disparity between his thought and the currents of his time—a measure, in one sense, of his genius—resulted in an almost total neglect in his lifetime. Giambattista Vico (1668–1744) was born in poverty and lived in obscurity. He took no part in public affairs. Tutoring and a modest income as professor of rhetoric at the University of Naples kept him alive. After writing three major works in Latin, he significantly shifted to Italian for his greatest treatise, *Principi di una scienza nuova intorno alla commune natura delle nazioni* (*Principles of a New Science Concerning the Natural Community of Nations*, 1725).[42]

The *Scienza nuova* is vast, complex, and often confusing. It moves in two apparently antithetical directions, creating a pervading tension. On the one hand, Vico is absorbed with infinite detail, the objective, concrete "reality" of history as conventionally understood. On the other hand, he is concerned with methodological principles, the theory of history, the subjective reality of history as it exists in the poetic memory of man. Against the cold, geometrical reason of the Enlightenment he puts an almost mystical reason working its way out of the long experience of the race: "Humanity's living consciousness of what it has done."[43] Against the optimistic hope for linear progress in history he puts a pessimistic theory of cyclical repetition in history. Against modern, scientific naturalism, which makes man a datum of nature, "Vico offers to modern man an alternative principle for the vindication of his own spirituality and subjectivity. That alternative is history."[44]

The "new science" was more a new approach, a psychological approach, to history than it was a new method. It was grounded on the belief that "the true history of the human race is the history of its progressive mental states."[45] In the *Scienza nuova* Vico wrote that the scholar must penetrate these mental states by poetic-mystical participation; he must "enter into the imaginations of the first men who founded the gentile world." There he finds man remaking the world in his own image: resinous trees weep, the wind whistles, fields are thirsty, the heavens smile. The "rational metaphysics" of most moderns does not take these transformations seriously but Vico does. "Rational metaphysics" teaches that "man becomes all things by understanding them." But Vico's "imaginative metaphysics" teaches that "man becomes all things by *not* understanding them . . . he makes the things out of himself and becomes them by transforming himself into them." This negation of rational understanding must take place if the scholar is to know the past and he must know the past to know the present. To do so is to "experience in his body a divine pleasure."

This participation in the past was more than a matter of capturing the mood of a given time. Vico actually tried to validate assertions about events and origins in this way. For example, after struggling to enter into the "primitive mind" of the Roman *plebs,* Vico concluded that it was impossible that they could have been governed by the laws of Solon. He thus denied the Greek origin of the Roman law of the Twelve Tables.

While basically a historian and historical methodologist, Vico qualifies as a political theorist on several grounds. One is his concern for law in its most exalted sense. The essence of humanity, he felt, was an indwell-

42 Translated by Thomas G. Bergin and Max H. Fisch as *The New Science of Giambattista Vico* (Ithaca: Cornell Univ. Press, 1948). Subsequent quotations are from this first and only English translation.

43 Benedetto Croce, "Vico," in *Encyclopaedia of the Social Sciences* (New York: Macmillan, 1935), Vol. XV, p. 249.

44 A. R. Caponigri, *Time and Idea, the Theory of History in Giambattista Vico* (Chicago: Regnery, 1953), p. 3.

45 H. P. Adams, *The Life and Writings of Giambattista Vico* (London: Allen & Unwin, 1935), p. 152.

ing desire for law: ". . . man, fallen into despair of all the succors of nature, desires something superior to save him." This was a rational desire and the root of man's progress but it was continually being transformed and cancelled out by the passions. Vico had a strong sense of the "fallen" nature of man, struggling half-consciously toward the right and immortality. This aspiration for law is expressed in religion, customs, the whole "vulgar wisdom" (as contrasted with "the esoteric wisdom of the philosophers") of the race. In the course of this history-long quest, "Providence" has educated mankind. Part of this educative process involves the gradual realization in history of the meaning of justice, an eternal and universal idea that is in part embodied in, but also in part negated by, courts, judges, and lawmakers, and every concrete political structure.

There is some difficulty here. In discussing justice, Vico suggests a uniformity of historical development that does not altogether coincide with his cyclical theory. He displays a Platonic concern with the ideal form of justice, a concern that is inconsistent with his criticism of Plato's "learned error," namely Plato's attribution of reality to products of speculation and his failure to see that ideas are products of history. "The nature of things is nothing but their coming into being at certain times and in certain fashions."

Vico has some interesting things to say about the origins of states. Like Carlyle, he rejects the view that force accounts for the great movements of history and he places heavy emphasis on the decisive role of great men. The state itself originates in the relationship between "giants," or "heroes," and their "clients," those who are protected or rescued by the hero. The hero may be cruel, his rages are often childish, but magnanimity is the trait that establishes his position. Not that Vico operates from the assumption of an idyllically innocent state of nature: the hero is feared, too, and fear plays its part in the growth of the state as it does in the growth of religion. But, says Vico, in the long run the stability of a political regime owes more to the ruler's contribution to progress than to his skill at repression.

Vico is not without ambiguities resulting from his inspired but lonely scholarship. He sometimes uses the word "Providence," for example, to mean the divine power of God shaping events. At other times "Providence" seems to be man's *belief* in this divine power. Men both are and are not in control of history. All in all, Vico with difficulty escapes the pitfalls of pantheism. But we can hardly underestimate his precociousness in relation to some key movements of thought in twentieth-century social science. Two centuries before Mannheim and the "sociology of knowledge" he developed a theory about the way in which our location in the historical stream conditions the very modes of our thought: ". . . we know only what we do . . . action and truth are mutually convertible."[46] In a day when the Enlightenment was pushing everything earlier than the eighteenth century into a box marked "superstitions of the past" and sealing it off, Vico was examining with great sensitivity the problems of language and myth in primitive culture as a clue to his own intellectual consciousness, an enterprise worthy of today's most sophisticated anthropologists and social psychologists.

LAW AND CONSTITUTIONALISM

If the eighteenth century was not a constitutional age, it was at least an age of constitutionalism. The faith in fundamental charters was a reflection of the faith in fundamental laws of nature, the "self-evident truths" of the American Declaration of Independence, and the "simple and incontestable principles" of the French Declaration of the Rights of Man and Citizen. Even in Germany, where the Prussian king was still consolidating his autocratic power over the representative assemblies (*Landtage*), speculation on law was flourishing. Although the aim was not nec-

[46] Croce, p. 249.

essarily libertarian, the trend was at least toward systematization and a measure of equity.

Germany

Thomasius

Christian Thomasius (1655–1728) qualifies as a man of the Enlightenment for both his religious toleration and his stout resistance to witch hunts and the use of torture in criminal proceedings. He was also the first important professor to lecture in German (at Leipzig and Halle), an innovation that led to the appellation "the second Luther." Although he sought the same kind of systematization of law that Pufendorf had worked for, Thomasius made a much sharper distinction between law and morals. He elaborated on the law of nature, relating it more specifically to the common-sense element in reason than had many of his predecessors. But this law he regarded as a command of God, which teaches wisdom and is not connected in any direct way with positive law. The commands of governments embodied in statutory law are not necessarily related to these commands of God embodied in reason; and the systematization of positive law, desirable as this may be, does not necessarily establish the reign of natural law on earth.[47]

Wolff

A later professor at Halle, Christian Wolff (1679–1754), blurred the distinction Thomasius had so carefully made by developing a theory of duty intended to synthesize Pufendorf, Thomasius, and Leibnitz.[48] Through this concept, Wolff sought to express a fundamental unity of law and nature. The result was egalitarian, in a way, but not at all democratic. He optimistically asserted that "inborn human duties" are the same for all men; consequently men are essentially equal and the state is obligated to treat them as such. A network of moral obligation binds together state, citizen, and law in a continuing quest for perfection. The substitution of a Stoic perfection for happiness as a goal of life fitted neatly with Wolff's predilection for benevolent despotism. Basically, Wolff was more interested in ethics than in jurisprudence; however, both his legal and his ethical writings were widely read and much admired. For a time his philosophy became almost authoritative for German scholars.

For our purposes the important influence of Thomasius and Wolff was on the codification and systematization of positive law. Combined with Frederick the Great's penchant for order and efficiency, this influence had a practical effect in the Germanic states, where codes were adopted in Bavaria in 1756, Prussia in 1794, and Austria in 1811. And though these codes had many feudal, corporative elements still clinging to them, separating them from the egalitarian, entrepreneur-oriented Code of Napoleon (1804), the latter was not wholly uninfluenced by German constitutionalism.[49]

Frederick the Great

Like Bolingbroke, Frederick II of Prussia (1712–86) is more important for what he did than for what he wrote. But it is impossible to ignore his writings: in addition to the political and military treatises there were histories, essays, poems, musical compositions, and sixty volumes of correspondence—and all of this on top of an exceedingly full life as military conqueror and conscientious autocrat. His precociousness is illustrated by his first political writing, produced at the age of nine-

[47] See Carl J. Friedrich, *The Philosophy of Law in Historical Perspective* (Chicago: Univ. of Chicago Press, 1958), pp. 116–19.

[48] Gottfried Leibnitz (1646–1716), a great metaphysician who also touched on the theory of law, had sharply criticized Pufendorf's attempt to secularize the law of nature. Leibnitz' view that the world is the best of all possible worlds—a much maligned view immortalized in *Candide* by Voltaire's viciously satirical characterization of Dr. Pangloss—his determinism, and his monism required the assumption of an underlying unity between positive law and the system of eternal ideas that he called the law of nature.

[49] Friedrich, p. 121. The Napoleonic Code, it should be noted, was not the first French code. The codes of 1667 and 1670, under Louis XIV, were significant predecessors.

teen in the prison where his father had thrown him for trying to flee the anti-intellectual environment of the court. In this *cahier* he not very modestly outlined his system for gaining political control of Europe. In 1740, the year he ascended the throne and marched into Silesia against Maria Theresa, he wrote *L'Antimachiavel,* a moralistic and not altogether fair critique of Machiavelli's *The Prince.* This was followed by his two *Political Testaments,* the first in 1752 and the second in 1768. While, again, the range of these works is impressive—touching on finances, the organization of the army, foreign policy, the training of princes, and so on—what is significant is the degree to which Frederick, the absolute monarch, was moved by considerations of natural law and "natural equity" to a clear position of monarchical self-restraint. A king, he argued in the *First Political Testament,* should never interfere in a law case: ". . . in the tribunals the law must speak and the sovereign be silent."[50] But the monarch must keep an eagle eye on the judges and be prepared to remove them if they do not measure up.

Affecting and affected by the Kameralists' views of natural law and administrative science, especially those of Von Justi, Frederick was willing to put upon himself not only the burdens of absolute autocracy but the burdens of legal restraint. *L'état c'est moi* was his slogan as much as it was Louis XIV's but to Frederick it was a weight of responsibility rather than a badge of complacency. The extent of his detailed supervision of the Prussian bureaucracy is astounding. His bureaucrats—selected by examination, well trained, and omnisciently watched—stand in marked contrast to their class- and graft-ridden counterparts to the west. This contrast helps explain German "autocratic" respect for bureaucracy and French "democratic" disrespect for bureaucracy, a difference that has carried down to the twentieth century. Frederick's early reputation was undoubtedly excessively enhanced by the praise of his French admirers, especially Voltaire and Diderot. Their praise, it should be recognized, was not entirely gratuitous; in fact, it can be compared to a well-paid public-relations job. But the fact that Frederick was shrewd enough to exploit a newly self-conscious public opinion in this way is merely another evidence of his imaginativeness.

The fatal flaw in Frederick's system of "everything for the people, nothing by the people" was the problem of succession. The system could work only as long as a man like Frederick was on the throne and even one such man in a century is rare. Frederick sensed this flaw—note his lamentations over the weak nephew who would succeed him—but was unable to draw the logical conclusion of a truly constitutional monarchy. In the history of modern politics Frederick was a significant bridge between the autocratic and the modern constitutional state but in the history of political theory he appears mainly as a fascinating anomaly. It was not until after the French Revolution that Frederick's absolutism was seen as the fragile thing it really was. Only then, in the writings of Stein, Hardenberg, and Humboldt, would German constitutionalism develop deeper roots.

England: Blackstone

What William Blackstone (1723–80) illustrates is not a new set of ideas or even a new depth in legal analysis but the spread of a sense of law to the furthermost arteries of the English-speaking body politic. The influence of Blackstone's *Commentaries on the Laws of England* (which appeared in four volumes from 1765 to 1769) was phenomenal and as great in America as in England, where the roots of the common law already ran deep. The mental picture of ambitious young Abe Lincoln reading his Blackstone reminds us of countless other nineteenth-century lawyer-politicians developing or expressing a reverence for law by reading Blackstone.

If the *Commentaries* do not strike us as

[50] Quoted in G. P. Gooch's excellent study, *Frederick the Great* (New York: Knopf, 1947), p. 293.

profound, we should remember that they were written for the layman as well as the law student, out of Blackstone's conviction that everyone ought to know some law. In many ways this work can be called an introductory textbook. Blackstone's often-criticized inconsistencies stem in part from his strained attempt to be comprehensive and from the fact that the textbookish definitions of Volume I are not always taken seriously in subsequent pages. Perhaps Blackstone's most serious running fault was that he repeatedly confused government and society. Partly because Blackstone was trying only to describe the law as it was, his former student Bentham, moved by a new conception of a science of law as it should be, attacked him with special virulence. Referring to the *Commentaries,* Bentham spoke of "the capital blemishes of that work, particularly this grand and fundamental one, the antipathy to reformation . . . [in addition to] the universal inaccuracy and confusion which seemed to my apprehension to pervade the whole."[51] Blackstone did indeed present certain structures of law as if they exhausted reality, while legal practice was in fact quite another thing:

> He must have known that to talk of the independence of the branches of the legislature was simple nonsense at a time when king and peers competed for the control of elections in the House of Commons. . . . It was ridiculous to describe the Commons as representative of property so long as places like Manchester and Sheffield were virtually disfranchised. . . . What he did was to produce the defense of a nonexistent system which acted as a barrier to all legal, and much political progress in the next half-century.[52]

Nor can all the inconsistency be attributed to faulty definition. Within a few pages he seems to speak for both the supremacy of natural law and the absolute supremacy of the legislature. The purpose of society, says Blackstone, is to protect the "absolute rights" of individuals "vested in them by the immutable laws of nature."[53] If they are contrary to these laws of nature, "no human laws are of any validity." Elsewhere, however, Blackstone says that the legislature, "being in truth the sovereign power, is . . . always of absolute authority: it acknowledges no superior on earth." Blackstone meant by "legislature" more than Parliament alone. He meant the whole lawmaking power, the king in Parliament. But he certainly meant to defend the legislature so conceived from any superior power in the people. He specifically criticized Locke's grant of authority to the people to remove an offending legislature. Two absolutes can hardly exist side by side; but Blackstone may not have been quite as inept as Bentham and Laski imply. Gough suggests[54] that Blackstone is making a sharper distinction between law and morals than Bentham is capable of recognizing. If natural law is *morally* absolute, the legislature may still be *legally* absolute. Blackstone assumed that Parliament had an obligation under natural law but he also blandly assumed that Parliament always had and always would fulfill that obligation. This complacency explains his tremendous appeal to visceral conservatives.

Complacent conservatism has always been an element of constitutionalism and is today. The law and order that stems from an unwillingness to rock the boat is at least a part of all law and order. Even in a century smitten with revolutionary ideals its influence was extensive. Today, in the more frantic twentieth century, the "new conservatives" or "radical conservatives," the zealous men who try to save us from ruin, make more noise but have less influence than the Blackstonian, let-us-count-our-blessings conservatives.

[51] Jeremy Bentham, *Fragment on Government,* Wilfred Harrison, ed. (Oxford: Blackwell, 1948), p. 4.

[52] Laski, p. 120. See also Wilfred Harrison, *Conflict and Compromise: History of British Political Thought, 1593–1900* (New York: Free Press, 1965), pp. 105–08.

[53] This quotation and the two immediately following are from the *Commentaries on the Laws of England,* 8th ed., William G. Hammond, ed. (San Francisco: Bancroft Whitney, 1890), Vol. I, pp. 290, 69, and 197, respectively.

[54] John Gough, *Fundamental Law in English Constitutional History* (Oxford: Clarendon Press, 1955), pp. 188–91.

Constitutionalism in America

Strange, perhaps, that the young and revolutionary United States, whose example was an inspiration to the French Revolution, should turn out to be the standard-bearer to the world of sane and sensible constitutionalism. This is no place to expatiate once more on the miracle of the founding fathers or to analyze the document they brought forth. But we can afford to observe, with many other writers, that they were great constitution-makers not merely because they were Americans but because they were Americans steeped in the tradition of English law and Lockean liberalism. Although his own constitutional plan for America was not adopted, Hamilton was not greatly at odds with his brethren in declaring, "I believe the British government forms the best model the world has ever produced. . . . this government has for its object *public strength* and *individual security*.[55]

Even monarchically inclined Hamilton felt that a mixed government, with power divided between the one, the few, and the many, did not depart too far from English practice. And even in the Revolutionary period the dominant American arguments were drawn from English legal precedents. This is support enough for the common judgment that the American Revolution was the most conservative revolution in history. James Otis of Massachusetts[56] was particularly eloquent in grafting the writings of Coke and Locke onto the English Constitution and from this base challenging the constitutionality of Parliament when it enacted such measures as the Sugar Act (1764) and the Stamp Act (1765). Since government rests on a contract drawn to ensure protection of life, liberty, and property, Otis argued, by taking property without granting representation to the property-holder the English Parliament was violating the basic charter of government.

Ultimately, of course, it was up to the English king and Parliament to define the scope of the Constitution;[57] but the colonials did try very hard to keep their objections within a constitutional framework. They did not want a revolution; but if it had to come, they wanted to make it a revolution by due process of law. In mid-1774, when the more radical elements had infiltrated the Continental Congress, James Wilson of Pennsylvania[58] excoriated Parliament but still swore allegiance to the English king. He expounded what amounts to a theory of the British Commonwealth as it ultimately came to be. And even in 1776, when blood was being shed, the idea was still prevalent that America was merely asserting a legal claim against England.

Its reluctant revolutionaries illustrate the degree to which America identified with English traditionalism and the Blackstonian-conservative element in constitutionalism. But there were other constitutional influences at work. One was the typical eighteenth-century view of the universe and its natural laws—a mechanistic, optimistic view already aired a number of times in these pages. Its presence in the New World is nowhere better illustrated than in the justifiably famous *Federalist,* one of the few pieces of election propaganda to become a classic of political theory. "The science of politics," wrote Hamilton in *The Federalist,*

> like most other sciences, has received great improvement. The efficacy of various principles is now well understood, which were either not known at all, or imperfectly known to the ancients. The regular distribution of power into distinct departments; the introduction of legis-

[55] Alexander Hamilton, at the Constitutional Convention (June 18, 1787), in Max Farrand, ed., *The Records of The Federal Convention of 1787* (New Haven: Yale Univ. Press, 1911), Vol. I, p. 299.

[56] See his *Rights of the British Colonies Asserted and Proved* (1764) (London: J. Williams, 1766).

[57] Which they did to the colonials' disadvantage. But by claiming that the Americans had "virtual representation" in Parliament even without having flesh-and-blood members sitting there, the British showed that they, too, wanted to be constitutional, if at all possible.

[58] See his *Considerations on the Nature and Extent of the Legislative Authority of the British Parliament* (1774), in J. D. Andrews, ed., *The Works of James Wilson* (New York: Callaghan, 1896), Vol. II, pp. 505–43.

lative balance and checks. . . . These are wholly new discoveries, or have made their principal progress towards perfection in modern times.[59]

The secret of the American Constitution's sure success, wrote Madison, was in properly "combining the requisite stability and energy in government with the inviolable attention due to liberty and to the republican form."[60] The Constitution would work because it was designed to work; and it was designed according to natural principles of government discovered by rational men.[61]

The same spirit, as we have seen, animated the *philosophes* and sustained the hopes of the French revolutionaries. But there was an important difference between the French and American students of constitutionalism, a difference that gave the Americans an infinitely stronger constitutional tradition. The American leaders tended to be realists, while the French leaders tended to be visionaries. Despite the inherent optimism of their natural-law assumptions, Madison, Hamilton, and even Jefferson knew that "if men were angels no government would be necessary" and that men are not angels. Or again: "Why has government been instituted at all? Because the passions of men will not conform to the dictates of reason and justice, without restraint." John Adams tended to focus his suspicions on the poor: "the idle, the vicious, the intemperate" who, without legal restraints, "would rush into the utmost extravagance of debauchery."[62] But he was hardly sentimental about the rich, either. For his part, Madison was able to look unblinkingly at the evils of "faction . . . the most common and durable source of [which] has been the various and unequal distribution of property" and, while giving up the hope of eliminating its cause, still work diligently and hopefully to control its effects.

The steady balance between the extremes of utopianism and despair has been the keynote of American political thinking from the beginning. It helps account for both the viability of our political institutions and the conventionality of our political theorizing.[63] Even in the colonial period our theorists tended to be men who had carried the burdens of governmental responsibility on their own shoulders. This practical experience of self-government had not been granted to the French revolutionaries, a deficiency that fostered their incipient utopianism and added to the consequent fragility of the French constitutional tradition.

THE THEORY OF REVOLUTION

While the anatomy of revolution is strikingly constant, theories justifying revolution are highly volatile. From Aristotle to Brinton[64] the standard pattern of revolutionary activity has been cataloged. An oppressive, inflexible ruling class is unable to recognize the demands a changing society makes upon it. Discontent produces more oppression, which produces more discontent. Finally the vicious circle is broken by a *coup d'état*. The offending regime is expelled and the moderates attempt to take control. But the pent-up forces

[59] Alexander Hamilton, John Jay, and James Madison, *The Federalist,* No. 9 (New York: Random House, Modern Library, 1937). Subsequent quotations from *The Federalist* are from this edition.

[60] That *The Federalist* was not antidemocratic in the present-day sense of the term "democracy" is convincingly shown by Martin Diamond, "Democracy and *The Federalist:* A Reconsideration of the Framers' Intent," *American Political Science Review,* Vol. 53 (1959), pp. 52–68.

[61] See Robert A. Dahl's imaginative critique of Madisonian theory in *A Preface to Democratic Theory* (Chicago: Univ. of Chicago Press, 1956), Ch. 1.

[62] *A Defense of the Constitutions of Government of the United States of America,* 1787. Quoted in Alan P. Grimes, *American Political Thought* (New York: Holt, Rinehart and Winston, 1955), p. 110. This work was a reply to Turgot's criticisms of the American state constitutions, especially their reliance upon separation of powers. Turgot regarded this principle as productive of inequality and division within the community.

[63] See Louis Hartz, *The Liberal Tradition in America* (New York: Harcourt, Brace, & World, 1955).

[64] Aristotle, *Politics,* Bk. V; Crane Brinton, *The Anatomy of Revolution* (New York: Norton, 1938). More penetrating than Brinton is Hannah Arendt, *On Revolution* (New York: Viking, 1963).

of revolt, suddenly released, surge beyond the control of the moderates, carrying them along on the tide for a while until the militarists or extremists replace them: Cromwell replaces Pym, Robespierre replaces Mirabeau, Lenin replaces Kerensky. Then, while idealistic programs and radical ideals are held aloft for public edification, consolidation through growing dictatorship takes place below. Finally, disillusionment sets in and the Thermidorian Reaction[65] takes place. Old forms creep back under new names: Charles II replaces Cromwell, Napoleon replaces Robespierre, Stalin replaces Lenin.

The particular doctrines that become the ideological weapons of a revolution cannot be classified in any such neat pattern. Revolutions are waged primarily against a great evil. They are negative efforts. And the positive ideas that become rallying cries are often taken up in catch-as-catch-can fashion. Therefore, while revolutionary eras seem to produce the greatest political theorizing, actual revolutions themselves rarely produce great ideas. They feed upon the ideas of the recent past.

The French Revolution is a prime example of these common patterns. With very little political experience (the Estates-General had not been called since 1614!), the Third Estate tried to drive a wedge between the monarchy and the nobility. When both collapsed and the Third Estate was on its own, the ideas it turned to for guidance were naturally those of the *philosophes*. But for all the sparkling profusion of ideas associated with these men, not many were helpful to an ongoing parliamentary government. The *philosophes* had, at best, hoped for an enlightened despot like Frederick the Great, who could eliminate abuses of privilege, cut down inequalities of status, and reform the law. But an enlightened despot was not a practical possibility in 1789 and the bland trust in the goodness of man characteristic of some *philosophes,* like Condorcet, was especially inappropriate to the passions of a revolution. For a time the great general Lafayette had hoped that the ideals of moderation, balance, and law developed by Montesquieu and applied, he thought, in America might find a reception in the form of a constitutional monarchy, with a responsible aristocracy serving as a mediator between monarch and Third Estate. But the collapse of monarchy made this view irrelevant. Thus, almost by default, Rousseau emerged as the philosopher of the Revolution, his poorly understood concept of the general will becoming a watchword.

Possibly the most revolutionary writer in France in the eighteenth century was Morelly. But the proposed communism of his *Code de la nature* (1755) was so radical and his critique of the whole structure of society was so fundamental that it had little effect on the exigencies of the French Revolution.[66]

Mably

One who shared many of Morelly's ideas but had a more direct effect on the Revolution was Gabriel de Mably (1709–85). Far more pessimistic than Morelly, Mably nevertheless felt that men had a natural, innate goodness, a harmonious bond with other men, which had been corrupted by the institutions of civilization, especially private property. To Mably equality was more important than liberty—a belief that he seemed to apply in his own life as he repeatedly refused posts, honors, and preferments and lived a frugal, constrained life rather than acknowledge the position of men he deemed unworthy or participate in the degrading system of rank and status. His *Rights and Duties of Citizens* (1758), one of fourteen major works, was not published until the eve of the Revolution. Some of the reforms he there proposes actu-

[65] Thermidor was the "month of heat" on the new Revolutionary Calendar. It began July 19 on the Gregorian Calendar. With the execution of Robespierre on July 28, 1794, the Jacobian dictatorship and Reign of Terror ended.

[66] Morelly, whose first name no one seems to know, anticipates many of the ideas of Fourier. Fourier is reviewed in Chapter 18, below. See Kingsley Martin, *The Rise of French Liberal Thought,* 2nd ed. (New York: New York Univ. Press, 1954), pp. 242–47, and C. H. Driver, "Morelly and Mably," in Hearnshaw, pp. 217–51.

ally were attempted thirty years later, for example, the calling of the Estates-General and the formation of executive committees. His advocacy of a mixed government, reflected in his phrase "republican-monarchy," found much support and the phrase was widely quoted in the early days of the Revolution. He favored cuts in state spending, a curb on land holdings, and various sumptuary laws.

But more significant than the specifics of Mably's reforms, which provided fodder for the Revolution, was the underlying doctrine in both Morelly and Mably of man's natural goodness and the evil character of certain institutions that were corrupting him. The idealistic phase of the Revolution was bursting with such sentiments, was full of a tingling spirit of newness. France, not only in the name of France but in the name of mankind, was sloughing off a decadent past and presenting a fresh face to the world. One cannot but note how in all innocence these men were offering categories in secular dress that were very close to traditional concepts of Christian theology: an original state of innocence, the Fall, and now, after despair—at least in Mably—a shattering regeneration and the emergence of a "new being." No wonder some Frenchmen acted as if the Revolution were Armageddon.

Sieyès

Among those who participated directly in the Revolution, only Condorcet had as much influence as Mably and neither could touch the influence of Rousseau. But two other vigorous intellects stand cut in the frenzied currents and countercurrents of the Revolution, Sieyès and Mirabeau. The Abbé Emmanuel Joseph Sieyès (1748–1836) is a phenomenon typical of Enlightenment France —the antireligious abbé. He is often passed by with a nod, although Lord Acton called him "the first political intellect of his age." His immediately popular yet unsuccessful attempt in *Qu'est-ce que la Tiers État?* (*What Is the Third Estate?*) to transform Rousseau's general will into majority rule, his odd mixture of passionate concern for the ideal state with short-run cynicism,[67] and his undistinguished writing explain his lack of influence. But the combination of his moralistic zeal and realistic insight was, and is, unusual: "He understood politics as the science of the State as it ought to be, and he repudiated the product of history, which is things as they are. . . . [He] was essentially a revolutionist because he held that political oppression can never be right and that resistance to oppres-
ture of passionate concern for the ideal state
sion can never be wrong."[68] But he was not a rabid democrat: he favored indirect elections and a suffrage limited to taxpayers. Although a republican, he admitted that a properly checked monarchy could maintain individual liberties. He proposed one interesting constitutional check in the form of a supreme court composed not of judges, whom he distrusted as reactionaries, but of veteran politicians. No contractualist, for him it was society and not "nature" that gave men their liberty. Yet Sieyès regarded his "society" as no more automatically wise than was the *philosophes*'s "nature." The valid national will, he felt, did not spring full blown from the process of election but arose from the give-and-take of sustained discussion. What a country thinks is less important than what it would think after enlightened men had debated the issues. In this view Sieyès is not so far from what some present-day critics have said about the public-opinion polls.

Mirabeau

An outstanding orator, Honoré Gabriel Victor Riqueti, Comte de Mirabeau (1749–91), son of the Physiocrat, was perhaps as close to what some people call a statesman as any other figure of the Revolution.[69] He opposed

[67] Asked what his greatest accomplishment was in the Revolution, Sieyès answered, "I survived." After his survival, he composed the Napoleonic Constitution of 1799, was made President of the Senate, and then passed into obscurity.

[68] John E. E. D. Acton, *Lectures on the French Revolution* (London: Macmillan, 1910), p. 161.

[69] See J. P. Thompson, *The French Revolution* (New York: Oxford Univ. Press, 1945), pp. 208–16, and Lord Acton, *Lectures*, Ch. 10.

Sieyès' republicanism and hoped to negotiate a new constitution with Louis XVI but failed. Knowing England well, Mirabeau also opposed followers of American precedent, such as Lafayette, who wanted a system of "checks and balances." Mirabeau wanted, rather, a parliamentary ministry that would bind together king and legislature. He was attracted even by Bolingbroke's idea of a patriot king under whom a national party might rally. But the chance for an English form of government was cut off by the Constituent Assembly vote of November 7, 1789, to exclude deputies from the ministry, a measure aimed directly at Mirabeau.

Despite the diversity of their positions, Condorcet, Lafayette, Sieyès, and Mirabeau all published their own model Declaration of Rights and all had some influence on the Declaration of the Rights of Man and Citizen proclaimed by the Constituent Assembly on August 26, 1789. The Declaration[70] was quite similar in aim to the American Bill of Rights, though without the same practical bearing or legal effect. A wide variety of influences can easily be read into it: Rousseau's general will appears in Article VI; Blackstone's stress on innocence until proven guilty appears in Article IX; the Italian prison-reformer Beccaria's hostility to ex post facto laws appears in Article VIII. Events of the times are also reflected: the storming of the Bastille in July can be read into Article VII, which prohibits arbitrary imprisonment; the attack on social distinctions in Article I mirrors the spirit of the day as well as records Mably's basic theme; "the source of all sovereignty is essentially in the nation," in Article III, was a declaration of self-authorization by the National Assembly. But the underlying assumption of the whole document and, indeed, of an entire age appears in the preamble: ". . . ignorance, forgetfulness or contempt of the rights of man are the sole causes of the public miseries and of the corruption of governments."

[70] The Declaration is reprinted in English in Lionel Laing, Manfred C. Vernon, and others, eds., *Source Book in European Governments* (New York: Sloane, 1950), pp. 79–81.

The American Revolution, as we have seen, was almost unique in its departure from the pattern of other revolutions. It was not a class revolution, a social revolution, or even an overturning of the men who had held governmental positions in the colonies. It had similarities to present-day nationalistic revolts but was without most of the egalitarian mass-democracy overtones of the colonial revolutions of the twentieth century.[71] Yet it may be significant that the two best-known "revolutionary theorists" in colonial America, Paine and Jefferson, were, in one way or another, associated with France.

Paine

Thomas Paine (1737–1809) was an Englishman who did not arrive in America until 1774. Although he eventually found himself in a French jail, his greatest popular adulation came when he visited France in the 1790s. Paine was more of a journalist than a theorist. He was an indefatigable pamphleteer and gadfly, with the simplistic bias essential to the true revolutionary. His pamphlet *Common Sense* (January, 1776) sold over 100,000 copies in a few months. An appeal more to emotion than to common sense, it did not hesitate to call for armed conflict with England and helped arouse the colonials to fighting temper. In it Paine pungently ridiculed monarchy, attacked the English Constitution, and criticized the separation of powers, the last two of which he, like a good many others at that time, tended to confuse. Monarchy and the separation of powers were, for Paine, mere encumbrances, since, "The more simple any thing is the less liable it is to be disordered." The simple life of Paine's state of nature was a glorious condition for its residents: "Some convenient tree will afford them a State House." But a series of at least superficially depressing moral failures leads to the present condition, wherein "Society . . . is a blessing, but Government,

[71] See Louis Hartz, "American Political Thought and the American Revolution," *American Political Science Review,* Vol. 46 (1952), pp. 321–42.

even in its best state, is but a necessary evil."[72] Later, when Paine tried to be more profound, he became less effective.

Jefferson

We can call Thomas Jefferson (1743–1826) a revolutionary theorist only because of circumstantial evidence. He wrote "A Summary View of the Rights of British America," a paper too revolutionary for the Virginia Convention to approve in 1774. In drafting the Declaration of Independence he substituted "the pursuit of happiness" for "property" in the Lockean phrase, "life, liberty, and property." He once wrote to Madison, "I hold it that a little rebellion, now and then, is a good thing."[73] Jefferson was a consorter with Parisian radicals while ambassador to France. But one who at the age of thirty-six is able to get himself elected governor of old Virginia is not likely to be regarded by his peers as a congenital insurrectionist. In his letter to Madison he was talking especially of "governments of force," or—with an unmistakable allusion to France—"a government of wolves over sheep." His advice to republican governors to keep their punishment of rebels "mild" was on the cautiously pragmatic ground that excessive repression is more dangerous than some "turbulence." "The pursuit of happiness" was not, as we have seen, at odds with Locke's conception of "property" and both phrases had appeared side by side in George Mason's Virginia Bill of Rights. As ambassador to France in the 1780s, Jefferson almost indiscreetly supported Lafayette's efforts to gain a compromise between absolute monarchy and a republic.

Jefferson was a respecter of law and order, a country gentleman, a patron of the arts and sciences, a believer in the natural rights of man, and a liberal. His sensitivity to humane values led him to resent the autocratic pretensions of New York City aristocrats, just as it led him to fear the outcroppings of urban, "artisan," leveling democracy. His view of revolution was essentially Lockean, that is, he believed that government should be the servant of the people, advancing the general interest while also protecting individual rights; when rulers forget this purpose and go astray, they may properly be regarded as tyrants and men of good sense and sound judgment have every right—even a natural right—to throw the rascals out as adroitly as possible.[74]

CONCLUSION

For the following reasons we cannot understand twentieth-century politics without understanding eighteenth-century political theory:

(1) The urgent hope embedded in the secularized natural law of the Enlightenment, the hope that man can rationally know and rationally control his universe, is one important source of nineteenth-century utopi-

[72] The quotations are from *Common Sense,* in *Political Works* (New York: Eckler, 1892), pp. 3, 1. Paine's other major works are *The Rights of Man* (1791–92), a reply to Burke's *Reflections on the Revolution in France; The Age of Reason* (1794), a critique of Christianity; and *Agrarian Justice* (1797), a plea for welfare measures financed by a heavy tax on the inheritance of land. See M. D. Conway, ed., *The Writings of Thomas Paine* (New York: Putnam's, 1894–96), and Cecilia Kenyon, "Where Paine Went Wrong," *American Political Science Review,* Vol. 45 (1951), pp. 1086–99.

[73] From Paris (January 30, 1787). Quoted in Adrienne Koch and William Peden, eds., *The Life and Selected Writings of Thomas Jefferson* (New York: Random House, Modern Library, 1944), p. 413.

[74] The many other facets of Jefferson's thought must be left to other studies. The literature on Jefferson is voluminous—as is literature *by* Jefferson. See Julian P. Boyd, ed., *The Papers of Thomas Jefferson* (Princeton: Princeton Univ. Press, 1950–   ). Seventeen of a projected fifty volumes are presently available. See also Max Beloff, *Thomas Jefferson and American Democracy* (London: Hodder & Stoughton, 1949); Edward Dumbauld, ed., *Political Writings* (New York: Liberal Arts Press, 1955); Paul L. Ford, ed., *The Works of Thomas Jefferson* (New York: Putnam's, 1904–05); Adrienne Koch, *The Philosophy of Thomas Jefferson* (New York: Columbia Univ. Press, 1943); Merrill D. Peterson, *The Jefferson Image in the American Mind* (New York: Oxford Univ. Press, 1960); and Charles M. Wiltse, *The Jeffersonian Tradition in American Democracy* (New York: Hill & Wang, 1960).

anism and twentieth-century social science. The collapse of the hope has helped turn utopianism into totalitarianism and threatens to turn social science into social statistics.[75]

(2) The rise of the middle class, the triumph of the market economy, and the birth of economic science were aspects of a newly dynamic economy and heralded a new kind of political interpenetration with the economy. Coeval with this development came a theoretical separation of politics and economics. The separation has produced problems not yet fully faced by the "capitalist West" and inadequately resolved by the "communist East."

(3) Western men for certain—all men perchance—are creatures of history. Darwin, Marx, and Freud; psychoanalysis, rockets to the moon, and presidential speeches only make us more self-conscious creatures of history. We can wish-fulfill with history like Condorcet, or play politics with history like Bolingbroke, or think with history like Vico. We can and we do.

(4) The failure of men in the form of eighteenth-century enlightened despots transferred confidence to laws in the form of codes, bills of rights, and constitutions. But by the eighteenth century the medieval mystique that sanctified and dehumanized law was shattered by skepticism. The recurring controversies over the role of our own Supreme Court suggest that we have not yet found a simple answer to the question, If you cannot trust men, how can you trust the laws they make?

(5) We study revolutions because we cannot help it. We are drawn to revolutions as we are drawn to fights, wrecks, murders, and violence of all kinds because of something deep and dark within us. And so we learn about ourselves from studying revolutions. We learn that America is basically conservative and law-abiding—or at least law-respecting—because even her revolution was conservative and law-respecting. From studying political *theories* of revolutionary periods we learn that ideologies come and ideologies go but tyrants go on forever.

[75] See Judith Shklar, *After Utopia; The Decline of Political Faith* (Princeton: Princeton Univ. Press, 1958); J. L. Talmon, *The Origins of Totalitarian Democracy* (New York: Praeger, 1960); Hannah Arendt, *The Origins of Totalitarianism* (New York: Harcourt, Brace & World, 1951); and Glenn Tinder, *The Crisis of Political Imagination* (New York: Scribner's, 1964). To balance the gloom of Talmon and Arendt, one should try the bracing liberalism of Charles Frankel, an Enlightenment scholar who still believes in the Enlightenment. See his *The Case for Modern Man* (New York: Harper & Row, 1956), or *The Democratic Prospect* (New York: Harper & Row, 1962).

14

MONTESQUIEU

Charles Louis de Secondat, Baron de la Brède et de Montesquieu, is a somewhat enigmatic figure in the history of political theory. He was in but not of the Enlightenment, identified with but not attached to the *philosophes,* a mixer of ancient lore with modern sociology, an empirical but still unscientific historian. He poured years of work into *L'esprit des lois,* "that apparently incoherent and alternately simplistic and obscure masterpiece of profound and benevolent guile."[1]

LIFE

Montesquieu's life is without the fascination of many eighteenth-century French lives and can be dealt with rather briefly. He was born in 1689 of a noble family at La Brède, near Bordeaux. His mother died when he was seven and at eleven he was sent to a school near Paris for a classical education. Perhaps because of his limited home life, he was shy and somewhat aloof even as an adult. But he was always a good student, with a strong attraction to languages and the classics. His admiration for the Stoic philosophers is explicit in an essay written when he was twenty-two in which he argued that the Church was wrong in its position that the Stoics could not know salvation. He also displayed an early interest in natural science, studying and writing on botany, anatomy, physics, and related subjects.

In 1716 the uncle of M. de la Brède, as Montesquieu was then named, died and bequeathed to him the presidency of the *parlement* of Bordeaux. We would describe the post today as the chief justiceship of a local court. The *parlements,* of which the one at Bordeaux was the most venerated of all those outside Paris, had at one time been the agencies by which the centralized monarchy gained ascendancy over the feudal nobility and the clergy. Later, because seats were gained by hereditary right, the *parlements* were able to become more independent of the king. Some of this independence rubbed off on Montesquieu and he was to become, in his way, a champion of the provincial *parlements* in their essentially conservative resistance to the monarchy. He kept this post for

[1] David Lowenthal, "Book I of Montesquieu's *The Spirit of the Laws,*" *American Political Science Review,* Vol. 53 (1959), p. 487.

ten years but sold it and moved to Paris after the literary fame brought about by the publication of *Les lettres persanes* (*The Persian Letters*) in 1721.

Les lettres persanes were published anonymously in Cologne and purported to be the account of two Persian travelers visiting France. The format was devious enough to permit Montesquieu to get away with some sharp criticisms of French government and Parisian society and his inclusion of both French and allegedly Persian erotica was then, as it would be now, conducive to sales. The book was a literary sensation; when the author was identified, Montesquieu was famous. That the court was displeased with *Les lettres persanes* may be inferred from the objection raised to the initial proposal of Montesquieu's name for membership in the French Academy. (In 1728 he was finally elected to this select circle of literary men.)

In 1729 Montesquieu departed for a lengthy trip through Europe, terminating in England, where he stayed for two years. There he studied English government with diligence and restrained admiration—though he ignored social problems—was a favorite at the court of Queen Caroline, and was elected to the Royal Society. Upon his return to France he spent more time at the family estate at La Brède; in 1734 he produced *Considérations sur les causes de la grandeur des Romains et de leur décadence* (*Considerations on the Greatness and Decline of Rome*).

After a lifetime of study, in 1748 Montesquieu published his great book, *L'esprit des lois*. A work of apparently formless design, it exerted a profound influence on historical method and the study of the sociological basis of forms of government. The Jesuits attacked its apparent determinism. The *philosophes* welcomed much of the book but were unhappy with its conservative implications.[2] Voltaire was provoked to list, in his *Sur l'esprit des lois,* all Montesquieu's historical inaccuracies—or at least all those Voltaire knew about.

In 1755, only a few years after the publication of *L'esprit des lois,* Montesquieu, his sight failing, died in Paris.

L'ESPRIT DES LOIS: ORGANIZATION AND AIM

Organization and Aim

Scholars are still not agreed on the organizational logic of *L'esprit des lois,* or on the relationship of the organization to the work's underlying purpose, or, indeed, on what this underlying purpose may be. Sabine, on the one hand, professes to find very little by way of an orderly pattern in *L'esprit des lois:* "There is not in truth much concatenation of subject matter and the amount of irrelevance is extraordinary." Lowenthal, on the other hand, finds a rigorous design deliberately hidden from the "vulgar reader" (to use D'Alembert's phrase in dealing with the same problem). Vaughn sees in the opening chapter a forthright declaration of "the vital principle which gives unity to the necessarily scattered details, the torch, in the light of which every detail is seen to take its place as part of an ordered and intelligible whole." Cabeen finds the disorder, or better, the irregularity of Montesquieu's writing an inevitable result of the elusive concept of *l'esprit,* which it was his aim to communicate.[3]

[2] For Montesquieu's influence on the *philosophes* see Kingsley Martin, *The Rise of French Liberal Thought,* 2nd ed. (New York: New York Univ. Press, 1954), pp. 137–62, and Joseph Dedieu, *Montesquieu; L'Homme et l'oeuvre* (Paris: Boivin, 1943), Ch. 11.

[3] The above quotations are from George Sabine, *History of Political Theory* (New York: Holt, Rinehart and Winston, 1937), p. 556; David Lowenthal, p. 486; C. E. Vaughn, *Studies in the History of Political Philosophy* (Manchester: Manchester Univ. Press, 1925), Vol. I, p. 257; David Cabeen, "The *Esprit* of the *Esprit des Lois,*" *Publications of the Modern Language Association,* Vol. 54 (1939), pp. 439–53. See also Gustave Lanson, *Montesquieu* (Paris: Alcan, 1932), pp. 5–7, and Franz Neumann's Introduction to his edition of *The Spirit of the Laws,* trans. by Thomas Nugent (New York: Hafner, 1949), pp. XXIX–XXXV. Subsequent quotations are from this edition.

Part of the problem of the organization of *L'esprit des lois,* therefore, is whether it needs to be taken as a problem. A quick outline of the work is enough to indicate that as written it is not what one would call conventionally systematic. Montesquieu begins with a short book (the *livres* are generally of chapter length), *"Des lois"* ("Of Laws in General"), and is soon immersed in more or less practical considerations pertaining to three basic forms of government—monarchy, republic, and despotism—including the relation of each of the three forms to "sumptuary laws, luxury, and the condition of women" (Bks. II–VIII). There follow two books (IX and X) on defense and the laws of war, and three (XI, XII, and XIII) on the subject of liberty. Perhaps the most famous part of the whole work is Book XI, in which the principle of separation of powers is developed, related to the subject of liberty, and illustrated in large part by reference to the English Constitution.

Books XIV–XXV, which have been shuffled around in a variety of ways by different students of Montesquieu, all relate in one way or another to the influence of environmental factors, especially geography and climate, on forms of government, social and economic forces, morals and manners, and religion. The last books, XXVI–XXXI, have been called the work of the pure historian, or fragmentary contributions to the history of law, or the incidental residue of Montesquieu's legal interests. He discusses the Roman law of succession, the origins of feudal law in France, and, in a rather technical treatment, "Of the Manner of Composing Laws" (XXIX).

Vaughn feels that the first eight books are of secondary importance but that Montesquieu put them first because they dealt with some of the more practical aspects of statesmanship and were therefore more likely to be read. The heart of *L'esprit des lois,* in Vaughn's view, is Books XIV–XXV (despite the greater fame of XI–XIII), in which the influence of geographic environment on cultural life is developed. The final books, in this analysis, are intended to make up for the neglect of historical continuity in the earlier books, which tended—though much less than did the writings of the *philosophes*—to stress cultural unity from a nonlinear point of view. Others feel that the concept of liberty and its relation to forms of government is, as its position would indicate, the central concern of the work. But to decide what is most important we must, temporarily at least, forget about organization and first take seriously the title of this strange work, *L'esprit des lois.*

Des lois

Montesquieu begins Book I, *"Des lois,"* as follows:

> Laws, in their most general signification, are the necessary relations arising from the nature of things. In this sense all beings have their laws: The Deity His Laws, the material world its laws, the beasts their laws, man his laws.
>
> They who assert that a blind fatality produced the various effects we behold in this world talk very absurdly; for can any thing be more unreasonable than to pretend that a blind fatality could be productive of intelligent beings?
>
> There is, then, a prime reason; and laws are the relations subsisting between it and different beings, and the relations of these to one another.[4]

God's creation and preservation of the universe, Montesquieu explains, presuppose invariable laws. Among "particular intelligent beings" the term describing their proper relations is "justice":

> To say that there is nothing just or unjust but what is commanded or forbidden by positive laws is the same as saying that before the describing of a circle all the radii were not equal.
>
> We must therefore acknowledge relations of justice antecedent to the positive law by which they are established.[5]

The intelligent world is not so well governed as the physical, since particular intelligent beings are finite and liable to error. Beasts are governed by natural laws (here Montesquieu is using the term "natural law[s]" in the nontraditional sense of descriptive behavioral laws) but not positive laws, since beasts do not have knowledge as humans do:

[4] *The Spirit of the Laws,* Bk. I, Ch. 1.
[5] *Ibid.*

Man, as a physical being, is like other bodies governed by invariable laws. As an intelligent being, he incessantly transgresses the laws established by God, and changes those of his own instituting. He is left to his private direction, though a limited being, and subject, like all finite intelligences, to ignorance and error: even his imperfect knowledge he loses; and as a sensible creature, he is hurried away by a thousand impetuous passions. Such a being might every instant forget his Creator; God has therefore reminded him of his duty by the laws of religion. Such a being is liable every moment to forget himself; philosophy has provided against this by the laws of morality. Formed to live in society, he might forget his fellow creatures; legislators have, therefore, by political and civil laws, confined him to his duty.[6]

First of all we must note that, while Montesquieu is speaking of laws in general, he is not speaking of law in the abstract. Every reference to law in this chapter is plural. Montesquieu is developing a theme rather than proving a proposition. In his reference to justice he is clearly conscious of the natural-law tradition behind the term, and in the analogy of the circle and its radii he seems to adopt a Grotius-like, rationalistic, deistic view of natural law. But it is also clear from the last paragraph quoted above that he does not share the traditional optimistic view of man as a rational being. Although possessed of intelligence, man forgets God in using his intelligence; he forgets his own knowledge when hurried by a thousand passions; and he forgets his fellows. Law is used in three senses in this paragraph: there are physical laws, which cannot be violated; there are religious laws of God—who here seems rather isolated from physical laws—and moral laws of philosophers, which can be and are violated; finally there are "political and civil laws" of the legislator, which can confine men to their duty.

Antecedent to these three types of laws, continues Montesquieu in Chapter 2, "are those of nature, so called," derived entirely "from our frame and existence." In this chapter Montesquieu looks at natural man and finds him to be one who thinks first of self-preservation, as Hobbes contended, but who is weak and without the strong power impulse that Hobbes found. Indeed, war, said Montesquieu, was not possible until *after* man entered society, since before society was formed each man would be isolated and "would fancy himself inferior." The natural laws Montesquieu talks about at this point are simply nonmoral drives, such as sex and gregariousness. Montesquieu's view of man, Lowenthal concludes from this chapter, lies somewhere between Hobbes's egoism and the traditional natural-law view.

In Chapter 3, "Of Positive Laws," Montesquieu explains the distinction between political and civil laws referred to at the end of Chapter 1. Here, for the first time, *droits* replaces *lois*—although not in the chapter title. Political laws (rights) deal with the constitutional structure, the relations of the governors to the governed, and the union of strengths, forces, and powers. Civil laws (rights) stem from the conjunction of individual wills. Montesquieu is obscure at this point but the civil would seem to be an ideological substructure or prerequisite to the political. Though both types of law are aspects of the same society, each is a product of a different kind of state: the "political state," or constitutional body politic, on the one hand, and the "civil state"—perhaps we could say consensual state—on the other. A third type of law is the law (right) of nations, whose principle is to do as much good in peace and as little harm in war as is possible "without prejudicing . . . real interests." By this law, nations are united in their relations to each other, even though there is between them no common state.

Given the specialized and esoteric character of these conceptions, it is all the more surprising to find that Montesquieu concludes the chapter and the book by stating:

Law in general is human reason, inasmuch as it governs all the inhabitants of the earth: the political and civil laws of each nation ought to be only the particular cases in which human reason is applied.

They should be adapted in such a manner

[6] *Ibid.*

to the people for whom they are framed that it should be a great chance if those of one nation suit another.

They should be in relation to the nature and principle of each government: whether they form it, as may be said of politic laws; or whether they support it, as in the case of civil institutions.

They should be in relation to the climate of each country, to the quality of its soil, to its situation and extent, to the principal occupation of the natives. . . . In all of which different lights they ought to be considered.

This is what I have undertaken to perform in the following work. These relations I shall examine, since all these together constitute what I call the Spirit of the Laws.

I have not separated the political from the civil institutions, as I do not pretend to treat of laws, but of their spirit; and as this spirit consists in the various relations which the laws may bear to different objects, it is not so much my business to follow the natural order of laws as that of these relations and objects.[7]

This passage shows Montesquieu's almost paradoxical combination of universalism and relativism. It also shows that he is neither unaware of what he is about nor careless of the reader's expectations. If the reader is subseqently bothered by Montesquieu's purpose, it may be the result of a misunderstanding of *l'esprit.*

L'esprit

Given the subject of the spirit of the laws—or, as Mme. de Deffand revised it, "Of the spirit in the laws"—Montesquieu was bound to follow the elliptical, uneven, ambiguous approach that marks his writings. *L'esprit* cannot be pursued directly. Montesquieu himself said, "When one runs after spirit, one catches foolishness [la sottise]."[8] Cabeen has listed the stylistic techniques Montesquieu necessarily employs in trying to communicate *l'esprit:* "irony (rarely), sarcasm, affected naïveté, *pointes* (sometimes with a trace of *préciosité*), an occasional paradox, metaphor or gasconnade, with some humor of understatement or dryness."[9] Montesquieu operates from the assumption that he can omit nonessentials for the reader who is also seeking *l'esprit* rather than the mere forms of knowledge. Only such a reader can, in any case, grasp what the writer is after: "My business is not to make people read, but to make them think." This helps explain the many abrupt starts and stops in *L'esprit des lois.* Cabeen feels that Montesquieu was often led to restrain his natural brilliance deliberately in order to win the wide readership he knew the book deserved and thus to impart its liberalizing effect both to those who did and to those who did not also truly seek *l'esprit.*

But still we are not completely sure what *l'esprit* means. It must be a word able to signal the paradoxes that delighted or perhaps only fascinated Montesquieu. In the rules of the physical universe, he says, "each diversity is uniformity, each change is constancy." Everything seems to act in relation to everything else, in physical and nonphysical worlds; yet somehow Montesquieu hoped to find an element of constancy in this fluid network of relationships. The word *esprit* has many English translations—*wit, mind, intellect, character, spirit,* even *bodily fluids* (compare *âme,* "soul" or "mind"). But its protean character should not be allowed to obscure its systematic possibilities:

Something like intelligence or reason is only one level within "esprit." Temperament or disposition typify another and more physical level, and animal spirits another and even more evidently physical level. . . . There is reason to believe that the psychology and physiology of man, set within a wider natural philosophy, supply a continuing framework to Montesquieu's analysis. And to indicate these various ingredients of his concern, the word "esprit" was admirably chosen.[10]

A search for *the* definitive objective of *L'esprit des lois* runs the risk of what Montesquieu warned against, chasing *l'esprit* only to catch *la sottise.* But if his opening

[7] *Ibid.,* Ch. 3.

[8] *Pensées et fragments inédite,* quoted in Cabeen, p. 440.

[9] *Ibid.,* pp. 447–48.

[10] Lowenthal, p. 498.

declaration of purpose is to have any meaning at all, the assumption of underlying unity of purpose must be granted. The scope of this purpose is, in any case, more definable than its substance, ranging through the relations of climate to political structure and of political structure to "liberty." As students of politics, we have been given ample material.

Climate and Causation

> Cold air constringes the extremities of the external fibres of the body; this increases their elasticity, and favors the return of the blood from the extreme parts to the heart. It contracts those very fibres; consequently it increases also their force. On the contrary, warm air relaxes and lengthens the extremes of the fibres; of course it diminishes their force and elasticity. People are, therefore, more vigorous in cold climates.[11]

People are, in Montesquieu's view, many other things in cold climates: they are more courageous, industrious, liberty-minded, and capable of bearing pain, but also more likely to commit suicide. They are less erotic, romantic, indolent, and otherworldly than their southern brethren. In northern climates one needs a certain amount of strong liquor, "without which the blood would congeal." In the south, where "the aqueous part of the blood loses itself greatly by perspiration," the Moslem law properly forbids wine.

Some of Montesquieu's observations about climate and soil are now obviously incorrect; but others are still illuminating: the greater relative equality of women in Europe results from monogamy; monogamy results from climate; in warmer climates, girls mature more rapidly and are suitable for marriage at an earlier age, which makes them grow old and wrinkled faster, which leads to the practice of adding a new wife every so often. The great plains of Asia make for despotic rule; but the natural subdivisions created by rivers and mountains in Europe encourage less centralized authority: "Monarchy is more frequently found in fruitful countries, and a republican government in those which are not so." "The inhabitants of islands have a higher relish for liberty than those of the continent." A trading and navigating people require a much more extensive code of laws than agrarian peoples. The advent of a money economy increases the kinds and degrees of injustice. The Moslem religion is conducive to despotism, the Catholic to monarchy, the Protestant to republicanism.

Climate is made to explain almost everything in Montesquieu: morals, economics, religion, and forms of government. Much of this strikes us as a bit silly. But, on the one hand, we are never quite sure how much of it Montesquieu himself takes seriously. And, on the other hand, at the level of every general causal explanation in history, climate is certainly no less absurd than any of the other single-factor explanations of historical process that men have advanced. Montesquieu at least warns his readers

> to notice that there is a vast difference between saying that a certain quality, modification of the mind, or virtue, is not the spring by which government is actuated, and affirming that it is not to be found in that government. Were I to say such a wheel or such a pinion is not the spring which sets the watch going, can you infer thence that it is not to be found in the watch?[12]

Montesquieu was sensible enough to see that the factors of climate and soil were more determining in the earlier stages of civilization than in the later stages. If climate is implausible as an overall explanatory cause, in time the economic influences that are now weighed so heavily in the causal scales may seem equally implausible.

Montesquieu drew from his observations the logical conclusion that the institutions of a particular nation are not easily changed. Indeed, he could scarcely have drawn any other. Not only was he skeptical about change but pessimistic as well. A strong strain of pessimism runs through *Les lettres persanes.* Progress is seen as ambiguous: "Of what advantage has the invention of the mariner's

[11] *The Spirit of the Laws,* Bk. XIV, Ch. 2.

[12] *Ibid.,* Bk. XVIII, Ch. 16, Author's Explanatory Notes, No. 2.

compass been to us, and the discovery of so many nations who have given us more diseases than wealth?"[13] The best councils of France did not last long and neither did the good they accomplished. Every man ought to have a right to commit suicide; in fact, "men should be bewailed at their birth and not at their death." Statesmen, it would appear from both *L'esprit des lois* and *Considérations sur les causes de la grandeur des Romains et de leur décadence* have a limited capacity to control history. Time moved too rapidly for Roman emperors. Rome grew too fast for effective management and crumbled. Unforeseen reactions and counterreactions thwart the shrewdest calculations, as when Henry VIII broke from Rome and hoped thereby to strengthen the monarchy, only to help create a Protestant force that eventually weakened the monarchy.

Yet Montesquieu was not a blind fatalist. As man increased his control of nature the possibility of more libertarian political forms was enhanced. Political change could not be abrupt but it was not impossible. He wrote in *L'esprit des lois* that, "when a prince would make great alterations in his kingdom, he should reform by law what is established by law, and change by custom what is settled by custom; for it is very bad policy to change by law what ought to be changed by custom." In a famous illustration Montesquieu noted the futility of Peter the Great's law ordering the Muscovites' beards to be cut off. Laws (here Montesquieu means positive laws) apply to the actions of subjects. Manners and customs apply to the actions of men as men rather than as subjects. Manners relate to interior conduct and custom to exterior conduct. The wise legislator, says Montesquieu, is aware of these distinctions. It is clear that positive laws are but a junior part of the family of laws whose *esprit* Montesquieu is exploring; but it is also true that positive laws have a constructive, possibly even a progressive, role to play in the life of man.

[13] *Persian and Chinese Letters,* trans. by John Davidson (New York: Dunne, 1907), *Persian Letters,* No. 106. Subsequent quotations are from this edition.

Relativism and Justice

That what works in one society will not necessarily work in another is a judgment of common sense that few men would now question. If this is all that is meant by Montesquieu's relativism, it does not amount to much. What is today called ethical relativism implies that no truly independent judgment of moral worth can be made in comparing different societies or cultures. Every moral judgment grows out of, is relative to, and is valid for a particular culture only. Is Montesquieu a relativist in this sense?

Montesquieu sought to isolate the nature and the principle of different types of governments and evaluate them largely in their own terms. "Nature" and "principle" in his context are not the same:

> There is this difference between the nature and principle of government, that the former is that by which it is constituted, the latter that by which it is made to act. One is its particular structure, and the other the human passions which set it in motion.
>
> Now, laws ought not less to relate to the principle than to the nature of each government.[14]

The three basic types of government are republican, monarchical, and despotic. Their special nature is that, in the first, the whole people or a part have supreme power (a republic may be a democracy or an aristocracy depending upon the size of the ruling group); in the second, one person rules by fixed laws; and in the third, a single person rules by caprice (Book II). The "principles" these forms require are, for the republic, virtue; for monarchy, honor; and for despotism, fear. Education (IV) and legislation (V) must be calculated to support and advance the relevant principle of government if it is to survive. If the principle becomes corrupted, the best laws can do little to preserve the system (VIII).

By comparison with his contemporaries Montesquieu symbolizes a remarkable detachment in trying to understand and not

[14] *The Spirit of the Laws,* Bk. III, Ch. 1.

simply pass judgment on diverse institutions. If Cassirer is correct, Montesquieu was the first in history to grasp the concept of *ideal-types* as used in the twentieth century by Weber and others, that is, abstracted but nonutopian, historical-sociological models.[15]

Nevertheless, despite his sensitive awareness of diversity, Montesquieu would seem to depart in at least three respects from any kind of strict ethical relativism. In the first place, there are scattered in profusion throughout *L'esprit des lois* what we would call *personal value judgments,* or statements whose factual content is low and whose emotional content is fairly high: a despot "is naturally lazy, voluptuous, and ignorant"; despotism "glories in the contempt of life"; it has produced "horrid cruelties." The people in a democracy are "always either too remiss or too violent." The establishment of unlimited power is one remedy to prevent the dissolution of an empire, "but how dreadful the remedy." A full listing of such statements would be endless and perhaps without very great significance, in any case. Montesquieu was, like almost every eighteenth-century writer, something of a moralist, influenced by the belletristic tradition of such writers as Montaigne. Stylistic intrusions of moral judgments, as well as his failure to be wholly detached, are not necessarily a failure of his fundamental orientation.

In the second place, Montesquieu was unable to be wholly detached from the gross evils and extravagances of the French monarchy under Louis XIV and Louis XV. Lightly concealed beneath the analytic surface of *L'esprit des lois* lie a series of barbs aimed directly at that target. Repeatedly Montesquieu assures his readers that to designate honor as the principle of monarchy is not to suggest that virtue is absent therefrom. His assurances are not altogether convincing; or perhaps it is better said that they convince us only that Montesquieu was anxious about the reactions of certain monarchists. Certainly most of Book VIII, Chapter 6, "Of the Corruption of the Principle of Monarchy," can be regarded as an elliptical attack on the Louises. China is the ostensible source of the illustrative material but, when Montesquieu says that monarchy "is destroyed when the prince, directing everything entirely to himself, calls to the state his capital, the capital to his court, and the court to his own person," it is not hard to imagine whom he is talking about. The privileges of provincial cities are regarded tenderly and effeminacy in the ancient Lydian court is criticized pointedly and unhistorically.

Scholars have challenged the accuracy of much of Montesquieu's historical evidence. To prove by historical example that the institution of the *grand vizier,* or the Turkish prime minister, is the "fundamental law" of despotism is an effort that suggests either that Montesquieu was not the best of historians or that he had objectives other than merely writing history as it really was. Both suggestions are undoubtedly correct and, indeed, the latter partly explains the former. That Montesquieu was less than accurate on many historical points reflects in part, of course, the limitations of the sources available to him and especially the dubious character of many Asian chronicles. But it was more the character of his interest than a defect in his talent that affected his historiography. His long excursion into the Salic Law of France demonstrates his prowess as a historian. If the grand vizier became a slightly exaggerated target, it makes sense to believe that Richelieu and not a horde of Moslem functionaries was being delicately deflated. As in most other political writers, there is in Montesquieu a quantity of polemics mixed with history and social theory.

The third departure from ethical relativism is the most significant. It lies in Montesquieu's acknowledgment of a standard of justice that, being based on the "relations of justice anterior to the positive law by which they are established," transcends the differ-

[15] Ernst Cassirer, *The Philosophy of the Enlightenment,* trans. by Fritz C. A. Koelln and James P. Pettegrove (Boston: Beacon Press, 1955), p. 210. While representing a brilliant insight into the spirit of types, Montesquieu's accomplishment, says Cassirer, is essentially static. Principles of functions as distinct from forms elude him.

ences of place and time. It is his feeling about this standard that permits and encourages his personal judgments against despotism in general and the French monarchy in particular. Montesquieu's condemnation of dehumanizing practices is evident throughout *Les lettres persanes*. In Book XV of *L'esprit des lois* his mock defense of slavery is one of the most biting satires one could imagine; and in Book XXV his attack on religious persecutions is equally devastating. Montesquieu is incapable of saying, "To each culture its own." Yet he still recognizes the irremediable fact of moral diversity. What we have, then, is a tension between an eternal standard of justice and the passionate creature man, who in practice seems continually to ignore it. One of *Les lettres persanes* is most graphic on the contrast:

Justice is a true relation existing between things, a relation which is always the same, whoever contemplates it, whether it be God or an angel, or, lastly, man himself.

It is true that men do not always perceive these relations: often indeed, when they do perceive them, they turn aside from them, their own interest being always that which they perceive most clearly. Justice cries aloud; but her voice is hardly heard in the tumult of the passions.[16]

There would seem to be in Montesquieu a fundamental distinction parallel to that drawn in Book I between the political state and the civil state. At one level there are various political rights (*droits*) peculiar to given bodies politic, rights that from historical necessity must be accepted as natural reflections of national differences. At this level —and it is a fairly inclusive one—Montesquieu's advice seems to coincide with that of a gentleman he quotes: "Leave us as we are . . . and nature will repair whatever is amiss."

Yet there linger over or behind or in all bodies politic more fundamental human rights, especially rights of freedom of movement, individual expression, and personal justice derived from the "relations of justice antecedent to . . . positive law." Such rights cannot be neatly codified or easily isolated from standards of personal morality, yet it is clear that for Montesquieu they have a universal and not merely national sanction. These, too, are touched by necessity; indeed, they would seem to be necessary in a more profound sense than merely historical-political rights: "If I know of a thing useful for my nation which, however, would be ruinous to another, I would not propose it to my Prince, because I am a man before being a Frenchman, or, better, because I am a man by necessity and a Frenchman only by accident."[17]

On the record, we cannot call Montesquieu a moral relativist.

The Separation of Powers and Liberty

In dozens of books and hundreds of lectures and thousands of examination papers the name Montesquieu means one thing—separation of powers. Folklore has it that we Americans owe the separation of powers to Montesquieu via Madison and the founding fathers and that Montesquieu owes it to a misunderstanding of the English Constitution. A man's reputation tends to be made by his followers and we cannot deny that Montesquieu's significance for us necessarily reflects the importance we attach to the principle of the separation of powers. Let us give the subject its due, but let us also avoid exaggeration if possible.

With the taste for cultural variety that has become his trademark, Montesquieu begins Book XI of *L'esprit des lois* by noting the tremendously wide range of conceptions of liberty. (Once again he "makes hay with a beard" by noting the fact that for the Russians under Peter the Great the greatest liberty was the privilege of wearing a long beard.) But liberty, even in a democracy, does not consist of doing anything one pleases to do: "We must have continually present to our minds the difference between independence and liberty. Liberty is the right of do-

[16] *Persian Letters*. No. 84.

[17] *Cahiers* (1716–55), quoted by Neumann, Introduction, p. xv.

ing whatever the laws permit, and if a citizen could do what they forbid he would no longer be possessed of liberty, because all his fellow citizens would have the same power."

Montesquieu specifically dismisses "philosophical" conceptions of liberty from his concern. He is here interested in the well-ordered society, not the deep places of the individual psyche. Moreover, as Neumann observes, he is without a counterpart to Rousseau's concept of general will or to any other concept that might justify the subordination of individual interests to general law without the abandonment of liberty as a goal. Unlike his conception of justice, Montesquieu's conception of liberty is basically negative. If we remember his general attitude toward toleration, it is clear to us that he really wants to authorize not only those acts that the laws permit but all acts that the laws do not forbid. This is close to the traditional liberal view of liberty, quite consonant with Locke, for example.

In particular, Montesquieu found in the principle of separation of powers a guarantee of the kind of restraint on government that, given the right setting, could assure *liberty*, that is, a condition in which the laws were appropriate to a well-ordered society and also permitted a considerable degree of individual and group independence.

Although all seem to seek self-preservation, different governments have many different ends: war, commerce, tranquillity, princely pleasure, and the like. But one eighteenth-century nation has as its end political liberty, thinks Montesquieu, and that nation is England. Chapter 6 of Book XI is entitled "Of the Constitution of England" and begins: "In every government there are three sorts of powers: the legislative; the executive in respect to things dependent on the law of nations; and the executive in regard to matters that depend on civil law." This terminology at first glance seems to correspond to Locke's separation of powers into legislative, executive, and "federative" in Chapter 12 of his second of *Two Treatises of Government*. But Montesquieu, it appears, combines Locke's executive and federative into one and calls the executive in regard to matters that depend on the civil law the "judiciary."

The heart of Montesquieu's theme was that where these three functions were combined in the same person or body of magistrates there would be the end of liberty. Not only did he point to the dangers of allowing one agency to be prosecutor and judge but he argued for the safety of having popular feeling represented in one house of a legislature and "persons distinguished by their birth, riches, or honors" represented in another. They would have "a right to check the licentiousness of the people, as the people have a right to oppose any encroachment of theirs." Plausible arguments are offered for frequent but not continuous meetings of parliaments and for entrusting the power of summoning and proroguing to someone outside the legislative body. The American founding fathers were influenced by Montesquieu's arguments for both separation of powers and bicameralism, though, of course, the parallelism between Lords and Commons and Senate and House is not exact.

What Montesquieu was describing was not the English government as it actually operated but the English government as it might operate. He was fully aware of the distinction. His *Notes on England* shows that he was familiar with the realities of English politics, including the use of bribes and influence in high places. He had heard the famous Dunkirk debate in the House of Commons, during which Bolingbroke and Walpole argued the theory of the separation of powers. If he attached great weight to this theory, which came to earth more concretely in America than ever it did in England, it is partly because the system of centralized cabinet government that we have come to know in modern Britain was, at the time of Montesquieu's visit, in barely nascent form. It is also because he avowedly cared more about the theory than the practice: "It is not my business to examine whether the English actually enjoy this liberty or not," he wrote in *L'esprit des lois*. "Sufficient it is for my purpose to observe that it is established by their laws; and I inquire no further."

Actually, much more space is devoted to the principle of separation of powers in the early Roman government than to this principle in England. But with that, Montesquieu stops: "I should be glad to inquire into the distribution of the three powers in all the moderate governments we are acquainted with, in order to calculate the degree of liberty which each may enjoy. But we must not always exhaust a subject, so as to leave no work at all for the reader." The work given to the reader was the contemplation of an ideal-type construction of a system of liberty built on the separation of powers. Though rooted in historical contingency, it had no exact counterpart in England or anywhere else. Certainly it could not serve as a blueprint for the reform of political societies wholly unlike England. But it did provide a standard of orderly and liberal government by which different existing governments could be compared—a measuring stick, so to speak. Montesquieu could hardly have been unaware of the likelihood that such comparison would be disadvantageous to the French monarchy.

CONCLUSION

It is the fate of men of genius who do not fit into conventional categories to be neglected until such time as new categories emerge. Perhaps this has been the fate of Montesquieu. As Vaughan has observed,[18] Montesquieu was neither in the camp of the *philosophes* with their emphasis on abstract rights and their antihistorical bias nor was he at one with the mechanical "expediency" of the utilitarians. Like later conservatives—and Montesquieu's influence on Burke and De Maistre was profound—he saw the individual not as an atomistic entity but as a member of an ineluctable community. The variety of communities fascinated Montesquieu; the concept of immutable, inalienable, and universal rights to be hurled against these communities was not compatible with his mentality. Moreover, as an aristocrat he defended the privileged position of aristocratic classes, where he did not take it for granted.

Yet justice and liberty meant a great deal to him and he had a sensitivity for organic growth toward or away from such ideals, ideals that had a kind of universality similar to, yet distinct from, traditional natural-law principles. As we have seen, he was not an ethical relativist and was capable even of rousing moral denunciation. If such moralistic exercises seem inconsistent with the image of Montesquieu as an inductive scientist describing the diversities of cultures with an air of utter detachment, it is well to note that this was not necessarily the image Montesquieu had of himself. On the one hand, he knew that amidst the vast sea of uncertain and often unreliable historical data he could not conform to the rigorous canons of Baconian induction. On the other hand, he was interested in much more than mere description and correlation. The spirit of those necessary relations that he called laws was much too elusive for a two-dimensional exposition. "I have laid down the first principles," he says in the Preface to *L'esprit des lois,* "and have found that the particular cases follow naturally from them." This is not induction; Montesquieu was subtly interweaving the general with the particular and offering a complex series of judgments about the "necessary relations" of many things. Vaughan quaintly but perhaps accurately calls this process divination. This accounts for the difficulty of summarizing Montesquieu and the difficulty of appreciating him in capsule form.[19] Montesquieu requires an inquisitive, thorough, and leisurely reading.

Such a reading can be viewed almost as

[18] C. E. Vaughan, *Studies in the History of Political Philosophy Before and After Rousseau* (London: Longmans, Green, 1925), Vol. 1, pp. 260–63, 296.

[19] *Ibid.,* p. 293. See also A.-J. Grant, "Montesquieu," in F. J. C. Hearnshaw, ed., *The Social and Political Ideas of Some Great French Thinkers in the Age of Reason* (London: Harrap, 1930), pp. 114–35. This article is an example of the distortion and even caricaturization that can result from overcondensed summaries of too many points. By such means Grant is able to say that in Montesquieu "the English constitution is traced to the London fogs"!

an end in itself. The political thought it reveals is not by itself compelling in the way that Hobbes's political system is compelling. But there emerges from the pages the voice of a wise and witty man who saw, as did almost none of his contemporaries save Vico, the degree to which we are prisoners of our historic situation. Despite this perception, which at times bred a deep pessimism, he was able to communicate with genuine moral conviction a sense of justice and a sense of liberty. Politically they could be expressed only in different institutional forms in different places and times, but in *l'esprit* they could unite the parts into a whole. By looking intently and separately at Frenchmen, Englishmen, Indians, and Chinese, Montesquieu was finally able to see them all as men.

15

ROUSSEAU

Jean-Jacques Rousseau is an endlessly fascinating character. Few respect him as a man. Some do not respect him as a thinker. But almost everyone seems impelled to pay attention to him. The man is better known and discredits the thinker. But the thinker breaks through again and again and redeems the man. Rousseau's life and writings both are and are not at odds. The life seems amoral, the writings seem moralistic; yet the erratic character of his life seems also to have a parallel in the apparently inconsistent development of his thought. Rousseau recognized this self-contradiction as well as any of his critics and, as usual, bared it to the world in the strikingly titled *Rousseau juge de Jean-Jacques* (*Rousseau Judges Jean-Jacques*).

What did he really believe? Did he believe that society is the enemy or the savior of man, that objective law kills or liberates the spirit, that the supreme good is virtue or happiness? Is there consistency in either his life or his thought? Many commentators on Rousseau—John Morley, Émile Faguet, and Irving Babbitt, to name three—have found him in confusion and have left him there, a colorful and influential but second-rate figure in the history of ideas. Other scholars—Gustave Lanson, E. H. Wright, Albert Schinz, Ernst Cassirer, and Alfred Cobban—have found an underlying unity and profundity in Rousseau's thought.[1] But our first problem in dealing with Rousseau is to do justice to the relationship between his life and writings without getting wholly carried away by morbid fascination with his life.

LIFE

Early Life

Rousseau was born in Geneva, the center of Calvinism, in 1712. His mother died at his birth. His father, a watchmaker who preferred to be a dancing master when he could get away with it in that austere environment, was apparently a man of flabby character.

[1] C. E. Vaughn found unity in the movement from one extreme to the other, from Rousseau's individualism to his final collectivism. For a cogent discussion of these and other Rousseau interpreters see Peter Gay's Introduction to his translation of Ernst Cassirer, *The Question of Jean-Jacques Rousseau* (New York: Columbia Univ. Press, 1954), pp. 3–30. For works by the above-named men, see "Selected Readings," below.

Among other things, he kept young Jean-Jacques up till all hours of the night reading adult romances to him. A good time was had by all but "I soon acquired by this dangerous practice," wrote Rousseau,

> not only an extreme facility in reading and comprehending, but, for my age, a too intimate acquaintance with the passions. An infinity of sensations were familiar to me; without possessing any precise idea of the objects to which they related—I had conceived nothing—I had felt everything. The impact of this confused succession of emotions did not retard the future efforts of my reason, but through them I was given some extravagant, romantic notions of human life of which experience and reflection have never been able to cure me.[2]

When Jean-Jacques was ten, his father, who after a brawl felt it necessary to flee Geneva, abandoned him. Jean-Jacques drifted from job to job, learning how to lie and steal with considerable proficiency. When he was sixteen, he found himself locked out of the city of Geneva one night, so he left for France. His natural charm and wit found him many friends, especially women friends, but his capacity to attract was matched only by his capacity to infuriate and most of his friendships broke up after bitter quarrels.

Rousseau's greatest benefactress was Mme. de Warens, his beloved "Mamma," who time after time took him back into her country estate at Chambéry. At Mme. de Warens' establishment Rousseau took advantage of the opportunity to absorb the book learning that was essential to his later literary conquests. For a time he was one of two paramours living amicably in the household, but Rousseau could not accept as blandly another, later one of his mistress' lovers and thus departed for Paris in 1742.

In Paris Rousseau was, for a time, a different person. In the big city he was aware of the time of day. He was orderly and dutiful and unchildlike. But though he had secured letters of introduction to various salons, he was only tolerated and never fully accepted into the tight circle of conventional society. He wrote an opera and invented a system of musical notation that was politely rejected by the French Academy. Finally in 1743, to get rid of him, someone secured for him a job at the French Embassy in Venice. Rousseau did his routine chores with considerable diligence but soon quarreled with his employer, the wanton ambassador, and with magnificent disdain walked out of the embassy, never to return. He stayed in Venice awhile to taunt the ambasador with his presence and to taste, with mixed feelings, a bit of Venice's vaunted vice.

Returning to Paris, where he alienated more people by expounding the superiority of Italian to French music, he formed a liaison with an ignorant housemaid named Thérèse Levasseur. Devoted to each other in their fashion, they lived as common-law man and wife from that time on. Rousseau actually worked to support both her and her innumerable voracious relatives. But also during this time, in his most universally condemned action, he turned all five of his children over to a foundling home as soon as they were born, despite the tears of their mother. With a slight trace of remorse, he explains in the *Confessions* that they probably had a better life being reared by the state and even cites the authority of Plato's *Republic* for this policy. Yet, even though in debt, this warm-hearted irresponsible, who was prone to gush tears at the drop of an eyelid, sent money to the now impoverished Mme. de Warens. To make a living he copied music—mostly wrongly, says Hearnshaw—and wrote some hasty articles on music for Diderot's *Encyclopédie.*

A Crucial Essay

In 1749 the Academy of Dijon sponsored an essay contest on the subject "Has the Progress of the Sciences and the Arts Contributed to Corrupt or Purify Morals?" With the perversity of his genius, Rousseau took an antiprogressive stance and won the prize. (Diderot later claimed that he had suggested this approach to Rousseau; but Diderot was

[2] *Confessions,* Bk. I, Louis Martin-Chauffier, ed. (Paris: Gallimard, 1951), p. 8.

angry when he claimed it and was given to lying.) This was perhaps the decisive point in Rousseau's life. "In a moment," he said, "I saw a new world and became a new man." Rousseau's defense of the simple life, of the natural innocence and goodness of man that had been corrupted by civilization, struck the artificial, effete Paris society with tremendous force. Now that he had rejected society, society at last sought him out. He was lionized, fêted, and bothered by the curious. But seeking vengeance, he churlishly abused them. Once again heedless of time and regularity, he sold his watch. Deliberately dressing sloppily, he gave up his favorite linen shirts—with the help of Thérèse's brother, who stole them. His opera *Le devin du village* was now produced. The king attended the opening and asked to see the composer; but Rousseau did not bother to drop around.

In 1754 came the so-called *Second Discourse,* "On the Origin of Inequality," also written for a Dijon Academy contest. It did not win the prize, but it became even more famous than its predecessor; and justly so, for there Rousseau revealed his basic principles, so he said, "with the greatest boldness." In 1755 he wrote for the *Encyclopédie* the "Discourse on Political Economy," which, in its original form, anticipated much of *The Social Contract.* In 1756 he left Paris for a cottage in the country, The Hermitage, prepared for him by Mme. d'Épinay, a longtime admirer. For a while his existence was quite idyllic and his humor good, except for the insidious depredations and backbiting of his mother-in law—or mother-out-of-law.

Disputes and Derangements

With the terrible Lisbon earthquake of 1755 came shocked debates over the role of Providence in this disaster. This was the occasion of Rousseau's first dispute with Voltaire and a revelation of his concern with the problem of theodicy. He penned his *Lettre sur la Providence* to uphold an optimistic view of a beneficent Divinity against Voltaire's forthright pessimism. About this time, during his morning stroll in the woods, the time usually devoted to writing, Rousseau began to experience amatory daydreams and delusions. Some of these emerged on paper in the novel *Julie, ou la nouvelle Héloïse.* Also at this time came Rousseau's last grand passion, an affair with the sister-in-law of his hostess, which led to not a few quarrels and misunderstandings between Mme. d'Épinay and her "dear bear." When Diderot kept badgering him to return to Paris, Rousseau's emotional distress turned to paranoia. Had Rousseau lived in the twentieth century, much of his later life would no doubt have been spent in a mental hospital. What this would have done to his literary output no one knows.

In 1758 Mme. d'Épinay happily got rid of Rousseau and Rousseau happily got rid of Mme. Levasseur. He left The Hermitage for —as always—a borrowed cottage at Mont-Louis and sent Mme. Levasseur to Paris. Soon thereafter Rousseau found himself in a spirited exchange of letters with D'Alembert over the wisdom of establishing a theater in Geneva. Rousseau's opposition, on the grounds that the arts in general contaminated morality, placed him in company with the most conservative religious groups. This alliance, in turn, led to further and more intemperate exchanges between Voltaire and Rousseau. Those who explain Rousseau as a lifelong seeker after status can no doubt see in this episode an attempt to identify himself with the hidebound town of his youth, a town that had rejected him.

La nouvelle Héloïse (1760) was an immediate success. It gave jaded Parisians what they had long been wanting, a good cry. Riding the crest of popularity, Rousseau in 1762 published his two best-known works, *The Social Contract* (which had originally been intended as part of a greater but now abandoned work, *Institutions politiques*) and *Émile. Émile,* the story of an orphan correctly tutored by Rousseau himself, expounded a theory of child-centered, naturalistic education in which rationalistic, second-hand, or mere "verbal" knowledge would be deliberately kept at bay so that through a constant intercourse with "nature" the child could learn by himself and for himself. "Society" was still a culprit for Rousseau. The unorthodox opinions, especially about religion, that *Émile* contained led the Parliament of Paris to order it burned and its author arrested. Rousseau had to flee to Mont Louis, leaving Thérèse behind. He went first to Berne but was driven out. He went then to Neuchâtel, where, thanks to the tolerance of Frederick the Great, whom Rousseau had earlier criticized, he was able to stay three years; Thérèse joined him here.

Last Days

This period saw little literary work. The *Constitution for Corsica* was one of the few substantial enterprises. Rousseau did write a vigorous reply to Archbishop Beaumont of Paris, who had denounced *Émile,* and was drawn into the colorful dispute between factions in Geneva over whether the ban there on Rousseau's person and books should be lifted. The center of violent controversy, denied the sacraments by the Reformed Church —whose services he regularly attended— Rousseau finally had to leave Neuchâtel. He lived happily for a while on an island in Lake Bienne until he was driven on again, this time into Germany. Finally, he accepted Hume's invitation to visit England in 1766. Inevitably the two men quarreled as Rousseau's paranoia grew more and more out of control and Hume unwisely chose to make public his defense against Rousseau's charge of a conspiracy to humiliate him. Rousseau left England the next year, and until 1770 lived here and there about Europe. In 1768, to impress the bored, alcoholic, and now neglectful Thérèse, he married her—at least he recited a ceremony in the presence of two witnesses. Thérèse, however, was not impressed.

In 1770 he returned to Paris, where he was given to understand that if he did not make a nuisance of himself he would not be bothered by the authorities. He gave up the quaint Armenian dress he had adopted and settled down to his old vocation of copying music at ten *sous* a page. As many expected, however, he was unable not to make a nuisance of himself. Partly for self-vindication he began giving readings from his *Confessions* to private groups—one lasted seventeen hours—until Mme. d'Épinay, in self-defense, had the police put a stop to it. He composed *Rousseau juge de Jean-Jacques,* in which the signs of persecutory paranoia are unmistakable. Yet the work was also a penetrating self-analysis with passages of some philosophic significance.[3] He then wrote the *Dialogues,* the *Réveries d'un promeneur solitaire,* and the *Considérations sur le gouvernement de Pologne,* a sober, workmanlike job. For eight years he remained in Paris; but, ill and tormented, he finally took to the country again, living at Ermonville, ten miles from Paris, in a little cottage lent to him by the Marquis de Girardin. In May, 1778, his old enemy Voltaire died. Rousseau felt that somehow his existence was tied up with Voltaire's: "He is dead, and I shall soon follow," he wrote. Scarcely two months later, on July 2, he did. Thérèse, stupid and coarse to the end, lived on until 1801.

Conflicting Evaluations

It is easy, too easy, to make fun of this sad life and, worse, to explain too much of Rousseau's writings in terms of it. Hearnshaw, for example, divides Rousseau's life into five periods: "the undisciplined boy," "the super-tramp," "the would-be man of the world," "the inspired maniac," and "the hunted fugitive." "So intimately," writes Hearnshaw, "were Rousseau's writings associated with his life that it is impossible to comprehend them without a detailed knowledge of his curious and remarkable career."[4] In the view of Hearnshaw and others, Rousseau's glorification of the simple presocial state of nature was but the outward mani-

[3] To foil his delusory "enemies" Rousseau planned to leave the manuscript on the altar in Notre Dame Cathedral; but when he found a gate locked against him, he knew that even God was on their side.

[4] F. J. C. Hearnshaw, "Rousseau," in F. J. C. Hearnshaw, ed., *The Social and Political Ideas of Some Great French Thinkers of the Age of Reason* (London: Harrap, 1930), p. 172.

festation of his inner rejection of a society that had rejected him. The contradiction between the individualism of the *First* and *Second Discourses* and the collectivism of the *Third Discourse,* and the latter parts of *The Social Contract,* as well as many other contradictions, are found to be reflections of his erratic personality. "He was an unsystematic thinker, untrained in formal logic. He was an omnivorous reader with undeveloped powers of assimilation. He was an emotional enthusiast who spoke without due reflection. He was an irresponsible writer with a fatal gift for epigram."[5] There is some truth to this, of course, but the "fatal gift for epigram" may also have been fatal to many of Rousseau's critics. Gay writes,

> it was Rousseau's eloquence rather than his extravagance that created difficulties for the commentators. Rousseau was, unhappily, the coiner of happy phrases. Read in context, they were usually elucidated by the argument in which they were embedded. Taken out of context, their rhetorical power obscured the fact that they were only elliptical pronouncements. Used as slogans, they twisted or destroyed his meaning.[6]

Gay believes that Rousseau was neither confused nor inconsistent in the essentials of his thought but, like another inspired madman, Nietzsche, *invited* misunderstanding. Given such a challenge, can we do less than seek for consistency—and understanding?

NATURE AND SOCIETY

From the time of his prize-winning essay, Rousseau is absorbed by the conflict between something called nature and something called society. Compared to the *philosophes*'s easy assumptions about natural law and their often shallow individualism, Rousseau's position was highly original. It was also boldly stated: "I shall be at no pains to please either intellectuals or men of the world," he wrote in the *First Discourse.*[7] (However, he flattered the Academy of Dijon to an extent the twentieth century would call inordinate.)

"Nature" for Rousseau did not refer to man as he is so much as to man as he might have been: ". . . nature makes man happy and good, but . . . society causes him to be depraved and miserable," he wrote in *Rousseau juge de Jean-Jacques.*[8] The famous openings of his most famous works strike the same note. Book I of *Émile:* "Everything is good as it comes out of the hands of the Author of things, everything degenerates in the hands of man."[9] Book I of *The Social Contract:* "Man is born free but yet we see him everywhere in chains."[10] Note well that Rousseau does not promise to remove these chains. "Those who believe themselves the masters of others cease not to be even greater slaves than the people they govern. How this happens I am ignorant; but if I am asked what renders is justifiable [*légitime*], I believe it may be in my power to resolve the question." Society has forged the chains that are the condition of our lost innocence and in so doing has helped destroy something precious; but at least in *The Social Contract* and *Émile,* Rousseau is trying mainly to teach us how to live in our state of lost innocence, for, once lost, innocence can never be recaptured.

Nor was there a period in his life, as some have thought, when Rousseau, his Armenian dress notwithstanding, took seriously a literal back-to-nature movement. The *First Discourse* does deal with a state of nature but

[5] *Ibid.,* p. 86.

[6] In the Introduction to his translation of Cassirer.

[7] All quotations from the three *Discourses* are taken from *The Social Contract and Discourses,* trans. by G. D. H. Cole (London: Dent, Everyman, 1913).

[8] *Oeuvres complètes de J.-J. Rousseau,* Vol. IX (Paris: Hachette, 1909), p. 287. Subsequent quotations from *Émile* and *Rousseau juge de Jean-Jacques* are from this edition. There is a certain parallel between Rousseau's nature-society distinction and Aristotle's *physis-nomos* distinction.

[9] *Ibid.,* Vol. II, p. 3.

[10] All quotations from *The Social Contract* are from an eighteenth-century translation rev. and ed. by Charles Frankel, trans. by G. D. H. Cole (New York: Hafner, 1947).

it is not simply a foolish idealization of the happy savage. If Rousseau does idealize the ancient primitives in passing, he also parades before us some historical facts about the depravities of advanced civilizations. If he twists Socrates' praise of ignorance slightly, he also uses him well against civilized vanities. The significance of Rousseau's assertion that "the arts and sciences owe their birth to our vices" —astronomy to superstition, geometry to avarice, moral philosophy to human pride, and so on,—is a contention the significance of which many learned men never grasp. He overdoes, to be sure, the decline of military courage and fortitude and the pernicious character of most philosophizing; yet, if he does not quite prove his case that good morals are injured by the arts and sciences, he does—and his slightly ironic, biting tone helps —make the reader reflect seriously on the proposition that the moral quality of man's life is very little improved by the advances of society, that is, by scientific information, elegant architecture, or personal luxury.

The very proposition flew in the face of the prevailing optimism of the eighteenth century and also the material hopes that underlay it, hopes that Rousseau was not above ridiculing: "The politicians of the ancient world were always talking of morals and virtue; ours speak of nothing but commerce and money. . . . According to them, a man is worth no more to the State than the amount he consumes; and thus a Sybarite would be worth at least thirty Lacedaemonians."

Those who chide Rousseau for the idyllic raptures of his state of nature overlook the hypothetical-imaginative character of almost all Rousseau's writings save his model constitutions. In the *Second Discourse* he suggests most clearly of all what he is doing: trying to look not at men but at man in order to arrive at a standard of his true nature that can be set against almost all forms of contemporary knowledge. In the first two *Discourses* Rousseau is more radical than any naive state-of-nature literalist. His call for a return to nature is a call to purge ourselves of moral dependence upon social convention and to consult only the uncorrupted conscience hidden in our innermost being. This is an "impossible possibility" comparable only to the Christian understanding of redemption. Even theoretical statements on natural right and natural law, Rousseau points out in the *Second Discourse,* are developed with the language and the conceptions that are products of society's artifice. Most natural-law theories, therefore, are really artificial rather than natural.

The state of affairs Rousseau wishes to look at "perhaps never did exist, and probably never will exist." His is a hypothetical history of government. "Let us begin," he says, "by laying facts aside, as they do not affect the question. The investigations we may enter into in treating this subject must not be considered as historical truths, but only as mere conditional and hypothetical reasonings, rather calculated to explain the nature of things than to ascertain their actual origin." In one sense the bulk of Rousseau's literary effort is a gigantic "as if."

This distinction between historical truth and nature is fundamental to Rousseau and little sense can be made of him until it is understood. He considers what man ought to be as much a part of his nature as what man does. To this extent Rousseau parallels most natural-law thinkers. But for several reasons Rousseau does not fit into the category of natural-law thinker. He does not agree with the classical natural-law view that was without the state-of-nature concept and held that man is naturally a social animal. Man for Rousseau is naturally independent of society. This does not mean that man can be studied empirically outside society. Indeed, in Émile Rousseau says the reverse: "It is necessary to study society through men and men through society: those who would wish to treat separately politics and morals will never understand a thing about either." Rousseau accepts the fact of society—far more, indeed, than did the *philosophes*—but wishes to set the individual off from it, to give him a vision of radical independence that can preserve him from submersion in society. The state of nature was a literary device used toward this end.

But Rousseau does not conform to either the secular or religious forms of modern natural law. Rejecting a theological base for law, his intuitionist naturalism is at odds with what we have come to call the Thomistic view. And he does not regard the pursuit of happiness and its derivatives as a natural right in the fashion of Locke or Paine. On this point Rousseau sided with the classicists, for he was more concerned with goodness and virtue than with happiness or even the prudential security of Hobbes. But basically he does not agree with either classical or modern schools of natural law because he rejects reason as nature's ultimate standard for moral guidance.[11]

FEELING, CONSCIENCE, AND REASON

In the *Second Discourse* reason is artificial in the sense that it is a part of man's advanced cultural heritage. Conscience, or compassion, reveals the essence or nature of man: "I think I can perceive in [the human soul] two principles prior to reason, one of them deeply interesting us in our own welfare and preservation, and the other exciting a natural repugnance at seeing any other sensible being, and particularly any of our own species, suffer pain or death." From these, "all the rules of natural right appear to me to be derived—rules which our reason is *afterwards* [our italics] obliged to establish on other foundations." It follows that "if I am bound to do no injury to my fellow creatures, this is less because they are rational than because they are sentient beings [*un être sensible*]."[12]

Likewise in the first part of the *First Discourse* Rousseau is ostensibly describing the state of nature. But the form scarcely conceals his intent of demonstrating the priority of the passions to reflective thought without reference to time or place. Physical prowess is, but intellectual discrimination is not, required of the natural man. While the proliferation of speech and its application to general ideas require intellect (indeed general ideas are impossible without speech) the origin of speech is probably the work of children trying to communicate with their mothers rather than the deliberate act of learned men. So much that we know depends upon society and the arts that very little can be assumed about the natural state—not even Hobbes's assumption about egotistical warring. But the essence of what does appear is the "force of natural compassion": "It is . . . certain that compassion is a natural feeling which, by moderating the violence of love of self in each individual, contributes to the preservation of the whole species." This natural compassion is utterly divorced from thought: ". . . a state of reflection is a state contrary to nature . . . a thinking man is a depraved animal [*l'homme qui médite est un animal dépravé*]."[13] This statement is frequently castigated, and perhaps justly so, as an example of Rousseau's tendency to hyperbole. But the phrase cannot be dismissed as mere exaggeration. Rousseau was fully aware of the audacity of his position at the very start of his literary career: "Will we dare take the side of instinct against reason? That is precisely what I ask."[14] And at the very end of his life he could write to Mirabeau the elder: ". . . I am perfectly sure that my heart loves only that which is good. All the evil I ever

[11] Yet even on this conclusion there is no consensus on Rousseau. Robert Derathé has traced traditional natural-law influences on Rousseau and concludes that he is really a rationalist, although one who is unusually sensitive to the limits of reason. See his *Le Rationalisme de J.-J. Rousseau* (Paris: Presses Universitaires de France, 1948).

[12] French interpolations in all quotations are from *Oeuvres complètes*.

[13] *Ibid.*, Part 1.

[14] "Dernière Réponse à A. M. Bordes" [in defense of the *First Discourse*]. *Oeuvres complètes,* Vol. I, pp. 62–63.

did in my life was the result of reflection; and the little good I have been able to do was the result of impulse."[15]

Rousseau has, of course, been most severely attacked at this very point. In making feeling, sentiment, or emotion rather than reason the test of the good, he is said to have thrown away all hope for a well-ordered society with dutiful, self-restrained citizens. His emotional subjectivism leads to anarchy, it is claimed, which in turn leads to the kind of oppressive external restraints suggested by Rousseau himself in *The Social Contract.*

This, indeed, is a fundamental issue in Rousseau. We will examine the character of these restraints in a moment. But first, what does Rousseau really mean to do in putting impulse, instinct, and sentiment ahead of reason? What are the obligations between men arising from the fact that they are naturally sentient beings rather than rational beings? Two things must be said:

(1) To make reason subsidiary is not to eliminate reason. Were we to change Rousseau's famous statement to "a man who thinks *only* is a depraved animal," it would make more sense and would not be at odds with his general argument. Rousseau does not belittle every act of reason or disregard the need for laws to restrain men's unruly emotions. In the *Second Discourse* he writes, "the more violent the passions are, the more are laws necessary to keep them under restraint." This is not the "deliberately courted giddiness" that Babbitt accuses Rousseau of elevating into a principle. Whatever his ambiguities, Rousseau's guide to the good life was not a function of adrenal secretions.

(2) "Sentiment" had a double meaning in Rousseau. On the one hand, it meant mere feeling, a psychological affect stemming from memory or sensory stimuli (*sens*). On the other hand, it meant a spontaneous impulse or action of the soul with genuine ethical content and with overtones almost of divinity. This impulse was part of natural man but not simply physical man: ". . . my will is independent of my senses," Rousseau wrote in the controversial *"Profession de foi du Vicaire Savoyard"* in Book IV of *Émile.* In what could be only a deliberate metaphorical transplanting of the organ of thought, the Savoyard vicar revealed what "I think in the simplicity of my heart" and asked his auditor to do likewise. "It is said that conscience is the product of prejudice; however, I know by my experience that it insists on following the order of nature against the laws of men." Although it is not that of logic or calculation, there is a kind of rationality, or at least a self-evidence, in this "order of nature." And it is directly related to man's destiny in society, for it would appear that the innocent savage in the state of nature scarcely has need of such insights. His passions, Rousseau holds in the *Second Discourse,* are *less* violent than those of modern man, especially as related to sexual conquests, because they are more simply animalistic and prosaic. The more imaginative and "moral" and less simply physical aspects of love are the marks of man in society. But the impetuosity of modern lovers is a source both of greater delight and of more violent trouble than the savage knows.

Cassirer, Platonizing Rousseau somewhat, makes this distinction between simple animal feeling and natural moral sentiment fundamental to the understanding of Rousseau:

> Beside the self-evidence of feeling, then, there stands the self-evidence of ethical insight; but the two do not have the same origin. For one is a passive, the other an active power of the soul. In the case of self-evidence of feeling, our faculty of devotion is at work; it alone can unlock nature to us, and it allows us to blot out our own existence, so that we may live solely in and with nature. In the case of self-evidence of ethical insight, we are concerned with elevating and intensifying this existence of ours; for thus only may we survey the task of man in its true magnitude. This task remains insoluble for the individual as such; it can be accomplished only within the community and by means of its powers.[16]

[15] Letter of March 25, 1767. In Theophile Dufour, ed., *Correspondance générale de J.-J. Rousseau,* Vol. XVII (Paris: Colin, 1934), pp. 2–3. Quoted in Cassirer, p. 127.

[16] *The Question of Jean-Jacques Rousseau,* p. 108.

The two elements may be seen concretely in, first, the image of Jean-Jacques on his solitary morning walks, losing himself in the sound of singing birds. Here self-love (*amour de soi*) is an innocent and natural instinct for self-preservation. And it may be seen, secondly, in the image of Rousseau in the afternoon, taking pen in hand to wage regretfully necessary battles for equity and justice—battles in which "society" complicates everything unmercifully, self-love is corrupted into selfish love (*amour-propre*), and pride and vanity are at stake. Here the "order of nature" is infinitely harder to follow but no less authoritative.

As Rousseau is pulled reluctantly but inexorably from morning to afternoon, so mankind is driven or led to its present state. There is both irony and a double paradox in this development: ". . . human *perfectibility*, the social virtues, and the other faculties which natural man potentially possessed," he writes in the *Second Discourse*, were developed only by "the different accidents which may have improved the human understanding while depraving the species and made man wicked while making him sociable." There is a paradox in man's becoming simultaneously wicked and sociable and there is a paradox in his being "perfected" in this way by historical "accidents": man's capacity to perfect himself is shown by that which fortuitously happens to him to make him less perfect! What are we to make of this?

Obviously we can say that Rousseau is confused or we can say that he has struck deep into the paradox of life: the better we are the worse we are; we make ourselves yet we are made; we are individuals only in a group; society and the individual are simultaneously guilty of evil. The Christian relates this same complex of ideas to the doctrine of original sin but Rousseau was too much a child of the Enlightenment, albeit a precocious and spoiled child, to use this terminology. Rousseau sought a way out of this, man's condition, not through divine grace but through education and political reorganization. The tangible goal was the achievement of a special kind of freedom for man.

FREEDOM

Natural man is perfectible precisely because he is in a state of innocence, without pride; but being innocent, he is also without freedom. In being perfected, man loses his innocence and becomes infected with artificiality. He now has the capacity to become free but is nevertheless a slave to his own spurious appetites and those of his fellows. His condition, we have seen, is both better and worse than that of natural man; but in any event there is no turning back. What one must strive for is freedom (*liberté*), which Rousseau defines many times, as in *The Social Contract,* as freedom "to obey a law which we prescribe for ourselves."

This conception of freedom is subjectivistic, for it points back into the individual. But, as we have seen, the law man prescribes for himself as a sentient being is not the product of mere emotional whim. Rousseau was not an Epicurean. His quest for freedom did not lead to pleasure; nor, in one sense, did it lead to "goodness"—which he tended to associate with the state of innocence—but rather to virtue in the classical sense of *virtus*—manly strength, excellence, and self-control. This goal was made necessary by society but was also in part made possible by society. Rousseau's frequent praise of ancient Sparta was not accidental. Nor could Kant have been as impressed as he was by Rousseau had his freedom meant only lack of restraint: "Rousseau's ethics is not an ethics of feeling, but the most categorical form of a pure ethics of obligation [*Gesetzes-Ethik*] that was established before Kant."[17]

It was the nineteenth-century romantic literary movement, the *Sturm und Drang,* that later perverted Rousseau's writings into a symbol of irrationalism and irresponsible individ-

[17] Cassirer, p. 96. See also Immanuel Kant's "Idea for a Universal History" (1784), in Carl J. Friedrich, ed., *The Philosophy of Kant* (New York: Random House, Modern Library, 1949), p. 126; Gordon H. McNeil, "Anti-Revolutionary Rousseau," *American Historical Review,* Vol. 58 (1958), pp. 808–23; and Joan McDonald, *Rousseau and the French Revolution 1762–1791* (London: Athlone Press, 1965).

ualism. That freedom is not a synonym for license for Rousseau is made clear in the dedicatory section of the *Second Discourse:* "I should have wished to live and die free, that is, so far subject to the laws that neither I nor anybody else should be able to cast off their honorable yoke. . . . No one within the State should be able to say he was above the law." Nor was Rousseau, that great revolutionary influence, one who encouraged revolutions: "Peoples once accustomed to masters are not in a condition to do without them. If they attempt to shake off the yoke they still more estrange themselves from freedom, as, by mistaking for it an unbridled license to which it is diametrically opposed, they nearly always manage, by their revolutions, to hand themselves over to seducers, who only make their chains heavier than before."

Many critics of Rousseau have ignored all this qualification of freedom and by mixing the right proportions of his life with his teachings have managed to come to a conclusion the exact opposite of the foregoing. Babbitt said that Rousseau's "general readiness to subordinate his ethical self to his sensibility is indubitable."[18] And Hudson wrote, "he talked unceasingly of freedom; but freedom for him meant not that true liberty which is to be achieved only through cheerful obedience to the eternal laws of life, but simply absence of obligation and responsibility. He had no will-power and no moral fibre."[19]

Rousseau's ethical position was, to be sure, relativistic: he appealed to no fixed metaphysical standard. But this lack of absolutes merely strengthened the logic of his call for community. For without a metaphysical base from which to challenge the norms of a given society, Rousseau's individual found his salvation in community or nowhere.[20] The individual alone can never be emancipated from his slavery. All of us in a given society are free or we are all slaves. Politics for Rousseau was thus central to the very existence of the individual, central in a way minimal-government liberals were never quite able to understand.

THE SOCIAL CONTRACT

Sovereignty and the General Will

Standing alone, *The Social Contract,* Rousseau's most famous political work, is something of a puzzle. In the context of his problem of freedom, however, it can be understood as an unsuccessful yet inspired attempt to make man free while in society, that is, to make legitimate his chains. Seen in this light, the alleged contradiction between the "individualist" first part and the "collectivist" second part dissolves, or at least resolves into an understandable tension.

Rousseau is concerned with what is right in society: "I shall endeavor to unite what right [*droit*] permits with what interest prescribes," a hopeless task, no doubt, but well worth the effort. He first establishes that society, while basic, is nevertheless artificial: ". . . the social order is a sacred right which serves as a basis for all other [rights]. Yet this right comes not from nature; it is therefore founded on conventions. The question is, what those conventions are."[21] Immediately we see that the convention known as the social contract does not serve the same purpose at all that it did for Hobbes, Locke, or Paine, that is, to preserve natural rights. For Rousseau, all rights are born of the social order. And we already know that man has no real choice of whether to be brought

[18] Irving Babbitt, *Rousseau and Romanticism* (New York: Noonday Press, Meridian, 1955), p. 130.

[19] William Henry Hudson, *Rousseau and Naturalism in Life and Thought* (Edinburgh: Clark, 1903), p. 111.

[20] Of course it is just as plausible to say that his avoidance of metaphysics was a deliberate result of his faith in community as to say that the absence of a metaphysical base left him with no alternative but faith in community.

[21] Theodore Waldman argues that we understand Rousseau better by translating *droit* as "what is procedurally correct" rather than as "what is morally right in a universal sense." See his "Rousseau on the General Will and the Legislator," *Political Studies,* Vol. 8 (1960), pp. 221–30. The view is challenged in the same journal by Vivienne Mylne, Vol. 9 (1961), pp. 309–10.

out of the state of nature; the accidents of history drag him out. *The Social Contract* is not, therefore, an aptly titled work.

Natural society

Since civil society is not natural, the family is the only natural society. But even families are natural only so long as the children need the father's protection. If they manage to hang together after that time, they become for Rousseau conventional. Although in the *Second Discourse* Rousseau had opposed the paternalism of Filmer and Bossuet, he was not opposed to the family as an institution; but, perhaps on the basis of personal experience, he could not regard it as the kind of purely ethical community he was seeking. Thus, if Rousseau's concept of nature was deeper than Locke's, it was narrower than Aristotle's. When Aristotle spoke of natural slaves, for example, he mistook, said Rousseau, the effect for the cause: that society can give a man a slavish mentality is no proof that it was natural and proper that it should have done so. Grotius opposes slavery but on equally specious grounds: Grotius seeks to establish rights by appeal to fact, says Rousseau, not entirely accurately. Rousseau, ever the moralist, does not appeal to "facts." He wants to establish what is right, it would seem, not simply what is existent. His critique of the position of might makes right is classic in its simplicity, a model for all who follow: "Force is a physical power; I do not see what morality can result from its effects. . . . If it is necessary to obey by force, there can be no occasion to obey from duty. . . . If in saying, 'Let us obey the powerful,' they mean to say 'Let us yield to force,' the precept is good, but it is superfluous, for it never is or can be violated." Nor can a man voluntarily give up his liberty, says Rousseau in a direct rebuttal to Hobbes, for liberty is of the essence of the "quality of man" and to give up liberty is to give up being a man.

Contract and sovereign

In Chapters 6, 7, and 8 of Book I Rousseau takes up the social contract, the establishment of the sovereign, and the civil state. The contract amounts to an "act of association" that "produces a moral and collective body" and involves "the total alienation of each associate, and all his rights, to the whole community." What is formed by this association is a "public person, which took formerly the name of 'city'[22] and now takes that of 'republic' or 'body politic.' It is called by its members 'State' when it is passive, 'Sovereign' when in activity." Rousseau's political community is really a modern version of the ancient Greek *politeia,* or "soul of the *polis.*" In describing it, he is clearly reacting against the excessive individualism and atomism of the English contractualists. For the latter, the body politic was an artificial, constitutional structure; for Rousseau, it is a natural, moral association.

The sovereign created by this association is not the determinate figure it was for Hobbes but is rather the whole body of citizens. The concept gives rise to the same questions of the moral basis for obedience by subjects and command by sovereigns that we discussed in connection with Hobbes but, in addition, Rousseau's "popular sovereignty" raises the special problem of protecting individuals from themselves. Each individual "contracting, as it were, with himself, is engaged under a double character," as a member of the state acted upon and the sovereign acting. The sovereign cannot be bound by law, since it is the source of law. There is no cause for alarm here, Rousseau assures us somewhat too hastily, because "the Sovereign, being formed only of the individuals who compose it, neither has, nor can have, any interest contrary to theirs. . . . The Sovereign, by its nature, is always everything it ought to be."

Forced to be free

It is difficult to accept the notion that the individuals who compose the sovereign are always everything they ought to be. Rousseau thinks they are, however, when in their sov-

[22] Houses do not make a city, houses make a town. *Citizens* make a city; but few French authors seem to realize this, says Rousseau in a stern footnote.

ereign capacity, for then they are guided by the general will and then only are they true citizens. The general will (*volonté général*) is the perfect expression of common interest. Each individual partakes of it but each individual also has a private will (*volonté particulière*), which is the expression of noncommon, particular, selfish, and hence potentially dangerous interests, which if given sway could "cause the ruin of the body politic . . . therefore, to prevent the social compact from becoming an empty formula . . . whoever refuses to obey the general will shall be compelled to it by the whole body: this in fact only forces him to be free. . . . This alone renders all civil engagements justifiable, and without it they would be absurd, tyrannical, and subject to the most enormous abuses." This is the most significant of the several contradictions with which Rousseau has been charged: Force can have no moral effect but man can be forced to be free; to prevent tyranny, individuals may have to be tyrannized. Though possibly mistaken, Rousseau was not venally deceptive and we have no grounds for questioning the genuineness of his objective of a free individual in a free society. We must give him the chance to follow through.

By entering the social contract the individual gives up his "natural liberty," the "unlimited right to all which tempts him," but he exchanges it for

> civil liberty, which is limited by the general will. . . . In addition we might add to the other acquisitions of the civil state that of moral liberty, which alone renders a man master of himself; for it is *slavery* to be under the impulse of appetite, and *freedom* to obey a law which we prescribe for ourselves. But I have already said too much on this head, and the philosophical sense of the word "liberty" is not at present my subject.[23]

Rousseau takes us into some murky waters but deliberately avoids the "philosophical" discussion that seems necessary if we are to follow through. Actually, the problem is not so much how force, which is unfree, can free a man. (We know, do we not, how students can be forced to read books by the threat of an examination and by this process learn to read books of their own volition?) It is a simple case of immoral but necessary means being used toward a moral end. The problem is much more the practical one of deciding whether the process of forcing to be free is the action of one group—the sovereign citizens—on another group—the nonsovereign, nonfree, noncitizens—or the action of one part of the individual's psyche—that motivated by the general will—acting upon another part—that motivated by the particular will. Rousseau also leaves somewhat obscure whether this process is an ideal not yet attained or an ongoing function existing in some sense in actual bodies politic. In one of his most controversial statements Rousseau says that "the general will is always right and tends always to the public advantage." Does he mean that the general will is a standard of rightness by which to judge the imperfections of present policies? Or does he think the general will is actually embodied in some present policies? Does he think there is a mysterious force—it cannot be a rational idea, for *volonté* and *raison* can scarcely be made synonyms—actually at work in society leading all of us to do what is right?

Rousseau apparently meant all these things —and more, for the "Legislator" is yet to be heard from. He characteristically wanted to have his cake and eat it too. In the fashion of a romantic who distrusts abstract formulas, he wanted to go to the heart of reality, to deal with the concrete actualities of life. At the same time he was driven by a vision of the good society and the good individual in that society that had a counterpart nowhere on earth.[24] He invented a new term, "general will," and, perhaps without quite knowing what he was doing, he used it in two different ways. Who or what is forcing us to be free makes a great deal of difference. If

[23] *Social Contract,* Bk. I, Ch. 8.

[24] He also thought, however: "There is still in Europe one country capable of receiving legislation: it is the island of Corsica. . . . I have a presentiment that this little island will some day astonish Europe." One is reminded of Plato's temporal hopes for Syracuse.

it is our better selves winning a battle over our worse selves, that is one thing. If it is a mob or a man with shiny buttons and a rubber truncheon, that is quite another thing. It is in many ways unfortunate that the power of Hobbesian logic pressed Rousseau into a mold not best adapted to his argument.

The general will illustrated

There are many helpful illustrations of the general will conceived as our better self: our general will tells us that we ought to get up at seven A.M.; our particular will leads us to turn off the alarm and roll over. Our general will tells us that we need a strong army; our particular will wants to keep us out of the draft. The drunkard's general will tells him that he should have stopped drinking several hours ago; his particular will gives him one more for the road. If the police throw him in jail, he is really throwing himself in jail. And he is free because his restraint is self-imposed. He really wants to do right and in his heart of hearts knows better. That is why, when sober, he accepted the law against public drunkenness and chose to remain a member of the community that adopted this law. So far so good. But we are talking about this or that individual. When we bring the sovereign into the picture, when we try to institutionalize the operation of the general will and make it produce binding rules for all men, then confusion returns. It has been said that the sovereign is like the quarterback on a football team. When he calls the signals, every team member carries out the play to the best of his ability, even though other players might have called different signals. The players know and accept the facts that someone has to call signals and the whole team has to follow them or be ruined. Thus every signal represents the operation of the general will for that miniature society.

The trouble is, of course, that the political society of, say, France is not a football team with its single, simple objective and face-to-face relationships. And the sovereign is not a quarterback but "a collective being" that cannot be represented except by itself: "The power may be transmitted but not the will." Rousseau was firm in denying the possibility of delegating sovereignty. If a people give themselves a representative, they are no longer free, for their laws are no longer self-prescribed. The "city" is destroyed. It is interesting to note that Rousseau identifies representation with the "absurd and iniquitous" feudal system and is led back to the classical ideal of a state small enough for all citizens to participate. In such a state, public affairs more and more replace merely private affairs "in the minds of the citizens."[25] Sovereignty is hence "inalienable." It is also "indivisible." "For the will is general or it is not; it is either the will of the whole body of people, or only of a part." Law and the general will must be absolutely general and many things that have been regarded as acts of sovereignty are not so. They are not acts of law but particular applications of law. Declaring war is one example.

It would seem, then, that the sovereign is the body of people as a whole *when* they agree on a general policy for the common good, which may be called law. In this sense, he writes in the *Third Discourse,* "the voice of the people is in fact the voice of God." But when it comes to the practical determination of this will, Rousseau runs into trouble. In an important footnote to *The Social Contract,* for example, he says, "To make the will general it is not always necessary that it should be unanimous, but it is indispensably necessary that every vote be counted: any formal exclusion destroys generality." Again, after saying that the general will is always right, he says, "but it does not follow that the

[25] That thought, morality, and excellence were above all aspects of the public as opposed to the private realm in the classical world, by contrast with the reverse in modern times, is a point made with much force by Hannah Arendt in *The Human Condition* (Chicago: Univ. of Chicago Press, 1958), Ch. 2. She attaches the greatest significance to Rousseau as the theorist of the intimate, who, for the sake of protecting the intimate, resurrected a classical ideal of politics to be used against the "leveling demands of the social." After Rousseau came the rise of the novel, "the only entirely social art form," and a "decline of all the more public arts, especially architecture."

deliberations of the people have always the same rectitude. Our will always seeks our own good, but we do not always perceive what it is. The people are never corrupted, but they are often deceived, and only then do they seem to will what is bad." He then distinguishes between the general will and the will of all, which is the "sum of private wills."

Thus the general will not only does not have to be discovered through unanimity, it is not assured even through unanimity: ". . . the generality of the will depends less on the number of voters than on the common interest which unites them. It must be general in its object as well as its essence." Every vote must be counted but in the last analysis the votes do not tell us anything. Rousseau is reluctant to transform mere quantity into quality, yet he does not give us any test beyond generality by which to recognize the general will when we see it. It cannot be represented, yet its power may be delegated.[26] No wonder that both the ideal of popular sovereignty and the ideal of totalitarian uniformity have been found in the concept of the general will; and no wonder that hard-headed analysts have for generations been suspicious of its vagaries.

Voting, unanimity, and general will

Rousseau himself seems to backtrack in Book IV of *The Social Contract* when he discusses suffrage: ". . . the general will is found by counting the votes. When, therefore, the motion which I oppose carries, it only proves to me that I was mistaken, and that what I believed to be the general will was not so."

[26] Kant overcame most of these difficulties by simply lifting the general will unequivocally into the normative realm and declaring that only what is always right can be the general will. Given a social order symbolized by a wholly normative general will and given the existence of a government somewhat at odds with this symbol because it must, as a practical matter, be involved with representation, we can see in this situation what Frederick Watkins has seen, a counterpart of medieval dualism. See his *Political Tradition of the West* (Cambridge, Mass.: Harvard Univ. Press, 1948), pp. 104–05. Chapter 4, on the general will, is excellent.

If a reconciliation of this statement with earlier ones is in any way possible, it is by looking carefully at the context of the second statement. In the first place, Rousseau is trying, almost against his nature, to appeal to his reader at a practical level. It is also clear that, although the distinction is not mentioned here, Rousseau is still very conscious of the substantive difference between the general will and the will of all, a difference that belies their surface similarity. He cites elections in the Roman Republic, where from fear or flattery the people abandoned deliberation. On such occasions their votes, while unanimous, were not true votes at all but became mere acclamations. The general will is not found by such a vote. Careful precautions, precautions "which must vary as the general will is more or less easy to ascertain," must be taken to prevent such invalid demonstrations. The larger the groups and the more factions there are the harder it is to ascertain the general will. And again the generality of the object of the general will must be recalled: "When the people of Athens, for example, nominated or cashiered their chiefs, decreed honors to one, imposed punishments on another . . . the people, properly speaking, had then no longer a general will; they acted no longer as Sovereign but as magistrate."

Yet there is only one law that requires unanimous consent and that is the social contract. He who opposes the social contract is simply a foreigner, a noncitizen. Thereafter, as in Locke, residence constitutes consent. (Note, however, that the dissidents are never referred to as being put back into a state of nature; society will exist regardless.) In other votes a majority is necessary to bind the voter. Rousseau is not blind to the problem this requirement raises in light of the priority he attaches to his particular conception of freedom in society. He poses the question himself: "How are the opposers free when they are in submission to laws to which they have never consented?"

I answer that the question is not fairly stated. The citizen consents to all the laws, to those which are passed in spite of his opposition, and even to those which sentence him to punishment if he violates any one of them. The constant will of all the members of the State is the general will; it is by that they are citizens and free. When any law is proposed in the assembly of the people, the question is not precisely to inquire whether they approve the proposition or reject it, but if it is conformable or not to the general will, which is their will.[27]

Even if the theory is not ambiguous, the practice most certainly is. The general will seems clearly relevant only to acceptance of the idea of law itself, yet Rousseau speaks as if many propositions could be passed in conformity to it. But at this level the voter's will is somehow made separable from his preference for or against any concrete proposal and a practical test whether a vote is cast in the true spirit of the general will or as an unreflective piece of selfishness is never offered. Rousseau does offer two practical rules of thumb: the more serious and important the deliberations are the closer the number of votes should approach unanimity; and the greater the necessity for swift action the smaller may be the majority. Any skillful politician would be delighted to use these as loopholes by which to jam or railroad suggested legislation.

The Legislator and Civil Religion

Early in *The Social Contract* Rousseau urges the necessity of avoiding factions or "partial societies" in order that "every citizen should speak his opinion entirely from himself." But apparently many citizens or potential citizens are incapable of grasping and expressing the general will that is within them. The problem of counting votes, thus, is not the only practical problem connected with the general will.

Men can be made moral and free by obedience to the general will but not until they have seen it—or felt it. All men are equal as citizens but not until the city has been achieved. This achievement does not fall willy-nilly on the people but upon one among them who is superior, the legislator. He must protect the people from "the seducing voice of private wills." The challenge to the legislator, therefore, is no small one:

Those who dare to undertake the institution of a people must feel themselves capable, as it were, of changing human nature, of transforming each individual, who by himself is a perfect and solitary whole, into a part of a much greater whole, from which he in some measure receives his being and his life . . . of substituting a moral and partial existence instead of the physical and independent existence which we have all received from nature.[28]

The legislator is a man of "superior intelligence, acquainted with all the passions of men but liable to none of them . . . whose happiness [is] independent of ours, but who still condescend[s] to make us the object of his care." The image is strikingly similar to that of Plato's philosopher-king and it is significant that, with the exception of Calvin, all Rousseau's examples of great lawmakers are taken from antiquity. When we understand the magnitude of Rousseau's problem and the daring of his solution, we are not surprised by his statement that "legislation is at the highest point of perfection which human talents can attain."

Nevertheless, unlike Plato's philosopher-king, this genius among men must propose laws only and not command men directly, or else "private aims" might "defile the sanctity of his work." He is not the sovereign, for his proposed laws in each case must be submitted to the free vote of the people so that each citizen has the opportunity to be free by imposing his own restraints. No dictator here, apparently.

But such wise men who try to address themselves to the vulgar in their own language instead of the language of the vulgar "cannot possibly make themselves understood." And not being understood, they will be rejected. "It is not enough to say to the citizens, *be good;* they must be taught to be so; and even example, which is in this respect the first lesson, is not the sole means to be employed; patriotism is the most efficacious."

[27] *Social Contract,* Bk. IV, Ch. 2.

[28] *Ibid.,* Bk. II, Ch. 7.

And the most efficacious form of patriotism is "civil religion." The legislators' wisdom must be clothed in the authority of divine sanction. They must "attribute to the gods what has proceeded from their own wisdom."

Whatever its potentialities, Rousseau's "civil religion" was conceived as a device not to enslave people but to free them. It was the necessary tool of communication by which the legislature could channel popular feeling toward the general will and away from particular wills. It was also a reflection of Rousseau's classicism, a harking back to the period when "each State, having its peculiar cult as well as its own form of government, did not distinguish its gods from its laws." In that time men did not fight for their gods, since each nation had its own gods, which were not assumed to watch over other nations or require the conversion of foreigners. Men fought wars for themselves. Israel was a limited exception; but Christianity, of course, was the great exception, bringing with it "a perpetual conflict for jurisdiction which has made any system of good polity impossible in Christian states." Rousseau praises the intention of Hobbes's clear-cut Erastian solution to this problem but almost wistfully observes that the interest of the priesthood would in fact defeat it. Rousseau sets apart from the religion of the priest the "simple religion of the Gospel, the true theism," which is the "religion of man" as distinguished from the "religion of the citizen." The former should be no bother at all to the latter and, presumably, vice versa. The religion of the priest is a dangerous confusion of the two. Rousseau makes a plausible case that a society of dedicated Christians with their eyes focused on only the other world would fly to pieces, indeed would probably be impossible.

What remains for Rousseau is

> a purely civil profession of faith, the articles of which it is the business of the Sovereign [Legislator? Magistrate?] to arrange, not precisely as dogmas of religion, but as sentiments of sociability, without which it is impossible to be either a good citizen or a faithful subject. The Sovereign has no power by which it can oblige men to believe them, but it can banish from the State whoever does not believe them, not as an impious person, but as an unsociable one. . . . But if any one, after he has publicly subscribed to these dogmas, shall conduct himself as if he did not believe them, he is to be punished by death. He has committed the greatest of all crimes: he has lied in the face of the law.[29]

The civil religion was not conceived as preempting the rights of all religions: ". . . all religions that tolerate others ought to be tolerated, so long as their dogmas discover nothing contradictory to the duties of a citizen." This tolerance, Rousseau made perfectly clear, did not apply to the Roman Church, which, he said, holds that there is no salvation outside its confines.

It is not hard to imagine how an elite group can control a populace by manipulating the symbols of an ingenious ideology. It has been done before and it will be done again. But even the most vigorous of Rousseau's defenders are hard put to explain, let alone justify, how the sovereign, that is, all the citizens motivated by a general will, can put over an ersatz religion on all the people and punish by death the somewhat subjective crime of lying about one's beliefs, without surrendering entirely the condition of every citizen speaking his opinion "entirely from himself."

There is no reason to question Rousseau's goal at this point: he thought that civil religion was a necessary mythological mechanism for deceiving the unfree into freedom. But the relationship created suggests that of oppressor-oppressee much more than teacher-pupil; belief would not be induced so much as the outward appearance of belief would be compelled. Thus, in a work that skillfully defends the thesis that Rousseau is a liberal, Chapman nevertheless grants that "the purpose of the civil religion may be to preserve man's political freedom, but it is a means which destroys his moral freedom and dignity. This is surely sufficient to make it totalitarian."[30]

[29] *Ibid.*, Bk. IV, Ch. 8.

[30] John W. Chapman, *Rousseau—Totalitarian or Liberal* (New York: Columbia Univ. Press, 1956), p. 86.

CONCLUSION

All things begin in mystique and end in politics, said Péguy. Rousseau had good reason to believe this. Preoccupied with the torments of his own soul, he could nevertheless say toward the end of the *Confessions,* "Everything is related to politics." His drive to make life whole, to reconcile the warring demands of individuality and sociability, was overwhelming. The goodness, not to say the holiness, of unity was his underlying theme and this led him inevitably to attempt political-historical solutions.

The "solution" of the general will was not enough to bridge all disunities and answer all questions. Many lines of Rousseau's thought were truncated and incomplete. For one thing, there was the problem of his relativism, which can be illustrated at both ends of the political scale. Each human group, Rousseau recognized in the *Discourse on Political Economy,* has its own general will; but this general will, judged by the interests of a higher community, becomes a particular will. Thus factions were a great social evil for Rousseau because they threatened unity. But the unity of the general will itself is destroyed if general wills in one context become particular wills in another. Do big general wills from little general wills grow, or don't they?

The city-state—or, at the most, national—limits of Rousseau's political community seemed to preclude any general will for the world. Is the problem of law, then, irrelevant to the world as a whole? Must war be the normal method for determining international policy? Rousseau had no answer; but his scattered speculations on the point were profoundly pessimistic.[31] He seemed less cramped by temporal limits, however, than he did by spatial limits. His thought leaped about history more easily than it leaped about the eighteenth-century world. In shielding Émile from the influence of his own society, for example, Rousseau may merely have been preparing him for life in a future and greater society.

Another problem is the subjectivism of Rousseau's religious, metaphysical, and epistemological views—insofar as he had any. Every man, in a sense, stands alone. Although he can find freedom only in a community, the more free he is the more alone he is: he must vote for himself, speak for himself, think for himself, believe for himself. The virtuous man, like the natural man, listens to his own heart and that is enough. Man is made free in this way, as he is for the twentieth-century existentialist; but is such freedom conducive to the particular kind of social unity Rousseau wanted?

A third problem is presented by a strongly stated but weakly reinforced goal of equality. As freedom was Rousseau's great positive goal, inequality was his great negative evil. As did the early liberals, however, Rousseau treated equality and inequality as political concepts having little to do with economics. Although he denounced the rich for their political machinations, he was plainly uninterested in the inequalities of property per se or even in the plight of the poor. But can an economically divided community be a politically united community?

These and many other questions Rousseau leaves unanswered. Nevertheless, his enduring greatness derives from his having raised the right questions, not from his having answered them. His vision of a long outdated and even irrelevant *polis* was so graphic, his attempt to erect a community that could absorb the individual while still freeing him was so poignant, that his influence is still felt.

The French Revolution, only half understanding Rousseau, clumsily tried to make the new society and the new man he called for. Romantic poets and novelists tried to ascertain the quality of the "real man" and to lay his inner self before the public, in part because Rousseau had done so. Criminolo-

Chapman argues that despite Rousseau's divergence from the early so-called classical liberalism, his theory of the general will is "remarkably similar to the modern liberal doctrine of the deliberative state."

[31] See Stanley Hoffman, "Rousseau on War and Peace," *American Political Science Review,* Vol. 57 (1963), pp. 317–33.

gists and educators began to consider the power and guilt of society in producing individual behavior, kindergartens were started, and child-centered education eventually developed, in part because Rousseau had raised some questions. At second or third or twentieth hand, perhaps, dictators adapted Rousseau's "civil religion" to their own use. And democrats were given a concept of law and a standard of popular participation in politics that still have much to commend them, for we still worry—or perhaps we have only begun to worry—about passive conformism, political apathy, and a weak sense of community as problems for the "highly civilized" democratic nations.

16

HUME

David Hume's cool skepticism appears to be equally characteristic of his philosophy and his life. To the age of rationalist enthusiasm he was a brake. But to the subsequent age of empiricist enthusiasm he was a stimulus. Always he seemed to fit into a position of dual influence: a liberal who was conservative, a secularist who accepted religion, a man of the Enlightenment with doubts about the source of light.

LIFE

Thirst for Fame

Hume was born in Edinburgh, Scotland, on April 26, 1711, the son of Joseph Hume (or, as it was then spelled, Home), offspring of a long and distinguished Scottish line, which he mentions with pride in his briefest of brief autobiographies.[1] His genius, his love of learning, and his "thirst for literary fame" (which, he tells us, was his life's "ruling passion") appeared early in life. Yet Hume was a long time in finding himself. The schools of Scotland did not challenge him; the profession of the law, which his family sought for him, did not excite him, though his skill at handling legal phraseology was unquestionable. For a brief time he tried employment as a clerk to a trader in Bristol, with little satisfaction. Overcoming a great melancholy and an attack of scurvy, he finally left England for France, where, following a plan of "very rigid frugality," he stayed for three years and wrote his greatest work, the *Treatise of Human Nature*. This young man who was so slow to find himself had written one of the world's masterpieces of philosophy by the age of twenty-five. Book I, "Of the Understanding," and Book II, "Of the Passions," were published in January, 1739; Book III, "On Morals," the next year. "Never literary attempt was more unfortunate than my *Treatise of Human Nature*. It fell *deadborn from the press.*" Hume exaggerated. By those who read it, the work was well received; but its author had hoped for a best-seller.

Later, Hume condensed and rewrote Book I of the *Treatise* as the *Essay Concerning Hu-*

[1] *My Own Life,* reprinted as Appendix A to Ernest Campbell Mossner, *The Life of David Hume* (Austin: Univ. of Texas Press, 1954). The discussion above is indebted to this distinguished recent work.

man Understanding. The book was more readable but less substantial and it is one of the sad facts of Hume's life that his concern for popular literary fame seemed to lead him away from the continuing extension, testing, and development of the ideas in the *Treatise,* a task of which he was fully capable. Fame was, at least in part, the spur that induced Hume to spend his later years on political and historical subjects at the expense of deeper philosophical penetration. Political theory has been blessed in this way and perhaps we should ask no more than one masterpiece from any man. But neither can we deny the fact of unfulfilled promise.

Back in Edinburgh, Hume published anonymously *Essays Moral and Political* (in two volumes, 1741 and 1742). Of the twenty-seven essays in that collection, some of the lighter, Addison-like efforts were purged by the author in the long series of later editions. Of the rest, the political essays—"Of the First Principles of Government," "That Politics May Be Reduced to a Science," "Of the Parties of Great Britain," and so on—were more popular than the philosophic ones. Hume has been accused of deleting indiscreetly democratic passages from his essays as they moved through subsequent editions. Although, through cutting and reediting, he moved continually in the direction of greater political caution, it is fair to say that he did not seriously alter any expressions of his basic convictions.

Travels and Further Publications

In 1746 Hume joined General St. Clair in his ill-fated expedition to Canada, serving him as secretary and later as judge advocate. When St. Clair went to the court of Turin, Hume went along with him as aide-de-camp, "so that the philosopher was obliged to encase his more than portly, and by no means elegant, figure in a military uniform."[2] The *Enquiry Concerning Human Understanding* (first titled *Philosophical Essays*) was published in 1748, while Hume was away from England. Between 1749 and 1751, Hume was back at the family home in Ninewells, in Berwickshire along the Tweed River valley, writing the *Dialogues of Natural Religion, Enquiry Concerning the Principles of Morals,* and the *Political Discourses.* The last-named, published in 1752, contained twelve essays, seven of which dealt with economics from a free-market perspective, reflecting and affecting Hume's friendship with the young Adam Smith.

In that same year Hume was elected librarian of the Edinburgh Faculty of Advocates, despite the charges of irreligion made against him, charges that had kept him from an Edinburgh University post years before. The new post was negligible except that it gave him access to a large library, which he used to good advantage in writing the *History of England,* published in volume after volume between 1754 and 1762. During this period he also wrote the *Natural History of Religion,* published in 1757.

In 1763 Hume went to France as secretary to Lord Hertford, the new ambassador. The bland countenance of *"le gros David, le bon David"* was the delight of Parisian society, for whom any visiting philosopher was a good show. His acquaintance there with Rousseau led to Rousseau's nightmarish trip to England, referred to in Chapter 15, and his introduction to the Comtesse de Boufflers led to a delicate but hopeless love affair. Moving up the administrative ladder, Hume became Under-Secretary of State in London for two years, beginning in 1767. By contrast with our twentieth-century image of the life of the harried bureaucrat, Hume's life in this post was quiet and leisurely and he casually mixed wide reading and personal correspondence with affairs of state.

He returned to Edinburgh in 1769, more or less to retire; he built his own house there the next year in order to live the comfortable and somewhat complacent life of a bachelor, whose hobby, incidentally, was cooking. In correspondence he fulminated against the

[2] Thomas Huxley, *Hume* (London: Macmillan, 1881), p. 28.

English and radicals like Wilkes[3] and worked over another edition of the *History* to "soften or expunge [he said] many villainous seditious Whig strokes which had crept into it." There he died, on August 25, 1776, of an intestinal disorder, after writing his will and the memorable five-page autobiography, *My Own Life*.

SKEPTICISM, EMPIRICISM, AND CAUSATION

Hume was a skeptic, which meant that he asked doubting questions about everything imaginable. But he was also part of a philosophic tradition. The critics of rationalism and its religious offshoot, deism, included some of the most distinguished men of Hume's century: the earl of Shaftesbury, Bishop Berkeley, and the professor of moral philosophy at the University of Glasgow, Francis Hutcheson, prominent member of the "moral-sense" school. Hume was respectful of this tradition but his originality would not be contained by it. Back to Locke, Newton, Hobbes, Descartes, Bayle, Bacon, Cicero, and Seneca he went in his readings; and from the richness of his knowledge came a dedication to detached analysis that pruned away the theological speculations that marked Berkeley's and Hutcheson's attack on rationalism. Hume sent Hutcheson the manuscript of Book III of the *Treatise*. The older man commented that it "wants a certain warmth in the Cause of Virtue," to which Hume replied, ". . . I am perswaded, that a Metaphysician may be very helpful to a moralist; tho' I cannot easily conceive these two Characters united in the same work. Any warm Sentiment of Morals, I am afraid, wou'd have the air of Declamation amidst abstract reasonings, & wou'd be esteemed contrary to good Taste."[4] Cool and cautious—that was Hume.

The caution that restrained his own passion enabled him to see and accept more readily the passions of others. "Reason is, and ought only to be, the slave of the passions," he wrote in the *Treatise of Human Nature*.[5] Despite his differences from the moral-sense school, he agreed with them that a priori reason is not the source of morality and also that man is a naturally sympathetic creature and not one of Hobbes's warring beasts. However, by his close attention to Berkeley's argument for God, Hume was able to carry nontheological empiricism to a point of independence scarcely yet exceeded. By disproving the reality of the external world apart from our own perceptions, Berkeley had found God to be the inescapable ordering principle. Granting the irreducibility of our disconnected perceptions, Hume went further to ask the question: Is not the idea of God, like the idea of Matter, necessary to hold our perceptions together only so long as we assume the necessity of a continual operation of cause and effect in the world? Can we get along without assuming that everything is caused? Hume thought that we could.

The sweeping character of this assertion can hardly be exaggerated. All conclusions based on causal inference—obviously an overwhelming number of conclusions—become uncertain. Hume himself spoke of this proposition as a "revolution in philosophy." Ironically, Hume's doubts about causal inference, which would seem to imply abandoning the quest for universal knowledge and living from experiment to experiment, were developed in the *Treatise of Human Nature* as part of a more or less traditional attempt to systematize all human knowledge. Moreover, in some ways, even his radical empiricism leaned heavily on the past. Hume's distinction between "impressions"—we might say "feelings"—and "ideas" was largely a reaffirmation of Locke's empiricism and therefore retained the tincture of rationalist faith lurking in Locke's "true ideas."

Hume's unique contribution rested on

[3] See Chapter 17 below.

[4] Mossner, p. 134.

[5] L. A. Selby-Bigge, ed., *Treatise of Human Nature*, Bk. II, Part III, sec. 3 (Oxford: Clarendon Press, 1896).

another distinction, one that is crucial for all modern logical empiricism: that between "demonstrable" and "moral"—we might say "experiential"—knowledge. The former deals with the logical relations of ideas and is governed by rules of mathematics. The latter deals with matters of fact. In this realm there are no absolutely necesary propositions. Logically there is no logic of facts, and anything is possible. This, says Hume, is the realm of experience. In experience we *assume* a future conformable to the past. From causes that appear similar, we have come to expect similar effects. But our causal inferences cannot be proven by logical demonstration or even validated by intuition. They are based, says Hume, on custom or habit.

However unprovable causal inferences may be, we nevertheless lean on them to survive. We piece together and make sense of our perceptions by noting their resemblance, their contiguity in space and time, and their constant conjunction. The operation of these three principles appears to Hume to be an invariable tendency of the human mind, a tendency that makes possible a belief in the external world and in true causation (i. e., a *necessary* connection between events). But it is habitual belief and natural impulse, not necessity, that permit us to act on these causal assumptions, just as it is individual preference and not necessity that designates our values. Each human being constructs his own world.

Hume was not fully content with his system of "moderate skepticism," especially in coping with the problem of the self and self-consciousness; and he was reluctant to draw radical conclusions from it. As he demonstrated in the *Dialogues Concerning Natural Religion,* his disinclination to be dogmatic led him to grant the tenability of common beliefs about religion.

THE CRITIQUE OF THE CONTRACTUALISTS

Such skepticism not only tended to eliminate the easy faith in natural law characteristic of many Enlightenment writers but also seemed to eliminate the historical optimism that was a part of that faith. This Hume accomplished without an appeal to a supernatural mystique, simply by using the tools of critical analysis so favored by the Enlightenment. "Hume was something more than the Enlightenment incarnate, for his significance is that he turned against the Enlightenment its own weapons. And herein lies his importance as a conservative thinker."[6] He was a conservative without sentimental emotion. He was a utilitarian without grand schemes of reform. Using a variation of the associationist psychology adopted by Locke and later by the English utilitarians, he came to more realistic conclusions than either concerning the possibility of rational self-interest operating toward social harmony.

> What strikes upon [men] with a strong and lively idea commonly prevails above what lies in a more obscure light . . . as everything that is contiguous to us, either in space or time, strikes upon us with such an idea . . . and commonly operates with more force than any object that lies in a more distant and obscure light.
>
> This is the reason why men so often act in contradiction to their known interest; and in particular why they prefer any trivial advantage, that is present, to the maintenance of order in society, which so much depends on the observance of justice. The consequences of every breach of equity seem to lie very remote, and are not able to counterbalance any immediate advantage that may be reaped from it. They are, however, never the less real for being remote; and as all men are, in some degree, subject to the same weakness, it necessarily happens that the violations of equity must become very frequent in society, dangerous and uncertain.[7]

If men's interests cannot be assumed to be clearly perceptible to them, if natural sympathy rather than rational calculation draws men together, it follows that the contractualist view of society is defectively simple. Hume addresses himself to the subject in the essays "Of the Origin of Government" and "Of the

[6] Sheldon Wolin, "Hume and Conservatism," *American Political Science Review,* Vol. 48 (1954), p. 1001.

[7] *Treatise,* Bk. III, Part II, sec. 7.

Origin of Contract."[8] "Man, born in a family, is compelled to maintain society from necessity, from natural inclination, and from habit," Hume begins the first-named essay. All men are conscious of the need to maintain peace and order and of the contribution of justice to this end, he goes on. Yet because of "the frailty or perverseness of our nature" men do not follow the paths of justice unerringly. Sometimes a man's interest is promoted by fraud or rapine but more often, as the foregoing quotation from the *Treatise* argued, present transient interests overshadow greater and more important ones. "This weakness is incurable in human nature." As an agency to induce habits of obedience in support of justice, "government commences . . . casually and . . . imperfectly." And though strong and superior leaders may develop habits of good order, "in all governments there is a perpetual intestine struggle, open or secret, between Authority and Liberty, and neither of them can ever absolutely prevail in the contest." While liberty may be in one sense the principle of perfection in a civil society (Hume was not much bothered to distinguish between state and society), "still authority must be acknowledged essential to its very existence." Consequently, those governments commonly called "free"—the quotation marks are Hume's—are those that have managed to divide power and can keep the monarch in check without overturning him.

In "Of the Original Contract" Hume examines more systematically first the divine-right theorists then the contractualists. With surprising sympathy and patience he neatly demolishes the theory of divine right. All men are under God and no "peculiar sacredness" can be discovered in the persons of kings. Again, seeking agreement rather than exploiting disagreement with the position he examines, Hume grants that in a sense there must have been a kind of consent exercised for primitives to have banded together for protection; however, "no compact or agreement, it is evident, was expressly formed for general submission, an idea far beyond the comprehension of savages." And the idea of rational consent to government in the contemporary world is even more hypothetical: in a sly dig at Locke, Hume refers to "philosophers who have embraced a party—if that be not a contradiction in terms." If these men would "look abroad in the world," they would find, whether in Persia or China, France or Spain, Holland or England, that political connections are "independent of our consent." "Obedience or subjection becomes so familiar that most men never make any inquiry about its origin or cause, more than about the principle of gravity." Moreover, "were you to preach, in most parts of the world, that political connections are founded altogether on voluntary consent or a mutual promise, the magistrate would soon imprison you as seditious." The simple and incontestable fact is that almost every present and past government has been "founded originally either on usurpation or conquest or both, without any pretence as a fair consent or voluntry subjection of the people."

Hume points out that the much-feted Glorious Revolution of 1688 was really less of a revolution than a change in the succession and involved no contractual arrangement with the people. The bulk of ten million people acquiesced, to be sure, but did they have any choice in the matter? Hume thinks not, and his examination of governments of the past leads him to conclude that they were not much different in this respect. "My intention here is not to exclude the consent of the people from being one just foundation of government. . . . I only contend that it has very seldom had place in any degree, and never almost in its full extent and that, therefore, some other foundation of government must also be admitted."

Locke, of course, had said that acquiescence could be regarded as consent, since a man was free to depart and live under an-

[8] *David Hume, Political Essays,* Charles W. Hendel, ed. (New York: Liberal Arts Press, 1953), pp. 39–61. All quotations from the *Essays* in the remainder of this chapter are taken from this book, which is reprinted from the last edition in Hume's lifetime (1777) of *Essays Moral and Political.* See also *Treatise,* Bk. III, Part II, secs. 7–8.

other government. Again, Hume the realist speaks: "Can we seriously say that a poor peasant or artisan has a free choice to leave his country when he knows no foreign language or manners and lives from day to day by the small wages he acquires?"

Hume is concerned with reality but also with what is justifiable. And so, in a quite Burkean paragraph, he shows how a constant stress on individual consent would rip open the social fabric and lead to violence. The process of history cannot be stopped dead in its tracks to take a vote: ". . . as human society is in perpetual flux, one man every hour going out of the world, another coming into it, it is necessary in order to preserve stability in government that the new brood should conform themselves to the established constitution." Hume is careful not to base his conception of civic duty on a monistic conception of moral duties. He contrasts natural moral impulses—love of children, gratitude to benefactors, pity of the unfortunate, et cetera—with moral duties arising only out of a sense of obligation—the keeping of promises, respect for others' property, and so on. Civil authorities are needed precisely because the latter actions, while moral, do not arise spontaneously; a bit of prodding is sometimes necessary. The authorities cannot rely on our promise to obey, given in some hypothetical contract, because we can and often do fall short of our promises; the authorities need power as well as a promise. On the question "But to whom is allegiance due . . . who is our lawful sovereign?" Hume hedges a bit. He retreats into historical examples of usurpation, conquest, and succession and concludes that in sovereignty, as in property, possession seems to be nine points of the law—which does not tell us whether it should be. Such a conclusion appears to be more statically conservative than Hume elsewhere appears. But the gist of his argument is not affected by this evasion. It can be summed up by his answer to the question of why government must be obeyed: "I readily answer, 'Because society could not otherwise subsist.'"

POLITICS AS A SCIENCE

The skepticism that shattered the bland Lockean assumptions about the origins of government might easily be thought to have dissolved as well the Lockean hope for a science of morals and, by implication, a science of politics. But in this respect, Hume seems more a child of the Enlightenment than its critic. He addresses himself to this question in the essay "That Politics May Be Reduced to a Science."

The title may be deceptive unless we note carefully what Hume means by "science." Hume's conception of a science of politics is not in accord with that of some of our more mathematically inclined contemporaries. Sophisticated algebraic formulas for handling questionnaire responses and voting statistics were not yet relevant. Basically, he was trying to prove, like Aristotle, that forms of government have certain predictable influences on the course of political development—influences that, if not absolutely causative, may be more determinative than the personalities of specific leaders. Nevertheless, the image of mathematical certainty does creep into his usage: "So great is the force of laws and of particular forms of government, and so little dependence have they on the humors and tempers of men, that consequences almost as general and certain may sometimes be deduced from them as any which the mathematical sciences afford us."

Note the prudent qualifications: "*almost* as general and certain may *sometimes* be deduced." The empirical evidence to support such generalizations about politics was to be drawn from the common materials of history. For example, Hume shows how, as was true in the Roman Republic before the Caesars, a democratic form that vests power in a collective rather than a representative body leads with almost complete certainty to tumult, licentiousness, and anarchy. The methodology of this science of politics is the methodology of history, with the canons of sound evidence being very close to common sense. From the experience of England and Ireland he generalizes that "free governments" are likely to be the most oppressive to their provinces. "And this observation may, I believe, be *fixed* as a maxim of the kind we are here speaking of."

For all his caution, Hume was hoping for a kind of fixity that contemporary social scientists would be unlikely to expect. Moreover, he was seeking a science of morals antithetical to the value-free methodology of the contemporary social scientist and seemingly antithetical to his own epistemology, with its sharp distinction between matters of fact and matters of value. At least at a low level, an understanding of the good as well as the real was to be accomplished by Hume's method: "It may, therefore, be pronounced as a universal axiom in politics *that a hereditary prince, a nobility without vassals, and a people voting by their representatives form the best monarchy, aristocracy, and democracy.*" He cites an observation of Machiavelli concerning Alexander the Great as "one of those eternal political truths which no time nor accidents can vary."

This concern for the good and the wise and the eternal in political relationships is in keeping with a distinguished tradition of political speculation as well as with some of the special assumptions of the Enlightenment. But it does not always seem in keeping with Hume's analysis of causation earlier discussed. Is it a lapse of judgment or methodological schizophrenia that permits him to say in the essay "That Politics May Be Reduced to a Science": "Effects will always correspond to causes, and wise regulations in any commonwealth are the most valuable legacy that can be left to future ages"?

We would do well to remember that, on the one hand, in the eighteenth century "science" was still roughly a synonym for "philosophy" and philosophy was the term attached to the love of wisdom, not merely the pursuit of empirical truth. Science had not yet become essentially experimental nor philosophy largely analytical. Hume could scarcely draw all the skeptical implications out of his epistemology that later students did. On the other hand, there is unquestionably a gap between his epistemology and his social theorizing. To say in one place that causality is an inference not amenable to rational proof and in another place that a science of politics can prove that nonrepresentative democracy is a cause of anarchy does seem rather contradictory. Technically, Hume has no right to talk about historical causes in the way that he does. But he never questioned the inevitability of causal inference nor the fact that there were more and less reliable causal inferences. He simply denied their rational certitude.

His antirationalism does not, of course, make Hume "value-free." His attack on partisan zeal as a source of social instability becomes almost partisan in its zeal. And, ironically, it was probably this conception of the danger of faction that, sanctified as a conclusion of "science," most influenced James Madison's famous position on factions in the *Federalist* and afterward.[9] But if we rule Hume and other members out of the fraternity of social scientists on the grounds of partisanship, there would be few left.

Lest we oversimplify the contrast between Hume's political science and his epistemology, three things ought to be said. First, his philosophical works, especially Book III of the *Treatise* and parts of the *Essay Concerning Human Understanding,* are not devoid of the considerations raised in the essay on politics as a science. In the *Essay Concerning Human Understanding* he asks, "How could *politics* be a science, if laws and forms of government had not a uniform influence upon society?" And he argues that the chief use of history "is only to discover the constant and

[9] See Douglass Adair, " 'That Politics May Be Reduced to a Science': David Hume, James Madison, and the Tenth *Federalist,*" *Huntington Library Quarterly,* Vol. 20 (1957), pp. 343–60. Adair effectively shows how Madison and his colleagues in the Convention were, in the eighteenth-century sense of the term, "making a genuinely 'scientific' attempt to discover the 'constant and universal principles' of any republican government in regard to liberty, justice, and stability."

universal principles of human nature, by showing men in all varieties of circumstances and situations, and furnishing us with materials from which we may form our observations and become acquainted with the regular springs of human action and behavior." There is a basic unity to all Hume's work.

Second, like Locke, Hume displayed a practical bent, a bias toward action that led him into the world of affairs and kept the man of thought at least familiar with the man of action. This propensity tended to restrain any tendency toward a wholly radical and irresponsible subjectivism. Or perhaps a better way to put it would be to say that Hume was skeptical enough to be skeptical even of skepticism itself. In the final pages of the *Essay Concerning Human Understanding* he criticizes what he calls Pyrrhonism, or excessive skepticism. And it is interesting to note that what overcomes Pyrrhonism is "action," "employment," and "the occupations of common life." Hume was neither a visionary nor an intellectual escapist. "Be a philosopher," he wrote, "but amidst all your philosophizing, be still a man."

Third, having noted Hume's consistency and down-to-earthness, we are obliged also to recognize that both fail when Hume discusses natural law and his idea of a perfect commonwealth.[10] For one thing, reason, which has been eliminated as a source of morality and subordinated to passion, creeps back in disguise. "Calm" passions, which permit far-sighted judgments, are recognized as superior to "violent" passions, which do not. This distinction reinforces Hume's conservatism, for he finds that men of education and property tend to be the most calm. And it is a requirement of Hume's political science that such calm judgments are necessary for the perception of "general and Universal rules." Moreover, while Hume's epistemology undermines natural law, it does not do so with finality. Rules of natural law, says Hume, are "invented" by man to cope with what may, without such rules, be natural and unrestrained appetites. Although for Hume they seem to have prudential rather than metaphysical sanction, he appears to believe in their necessity as strongly as any natural-law thinker. Yet their scope is narrowly conservative in that they are confined exclusively to the domain of property rights. The "three fundamental laws of nature" are those *"of the stability of possession, of its transference by consent,* and *of the performance of promises.* It is on the strict observance of those three laws that the peace and security of human society entirely depend. . . . Society is absolutely necessary for the well-being of men; and these are as necessary to the support of society."[11]

THE BALANCE OF POWER

The political theorist is sometimes accused of spending all his time talking about what can and cannot be done while the political scientist is, figuratively at least, out in the world doing it. By this test, Hume should be more acceptable as a colleague of political scientists than most of the men discussed in these pages. That Hume had an insight into the realities of politics transcending most of the legalistic and prescriptive theories of his day may be illustrated by looking at his discussions of the balance of power and the system of influence in English politics.

The term "balance of power," which to-

[10] *Treatise,* Bk. II, Part II, secs. 1–6; "Idea of a Perfect Commonwealth," in *Political Essays.*

[11] *Treatise,* Bk. II, Part II, sec. 6. Watkins observes that this is by no means an outmoded point of view: "Under the influence of scientific empiricism liberal theorists have been prone to adopt a position of mildly conservative utilitarianism. Rejecting *a priori* standards of political morality, they have tried to defend the institutions and practices of constitutional government as empirically superior manifestations of historical evolution. An aristocratic and conservative bias quite similar to that of Hume has normally been characteristic of the Western liberal attitude toward the traditions and aspirations of the non-Western majority of mankind" (Frederick Watkins, ed., *Hume: Theory of Politics* [Austin: Univ. of Texas Press, 1953], p. xxv). See also Laurence L. Bongie, *David Hume: Prophet of the Counter-Revolution* (Oxford: Clarendon Press, 1965).

day is usually applied to the relations between nations, was applied by Hume in the same way in his essay "Of the Balance of Power" (1752). In the essay he was able to point to the necessity of balancing nation against nation in the ancient world as a "desirable check" against top-heavy concentrations of power, and also to see England's military policy as an attempt to contain the assertive power of Austria and France. But he was detached enough to observe that England tends to err on the side of excess rather than prudence once a war has begun.

The balancing, moderating tendency that Hume both described and praised was found to operate not only in the realm of international relations but in domestic politics and the economy. Hume, the friend of Adam Smith, shared some of Smith's optimism about the balancing process that was supposed to take place automatically in a free market unhampered by mercantilist restrictions. But he also saw, as few of the early economic liberals did, the fact of and the necessity for a reciprocal relationship between public state power and private economic power: "As the ambition of the sovereign must entrench on the luxury of individuals, so the luxury of individuals must diminish the force and check the ambition of the sovereign."[12] His defense of equal opportunity in acquisition of property and the enjoyment of the fruits of one's labor was based not upon abstract rights of the individual but upon the contention that "a too great disproportion among the citizens weakens any state."

The results, if not the rationale, behind Hume's preference for balance and moderation often place him close to the liberal tradition. It is the praiseworthy attribute of "civilized monarchies" as of republics that *"they are a government of laws, not of men."*[13] The liberty of the press is to be stoutly defended not because it is a right but because it is an advantage. Liberty of the press and mixed government mutually support each other. The spirit of the people must frequently be roused in order to curb the ambition of the court; "the liberty of the press is so [thoroughly] essential to the support of our mixed government, this sufficiently decides the . . . question: *Whether this liberty be advantageous or prejudicial,* there being nothing of greater importance than the preservation of the ancient government, especially if it be a free one." The common sense of Hume's approach is conspicuous. "A man reads a book or pamphlet alone and coolly. . . . The liberty of the press . . . however abused, can scarce ever excite popular tumults or rebellion. . . . the *people* are no such dangerous monsters as they have been represented, . . . it is in every respect better to guide them like rational creatures than to lead or drive them like brute beasts."[14]

Though Hume was calm about the threat of a wholly popular government, he did conceive of it as a threat if unchecked by another power. Popular government would see the tyranny of faction subdivided into new factions. But he also believed that absolute monarchy would be a less spectacular but equally certain cause of death to the English Constitution, a "true Euthanasia" he called it: ". . . we have also reason to be more jealous of popular government because that danger is more terrible. This may teach us a lesson of moderation in all our political controversies."[15] Hume's opposition to parties, therefore, was not based on their challenge to monarchical power, which he regarded as healthy, but on their tendency to be immoderate.

POWER AND THE SYSTEM OF INFLUENCE

Since, in terms of numbers, force is always on the side of the governed rather than the

[12] "Of Commerce" (1752).

[13] "Of Civil Liberty."

[14] "Of the Liberty of the Press."

[15] "Whether the British Government Inclines More to Absolute Monarchy or to a Republic."

governors, the ultimate power and authority of governments, says Hume, always rest on opinion. In "Of the First Principles of Government" Hume finds this base of opinion to be composed of three aspects—opinion of "public interest," opinion of the "right to power," and opinion of the "right to property." He shows, with perhaps somewhat more realism than Machiavelli, the limits of fear as an instrument of governance but he also deals with the limits of affection. More significant than either, thinks Hume, is the individual's capacity to invest the acts of governments with his own self-interest.

The remarkable perceptiveness of Hume the political analyst is nowhere better shown than in his explanation and defense of the system of influence in the English government. Like Madison, Hume accepted factions or parties as necessary evils that ought to be tolerated because to eliminate them would be a remedy worse than the disease. What could be hoped for was to keep them in check. Most dangerous were parties or factions of principle, for they tended to crystallize opinion around inflexible positions and to generate the intractable "enthusiasm" that Hume saw as the bane of orderly political life. In "Of the Parties of Great Britain" he found the Whigs and Tories to be far more agreed on fundamental assumptions than was commonly thought. The ambiguity of principle, the tendency to follow men rather than ideas, the pressures toward moderation, Hume approved of. "The Tories, as men, were enemies to oppression; and also, as Englishmen, they were enemies to arbitrary power. Their zeal for liberty was perhaps less fervent than that of their antagonists, but was sufficient to make them forget all their general principles when they saw themselves openly threatened with subversion of the ancient government."[16]

As Wolin has pointed out,[17] admirers of the "balanced" English Constitution, such as Blackstone and Burke, failed to see as Hume did the degree to which the system of influence—patronage, bribes, ties of family, contracts, and so on—was an integral part of the balancing process between king and Commons. It was partly because this network of influence was hidden from view and involved with deeply habitual behavior that Hume could say,

> To tamper . . . or try experiments merely upon the credit of supposed argument and philosophy can never be the part of the wise magistrate, who will bear a reverence to what carries the marks of age; and though he may attempt some improvements for the public good, yet will he adjust his innovations as much as possible to the ancient fabric and preserve entire the ancient pillars and supports of the constitution.[18]

THE HISTORY OF ENGLAND AND THE USES OF HISTORY

At about the age of thirty-five, Hume shifted from philosophy to history as his primary preoccupation. Even before, however, he had been more concerned than were most thinkers identified with the Enlightenment with the methodology of history.[19] As against some who would use his own skepticism to discredit historical studies altogether, Hume was able to vindicate historical knowledge by showing it to be a system of reasonable beliefs based on testimony. If such knowledge did not have absolute certitude, neither, in Hume's view, had any other kind of knowledge.

But when it came to *writing* history, Hume's accomplishments are more equivocal. In the first place, he was rather careless about sources, especially in dealing with the period before the Tudor monarchs. Sharing to some degree the antireligious and antihistorical bias of the Enlightenment, he was not really interested in historical epochs prior to his own.

[16] In *Political Essays.* See also "Of Parties in General," reprinted in Watkins, *Hume: Theory of Politics,* pp. 168–76.

[17] In "Hume and Conservatism."

[18] "Idea of a Perfect Commonwealth."

[19] See *Treatise,* Bk. I, Part III, secs. 4, 13.

Hume's somewhat parochial history certainly did not always square with the tone of detachment he urged in many of his other writings: ". . . there is no subject in which we must proceed with more caution than in tracing the history of the arts and sciences, lest we assign causes which never existed and reduce what is merely contingent to stable and universal principles."[20]

Hume's reputation as a historian is blemished by the belief that he was mainly a Tory partisan. Such a judgment is derived not so much from the work itself as from the reaction to the work in some Whig quarters and Hume's exaggerated and somewhat bitter statement in his autobiography that after the "senseless clamour" of the Whigs over his book, alterations in future editions were "made all of them invariably to the Tory side." Hume's volume on the Stuarts had been greeted by the more rabid Whigs with charges of being Jacobite. But Horace Walpole himself wrote that the book, though "certainly with faults, I cannot help liking much. It is called Jacobite, but in my opinion it is only not *George-abite*." And Hume's publisher had early been impressed that "it is neither whig nor tory but truely imparshal." This was Hume's feeling also: "I have the impudence to pretend that I am of no party and have no bias. . . . With regard to politics . . . I think I am very moderate. My views of *things* are more conformable to Whig principles, my representations of *persons* to Tory prejudices."[21]

Hume also produced reactions from some of the clergy, who charged him with irreligion. But the *History* much more than the *Treatise* was written with income in mind and Hume was not ashamed to admit that he wrote with an awareness of his audience: "A few Christians (and but few) think I speak like a Libertine in religion; be assured I am tolerably reserved on this head. . . . I composed it *ad populum* as well as *ad clerum*, and thought that scepticism was not in its place in a historical production."[22] In a later edition Hume actually removed two passages that had offended the clergy.

By our standards the *History* is neither dispassionate nor a testament to original research. But although it is a work based largely on the synthesis of others' research and is loaded with what we would call value-judgments, it is by no means a mere partisan tract. The work has great literary merit and this distinction overshadows its shortcomings as a history. In addition to the technical defects of Hume's history, however, there is a deeper difficulty, as Collingwood has pointed out. There was in the Enlightenment quest for a science of an unvarying human nature a remnant of what Collingwood calls classical "substantialism," that is, the view that only what is unchanging is knowable. Because the essence of history is change, substantialism is antithetical to any view that takes the problem of history seriously. "Hume substituted for the idea of spiritual substance the idea of constant tendencies to associate ideas in particular ways, and these laws of association were just as uniform and unchanging as any substance."[23] Hume could not simultaneously think historically and in terms of constants of human nature; and in the balance his treatment of history suffered.

Nevertheless, we must grant that Hume was more sophisticated about the historical process than most of the conservatives *or* Enlightenment progressives of his day. On the one hand, Blackstone found in the mere longevity of institutions a sign of their naturalness and rationality. The rationality of habitual institutions was not so clear to Hume. On the other hand, the progressives assumed that a science of politics applied to the world would automatically lead to reform. Hume made no such assumption and did not pretend to possess the key to the

[20] "Of the Rise and Progress of the Arts and Sciences."

[21] Quotations are from Mossner, *Hume*, pp. 614, 310, 303, and 311, respectively. See E. C. Mossner, "Was Hume a Tory Historian? Facts and Reconsiderations," *Journal of the History of Ideas*, Vol. 2 (1941), pp. 225–36.

[22] Mossner, *Hume*, p. 305.

[23] R. G. Collingwood, *The Idea of History* (Oxford: Clarendon Press, 1946), p. 83. What to us are historically conditioned traits of Western man, to Hume were trans-historical constants of human nature.

good life on earth. If his historical skepticism was not pure, neither was it naive.

CONCLUSION

In the eighteenth-century sense of "moral," Hume's political writings were moral through and through. The whole thrust of his social thought was to find a basis for distinguishing between justified and unjustified institutions. From his empirical and experimental premise Hume sought to extract reliable principles from both the psychological and the social worlds. From the former came his "natural principles" of human nature expounded in the *Treatise*. On the basis of these plus further observations of whole societies came his "artificial principles" of society sketched in the *Political Essays*. Like the later utilitarians, Hume believed that the natural obligation in social relationships was the obligation of interest. But he also believed that this interest was a function of passions less mechanical and more elusive than, say, Bentham would admit. He further assumed that individual interests and social interests are ultimately—though he would not have liked this word—capable of harmonious adjustment. Hume found no evidential basis for believing in a natural disharmony of individual and society. But his subjectivism was such that he saw more clearly than Bentham the scope of individual differences in values; and he could explain a great many social disharmonies by noting the dominance of immediate interest over the possibly greater but more distant interest in the affairs of men.

Using the general criterion of utility, Hume concluded that social stability must be the cardinal goal of policy. Such stability was not, for him, accidental, the result of the simple operation of natural principles of human nature, or the result of superimposed rules. It was rather the result of a system of "conventions," which were the product of both human understanding and natural human affections.[24] In this view he anticipated much of Burke's reverence for the human community. Hume is in the unique position of influencing Bentham's radicalism and Burke's conservatism by virtue of categories that transcend them both. Rousseau's paradoxical blend of radicalism and conservatism may also owe something to Hume. By divorcing the demands of community from a rational sanction, Hume left the way open for his contemporary Rousseau to introduce a nonrational "civil religion" as the ideological basis of a romanticized community

Hume's methodological skepticism, meanwhile, turns out not to be so skeptical after all. He was cautious about grand schemes and fixed models; he had little faith in radical transformations based on rational plans. The passionate character of men's interests was most real to him. These qualities made him a conservative with a probing concern for the consequences of each new social step and a deep affection for social stability. But, despite this outlook, he was an optimistic conservative, a man with limited hopes, perhaps, but virtually no sense of despair. After the French Revolution, this relaxed brand of conservatism would no longer suit the times and urgent metaphysical varieties would take its place.

[24] See W. Gordon Ross, *Human Nature and Utility in Hume's Social Philosophy* (Garden City, N. Y.: published by the author, 1942), pp. 98–101.

17

BURKE

In Edmund Burke we have the theorist as statesman, or, to be more precise, the statesman as theorist. We also have a man who has become a symbol of conservatism. Put the two together and we have the myth that the man of affairs, the responsible man, the man in constant daily touch with political reality, tends to be conservative. The myth is not necessarily false; but it *is* a myth, a proposition more easily believed than proved. Thus arises the problem of the relationship of political thought to political action, a problem that makes the biography of Burke especially relevant.

LIFE

Education and Early Works

Burke was born in Dublin, Ireland, January 12, 1729, one of several offspring of an irritable Church of Ireland (Anglican) attorney and a gentle Catholic housewife. The mother was a remote descendant of Edmund Spenser, whence came our subject's name. In delicate health, Edmund spent periods of physical quiet studying history and dreaming dreams of the past, a romantic fascination that affected his whole life. From his mother he learned to tolerate Catholics, from his Quaker schoolmaster at Ballitore School, Dublin, he learned to tolerate Quakers, and from the many French Huguenot boys enrolled there he learned to tolerate Calvinists. But he was always a strong Church of England man and never comfortable in the presence of the irreligious.

In 1744 Burke entered Trinity College, Dublin University, at that time a better school than either Oxford or Cambridge. He went through a series of infatuations and disillusionments with mathematics, metaphysics, history, and poetry, of which only the last two left a positive mark. Metaphysics became Burke's chief whipping boy, a "Serbonian bog" he called it. While an undergraduate, he wrote a play and in 1748, the year of his Bachelor of Arts, he produced pamphlets attacking mercantilism and examining Bolingbroke's *Idea of a Patriot King*. He also wrote but did not publish a treatise on aesthetics, *The Sublime and the Beautiful,* and edited thirteen issues of a periodical called—ironically enough, considering his subsequent reputation—the *Reformer*. The journal paid special attention to economics and the drama.

Altogether not a bad start for a boy of nineteen.

In 1750 Burke entered the Inn of the Middle Temple in London to study law but spent as much or more time studying literature. By 1755, fearing that he had become a wastrel, his disgusted father cut off his allowance. Burke never was admitted to the bar. But fame and his own income began with the publication of his *Vindication of Natural Society* (1756). History, he maintained, is a history of wars. Wars are mainly the result of the subversion of "natural society" by atheists, divines, and politicians. In a natural society, labor produces the ownership of goods. In an artificial or "political" society, those who labor the most tend to have the least—witness, said Burke, the terrible conditions of the miners in northern England. (When, in 1765, a mellower and more "political" Burke was running for Parliament, he felt it necessary to issue a preface to the new edition of *The Vindication of Natural Society* assuring readers that the design of the work was "entirely ironical.")

The success of the *Vindication* led Burke to publish in the same year *The Sublime and the Beautiful.* But suddenly his health broke. Fortunately, he found in Bath a skilled—though Presbyterian—doctor with a gentle, charming daughter. The doctor cured him, the daughter married him, and Burke managed to get his father-in-law to pay some of his mounting bills. In the same year he published *An Abridgement of English History,* which, by contrast with most of the histories of the Enlightenment period, did not disparage the past.

From 1758 to 1791 Burke was the unacknowledged editor of the *Annual Register,* a journal devoted to the review of major events in history, politics, and literature.[1] Journalists were looked down upon in the eighteenth century and Burke's self-chosen anonymity left a cloud of obscurity over much of this journal's authorship.[2] But it can be said that the tone of the publication was consistently moderate and dispassionate. Here is evidence that the man of thought and the man of action can to some degree exist in the same person at different times—for whatever else Burke's oratory and political tract-writing were, they could not be called dispassionate. The mixture of moderate reason and immoderate passion is perhaps a large part of Burke's fascination.

Introduction to Politics

In 1759 Burke was introduced to William Gerald "Single Speech" Hamilton.[3] This was his first contact with statesmanship. He became Hamilton's secretary and, when Hamilton went to Ireland in 1761 as chief secretary of the Lord Lieutenant, Burke went with him. Fascinated by politics, Burke soon faced a dilemma: whether to become an Irish politician, in which case his Catholic sympathies would be an asset, or to strive for greater rewards by going back to England to become an English politician, in which case his Catholic sympathies would be a liability. He chose the latter. While his choice gave England one of its greatest parliamentarians, it also imposed tragic elements on Burke's life.

Burke was not one to shun an unpopular cause. During his Irish stay he wrote his *Tracts on the Popery Laws,*[4] which attacked the terribly oppressive—even if largely unenforced—laws against Catholics in Ireland. Schools, professions, and politics were closed to Catholics by these laws. Special taxes lay

[1] The *Register* had limited space for reviews, but Burke's careful choice of books for review brought to the reader's attention almost all those contemporary works that time has vindicated as great, works by such men as Rousseau, Hume, Sterne, Samuel Johnson, and Adam Smith. See Robert H. Murray, *Edmund Burke, A Biography* (New York: Oxford Univ. Press, 1931), pp. 83–84. This biographical section draws heavily on Murray's book.

[2] See Thomas W. Copeland, *Edmund Burke, Six Essays* (London: Cape, 1950), Chs. 3–4.

[3] Hamilton, who subsequently held many administrative posts, attracted Prime Minister Walpole's attention with his maiden speech in the House of Commons, November 13, 1755. According to legend, he never again spoke in the House. The legend is false.

[4] In *The Writings and Speeches of Edmund Burke* (Boston: Little, Brown, 1901), Vol. VI, pp. 301–60. Hereinafter referred to as *Works.*

against them. The Mass was forbidden. Attempts to gain conversions were considered high treason. The nearest Protestant relative could claim an inheritance ahead of a Catholic heir. Burke's consistent position against such measures was later to encourage political reprisals against him.

In 1763 Burke went back to London with Hamilton and joined a notable fellowship called simply The Literary Club, founded by the painter Sir Joshua Reynolds. Meeting once a week for supper at the Turk's Head in Soho, the society debated issues of the day, enabling Burke to sharpen his wit and try out his flow of bad puns on such friends and fellow raconteurs as Samuel Johnson and Oliver Goldsmith. (Later the group came to include such distinguished men as Boswell, Gibbon, Adam Smith, Fox, Windham, Sheridan, and Garrick, the actor.) At this time, after some unpleasant disagreements, Burke broke with Hamilton. He was poor again, despite which he, and even more his brother Dick and cousin Will Burke, ran up great debts and generously befriended all sorts of acquaintances.[5]

In 1765 a new career began for Burke. He became private secretary of Lord Rockingham, leader of the Whigs, and entered Parliament. Burke could not have chosen a more critical time. William Pitt the Elder, under whose aggressive leadership Britain had defeated the French in the Seven Years' War, had been abruptly dismissed by George III in 1761, almost two years before the Treaty of Paris had ended the war. No one got along very well with the king, that man of "unforgiving piety," as Junius called him, that "conscientious bull in a china ship."[6] Seven ministries came and went in less than ten years: those of Pitt, Bute, Grenville, Rockingham, Grafton (twice), and North. It was during Rockingham's ill-starred government that Burke became his secretary and also became a member of the House of Commons from Wendover in Buckinghamshire, a pocket borough of Lord Verney that Cousin Will had helped Burke line up.

Orator for the Underdog

The Rockingham government is remembered for repealing the Stamp Act, which had so infuriated the Americans when first passed, and for "an almost suicidal incorruptibility"[7] in an age of awesome corruption. Among the first speeches Burke made in the House were those for repeal of the Stamp Act. The speeches, said Dr. Johnson, were so impressive they "filled the town with wonder."[8] Until 1794, for virtually the rest of his life, Burke was, as every writer seems to term it, "mentor, guide, and philosopher" of the Whig Party, or at least that faction of it originally led by Rockingham. Yet for all his fame and prestige, Burke was more often on the losing than the winning side and never became a minister.

Burke's first major political publication was *Thoughts on the Cause of the Present Discontents* (1770). King George, no longer worried about a Jacobite restoration, was actively seeking to build up the Tories in hopes of making them a personal court party. The beleaguered Whigs were split into factions. The *Present Discontents* was an eloquent critique of the ideas used by the court cabal to advance their cause. The separation of the court from "the sentiments and opinions of the people," argued Burke, and the system of corruption and favoritism that had grown up around the cabal were threatening the Constitution itself. The traditional balance of the

[5] Burke assisted for years one Joseph Emin, an Armenian refugee he happened to encounter in St. James Park. Copeland has documented how much of the scathing personal criticism Burke received during his life was due to the reputation of his relatives, especially Dick and Will, who were virtually part of the family. "The Burkes" as a whole were commonly regarded as erratic, irresponsible, sly, and quite charming.

[6] Richard Pares, *King George III and the Politicians* (Oxford: Clarendon Press, 1953), p. 67. The anonymous *Letters of Junius* (1769–72) attacked George III and defended John Wilkes.

[7] Quoted in Ross J. S. Hoffman and Paul Levack, eds., *Burke's Politics, Selected Writings and Speeches of Edmund Burke on Reform, Revolution, and War* (New York: Knopf, 1949), p. 3. This excellent collection is a good introduction to Burke.

[8] *Ibid.*, p. 4.

English Constitution required Parliamentary men of independent judgment, working together in political parties, responsible to the people, though not necessarily subservient to them. George's efforts to dominate Parliament were largely frustrated by his own bungling. "Yet," says Laski, "in the long run, the real weapon which defeated George was the ideas of Edmund Burke, for he gave to political conflict its real place in philosophy."[9]

In 1771 Burke became the English agent for the colony of New York.[10] This position furthered his identification with the American colonists, in whose interests some of his greatest speeches were made. The Irish also benefited from Burke's sometimes outraged solicitude for their rights, although the cause of Ireland was the source of major political headaches for Burke. In 1774 Burke became Member of Parliament for the industrial city of Bristol in western England. In that year Lord Verney, a bit short of cash, had put up for sale his four Parliamentary seats, and Burke, one of the incumbents, was unfortunately too poor to buy his own. He was therefore much pleased to be asked to run in a genuine election in Bristol. The city fathers liked his views on trade with America and he was elected. But Burke's principled independence, especially as regarded Ireland, was too much for them. Not only Bristol's anti-Catholicism but its ardent support of trade restrictions on Ireland harmed Burke, for he went on pressing for relief of Catholic disabilities and, loyal to the economic views of his friend Adam Smith, opposed restrictions on Irish commerce. When the Savile Act for the relief of Catholics was passed in 1778, the so-called Gordon riots broke out in London. Over three hundred people were killed and at one point Parliament was invaded. Burke was one of the major objects of hostility. By the time of the election of 1780 Burke knew it was hopeless to stand for reelection from Bristol. He abandoned the seat and picked up one in Malton, Yorkshire, a family borough of Lord Rockingham. Thus ended Burke's direct encounter with grassroots democracy.

India and France were two other stimuli to Burkean thought and action. Many Englishmen were disturbed by the plunder of India and the mismanagement in the East India Company, though their concern was sometimes as much fiscal as humanitarian. Burke, concerned as always with the dignity of the British heritage, also spoke of Indian rights. One of his rare references to the "natural rights of mankind" came during the debate on Charles James Fox's East India Bill of 1783. Not that Burke was free of partisan influences: he had opposed Lord North's India reform bill in 1773 on the grounds that it would violate the East India Company's charter rights and create a source of government patronage. When the Whigs later came to power under Fox and attempted a similar reform, the same arguments could be and were used against Fox and Burke. But part of the forensic ammunition in the debate was a Parliamentary committee report drafted by Burke that bluntly revealed the injustices heaped on Indian natives and the collusion of East India Company officials with native princes. It was Burke who, from 1788 to 1794, pushed through the impeachment of Warren Hastings, governor general of Bengal, on grounds of extortion, brutality, and other crimes. Hastings was in the end acquitted but the trial was nevertheless a landmark in the reform of the British Empire.

Closing Years

The work for which Burke is most widely known is *Reflections on the Revolution in France* (1790), a book that might best be described as a protracted explosion. Important as it is in the history of ideas, perhaps too much of Burke's popular reputation depends upon this one tract. At any rate, it made him many friends and many enemies and touched off one of the most vigorous running debates in modern times. Burke was shocked in 1791 when his friend Fox praised the new French constitution as "the most stupendous and

[9] H. J. Laski, *Political Thought in England, Locke to Bentham* (New York: Oxford Univ. Press, 1920), p. 146.

[10] See Ross J. S. Hoffman, *Edmund Burke, New York Agent* (Philadelphia: American Philosophical Society, 1956).

glorious edifice of liberty." The resultant conflict between the two men led to an open break that never healed. The Whigs voted to follow Fox rather than Burke and he was, in effect, read out of the party he had served for almost thirty years. In this context he wrote *An Appeal from the New to the Old Whigs* (1791), the classic statement of Burke's "idea of a people" and defense of "natural aristocracy."

The year 1794 appeared to be a sad, depressing end of the road for Burke. His beloved son died on the eve of a promising career. Hastings was acquitted. Old and weary, repudiated by his party, Burke retired from political life. But until his death in 1797 he continued to write, with no reduction of his literary powers. His last work was *Letters on a Regicide Peace* (1796), which developed his conception of the whole of Europe as a Christian commonwealth threatened by the rise of Jacobinism. *A Letter to a Noble Lord* (1796) has been called his valedictory. It was a reply to the duke of Bedford's petty attack on the pension Burke received upon retirement. Burke was masterfully satirical and ironic, joining the issue with vigor yet without loss of humor or perspective. He demonstrated what his friends knew by experience, that strong-willed and testy as he was, he was incapable of being petty. They knew that he was a great man as well as a great politician. To the very end, the man of thought and the man of action remained united.

"Burke's magnificent speeches," wrote Stephen, "stand absolutely alone in the language. They are, literally speaking, the only English speeches which may still be read with profit when the hearer and the speaker have long been turned to dust."[11] Burke's dazzling command of the English language and his principled avoidance of systematization create a strong temptation to deal with his political theory by simply stringing together a long series of pungent epigrams. Though contrary to his own belief, it has been necessary for the sake of exposition to impose an external, somewhat abstract structure on the Burkean materials discussed in the pages that follow; we shall quote frequently within that structure. The temptation to quote at length Burke's flowing prose is irresistible. Of this, Burke would no doubt approve. For him, the mode of action was always as important as the end of action, and flowing prose was his primary mode of action.

[11] Sir Leslie Stephen, *English Thought in the Eighteenth Century,* 2nd ed. (London: Smith, Elder, 1881), Vol. II, p. 219.

NONCONSERVATIVE ELEMENTS IN BURKE

Edmund Burke is almost universally regarded as the archetypal conservative.[12] In the vernacular of our day, "conservative" is regarded as the opposite of "liberal." A conservative supposedly opposes and a liberal supposedly favors innovation (even though a self-designated conservative may argue for a wholly new tax structure and a self-designated liberal may labor to conserve civil liberties). The confusion presently surrounding these terms suggests that their use as antitheses may be unwarranted. If so, to call Burke antiliberal, hence conservative, may be too simple.

Liberalism—if we may digress a moment —more clearly than conservatism refers to a particular movement of thought occurring within a given historical period. Although the name was not used until the early nineteenth century,[13] scholars now apply it to the general body of Western European thought deriving from the attempt to justify the "liberation"

[12] See footnote 26 below.

[13] By the *Liberales,* a Spanish party. See J. Salwyn Schapiro, ed., *Liberalism: Its Meaning and History* (Princeton: Van Nostrand, 1958), p. 9; Guido de Ruggiero, *The History of European Liberalism,* trans. by R. G. Collingwood (Boston: Beacon Press, 1959); Harold J. Laski, *The Rise of European Liberalism* (London: Allen & Unwin, 1936); John H. Hallowell, *The Decline of Liberalism as an Ideology* (Berkeley: Univ. of California Press, 1943); Louis Hartz, *The Liberal Tradition in America* (New York: Harcourt, Brace & World, 1955).

of the individual from the confinements of feudal status and privilege. Three characteristics of liberal thought are basic: (1) Private interest (or conscience) is given priority over public (governmental) authority. That is, individualism replaces communitarianism.[14] (2) Scientific judgments are given priority over religious insight. Liberalism has almost always been sympathetic to scientific inquiry and even when not antireligious has been anticlerical. (3) The economy is given priority over the polity. The liberal movement is identified with the middle classes of industrial civilizations for whom the maximization of economic productivity takes precedence over noneconomic public goods. By these three tests, Burke is clearly nonliberal.

In one of its aspects, conservatism is not so much a definable body of social thought as it is a temperamental predisposition in favor of caution. We speak of conservative tastes in music and architecture but we do not speak similarly of liberal tastes. There will be conservatives even in societies where the term "liberalism" has no meaning. In its more clearly political connotations, conservatism suggests a reverence for tradition but often the plurality of traditions appealed to generates confusion and even a lack of caution. Burke, for all his reverence for tradition, could be incautious. In his attitude toward religion, class, and community Burke was no liberal. But in his defense of the free-market economy, the rights of free speech, and justice for underprivileged colonies he shared some of the policies born of liberal assumptions. Though not a liberal, he could sometimes be a nonconservative reformer.[15]

[14] One student of liberalism has argued that faith in the "autonomy of human reason" is the key to liberal individualism (John H. Hallowell, *Main Currents in Modern Political Thought* [New York: Holt, Rinehart and Winston, 1950], Ch. 4). Sheldon Wolin argues convincingly that faith in mechanism rather than faith in reason characterizes the liberal tradition (*Politics and Vision* [Boston: Little, Brown, 1960], Ch. 9).

[15] Arnold A. Rogow argues convincingly that Burke has little in common with the American conservatives who invoke his name most fervently, those who define the right "by what economic man does to achieve success" ("Edmund Burke and the American Liberal Tradition," *Antioch Review*, Vol. 17 [1957], pp. 255–65).

A Free Parliament: George III and the Wilkes Case

It was Burke's great virtue to deal with general moral principles without ever losing touch with the situation at hand. Or perhaps it is better to say that he dealt with a prodigious quantity of practical political issues without losing sight of their moral dimensions. In every dispute, save one, said Stephen, Burke had "taken the generous side." The exception Stephen granted was the dispute over the French Revolution, to which ought to be added the proposed reform of the rotten boroughs. In the Wilkes case he was on a generous and courageous side but also, this time, the popular, underdog side. John Wilkes was expelled from the House of Commons in 1764 for libeling the king and was prejudicially convicted at King's Bench for publishing an allegedly obscene poem. He first fled to France but returned, served his sentence, and was elected to Parliament from Middlesex in 1768. But Parliament, cowed by the king, refused to seat him. Three more times he went back to his constituency and was reelected and three more times Parliament refused to seat him. His plight became a *cause célèbre* and Burke took his stand with Wilkes.[16] With qualifications, Burke at the same time took his stand with the people:

> I am not one of those who think that the people are never in the wrong. They have been so, frequently and outrageously, both in other countries and in this. But I do say that in all disputes between them and their rulers the presumption is at least upon a par in favor of the people. . . . the people have no interest in disorder. When they do wrong, it is their error and not their crime. But with the governing part of the state, it is far otherwise.[17]

[16] See *Speech on Wilkes* in *Works*, Vol. VII, pp. 61–67; *Thoughts on the Cause of the Present Discontents* (1770), in *ibid.*, Vol. I, pp. 435–537.

[17] *Present Discontents*, pp. 440–41. At times Burke's words could be used to make him out a revolutionary: ". . . a decent attention to public interest in representatives [may require] *the interposition of the body of the people itself*. [The remedy is] most unpleasant. But if it be a legal remedy, it is intended on some occasion to be used; to be used then only when it is evident that nothing else can hold the constitution to its true princi-

Is this conservatism or liberalism? Maybe it is only a debater's point. Maybe it is only good sense. But in the context of the times it did not please the powers that be, and the powers that be were crudely suppressing an individual politician and his individual supporters. The persecution of Wilkes, Burke observes—nay, demonstrates—was but a pretense to achieve the "separation of the representatives from their constituents. . . . a precedent . . . tending to show *that the favor of the people was not so sure a road as the favor of the court even to popular honors and popular trusts.*" Such a precedent would be disastrous for good government. "The power of the people, within the laws, must show itself sufficient to protect every representative in the animated performance of his duty, or that duty cannot be performed." The court party, to be sure, says that this power to disqualify is in good hands and will not be abused: "Until I find something in this argument differing from that on which every mode of despotism has been defended, I shall not be inclined to pay it any great compliment. The people are satisfied to trust themselves with the exercise of their own privileges."

The argument is characteristic of Burke's method of operation, which is the same in his writings as in his speeches. As his friend Goldsmith said, he winds into his subject like a serpent. The values to which he appeals are implicit rather than explicit. In many men this approach would be a sign of superficiality or confusion but in Burke it was a way of life. The appeal to reason is not dogmatic, axiomatic, or geometrical. The good sense of what he says insinuates itself in a series of pithy, medium-level generalizations until the hearer finds himself lured into thinking the speaker is expressing sentiments with which he, the hearer, has agreed all along. This particular skill with words is the trait of the good politician. The good politician does not bludgeon his hearers with logic. Cold logic pitted against warm emotion wins only perfunctory assent and loses votes. Nor does he put them to sleep with a catalogue of dusty bits of data. He charms them. He woos them.

Yet even subtle, insinuating logic does not produce the values Burke ultimately appeals to. These are either shared or not shared. They cannot be demonstrated. These values —that the blatant persecution of Wilkes is wrong, that a constituency's right to pick its own representative should not be trampled on—are "givens," products of the historical community in which both Burke and his hearers reside. This pointed view raises the fundamental problem of the political community as a source of values, a problem to be examined later in this chapter.

The Responsibility of Authority: America and India

If solicitude for the rights of constituencies and the integrity of Parliament in their struggle against external control reflects a nonconservative side of Burke, so does the corollary of these rights—the *duty* of Parliament to grant the same kind of integrity to other governing bodies that it would wish for itself. Those in authority do not have to keep everyone happy. Burke would grant them no authority to do wrong in order to be popular. But political wisdom, Burke's everlasting goal, does not sanction paternalistic interference with orderly governments run by grown men. To claim a right is also to claim a responsibility but, if the responsibility is accepted, it ought to be respected by others.

As usual, the principle is not stated by Burke in the abstract but emerges from the discussion of tangible disputes, such as those concerning America and India. Burke's first major utterance on the American colonies occurs in the long pamphlet, *Observations on a Late Publication Intitled "The Present State of the Nation."* Written in early 1769, it was a reply to Lord Grenville's attack on the Rockingham Whigs in the preceding year. The pamphlet was not his best but it reveals his warm, almost elegiac feeling for the worth of the American colonies in the course of contending what a mistake the Stamp Act

ples." Or again, in defense of party government: ". . . he that supports every administration subverts all government."

and the Townshend Acts were. It is important to note that the affection for America was not an affection for all mankind. Burke was parochial enough and patriotic enough to be moved by the fact that Americans were not just anybody:

the people who are to be the subjects of these restraints are descendants of Englishmen, and of a high and free spirit. To hold over them a government made up of nothing but restraints and penalties, and taxes in the granting of which they have no share, will neither be wise nor long practicable. . . . The British colonist must see something which will distinguish him from the colonists of other nations.[18]

There is dignity without crass sentimentality in this statement; and if there is also a tincture of British chauvinism, we can at least remember that most of Burke's colleagues had greater difficulty identifying with white-skinned, English-speaking colonials three thousand miles away, not to mention dark-skinned Eastern natives six thousand miles away in India.

On April 19, 1774, Burke offered the House his *Speech on American Taxation*. In it he stressed the critical function in political relations of confidence—what today we would call rapport, a quality that the *philosophes,* with their concern for the geometrically precise statement of equity, tended to overlook. "The spirit of practicability, of moderation and mutual convenience will never call in geometrical exactness as the arbiter of an amicable settlement. Consult and follow your experience."[19] Burke's experience revealed to him that the Americans could not be browbeaten into subservience. If told "that sovereignty and their freedom cannot be reconciled, which will they take? They will cast your sovereignty in your face. Nobody will be argued into slavery."

On March 22, 1775, Burke gave one of his greatest speeches, the *Speech on Conciliation with the Colonies.* Its pervasive flavor is the delicate combination of passionate involvement and detached observation that we associate with Burke's kind of political responsibility and that, in fact, is the necessary art of political leadership. It is remarkable to find an analysis of the American situation, made in the heat of debate, that after two hundred years is still a sound and perceptive exposition. Burke outlines six major causes for America's "fierce spirit of liberty." If the accent falls somewhat more heavily on the moral than ours would, Burke does not therefore neglect hard economic realities. But it is the keen sensitivity to the moral interdependence of nations that strikes us: ". . . in order to prove that the Americans have no right to their liberties, we are every day endeavoring to subvert the maxims which preserve the whole spirit of our own. To prove that the Americans ought not to be free we are obliged to depreciate the value of freedom itself."[20] At the same time, Burke cautions against attempting to weaken the Southern states by declaring the slaves to be free, as some had suggested. No friend of slavery, Burke could nevertheless make highly practical arguments for the inexpedience of such a dictate from London. As to criminal charges against the Americans, "I do not know the method of drawing up an indictment against a whole people."

After eliminating all other alternatives, Burke concludes that the only solution is "to admit the people of our colonies into an interest in the constitution." Had Burke's advice been followed, the United States might

[18] *Observations on a Late Publication Intitled "The Present State of the Nation,"* in *Works,* Vol. I, pp. 395–96.

[19] *Speech on American Taxation,* in *Works,* Vol. II, p. 71. To the objection that Parliament should worry about the solution of the problem and not its origin, Burke posed a sarcastic restatement, "We are to consult our invention and reject our experience." He refused to be drawn into categorical definitions of rights and their limits. "I do not enter into these metaphysical distinctions; I hate the very sound of them."

[20] *Speech on Conciliation with the Colonies,* in *Works,* Vol. II, p. 130. The implied prophecy was fulfilled when, after the Revolution began, England suspended habeas corpus for the colonies. Burke attacked this action in his *Letter to the Sheriffs of Bristol,* April 3, 1777 (*Works,* Vol. II, pp. 187–245).

today be a Dominion of the Commonwealth. By "an interest in the constitution," however, Burke does not mean perfect equality with England. Though he raises questions about the concept of "virtual representation," in the end he sanctions it, being unable seriously to propose Parliamentary representation for America. The heart of his six resolutions is that the taxation of America should be by grant of colonial assemblies and not by "imposition."

India was, as we have seen, a somewhat different case, the honor of English officials being as much at issue as the rights of distant subjects. Yet, though Burke's references to India are often in terms of interest rather than some other standard, it is interest in its most refined and inclusive sense, a conception that calls for men of circumscribed mind to stretch their imaginations:

> The scene of the Indian abuse is distant, indeed; but we must not infer that the value of our interest in it is decreased in proportion as it recedes from our view. In our politics, as in our common conduct, we shall be worse than infants if we do not put our sense under the tuition of our judgment, and effectively cure ourselves of that optical illusion which makes a brier at our nose of greater magnitude than an oak at five hundred yards distance.[21]

Parliament was made to remember and Warren Hastings was not allowed to forget the "scene of the Indian abuse." Through them the whole nation was reminded that authority and power are not synonyms. Burke's intense personal hatred of all forms of cruelty had nothing to do with partisan politics, but the consequences he drew in political action were not unlike those drawn by many who later called themselves liberals.

[21] *Speech on the Nabob of Arcot's Debts,* in *Works,* Vol. III, p. 15. To get around the rule against accepting gifts from native princes, East India Company men often loaned money to them at fantastic rates of interest, sometimes without any initial cash transfer whatsoever. Such graft was involved in the case Burke was discussing: ". . . the Nabob of Arcot and his creditors are not adversaries but collusive parties . . . the whole transaction is under a false color and false names."

BURKE AS A CONSERVATIVE

If Burke's concern for the national interest was more compatible with a sensitivity to individual rights than some have imagined, other facets of his thought seem to fit appropriately under the conservative label—though we would do well to remember that Burke never called himself a conservative. Three facets seem central in this connection —Burke's conceptions of (1) the limits of abstract reason, (2) representation, and (3) the nature of social freedom.

The Limits of Abstract Reason

There are points of contact between almost all schools of thought. Though he would have been alarmed by the tinkering propensity of the contemporary pragmatist, Burke would share with him a distrust of metaphysical speculation and abstract reason.[22] As Godwin or Condorcet was the man of principle, Burke was the man of experience. Principled men are not blind to experience; experienced men cannot ignore every principle. But there is a difference.

Burke's final thoughts on the dangers of metaphysical abstractions in politics were violently pulled out of him by the events of the French Revolution. Not that he had concealed them before this time. In one of his earliest speeches, the Commination Service speech, he referred disparagingly to "refining speculatists," "political aeronauts," "smugglers of adulterated metaphysics," and "metaphysical knights of the sorrowful countenance."[23] In his *Letter to the Sheriffs of Bristol* (1777) he observed that the propensity of a people to

[22] Charles Parkin, in *The Moral Basis of Burke's Political Thought* (London: Cambridge Univ. Press, 1956), however, subtly infers the existence of an abstract design in Burke's writings tantamount to natural law. See also Peter Stanlis, *Edmund Burke and Natural Law* (Ann Arbor: Univ. of Michigan Press, 1959), and Hans Barth, *The Idea of Order,* trans. by E. W. Hankamer and W. M. Newell (Dordrecht, Holland: Reidel, 1960), Ch. 2.

[23] Quoted in John MacCunn, *The Political Philosophy of Burke* (New York: Longmans, Green, 1913), p. 1.

resort to theories is "one sure symptom of an ill-conducted state." "Civil freedom, Gentlemen, is not, as many have endeavored to persuade you, a thing that lies hid in the depth of abstruse science. It is a blessing and a benefit, not an abstract speculation."[24] "Abstract liberty," he said in his *Speech on Conciliation with the Colonies,* "like other mere abstractions, is not to be found. Liberty inheres in some sensible object."

The continuity of Burke's opposition to abstract principles is clear. Yet this antimetaphysical position did not, in his earlier days, automatically parallel a hostile attitude toward a possible French revolution, as it later bolstered opposition to the actual French Revolution in 1789. In *Observations on a Late Publication* (1769) he had referred to "injudicious" and "oppressive" taxation in France. In the *Annual Register* for 1770, he wrote sympathetically of the forces struggling against the oppressive French monarchy. Of the latter he wrote, "How long this destructive power may continue to desolate the country, or whether, as has frequently been the case, it may at length fall by its own enormous weight must be left to time to disclose."[25] Finally, once when discussing the American Revolution he noted that "revolts of a whole people. . . . are always provoked."[26]

These sentiments would seem to lead in a direction other than his thoroughgoing condemnation of the Revolution in the *Reflections.* Indeed, it required for Burke an uncharacteristic narrowness of view to blame the Revolution solely on a conspiracy of men, particularly one that included such moderates as Mirabeau and Lafayette. Burke was usually especially keen on the deep historic roots of any emerging conflict. Was it a sign of age or the frustrations of repeated Parliamentary defeats that led Burke to vitriolic denunciation: "Is it because liberty in the abstract may be classed among the blessings of mankind that I am to felicitate a mad-man who has escaped from the protecting restraint and wholesome darkness of his cell, on his restoration to the enjoyment of light and liberty?"[27]

Burke's first task in the *Reflections* was to show, as against the Reverend Dr. Richard Price and other English admirers of the Revolution, that the Glorious Revolution of 1688, which had given the Whigs their charter, had little in common with the French Revolution. James II was "a bad king with a good title," who, confronted with a true charge of papist subversion, chose to abdicate at an auspicious moment. "No experience has taught us that in any other course or method than that of an *hereditary crown* our liberties can be regularly perpetuated and preserved sacred as our *hereditary right.* An irregular, convulsive movement may be necessary to throw off an irregular, convulsive disease. But the course of succession is the healthy habit of the British Constitution." If the French admirers in England can restrain themselves, said Burke, law and order is secure in England. France, meanwhile, has burst asunder. The new principle of absolute equality, which made France "let loose the reins of regal authority," has "doubled the licence of a ferocious dissoluteness in manners, and of an insolent irreligion in opinions and practices." Authority has been placed in the hands of men "not taught habitually to respect themselves" and so now "intoxicated with their unprepared greatness. . . . a handful of country clowns, who have seats in [the] assembly, some of whom are said not to be able to read and write . . . and by not a greater number of traders who . . . had never known anything beyond their counting-house." The National Assembly is a body "with every possible power and no possible external control . . . a body without fundamental laws, without established maxims, without respected rules of proceeding." And

[24] *Letter to the Sheriffs of Bristol,* in *Works,* Vol. II, pp. 230, 229.

[25] *Annual Register,* 1770, p. 53. Quoted in Alfred Cobban, *Edmund Burke and the Revolt Against the Eighteenth Century* (New York: Macmillan, 1929), p. 120.

[26] Cobban, p. 120.

[27] *Reflections on the French Revolution,* in *Works,* Vol. III, p. 241.

due to the manner of election, "If possible, the next Assembly must be worse than the present." Of the men in the *Tiers État* some had rank and talent, "but of any practical experience in the state, not one man was to be found. *The best were only men of theory* [our italics]." The army, a result of "mixing mutinous soldiers with seditious citizens," has gone to pot. The officers are only able "to manage their troops by electioneering arts. They must bear themselves as candidates, not as commanders."

The mistreatment of Marie Antoinette touches off Burke's most agonized lament:

little did I dream that I should have lived to see such disaster fallen upon her in a nation of gallant men, in a nation of men of honor, and of cavaliers. . . . But the age of chivalry is gone. That of sophisters, economists, and calculators has succeeded; and the glory of Europe is extinguished forever. . . . The unbought grace of life, the cheap defense of nations, the nurse of manly sentiment and heroic enterprise, is gone! It is gone, that sensibility of principle, that chastity of honor, which felt a stain like a wound, which inspired courage whilst it mitigated ferocity, which ennobled whatever it touched, and under which vice itself lost half its evil, by losing all its grossness.[28]

But how can one whose very philosophy is to operate from the facts ignore the facts of monarchical oppression and a successful revolution? In distinguishing France in 1789 from England in 1688, why does he ignore England in 1641? Is not what Burke laments in France the loss of principle, the destruction of standards? How can the loss of principle be blamed on the love of principles? Is Burke's rage so apoplectic that he does not know or care that he is contradicting himself right and left?

There is in this situation a triple irony. The first is that, despite his continuing criticism of reliance on abstractions and principles, Burke's peculiar genius as a political thinker was to take concrete, mundane political events and appraise them in the light of general principle: "A mere politician he could not be. When he encountered a political problem it was not in him to deal with it in ordinary fashion. . . . No politician, either in ancient or in modern times, has had so irrepressible a faculty of lifting even the passing incidents of the political hour into the region of great ideas."[29] Even where the futility of mere theory was his theme, he could not but place his confidence in theories, and uphold right principles: "The pretended rights of these [French] theorists are all extremes; and in proportion as they are metaphysically true, they are morally and politically false. The rights of men are in a sort of *middle,* incapable of definition, but not impossible to be discerned." Politics, Burke said elsewhere, is not so much concerned with the true and the false as with the good and the evil. But this does not mean reason has no place in politics. Quite the contrary. He tells his French friend Dupont in 1789, "The moment *will* is set above reason and justice, in any community, a great question may arise in sober minds in what part or portion of the community that dangerous dominion of will may be the least mischievously placed."[30] This question was at the heart of his dispute with Rousseau. We know that Burke is, despite himself, a theorist. But he is not even a thoroughly antitheoretical theorist. For an antitheoretical theorist could never put those abstractions "reason and justice" ahead of "will."

The second irony is that this advocate of caution, deliberation, and concrete facts was, in his attacks on the French Revolution, highly incautious in his assertions and without reliable information to support his "facts." Yet his prophecies, constructed from confused bits of data in 1790, in the long run proved right. From a mixture of intuition and analysis he sensed that France was headed for ever more serious trouble that would lead eventually to armed conflict with England. It is dubious logic to say, as Cobban does,

[28] *Ibid.,* pp. 331–32. Thomas Paine, commenting on this passage in his *Rights of Man,* said of Burke, "He pities the plumage but forgets the dying bird" (*Political Works* [New York: Eckler, 1892], Part II, p. 25).

[29] MacCunn, p. 3.

[30] Hoffman and Levack, p. 279.

that the success of Burke's prediction "is a vindication of the virtue of just theory."[31] Cobban does, however, call our attention to what is often overlooked, that Burke's concern was not only domestic but was directed as well at the international consequences of the Revolution and the possibility of just such an expansively nationalistic force as Napoleon's troops turned out to be. The concern was more implicit than explicit but it was there. Burke quotes the French Secretary of State for War to the effect that the domestic disorders are not the greatest evil: "*The nature of things requires* that an army should never act but as *an instrument.* The moment that, erecting itself into a deliberative body, it shall act according to its own resolutions, *the government, be it what it may, will immediately degenerate into a military democracy.*" Burke comments, "It is not necessary to add much to this finished picture." Burke might have been just as vigorous had the internal factors been discussed in isolation, but his half-concealed perception of their relation to external factors is what gives his work a special kind of historical significance. Indeed, in the view of Cobban, this significance is what makes the *Reflections* "the greatest and most influential political pamphlet ever written."[32]

In this significance is our third irony. Against the new nationalism of Frenchmen Burke was appealing to a not-quite-so-new nationalism of Englishmen. Because aristocratic leaders in England, William Pitt and others, could not see the potential threat in France that Burke saw, he spoke in the *Reflections* over the heads of the aristocrats and directly to the English public—on behalf of an aristocratic cause. Without implying a blatant, manipulative intent on his part, it may be suggested that Burke's emotion and not his reason was what weighed most heavily with his readers. He employed terms of abstract reason—"justice," "equity," "rights"—to disparage reliance on abstract reason. Many theorists have done the same. But Burke used the terms in a particularly forceful and emotional way. Just as Burke always insisted, the how is as important as the what. The act, not the word, validates the principle of the limits of abstract reason in political affairs. Perhaps Burke's greatest contribution, then, was not in exalting the concrete over the abstract in politics but in showing in the concrete how false is the dichotomy between abstract reason and concrete emotion.

Representation and the People

Just after they had elected him to Parliament, on November 3, 1774, Burke faced his new constituents at Bristol and told them that as their representative he would do his own thinking:

> Certainly, Gentlemen, it ought to be the happiness and glory of a representative to live in the strictest union, the closest correspondence, and the most unreserved communication with his constituents. Their wishes ought to have great weight with him; their opinions high respect; their business unremitted attention. It is his duty to sacrifice his repose, his pleasure, his satisfactions, to theirs—and above all, ever, and in all cases, to prefer their interests to his own.
>
> But his unbiased opinion, his mature judgment, his enlightened conscience, he ought not to sacrifice to you, to any man, or to any set of men living. These he does not derive from your pleasure—no, nor from the law and the constitution. They are a trust from Providence, for the abuse of which he is deeply answerable. Your representative owes you, not his industry only, but his judgment; and he betrays, instead of serving you, if he sacrifices it to your opinion.
>
> . . . Parliament is not a *congress* of ambassadors from different and hostile interests . . . but Parliament is a *deliberative* assembly of *one* nation, with *one* interest, that of the whole. You choose a member, indeed; but when you have chosen him he is not a member of Bristol, but he is a member of *Parliament.* If the local constituent should have an interest or should form a hasty opinion evidently opposite to the real

[31] Cobban, p. 123.

[32] Cobban, p. 129. As Cobban notes, however, along with his prescience, Burke conspicuously fails to see that, though France might be less of a state after the Revolution, it might also be more of a nation. Given his nationalistic and generally peaceful premises, Burke could not otherwise have called for the invasion of France.

good of the rest of the community, the member for that place ought to be as far as any other from any endeavor to give it effect. . . . Your faithful friend, your devoted servant, I shall be to the end of my life: a flatterer you do not wish for.[33]

Here is a man of independent judgment, the kind of man we say we want for our congressman, and the kind of man we consistently vote against, especially if he is bold enough to speak as Burke spoke. Burke could get away with this kind of talk partly because it was the eighteenth century and partly because he was Burke, but even he did not get away with it for long in Bristol, as we saw. What Burke was speaking against was the practice of constituencies instructing their M.P.'s how to vote on specific measures. After the Wilkes agitation in Middlesex, a number of the more radically democratic constituencies had begun to do this. Bristol was such a constituency and Burke was not pleased by the fact. He clearly felt himself above the kind of errand-running that democratic constituencies require their representative to do. (Representatives of pocket boroughs had a different kind of errand-running.) It is, at any rate, a tribute to the man's influence that the practice of instructed M.P.'s almost died out. And even though a flatterer is what most constituencies *do* wish for, especially in less "deferential" nations than England—to use Walter Bagehot's phrase—the idea that members of a legislative body must have more freedom to deliberate than ambassador-delegates to an international conclave is fairly well fixed in the Western democracies.

Yet, as Carl Friedrich has pointed out, the deliberative and the representative functions of legislative bodies are never easily compatible, since the former reflects the reason of the expert and the latter the will of the masses. The problem of democratic leadership remains one of the thorniest of all contemporary political problems: how can a man lead the public and still follow it? Burke leaned on the side of strong leadership and was, at least verbally, a bit too hopeful that the national interest existed as a clearly visible guide that could triumph over the legislator's self-interest as well as over local interest. His plea for deliberation overlooked the value in the tension between aristocratic deliberation and democratic representation.

On these aristocratic grounds Burke opposed a bill for triennial elections in 1780, believing that too many elections were a disturbance to orderly government. In 1782 he opposed Pitt's plan to eliminate rotten boroughs. The argument for "virtual representation" on which this opposition rests is the one argument among all aristocratic arguments that many of us find most difficult to accept today. The theory was that the areas without men in Parliament could count on the faithful service of others in Parliament just as much as their voting brethren who had "actual representation." The theory smacks of rationalizing paternalism and that is what it was. Burke nevertheless claimed advantages for the system: "It corrects the irregularities in the literal representation, when the swifting currents of human affairs . . . carry it obliquely from its first line of direction. The people may err in their choice, but common interest and common sentiment are rarely mistaken."[34] The argument no doubt benefits if seen as an admonition to the M.P. to take seriously his responsibilities even for those who cannot vote for him. As a message to the unrepresented that they are really better represented than those who elect their men, the argument does not make much sense.

That the idea of virtual representation had some limits in Burke's mind is evident not only by his speeches on America but by his position on Ireland, where he included disfranchisement in his catalogue of protest. English laws, he said, had divided Ireland "into two distinct bodies, without common interest, sympathy or connexion. One of these bodies was to possess *all* the franchises, *all* the property, *all* the education: the other was to

[33] *Speech to the Electorate at Bristol,* in *Works,* Vol. II, pp. 95–97.

[34] *Letter to S. H. Langrishe,* quoted in Murray, p. 110.

be composed of drawers of water and cutters of turf for them. . . . If you treat men as robbers, why, robbers sooner or later they will become."[35] And if you treat men as incapable of significant electoral choice?

Burke was not an aristocrat by default. Indeed at the heart of his politics was the belief that a natural aristocracy was essential to keep society running. But it was a *natural* aristocracy he favored, not a propped-up, artificial aristocracy of unchecked and irresponsible privilege. He was honest enough to see that rulers as well as the ruled have passions requiring external checks. In *An Appeal from the New to the Old Whigs,* Burke's attack on arbitrary power and "the vulgar of every description" was not limited to the rampant majority but to their power-thirsty servants, willing victims of the fact that "the democratic commonwealth is the foodful nurse of ambition." The rule of a "true, natural aristocracy," however, requires men who have not only had good breeding and the leisure to read and who are habituated to command and possessed of the virtues of "diligence, order, constancy, and regularity," vital as these are, but also men who are "habituated to the censorial inspection of the public eye; [who] look early to public opinion; [and] stand upon such elevated ground as to be enabled to take a large view of the wide-spread and infinitely diversified combinations of men and affairs in a large society."[36]

Burke's description of "natural aristocracy" as well as his assertion of the priority of deliberation over representation may sound excessively idealistic to us. But were we to stop with that conclusion we might miss the most important point. Mansfield has recently shown us with telling precision how Burke's empirical, prudential concept of "prescriptive" rights (sharply opposed to Bolingbroke's abstract, rationalistic and often vacuously idealistic rights) made modern party government possible. Unsatisfied with merely factional rivalry, Burke was willing to abandon hope in the "actual virtue" of Aristotle's legislator and put his trust in the "presumptive virtue" of an English aristocracy. The public status of that aristocracy was presumptive because justified by reference to private, social status rather than vice versa. As long as the people were relatively deferential, differing interests could be represented through parties and a modicum of harmony could be achieved. Through "presumptive virtue" the aristocracy could lead, even though it lacked the "actual virtue" to "rule" in a Platonic or Aristotelian sense.[37]

The Nature of Social Freedom

Burke seems to stand most sharply at odds with the whole liberal tradition in his conception of the individual's proper relationship to the social fabric. The liberal tradition was and is concerned to liberate the individual from the chains of social restraint, to make him a "free man." Burke did not believe that the "autonomous individual" of the liberals could or should exist. All men are and inevitably will be bound by an elaborate network of social obligations not wholly of their own choosing. To seek to escape these obligations is, to put it bluntly, immoral. Not only should we accept them, we should accept them reverently. Man "should approach to the faults of the state as to the wounds of a father, with pious awe and trembling solicitude." Society is a contract, but not in the mechanical sense of the Lockeans. "It is," wrote Burke in his most famous statement,

> a partnership in all science; a partnership in all art, a partnership in every virtue, and in all perfection. As the ends of such a partnership cannot be obtained in many generations, it becomes a partnership not only between those who are living, but between those who are living, those who are dead, and those who are to be born. Each contract of each particular state is but a clause in the great primeval contract of

[35] *Ibid.*

[36] *An Appeal from the New to the Old Whigs,* in *Works,* Vol. IV, pp. 164, 175.

[37] See Harvey Mansfield, Jr., *Statesmanship and Party Government: A Study of Burke and Bolingbroke* (Chicago: Univ. of Chicago Press, 1965).

eternal society. . . . a necessity that is not chosen, but chooses, a necessity paramount to deliberation.[38]

The basic theme of the *Reflections* is that an individualist revolt against society is impossible and that the attempt can lead only to the crippled half-society of the mob. Against liberal clichés about liberty, Burke hurled brilliant metaphors: the commonwealth crumbling "into the dust and powder of individuality" or men severed from prior generations becoming "little better than the flies of a summer." In the *Appeal* he spoke of "a people" breaking up into "a number of vague, loose individuals, and nothing more." As against grand words about mankind in general, Burke spoke warmly of the necessity of loving "the little platoon" each of us belongs to. Clearly belongingness was essential to Burke. He saw man as a group being and a familial being and regarded speculation about him in a condition of isolation as unrealistic and dangerous.

Yet we should err to conclude from this that Burke was an organicist who gave society a life of its own. "The idea of a people is the idea of a corporation. It is wholly artificial, and made, like all other legal fictions, by common agreement."[39] Nor could he be regarded as scornful of the dignity of the individual. He lamented what the French Revolution had done to humanity, compassion, and "tenderness to individuals." His anguish over oppression anywhere and his personal life confirm the genuineness of this solicitude. Nevertheless, by focusing on the necessary restraints society imposes on the individual, Burke allied himself with those who had and would submerge the individual completely in an organismic conception of society. His frequent failure to distinguish between state and society furthered this alliance.

He also edged toward the Germanic Reaction in sometimes stressing freedom as an inner quality: "Men of intemperate minds cannot be free. Their passions forge their fetters."[40] The idea was in no sense novel; but it was a new emphasis for Whigs, who, like the *philosophes,* generally meant to refer to prisons, civil liberties, and the like when they spoke of "freedom." Burke, in his attack on the supposed libertarian excesses of Rousseau and the Revolution, put discipline ahead of absence of restraint. He was not in the least interested in developing a new, esoteric philosophy of internalized freedom, as Hegel was. He was simply impressed with how tenuous and valuable a creation society is. Prudence was his watchword:

to make a government requires no great prudence. Settle the seat of power; teach obedience: and the work is done. To give freedom is still more easy. It is not necessary to guide; it only requires to let go the rein. But to form a *free government;* that is, to temper together these opposite elements of liberty and restraint in one consistent work, requires much thought, deep reflection, a sagacious, powerful, and combining mind.[41]

Surprising, perhaps, that Burke should place as much faith as he did in party government to achieve this delicate end. If the philosopher discerns the ends of government, said Burke, the politician, who is the "philosopher in action," discovers the means to the end. And to reach that end, he must associate with others, even, Burke might have said, at the expense of his own individuality. Admitting the narrow bigotries that sometimes beset party factions, Burke's case for participation in political associations is still relevant and is couched in infinitely better prose than most "good citizenship" tracts of our day:

When bad men combine, the good must associate else they will fall, one by one, an unpitied sacrifice in a contemptible struggle. . . . it is not enough that [a man] never did an evil act, but always voted according to his conscience. . . . duty demands and requires that what is right should not only be made known, but made prevalent; that what is evil should not only be detected but defeated. . . . For my part, I find

[38] *Reflections,* pp. 359–60.
[39] *Appeal,* p. 169.

[40] *Letter to a Member of the National Assembly,* in *Works,* Vol. IV, p. 52.
[41] *Reflections,* pp. 559–60.

it impossible to conceive that anyone believes in his own politics or thinks them to be of any weight, who refuses to adopt the means of having them reduced into practice.[42]

Burke's famous definition of party—"a body of men united for promoting by their joint endeavors the national interest upon some principle in which they are all agreed"—is often held to be hopelessly idealistic. Read in the context of the *Present Discontents* it appears much less so. Politicians, it is true, talk more of principle and less of interest than the facts would warrant; but nonpoliticians often see more of interest and less of principle than the facts would warrant. Our inability to grant that men with sharply different principles from ours sincerely believe them helps to obscure the role that ideological principles play in the party politics of even "nonideological" political systems, such as that of the United States. Burke is not so naive but that he can note with a touch of skepticism the degree to which men confuse the desire for power with their own consciences. The well-run party is a counteractive to such confusions. That Burke suffered from his own party is insufficient reason to say that his own faith in party government was misplaced. It is this faith in "free parties" as a bulwark of "free government" that keeps Burke from complete identification with the group of thinkers known as the Reaction (Hegel, De Maistre, De Bonald, Müller, Schlegel, and so on). The Reactionaries who followed Hegel—even more than Hegel himself—allowed the concept of internalized freedom to become a cloak for despotism as Burke could never have done.

CONCLUSION: PRESCRIPTION AND RIGHTS

What Burke the conservative wished to conserve is the historic community, the partnership in all science, art, and virtue, the necessity that is not chosen, but chooses. The name that Burke gave to this necessity is "prescription." Prescription means that the past legitimizes what it produces, that a moral presumption rests in favor of "any settled scheme of government against any untried project," that "the individual is foolish . . . but the species is wise." The contemplation of prescription produces two problems whose consideration can serve to close our examination of Burke: What does prescription do to individual rights? What ground of value does prescription offer?

Prescription and Rights

Thomas Paine wrote *The Rights of Man* in 1791 as a reply to Burke's *Reflections*. With disarming directness, Paine granted the power of Burke's prescription but rejected its authority. "Paine's doctrine may be given in two words. Kings, like priests, are cheats and impostors."[43] Their power and that of aristocracies rest on superstition and should be swept away. Paine accused Burke of making dead men more important than live ones, of advocating rulers accountable to nobody because they ruled by prescription, and of treating the mass of men as contemptible fools. Paine's constructive theory of natural rights did little to advance earlier conceptions but his searing criticism of Burke sometimes came close to home.

Burke often spoke of rights. He spoke of "natural rights," "sacred rights," "*real* rights," "the great rule of equality grounded upon our common nature," "the fundamental rule" of all civil society that "no man should be a judge in his own cause," and so forth. The many references display very little consistency, which, no doubt, is itself consistent with Burke's most pervasive view of rights, that "their abstract perfection is their practical defect." As abstractions he was against them and as legal practices he very nearly took them for granted. The important thing for Burke was a clear perception of the national interest derived from the collective ex-

[42] *Present Discontents*, p. 526.

[43] Stephen, Vol. II, p. 262.

perience of the whole society. We should not waste time arguing over the precise boundary of the right to make people miserable, he said in the *Speech on Conciliation with the Colonies,* but explore our interest in making people happy.

John Locke took the rights in the English Constitution and by justifying them in natural-rights terminology made them central to his thought. Edmund Burke took the English Constitution and justified it by prescription, which made the Constitution central and the rights it contained peripheral to his thought.

Thus in answer to the question of what prescription does to individual rights, we can say that in theory it demolishes them and in practice it leaves them untouched—*if* the constitution history has prescribed happens to be the English Constitution.

Prescription and the Ground of Value

But what if the constitution is not the English Constitution? Or what if the English Constitution prescribes that all Whig babies be executed at birth, that M.P.'s shall own no property, or that only Jacobins may ascend the British throne? On what grounds could Burke challenge such a constitution if, hypothetically speaking, it were a genuine product of history? Burke would decline to answer on the grounds that, since constitutions are always here before us, we cannot speak hypothetically about them, even though metaphysicians may try.

In defense of his various policies Burke appealed at different times to "moral law," to "experience," to "the national interest," to "Providence," to "utility," and to "prudence." In all these cases what he was really appealing to was what we all know down deep to be right because we are, after all, Englishmen. In the case of Irishmen, Americans, Indians, and Frenchmen, they were judged *as if* they were Englishmen—which, if we may judge Burke *as if* he were an American, was not in the least uncharitable of him. Burke did not see his own ground of value—though he no doubt felt it—because he was too antiphilosophical to articulate the historical relativism he was continually forced to act on in good faith, if not blind faith. As men of action, we are not much different.

But as a man of thought, Burke was needlessly cramped. This inarticulate and—to the twentieth-century scholar—unsophisticated relativism more than any policy he did or did not support or any argument he did or did not use is what makes Burke a conservative. And it is this same relativism that dooms any attempt to make a philosophy out of the various ideological excrescences of modern conservatism. Though the conservative is often deeply troubled by the spectacle of diversity, diversity is exactly what this type of relativism produces. For if the established order is taken as the ultimate measure of political wisdom, there is no basis of choice among established orders.

In defense of his various policies Burke appealed at different times to "natural law," to "experience," to "the national interest," to "Providence," to "utility," and to "prudence." In all these cases what he was really appealing to was what we all know down deep to be right because we are, after all, Englishmen. In the case of Irishmen, Americans, Indians and Frenchmen, they were judged *as if* they were Englishmen—which, if we may judge [illegible] of he [illegible] Americans [illegible] [illegible] his own ground of value—though he [illegible] [illegible]—because he was too unorthodox [illegible] to articulate the historical relativism he was continually forced to act on in good faith, if not blind faith. As men of action, we are not much different.

But as a man of thought, Burke was [illegible] [illegible]. This [illegible] [illegible] to the [illegible] century scholar—[illegible] [illegible] [illegible] more than any policy he did or did not [illegible] or any [illegible] he did or did not use—is what makes Burke a [illegible]. And it is this same relativism that [illegible] to make [illegible] out of the [illegible] ideological [illegible] of modern conservatism. [illegible] [illegible] [illegible] exactly what this type of relativism produces. For if the established order is [illegible] as the ultimate [illegible] of [illegible] [illegible] there is no [illegible] of choice among established orders.

perience of the whole society. We should not waste time arguing over the precise boundary of the right to make people miserable, he said in the *Speech on Conciliation with the Colonies*, but explore our duty rather in making people happy.

John Locke took the rights in the English Constitution and in [illegible] them in natural-rights terms [illegible] [illegible] his thought [illegible] [illegible] Burke took the English [illegible] [illegible] [illegible] [illegible] [illegible] prescription, which [illegible] [illegible]

[illegible] [illegible] [illegible] [illegible] [illegible] we can [illegible] [illegible] [illegible] [illegible] [illegible] [illegible] [illegible] [illegible] [illegible] [illegible] [illegible] [illegible] [illegible] [illegible] [illegible] [illegible]

[illegible] and the Ground of Value

But [illegible] it is not the [illegible] what if the English Constitution [illegible] at all? What if [illegible] shall own [illegible] [illegible] may [illegible] [illegible] [illegible] product of history [illegible] on the [illegible] [illegible] spirit [illegible] though metaphysicians may [illegible].

SELECTED READINGS

Chapter 1 INTRODUCTION

BARKER, ERNEST. *Principles of Social and Political Theory.* London: Oxford Univ. Press (Galaxy Books), 1961.

BENN, S. J., AND R. S. PETERS. *Principles of Political Thought.* New York: Free Press, 1959.

BOWLE, JOHN. *Western Political Thought; An Historical Introduction from the Origins to Rousseau.* New York: Barnes & Noble (University Paperbacks), 1961.

EBENSTEIN, WILLIAM, ed. *Great Political Thinkers.* 3rd ed. New York: Holt, Rinehart and Winston, 1960. Selections from leading political theorists with prefatory statements. Good bibliography, pp. 869–974.

ELIADE, MIRCEA. *Myths, Dreams and Mysteries; The Encounter Between Contemporary Faiths and Archaic Realities.* New York: Harper & Row, 1960.

D'ENTREVES, ALEXANDER PASSERIN. *The Notion of the State: An Introduction to Political Theory.* New York: Oxford Univ. Press, 1967.

SABINE, GEORGE H. *A History of Political Theory.* 3rd ed. New York: Holt, Rinehart and Winston, 1961.

STRAUSS, LEO. *What Is Political Philosophy?* New York: Free Press, 1960.

———, AND JOSEPH CROPSEY, eds. *History of Political Philosophy.* Chicago: Rand McNally, 1964.

VEREKER, CHARLES. *The Development of Political Theory.* New York: Harper & Row (Colophon Books), 1965.

VOEGELIN, ERIC. *Order and History.* Vol. 1, *Israel and Revelation.* Baton Rouge: Louisiana State Univ. Press, 1956.

WOLIN, SHELDON S. *Politics and Vision; Continuity and Innovation in Western Political Thought.* Boston: Little, Brown, 1960.

Chapter 2 PLATO

Works by Plato

Collected Dialogues. Ed. by Edith Hamilton and Huntington Cairns. New York: Pantheon, 1961. The only one-volume edition in English.

Dialogues. Tr. by Benjamin Jowett. 4th ed. London: Oxford Univ. Press, 1953. 4 vols.

Euthyphro, Apology and Crito, and the Death Scene from Phaedo. Tr. by F. J. Church. 2nd rev. ed. New York: Liberal Arts Press, 1956.

Gorgias. Tr. by W. Hamilton. Baltimore: Penguin Books, 1960.

The Laws. Tr. by A. E. Taylor. London: Dent (Everyman's), 1960.

Parmenides, Theaitetos, Sophist, Statesman. Tr. by John Warrington. London: Dent (Everyman's), 1961.

The Republic. Tr. by F. M. Cornford. New York: Oxford Univ. Press, 1958.

The Republic. In Greek with Eng. tr. by Paul Shorey. Cambridge, Mass.: Harvard Univ. Press (Loeb Classical Library), 1953, 1956. 2 vols.

Statesman. Tr. by J. B. Skemp. New York: Liberal Arts Press, 1957.

Secondary Works

BARKER, ERNEST. *Greek Political Theory; Plato and His Predecessors.* New York: Barnes & Noble (University Paperbacks), 1960.

BOSANQUET, BERNARD. *A Companion to Plato's Republic.* New York: Macmillan, 1895.

CROSSMAN, R. H. S. *Plato Today.* Rev. ed. New York: Oxford Univ. Press, 1959.

FOSTER, MICHAEL B. *The Political Philosophies of Plato and Hegel.* Oxford: Clarendon Press, 1935.

GOULDNER, ALVIN W. *Enter Plato; Classical Greece and the Origins of Social Theory.* New York: Basic Books, 1965.

GRENE, DAVID. *Greek Political Theory; The Image of Man in Thucydides and Plato.* Chicago: Univ. of Chicago Press (Phoenix Books), 1965.

GRUBE, G. M. A. *Plato's Thought.* Boston: Beacon Press, 1958.

NETTLESHIP, RICHARD LEWIS. *Lectures on the Republic of Plato.* 2nd ed. London: Macmillan, 1901.

POPPER, KARL R. *The Open Society and Its Enemies.* Vol. 1, *The Spell of Plato.* 3rd ed. rev. London: Routledge & Kegan Paul, 1957.

TAYLOR, A. E. *Plato, The Man and His Work.* New York: World (Meridian Books), 1956.

———. *Socrates.* Garden City, N.Y.: Doubleday (Anchor Books), 1960.

THORSON, THOMAS L., ed. *Plato: Totalitarian or Democrat.* Englewood Cliffs, N.J.: Prentice-Hall (Spectrum Books), 1963.

VOEGELIN, ERIC. *Order and History.* Vol. 3, *Plato and Aristotle.* Baton Rouge: Louisiana State Univ. Press, 1957.

WILD, JOHN D. *Plato's Theory of Man; An Introduction to the Realistic Philosophy of Culture.* Cambridge, Mass.: Harvard Univ. Press, 1946.

Chapter 3 ARISTOTLE

Works by Aristotle

The Ethics of Aristotle. Tr. by J. A. K. Thomson. Baltimore: Penguin Books, 1958.

The Nicomachean Ethics. Tr. by D. P. Chase. New York: Dutton (Everyman's Library), 1915.

The Politics of Aristotle. Ed. and tr. by William L. Newman. Oxford: Clarendon Press, 1887–1902. 4 vols. Vol. 1 is Newman's introduction.

Politics and the Athenian Constitution. Tr. by John Warrington. New York: Dutton (Everyman's Library), 1961.

The Politics of Aristotle. Tr. by Ernest Barker. New York: Oxford Univ. Press, 1958.

The Works of Aristotle Translated into English. Ed. by W. D. Ross. Oxford: Clarendon Press, 1908–31. 11 vols.

Secondary Works

BARKER, ERNEST. *The Political Thought of Plato and Aristotle.* New York: Dover, 1959.

JAEGER, WERNER. *Aristotle.* 2nd ed. Tr. by Richard Robinson. New York: Oxford Univ. Press, 1962.

KAGEN, DONALD. *The Great Dialogue: A History of Greek Political Thought from Homer to Polybius.* New York: Free Press, 1964.

RANDALL, JOHN HERMAN, JR. *Aristotle.* New York: Columbia Univ. Press, 1962.

ROSS, W. D. *Aristotle.* 2nd ed. New York: World (Meridian Books), 1960.

TAYLOR, A. E. *Aristotle.* Rev. ed. New York: Dover, 1956.

WHEELWRIGHT, PHILIP. *Aristotle.* New York: Odyssey Press, 1951.

Chapter 4 THE STOICS AND ROME

Primary Works

AURELIUS ANTONINUS, MARCUS. *Communings with Himself.* Tr. by C. R. Haines. New York: Putnam's (Loeb Classical Library), 1916.

———. *Meditations* (with Epictetus, *Enchiridion*). Tr. by George Long. Chicago: Regnery (Gateway Editions), 1956.

CICERO, MARCUS TULLIUS. *De officiis.* With Eng. tr. by Walter Miller. Cambridge, Mass.: Harvard Univ. Press (Loeb Classical Library), 1951.

———. *De republica; De legibus.* With Eng. tr. by C. W. Keyes. New York: Putnam's (Loeb Classical Library), 1928.

———. *On the Commonwealth.* Tr. by George H. Sabine and Stanley B. Smith. New York: Liberal Arts Press, 1959.

EPICTETUS. *The Discourses and Fragments.* Tr. by W. A. Oldfather. New York: Putnam's (Loeb Classical Library), 1926, 1928. 2 vols. Vol. 2 reprinted by Harvard Univ. Press, 1952.

GAIUS. *The Institutes of Gaius.* Tr. by Francis de-Zulcuta. Oxford: Clarendon Press, 1946, 1953. 2 vols. Vol. 2 is commentary.

POLYBIUS. *The Histories of Polybius.* Tr. by Evelyn Shuckburgh. Bloomington: Univ. of Indiana Press, 1962. 2 vols.

Secondary Works

ARNOLD, EDWARD V. *Roman Stoicism.* London: Cambridge Univ. Press, 1911.

CARLYLE, R. W., AND A. J. CARLYLE. *A History of Medieval Political Theory in the West.* 2nd ed. 6 vols., Vol. 1. New York: Barnes & Noble, 1927. Part 1 is on the Stoics.

COCHRANE, CHARLES N. *Christianity and Classical Culture.* Rev. ed. New York: Oxford Univ. Press (Galaxy Books), 1957.

FRITZ, KURT VON. *The Theory of the Mixed Constitution in Antiquity: A Critical Analysis of Polybius' Political Ideas.* New York: Columbia Univ. Press, 1954.

HICKS, ROBERT D. *Stoic and Epicurean.* New York: Russell & Russell, 1962.

MURRAY, GILBERT. *Stoic, Christian and Humanist.* London: Allen & Unwin, 1940.

RICHARDS, GEORGE C. *Cicero, A Study.* Boston: Houghton Mifflin, 1935.

WALBANK, F. W. *A Historical Commentary on Polybius.* Oxford: Clarendon Press, 1957.

ZELLER, EDUARD. *The Stoics, Epicureans and Sceptics.* Tr. by Oswald J. Reichel. New and rev. ed. New York: Russell & Russell, 1962.

Chapter 5 AUGUSTINE

Works by Augustine

An Augustine Synthesis. Ed. by Erich Przywara. New York: Sheed & Ward, 1936; Harper & Row (Torchbooks), 1958.

Basic Writings of Saint Augustine. Ed. by Whitney J. Oates. New York: Random House, 1948. 2 vols.

City of God. Tr. by Marcus Dods. New York: Random House (Modern Library), 1950.

The City of God. Tr. by John Healey (1610). New York: Dutton (Everyman's Library), 1945.

Confessions. Tr. by Rex Warner. New York: New American Library (Mentor Books), 1963.

Confessions and Enchiridion. Ed. by Albert C. Outler. (Library of Christian Classics, Vol. 7). Philadelphia: Westminster Press, 1955.

Earlier Writings. Ed. and tr. by J. H. S. Burleigh. (Library of Christian Classics, Vol. 6). Philadelphia: Westminster Press, 1953.

Later Works. Ed. and tr. by John Burnaby. (Library of Christian Classics, Vol. 8). Philadelphia: Westminster Press, 1955.

Political Writings of St. Augustine. Ed. by Henry Paolucci. Chicago: Regnery (Gateway Editions), 1962.

Works. Ed. by Marcus Dods. Edinburgh: T. & T. Clark, 1872–1934. 8 vols.

Secondary Works

ANDRESON, CARL, ed. *Bibliographia Augustiniana.* Darmstadt, Germany: Wissenschaftliche Buchgesellschaft, 1962.

BATTENHOUSE, ROY, ed. *A Companion to St. Augustine.* New York: Oxford Univ. Press, 1955.

BROOKS, EDGAR H. *The City of God and the Politics of Crisis.* London: Oxford Univ. Press, 1960.

COMBES, GUSTAVE. *La Doctrine politique de Saint Augustin.* Paris: Librairie Plon, 1927.

CULLMANN, OSCAR. *The State in the New Testament.* New York: Scribner's, 1956.

D'ARCY, M. C., ed. *Saint Augustine.* New York: World (Meridian Books), 1957. A symposium.

DEANE, HERBERT A. *The Political and Social Ideas of Saint Augustine.* New York: Columbia Univ. Press, 1963.

FIGGIS, JOHN NEVILLE. *The Political Aspects of S. Augustine's City of God.* London: Longmans, Green, 1921.

GILSON, ÉTIENNE. *The Christian Philosophy of St. Augustine.* Tr. by L. E. M. Lynch. New York: Random House, 1960.

POPE, HUGH. *St. Augustine of Hippo.* London: Longmans, Green, 1954.

PORTALIÉ, EUGENE. *A Guide to the Thought of Saint Augustine.* Tr. by Ralph J. Bastian. Chicago: Regnery, 1960.

VERSFELD, MARTHINUS. *A Guide to the City of God.* New York: Sheed & Ward, 1958.

Chapter 6 AQUINAS

Works by Aquinas

On Kingship to the King of Cyprus. Tr. by Gerald B. Phelan. New ed., rev. by I. T. Eschmann. Toronto: Pontifical Institute of Medieval Studies, 1949. (1938 ed. titled *On the Governance of Rulers.*)

Philosophical Texts. Ed. and tr. by Thomas Gilby. New York: Oxford Univ. Press (Galaxy Books), 1960.

The Political Ideas of St. Thomas Aquinas. Ed. by Dino Bigongiari. New York: Hafner, 1953.

Selected Political Writings. Tr. by J. G. Dawson. Ed. by A. P. d'Entreves. Oxford: Blackwell & Mott, 1948.

Summa contra Gentiles. Tr. by English Dominican Fathers. London: Burns & Oates, 1928–29. 5 vols.

Summa Theologica. Tr. by English Dominican Fathers. Amer. ed. New York: Benziger, 1947–49. 3 vols.

Treatise on Law. Tr. by English Dominican Fathers. Chicago: Regnery (Gateway Editions), n.d.

Secondary Works

BRENNAN, ROBERT E., ed. *Essays in Thomism.* New York: Sheed & Ward, 1942.

CHESTERTON, G. K. *St. Thomas Aquinas.* Garden City, N.Y.: Doubleday (Image Books), 1956.

COPLESTON, FREDERICK C. *Aquinas.* Baltimore: Penguin Books (Pelican Books), 1955.

D'ARCY, MARTIN. *St. Thomas Aquinas.* Glen Rock, N.J.: Newman Press, 1955.

FARRELL, WALTER. *A Companion to the Summa.* New York: Sheed & Ward, 1939–42. 4 vols.

GILBY, THOMAS. *The Political Thought of Thomas Aquinas.* Chicago: Univ. of Chicago Press, 1958.

———. *Principality and Polity; Aquinas and the Rise of State Theory in the West.* London: Longmans, Green, 1958.

GILSON, ÉTIENNE. *The Christian Philosophy of Saint Thomas Aquinas.* Tr. by L. K. Shook. New York: Random House, 1956.

JAFFA, HARRY V. *Thomism and Aristotelianism; A Study of the Commentary by Thomas Aquinas on the Nicomachean Ethics.* Chicago: Univ. of Chicago Press, 1952.

MARITAIN, JACQUES. *St. Thomas Aquinas.* New York: World (Meridian Books), 1958.

MIHALICH, JOSEPH C. *Existentialism and Thomism.* New York: Philosophical Library, 1960.

SERTILLANGES, ANTONIN G. *Saint Thomas Aquinas and His Work.* Tr. by Godfrey Anstruther. London: Blackfriars, 1957.

Chapter 7 SOME MEDIEVAL LEGACIES

General

CARLYLE, R. W., AND A. J. CARLYLE. *A History of Medieval Political Theory in the West.* New York: Barnes & Noble, 1953. 6 vols.

COPLESTON, FREDERICK C. *Medieval Philosophy.* New York: Harper & Row (Torchbooks), 1961.

DUNNING, WILLIAM A. *A History of Political Theories: Ancient and Medieval.* New York: Macmillan, 1936.

D'ENTREVES, ALEXANDER PASSERIN. *The Medieval Contribution to Political Thought.* London: Oxford Univ. Press, 1939.

FIGGIS, JOHN NEVILLE. *The Divine Right of Kings.* 2nd ed. New York: Harper & Row (Torchbooks), 1965.

GIERKE, OTTO. *Political Theories of the Middle Age.* Tr. by F. W. Maitland. Boston: Beacon Press, 1958.

GILSON, ÉTIENNE. *A History of Christian Philosophy in the Middle Ages.* New York: Random House, 1955.

HEARNSHAW, F. J. C., ed. *The Social and Political Ideas of Some Great Medieval Thinkers.* London: Harrap, 1923.

JENKS, EDWARD. *Law and Politics in the Middle Ages.* New York: Holt, Rinehart and Winston, 1932.

KANTOROWICZ, ERNST H. *The King's Two Bodies; A Study in Medieval Political Theology.* Princeton, N.J.: Princeton Univ. Press, 1957.

KERN, FRITZ. *Kingship and Law in the Middle Ages.* Tr. by S. B. Chrimes. Oxford: Blackwell & Mott, 1939.

LERNER, RALPH, AND MUHSIN MAHDI, eds. *Medieval Political Philosophy: A Sourcebook.* New York: Free Press, 1963.

LEWIS, EWART K., ed. *Medieval Political Ideas.* London: Routledge & Kegan Paul, 1954. 2 vols.

McILWAIN, CHARLES H. *The Growth of Political Thought in the West.* New York: Macmillan, 1932, chs. 5 and 6.

MORRALL, JOHN B. *Political Thought in Medieval Times.* Rev. ed. New York: Harper & Row (Torchbooks), 1962.

RIESENBERG, PETER N. *The Inalienability of Sovereignty in Medieval Political Thought.* New York: Columbia Univ. Press, 1956.

ROSENTHAL, ERWIN I. J. *Political Thought in Medieval Islam.* London: Cambridge Univ. Press, 1958.

TIERNEY, BRIAN. *The Crisis of Church and State, 1050–1300.* Englewood Cliffs, N.J.: Prentice-Hall (Spectrum Books), 1964. With selected documents.

ULLMAN, WALTER. *History of Political Thought: The Middle Ages.* Baltimore: Penguin Books (Pelican Books), 1965.

———. *Medieval Papalism; The Political Theories of the Medieval Canonists.* London: Methuen, 1949.

WILKS, MICHAEL J. *The Problem of Sovereignty in the Later Middle Ages.* London: Cambridge Univ. Press, 1963.

John of Salisbury

JOHN OF SALISBURY. *Early Letters.* Vol. 1, *Letters.* Ed. by W. J. Millor and H. E. Butler. Rev. by C. N. L. Brooke. London: Nelson, 1955.

———. *Policraticus.* Ed. by C. C. J. Webb. Oxford: Clarendon Press, 1909. 2 vols.

———. *The Statesman's Book of John of Salisbury.* Tr. by John Dickinson. New York: Knopf, 1927.

LIEBESCHUTZ, HANS. *Medieval Humanism in the Life and Writings of John of Salisbury.* London: Univ. of London Press (Warburg Institute), 1950.

WEBB, CLEMENT C. J. *John of Salisbury.* London: Methuen, 1932.

Dante

DANTE ALIGHIERI. *The Divine Comedy.* Italian with Eng. tr. by Geoffrey L. Bickersteth. Cambridge, Mass.: Harvard Univ. Press, 1965.

———. *De Monarchia.* Tr. by Henry Aurelia. Boston: Houghton Mifflin, 1904.

———. *On World Government.* Tr. by Herbert W. Schneider. 2nd rev. ed. New York: Liberal Arts Press, 1957.

DAVIS, CHARLES T. *Dante and the Idea of Rome.* London: Oxford Univ. Press, 1957.

D'ENTREVES, ALEXANDER PASSERIN. *Dante as a Political Thinker.* Oxford: Clarendon Press, 1952.

GILSON, ÉTIENNE. *Dante and Philosophy.* Tr. by David Moore. New York: Harper & Row (Torchbooks), 1963.

LENKEITH, NANCY. *Dante and the Legend of Rome.* London: Univ. of London Press (Warburg Institute), 1952.

ROLBIECKI, JOHN J. *The Political Philosophy of Dante Alighieri.* Washington, D.C.: Catholic Univ. of America Press, 1921.

Marsilio of Padua

ALLEN, J. W. "Marsilio of Padua and Medieval Secularism." In F. J. C. Hearnshaw, ed., *The Social and Political Ideas of Some Great Medieval Thinkers.* London: Harrap, 1923, ch. 7.

EMERTON, EPHRAIM. *The Defensor Pacis of Marsilio of Padua: A Critical Study.* Gloucester, Mass.: Peter Smith, 1951.

D'ENTREVES, ALEXANDER PASSERIN. *The Medieval Contribution to Political Thought.* London: Oxford Univ. Press, ch. 2.

MARSILIUS OF PADUA. *The Defender of Peace.* Ed. and tr. by Alan Gewirth. New York: Columbia Univ. Press, 1951. 2 vols. Vol 1 is commentary.

PREVITÉ-ORTON, C. W. *Marsilius of Padua.* London: Milford, 1935.

Nicholas of Cusa

BETT, HENRY. *Nicholas of Cusa.* London: Methuen, 1932.

MORRALL, JOHN B. *Gerson and the Great Schism.* Manchester, Eng.: Manchester Univ. Press, 1960.

NICOLAI DE CUSA. *De Concordantia Catholica.* Ed. by Gerhard Kallen. Hamburg: Meiner, 1964–65. 2 vols.

———. *Unity and Reform: Selected Writings of Nicholas de Cusa.* Ed. by John P. Dolan. Notre Dame, Ind.: Univ. of Notre Dame Press, 1962.

SIGMUND, PAUL. *Nicholas of Cusa and Medieval Political Thought.* Cambridge, Mass.: Harvard Univ. Press, 1963.

TIERNEY, BRIAN. *Foundations of the Conciliar Theory.* New York: Cambridge Univ. Press, 1955.

WATANABE, MORIMICHI. *The Political Ideas of Nicholas of Cusa.* Geneva: Libraire Droz, 1963.

Chapter 8 MACHIAVELLI

Works by Machiavelli

Chief Works and Others. Ed. and tr. by Allan H. Gilbert. Durham, N.C.: Duke Univ. Press, 1965. 3 vols.

The Discourses. Tr. by Leslie J. Walker. New Haven, Conn.: Yale Univ. Press, 1950. 2 vols.

The Historical, Political and Diplomatic Writings of Niccolo Machiavelli. Tr. by Christian E. Detmold. Boston: Houghton Mifflin, 1882–91. 4 vols.

History of Florence and of the Affairs of Italy. Intro. by Felix Gilbert. New York: Harper & Row (Torchbooks), 1960.

The Prince and The Discourses. Tr. by Luigi Ricci and Christian Detmold. New York: Random House (Modern Library), 1940.

Secondary Works

BUTTERFIELD, HERBERT. *The Statecraft of Machiavelli.* New York: Macmillan (Collier Books), 1962.

CHABOD, FREDERICO. *Machiavelli and the Renaissance.* Tr. by David Moore. Cambridge, Mass.: Harvard Univ. Press, 1958.

GILBERT, ALLAN H. *Machiavelli's Prince and Its Forerunners.* Durham, N.C.: Duke Univ. Press, 1938.

GILBERT, FELIX. *Machiavelli and Guicciardini; Politics and History in Sixteenth-Century Florence.* Princeton, N.J.: Princeton Univ. Press, 1965.

GUICCIARDINI, FRANCESCO. *Maxims and Reflections of a Renaissance Statesman.* Tr. by Mario Domandi. New York: Harper & Row (Torchbooks), 1965.

HALE, JOHN RIGBY. *Machiavelli and Renaissance Italy.* New York: Macmillan, 1960.

MEINECKE, FRIEDRICH. *Machiavellism; The Doctrine of Raison D'Etat and Its Place in Modern History.* Tr. by Douglas Scott. London: Routledge & Kegan Paul, 1957.

RIDOLFI, ROBERTO. *The Life of Niccolo Machiavelli.* Tr. by Cecil Grayson. Chicago: Univ. of Chicago Press, 1963.

STRAUSS, LEO. *Thoughts on Machiavelli.* New York: Free Press, 1958.

WHITFIELD, JOHN H. *Machiavelli.* Oxford: Blackwell & Mott, 1947.

Chapter 9 THE REFORMATION

General

ALLEN, J. W. *Political Thought in the Sixteenth Century.* Rev. ed. New York: Barnes & Noble, 1957.

AMES, RUSSELL A. *Citizen Thomas More and His Utopia.* Princeton, N.J.: Princeton Univ. Press, 1949.

BAINTON, ROLAND H. *The Reformation of the Sixteenth Century.* Boston: Beacon Press, 1952.

CHURCH, WILLIAM FARR. *Constitutional Thought in Sixteenth-Century France.* Cambridge, Mass.: Harvard Univ. Press, 1941.

DALY, LOWRIE JOHN. *The Political Theory of John Wyclif.* (Jesuit Study, No. 17.) Chicago: Loyola Univ. Press, 1962.

DODGE, GUY H. *The Political Theory of the Huguenots of the Dispersion.* New York: Columbia Univ. Press, 1947.

DUNNING, WILLIAM A. *A History of Political Theory from Luther to Montesquieu.* New York: Macmillan, 1905.

ERASMUS, DESIDERIUS. *The Education of a Christian Prince.* Tr. by Lester K. Born. New York: Columbia Univ. Press, 1936.

HAMILTON, BERNICE. *Political Thought in Sixteenth-Century Spain.* Oxford: Clarendon Press, 1963.

HARBISON, E. HARRIS. *The Age of Reformation.* Ithaca, N.Y.: Cornell Univ. Press, 1955.

KAUTSKY, KARL. *Thomas More and His Utopia.* New York: Russell & Russell, 1959.

MORE, THOMAS. *Utopia.* Tr. by H. S. V. Ogden. New York: Appleton-Century-Crofts, 1949.

MOSSE, GEORGE L. *The Holy Pretence; A Study in Christianity and Reason of State from William Perkins to John Winthrop.* Oxford: Blackwell & Mott, 1957.

MURRAY, ROBERT H. *The Political Consequences of the Reformation.* London: Benn, 1926.

REYNOLDS, E. E. *St. Thomas More.* New York: Kenedy, 1953.

SMITH, PRESERVED. *Erasmus.* New York: Harper & Row, 1923.

TAWNEY, R. H. *Religion and the Rise of Capitalism.* New York: New American Library (Mentor Books), 1958.

TROELTSCH, ERNST. *The Social Teaching of the Christian Churches.* Tr. by Olive Wyon. New York: Macmillan, 1950. 2 vols.

Vindiciae contra tyrannos. Tr. by H. J. Laski. London: Bell, 1924.

WEBER, MAX. *The Protestant Ethic and the Spirit of Capitalism.* Tr. by Talcott Parsons. New York: Scribner's, 1950.

Luther

BAINTON, ROLAND H. *Here I Stand: A Life of Martin Luther.* New York: New American Library (Mentor Books), 1955.

CRANZ, FERDINAND EDMUND. *An Essay on the Development of Luther's Thought on Justice, Law and Society.* Cambridge, Mass.: Harvard Univ. Press, 1959.

ERIKSON, ERIK H. *Young Man Luther.* New York: Norton, 1958.

FORELL, GEORGE. *Faith Active in Love: An Interpretation of Principles Underlying Luther's Social Ethics.* New York: American Peoples Press, 1954.

LUTHER, MARTIN. *Reformation Writings.* Tr. by Bertram Lee Wolf. London: Lutterworth Press, 1952, 1956. 2 vols.

———. *Selections from His Writings.* Ed. by John Dillenberger. Garden City, N.Y.: Doubleday (Anchor Books), 1961.

———. *Works.* Ed. by Jaroslav Pelikan and Helmut T. Lehman. St. Louis, Mo.: Concordia; Philadelphia: Muhlenberg Press. 1955 et sec. 55 vols.

MUELLER, WILLIAM A. *Church and State in Luther and Calvin.* Nashville, Tenn.: Abingdon, 1954.

RITTER, GERHARD. *Luther, His Life and Work.* Tr. by John Riches. New York: Harper & Row, 1963.

SCHWEIBERT, ERNEST G. *Luther and His Times.* St. Louis, Mo.: Concordia, 1950.

WARING, LUTHER H. *The Political Theories of Martin Luther.* New York: Putnam's, 1910.

Calvin

CHENEVIERE, MARC-EDOUARD. *La Pensée politique de Calvin.* Geneva: Éditions Labor, 1937.

CALVIN, JOHN. *Institutes of the Christian Religion.* Ed. by J. T. McNeill. Tr. by F. L. Battles. (Library of Christian Classics, Vols. 20, 21.) Philadelphia: Westminster Press, 1960. 2 vols.

———. *Tracts Relating to the Reformation.* Tr. by H. Beveridge. Grand Rapids, Mich.: Eerdmans, 1957. 3 vols.

HARKNESS, GEORGIA. *John Calvin: The Man and His Ethics.* Nashville, Tenn.: Abingdon (Apex Books), 1958.

MACKINNON, JAMES. *Calvin and the Reformation.* London: Longmans, Green, 1936.

MCNEILL, JOHN T. *The History and Character of Calvinism.* New York: Oxford Univ. Press, 1954.

MOSSE, GEORGE L. *Calvinism, Authoritarian or Democratic?* New York: Holt, Rinehart and Winston, 1957.

Bodin

BODIN, JEAN. *Method for the Easy Comprehension of History* (1566). Tr. by Beatrice Reynolds. New York: Columbia Univ. Press, 1945.

———. *Oeuvres philosophiques.* Tr. by Pierre Mesnard. Paris: Presses Universitaires de France, 1951, 1952. 2 vols.

———. *The Six Bookes of a Commonweale* (Eng. tr. of 1606). Ed. by Kenneth D. McRae. Cambridge, Mass.: Harvard Univ. Press, 1962.

———. *Six Bookes of the Commonwealth.* Abridged ed. Tr. by M. J. Tooley. (Blackwell's Political Texts.) New York: Macmillan, 1955.

FRANKLIN, JULIAN H. *Jean Bodin and the Sixteenth-Century Revolution in the Methodology of Law and History.* New York: Columbia Univ. Press, 1963.

REYNOLDS, BEATRICE. *Proponents of Limited Monarchy in Sixteenth-Century France: Francis Hotman and Jean Bodin.* New York: Columbia Univ. Press, 1931.

Hooker

DAVIES, E. T. *The Political Ideas of Richard Hooker.* London: Society for Promoting Christian Knowledge, 1946.

HOOKER, RICHARD. *Works.* Ed. by John Keble. 7th ed. Oxford: Clarendon Press, 1888. 3 vols.

———. *Hooker's Ecclesiastical Polity, Book VIII.* Intro. by R. Houk. New York: Columbia Univ. Press, 1931.

———. *Of the Laws of Ecclesiastical Polity.* New York: Dutton (Everyman's Library), 1907. 2 vols.

MORRIS, CHRISTOPHER. *Political Thought in England, Tyndale to Hooker.* London: Oxford Univ. Press, 1953, ch. 9.

MUNZ, PETER. *The Place of Hooker in the History of Thought.* London: Routledge & Kegan Paul, 1952.

SHIRLEY, F. J. *Richard Hooker and Contemporary Political Ideas.* London: Society for Promoting Christian Knowledge, 1949.

Chapter 10 THE SEVENTEENTH CENTURY

General

BOULENGER, JACQUES. *The Seventeenth Century.* (The National History of France, No. 3.) New York: Putnam's, 1920.

CARRÉ, MAYRICK. *Phases of Thought in England.* Oxford: Clarendon Press, 1949.

CLARK, G. N. *The Seventeenth Century.* New York: Oxford Univ. Press (Galaxy Books), 1961. An intellectual survey of Europe.

GOOCH, G. P. *Political Thought in England from Bacon to Halifax.* London: Butterworth, 1914.

STANKIEWICZ, W. J. *Politics and Religion in Seventeenth-Century France.* Berkeley: Univ. of California Press, 1960.

WILLEY, BASIL. *The Seventeenth Century Background; Studies in the Thought of the Age in Relation to Poetry and Religion.* New York: Columbia Univ. Press, 1934; Garden City, N.Y.: Doubleday (Anchor Books), 1953.

The Political Obligation of Subjects

ALLEN, J. W. *English Political Thought, 1603–1644.* London: Methuen, 1938.

BACON, FRANCIS. *Essays or Counsels Civil and Moral.* London: Dent (Everyman), 1906. A reprint of the fifth and last edition written by Bacon and published in 1625. The first edition was published in 1597.

FIGGIS, JOHN NEVILLE. *The Theory of the Divine Right of Kings.* 2nd ed. New York: Harper & Row (Torchbooks), 1960.

FILMER, ROBERT. *Patriarcha and Other Political Works.* Ed. by Peter Laslett. Oxford: Blackwell & Mott, 1949.

Grotius, Hugo. *De juri belli et pacis.* London: Cambridge Univ. Press, 1853. 3 vols. Latin text of 1625 with tr. by William Whewell. The *Prolegomena* is published by Liberal Arts Press, 1957.

James I. *The Political Works of James I.* Ed. by Charles H. McIlwain. Cambridge, Mass.: Harvard Univ. Press, 1918.

Knight, W. S. M. *The Life and Work of Hugo Grotius.* London: Sweet & Maxwell, 1925.

Krieger, Leonard. *The Politics of Discretion: Pufendorf and the Acceptance of Natural Law.* Chicago: Univ. of Chicago Press, 1965.

Pufendorf, Samuel. *De officio hominis et civis* (1673). (Carnegie Classics in International Law.) New York: Oxford Univ. Press, 1921. 2 vols. Vol. 2 tr. by F. G. Moore.

———. *De jure naturae et gentium* (1688). (Carnegie Classics in International Law.) Oxford: Clarendon Press, 1934. 2 vols. Vol. 2 tr. by C. H. Oldfather and W. A. Oldfather.

Spinoza, Benedict de. *Writings on Political Philosophy.* Ed. by A. G. A. Balz. New York: Appleton-Century-Crofts, 1937. Contains the *Tractatus politicus* of 1677 in full in the R. H. M. Elwes tr. of 1883.

———. *The Political Works.* Ed. and tr. by A. G. Wernham. Oxford: Clarendon Press, 1958. Contains the *Tractatus politicus* in full and the *Tractatus theologico politicus* (1670) in part.

Sykes, Norman. "Bossuet." In F. J. C. Hearnshaw, ed. *The Social and Political Ideas of Some Great French Thinkers of the Age of Reason.* London: Harrap, 1930, ch. 2.

Vreeland, Hamilton. *Hugo Grotius.* New York: Oxford Univ. Press, 1917.

Restraints upon Rulers: Constitutionalism

Althusius, Johannes. *Politica methodica digesta.* Ed. by Carl J. Friedrich. Cambridge, Mass.: Harvard Univ. Press, 1932.

———. *The Politics of Johannes Althusius.* Abridged ed. Tr. by Frederick S. Carney. Boston: Beacon Press, 1964.

Barker, Arthur. *Milton and the Puritan Dilemma, 1641–1660.* Toronto: Univ. of Toronto Press, 1942.

Bowen, Catherine Drinker. *The Lion and the Throne; The Life and Time of Sir Edward Coke.* Boston: Little, Brown, 1956.

Coke, Edward. *The First Part of the Institutes of the Laws of England.* Ed. by Francis Hargrove and Charles Butler. London: Clarke, 1832.

Cromwell, Oliver. *The Writings and Speeches of Oliver Cromwell.* Ed. by Wilbur C. Abbott. Cambridge, Mass.: Harvard Univ. Press, 1937–47. 4 vols.

Gardiner, Samuel Rawson, ed. *The Constitutional Documents of the Puritan Revolution.* Oxford: Clarendon Press, 1889.

Gerbrandy, P. S. *National and International Stability; Althusius, Grotius, Van Vollenhoven.* London: Oxford Univ. Press, 1944.

Gooch, G. P. *English Democratic Ideas in the Seventeenth Century.* 2nd ed. New York: Harper & Row (Torchbooks), 1960.

Miller, Perry. *The New England Mind; The Seventeenth Century.* New York: Macmillan, 1939.

Milton, John. *Areopagitica.* New York: Dutton (Everyman's Library), 1927.

Perry, Ralph Barton. *Puritanism and Democracy.* New York: Vanguard, 1944.

Williams, Roger. *Works.* Providence, R.I.: Narragansett Club, 1866. 6 vols. The standard edition.

———. *Roger Williams; His Contribution to the American Tradition.* Indianapolis, Ind.: Bobbs-Merrill, 1953.

Woodhouse, A. S. P., ed. *Puritanism and Liberty; Being the Army Debates (1647–1649) from the Clarke Manuscripts.* 2nd ed. Chicago: Univ. of Chicago Press, 1951.

Zagorin, Perez. *A History of Political Thought in the English Revolution.* London: Routledge & Kegan Paul, 1954.

The Ground of Political Authority: Populism

Blitzer, Charles. *An Immortal Commonwealth: The Political Thought of James Harrington.* New Haven: Yale Univ. Press, 1960.

Frank, Joseph. *The Levellers; A History of the Writings of Three Seventeenth-Century Social Democrats: John Lilburne, Richard Overton, William Walwyn.* Cambridge, Mass.: Harvard Univ. Press, 1955.

Gibb, M. A. *John Lilburne the Leveller; A Christian Democrat.* London: Drummond, 1947.

Haller, William. *Liberty and Reformation in the Puritan Revolution.* New York: Columbia Univ. Press, 1955.

———, ed. *Tracts on Liberty in the Puritan Revolution, 1638–1647.* New York: Columbia Univ. Press, 1934. 3 vols.

———, and Godfrey Davies, eds. *The Leveller Tracts, 1647–1653.* New York: Columbia Univ. Press, 1944.

HARRINGTON, JAMES. *Political Writings; Representative Selections.* Ed. by Charles Blitzer. New York: Liberal Arts, 1955.

HARRISON, WILFRED. *Conflict and Compromise; A History of British Political Thought, 1593–1900.* New York: Free Press, 1965.

JONES, RUFUS M. *Mysticism and Democracy in the English Commonwealth.* Cambridge, Mass.: Harvard Univ. Press, 1932.

ROBERTSON, D. B. *The Religious Foundations of Leveller Democracy.* New York: Columbia Univ. Press, 1951.

WINSTANLEY, GERRARD. *Works.* Ed. by George H. Sabine. Ithaca, N.Y.: Cornell Univ. Press, 1941.

WOLFE, DON M. *The Leveller Manifestoes of the Puritan Revolution.* Camden, N.J.: Nelson, 1944.

Natural Law, Reason of State, and Comparative Politics

D'ENTREVES, ALEXANDER PASSERIN. *Natural Law.* New York: Hillary House, 1952.

GIERKE, OTTO. *Natural Law and the Theory of Society, 1500–1800.* London: Cambridge Univ. Press, 1934. 2 vols.; 1 vol. ed., 1950; Boston: Beacon Press, 1957.

HALIFAX, LORD (George Savile). *The Complete Works of George Savile, First Marquess of Halifax.* Ed. by Walter Raleigh. Oxford: Clarendon Press, 1912.

Chapter 11 HOBBES

Works by Hobbes

The English Works of Thomas Hobbes. Ed. by William Molesworth. London: Bohn, 1839–45, 11 vols.

Behemoth, or the Long Parliament. Ed. by F. Tonnies. London: Simpkin Marshall, 1889.

De cive, or The Citizen. Ed. by Sterling P. Lamprecht. New York: Appleton-Century-Crofts, 1949.

The Elements of Law, Natural and Politic. Ed. by F. Tonnies. London: Simpkin Marshall, 1889.

Leviathan. Ed. by A. D. Lindsay. New York: Dutton (Everyman's Library), 1950.

Leviathan. Ed. by Michael Oakeshott. Oxford: Blackwell & Mott, 1946.

Selections. Ed. by Frederick J. E. Woodbridge. New York: Scribner's, 1930.

Secondary Works

BOWLE, JOHN. *Hobbes and His Critics; A Study in Seventeenth-Century Constitutionalism.* London: Cape, 1951.

BROWN, KEITH C., ed. *Hobbes Studies.* Cambridge, Mass.: Harvard Univ. Press, 1965.

GOLDSMITH, M. M. *Hobbes's Science of Politics.* New York: Columbia Univ. Press, 1966.

HOOD, F. C. *The Divine Politics of Thomas Hobbes: An Interpretation of Leviathan.* Oxford: Clarendon Press, 1964.

JESSOP, THOMAS EDMUND. *Thomas Hobbes.* London: Longmans, Green, 1960.

LAIRD, JOHN. *Hobbes.* London: Oxford Univ. Press, 1934.

MACPHERSON, C. B. *The Political Theory of Possessive Individualism: Hobbes to Locke.* New York: Oxford Univ. Press, 1962.

PETERS, RICHARD. *Hobbes.* Harmondsworth, Eng.: Penguin Books, 1956.

STEPHEN, LESLIE. *Hobbes.* New York: Macmillan, 1904.

STRAUSS, LEO. *The Political Philosophy of Hobbes.* Tr. by Elsa M. Sinclair. Chicago: Univ. of Chicago Press (Phoenix Books), 1963.

WARRENDER, J. HOWARD. *The Political Philosophy of Hobbes; His Theory of Obligation.* Oxford: Clarendon Press, 1957.

WATKINS, J. W. N. *Hobbes's System of Ideas: A Study in the Political Significance of Philosophical Theories.* London: Hutchinson, 1965.

Chapter 12 LOCKE

Works by Locke

The Correspondence of John Locke and Edward Clarke. Ed. by Benjamin Rand. London: Oxford Univ. Press, 1927.

An Essay Concerning Human Understanding (1690). Ed. by Alexander Campbell Fraser. Oxford: Clarendon Press, 1894. 2 vols. A convenient abridged ed. is Russell Kirk, ed., Chicago: Regnery (Gateway Editions), 1956.

Essays on the Law of Nature (*c.* 1670's). Ed. by Wolfgang von Leyden. Oxford: Clarendon Press, 1954. Latin with Eng. tr.

A Letter Concerning Toleration (1685). Ed. by J. W. Gough. Oxford: Blackwell & Mott, 1947. See also entry below under *Two Treatises.*

The Reasonableness of Christianity (1695). Ed. by I. T. Ramsey. (Library of Modern Religious Thought.) Stanford, Cal.: Stanford Univ. Press, 1958.

Two Tracts on Government. Ed. and tr. by Philip Abrams. New York: Cambridge Univ. Press, 1967. Two early tracts on civil power and religion.

Two Treatises of Government. Intro. and Apparatus Criticus by Peter Laslett. London: Cambridge Univ. Press, 1960. The definitive edition, incorporating for the first time Locke's final revisions. See also Thomas I. Cook, ed. New York: Hafner, 1947; *A Treatise of Civil Government and A Letter Concerning Toleration.* Ed. by Charles L. Sherman. New York: Appleton-Century-Crofts, 1937; and *Of Civil Government.* Chicago: Regnery (Gateway Editions), 1955.

The Works of John Locke. London: Tegg, 1823. 10 vols.

Secondary Works

AARON, R. I. *John Locke.* 2nd ed. New York: Oxford Univ. Press, 1955.

COX, RICHARD H. *Locke on War and Peace.* New York: Oxford Univ. Press, 1960.

CRANSTON, MAURICE. *John Locke; A Biography.* New York: Macmillan, 1957.

CZAJKOWSKI, C. J. *The Theory of Private Property in Locke's Political Philosophy.* Notre Dame, Ind.: Univ. of Notre Dame Press, 1941.

FOX-BOURNE, H. R. *The Life of John Locke.* London: King & Jarrett, 1876. 2 vols.

GOUGH, JOHN W. *John Locke's Political Philosophy; Eight Studies.* Oxford: Clarendon Press, 1950.

LAMPRECHT, STERLING P. *The Moral and Political Philosophy of John Locke.* (Archives of Philosophy, No. 1.) New York: Columbia Univ. Press, 1918.

LASLETT, PETER. Intro. to his ed. of Robert Filmer's *Patriarcha.* Oxford: Blackwell & Mott, 1949.

O'CONNOR, D. J. *John Locke.* Baltimore: Penguin Books, 1952.

POLIN, RAYMOND. *La Politique morale de John Locke.* Paris: Presses Universitaires de France, 1960.

VAUGHN, C. E. *Studies in the History of Political Philosophy Before and After Rousseau.* Manchester, Eng.: Univ. of Manchester Press, 1925. 2 vols. Vol. 1, pp. 130–204.

YOLTON, JOHN Y. *John Locke and the Way of Ideas.* London: Oxford Univ. Press, 1956. Excellent bibliography.

Chapter 13 THE EIGHTEENTH CENTURY

The Enlightenment

BECKER, CARL L. *The Heavenly City of the Eighteenth-Century Philosophers.* New Haven, Conn.: Yale Univ. Press, 1932.

CASSIRER, ERNST. *The Philosophy of the Enlightenment.* Tr. by F. C. A. Koelln and J. P. Pettegrove. Boston: Beacon Press, 1955.

COBBAN, ALFRED. *In Search of Humanity: The Role of the Enlightenment in Modern History.* New York: Braziller, 1960.

DE TOCQUEVILLE, ALEXIS. *The Old Regime and the French Revolution* (1856). Tr. by Stuart Gilbert. Garden City, N.Y.: Doubleday (Anchor Books), 1955.

FLEISHER, DAVID. *William Godwin: A Study in Liberalism.* London: Allen & Unwin, 1951.

FRANKEL, CHARLES. *The Faith of Reason; The Idea of Progress in the French Enlightenment.* New York: Columbia Univ. Press, 1948.

GAY, PETER. *The Enlightenment: An Interpretation.* New York: Knopf, 1966. The bibliographic essay, pp. 423–555, is a tour de force.

———. *Voltaire's Politics; The Poet as Realist.* Princeton, N.J.: Princeton Univ. Press, 1959.

GODWIN, WILLIAM. *An Enquiry Concerning Political Justice.* Ed. by F. E. L. Priestly. 3rd ed. Toronto: Univ. of Toronto, 1946. 2 vols.

HAZARD, PAUL. *European Thought in the Eighteenth Century; From Montesquieu to Lessing.* Tr. by J. Lewis May. New Haven, Conn.: Yale Univ. Press, 1954.

HEARNSHAW, F. J. C., ed. *Social and Political Ideas of Representative Thinkers of the Revolutionary Age.* New York: Barnes & Noble, 1950.

———, ed. *Social and Political Ideas of Some Great French Thinkers of the Age of Reason.* New York: Barnes & Noble, 1950.

KANT, IMMANUEL. *Metaphysical Elements of Justice.* Ed. by John Ladd. New York: Liberal Arts Press, 1963.

KEGAN PAUL, C. *William Godwin.* London: King & Jarrett, 1876. 2 vols.

KETTLER, DAVID. *The Social and Political Thought of Adam Ferguson.* Columbus: Ohio State Univ. Press, 1965.

LASKI, HAROLD J. *The Rise of European Liberalism.* London: Allen & Unwin, 1936.

———. *Political Thought in England; Locke to Bentham.* London: Oxford Univ. Press (Home University Library), 1920.

MARTIN, KINGSLEY. *The Rise of French Liberal Thought; A Study of Political Ideas from Bayle to Condorcet.* Ed. by J. P. Mayer. New York: New York Univ. Press, 1954.

ROBBINS, CAROLINE. *The Eighteenth-Century Commonwealthman.* Cambridge, Mass.: Harvard Univ. Press, 1959.

ROCKWOOD, RAYMOND O., ed. *Carl Becker's Heavenly City Revisited*. Ithaca, N.Y.: Cornell Univ. Press, 1958.

ROWE, CONSTANCE. *Voltaire and the State*. New York: Columbia Univ. Press, 1955.

STEPHEN, LESLIE. *History of English Thought in the Eighteenth Century*. 3rd ed. New York: Harcourt, Brace & World (Harbinger Books), 1962. 2 vols.

VOLTAIRE. *Oeuvres Complètes*. Ed. by Louis Moland. Paris: Garnier, 1883–85. 52 vols.

———. *Philosophical Dictionary*. Sel. and ed. by H. I. Woolf. New York: Knopf, 1938.

———. *Selections*. Ed. by George R. Havens. New York: Century, 1925.

VYVERBERG, HENRY. *Historical Pessimism in the French Enlightenment*. Cambridge, Mass.: Harvard Univ. Press, 1958.

WILLEY, BASIL. *The Eighteenth-Century Background; Studies on the Idea of Nature in the Thought of the Period*. London: Chatto & Windus, 1940.

Economics and Politics

BEER, MAX. *An Inquiry into Physiocracy*. New York: Macmillan, 1940.

CROPSEY, JOSEPH. *Polity and Economy; An Interpretation of the Principles of Adam Smith*. The Hague: Nijhoff, 1957.

GINZBERG, ELI. *The House of Adam Smith*. New York: Columbia Univ. Press, 1934.

HEILBRONER, ROBERT L. *The Worldly Philosophers*. New York: Simon and Schuster, 1953, chs. 1–4.

HIGGS, HENRY. *The Physiocrats*. New York: Macmillan, 1897.

POLANYI, KARL. *The Great Transformation*. Boston: Beacon Press, 1957.

SCHUMPETER, JOSEPH A. *A History of Economic Analysis*. New York: Oxford Univ. Press, 1954, Part 2.

SMITH, ADAM. *Adam Smith's Moral and Political Philosophy*. Ed. by Herbert W. Schneider. New York: Hafner, 1948.

———. *An Inquiry into the Nature and Causes of the Wealth of Nations*. Ed. by E. B. Bax. London: Bell, 1896. 2 vols.

History and Politics

ADAMS, H. P. *The Life and Writings of Giambattista Vico*. London: Allen & Unwin, 1935.

BOLINGBROKE, LORD (HENRY ST. JOHN). *A Dissertation on Parties*. 10th ed. London: Davies and Cadell, 1775 (orig. ed., 1734).

———. *The Idea of a Patriot King* (1738). Ed. by Sydney W. Jackman. New York: Liberal Arts Press, 1965.

———. *Letters on the Study and Use of History*. 2nd ed. London: Cadell, 1770 (orig. ed., 1735).

CAPONIGRI, A. R. *Time and Idea; The Theory of History in Giambattista Vico*. Chicago: Regnery, 1953.

CONDORCET, MARQUIS DE (MARIE JEAN ANTOINE NICHOLAS DE CARITAT). *Outlines of an Historical View of the Progress of the Human Mind*. Philadelphia: Carey, Rice, Orwood, Bache, and Fellows, 1796.

CROCE, BENEDETTO. *The Philosophy of Giambattista Vico*. Tr. by R. G. Collingwood. New York: Macmillan, 1913.

PETRIE, CHARLES. *Bolingbroke*. London: Collins, 1937. A critical biography.

SCHAPIRO, J. SALWYN. *Condorcet and the Rise of Liberalism*. New York: Harcourt, Brace & World, 1934.

VICO, GIAMBATTISTA. *The New Science*. Tr. by Thomas G. Bergin and Max H. Fisch. Ithaca, N.Y.: Cornell Univ. Press, 1948. From 3rd ed. of 1744.

Law and Constitutionalism

ADAMS, JOHN. "A Defense of the Constitution." In *Works*. Ed. by Charles Francis Adams. Boston: Little, Brown, 1851. Vol. 6.

BECKER, CARL. *The Declaration of Independence: A Study in the History of Political Ideas*. New York: Random House (Vintage Books), 1957.

BLACKSTONE, WILLIAM. *Commentaries on the Laws of England*. Ed. by William G. Hammond. 8th ed. San Francisco: Whitney, 1890. Also Oxford: Clarendon Press, 1765–69. 4 vols.

BOORSTIN, DANIEL J. *The Mysterious Science of the Law; An Essay on Blackstone's Commentaries*. Boston: Beacon Press, 1958.

FARRAND, MAX, ed. *The Records of the Federal Convention of 1787*. New Haven, Conn.: Yale Univ. Press, 1911. 2 vols.

The Federalist. New York: Random House (Modern Library), 1937.

FRIEDRICH, CARL J. *The Philosophy of Law in Historical Perspective*. Chicago: Univ. of Chicago Press, 1958.

GOUGH, JOHN. *Fundamental Law in English Constitutional History*. Oxford: Clarendon Press, 1955.

HANDLER, EDWARD. *America and Europe in the Political Thought of John Adams*. Cambridge, Mass.: Harvard Univ. Press, 1964.

HARTZ, LOUIS. *The Liberal Tradition in America.* New York: Harcourt, Brace & World (Harvest Books), 1955.

LOCKMILLER, DAVID A. *Sir William Blackstone.* Chapel Hill: Univ. of North Carolina Press, 1938.

OTIS, JAMES. *Rights of British Colonies Asserted and Proved.* London: Williams, 1766.

WHITE, ANDREW DICKSON. *Seven Great Statesmen in the Warfare of Humanity with Unreason.* New York: Century, 1912. Ch. 3 is on Thomasius.

WILSON, JAMES. *Works.* Ed. by J. D. Andrews. Chicago: Callaghan, 1896. 2 vols.

Theory of Revolution

ACTON, LORD (JOHN E. E. D. ACTON). *Lectures on the French Revolution.* London: Macmillan, 1910.

BEST, M. A. *Thomas Paine; Prophet and Martyr of Democracy.* New York: Harcourt, Brace & World, 1927.

BRINTON, CRANE. *The Anatomy of Revolution.* New York: Norton, 1938.

CONWAY, M. C. *The Life of Thomas Paine.* New York: Putnam's, 1892. 2 vols.

JEFFERSON, THOMAS. *Life and Selected Writings.* Ed. by Adrienne Koch and William Peden. New York: Random House (Modern Library), 1944.

———. *Political Writings.* Ed. by Edward Dumbauld. New York: Liberal Arts Press, 1955.

PAINE, THOMAS. *The Complete Writings.* Ed. by Philip Foner. New York: Citadel Press, 1945. 2 vols.

TALMON, J. L. *The Origins of Totalitarian Democracy.* New York: Praeger, 1960.

WICKWAR, W. HARDY. *Baron d'Holbach: A Prelude to the French Revolution.* London: Allen & Unwin, 1935.

Chapter 14 MONTESQUIEU

Works by Montesquieu

Cahiers, 1716–1755. Ed. by Bernard Grasset. Paris: Grasset, 1941.

Considerations on the Causes of the Grandeur and the Decadence of the Romans. Tr. by Jehu Baker. New York: Appleton-Century-Crofts, 1894.

Oeuvres complètes. Ed. by Edouard Laboulaye. Paris: Garnier, 1875–79. 7 vols.

Persian and Chinese Letters. Tr. by John Davidson. New York: Dunne, 1901.

The Spirit of the Laws. Ed. by Franz Neumann. Tr. by Thomas Nugent. New York: Hafner, 1949. Many other editions.

Secondary Works

CABEEN, DAVID C. *Montesquieu Bibliography.* New York: New York Public Library, 1947. An extended and excellent annotated bibliography.

COURTNEY, CECIL PATRICK. *Montesquieu and Burke.* Oxford: Blackwell & Mott, 1963.

DEDIEU, JOSEPH. *Montesquieu; L'Homme et l'oeuvre* (1913). Paris: Boivin, 1943.

DURKHEIM, ÉMILE. *Montesquieu et Rousseau; Precurseurs de la sociologie.* Intro. by George Davy. Paris: Rivière, 1953. (Written 1892 and 1918.)

FAGUET, ÉMILE. *La Politique comparée de Montesquieu, Rousseau, et Voltaire.* Paris: Société d'Imprimerie et de Librairie, 1902.

GRANT, A. J. "Montesquieu." In F. J. C. Hearnshaw, ed., *The Social and Political Ideas of Some Great French Thinkers in the Age of Reason.* London: Harrap, 1930.

HOLMES, OLIVER WENDELL. "Montesquieu." In *Collected Legal Papers.* New York: Appleton-Century-Crofts, 1921.

LEVIN, LAWRENCE MEYER. *The Political Doctrine of Montesquieu's Esprit des Lois; Its Classical Background.* New York: The Institute of French Studies, 1936.

SHACKLETON, ROBERT. *Montesquieu: A Critical Biography.* London: Oxford Univ. Press, 1961.

STARK, W. *Montesquieu: Pioneer of the Sociology of Knowledge.* Toronto: Univ. of Toronto Press, 1961.

TEBERT, COURTNEY. *Montesquieu.* Oxford: Clarendon Press, 1904.

VAUGHN, C. E. *Studies in the History of Political Philosophy Before and After Rousseau.* Manchester, Eng.: Univ. of Manchester Press, 1939. 2 vols. Vol. 1, pp. 253–302.

Chapter 15 ROUSSEAU

Works by Rousseau

The Confessions. Tr. by Edmund Wilson. New York: Knopf, 1923. 2 vols. Many other editions.

Émile. Tr. by Barbara Foxley. New York: Dutton (Everyman's Library), 1948.

The First and Second Discourses. Ed. by Roger D. Masters and Judith R. Masters. New York: St. Martin's Press, 1964.

Oeuvres complètes. Paris: Hachette, 1886–1911. 13 vols.

The Political Writings of Jean-Jacques Rousseau. Ed. by C. E. Vaughn. New York: Wiley, 1962 (orig. ed., 1915). 2 vols. Note Vaughn's introduction.

Rousseau; Political Writings. Tr. by Frederick W. Watkins. London: Nelson, 1953.

The Social Contract and Discourses. Tr. by G. D. H. Cole. New York: Dutton (Everyman's Library), 1950. Note Cole's introduction.

The Social Contract. Ed. by Charles Frankel. New York: Hafner, 1947. An eighteenth-century translation revised by Frankel.

Secondary Works

Babbitt, Irving. *Rousseau and Romanticism.* Boston: Houghton Mifflin, 1919; New York: World (Meridian Books), 1955.

Broome, J. H. *Rousseau; A Study of His Thought.* London: Arnold, 1963.

Cassirer, Ernst. *The Question of Jean-Jacques Rousseau.* Trans., ed., and intro. by Peter Gay. New York: Columbia Univ. Press, 1954.

———. *Rousseau, Kant, and Goethe.* Princeton, N.J.: Princeton Univ. Press, 1945.

Chapman, John W. *Rousseau—Totalitarian or Liberal?* New York: Columbia Univ. Press, 1956.

Cobban, Alfred. *Rousseau and the Modern State.* Hamden, Conn.: Shoe String Press (Archon Books), 1961.

Derathé, Robert. *Jean-Jacques Rousseau et la science politique de son temps.* Paris: Presses Universitaires de France, 1950.

———. *Le Rationalisme de Jean-Jacques Rousseau.* Paris: Presses Universitaires de France, 1948.

Green, F. C. *Jean-Jacques Rousseau; A Critical Study of His Life and Writings.* London: Cambridge Univ. Press, 1955.

Grimsley, Ronald. *Jean-Jacques Rousseau; A Study of Self-Awareness.* Cardiff, Wales: Univ. of Wales Press, 1961.

Hendel, Charles W. *Jean-Jacques Rousseau, Moralist.* London: Oxford Univ. Press, 1934. 2 vols.

Høffding, Harald. *Jean-Jacques Rousseau and His Philosophy.* Tr. by William Richards and Leo Saidla. New Haven, Conn.: Yale Univ. Press, 1930.

McDonald, Joan. *Rousseau and the French Revolution, 1762–1791.* London: Athlone Press, 1965.

Morley, John. *Rousseau.* London: Macmillan, 1905. 2 vols.

Osborne, Annie M. *Rousseau and Burke.* London: Oxford Univ. Press, 1940.

Schinz, Albert. *La Pensée de Jean-Jacques Rousseau.* Northampton, Mass.: Smith College, 1929.

Starobinski, Jean. *Jean-Jacques Rousseau: La Transparence et l'obstacle.* Paris: Librairie Plon, 1957.

Wright, Ernest Hunter. *The Meaning of Rousseau.* London: Oxford Univ. Press, 1929.

Chapter 16 HUME

Works by Hume

David Hume's Political Essays. Ed. by Charles W. Hendel. New York: Liberal Arts Press, 1953. From the 1777 edition of *Essays, Moral and Political.*

Dialogues Concerning Natural Religion. Ed. by Norman Kemp Smith. 2nd ed. London: Nelson, 1947.

An Enquiry Concerning Human Understanding. Ed. by L. A. Selby-Bigge. Oxford: Clarendon Press, 1894. From the 1777 edition.

Essays and Treatises on Several Subjects. Edinburgh: Bell and Bradfate, 1800. 2 vols. Vol. 1 is *Essays, Moral, Political, and Literary.* Vol. 2 contains, among other works, *An Enquiry Concerning the Principles of Morals* and *The Natural History of Religion.*

The History of England from the Invasion of Julius Caesar to the Revolution of 1688. London: Cadell and Davies, 1802 (orig. ed., 1754–62). 8 vols.

The History of England from the Revolution to the Death of George II. Ed. by T. G. Smollett. London: Cadell and Baldwin, 1804. 5 vols.

Hume; Theory of Politics. Ed. by Frederick Watkins. Austin: Univ. of Texas, 1953. Note Watkins' introduction.

Moral and Political Philosophy. Ed. by Henry Aiken. New York: Hafner, 1948.

Treatise of Human Nature. Ed. by L. A. Selby-Bigge. Oxford: Clarendon Press, 1896.

Secondary Works

Bongie, Laurence L. *David Hume: Prophet of the Counter-Revolution.* Oxford: Clarendon Press, 1965.

Bryson, Gladys. *Man and Society; The Scottish Inquiry of the Eighteenth Century.* Princeton, N.J.: Princeton Univ. Press, 1945.

Huxley, Thomas. *Hume.* London: Macmillan, 1881.

Kydd, Rachel M. *Reason and Conduct in Hume's Treatise.* London: Oxford Univ. Press, 1946.

Laing, B. M. *David Hume.* London: Benn, 1932.

Laird, John. *Hume's Philosophy of Human Nature.* London: Methuen, 1932.

LETWIN, SHIRLEY R. *The Pursuit of Certainty: David Hume, Jeremy Bentham, John Stuart Mill, Beatrice Webb.* London: Cambridge Univ. Press, 1965.

MOSSNER, ERNEST C. *The Life of David Hume.* Austin: Univ. of Texas, 1954.

ROSS, WILLIAM G. *Human Nature and Utility in Hume's Social Philosophy.* Berea, Ky.: published by the author, 1942.

SMITH, NORMAN KEMP. *The Philosophy of David Hume.* London: Macmillan, 1941.

STEWART, JOHN B. *The Moral and Political Philosophy of David Hume.* New York: Columbia Univ. Press, 1963.

Chapter 17 BURKE

Works by Burke

Appeal from the New to the Old Whigs. Ed. by John M. Robson. New York: Liberal Arts Press, 1962.

Burke's Politics. Ed. by Ross Hoffman and S. J. Levack. New York: Knopf, 1949.

The Philosophy of Edmund Burke; A Selection from His Speeches and Writings. Ed. by L. I. Bredvold and R. G. Ross. Ann Arbor: Univ. of Michigan Press, 1961.

Reflections on the Revolution in France. Ed. by Russell Kirk. Chicago: Regnery, 1955.

Selected Writings of Edmund Burke. Ed. by Walter J. Bate. New York: Random House (Modern Library), 1960. *Appeal from the New to the Old Whigs* is a conspicuous omission from this collection.

Selected Writings and Speeches. Ed. by Peter J. Stanlis. Garden City, N.Y.: Doubleday (Anchor Books), 1963.

The Writings and Speeches of Edmund Burke. Boston: Little, Brown, 1901. 12 vols.

Secondary Works

CANAVAN, FRANCIS. *The Political Reason of Edmund Burke.* Durham, N.C.: Duke Univ. Press, 1960.

COBBAN, ALFRED. *Edmund Burke and the Revolt Against the Eighteenth Century.* New York: Macmillan, 1929.

COPELAND, THOMAS W. *Edmund Burke; Six Essays.* London: Cape, 1950.

HARRIS, RONALD W. *Political Ideas, 1760–1772.* London: Gollancz, 1963.

KIRK, RUSSELL. *The Conservative Mind; From Burke to Santayana.* Chicago: Regnery, 1953.

LASKI, HAROLD J. *Political Thought in England; Locke to Bentham.* London: Hutchinson, 1937, ch. 6.

MACCUNN, JOHN. *The Political Philosophy of Burke.* London: Longmans, Green, 1913.

MANSFIELD, HARVEY C., JR. *Statesmanship and Party Government; A Study of Burke and Bolingbroke.* Chicago: Univ. of Chicago Press, 1965.

MURRAY, ROBERT H. *Edmund Burke; A Biography.* Oxford, Clarendon Press, 1931.

PARKIN, CHARLES. *The Moral Basis of Burke's Political Thought; An Essay.* London: Cambridge Univ. Press, 1956.

STANLIS, PETER J. *Edmund Burke and the Natural Law.* Ann Arbor: Univ. of Michigan Press, 1958.

Chapter 18 THE NINETEENTH CENTURY

General

BARKER, ERNEST. *Political Thought in England, 1848–1914.* 2nd ed. London: Oxford Univ. Press (Home University Library), 1928.

BOWLE, JOHN. *Politics and Opinion in the Nineteenth Century.* New York: Oxford Univ. Press (Galaxy Books), 1964. See bibliography, pp. 500–02.

BRINTON, CRANE. *English Political Thought in the Nineteenth Century.* Cambridge, Mass.: Harvard Univ. Press, 1933.

FAGUET, ÉMILE. *Politiques et moralistes du dix-neuvième siècle.* Paris: Boivin, 1899. 3 vols.

HEARNSHAW, F. J. C., ed. *Essays in the Social and Political Ideas of the Age of Reaction and Reconstruction.* London: Harrap, 1932.

———, ed. *Social and Political Ideas of the Victorian Age.* London: Harrap, 1933.

KRIEGER, LEONARD. *The German Idea of Freedom.* Boston: Beacon Press, 1957. See bibliography, pp. 529–33.

LÖWITH, KARL. *From Hegel to Nietzsche.* Tr. by David E. Green. New York: Holt, Rinehart and Winston, 1964.

MAYER, J. P. *Political Thought in France from Sieyès to Sorel.* London: Faber & Faber, 1948.

MURRAY, R. H., ed. *Studies in English Social and Political Thinkers of the Nineteenth Century.* Heffer, 1929. 2 vols. Vol. 1 contains selections from Malthus, Bentham, James Mill, John Stuart Mill, Owen, Coleridge, Disraeli, Carlyle, Cobden, and Kingsley. Vol. 2 contains selections from Spencer, Maine, Ruskin, Arnold, Seeley, Bagehot, Green, Bryce, Maitland, and assorted socialists.

REISS, H. S., ed. *The Political Thought of the German Romantics, 1793–1815.* Oxford: Blackwell & Mott, 1955. Selections from Fichte, Novalis, Müller, Schleiermacher, Savigny.

RUGGIERO, GUIDO DE. *A History of European Liberalism.* Tr. by R. G. Collingwood. London: Oxford Univ. Press, 1927; Boston: Beacon Press, 1959. See bibliography.

SCHAPIRO, J. SALWYN. *Liberalism and the Challenge of Fascism; Social Forces in England and France, 1815–1870.* New York: McGraw-Hill, 1949. See bibliography, pp. 405–13.

SOLTAU, ROGER. *French Political Thought in the Nineteenth Century.* New Haven, Conn.: Yale Univ. Press, 1931.

English Utilitarianism [See also the bibliography for Chapter 19, "Bentham."]

AUSCHUTZ, R. P. *The Philosophy of John Stuart Mill.* Oxford: Clarendon Press, 1953.

AUSTIN, JOHN. *Austinian Theory of Law.* Ed. by W. Jethro Brown. London: Murray, 1906.

———. *The Province of Jurisprudence Determined; and, The Uses of the Study of Jurisprudence.* Ed. by H. L. A. Hart. London: Weidenfeld & Nicolson, 1954.

BRITTON, KARL. *John Stuart Mill.* Harmondsworth, Eng.: Penguin Books, 1953.

BULLOCK, ALAN, AND MAURICE SHOCK. *The Liberal Tradition: Fox to Keynes.* London: Oxford Univ. Press (Galaxy Books), 1967.

COWLING, MAURICE. *Mill and Liberalism.* New York: Cambridge Univ. Press, 1964.

HAMBURGER, JOSEPH. *Intellectuals in Politics: John Stuart Mill and the Philosophical Radicals.* New Haven, Conn.: Yale Univ. Press, 1965.

MILL, JAMES. *Essays on Government, Jurisprudence, Liberty of the Press, and Law of Nations.* Ed. by Philip Wheelwright. (Doran Series.) Garden City, N.Y.: Doubleday, Doran, 1935. Bound with works by Bentham and John Stuart Mill.

MILL, JOHN STUART. *Disquisitions and Discussions.* London: Longmans, Green, 1859–75. 4 vols.

———. *Essays on Politics and Culture.* Garden City, N.Y.: Doubleday, 1963.

———. *A Selection of His Works.* Ed. by John M. Robson. New York: St. Martin's Press, 1966.

———. *A System of Logic.* 8th ed. London: Longmans, Green, 1925, Book 6.

———. *Utilitarianism, Liberty, and Representative Government.* New York, Dutton (Everyman's Library), 1951. Many other editions.

Continental Liberalism

BASTID, PAUL. *Benjamin Constant et sa doctrine.* Paris: Colin, 1966. 2 vols.

CONSTANT, BENJAMIN. *Principes de politique,* in *Oeuvres.* Ed. by Alfred Roulin. Paris: Gallimard, 1957, pp. 1099–1249.

DE TOCQUEVILLE, ALEXIS. *Democracy in America.* Ed. by H. S. Commager. Tr. by Henry Reeve. London: Oxford Univ. Press, 1946. Many other editions.

———. *The Old Regime and the French Revolution.* Tr. by Stuart Gilbert. Garden City, N.Y.: Doubleday (Anchor Books), 1955. From 4th French ed. (1858).

GUIZOT, FRANÇOIS. *Democracy in France.* New York: Appleton-Century-Crofts, 1849.

HERR, RICHARD. *Tocqueville and the Old Regime.* Princeton, N.J.: Princeton Univ. Press, 1962.

LIVELY, JACK. *The Social and Political Thought of Alexis de Tocqueville.* London: Oxford Univ. Press, 1962.

MAZZINI, JOSEPH. *The Duties of Man and Other Essays.* New York: Dutton (Everyman's Library), 1929.

ROYER-COLLARD, PIERRE PAUL. *Les Fragments philosophiques.* Intro. by André Schimberg. Paris: Alcan, 1913.

SCHERMERHORN, ELIZABETH W. *Benjamin Constant.* London: Heinemann, 1924.

TALMON, J. L. *Political Messianism: The Romantic Phase.* New York: Praeger, 1961.

VON TREITSCHKE, HENRICH. *Politics.* Tr. by Blanche Dugdale and T. de Bille. New York: Macmillan, 1916. 2 vols.

Social Darwinism

BAGEHOT, WALTER. *Physics and Politics.* New York: Appleton-Century-Crofts, 1873.

DEWEY, JOHN. *The Influence of Darwin on Philosophy.* New York: Holt, Rinehart and Winston, 1910.

HOBHOUSE, LEONARD. *Social Evolution and Political Theory.* New York: Columbia Univ. Press, 1911.

HOFSTADTER, RICHARD. *Social Darwinism in American Thought.* Philadelphia: Univ. of Pennsylvania Press, 1944; Boston: Beacon, 1955. See bibliography.

RITCHIE, DAVID G. *Darwinism and Politics.* London: Sonnenschein, 1889.

RUMNEY, JUDAH. *Herbert Spencer's Sociology*. London: Williams and Norgate, 1934.

SPENCER, HERBERT. *First Principles*. New York: Appleton-Century-Crofts, 1864.

———. *The Man Versus the State*. Caldwell, Ida.: Caxton, 1940.

———. *Social Statics*. New York: Appleton-Century-Crofts, 1864.

STARR, HARRIS. *William Graham Sumner*. New York: Holt, Rinehart and Winston, 1925.

SUMNER, WILLIAM GRAHAM. *The Challenge of Facts and Other Essays*. New Haven, Conn.: Yale Univ. Press, 1914.

———. *Essays*. Ed. by A. G. Keller and M. R. Davie. New Haven, Conn.: Yale Univ. Press, 1934. 2 vols.

Conservatism [See also the bibliography for Chapter 20, "Hegel."]

BERLIN, ISAIAH. *The Hedgehog and the Fox; An Essay on Tolstoy's View of History*. New York: Simon and Schuster, 1953. Relates De Maistre to Stendahl and Tolstoy.

CAIRD, EDWARD. *The Social Philosophy and Religion of Comte*. London: Macmillan, 1885.

COMTE, AUGUSTE. *A General View of Positivism* (1848). Tr. by J. H. Bridges. Stanford, Cal.: Academic Reprints, n. d.

DE BONALD, LOUIS. *Legislation primitive*. 5th ed. Paris: Le Clere, 1857.

DEMAISTRE, JOSEPH. *The Works of Joseph deMaistre*. Ed. by Jack Lively. New York: Macmillan, 1965.

———. *On God and Society*. Tr. by Elisha Greifer. Chicago: Regnery (Gateway Editions), 1959.

FICHTE, JOHANN G. *Addresses to the German Nation*. Tr. by R. F. Jones and G. F. Turnbull. LaSalle, Ill.: Open Court, 1922.

GIANTURCO, ELIO. *Joseph de Maistre and Giambattista Vico*. Washington, D.C.: published by the author, 1937.

LASKI, HAROLD J. *Authority in the Modern State*. New Haven, Conn.: Yale Univ. Press, 1919, ch. 1.

MILL, JOHN STUART. *Auguste Comte and Positivism*. 3rd ed. London: Turner, 1882.

British Idealism

BOSANQUET, BERNARD. *Philosophical Theory of the State*. 4th ed. London: Macmillan, 1923.

BRADLEY, F. H. *Ethical Studies; Selected Studies*. Intro. by Ralph Ross. New York: Liberal Arts Press, 1951 (orig. ed., 1876).

GREEN, THOMAS HILL. *Lectures on the Principles of Political Obligation* (1879). Intro. by A. D. Lindsay. London: Longmans, Green, 1941.

———. *The Political Theory of T. H. Green*. Ed. by John R. Rodman. New York: Appleton-Century-Crofts, 1964.

HOBHOUSE, LEONARD. *The Metaphysical Theory of the State*. London: Allen & Unwin, 1918.

RICHTER, MELVIN. *The Politics of Conscience: T. H. Green and His Age*. Cambridge, Mass.: Harvard Univ. Press, 1964.

RITCHIE, DAVID G. *Natural Rights*. London: Allen & Unwin, 1894.

Elitism

CARLYLE, THOMAS. *Critical and Miscellaneous Essays*. 2nd ed. New York: Appleton-Century-Crofts, 1871.

———. *Heroes, Hero-Worship, and the Heroic in History*. New York: Burt, n. d. (orig. ed., 1841).

CASSIRER, ERNST. *The Myth of the State*. New Haven, Conn.: Yale Univ. Press, 1946, 1960. Ch. 15 is on Carlyle.

CHAMBERLAIN, HOUSTON STEWART. *The Foundations of the Nineteenth Century*. Tr. by John Lees. London: Lane, 1911. 2 vols.

DE GOBINEAU, ARTHUR. *The Inequality of Human Races*. Tr. by Adrian Collins. New York: Putnam's, 1915.

LIPPINCOTT, BENJAMIN E. *Victorian Critics of Democracy*. Minneapolis: Univ. of Minnesota Press, 1938. On Carlyle, Ruskin, Arnold, Stephen, Maine, and Lecky.

ROE, FREDERICK WILLIAM. *The Social Philosophy of Carlyle and Ruskin*. New York: Harcourt, Brace & World, 1921.

RUSKIN, JOHN. *The Seven Lamps of Architecture, Sesame and Lilies, Unto This Last*. Sterling ed. Boston: Estes, n. d.

Socialism and Anarchism [See also the bibliographies for Chapter 21, "Marx," and Chapter 24, "Lenin."]

AURICH, PAUL. *The Russian Anarchists*. Princeton, N.J.: Princeton Univ. Press, 1967.

BAKUNIN, MICHAEL. *Marxism, Freedom, and the State*. Tr. and ed. by K. J. Kenafick. London: Freedom, 1950.

———. *The Political Philosophy of Bakunin*. Ed. by G. P. Maxinoff. New York: Free Press, 1964.

BELLAMY, EDWARD. *Looking Backward* (1887). Memorial ed. Boston: Houghton Mifflin, 1898. Many other editions.

BERNERI, MARIE LOUISE. *Journey Through Utopia.* London: Routledge & Kegan Paul, 1950. See bibliography, pp. 320–29.

BRISBANE, ALBERT. *The Social Destiny of Man.* Philadelphia: Stollmeyer, 1840. By Fourier's chief American disciple.

BROGAN, DENIS W. *Proud'hon.* London: Hamilton, 1934.

BUBER, MARTIN. *Paths in Utopia.* Tr. by R. F. C. Hull. Boston: Beacon Press, 1960.

CARR, E. H. *Michael Bakunin.* London: Macmillan, 1937.

COLE, G. D. H. *A History of Socialist Thought.* London: Macmillan, 1953–60. 5 vols. A monumental work covering the period from 1789 to 1939. See the bibliographies in each volume.

———. *Robert Owen.* London: Benn, 1925.

COLE, MARGARET. *The Story of Fabian Socialism.* Stanford, Cal.: Stanford Univ. Press, 1962.

FOURIER, CHARLES. *Selections from the Works of Fourier.* Tr. by Julia Franklin. London: Swan, Sonnenschein, 1901.

GEORGE, HENRY. *Progress and Poverty* (1881). New York: Vanguard, 1929.

JAURÈS, JEAN, ed. *Histoire socialiste, 1789–1900.* Paris: Rouff, 1901–08. 4 vols.

KROPOTKIN, PETER. *Mutual Aid.* Rev. ed. London: Heinemann, 1904.

LLOYD, HENRY DEMAREST. *Wealth Against Commonwealth.* New York: Harper & Row, 1894.

MANUEL, FRANK E. *The New World of Henri Saint-Simon.* Cambridge, Mass.: Harvard Univ. Press, 1956.

———. *The Prophets of Paris: Turgot, Condorcet, Saint-Simon, Fourier, and Comte.* New York: Harper & Row (Torchbooks), 1965.

OWEN, ROBERT. *Book of the New Moral World.* London: Wilson, 1836.

———. *A New View of Society and Other Writings* (1813). New York: Dutton (Everyman's Library), 1927.

PROUDHON, PIERRE JOSEPH. *What Is Property?* Tr. by Benjamin R. Tucker. New York: Humboldt, 1876.

SAINT-SIMON, COMTE DE (CLAUDE DE ROUVROY). *Social Organization, The Science of Man, and Other Writings.* Ed. and tr. by Felix Markham. New York: Harper & Row (Torchbooks), 1966.

SCHAPIRO, J. SALWYN, ed. *Movements of Social Dissent in Modern Europe.* Princeton, N.J.: Van Nostrand (Anvil Books), 1962.

WILSON, EDMUND. *To the Finland Station; A Study on the Writing and Acting of History.* Garden City, N.Y.: Doubleday (Anchor Books), 1959, Part 2, chs. 1–4.

WOODCOCK, GEORGE. *Pierre-Joseph Proud'hon.* London: Routledge & Kegan Paul, 1956.

Chapter 19 BENTHAM

Works by Bentham

A Fragment on Government. Ed. by F. C. Montague. Oxford: Clarendon Press, 1891.

A Fragment on Government and Introduction to the Principles of Morals and Legislation. Ed. by Wilfred Harrison. Oxford: Blackwell & Mott, 1948.

Handbook of Political Fallacies. Ed. by Harold A. Larrabee. New York: Harper & Row (Torchbooks), 1962.

Introduction to the Principles of Morals and Legislation. Oxford: Clarendon Press, 1879. New ed., 1907.

Introduction to the Principles of Morals and Legislation. Ed. by Lawrence J. Lafleur. New York: Hafner, 1948.

Theory of Legislation. Ed. by C. K. Ogden. London: Routledge & Kegan Paul, 1950.

The Works of Jeremy Bentham. Ed. by John Bowring. Edinburgh: Tait, 1838–42. 22 vols.

Secondary Works

ALBEE, ERNEST. *A History of English Utilitarianism.* London: Swan, Sonnenschein, 1900.

BAUMGART, DAVID. *Bentham and the Ethics of Today.* Princeton, N.J.: Princeton Univ. Press, 1952.

DAVIDSON, WILLIAM L. *Political Thought in England; The Utilitarians from Bentham to J. S. Mill.* New York: Oxford Univ. Press, 1950.

EVERETT, CHARLES W. *The Education of Jeremy Bentham.* New York: Columbia Univ. Press, 1931.

HALÉVY, ELIE. *The Growth of Philosophic Radicalism.* Tr. by Mary Morris. Boston: Beacon Press, 1955. See bibliography, pp. 522–46.

KEETON, G. W., AND GEORGE SCHWARZENBERGER, eds. *Jeremy Bentham and the Law.* London: Stevens, 1948.

LEAVIS, F. R., ed. *Mill on Bentham and Coleridge.* London: Chatto & Windus, 1950.

MACK, MARY P. *Jeremy Bentham: An Odyssey of Ideas.* New York: Columbia Univ. Press, 1963.

OGDEN, C. K. *Bentham's Theory of Fictions.* New York: Harcourt, Brace & World, 1932.

PLAMENATZ, JOHN. *The English Utilitarians.* London: Oxford Univ. Press, 1949.

STEPHEN, LESLIE. *The English Utilitarians.* London: Duckworth, 1900. 3 vols. Vol. 1 is on Bentham.

Chapter 20 HEGEL

Works by Hegel

Early Theological Writings. Tr. by T. M. Knox. Chicago: Univ. of Chicago Press, 1948. Reprinted as *On Christianity.* New York: Harper & Row (Torchbooks), 1961. In the latter see Richard Kroner's introduction, pp. 1–66.

Hegel's Political Writings. Tr. by T. M. Knox. Intro. by Z. Pelczynski. London: Oxford Univ. Press, 1964.

Phenomenology of Mind. Tr. by J. B. Baillie. 2nd ed. rev. London: Allen & Unwin, 1961.

The Philosophy of Hegel. Ed. by Carl J. Friedrich. New York: Random House (Modern Library), 1954.

Philosophy of History. Tr. by J. Sibree. London: Bell, 1905; New York: Dover, 1955.

Philosophy of Right. Tr. by T. M. Knox. Oxford: Clarendon Press, 1942; Corrected eds., 1945, 1949, 1953.

Reason in History. Tr. by R. S. Hartman. New York: Liberal Arts Press, 1953. Contains introduction to *Philosophy of History.*

Sämtliche Werke. Vols. 1–27. ed. by G. Lasson. Vols. 28–30 ed. by J. Hoffmeister. Vols. 1–26, Leipzig, 1923–32; Vol. 27, Hamburg, n.d.; Vols. 28–30, Hamburg, 1952–58. All published by Meiner. A critical edition, the best of several collected works. 35 vols. projected.

Selections. Ed. by J. Loewenberg. Rev. ed. New York: Wiley, 1944.

Secondary Works

CAIRD, EDWARD. *Hegel.* Edinburgh: Blackwood, 1883.

CROCE, BENEDETTO. *What Is Living and What Is Dead in Hegel's Philosophy?* Tr. by D. Ainslie. London: Macmillan, 1915 (orig. Italian ed., 1906).

FINDLAY, JOHN N. *Hegel: A Re-examination.* New York: Macmillan (Collier Books), 1962.

FOSTER, MICHAEL B. *The Political Philosophies of Plato and Hegel.* Oxford: Clarendon Press, 1935.

KAUFMANN, WALTER. *Hegel: A Reinterpretation.* Garden City, N.Y.: Doubleday (Anchor Books), 1966.

LOEWENBERG, JACOB. *Hegel's Phenomenology: Dialogues on the Life of the Mind.* LaSalle, Ill.: Open Court, 1965.

MARCUSE, HERBERT. *Reason and Revolution; Hegel and the Rise of Social Theory.* Boston: Beacon Press, 1960.

MURE, G. R. G. *An Introduction to Hegel.* Oxford: Clarendon Press, 1940.

REYBURN, HUGH A. *The Ethical Theory of Hegel; A Study of the Philosophy of Right.* Oxford: Clarendon Press, 1921.

ROSENZWEIG, FRANZ. *Hegel und der Staat.* Munich: Oldenbourg, 1920. 2 vols.

STACE, W. T. *The Philosophy of Hegel.* New York: Dover, 1955.

TRAVIS, D. C., ed. *A Hegel Symposium.* Austin: Univ. of Texas Press, 1962.

WEIL, ERIC. *Hegel et l'état.* Paris: Vrin, 1950.

Chapter 21 MARX

Primary Works

ENGELS, FRIEDRICH. *Herr Eugen Dühring's Revolution in Science* [*Anti-Dühring*] (1877–78). London: Lawrence & Wishart, 1894. Three chapters of *Anti-Dühring* were published separately as *Socialism, Utopian and Scientific* in 1880 and subsequently. See Edward Aveling's tr. Chicago: Kerr, 1902.

———. *The Origin of the Family, Private Property, and the State* (1884). Tr. by Ernest Untermann. Chicago: Kerr, 1902.

Handbook of Marxism. Ed. by Emile Burns. New York: Random House, 1935.

MARX, KARL. *Capital* (1867–94). Tr. by Samuel Moore and Edward Aveling. Chicago: Kerr, 1904–09. 3 vols.

———. *The Civil War in France* (1871). Intro. by Friedrich Engels. New York: International Publishers, 1933.

———. *A Critique of the Gotha Program* (1891). Ed. by C. P. Dutt. New York: International Publishers, 1933.

———. *Critique of Political Economy* (1859). Tr. by N. I. Stone. Chicago: Kerr, 1904. From the 2nd German ed.

———. *Early Writings.* Ed. and tr. by T. B. Bottomore. New York: McGraw-Hill, 1964.

———. *The Poverty of Philosophy* (1847). Tr. by H. Quelch. Chicago: Kerr, 1920.

———, AND FRIEDRICH ENGELS. *Basic Writings on Politics and Philosophy.* Ed. by Lewis S. Feuer. Garden City, N.Y.: Doubleday (Anchor Books), 1959.

———. *The Communist Manifesto.* Tr. by Eden Paul and Cedar Paul. New York: International Publishers, 1930.

———. *The Communist Manifesto, with Selections from the Eighteenth Brumaire of Louis Napoleon.* Ed. by Samuel Beer. New York: Appleton-Century-Crofts, 1955. There are countless editions of the Manifesto.

———. *Selected Works of Marx and Engels.* Ed. by C. P. Dutt. New York: International Publishers, 1936. 2 vols.

Marx on Economics. Ed. by Robert Freedman. New York: Harcourt, Brace & World (Harvest Books), 1961.

Writings of the Young Marx on Philosophy and Society. Ed. and tr. by Loyd D. Easton and Kurt H. Guddat. Garden City, N.Y.: Doubleday (Anchor Books), 1967.

Secondary Works

BERLIN, ISAIAH. *Karl Marx; His Life and Environment.* 2nd ed. New York: Oxford Univ. Press, 1948 (Galaxy Books, 1959). See bibliography.

BÖHM VON BAWERK, E. *Karl Marx and the Close of His System.* Ed. by Paul M. Sweezy. New York: Kelley, 1949.

BOBER, M. M. *Karl Marx's Interpretation of History.* Rev. ed. Cambridge, Mass.: Harvard Univ. Press, 1948.

CARR, E. H. *Karl Marx; A Study in Fanaticism.* London: Dent, 1935.

CROCE, BENEDETTO. *Historical Materialism and the Economics of Karl Marx.* Tr. by C. M. Meredith. London: Allen & Unwin, 1922.

FROMM, ERICH. *Marx's Concept of Man.* New York: Ungar, 1961.

HOOK, SIDNEY. *From Hegel to Marx.* Ann Arbor: Univ. of Michigan Press, 1962.

HUNT, R. N. CAREW. *The Theory and Practice of Communism.* 5th ed. New York: Macmillan, 1957.

KAUTSKY, KARL. *The Economic Doctrines of Karl Marx.* London: Black, 1925.

LICHTHEIM, GEORGE. *Marxism; An Historical and Critical Study.* New York: Praeger, 1964.

LINDSAY, A. D. *Karl Marx's Capital: An Introductory Essay.* 2nd ed. London: Oxford Univ. Press, 1947 (orig. ed., 1925).

MAYO, HENRY B. *Introduction to Marxist Theory.* New York: Oxford Univ. Press, 1960. Note Mayo's excellent bibliography, pp. 310–25.

MEYER, ALFRED G. *Marxism.* Cambridge, Mass.: Harvard Univ. Press, 1954.

SCHUMPETER, JOSEPH A. *Capitalism, Socialism, Democracy.* 3rd ed. New York: Harper & Row, 1950, Part 2.

TUCKER, ROBERT M. *Philosophy and Myth in Karl Marx.* London: Cambridge Univ. Press, 1961.

WILSON, EDMUND. *To the Finland Station; A Study in the Writing and Acting of History.* New York: Harcourt, Brace & World, 1940; Garden City, N.Y.: Doubleday (Anchor Books), 1959.

WOLFE, BERTRAM D. *Marxism: One Hundred Years in the Life of a Doctrine.* New York: Dial Press, 1965.

Chapter 22 NIETZSCHE

See Herbert Reichert and Karl Schlechta, eds., *International Nietzsche Bibliography.* Chapel Hill: Univ. of North Carolina Press, 1960.

Works by Nietzsche

Beyond Good and Evil. Tr. by Helen Zimmern. New York: Boni and Liveright, 1917; tr. by Marianne Cowan. Chicago: Regnery, 1955.

The Birth of Tragedy; and The Genealogy of Morals. Tr. by Francis Golffing. Garden City, N.Y.: Doubleday (Anchor Books), 1956.

Complete Works. Tr. by Oscar Levy. New York: Macmillan, 1924. 18 vols.

The Genealogy of Morals; A Polemic. Tr. by Horace B. Samuel. New York: Macmillan, 1924.

The Joyful Wisdom. Tr. by Thomas Common. 2nd ed. London: Foulis, 1918.

The Philosophy of Nietzsche. New York: Random House (Modern Library), 1937.

The Portable Nietzsche. Ed. by W. Kaufmann. New York: Viking Press, 1954.

Thus Spake Zarathustra. Tr. by Thomas Common. New York: Macmillan, 1911; New York: Random House (Modern Library), n. d.

The Use and Abuse of History. Tr. by Adrian Collins. New York: Liberal Arts Press, 1949.

Werke. Leipzig: Naumann, 1899–1904. 15 vols.

The Will to Power. Tr. by Anthony M. Ludovici. Edinburgh: Foulis, 1910.

Secondary Works

BRINTON, CRANE. *Nietzsche.* Cambridge, Mass.: Harvard Univ. Press, 1941.

DANTO, ARTHUR C. *Nietzsche as a Philosopher.* New York: Macmillan, 1965.

JASPERS, KARL. *Nietzsche: An Introduction to the Understanding of His Philosophical Activity.* Tr. by C. F. Wallraff and F. J. Schmitz. Tucson: Univ. of Arizona Press, 1965.

KAUFMANN, WALTER A. *Nietzsche; Philosopher, Psychologist, Anti-Christ.* Princeton, N.J.: Princeton Univ. Press, 1950. See bibliography, pp. 383–95.

LEA, FRANK A. *The Tragic Philosopher; A Study of Friedrich Nietzsche.* New York: Philosophical Library, 1957.

MENCKEN, H. L. *The Philosophy of Friedrich Nietzsche.* 3rd ed. Boston: Luce, 1913.

MORE, PAUL ELMER. *Nietzsche.* Boston: Houghton Mifflin, 1912.

MORGAN, GEORGE ALLEN, JR. *What Nietzsche Means.* New York: Harper & Row, 1965.

REYBURN, HUGH A. *Nietzsche; The Story of a Human Philosopher.* London: Macmillan, 1948.

Chapter 23 THE TWENTIETH CENTURY

The multiplicity of books and the uncertainty of criteria of importance make this selection even more arbitrary than the selections for other chapters. For more extended bibliographies see Christian Bay, *The Structure of Freedom* (Stanford, Cal.: Stanford Univ. Press, 1958), pp. 391–408; Arnold Brecht, *Political Theory* (Princeton, N.J.: Princeton Univ. Press, 1959), pp. 499–574; Albert R. Chandler, ed., *The Clash of Political Ideals,* 3rd ed. (New York: Appleton-Century-Crofts, 1957), pp. 334–74; Henry S. Kariel, *In Search of Authority: Twentieth-Century Political Thought* (New York: Free Press, 1964), *passim;* William Kornhauser, *The Politics of Mass Society* (New York: Free Press, 1959), pp. 239–47; and J. Roland Pennock, *Liberal Democracy* (New York: Holt, Rinehart and Winston, 1950), pp. 373–94.

Totalitarianism

ARENDT, HANNAH. *The Origins of Totalitarianism.* New York: Harcourt, Brace & World, 1951; rev. and exp. ed., New York: World (Meridian Books), 1958.

CARSTEIN, F. L. *The Rise of Fascism.* Berkeley: Univ. of California Press, 1967.

EBENSTEIN, WILLIAM. *Totalitarianism: New Perspectives.* New York: Holt, Rinehart and Winston, 1962.

FRIEDRICH, CARL J., ed. *Totalitarianism.* Cambridge, Mass.: Harvard Univ. Press, 1954.

———, AND ZBIGNIEW BRZEZINSKI. *Totalitarian Dictatorship and Autocracy.* Cambridge, Mass.: Harvard Univ. Press, 1956.

GENTILE, GIOVANNI. *The Genesis and Structure of Society.* Tr. by H. S. Harris. Urbana: Univ. of'Illinois Press, 1960.

HARRIS, H. S. *The Social Philosophy of Giovanni Gentile.* Urbana: Univ. of Illinois Press, 1960.

HITLER, ADOLF. *Mein Kampf.* Tr. by Ralph Manheim. Boston: Houghton Mifflin, 1943.

HOFFER, ERIC. *The True Believer.* New York: Harper & Row, 1951.

MILOCZ, CESLAW. *The Captive Mind.* Tr. by Jane Zielonko. New York: Knopf (Vintage Books), 1953.

MUSSOLINI, BENITO. *The Political and Social Doctrine of Fascism.* Tr. by Jane Soames. London: Hogarth, 1933.

ROCCO, ALFREDO. "The Political Doctrine of Fascism." Tr. by D. Bigongiari in *International Conciliation Bulletin No. 223.* New York: Carnegie Endowment for International Peace, 1926.

SCHNEIDER, HERBERT W. *Making the Fascist State.* New York: Oxford Univ. Press, 1928.

SOREL, GEORGES. *Reflections on Violence.* Tr. by T. E. Hulme and J. Roth. New York: Free Press, 1950.

WEBER, EUGEN J. *Varieties of Fascism.* Princeton, N.J.: Van Nostrand (Anvil Books), 1964.

Liberalism-Conservatism [For Socialism, see the bibliography for Chapter 24, "Lenin."]

AUERBACH, MORTON. *The Conservative Illusion.* New York: Columbia Univ. Press, 1959.

BAY, CHRISTIAN. *The Structure of Freedom.* New York: Atheneum, 1965.

BERLIN, ISAIAH. *Two Concepts of Liberty.* Oxford: Clarendon Press, 1958.

CRANSTON, MAURICE. *Freedom; A New Analysis.* 2nd ed. London: Longmans, Green, 1954.

FRANKEL, CHARLES. *The Democratic Prospect.* New York: Harper & Row, 1962.

FRIEDMAN, MILTON. *Capitalism and Freedom.* Chicago: Univ. of Chicago Press (Phoenix Books), 1962.

GALBRAITH, JOHN KENNETH. *The Affluent Society.* Boston: Houghton Mifflin, 1958.

———. *American Capitalism.* Rev. ed. Boston: Houghton Mifflin, 1956.

———. *The New Industrial State.* Boston: Houghton Mifflin, 1967.

———. *Studies in Philosophy, Politics and Economics.* Chicago: Univ. of Chicago Press, 1967.

KENDALL, WILLMOORE. *The Conservative Affirmation.* Chicago: Regnery, 1963.

KEYNES, JOHN MAYNARD. *The Economic Consequences of the Peace.* New York: Harcourt, Brace & World, 1920.

———. *The General Theory of Employment, Interest, and Money.* London: Macmillan, 1936; New York: Harcourt, Brace & World, 1936.

LASKI, HAROLD J. *A Grammar of Politics.* London: Allen & Unwin, 1925.

———. *Liberty in the Modern State.* New York: Harper & Row, 1930.

———. *The State in Theory and Practice.* New York: Viking Press, 1935.

LIPPMANN, WALTER. *Essays in the Public Philosophy.* New York: New American Library (Mentor Books), 1957.

———. *The Essential Lippmann.* Ed. by Clinton Rossiter and James Lare. New York: Random House (Vintage Books), 1965.

———. *An Inquiry into the Principles of the Good Society.* Boston: Little, Brown, 1937.

———. *Public Opinion.* New York: Harcourt, Brace & World, 1922; Baltimore: Penguin Books, 1946.

MCGOVERN, WILLIAM M., AND DAVID S. COLLIER. *Radicals and Conservatives.* Chicago: Regnery, 1957.

MEYER, FRANK S., ed. *What Is Conservatism?* New York: Holt, Rinehart and Winston, 1964.

MINOGUE, KENNETH. *The Liberal Mind.* London: Methuen, 1963.

OAKESHOTT, MICHAEL. *Rationalism in Politics.* New York: Basic Books, 1962.

ORTEGA Y GASSET, JOSÉ. *The Revolt of the Masses.* New York: Nelson, 1932.

RUSSELL, BERTRAND. *Authority and the Individual.* New York: Simon and Schuster, 1945.

VON HAYEK, FRIEDRICH A. *The Constitution of Liberty.* Chicago: Univ. of Chicago Press, 1960.

Freudianism

BIRNBACH, MARTIN. *Neo-Freudian Social Philosophy.* Stanford, Cal.: Stanford Univ. Press, 1961.

BROWN, NORMAN. *Life Against Death; The Psychoanalytic Meaning of History.* New York: Random House (Vintage Books), 1961.

FREUD, SIGMUND. *Civilization and Its Discontents* (1930). Tr. by Joan Rivière. London: Hogarth, 1939, 1951.

———. *Civilization, War, and Death.* Ed. by John Rickman. London: Hogarth, 1939. Consists of three essays written in 1915, 1929, 1933.

———. *The Future of an Illusion.* Tr. by W. D. Robson-Scott. London: Hogarth, 1928; Garden City, N.Y.: Doubleday (Anchor Books), 1957.

FROMM, ERICH. *Escape from Freedom.* New York: Holt, Rinehart and Winston, 1941.

———. *The Sane Society.* New York: Holt, Rinehart and Winston, 1955.

HORNEY, KAREN. *The Neurotic Personality of Our Time.* New York: Norton, 1937.

JOHNSON, THOMAS. *Freud and Political Thought.* New York: Citadel Press, 1965.

JUNG, CARL G. *Modern Man in Search of a Soul.* London: Kegan Paul, Trench, Trübner, 1933.

MARCUSE, HERBERT. *Eros and Civilization.* New York: Random House (Vintage Books), 1962.

NELSON, BENJAMIN, ed. *Freud and the Twentieth Century.* New York: World (Meridian Books), 1957.

PROGOFF, IRA. *Jung's Psychology and Its Social Meaning.* New York: Grove Press, 1957.

RIEFF, PHILIP. *Freud: The Mind of the Moralist.* Garden City, N.Y.: Doubleday (Anchor Books), 1961.

SCHAAR, JOHN H. *Escape from Authority; The Perspectives of Erich Fromm.* New York: Basic Books, 1961.

Existentialism

ARENDT, HANNAH. *Between Past and Future; Six Exercises in Political Thought.* New York: Viking Press, 1961.

———. *The Human Condition.* Chicago: Univ. of Chicago Press, 1958.

———. *On Revolution.* New York: Viking Press, 1963.

BARRETT, WILLIAM. *Irrational Man.* Garden City, N.Y.: Doubleday (Anchor Books), 1962.

CAMUS, ALBERT. *The Myth of Sisyphus and Other Essays.* Tr. by Justin O'Brien. New York: Knopf, 1955.

———. *The Rebel.* Tr. by Anthony Bower. London: Hamilton, 1953; New York: Random House (Vintage Books), 1959.

———. *Resistance, Rebellion, and Death.* Tr. by Justin O'Brien. New York: Knopf, 1961.

CRANSTON, MAURICE. *Jean-Paul Sartre.* New York: Grove Press, 1962.

CRUICKSHANK, JOHN. *Albert Camus and the Literature of Revolt.* New York: Oxford Univ. Press (Galaxy Books), 1960.

DESAN, WILFRED. *The Marxism of Jean-Paul Sartre.* Garden City, N.Y.: Doubleday, 1965.

DOUGLAS, KENNETH. *A Critical Bibliography of Existentialism (The Paris School).* Yale French Studies, Special Monograph No. 1, 1950.

GREENE, NORMAN N. *Jean-Paul Sartre, The Existentialist Ethic.* Ann Arbor: Univ. of Michigan Press, 1960.

GRENE, MARJORIE. *Introduction to Existentialism.* Chicago: Univ. of Chicago Press (Phoenix Books), 1959.

HEINEMANN, FREDERICK. *Existentialism and the Modern Predicament.* 2nd ed. New York: Harper & Row (Torchbooks), 1958.

JASPERS, KARL. *The Future of Mankind.* Tr. by E. B. Ashton. Chicago: Univ. of Chicago Press, 1961.

———. *Man in the Modern Age.* Tr. by Eden Paul and Cedar Paul. Garden City, N.Y.: Doubleday (Anchor Books), 1957 (orig. German ed., 1931).

SARTRE, JEAN-PAUL. *Théorie des ensembles pratiques.* Vol. 1, *Critique de la raison dialectique.* Paris: Gallimard, 1960.

———. *Existentialism and Humanism.* Tr. by Philip Mairet. London: Methuen, 1948.

———. *Literary and Philosophical Essays.* Tr. by Annette Michelson. New York: Criterion Books, 1955.

———. *Search for a Method.* Tr. by Hazel Barnes. New York: Knopf, 1963.

WILLHOITE, FRED H., JR. *Beyond Nihilism: Albert Camus's Contribution to Political Thought.* Baton Rouge: Louisiana State Univ. Press. To be published in 1968.

Chapter 24 LENIN

Useful bibliographies may be found in Henry B. Mayo, *Introduction to Marxist Theory* (New York: Oxford Univ. Press, 1960), pp. 310–25; and Harry Overstreet and Bonaro Overstreet, *What We Must Know about Communism* (New York: Norton, 1958), pp. 314–24. See also works listed below by Daniels, Haimson, Hammond, and Meyer.

Works by Lenin

Collected Works. New York: International Publishers, 1927–42. Vols. 4, 13, 18–20, 21 only are translated (badly) into English.

Essentials of Lenin. London: Lawrence & Wishart, 1947. 2 vols.

Marx-Engels-Marxism. 3rd Eng. ed. Moscow: Foreign Language Publishing House, 1947. Includes excerpts from "State and Revolution," "What Is to Be Done?" and most of the major tracts.

Selected Works. New York: International Publishers, 1935–43. 12 vols.

Selected Works. Moscow: Foreign Language Publishing House, 1946. 2 vols.

Sochineniya (Works). 5th ed. Moscow: Marx-Engels-Lenin Institute, 1958–65. 55 vols. Many of the various Lenin tracts have been published separately in English by International Publishers, New York.

The Suppressed Testament of Lenin; The Complete Original Text with Two Explanatory Articles by L. Trotsky. New York: Pioneer, 1935. Lenin's famous criticism of Stalin, not published in the Soviet Union until 1956.

Secondary Works

APTHEKER, HERBERT, ed. *Marxism and Alienation: A Symposium.* New York: Humanities Press, 1965.

BARON, SAMUEL H. *Plekhanov, The Father of Russian Marxism.* Stanford, Cal.: Stanford Univ. Press, 1963.

BUKHARIN, NIKOLAI I. *Historical Materialism.* New York: International Publishers, 1925. Author's tr. from 3rd Russian ed.

CARR, EDWARD H. *The Bolshevik Revolution, 1917–1923.* New York: Macmillan, 1954. 3 vols.

CHEN, YUNG PING. *Chinese Political Thought: Mao Tse-tung and Liu Shao-chi.* The Hague: Nijhoff, 1966.

DANIELS, ROBERT V. *The Conscience of the Revolution; Communist Opposition in Soviet Russia.* Cambridge, Mass.: Harvard Univ. Press, 1960.

FISCHER, LOUIS. *The Life of Lenin.* New York: Harper & Row, 1964.

HAIMSON, LEOPOLD H. *The Russian Marxists and the Origins of Bolshevism.* Cambridge, Mass.: Harvard Univ. Press, 1955. See bibliography, pp. 235–40.

HAMMOND, THOMAS TAYLOR. *Lenin on Trade Unions and Revolution, 1893–1917.* New York: Columbia Univ. Press, 1957. See bibliography, pp. 130–50.

HILLQUIT, MORRIS. *From Marx to Lenin.* New York: Hanford, 1921.

History of the Communist Party of the Soviet Union (Bolsheviks): Short Course. New York: International Publishers, 1939. The so-called Stalin history.

KAUTSKY, KARL. *The Economic Doctrines of Karl Marx.* Tr. by H. J. Stenning. London: Black, 1925.

———. *Terrorism and Communism; A Contribution to the Natural History of Revolution.* Tr. by W. H. Kerridge. London: Allen & Unwin, 1920.

MAO TSE-TUNG. *Mao Tse-tung: An Anthology of His Writings.* Ed. by Anne Freemantle. New York: New American Library (Mentor Books), 1962.

MEYER, ALFRED G. *Leninism.* Cambridge, Mass.: Harvard Univ. Press, 1957. See bibliography, pp. 295–98.

PLAMENATZ, JOHN. *German Marxism and Russian Communism.* New York: Harper & Row (Torchbooks), 1965.

PLEKHANOV, GEORGI. *The Development of the Monist View of History* (1895). Tr. by Andrew Rothstein. Moscow: Foreign Language Publishing House, 1956.

POSSONY, STEFAN T. *Lenin: The Compulsory Revolutionary.* Chicago: Regnery, 1963.

SCHRAM, STUART A. *The Political Thought of Mao Tse-tung.* New York: Praeger, 1963.

STALIN, JOSEPH. *Problems of Leninism.* 11th ed. Moscow: Foreign Language Publishing House, 1941. Moscow-published works by Stalin tend to be unreliable.

TREADGOLD, D. W. *Lenin and His Rivals.* New York: Praeger, 1955.

TROTSKY, LEON. *Lenin.* Author's trans. New York: Minton, Balch, 1925.

———. *My Life; An Attempt at an Autobiography.* New York: Scribner's, 1931.

———. *The Permanent Revolution.* Tr. by Max Schachtman. New York: Pioneer, 1931.

ULAM, ADAM B. *The Unfinished Revolution.* New York: Random House, 1960.

WILSON, EDMUND. *To the Finland Station; A Study in the Writing and Acting of History.* Garden City, N.Y.: Doubleday (Anchor Books), 1959.

WOLFE, BERTRAM D. *Three Who Made a Revolution.* Boston: Beacon Press, 1956.

Chapter 25 DEWEY

Works by Dewey

Democracy and Education. New York: Macmillan, 1916.

Ethics, with James H. Tufts. Rev. ed. New York: Holt, Rinehart and Winston, 1932.

Experience and Nature. LaSalle, Ill.: Open Court, 1925.

Freedom and Culture. New York: Putnam's, 1939.

German Philosophy and Politics. New York: Holt, Rinehart and Winston, 1915; Boston: Beacon Press, 1945.

Human Nature and Conduct. New York: Holt, Rinehart and Winston, 1922; New York: Random House (Modern Library), 1930.

The Influence of Darwin on Philosophy. New York: Holt, Rinehart and Winston, 1910.

Intelligence in the Modern World. Ed. by Joseph Ratner. New York: Random House (Modern Library), 1939.

John Dewey and Arthur F. Bentley: A Philosophical Correspondence, 1932–1951. Ed. by Sidney Ratner and Jules Altman. New Brunswick, N.J.: Rutgers Univ. Press, 1964.

Liberalism and Social Action. New York: Putnam's, 1935.

The Public and Its Problems. New York: Holt, Rinehart and Winston, 1927; Chicago: Regnery (Gateway Editions), 1946; Denver, Colo.: Swallow, 1957.

The Quest for Certainty. New York: Minton, Balch, 1930.

Reconstruction in Philosophy. New York: Holt, Rinehart and Winston, 1920; enl. ed. Boston: Beacon Press, 1949.

School and Society. Rev. ed. Chicago: Univ. of Chicago Press, 1915.

Secondary Works

EDMAN, IRWIN. *John Dewey; His Contribution to the American Tradition.* Indianapolis, Ind.: Bobbs-Merrill, 1955.

Essays in Honor of John Dewey on the Occasion of His Seventieth Birthday. New York: Holt, Rinehart and Winston, 1929.

FELDMAN, W. T. *The Philosophy of John Dewey.* Baltimore: Johns Hopkins Press, 1934.

GEIGER, GEORGE R. *John Dewey in Perspective.* London: Oxford Univ. Press, 1958.

HOOK, SIDNEY. *John Dewey; An Intellectual Portrait.* New York: Day, 1939.

———, ed. *John Dewey; Philosopher of Science and Freedom.* New York: Dial Press, 1950.

JOHNSON, A. H., ed. *The Wit and Wisdom of John Dewey.* Boston: Beacon Press, 1949.

LAMONT, CORLISS, ed. *Dialogue on Dewey.* New York: Horizon Press, 1959.

LEANDER, FOLKE. *The Philosophy of John Dewey.* Göteborg, Sweden: Elanders, 1939.

MOORE, EDWARD C. *American Pragmatism; Peirce, James, and Dewey.* New York: Columbia Univ. Press, 1961.

RATNER, SIDNEY, ed. *The Philosopher of the Common Man.* New York: Putnam's, 1940.

SCHILPP, PAUL, ed. *The Philosophy of John Dewey.* Evanston, Ill.: Northwestern Univ. Press, 1939.

"Symposium on John Dewey," *Journal of the History of Ideas,* Vol. 20 (1959), pp. 515–76.

WHITE, MORTON G. *The Origin of Dewey's Instrumentalism.* New York: Columbia Univ. Press, 1943.

Chapter 26 NIEBUHR

For a complete bibliography of the writings of Reinhold Niebuhr see Harry R. Davis and Robert C. Good, eds., *Reinhold Niebuhr on Politics* (New York: Scribner's, 1960), p. 359. For a listing of Niebuhr's writings to 1956 see Kegley and Bretall, *Reinhold Niebuhr* (listed below), pp. 455–78. Issues of *Christianity and Crisis* from the early 1940's on provide a record of Niebuhr's political commentary.

Works by Niebuhr

The Children of Light and the Children of Darkness. New York: Scribner's, 1944.

Christian Realism and Political Problems. New York: Scribner's, 1953.

Christianity and Power Politics. New York: Scribner's, 1940.

Faith and History. New York: Scribner's, 1949.

An Interpretation of Christian Ethics. New York: Harper & Row, 1935.

The Irony of American History. New York: Scribner's, 1952.

Man's Nature and His Communities. New York: Scribner's, 1965.

Moral Man and Immoral Society. New York: Scribner's, 1932.

The Nature and Destiny of Man. New York: Scribner's, 1941. 2 vols.

Pious and Secular America. New York: Scribner's, 1958.

Reflections on the End of an Era. New York: Scribner's, 1934.

Secondary Works

BENNETT, JOHN C. *Christians and the State.* New York: Scribner's, 1958.

BINGHAM, JUNE. *The Courage to Change; An Introduction to the Life and Thought of Reinhold Niebuhr.* New York: Scribner's, 1961.

CARTER, PAUL A. *The Decline and Revival of the Social Gospel; Social and Political Liberalism in American Protestant Churches, 1920–1940.* Ithaca, N.Y.: Cornell Univ. Press, 1954. See bibliography, pp. 251–60.

GILL, THEODORE. *Recent Protestant Political Theory.* London: Hunt, Barnard, 1953.

HARLAND, GORDON. *The Thought of Reinhold Niebuhr.* New York: Oxford Univ. Press, 1960.

HOFMAN, HANS. *The Theology of Reinhold Niebuhr.* New York: Scribner's, 1956.

HUTCHISON, JOHN A., ed. *Christian Faith and Social Action.* New York: Scribner's, 1953.

KEGLEY, CHARLES W., AND ROBERT W. BRETALL, eds. *Reinhold Niebuhr; His Religious, Social, and Political Thought.* New York: Macmillan, 1956.

MARITAIN, JACQUES. *Man and the State.* Chicago: Univ. of Chicago Press, 1951.

MEYER, DONALD. *The Protestant Search for Political Realism, 1919–1941.* Berkeley: Univ. of California Press, 1960.

ODEGARD, HOLTAN P. *Sin and Science; Reinhold Niebuhr as Political Theologian.* Yellow Springs, Ohio: Antioch Press, 1956. See bibliography, pp. 221–34.

SCHNEIDER, HERBERT W. *Religion in Twentieth-Century America.* Cambridge, Mass.: Harvard Univ. Press, 1952.

TILLICH, PAUL. *Love, Power, and Justice.* New York: Oxford Univ. Press, 1954.

WHITE, MORTON G. *Social Thought in America; The Revolt Against Formalism.* Rev. ed. Boston: Beacon Press, 1958. Epilogue contains a critique of Niebuhr.

Chapter 27 POLITICAL THEORY AND THE SCIENCE OF POLITICS

CHARLESWORTH, JAMES C. *Contemporary Political Analysis.* New York: Free Press, 1967.

COWLING, MAURICE. *The Nature and Limits of Political Science.* New York: Cambridge Univ. Press, 1963.

EASTON, DAVID, ed. *Varieties of Political Theory.* Englewood Cliffs, N.J.: Prentice-Hall, 1966.

FRIEDRICH, CARL J. *Man and His Government; An Empirical Theory of Politics.* New York: McGraw-Hill, 1963.

FROHOCK, FRED M. *The Nature of Political Inquiry.* Homewood, Ill.: Dorsey, 1967.

RUNCIMAN, W. G. *Social Science and Political Theory.* London: Cambridge Univ. Press, 1963.

INDEX

Works discussed in depth are indexed under their titles. All other works are indexed under authors and are grouped alphabetically at the end of the author entries. Pages on which the chief discussion of a topic appears are printed in bold type.

A 0
B 1
C 2
D 3
E 4
F 5
G 6
H 7
I 8
J 9